12-13-99

THIRD EDITION

Ada 95

PROBLEM SOLVING AND PROGRAM DESIGN

Michael B. Feldman
The George Washington University

Elliot B. Koffman
Temple University

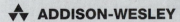

D0074596

▲▼ ADDISON-WESLEY

Addison-Wesley is an imprint
of Addison Wesley Longman, Inc.

Reading, Massachusetts   Harlow, England   Menlo Park, California
Berkeley, California   Don Mills, Ontario   Sydney   Bonn
Amsterdam   Tokyo   Mexico City

Sr. Acquisitions Editor: *Susan Hartman*
Associate Editor: *Katherine Harutunian*
Production Editor: *Patricia A. O. Unubun*
Cover Design: *Diana Coe*
Production Coordination: *Diane Freed*
Copy Editor: *Barbara Willette*

Access the latest information about Addison-Wesley books from our World Wide Web site: www.awl.com/cseng

Many of the designations used by manufacturers and sellers to distinguish their products are claimed as trademarks. Where those designations appear in this book, and the publisher was aware of a trademark claim, the designations have been printed in initial caps or in all caps.

The programs and the applications presented in this book have been included for their instructional value. They have been tested with care but are not guaranteed for any particular purpose. Neither the publisher nor the author offers any warranties or representations, nor do they accept any liabilities with respect to the programs or applications.

Library of Congress Cataloging-in-Publication Data

Feldman, Michael B.
  Ada 95 : problem solving and program design / Michael B.
Feldman, Elliot B. Koffman. — 3rd ed.
    p. cm.
  ISBN 0-201-36123-X
  1. Ada 95 (Computer program language) I. Koffman, Elliot B. II.
Title.
  QA76.73.A35 F43 1999
  005.13′3—dc21   99–11613
                                                          CIP

This book was typeset by Michael B. Feldman in FrameMaker 5.5 on an Apple Macintosh 7500. The fonts used were Christiana, Courier Pitch, and Helvetica. It was printed on New Era Matte.

1 2 3 4 5 6 7 8 9 10–MA–0302010099

PREFACE

This textbook is intended for the introductory course in problem solving and program design using Ada 95. It assumes no prior knowledge of computers or programming, and for most of its material, high school algebra is sufficient mathematical background. The first two editions of this book have been used with success in a large number of introductory courses.

While the book is generally oriented to the first-term student of programming, there is more material here than is usually covered in a first course. Chapters 11 through 17 focus on abstract data types, generics, recursion, dynamic data structures, inheritance-oriented programming, and concurrency. They can be used selectively in a fairly advanced first course or as part of a second-level course. The book covers the Ada 95 language thoroughly enough to serve as a useful introduction for professionals.

The Ada 95 language standard was adopted early in 1995 by the International Standards Organization and the American National Standards Institute. Ada is a foundation language in a growing number of institutions (about 150 at this writing). Ada is also a language of choice in many important industry sectors, especially commercial aviation and air traffic control, high-speed and metropolitan rail transportation, scientific and communications satellites, and manufacturing control. The consensus among teachers of Ada is that its pedagogical virtues are very similar to its industrial ones.

Problem Solving and Program Design

The primary focus of this book is problem solving with Ada 95, not a study of the Ada 95 programming language per se. We achieve this focus by selecting features of the language that lend themselves to good program design. We also emphasize abstraction and use the time-tested six-step approach to software development: problem specification, analysis, design, test planning, implementation, and testing. Each of the 35 case studies throughout the book follows this software development method.

New in the Third Edition

This edition includes a number of new end-of-chapter projects. Also, a new Chapter 2 uses an Ada 95 "spider" package—similar to the turtle graphics of Logo—to introduce the basics of algorithms and the fundamental sequential, loop, and test control structures, all in a platform-independent animated framework. Chapter 2 is independent of the others and thus provides flexibility to an instructor who sees real benefit in introducing all the major control structures together as early as possible. Instructors who were satisfied with the presentation order in the first two editions can simply skip from Chapter 1 to Chapter 3 without loss of continuity.

This edition also contains alphabetical indexes of syntax displays, case studies, and program style guides and a new Appendix A, *High-Resolution Color Graphics*. This appendix provides a platform-independent package for simple two-dimensional graphics and examples including a high-resolution color spider package.

Finally, this edition incorporates a CD-ROM, which is described in Appendix G. This CD-ROM contains

- the complete set of about 200 book programs, all in standard, platform-independent Ada 95

- the Appendix A software for various platforms

- platform-specific versions of the GNU Ada 95 Compiler (GNAT) and interactive development environments (IDEs) for Apple Macintosh, Microsoft Windows 95/98/NT, MS-DOS/PC-DOS, and Linux

- various browsable editions of the Ada 95 Reference Manual and Rationale and additional reference documents such as printable reference cards and graphical syntax diagrams

- a copy of Tenon's MachTen Code Builder system, a virtual UNIX environment for the Macintosh

General Organization of the Book

The order of presentation is designed to do justice both to modern programming concepts and to the power of Ada. *Each chapter beyond Chapters 1 and 2 presents a balanced mixture of a number of important language and computing issues.* These are organized in a number of categories; most chapter section headings give the main category of the section as well as the specific topic, to orient teacher and student alike to the flow of material in a given category from chapter to chapter. The categories are:

- *Problem Solving:* Here is where language-independent concepts of program design, algorithm development, and so forth, are introduced.

- *Control Structures:* Each of these sections introduces the program-level control structures of Ada: decisions, loops, assignments, and so on.

- *Data Structures:* In each of these sections appears a discussion of data types and their uses, in the usual order of scalar types followed by structured or composite (record and array) types.

- *System Structures:* Each of these sections introduces a concept that is useful in what is often called "programming in the large." These concepts help the student, right from the start, to realize that real-world programs really consist of many smaller pieces built up in systematic fashion. Included under System Structures are such things as functions and procedures, packages, and exception handling and propagation.

- *Tricks of the Trade:* These are the universal techniques that all programmers must learn in order to survive productively: debugging techniques, program tracing, documentation techniques, and the like.

Pedagogical Features

In this book we employ several proven pedagogical features:

- *Complete, compilable programs:* From the beginning, students see full, compilable, executable programs. These are captioned "Program x.y" to identify them clearly as compilable programs and not fragments, which are embedded in the text or numbered as figures. Each listing of a main program is immediately followed by a sample execution, to give the student an idea of the expected results.

  A particular advantage of Ada as a teaching language is that the strong standard ensures that program behavior will be nearly independent of the particular compiler or computer being used. The programs in this book have been fully tested and can be compiled and executed using any validated Ada 95 compiler.

- *Case Studies:* A case study is a program that is developed from specifications, step by step, from a statement of the problem to a complete working program. The software development method is taught, reinforced, and applied. We focus much attention on program testing and the development of test plans.

  Of the 35 case studies, some—especially in the early chapters—are presented in their entirety, while others are intentionally left incomplete so that their completion can be assigned as class projects.

- *Syntax displays:* A syntax display is a brief description, with words and examples, of the syntax and interpretation of a newly introduced structure. These are set apart typographically for ease of use, and they codify the language structures as they are first presented.

- *Programming style displays:* These are brief discussions, again set apart typographically, offering advice to the student about how to write good programs. Many of these are of course universal and language-independent; many are also Ada-specific.

- *End of section exercises:* Following most sections there are two kinds of exercises, self-check and programming.

- *End of chapter exercises:* Each chapter review contains a set of quick-check exercises with answers, review questions, and programming projects.

- *Error discussions and chapter review:* Each chapter ends with a section that discusses common programming errors and a review section that includes a table of Ada constructs introduced in that chapter.

Program Design Issues

Concepts of *object-oriented programming (OOP)* are introduced throughout the book as appropriate. While it is true that type extension and dynamic polymorphism are generally seen as *necessary* to "full" OOP, it is essential for the student to understand that these are not *sufficient*. Ada's strong support for packages, generics, exceptions, private types, and subprogram overloading—like their equivalents in other languages—play important roles as well. The idea that an object—even a scalar object—has state (value) and behavior (appropriate operations) is introduced beginning in Chapter 3, and "object thinking" is pervasive in the book. Type extension *per se* is an advanced topic that cannot be understood without a good grounding in the other topics, so it is deferred until Chapter 16.

We present *stepwise refinement* of an algorithm right from the start but make only rare use of top-down *implementation* through procedure stubs and the like. It is crucial to foster habits of design for *reusability* very early, and this argues for early emphasis of packages and the reusable functions and procedures they provide.

Functions are presented very early: They are used in Chapter 4 and written in Chapter 5. *Procedure calls* are introduced in Chapters 2 and 3 to support the spider package and Ada's input/output operations; procedures are *written* starting in Chapter 7. Functions are more intuitive than procedures, and, in Ada, cannot have IN OUT ("variable") parameters. Since functions in Ada are not restricted in their result type—arrays and records as well as scalars can be returned—this early exposure to functions will pay off later in encouraging students to use functional notation where possible. Introducing functions early allows us to introduce the writing of packages early (again in Chapter 5).

Enumeration types are introduced very early (Chapters 2 and 4). Enumerations are a useful structure for representing a set of values without regard to their internal representation. Students of other languages have a hard time seeing the utility of enumerations because they are so hard to read and display. In Ada, the input/output library provides a generic package for reading and displaying enumeration values. Furthermore, enumerations serve as a useful vehicle for motivating generic instantiation (for Enumeration_IO) and attributes (Pos, Val, Succ, Pred) very early in the game.

Records and arrays are presented together in Chapter 9, with records first. Other books have introduced arrays of scalars early, with arrays of records as an "advanced" topic. We prefer to teach that arrays of records are as natural as arrays of integers.

Design of *abstract data types (ADTs)* is introduced systematically beginning in Chapter 11. Ada.Calendar is seen as an ADT, and the discussion continues with ADTs for calendar dates, monetary quantities, employee records, and multiple spiders. *Unconstrained array types* are treated along with *generics* in Chapter 12; *multidimensional arrays* and *variant records* are introduced in Chapter 13. Chapter 14 presents an introduction to *recursion. Dynamic data structures,* in the form of one-way linked lists, as well as subunits and LIMITED PRIVATE types, are introduced in Chapter 15, with applications to stacks and queues. *Tagged records* are introduced in Chapter 16; these are seen to be supportive of the type extension (inheritance) that is now seen as essential to full object-oriented programming.

Finally, Chapter 17 introduces the important concept of *concurrent programming,* introducing Ada's task types and protected types as language-provided constructs for concurrency.

Preconditions and *postconditions* for subprograms are introduced at the start. We encourage the development of programs from their documentation; in case studies, the steps of the algorithm are written before the program is developed and become comments as the program is refined.

We encourage appropriate use of comments but do not get carried away with them; the programs and the book would be far too long if we used industrial-strength comment conventions.

Ada Issues

Ada 95 is a rich and powerful language. It is important to introduce the language to beginners, step by step, without overwhelming them. Here is a list of a number of Ada capabilities and how we have handled them:

- *Numeric Types:* Subtypes are introduced early in the book, as a way of specifying ranges of values that are sensible in the application. Where values shouldn't be negative, we always use a positive subtype, for example, and often use a subtype with range constraints where it makes sense not to allow the full range of integer.

  We have avoided the use of new and derived numeric types because the compatibility issues that arise from their use create more problems than they solve for beginners. It is range checking that is important to them, not the esoterica of type compatibility.

  Furthermore, using new or derived numeric types for simple beginning-level numerical problems gives completely counterintuitive results: Attempting to use types for distance, rate, and time, for example, to compute the old

  ```
  Distance := Rate * Time;
  ```

  formula leads to type-compatibility grief that no novice should have to endure.

- *Packages and related issues:* Using packages is introduced in Chapter 2 with the spider system and in Chapter 3 with the use of the various sublibraries of Ada.Text_IO. In Chapter 4, students learn how to use some of the capabilities of Ada.Calendar, which has a richness that is not often explored even by advanced Ada texts. Ada.Calendar is a recurring theme in this book, and is discussed in the absract data type material of Chapter 11, since Time and the various Time and Duration operations from Ada.Calendar serve as a particularly nice predefined example of a private ADT. Also, students understand times and dates intuitively; there is nothing esoteric about them. The year range of Ada.Calendar (1901–2099) provides an opportunity to discuss the Year 2000 problem.

  Also in Chapter 4, use of a simple screen-control package is introduced. Students will need to compile this before they use it, since it is provided with the book and is not part of most compiler distributions. Thus they will learn how to compile a package and understand specifications very early on, even if they don't yet understand the details of the package body, which are discussed at some length in Chapter 8. screen is used in a number of examples in the book, especially for menu handling, plotting, and the spider examples.

  By Chapter 5, students are writing simple packages; by Chapter 6 they are learning about overloaded function and procedure names. Private types and operator overloading appear in Chapter 11.

- *The USE clause:* This is introduced in Chapter 8. Ada industry practice generally avoids the USE clause for a number of good reasons. We avoid it here, in general, because qualifying all references to package resources helps the student to really understand which resources are provided by which libraries.

USE and its Ada 95 variant USE TYPE can be useful in taking advantage of the overloading of infix operators; this is discussed in Chapter 11. USE is a better solution for novices than the industry-favored device of renaming declarations.

- *Generic predefined libraries:* For numeric input/output, we use the Ada 95 Ada.Text_IO.Integer_Text_IO and Ada.Text_IO.Float_Text_IO. Using these new "preinstantiations" obviates the need for the student to instantiate numeric input/output packages. The new "preinstantiations" are introduced in Chapter 3 and are used consistently throughout. In Chapter 4 the student learns to instantiate Ada.Text_IO.Enumeration_IO for the desired enumeration type. The student instantiates Ada.Numerics.Discrete_Random beginning in Chapter 8.

- *Generics in general:* Some simple generic units appear starting in Chapter 12. Writing generics is really an advanced topic that should wait until CS2, when the student is better equipped to handle the underlying abstraction principles.

- *Exceptions:* Discussion of Ada's predefined exceptions occurs in Chapter 3, where compilation and run-time errors in general are introduced. Robust exception handling cannot be taken up until after the control structures have been presented, and so program level exception handling is first discussed in Chapter 6. Robust input loops are presented in Chapter 7, along with a package providing robust input operations. User-defined exceptions are introduced in Chapter 11, as a natural aspect of abstract data types.

- *Lexical style:* We have continued the practice of the earlier editions in using uppercase reserved words. We believe that beginners in programming should learn the structure templates through heavy reinforcement, and the uppercase reserved words make the structure templates stand out. Ada is not a case-sensitive language, and although reserved words are printed in the standard in lowercase, an uppercase convention is perfectly allowable and is, in our experience, pedagogically effective. It is emphasized in the text that teachers and students can, and should, develop their own coding styles and that consistency of style is more important than following any specific rule.

  Only one statement appears per line. We believe that this makes for more modifiable code and is a good habit for students to develop. Similarly, each variable and constant is declared in a separate declaration on its own line.

- *Procedure parameters:* Named association is used exclusively in the early chapters and almost exclusively thereafter. This is not only good Ada but also good pedagogy because—as our experience shows—the student has a much easier time understanding the formal/actual binding if the two always appear together.

- *Initialization expressions:* Initialization expressions are introduced in Chapter 8, along with record types, and the reader is advised to use initializations to ensure that record fields are always well defined. With some reluctance we have decided not to introduce initialization expressions for variables. It is true that a declaration with a static initialization such as

```
X: Float := 57.0;
```

contributes to program readability. However, an initialization such as

```
X: Float := 3.0 + Sqrt(Y);
```

is permitted but should not be used, because an exception that is raised if Y is negative will propagate unexpectedly. Instead of artificially limiting initializations to static expressions, we have simply chosen not to use them at all.

- *Private and limited private types*: Private types are covered in depth in Chapter 11, in the discussion of abstract data types. Specifically, a number of examples are given of situations in which giving a client access to the details of a type would allow the client inadvertently to violate the integrity of the abstraction. The exported types in this chapter all provide for default initialization so that assignment and equality test are always meaningful operations.

  In later chapters attention is paid to those situations—especially in the use of dynamic data structures—in which assignment and equality test can indeed be used misleadingly, for example, to copy just the headers of lists. The potential for abuse of these operations provides useful justification for limited private types, for objects of which assignment and equality test are prohibited.

- *Subunits and Ada stubs:* The list-handling packages of Chapter 15 serve as a way to introduce this concept, which is confusing if brought in too early. Besides being an interesting Ada technique for doing top-down testing, the use of subunits serves as a convenient way to present the operations of the packages as individual program displays and files.

- *Tasks and protected types:* Ada is unique among major programming languages in providing support for parallelism and concurrency within the language. Parallelism is now seen as a "recurring paradigm" in computing, and we think it important to introduce students to it as early as possible in their education. The material in Chapter 17 serves this purpose; we have made it independent of Chapters 12–16 so that a teacher desiring to introduce concurrency in a CS1-level course can do so after Chapter 11.

Instructor's Manual and Other Online Resources

Information regarding this text is available from the Addison-Wesley World Wide Web site at `http://www.awl.com/cseng/titles/0-201-36123-X`.

The Instructor's Manual is available electronically. The public part, containing chapter and section summaries and objectives, new terms, notes, and suggestions, as well as program libraries and errata, is at `http://www.seas.gwu.edu/faculty/mfeld-man/cs1book`. The private part, containing solutions to exercises and projects, is available to instructors only from Addison-Wesley. Contact your sales representative for access information.

It is intended that teachers make the full set of about 200 programs and packages available to their students so that they need not waste time keying them in. Of course the programs are available on the included CD-ROM; we hope that teachers will make them available centrally for courses using central systems for projects. The programs are also available from the above-named WWW sites.

Afterword

This book's earlier editions incorporated a great deal of new material that is intended to introduce the beginning programmer to the power of Ada while building on the successful pedagogy of the earlier Koffman works. The earlier editions' success among teachers of Ada—in a number of cases, even serving as critical "ammunition" in moving introductory courses to Ada—confirms the soundness of the approach.

The present edition builds on the success of the first two, serving as an important aid to teachers ready to introduce students to Ada 95.

Acknowledgments

All the programs have been tested using the GNU Ada 95 Translator (GNAT), running on an IBM-compatible computer under Windows, an Apple Macintosh under MachTen, and a Sun-SPARC computer under Solaris. The authors acknowledge the School of Engineering and Applied Science Computing Facility at The George Washington University for having provided the Solaris computing resources.

The authors are indebted to the following educators, who served as formal reviewers and provided unusually cogent and helpful assistance: Todd W. Breedlove, Jessica Lambert, Linda Null, David Nash, Ming Wang, and Phyllis Ann Williams. John Dalbey provided the original Spider package. We are further indebted to Chet Lund for some very creative project ideas; to Thibault Estier, Magnus Kempe, Laurent Pautet, and Paul Pukite for their Ada 95 electronic reference documents; to James Cross for GRASP; to Jerry van Dijk for the original AdaGraph package for Windows and other help; and to Martin Carlisle and James Hopper for their help in developing AdaGraph ports to other platforms. We offer thanks to Ada Core Technologies for providing the GNAT compilers, and to Tenon Intersystems for allowing us to distribute MachTen CodeBuilder.

The Addison-Wesley editorial and production staff, including Susan Hartman, Katherine Harutunian, Patricia Unubun, Diane Freed, Bob Woodbury, and Lynne Doran Cote, deserve hearty thanks for their expert and always good-natured assistance.

Finally, Ruth Feldman has earned a vote of gratitude for tender loving care and help on the index. Ben and Keith Feldman have, as before, always been there to cheer their father on through the development of (in their words) "yet another book."

Bethesda, Maryland
Philadelphia, Pennsylvania

Michael B. Feldman
Elliot B. Koffman

CONTENTS

CHAPTER 1

Introduction to Computers and Programming

In this chapter we introduce computers and computer programming. We begin with a brief history of computers and a description of the major components of a computer, including memory, central processor, input devices, and output devices. We also discuss how information is represented in a computer and how it is manipulated.

You are about to begin the study of programming using one of the richest and most interesting programming languages available today: the Ada language. This chapter begins a discussion of the main topics of this book: problem solving, programming, and Ada. We first discuss problem solving with a computer. Then languages for computer programming are described. We describe the process for creating a program and the roles performed by special programs that are part of a computer system. These programs include the operating system, compiler, editor, and loader. Finally, we take you through a first exercise in compiling a program and examining error listings.

1.1   Electronic Computers Then and Now

It is difficult to live in today's world without having some contact with computers. Computers are used to provide instructional material in schools, to print transcripts, to send out bills, to reserve airline and concert tickets, to play games, and to help authors write books. Several kinds of computers cooperate in dispensing cash from an automatic teller machine; "embedded" or "hidden" computers help to control the ignitions, fuel systems, and transmissions of modern automobiles; at the supermarket, a computer device reads the bar codes on the packages you buy, to total your purchase and help manage the store's inventory. Even a microwave oven has a special-purpose computer built into it.

However, it wasn't always this way. Computers as we know them did not exist at all before the late 1930s, and as recently as the early 1970s, they were fairly mysterious devices that only a small percentage of our population knew much about. Computer know-how turned around when advances in solid-state electronics led to cuts in the size and cost of electronic computers. Today, a personal computer (see Fig. 1.1) costs under $1000 and fits easily on a desk or in a briefcase. A computer that fits in the palm of one's hand costs only a few hundred dollars. These computers have computational power comparable to those of 15 years ago, which cost more than $100,000 and filled a 9-foot by 12-foot room. This price reduction is even more remarkable when we consider the effects of inflation over the last decade. It is said that if the development of automobiles had progressed at the same rate as that of computers, a luxurious car would cost only a few dollars and would be as fast as the Space Shuttle.

If we take the literal definition of *computer* as being a device for counting or computing, the abacus might be considered the first computer. However, the first electronic digital computers were designed in the late 1930s and 1940s.

An early large-scale, general-purpose electronic digital computer, called the ENIAC, was built in 1946 at the University of Pennsylvania with funding supplied by the U.S. Army. The ENIAC was used for computing ballistics tables, for weather prediction, and for atomic energy calculations. The ENIAC weighed 30 tons, occupied a space 30 by 50 feet, and could perform 5 multiplications per second (see Fig. 1.2).

A computer is basically a device for performing very simple computations and decisions, such as determining the alphabetical ordering of two words or summing two numbers, at incredible speeds (millions of these simple operations per second) and with great accuracy. To accomplish anything useful, a computer must be *programmed*, or given a sequence of explicit instructions (the *program*) indicating which simple operations to carry out, in which order, and how many times.

To program the ENIAC, hundreds of wires and thousands of switches had to be connected in a certain way. In 1946, Dr. John von Neumann of Princeton University proposed the concept of a *stored program computer* in which the instructions of a program would be stored in computer memory rather than be set by wires and switches. Because the contents of computer memory could be changed easily, it was much less difficult to reprogram this computer to perform different tasks than it was to reprogram the ENIAC. Von Neumann's design is the basis of the digital computer as we know it today.

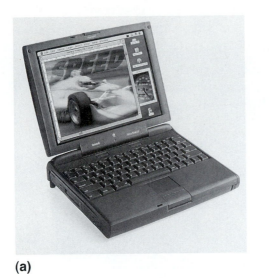

(a)

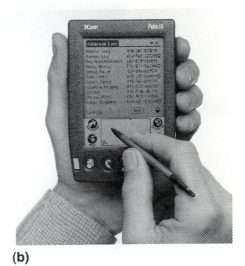

(b)

(c)

Figure 1.1   (a) Macintosh Powerbook G3 (photo courtesy of Apple Computer, Inc.;
Photographer: John Greenleigh)
(b) Palm III™ Connected Organizer (Palm Computing, Inc., a 3Com Company)
(c) IBM PC 300GL Desktop Computer (photo courtesy of IBM)

Figure 1.2   The ENIAC Computer (photo courtesy of Unisys Corporation)

A Brief History of Computers

Table 1.1 lists some of the important milestones along the path from the abacus to modern-day electronic computers. We often use the term *first generation* to refer to electronic computers that used vacuum tubes (1939–1958). The *second generation* began in 1958 with the changeover to transistors. The *third generation* began in 1964 with the introduction of integrated circuits. The *fourth generation* began in 1975 with the advent of large-scale integration. Since then, change has come so rapidly that we don't even count generations anymore. However, the late 1970s saw the beginning of the continuing "personal computer revolution" with computers that individuals and families could afford being sold at retail in computer stores.

Table 1.1   Milestones in the Development of Computers and Programming Languages

Date	Event
2000 B.C.	The abacus is first used for computations.
1642 A.D.	Blaise Pascal, in France, creates a mechanical adding machine for tax computations. It is unreliable.
1670	In Germany, Gottfried von Leibniz creates a more reliable adding machine, which adds, subtracts, multiplies, divides, and calculates square roots.
1842	Charles Babbage, in England, designs an Analytical Engine to perform general calculations automatically. Ada Byron, daughter of the poet Lord Byron and known later as Lady Lovelace, assists him in programming this machine.
1890	Herman Hollerith designs a system to record and tabulate data for the decennial U.S. census. The information is stored as holes on cards, which are interpreted by machines with electrical sensors. Hollerith starts a company that will eventually become IBM.
1939	Alan Turing and a team at Bletchley, England, begin developing a series of code-breaking computers culminating in the all-vacuum-tube Colossus.
1939	John Atanasoff at Iowa State University, with graduate student Clifford Berry, designs and builds an early digital computer. His project is funded by a grant for $650. Atanasoff is now generally credited with building the first electronic digital computer. However, he never filed for a patent for his invention.
1941	Konrad Zuse, in Berlin, develops Z3, possibly the first operational program-controlled calculating machine, based on electromechanical relays.
1943	Howard Aiken, at Harvard, develops the Mark I, essentially an electromechanical realization of Babbage's Analytical Engine.
1946	J. Presper Eckert and John Mauchly design, build, and patent the Electronic Numerical Integrator and Calculator (ENIAC) at the University of Pennsylvania. It uses 18,000 vacuum tubes and costs $500,000 to build.
1946	John von Neumann, at Princeton, proposes that a program be stored in a computer in the same form that data are stored. His proposal, called "von Neumann architecture," is still the basis of most modern computers.
1951	Eckert and Mauchly build the first general-purpose commercial computer, the UNIVAC.
1957	John Backus and his team at IBM complete the first FORTRAN compiler. This is a milestone in the development of programming languages.

Date	Event
1958	The first computer to use the transistor as a switching device, the IBM 7090, is introduced.
1958	Seymour Cray builds the first fully transistorized computer, the CDC 1604, for Control Data Corporation.
1959	Aided by the computer pioneer Grace Hopper of UNIVAC, the CODASYL Committee publishes the specification for COBOL. This is the first effort to standardize a programming language; it is followed by the development of the first procedures to validate a compiler.
1964	The first computer using integrated circuits, the IBM 360, is announced.
1965	The CTSS (Compatible Time-Sharing System) is introduced at MIT. It allows several users simultaneously to use, or share, a single computer.
1970	A first version of UNIX is running on the DEC PDP-7.
1971	The Pascal programming language is introduced by Niklaus Wirth of the Technical University of Zurich.
1972	Dennis Ritchie of Bell Laboratories develops the language C.
1973	Part of the UNIX operating system is developed in C.
1973	A court declares the ENIAC patent to be invalid, because ENIAC was derived from Atanasoff's invention. After 34 years, Atanasoff is recognized as having invented the first electronic digital computer.
1975	The first microcomputer, the Altair, is introduced.
1975	The first supercomputer, the Cray-1, is announced.
1975	The U.S. Department of Defense (DoD) High-Order Language Working Group (HOLWG) is created to find a solution to the DoD's "software crisis." The group's efforts culminate in the adoption of Ada.
1976	Digital Equipment Corporation introduces its popular minicomputer, the VAX 11/780.
1977	Steve Wozniak and Steve Jobs begin producing Apple computers in a garage.
1977	Radio Shack announces the TRS-80, one of the first fully packaged microcomputers to be sold in retail stores, in time for the Christmas season.
1978	Dan Bricklin and Bob Frankston develop the first electronic spreadsheet, called VisiCalc, for the Apple computer.
1979	After a competition lasting several years, the preliminary specification of Ada is published by the U.S. government. Ada's design team at CII-Honeywell-Bull is headed by Jean Ichbiah and includes about a dozen American and European language experts.
1979–82	Bjarne Stroustrup of Bell Laboratories introduces "C with Classes."
1981	IBM introduces the IBM Personal Computer. The business world now acknowledges that microcomputers are "real."

Date	Event
1982	Sun Microsystems introduces its first workstation, the Sun 100.
1983	The Ada language standard is adopted by the government and by the American National Standards Institute (ANSI).
1983–85	C with Classes is redesigned and reimplemented as C++.
1984	Apple introduces the Macintosh, the first widely available computer with a "graphical user interface" using icons, windows, and a mouse device.
1984	The Internet contains approximately 1,000 host computers.
1987	The Internet contains approximately 10,000 host computers.
1987	Ada is adopted as an international standard by the International Standards Organization (ISO).
1988	The Ada 9X project is begun, to consider extensions to the Ada language. Christine Anderson oversees the project for the U.S. government; the design team is headed by Tucker Taft of Intermetrics.
1989	The Internet contains approximately 100,000 host computers.
1990	Over 500 different Ada compilers have been validated. Compilers—all handling the same Ada language—are readily available for all categories of computers from laptops to supercomputers.
1992	The Internet contains approximately 1,000,000 host computers.
1992	The United States, Canada, and dozens of other countries around the world are redesigning their air traffic control systems using state-of-the-art computers running software written mostly in Ada.
1994	GNAT, the GNU Ada 95 Compilation System, is released as the first compiler to implement the evolving Ada 9X design. GNAT is distributed free to many thousands of users over the Internet and on CD-ROMs.
1995	The Internet, originally a university and defense research network started in the 1970s by the U.S. government, has hundreds of thousands of computers and millions of government, academic, commercial, and individual users and becomes a subject of widespread discussion in the public press. The World Wide Web, nonexistent in 1990, experiences explosive growth and popularity
1995	The Boeing 777, the most computer-dependent airliner to date, makes its first commercial flights. Its several million lines of software are written mostly in Ada.
1995	Ada 9X becomes Ada 95 when ISO and ANSI adopt the extended language as a U.S. and international standard. The first validated Ada 95 compilers appear.
1996	The Internet contains approximately 10,000,000 host computers.

Date	Event
1996	The Java Virtual Machine (JVM)—an "interpreter" program that runs applets, or small application programs distributed via the Internet—appears in World Wide Web browser programs for desktop personal computers. One of the programming languages used to produce applets is also called Java.
1996	Intermetrics AppletMagic, the first Ada 95 compiler that produces JVM applets, enters distribution.
1997	One of the authors of this book (Feldman) flies between Washington and Paris on a Boeing 777. It is a very nice airplane.
1997	GNAT is fully validated for the Ada 95 core language and all annexes.
1998	The "Year 2000 Problem"—an unknown but very large number of older computers and programs must be heavily modified so that they can distinguish between the year 1900 and the year 2000—is discussed nearly every day in newspapers and radio and TV news programs. It is still unknown just what the cost of solution—estimated at many billions of dollars—will be or just how many people will be affected when 2000 arrives.
1998	GNAT for the Java Virtual Machine enters distribution.
1998	The cost of a typical personal computer is just over $1,000.
1998	The Internet contains an estimated 30,000,000 host computers.

Categories of Computers

Modern-day computers are classified according to their size and performance. The three major categories of computers are mainframes, minicomputer, and microcomputers. These categories are useful but rough: As technology continues to improve, the categories increasingly blur into one another.

Businesses, research laboratories, and university computing centers often use larger computers called *minicomputers* and *mainframes*. These are most noticeable in that they can be used simultaneously by many individuals, all working on separate problems. *Supercomputers,* the most powerful mainframes, can perform in seconds computations that might take hours or days on a smaller computer or years with a hand calculator.

You are probably most familiar with desktop computers such as the Apple Macintosh or the "IBM-compatible" models from many manufacturers. The latter are called "IBM-compatible" because they were originally imitators, or "clones" of the IBM Personal Computer. Currently, they are often called "Wintel" computers—they run Microsoft Windows software and are based on a hardware design by Intel.

When these computers first appeared in the early 1980s, they were called *microcomputers* or *personal computers* because they were usually used by one person at a time and were small enough to fit on or next to a desk. They were also "micro" because they did not have much computing power compared to the physically larger ones. The most powerful microcomputers, called *workstations*, are commonly used by engineers to produce engineering drawings and to assist in the design and development of new products. The smallest general-purpose microcomputers are often called *laptops* or *notebooks* because they can fit into a briefcase and are often used on one's lap in an airplane. Finally, at this writing, *palmtop* computers—hand-held, pocket-sized devices originally designed for maintaining one's telephone list and appointment calendar but increasingly running general-purpose software—are selling for just a few hundred dollars and are becoming extremely popular.

Often, the term *embedded computer* is used to refer to a computer that is built into a larger system and not operated directly by a human user. Embedded computers are found in automobiles, automatic teller machines, cash registers, and so on.

This book was written by using an Apple Macintosh microcomputer; the programs were tested on a Macintosh, an IBM-compatible personal computer running Microsoft Windows 95, and a Sun workstation.

1.2 Hardware Components of a Computer

Despite significant variations in cost, size, and capabilities, digital computers have been remarkably similar throughout their 50-year history. They all consist of *hardware,* the physical equipment, and *software,* the programs that are loaded into the hardware to perform computational tasks.

Most computers consist of the following hardware components:

- main memory

- secondary memory, which includes storage devices such as hard disks, floppy disks, CD-ROMs, and writable CDs

- the central processing unit

- input devices, such as scanners, keyboards, and mice

- output devices, such as monitors and printers

Figure 1.3 shows how these components interact, with arrows showing the direction of information flow.

All information that is to be processed by a computer must first be entered into the computer memory via an input device. The information in memory is manipulated by the *central processing unit (CPU),* and the results of this manipulation are stored in memory. Information in memory can be displayed through an output device. A secondary storage device is often used for storing large quantities of information in a semipermanent form.

Main Memory

Main memory—often called *random-access memory,* or *RAM*—is used for storing information and programs. All types of information—numbers, names, lists, and even pictures—can be represented and stored in main memory.

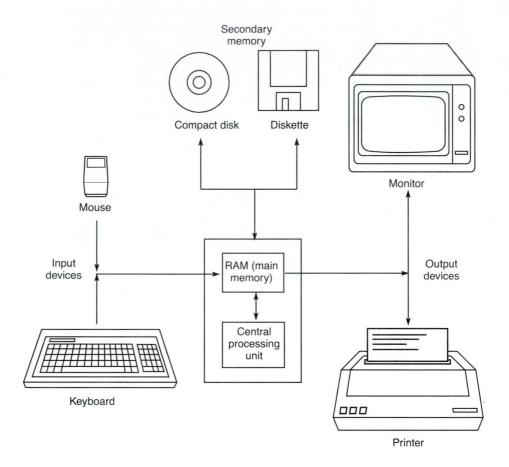

Figure 1.3 Hardware Components of a Computer

Imagine the memory of a computer as an ordered sequence of storage locations called *memory cells*. To be able to store and retrieve (access) information, there must be some way to identify the individual memory cells. To accomplish this, each memory cell has associated with it a unique *address*, which indicates its relative position in memory. Figure 1.4 shows a computer memory consisting of 1000 memory cells with addresses 0 through 999. Today's personal computers often have several million individual cells. Main memory—RAM—is conventionally measured in *megabytes,* where one megabyte is approximately one million cells.

The information stored in a memory cell is called the *contents* of a memory cell. Every memory cell always contains some information, although we may have no idea what that information is. Whenever new information is placed in a memory cell, any information that is already there is destroyed and can no longer be retrieved. In Fig. 1.4 the contents of memory cell 3 is the number –26, and the contents of memory cell 4 is the letter H.

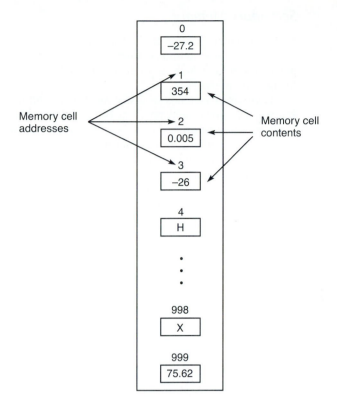

Figure 1.4   A Computer Memory with 1000 Cells

Although not shown in the figure, a memory cell can also contain a program instruction. The ability to store programs as well as data in the same physical memory is called the *stored program concept,* first developed by John von Neumann. A program's instructions must be loaded into main memory before that program can be executed. The great benefit of a stored program computer is that its operation can be changed by simply loading a different program into memory.

A memory cell as shown in Fig. 1.4 is actually a grouping of smaller units called *bytes*. A byte is the amount of storage required to store a single character. The number of bytes in a memory cell depends on the kind of information stored in that cell and varies from computer to computer. A byte is an aggregate of an even smaller unit of storage called a bit; a *bit* is a binary digit (0 or 1). In most computers, there are eight bits to a byte.

Each value stored in memory is represented by a particular pattern of 0s and 1s. To store a value, the computer sets each bit of a selected memory cell to 0 or 1, thereby destroying what was previously in that bit. Each value is represented by a particular pattern of 0s and 1s. To retrieve a value from a memory cell, the computer copies the pattern of 0s and 1s stored in that cell to another area where the bit pattern can be processed. The copy operation does not destroy the bit pattern that is currently in the memory cell. The process described above is the same regardless of the kind of information—character, number, or program instruction—stored in a memory cell.

Secondary Memory

Most computers have a limited amount of main memory. Consequently, *secondary memory* provides additional storage capability on most computer systems. For example, a *disk drive,* which stores data on a disk, is a common secondary storage device for today's computers.

There are two kinds of disks: *hard disks* and *floppy disks* (sometimes called *diskettes*); a computer may have one or more drives of each kind. A hard disk cannot normally be removed from its drive, so the storage area on a hard disk is often shared by all users of a computer. On the other hand, each computer user may have his or her own floppy disks that can be inserted in a disk drive as needed. Hard disks can store much more data than floppy disks and operate much more quickly, but they are also much more expensive. Floppy disks are called "floppy" because the actual recording surface is a flexible piece of magnetically coated plastic.

The currently popular 3.5-inch-diameter floppy disks are encased in a hard plastic outer shell to protect them from damage. The older 5.25-inch-diameter disks, which are rapidly disappearing from the scene, were encased in a (usually) black sealed envelope of heavy paper or flexible plastic. One inexperienced user once called the university's computer support organization to report that files were repeatedly disappearing from the floppy disk. On arriving at the user's office, the support technician immediately noticed that the user was keeping the disk from getting lost by sticking it to a metal file cabinet with magnets. Of course, the magnets erased the data on the disk. This user was not unintelligent, merely inexperienced, and had never been told not to use magnets near a floppy disk!

Many types of information can be stored on disk, for example, a term paper, a computer program, payroll data from a business, or data from earthquake seismic readings taken by a research center. Each of these collections of information is called a *file.* You must give a file a unique name when you first store it on a disk so that you can retrieve the file at a later date.

Comparison of Main and Secondary Memory

Main memory is much faster and more expensive than secondary memory. For example, a typical 3.5-inch floppy disk holds approximately one megabyte (1 million bytes) of data and costs less than a dollar. Currently, main memory comes in modules of up to 64 megabytes and costs several dollars per megabyte. At this writing, a personal computer hard disk can store several gigabytes (a gigabyte is a billion bytes) and costs a dollar or less per megabyte.

An increasingly popular form of memory is called *CD-ROM (compact disk read-only memory).* CD-ROMs are plastic disks similar to audio CDs. CD-ROMs are very inexpensive: a CD-ROM containing hundreds of megabytes of programs or other information may cost as little as a few dollars. The disadvantage of CD-ROMs is that your computer cannot store new information on them. This is why they are called "read-only."

New forms of secondary memory appear with increasing frequency. A Zip hardware unit costs about $100 and uses floppy disks with 100-megabyte capacity. Also, for a few hundred dollars you can purchase a writable compact disk unit, capable of storing, as well as reading, information on a CD.

The CPU normally transfers data between secondary memory and main memory; it manipulates the data in main memory only. Data in main memory are *volatile*: They disappear when you reset or switch off the computer. Data in secondary memory are *nonvolatile:* They do not disappear when the computer is switched off and are magnetically "erased" only by a program operating under an explicit command from the user. You can remove a floppy disk from the computer and set it aside for later use; the data will remain on the disk until explicitly erased.

Central Processing Unit

The CPU has two roles: coordinating all computer operations, and performing arithmetic and logical operations on data. The CPU follows the instructions contained in a program which has been loaded into memory. These instructions specify which operations should be carried out and in what order; the control unit then transmits coordinating control signals to the computer components. For example, if the instruction requires reading a data item, the CPU sends the necessary control signals to the input device.

To process a program stored in memory, the CPU retrieves each instruction in sequence (*fetches* the instruction), interprets (*decodes*) the instruction to determine what should be done, and then retrieves any data necessary to carry out that instruction. Next, the CPU performs the actual manipulation of the data it retrieves from memory (*executes* the instruction). Finally, the CPU can store the results of these manipulations back in memory for later use.

The CPU can perform such arithmetic operations as addition, subtraction, multiplication, and division. It can also compare the contents of two memory cells, for example, to determine which is the larger value or to determine whether the two values are equal. On the basis of the result of the comparison, the CPU can make a simple *decision* about which instruction to execute next. The ability to make simple decisions is the basis of a computer's real power.

A typical modern CPU can perform each operation in much less than one millionth of a second.

Input and Output Devices

We use *input/output (I/O)* devices to communicate with the computer. Specifically, they allow us to enter data for a computation into memory and to observe the results of the computation.

You will be using a *keyboard* (see Fig. 1.5) as an input device and a *monitor* or *display screen* as an output device. When you press a key on the keyboard, a binary-coded version of that character is sent to main memory and is also displayed (*echoed*) on the monitor at the position of the *cursor,* a moving place marker. A computer keyboard resembles a typewriter keyboard except that it has some extra keys for performing special functions. On the keyboard shown in Fig. 1.5, the row of keys at the top (labeled F1 through F12) are *function keys*. The function performed by each of these keys depends on the program that is executing.

Another common input device is a *mouse*. This is a device you hold in your hand, moving it around a pad on your desk. Several different mechanisms are used for mice. In one common one, as you move the mouse, a rubber ball attached to its bottom rotates, causing small rollers inside the mouse to send a signal to the computer. The

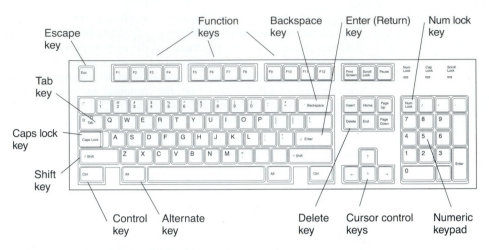

Figure 1.5 A Computer Keyboard

computer then moves the *mouse cursor* (normally a small box or arrow) around the screen to follow your hand motion. You select an operation by moving the mouse cursor to a particular word or picture, then pressing (*clicking*) a button on the mouse.

Humorous stories abound regarding new users' inexperience with using a mouse. In one case, a user picked up the mouse, pointed it at the computer screen, and clicked the button. This user, reasoning from experience with TV remote-control devices, was quite surprised when the computer did not respond. Another story tells of a user who placed the mouse on the floor, then stepped on the button without moving the mouse. This user was evidently thinking of the mouse as being similar to the foot pedal that comes with a sewing machine. These stories, funny as they are, are worth remembering as further examples of the observation that "inexperience does not equate to stupidity."

A *trackball* is a variant of a mouse that is commonly installed on laptop computers. The rotating ball is fixed in place on the keyboard; you roll it with your fingertip. An even newer mouse variant is the *trackpad*, a touch-sensitive pad built into the lower edge of the keyboard; you move the cursor by simply moving your fingertip across the pad.

A *monitor* is similar to a television screen. It provides a temporary display of the information that appears on the screen. If you want paper, or *hard-copy,* output, you must send your computational results to an output device called a *printer*.

Computer Networks

Often, several individual computers are interconnected as a *computer network*. The network usually comprises a number of personal computers or workstations, one or more central *file servers,* each with a very large hard disk, and perhaps a high-quality central *print server*. Many computer laboratories arrange their computers in a network.

You have probably heard of the *Internet*. This is a huge network of networks, interconnecting most university computers all over the world and many business, government, and individually owned computers as well. The Internet provides many very large file servers, as well as electronic bulletin boards and mail services. The Internet is a fascinating, ever-changing collection of resources, and if you have access to it, you will enjoy sending messages to friends in far-away places, looking up source material in libraries, and bringing interesting programs and other files into the computer you are using.

A risk in using the Internet is that you will become "hooked" on it, spending so much time "net surfing" that you neglect other work. Be careful! Also keep in mind that the Internet is the only medium in which *anyone* can be a publisher. Since there is no reliable way to sort out good information from useless information or outright lies, you must learn how to evaluate what you read on the Internet. Don't be misled into thinking that because it's on the Web, it must be true!

Discussion

By the time you read this book, new computers, new kinds of secondary memory, and new input/output devices will have emerged on the market, and prices will have dropped enough to make our price indications obsolete. It might seem that the changes are too frequent for mere humans to follow, but in fact, the basic hardware structure of a computer remains: A computer consists of main and secondary memory, a CPU, and input/output devices. If you keep this in mind, you will able to keep the amazing technological changes in perspective.

EXERCISES FOR SECTION 1.2

Self-Check

1. What are the contents of memory cells 0 and 999 in Fig. 1.4? What memory cells contain the letter X and the fraction 0.005?

2. Explain the purpose of the memory, CPU, and disk drive and disk. What input and output devices will be used with your computer?

1.3 Computer Software

Like computer hardware, software is changing rapidly, and categorizations are increasingly blurry. On the other hand, it is usually workable to divide software into *operating systems, application programs,* and *software development tools.*

Operating Systems

Some of you will be using a time-shared computer. In this environment many users are connected by terminals to one large, central computer, and all users share the central facilities.

Many of you will be using a personal computer. A personal computer is a smaller, desktop computer that is used by one individual at a time. Personal computers are often connected together in a computer network. Regardless of what computer you are using, it will be necessary to interact with a supervisory program that is within the computer called the *operating system (OS)*. In time-shared computers, it is the responsibility of the operating system to allocate the central resources among many users. Some tasks of the operating system are:

- validating the user's identification and password;

- making application programs and software development tools available to users;

- allocating memory and processor time;

- providing input and output facilities;

- retrieving needed files; and

- saving new files.

The operating system on a personal computer performs these tasks as well; the only difference is that often there is no user validation. In a computer network, managing the communication among the various computers and devices is an operating system responsibility.

Some of today's commonly used operating systems are:

- Macintosh OS, developed by Apple Computer and currently available only on Apple's own Macintosh computers;

- Windows 95, Windows 98, and Windows NT, developed by Microsoft and installed on computers from many companies using CPUs based on an Intel design;

- MS-DOS, an older Microsoft design whose use is declining in favor of the Windows variants; and

- UNIX, developed in the 1970s by Bell Laboratories and the University of California at Berkeley and currently available in many variants, including Sun's Solaris, Tenon's MachTen, Hewlett-Packard's HP/UX, IBM's AIX, Silicon Graphics' IRIX, and several freely distributed ones such as FreeBSD, BSD386, and Linux.

Application Programs

An application program is simply one we use directly to do some work on a computer. Word processors, spreadsheet programs, electronic-mail handlers, World Wide Web browsers, music composition programs, and computer games are all examples of applications. So are programs for power plant control, automatic teller machines, grocery checkout, and automobile fuel management and antilock braking. These programs have an amazing variety of purposes, but they all use services provided by an operating system, and they were all developed by using a special category of applications called software development tools.

Software Development Tools

A software development tool is an application program whose purpose is to aid a software developer in producing other programs. You will probably use the following software development tools in connection with this book:

- the *editor* or *interactive development environment* to enter or modify a program;

- the *compiler* to translate your program into hardware instructions;

- the *binder/linker* to link your program together with other modules to form an executable whole; and

- the *debugger* to help you find errors that arise from the execution of your program.

Discussion

When mainframes were the only computers in existence, the operating system and software tools were generally supplied by the builder of the hardware. This was called *bundling*. At that time, therefore, most people viewed software tools as a part of the OS. More recently, however, the software industry has grown independently of the hardware industry, and there is active competition in the production of programs of all kinds. Since the software on a given computer now generally comes from a variety of sources—preinstalled when you buy the computer, purchased separately, installed from a CD collection, or downloaded from the Internet—it is obvious that software development tools are just a special kind of application.

Having completed our general introduction to computer history, hardware, and software, we can move on to the specific focus of this book, namely, software development and the problem-solving process that is so essential to effective software.

EXERCISE FOR SECTION 1.3

Self-Check

1. Explain the different categories of software and give examples of each.

1.4 Problem Solving and Programming

Computer problem-solving ability is a combination of art and science, the transformation of a description—in English or another human language—of a problem into a form that permits a mechanical solution and the implementation of that solution on a computer. A relatively straightforward example of this process is transforming a word problem into a set of algebraic equations that can then be solved for one or more unknowns.

Most problems are not so easily solved. The problem-solving process is more difficult because problem descriptions are often incomplete, imprecise, or ambiguous. The successful problem solver needs to learn the following skills:

1. Ask the right questions to clarify the problem and obtain any information that is missing from the problem statement (this process is called *problem specification*).

2. Analyze the problem, attempting to extract its essential features and identify what is provided (the *problem inputs*) and what is required (the *problem outputs*).

3. Determine whether there are any *constraints* or *simplifying assumptions* that can be applied to facilitate the problem solution. We often cannot solve the most general case of a problem but must make some realistic assumptions that limit or constrain the problem so that it can be solved.

4. Apply knowledge of the problem environment and the formulas or equations that characterize it, to develop a series of steps whose successful completion will lead to the problem solution, eventually implementing or *coding* these steps in a form that can be submitted to a computer.

5. Once the solution is obtained, verify its accuracy by developing and carrying out a plan for testing it.

1.5 The Software Development Method

Students in many subject areas receive instruction in specific problem-solving methods. For example, business students are encouraged to follow a *systems approach* to problem solving; engineering and science students are encouraged to follow the *engineering and scientific method*. Although these problem-solving methods are associated with very different fields of study, their essential ingredients are quite similar. We will describe one such method below.

This book is concerned with a particular kind of problem solving, namely, developing solutions that use computers to get results. We mentioned earlier that a computer cannot think; therefore, to get it to do any useful work, we must provide a computer with a program that is a list of instructions. Programming a computer is a lot more involved than simply writing a list of instructions. Problem solving is an important component of programming. Before we can write a program to solve a particular problem, we must consider carefully all aspects of the problem and then organize its solution.

A *software developer* is someone who is involved with the design and implementation of reliable software systems. This title emphasizes the fact that programmers, like engineers, are concerned with developing practical, reliable solutions to problems. However, the product that a software developer produces is a software system rather than a physical system.

To highlight the analogy with engineering, some people refer to this method as *software engineering* and to software developers as *software engineers*. To emphasize the fact that one need not be an actual engineer or even an engineering student to develop good software, we instead use the terms *software development* and *software developer* in this book.

Steps in the Software Development Method

Software can be complicated, so software development requires the developer to use a methodical working style. Details of different methods vary somewhat, but these methods have in common that they are systematic, step-by-step approaches. The software development method that is used in this book is typical of the methods used in industry. Here are the major steps:

1. *Problem specification*: State the problem and gain a clear understanding of what is required for its solution. This sounds easy, but it can be the most critical part of problem solving. A good problem solver must be able to recognize and define the problem precisely. If the problem is not totally defined, you must study the problem carefully, eliminating the aspects that are unimportant and zeroing in on the root problem.

2. *Analysis*: Identify problem inputs, desired outputs, and any additional requirements of or constraints on the solution. Identify what information is supplied as problem data and what results should be computed and displayed. Also, determine the required form and units in which the results should be displayed (for example, as a table with specific column headings).

3. *Design*: Develop a list of steps (called an *algorithm*) to solve the problem and verify that the algorithm solves the problem as intended. Writing the algorithm is often the most difficult part of the problem-solving process. Once you have the algorithm, you should verify that it is correct before proceeding further.

4. *Test plan*: Develop a strategy for proving to yourself and to others that your algorithm will get the proper results. It is highly advisable to write a plan for testing the program you will write, even before you have written it. Which test cases will you choose? What are the special cases that must be tested? Pretend you are a potential purchaser of the program and ask, "Which tests would I require to be convinced that this program behaves as advertised?"

5. *Implementation or coding*: Implement the algorithm as a program. This requires knowledge of a particular programming language. Each algorithm step must be converted into a statement in that programming language.

6. *Testing*: Run the completed program, testing it with the test cases specified in the test plan.

If the first three steps in the list above are not done properly, you will either solve the wrong problem or produce an awkward, inefficient solution. To perform these steps successfully, it is most important that you read the problem statement carefully before attempting to solve it. You may need to read each problem statement two or three times. The first time, you should get a general idea of what is being asked. The second time, you should try to answer the questions:

- What information should the solution provide?

- What data do I have to work with?

The answer to the first question will tell you the desired results, or the *problem outputs*. The answer to the second question will tell you the data provided, or the *problem inputs*. It may be helpful to underline the phrases in the problem statement that identify the inputs and outputs.

As was indicated above, the design phase is often the most difficult part of the problem-solving process. When you write an algorithm, you should first list the major steps of the problem that need to be solved (called *subproblems*). Don't try to list each and every step imaginable; instead, concentrate on the overall strategy. Once you have the list of subproblems, you can attack each one individually, adding detail or *refining the algorithm*. The process of solving a problem by breaking it up into its smaller subproblems, called *divide and conquer*, is a basic strategy for all kinds of problem solving activities.

If you do not develop a proper test plan, you risk just running the program with casually chosen inputs, thereby missing important test cases which, should they arise after the program is completed and delivered, may cause the program to fail unexpectedly. A program's behavior must be, to the greatest extent possible, *predictable,* even if the user makes errors in operating it.

The *principle of predictable performance* requires that a test plan should include cases of "bad" as well as "good" input. An especially tragic, and true, story of unpredictable software is a certain radiation machine that, in treating several cancer patients, responded to some unexpected operator keystrokes by giving the patients lethally high radiation dosages, killing them instead of treating their cancer.

The software development method can be used with any actual programming language; indeed, only the implementation phase really requires detailed knowledge of a language or a particular computer. Even the testing phase is, in industry, often carried out by individuals who do not know programming but specialize in developing good tests of programs.

In this book you will see numerous examples of the software development method, with each step spelled out in some detail. To get us started, here is an example of the method applied to a real-life problem. This illustrates that while our method is especially useful in developing software, the systematic, step-by-step approach is certainly not limited to software development.

CASE
STUDY

CHANGING A FLAT TIRE

Problem Specification
You are driving a car with two friends and suddenly get a flat tire. Fortunately, there is a spare tire and jack in the trunk.

Analysis
After pulling over to the side of the road, you might decide to subdivide the problem of changing a tire into the subproblems below.

Design
Here are the main steps in the algorithm to change a tire.

Algorithm
1. Loosen the lug nuts on the flat tire; don't remove them yet.

2. Get the jack and jack up the car.

3. Remove the lug nuts from the flat tire and remove the tire.

4. Get the spare tire, place it on the wheel, and tighten the lug nuts.

5. Lower the car.

6. Secure the jack and flat tire in the trunk.

Because these steps are relatively independent, you might decide to assign subproblem 1 to friend A, subproblem 2 to friend B, subproblem 3 to yourself, and so on. If friend B has used a jack before, the whole process should proceed smoothly; however, if friend B does not know how to use a jack, you need to refine step 2 further.

Step 2 Refinement
2.1. Get the jack from the trunk.

2.2. Place the jack under the car near the flat tire.

2.3. Insert the jack handle in the jack.

2.4. Place a block of wood under the car to keep it from rolling.

2.5. Jack up the car until there is enough room for the spare tire.

Step 2.4 requires a bit of decision making on your friend's part. Because the actual placement of the block of wood depends on whether the car is facing uphill or downhill, friend B needs to refine step 2.4.

Step 2.4 Refinement
2.4.1 If the car is facing uphill, then place the block of wood in back of a tire that is not flat; if the car is facing downhill, then place the block of wood in front of a tire that is not flat. This is actually a conditional action: One of two alternative actions is executed, depending on a certain condition.

Finally, step 2.5 involves a repetitive action: moving the jack handle until there is sufficient room to put on the spare tire. Often, people stop when the car is high enough to remove the flat tire, forgetting that an inflated tire requires more room. It may take a few attempts to complete step 2.5.

Step 2.5 Refinement

2.5.1. Move the jack handle repeatedly until the car is high enough off the ground that the spare tire can be put on the wheel.

Refined Algorithm

Here is the refined algorithm thus far. You can continue refining it until you are satisfied that every detail has been properly specified.

1. Loosen the lug nuts on the flat tire; don't remove them yet.

2. Get the jack and jack up the car.

   2.1. Get the jack from the trunk.

   2.2. Place the jack under the car near the flat tire.

   2.3. Insert the jack handle in the jack.

   2.4. Place a block of wood under the car to keep it from rolling.

      2.4.1. If the car is facing uphill, then place the block of wood in back of a tire that is not flat; if the car is facing downhill, then place the block of wood in front of a tire that is not flat.

   2.5. Jack up the car until there is enough room for the spare tire.

      2.5.1. Move the jack handle repeatedly until the car is high enough off the ground that the spare tire can be put on the wheel.

3. Loosen the lug nuts from the flat tire and remove the tire.

4. Get the spare tire, place it on the wheel, and tighten the lug nuts.

5. Lower the car.

6. Secure the jack and flat tire in the trunk.

The algorithm for changing a flat tire has three categories of action: *sequential execution, conditional execution,* and *repetition.* Sequential execution simply means to carry out steps 2.1 through 2.5 in the sequence listed. Step 2.4.1 illustrates conditional execution in that placement of the block of wood depends on the angle of inclination of the car. Step 1.5.1 illustrates repetition.

In general, the order of steps in an algorithm is very important. For example, the car cannot be lowered before it has been raised. Sometimes, there are several sequences for the steps in an algorithm, any one of which will produce a proper result, but in any case the steps cannot be written in a careless, arbitrary order. To succeed in software development, you must be willing to focus on solving problems in a careful, step-by-step fashion.

1.6   Programming Languages

Writing a computer program requires knowing a system of instructions for the computer. There are many such systems; these have come to be called *programming languages*. Like human languages (often called *natural languages* by computer people), programming languages have vocabularies—sets of acceptable words and grammars—and rules for combining words into larger units analogous to sentences and paragraphs.

There is an important distinction between programming languages and natural languages. Because a person can think, he or she can understand or "make sense" of another person's communication, even if the second person's grammar or usage is poor. Because a computer cannot think, it is far less tolerant of a programmer's poor grammar or usage and will usually stop and refuse to proceed until the errors are corrected. This is not as difficult as it may seem: Although natural languages grew over many centuries and are filled with irregularities and strange constructions, programming languages were *designed* by humans expressly to be consistent and regular and are therefore easier to learn and use than natural languages.

There are many different programming languages, which fall into three broad categories: machine, assembly, and high-level languages.

Machine Languages

Machine language is the native tongue of a computer. Each machine-language instruction is a *binary sequence* (string of 0s and 1s) that specifies an operation and the memory cells involved in the operation. Three instructions in a machine language might be:

```
0010 0000 0000 0100
0100 0000 0000 0101
0011 0000 0000 0110
```

Obviously, what is easiest for a computer to understand is most difficult for a person to understand and vice versa. Each type of central processor has its own system of machine instructions. The Motorola Power PC, the Intel Pentium, and the Sun SPARC are examples of different CPU types whose machine-language programs are *not* interchangeable.

Assembly Languages

Assembly language allows us to use descriptive names to reference data and instruction; however, each operation is typically a very small and specific one. The machine language above might have been written as

```
LOAD Cost
ADD Profit
STORE Price
```

in an assembly language. Generally, each assembly-language instruction represents one machine-language instruction for a specific type of computer. A program called an *assembler* is used to translate assembly language to machine language.

High-Level Languages

High-level languages (also called high-order languages, mostly by the U.S. government) are most often used by *programmers* (program writers). High-level languages are much easier to use than machine and assembly languages. A high-level language program is more *portable*. This means that it can be made to execute with little or no modification on many different types of computers.

Some common high-level languages are BASIC, FORTRAN, COBOL, Pascal, C, C++, Java, and Ada. Each of these languages was designed with a specific purpose in mind. FORTRAN is an acronym for FORmula TRANslation, and its principal users have been engineers and scientists. BASIC (Beginners All-purpose Symbolic Instructional Code) was designed in the 1960s to be learned and used easily by students. COBOL (COmmon Business Oriented Language) is used primarily for business data-processing operations. Pascal (named for Blaise Pascal) was designed in the early 1970s as a language for teaching programming. C (whose developers designed B first) combines the power of an assembly language with the ease of use and portability of a high-level language. C++ is an extension of C that supports object-oriented programming. Java is an object-oriented language that combines many of the aspects of C++ and Ada.

One of the most important features of high-level languages is that they allow us to write program statements that resemble human language or everyday mathematics. We can reference data that are stored in memory using descriptive names (e.g., `Name`, `Rate`) rather than numeric memory cell addresses. We can also describe operations that we would like performed using familiar symbols. For example, in several high-level languages the statement

```
Price = Cost + Profit
```

means add `Cost` to `Profit` and store the result in `Price`.

Because a computer can execute only programs that are in its machine language, a high-level language program must be converted or *translated* into machine language before it can be executed. A program called a *compiler* carries out the translation; sometimes, the compiler produces assembly language, which is then further translated by the assembler. The original high-level language program is called the *source program;* the resulting machine-language program is called the *object program*. Section 1.8 describes the steps required to process a high-level language program.

Armed with a general introduction to progrmming languages, we begin our study of one specific programming language: Ada 95.

EXERCISE FOR SECTION 1.6

Self-Check

1. What do you think the following high-level language statements mean?

```
X := A + B + C
X := Y / Z
D := C - B + A
```

1.7   About Ada

The name *Ada* honors Augusta Ada Byron (1815–1852), Countess of Lovelace, the daughter of the English poet Lord Byron. Ada assisted the computer pioneer Charles Babbage in "programming" his early machines; she is therefore sometimes credited with having been the first programmer. In learning Ada you will be learning a computer language that can be used equally well for teaching introductory programming concepts and for developing large practical computer systems. Programs in Ada are relatively easy to read, understand, and maintain (keep in good working order).

The richness of Ada is such that you are learning a language that can serve you very well throughout your career, no matter how large or complex the programs you will need to write. This book introduces you to a large and useful part of the language; you will undoubtedly learn the more advanced features as your experience and interest grows. The standard nature of Ada ensures that you will be able to use everything you learn in this book about Ada, regardless of the computer or Ada compiler you use.

Ada was developed in the late 1970s and early 1980s at the direction of the U.S. Department of Defense (DoD). Although it seems hard to believe, in the mid-seventies *several hundred languages* were in use in defense-oriented computer systems. DoD determined that the use of a modern and strongly standardized programming language might result in more reliable and portable software at lower cost to the taxpayer and therefore organized a competition for the best design of a new language for its needs.

The result of this competition was a language, designed by the French engineer Jean Ichbiah and his international team of language experts, that is rich in capabilities for building software systems for general as well as defense purposes.

Ada's Capabilities

The capabilities of high-level languages like Ada can be organized in a way similar to the way sections are titled in chapters of this book:

- *Control structures* are, as we discussed above, those structures that allow the programmer to instruct the computer precisely which operations to carry out in which order. In this book you will study all the important control structures of Ada.

- *Data structures* provide ways to organize data—numbers, letters, sequences of letters, records, and other groupings—so that they can be processed by the control structures of the program. Most of the data structures—*scalar types, records,* and *arrays*—of Ada are presented in this book.

- *System structures* provide ways to organize control structures and data structures into units of appropriate size so that systems of programs can be built reliably and without great difficulty. *Procedures* and *functions* allow grouping of data and control statements into small, cohesive units; *packages* allow procedures, functions, and other resources, such as data type declarations, to be organized into larger units or *modules* so that they can be put in libraries for you and others to use in many applications. We consider *exception handling* to be a system structure because exception handling provides a standard way to control the flow of error information from one part of a system to another.

The facilities of Ada also include *tasking*—a powerful capability for building *concurrent programs* (programs containing segments that execute, or appear to execute, simultaneously)—and *representation specifications*—which explicitly associate high-level constructs with the lowest levels of the computer hardware. Tasking is introduced briefly in Chapter 17; representation specifications do not appear in this book. You will learn about both subjects as you continue your education in this interesting language.

The Ada Standard

A *standard* is a document describing a common way to do or build something. Engineering standards developed early in the twentieth century covered the sizes and shapes of mechanical fasteners such as nuts and bolts. The ability to attach a nut from one manufacturer to a bolt from another was an important advance in the Industrial Revolution; the automobile industry owes much of the success of mass production to standards. Standards play a role in your own life, too. For example, because of standards, you can buy a replacement for a burned-out light bulb without worrying whether or not it will screw into the socket in your study lamp.

In the computer industry, standards have governed the formulation and dimensions of physical media such as punched cards and magnetic tape; as computer software has grown and matured since the 1940s, so has the industry's attention to standards for programming languages. A language standard describes the structure of valid and invalid programs in the language and therefore serves as a defining document for users and compiler writers alike.

Some language standards are voluntary and represent a "lowest common denominator" subset of the language facilities. The "subset" nature of these standards makes it difficult to move a program from one compiler to another, even if both theoretically accept the same language. The Ada standard is an exception to this rule: DoD, in the interest of encouraging programs to be written in a truly common language, irrespective of computer or compiler supplier, took measures accordingly.

The reference manual for Ada (usually abbreviated RM) was adopted by the American National Standard Institute (ANSI) in January 1983, and by the International Standards Organization (ISO) in 1987. By 1991, more than 400 different Ada compilers had been *validated,* which means that they successfully passed a series of several thousand small test programs (known as the Ada Compiler Validation Capability, or ACVC) designed to evaluate their conformance to the standard. This unusually high degree of conformance to a language standard means that Ada programs are usually quite easy to *port*, or move to a different compiler on the same computer or to a different computer. To an extent unprecedented in the history of computers, Ada compilers all accept the same language.

From Ada 9X to Ada 95

In 1988 the process was begun to determine whether the Ada standard should be revised to extend the language and, if so, to design the necessary extensions. This project was called "Ada 9X": the 9X designation meant that it was intended to be completed sometime in the 1990s. This time the design team was headed by the American Tucker Taft, a language expert at Intermetrics.

The Ada 9X standard was completed at the end of 1994, and the revised standard, now called Ada 95, was adopted in 1995 by ISO (February) and ANSI (April). Six or seven years may seem a long time to revise a language standard, but in fact, every other major language revision has taken even longer. Designing a language is complex and highly specialized, and convincing a large number of organizations to approve the design and vote favorably on a national or international standard is time-consuming and requires much skill in the art of human persuasion.

The Ada 95 extensions are very interesting and useful, and many of the new features will be covered in this book. These include, among others, many changes and additions to the standard libraries as well as language constructs for object-oriented programming. In fact, Ada 95 is the first internationally standardized object-oriented programming language.

This book introduces Ada 95 throughout. In the text we refer simply to Ada in most cases, using the terms Ada 83 and Ada 95 for those few situations in which we deem it important to distinguish between the earlier standard and the current one.

Ada's Use around the World

At this writing, Ada is being actively used by the defense software industry whose needs inspired Ada's creation. More directly relevant to you in your everyday lives, Ada is used in

- the control software of nearly every new commercial aircraft model, including the Boeing 777, the Airbus 340, and many regional airliners;

- nearly every country's air traffic control system;

- high-speed railroads, including the French TGV and the French/British Channel Tunnel system;

- urban rail systems, including those of Paris, London, Caracas, Cairo, Calcutta, and Hong Kong;

- electronic funds transfer and other banking applications;

- a number of communications and navigational satellites and ground-based equipment, including the Global Positioning System (GPS) navigational terminals now becoming popular in rental and private automobiles; and

- steel mills, industrial robotics, medical electronics, and telecommunications.

These software applications share a common attribute: They are less visible than those running on your desktop computer, but they are of vital importance in the smooth, safe operation of our transportation, communication, and business systems. Many of these are called *safety-critical* software systems: They *must* function properly because lives and property are at stake.

As it happens, the same language attributes that make Ada a language of choice in these important systems also make it a desirable language for education. Whether or not you actually write defense or safety-critical software in your career, your knowledge of Ada will serve you well, providing a solid foundation for further knowledge of other languages and many application areas.

1.8 Processing a High-Level Language Program

Before it can be processed, a high-level language program must be entered at the terminal, then translated, and finally loaded into memory for execution. As was discussed in Section 1.3, a number of *software development tools*—programs that help us develop other programs—assist in this task. These are described next, and the process is summarized in Fig. 1.6.

The mechanics of entering a program as a source file and translating and executing it differ somewhat from system to system, although the general process is the same. In this section we describe this general process.

Each computer has its own special control language for communicating with its operating system. In many common systems, such as the Apple Macintosh, Microsoft Windows, or X-windows, the line-oriented command language is replaced by a *graphical user interface (GUI),* in which you select operations from menus, using a mouse to do the selection. Although space does not allow us to provide all the details here, we will discuss the general process. Your instructor will provide the specific commands for your system.

Logging On or Booting Up

Before you can use a time-shared or networked computer, you must *log on,* that is, identify yourself to the operating system, which may check to determine that you have a valid account on the system. To use a personal computer, you must switch it on, then wait for a brief period while it starts, or *boots up*. The startup process begins with a very small program that loads the operating system. Because one small program loads the next, the process is called *booting up,* from the expression "picking yourself up by your bootstraps."

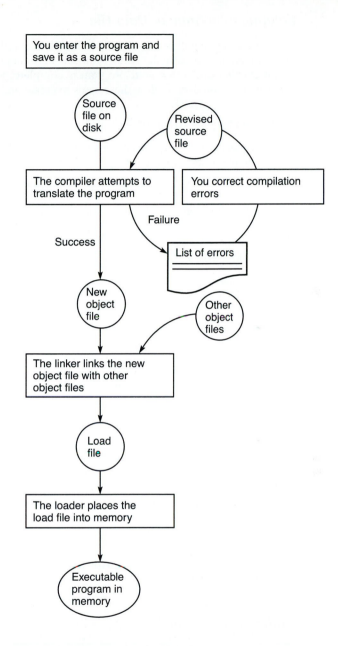

Figure 1.6 Preparing a Program for Execution

Creating a Program or Data File

In most cases you will use a software tool called an *editor* to enter or modify your Ada program. After accessing the editor, you can start to enter a new Ada program, or modify an existing one. Once your program is complete, you must save the program as a permanent file on disk. Follow these steps to create and save a program file:

1. access the editor program;

2. indicate that you are creating a new file and specify its name, or specify the name of the existing program to be modified;

3. enter each line of your program, or make the necessary changes; and

4. save your program as a permanent file in secondary memory.

Compiling Your Program

Once you have created your program and you are satisfied that each line is entered correctly, you can attempt to compile it. Some Ada compilers require that before you can use the compiler for the first time, you must set up a *project* or *library*. The command to do this depends on the specific compiler, and it is not repeated each time you log on or boot up. The Ada system will create some files or directories on your file system; they are for use by the compiler and linker, and you should not disturb them!

If your program will not compile because it contains errors, the compiler produces a list of errors for your information. You must reedit the program to eliminate the errors before going further. Follow these steps to correct and reexecute a program file:

1. reaccess the editor program;

2. get your program file;

3. correct those statements that contained errors;

4. save your edited program file; and

5. compile the saved program file.

When the source program is error-free, the compiler saves its machine-language translation as an object file.

Binding and Linking

Your next step is to call the *binder* program (sometimes called *linker*) to combine your object program with additional object files needed for your program to execute. These may be system files, such as input/output modules, or other application modules (*packages,* in Ada terms) that you or others have written. Generally, the binder needs only to be told the name of your main program; it then proceeds to save the final result as a *load file,* or *executable program,* on disk.

Executing a Program

Once a program has been linked into an executable file, you can execute it repeatedly. Depending on your operating system, you either just type the name of the program, or select it from a menu of programs. Doing this actually invokes an operating system module called the *loader,* which copies the program from secondary storage to RAM and then the CPU executes the program.

In executing a program, the CPU examines each program instruction in memory and sends out the command signals required to carry out the instruction. Although the instructions are normally executed in sequence, as we will see later, it is possible to have the control unit skip over some instructions or execute some instructions more than once.

During execution, data can be entered into memory and manipulated in some specified way. Special program instructions are used for requesting the user to enter *input data,* then reading the data into memory. After some manipulation of the input data, instructions are used for displaying or printing result values—*program output*—from memory.

Figure 1.7 shows the effect of executing a payroll program stored in memory. The first step of the program requires entering data into memory that describe the employee. In the second step, the employee data are manipulated by the central processor and the results of computations are stored in memory. In the final step, the computational results may be displayed as payroll reports or employee payroll checks.

EXERCISES FOR SECTION 1.8

Self-Check

1.   What is the role of a compiler?

2.   What is the difference between the source file and the object file? Which do you create and which does the compiler create? Which one is processed by the linker? What does the loader do?

1.9   A Step-by-Step Compilation Exercise

Now that you have read about the steps in creating, compiling, and executing a program file, you probably want to try one. After getting the detailed instructions for using your computer, operating system, and Ada compiler, try the program given in Program 1.1.

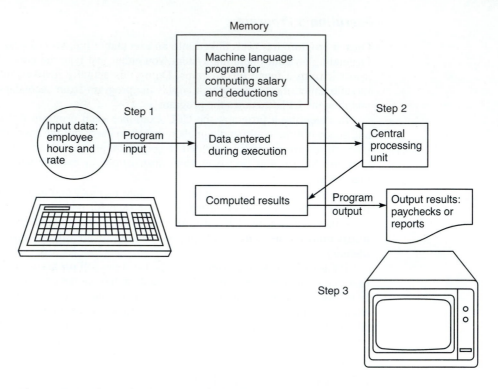

Figure 1.7 Flow of Information during Program Execution

Program 1.1 A First Ada Program

```
WITH Ada.Text_IO;
PROCEDURE Hello IS
-------------------------------------------------------------
--| A very simple program; it just displays a greeting.
--| Author: Michael Feldman, The George Washington University
--| Last Modified: June 1998
-------------------------------------------------------------
BEGIN -- Hello

  Ada.Text_IO.Put(Item => "Hello there. ");
  Ada.Text_IO.Put(Item => "We hope you enjoy studying Ada!");
  Ada.Text_IO.New_Line;

END Hello;
```

Do not be concerned at this point about what each of the statements in this program means; just enter it exactly as given (or copy it from a program distribution supplied with this book) and take it from there. Compile it, bind (link) it, and execute it. When the program is executed, the following line should appear on your display screen:

```
Hello there. We hope you enjoy studying Ada!
```

Listing Files

Compilers usually provide an option to create a *listing file* at the time of compilation. The listing file serves two important purposes:

1. It displays your source text, usually with line numbers, and identifies any errors the compiler may have found in your program;

2. It serves as an "official" record of the compilation, marked with the name of the compiler and the date and time of compilation. If you are taking a course, you may be required to submit listing files for your programming exercises or projects.

Find out how to request a listing file from your compiler, then recompile Program 1.1 and examine the listing by displaying or printing it. For example, Figure 1.8 shows a listing file from the author's compilation with GNAT.

Figure 1.8   Listing from an Error-Free Program Compilation

```
GNAT 3.10p (970814)
Copyright 1992-1997 Free Software Foundation, Inc.

Compiling: hello.adb (source file time stamp: 1998-06-28 19:24:19)

 1. WITH Ada.Text_IO;
 2. PROCEDURE Hello IS
 3. -------------------------------------------------------------
 4. --| A very simple program; it just displays a greeting.
 5. --| Author: Michael Feldman, The George Washington University
 6. --| Last Modified: June 1998
 7. -------------------------------------------------------------
 8. BEGIN -- Hello
 9.
10.    Ada.Text_IO.Put(Item => "Hello there. ");
11.    Ada.Text_IO.Put(Item => "We hope you enjoy studying Ada!");
12.    Ada.Text_IO.New_Line;
13.
14. END Hello;

14 lines: No errors
```

Examining the Program

Let us briefly go through the listing file in Fig. 1.8 to get a quick idea of the structure of this program.

Line 1 informs the compiler that this program will be making use of a *package* called Ada.Text_IO. A statement like this almost always precedes the rest of an Ada program file. A fuller explanation of packages will appear in the next few chapters; for now you should know that input and output are done in Ada by means of standard packages. Ada.Text_IO is the most used standard package.

Line 2 informs the compiler that this program is to be called `Hello` (in Ada a program is called a PROCEDURE). Lines 3 through 7 are *comments,* or remarks for the human reader of the program. Comments are not processed by the compiler. The start of a comment is indicated by `--`, that is, by two hyphens; the comment always includes all remaining text on that line. Note, for example, that line 8 has a comment following the initial BEGIN.

Lines 9 and 13 are left blank just to make the program easier to read. The section of the program between BEGIN (line 8) and END (line 14), called the *body,* or *executable statements section,* contains a list of actions the program is to perform. Each *statement* or action ends with a semicolon. In this program there are three statements, all calling for *output* actions. The statements in lines 10 and 11,

```
Ada.Text_IO.Put(Item => "Hello there. ");
Ada.Text_IO.Put(Item => "We hope you enjoy studying Ada!");
```

display the strings enclosed in quotes on the screen. The statement in line 12,

```
Ada.Text_IO.New_Line;
```

terminates the line displayed on the screen by advancing the *cursor* (a blinking place marker) to the first position of the next line. All these statements are prefixed by `Ada.Text_IO` as our way of indicating to the compiler (and to the reader of this program) that the operations in question are meant to be the ones provided by the `Ada.Text_IO` package. More about this later.

1.10 Tricks of the Trade: Common Programming Errors

One of the first things you will discover in writing programs is that a program often does not compile or run correctly the first time that it is submitted. When you are learning to develop programs, you will probably make mistakes in your programs. Learning a programming language is a lot like learning another human language: There are rules of grammar, spelling and usage that you must learn. You will get better at it as your experience grows, but even very experienced developers make programming errors, and you should not be discouraged by the ones you make when you are starting out.

Programming errors are so common that they have their own special name—*bugs*—and the process of correcting them is called *debugging a program.* To alert you to potential problems, a section on common errors appears near the end of many chapters of this book.

There are three basic categories of errors:

- *Compilation errors* are detected and displayed by the compiler as it attempts to translate your program. Compilation errors are mistakes in following the language's rules of *syntax* (grammar) or *semantics* (meaning). If a statement has a compilation error, it cannot be translated and your program cannot be executed. When a compilation error is detected, an *error message* appears in your listing file indicating that you have made a mistake and what the cause of the error might be. As you gain some experience, you will become more proficient at understanding error messages.

- *Run-time errors* are detected during execution of a program. A run-time error, called an *exception* in Ada, occurs as a result of directing the computer to perform an illegal or inappropriate operation, such as dividing a number by 0 or attempting to store in a variable a number that is outside the acceptable range for that variable. When an exception is raised—that is, when an error occurs—the computer stops executing your program and a diagnostic message is displayed that sometimes indicates the line of your program where the exception was raised. One of the interesting features of Ada is that it provides a way for programmers to predict the occurrence of exceptions and to *handle* them when they arise. In this manner a programmer can prevent the computer from halting the program. We will return later to the matter of handling exceptions in programs.

- *Logic* or *algorithm* errors result from developing an incorrect algorithm to solve a problem or translating a correct algorithm into a program incorrectly. These are errors in problem solving rather than programming. Such errors cannot be detected automatically—because the program compiles successfully and runs without terminating on an error message—but gets an incorrect or unexpected answer. The computer did exactly what you told it, which was not necessarily what you meant for it to do! Detecting and correcting logic errors can be done only by careful and thorough testing.

In this section we will limit our discussion to compilation errors; we will take up the other categories later.

Syntax Errors

Program 1.2 shows a program similar to `Hello` but containing three *syntax errors* that we have intentionally put in the file. A syntax error is a mistake in the use of the language's *syntax,* or rules of grammar.

Program 1.2 A Program with Syntax Errors

```
WITH Ada.Text_IO;
PROCEDURE Hello_Syntax IS
------------------------------------------------------------
--| A very simple program; it just displays a greeting.
--| Author: Michael Feldman, The George Washington University
--| Last Modified: June 1998
------------------------------------------------------------
BEGIN -- Hello_Syntax

  Ada.Text_IO.Put(Item => "Hello there. ");
  Ada.Text_IO.Put(Item => "We hope you enjoy studying Ada!");
  Ada.Text_IO.New_Line

EMD Hello_Syntax;
```

Figure 1.9 shows the relevant part of the listing file generated by GNAT.

Figure 1.9 Listing from a Program with Syntax Errors

```
 1. WITH Ada.Text_IO;
 2. PROCEDURE Hello_Syntax IS
 3. -----------------------------------------------------------------
 4. --| A very simple program; it just displays a greeting.
 5. --| Author: Michael Feldman, The George Washington University
 6. --| Last Modified: June 1998
 7. -----------------------------------------------------------------
 8. BEGIN -- Hello_Syntax
 9.
10.    Ada.Text_IO.Put(Item => "Hello there. ");
11.    Ada.Text_IO.Put(Item => "We hope you enjoy studying Ada!";
                                                                |
       >>> missing ")"

12.    Ada.Text_IO.New_Line
                            |
       >>> missing ";"

13.
14. EMD Hello_Syntax;
       |
       >>> incorrect spelling of keyword "END"
```

The actual format of the listing and error messages produced by your compiler may differ from Fig. 1.9. In this GNAT listing, whenever an error is detected, the compiler inserts a line starting with >>>. A vertical line (|) points to the position in the preceding line where the error was detected. This is usually, but not always, where the error occurred. The error is explained on the next line.

In attempting to compile this program, the compiler discovered that:

- in line 11, a left parenthesis is not matched by a corresponding right parenthesis;

- in line 12, a semicolon is missing at the end of the statement on that line;

- in line 14, END is misspelled as EMD.

The nature of these errors highlights an essential difference between human communication in languages like English and programming in languages like Ada. In human communication a speaker or writer sometimes makes grammatical errors, but the listener or reader can usually understand the content anyway. In programming languages the rules of grammar are much simpler than those of human languages, but they must be observed exactly.

A compiler is designed to discover syntax errors and does so mechanically and slavishly, without emotion. The compiler is just a program, and can process only what you submit to it. It has no idea what you *meant* to write, and so while it is quite good at discovering errors, it often guesses imperfectly at the desired correction. In this example we were lucky and the messages were obvious.

One of the purposes of this book is to teach you the syntax of Ada little by little. You'll see a lot of correct examples and read *syntax displays* that state the rules. You'll find that—as with the human languages you know—as your experience with programming grows, you'll know more and more syntax and make fewer and fewer errors.

Semantic Errors

In Program 1.3 we have properly followed the syntax rules—rules of punctuation, keyword spelling, and "word order"—but have intentionally coded two *semantic errors*, or errors in meaning. A semantic error is an inconsistency in the use of values, variables, packages, and so on.

Program 1.3 A Program with Semantic Errors

```
WITH Ada.Text_IO;
PROCEDURE Hello_Semantic IS
----------------------------------------------------------------
--| A very simple program; it just displays a greeting.
--| Author: Michael Feldman, The George Washington University
--| Last Modified: June 1998
----------------------------------------------------------------
BEGIN -- Hello_Semantic

  Ada.Text_IO.Put(Item => 12345);
  Ada.Text_IO.Put(Item => "We hope you enjoy studying Ada!");
  Ada.Txt_IO.New_Line;

END Hello_Semantic;
```

Figure 1.10 shows the listing, with the errors indicated by the compiler.

Figure 1.10 Listing from a Program with Semantic Errors

```
 1. WITH Ada.Text_IO;
 2. PROCEDURE Hello_Semantic IS
 3. ------------------------------------------------------------
 4. --| A very simple program; it just displays a greeting.
 5. --| Author: Michael Feldman, The George Washington University
 6. --| Last Modified: June 1998
 7. ------------------------------------------------------------
 8. BEGIN -- Hello_Semantic
 9.
10.   Ada.Text_IO.Put(Item => 12345);
                          |
      >>> invalid parameter list in call
      >>> possible missing instantiation of Text_IO.Integer_IO

11.   Ada.Text_IO.Put(Item => "We hope you enjoy studying Ada!");
12.   Ada.Txt_IO.New_Line;
          |
      >>> missing with for "Ada.Txt_IO"

13.
14. END Hello_Semantic;
```

Here the compiler discovered that:

- in line 10, we inadvertently provided an invalid parameter—a numerical one instead of the expected character string—to a procedure call;

- in line 12, we neglected to supply a WITH statement for the package `Ada.Txt_IO`. In this case, the compiler detected the error but guessed the wrong cause—We simply misspelled `Ada.Text_IO` as `Ada.Txt_IO`.

This last case shows how in programming, sometimes you make a certain error but the compiler interprets it as something entirely different. Remember, the compiler is only a computer program and is not as good a detective as you are! This can be frustrating at the start, but your skill at detective work will grow with experience.

Generally, the compiler will discover syntax errors, then stop the compilation and produce a listing file so that you can correct those. When you recompile, the compiler may then discover semantic errors it missed while it was checking the syntax.

Propagation Errors

Because the compiler cannot always determine the exact cause of an error, one syntax or semantic error sometimes leads to the generation of a number of error messages. (These "extra" errors are often called *propagation errors*.) It can be intimidating to look at a listing file containing dozens of error messages, but often all the messages really stem from just a couple of errors. For this reason, it is often a good idea to concentrate first on correcting the first one or two errors in a program and then to recompile, rather than to attempt to fix all the errors at once.

A Last Bit of Advice

This section's purpose has been to introduce you to the nature of compilation errors and the kinds of messages you can expect from your compiler. The Ada standard requires compilers to be "fussy"—to detect as many errors as possible before a program is executed. This "fussiness" may irritate you at first, but in fact, Ada programmers appreciate that once their programs are accepted by the compiler, they are very likely to execute properly. This helps them to develop software that *works*.

Finally, you must keep in mind that an operating system, compiler, or other computer program is *just* a computer program. It is very good at its mechanical job, but it has no real intelligence, and no emotions at all. Unlike a parent, teacher, or colleague, it will never get angry at you, but will continue slavishly to point out your mistakes in following its rules. We cannot emphasize too strongly that programming errors come from lack of experience—or lack of sleep—and not from "stupidity" or lack of ability.

CHAPTER REVIEW

This chapter described the basic components of a computer: main and secondary memory, the central processor or CPU, and the input and output devices. Remember these important facts about computers:

1. A memory cell is never empty, but its initial contents may be meaningless to your program.

2. The current contents of a memory cell are destroyed whenever new information is placed in that cell.

3. A program must be copied into the memory of the computer before it can be executed.

4. Data cannot be manipulated by the computer before they are first read into memory.

5. A computer cannot think for itself; you must use a programming language to instruct it in a precise and unambiguous manner to perform a task.

6. Programming a computer can be fun—if you are patient, organized, and careful.

Quick-Check Exercises

1. The _____ translates a _____ language program into _____.

2. After a program is executed, all program results are automatically displayed. True or false?

3. Specify the correct order for these four operations: execution, linking, translation, loading.

4. A high-level language program is saved on disk as a _____ file or a _____ file.

5. The _____ finds syntax errors in the _____ file.

6. A machine-language program is saved on disk as an _____ file.

7. The _____ is used to create and save the source file.

8. The _____ creates the load file.

9. The _____ program is used to place the _____ file into memory.

Answers to Quick-Check Exercises

1. Compiler, high-level, machine language

2. False

3. Translation, linking, loading, execution

4. Source, program

5. Compiler, source

6. Object

7. Editor

8. Linker

9. Loader, load

Review Questions

1. A computer can think. True or false?

2. List the three categories of programmming languages.

3. Give three advantages of programming in a high-level language such as Ada.

4. What processes are needed to transform an high-level language program to a machine-language program ready for execution?

5. List the five phases in the software development method. Which phases require actual use of a computer?

Programming Projects

1. This three-part project will help you to become familar with the development tools that are available to you.

   a. Find out how to use the software development tools on your computer. Compile, bind, and execute Program 1.1, and compile Programs 1.2 and 1.3 to see just how your compiler reports errors to you. Is there a listing file? A special window in the editor?

   b. Now use your editor to correct the errors in Programs 1.2 and 1.3. Recompile, bind, and execute these programs.

   c. Finally, use your editor to introduce some deliberate errors into Program 1.1. Don't be concerned that you don't know Ada yet; just try changing some of the statements. Compile your modified program and observe the messages.

CHAPTER 2

Introducing Algorithms: Adventures of the Spider

The purpose of this chapter is to introduce you to algorithms through programming a simple picture-drawing creature called the spider. This chapter is the first of several installments in a "continuing saga," an example that begins here and recurs in some sections of later chapters. We introduce an imaginary spider that steps around an imaginary room drawn on the screen. The spider recognizes a number of commands, which we can issue by writing, compiling, and executing spider programs.

We use the spider to introduce a number of algorithmic concepts, including control structures and parameters. We'll return to these much more formally and completely beginning in Chapter 3; the goal here is to just give you a quick introduction, to get you started writing some "fun" programs while you continue to read the more thorough chapters that follow.

This chapter and the other spider sections in the book are optional in the sense that no other parts of the book depend upon them. However, because they introduce programs that are very simple and clear and give you obvious feedback on the screen, we think you will find them useful in understanding algorithms and a number of Ada program constructs. We urge you to compile and run these examples on a computer, observe their behavior, and experiment with them by making changes as you see fit.

2.1 Introducing the Spider

This section introduces an imaginary spider that steps around an imaginary room drawn on the screen. The spider recognizes a number of commands, which we can issue by writing, compiling, and executing spider programs.

The spider is simulated by an Ada *package* within which is the set of commands that the spider recognizes and obeys. The package is a very important construct in Ada; it provides a way of *encapsulating,* or grouping, a set of related *operations.* Most Ada programs consist of a main procedure and a number of packages. We'll be using many packages in this book; some are standard Ada packages, and others are specific to the book. The spider package is one of the latter.

An Ada package is divided in two parts: the *interface* or *specification,* which gives a "table of contents" for the set of resources it provides, and the *implementation* or *body,* which contains the actual program segments for the various operations. Everything you need to know to *use* an Ada package is generally contained in the interface: There are specifications for the various resources and (in a well-written package) comments indicating how these are to be used.

The standard Ada packages are "built in," that is, provided with the compiler and ready to use. Generally, the interface and implementation for a nonstandard package like `spider` are provided in the form of two Ada source files; we assume that you have access to this book's packages on the computer you are using.

The `spider` specification is shown as Program 2.1 and explained in this chapter. We will study the body of the spider package in detail in Chapter 8. In this chapter, we just show and explain 14 programs that *use* some of the commands in the spider package; you don't need to understand yet just how the package works. By the time you've completed Chapter 8, you will be able to understand the spider package's internal mechanisms.

Before you can use the spider package, you must compile (but not link) both the specification and the body. If you have a collection of this book's programs available on disk or CD-ROM, now is a good time to find and compile the two files. File names are not part of the Ada standard, but some compilers require certain naming conventions. The Spider specification and body files will probably be called `spider.ads` and `spider.adb`, respectively (ads = Ada specification; adb = Ada body). but the file names may vary. You will also need to compile the package `screen`, whose file names are (most likely) `screen.ads` and `screen.adb`.

Program 2.1 The Spider Package

```
PACKAGE Spider IS
-----------------------------------------------------------------
--| This package provides procedures to emulate "Spider"
--| commands. The spider can move around
--| the screen drawing simple patterns.
--| Author: John Dalbey, Cal Poly San Luis Obispo, 1992
--| Adapted by M. B. Feldman, The George Washington University
--| Last Modified: December 1998
-----------------------------------------------------------------
   -- These are the spider's simple parameterless methods

   PROCEDURE Start;
   -- Pre:  None
   -- Post: Spider's room appears on the screen
   --    with spider in the center.

   PROCEDURE Quit;
   -- Pre:  None
   -- Post: End the drawing
```

```
    PROCEDURE Step;
    -- Pre:  None
    -- Post: Spider takes one step forward in the direction it is facing.
    -- Raises: Hit_the_Wall if spider tries to step into a wall.

    PROCEDURE TurnRight;
    -- Pre:  None
    -- Post: Spider turns 90 degrees to the right.

    -- now some types, and methods that use the types

    TYPE Directions IS (North, East, South, West);
    TYPE Colors     IS (Red, Green, Blue, Black, None);
    SUBTYPE Steps IS Integer RANGE 1..20;

    PROCEDURE Face (WhichWay: IN Directions);
    -- Pre:  WhichWay has been assigned a value
    -- Post: Spider turns to face the given direction.

    FUNCTION IsFacing RETURN Directions;
    -- Pre:  None
    -- Post: Returns the direction the spider is facing.

    FUNCTION RandomDirection RETURN Directions;
    -- Pre:  None
    -- Post: Returns a random direction

    PROCEDURE ChangeColor (NewColor: IN Colors);
    -- Pre:  NewColor has been assigned a value
    -- Post: Spider leaves its tracks in the new color

    FUNCTION IsPainting RETURN Colors;
    -- Pre:  None
    -- Post: Returns the color in which the spider is painting

    FUNCTION RandomColor RETURN Colors;
    -- Pre:  None
    -- Post: Returns a random color

    FUNCTION AtWall RETURN Boolean;
    -- Pre:  None
    -- Post: Returns True if the spider is standing next to a wall

    FUNCTION RandomStep RETURN Steps;
    -- Pre:  None
    -- Post: Returns a random number in the range 1..20

    Hit_The_Wall: EXCEPTION;

    TYPE Switch IS (On, Off);

    PROCEDURE Debug (Setting: IN Switch);
    -- Pre:  None
    -- Post: Turns on or off single stepping through the program.

    FUNCTION  Debugging RETURN Switch;
    -- Pre:  None
    -- Post: Returns on or Off depending on Debug setting

END Spider;
```

2.2 Straight-Line Algorithms

In this section we use the spider to introduce you to *straight-line algorithms*. A straight-line algorithm is one that is just a straight sequence of instructions, with no decisions or "forks in the road" and no backtracking to an earlier point in the algorithm. The algorithm just moves in one direction.

Let's look at a very simple spider program, Program 2.2. As you can see, it just calls the spider's start and stop commands. The sample run shows that calling `Spider.Start` draws a "room" on the screen, placing the spider icon (an asterisk) in the center. The spider starts out facing north (up the screen). Calling `Spider.Quit` just ends the program.

Program 2.2 The Simplest Spider Program

```
WITH Spider;
PROCEDURE Startup IS
------------------------------------------------------------------
--| Very simple Spider program; just starts and stops
--| Author: M. B. Feldman, The George Washington University
--| Last Modified: July 1998
------------------------------------------------------------------
BEGIN -- Startup
  Spider.Start;
  Spider.Quit;
END Startup;
```

Sample Run of Program 2.2

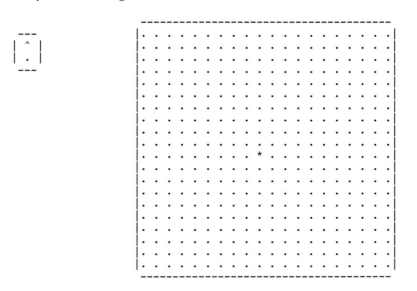

In Program 2.3 the spider takes five steps forward. You can see this from the five commands, each reading `Spider.Step`. The sample run shows the spider in a location five rows north (upward) from the starting point.

Program 2.3 The Spider Walks a Line

```
WITH Spider;
PROCEDURE Walk_Line IS
------------------------------------------------------------------
--| Walk line with spider
--| Author: M. B. Feldman, The George Washington University
--| Last Modified: July 1998
------------------------------------------------------------------

BEGIN -- Walk_Line

  Spider.Start;

  Spider.Step;
  Spider.Step;
  Spider.Step;
  Spider.Step;
  Spider.Step;

  Spider.Quit;

END Walk_Line;
```

Sample Run of Program 2.3

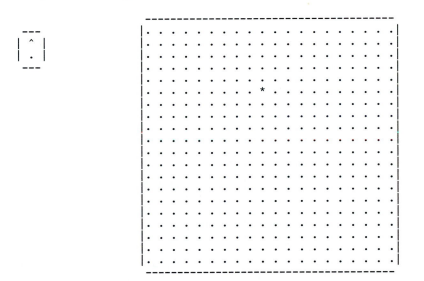

In Program 2.4 the spider walks around a square box, taking three steps forward, then turning right, then taking more steps, turning right again, and so on. Since it ends up back where it started from, there's nothing to show in the sample run. If you run the program, though, you'll observe the spider walking around the square.

Program 2.4 The Spider Walks around a Box

```
WITH Spider;
PROCEDURE Walk_Box IS
-----------------------------------------------------------------
--| Walk 4 x 4 box with spider
--| Author: M. B. Feldman, The George Washington University
--| Last Modified: July 1998
-----------------------------------------------------------------

BEGIN -- Walk_Box

  Spider.Start;

  Spider.Step;
  Spider.Step;
  Spider.Step;
  Spider.TurnRight;

  Spider.Step;
  Spider.Step;
  Spider.Step;
  Spider.TurnRight;

  Spider.Step;
  Spider.Step;
  Spider.Step;
  Spider.TurnRight;

  Spider.Step;
  Spider.Step;
  Spider.Step;
  Spider.TurnRight;

  Spider.Quit;

END Walk_Box;
```

Spider Commands with Parameters

So far, we've used four spider commands: `Start`, `Quit`, `Step`, and `TurnRight`. In Program 2.5 we introduce two more commands: `Face` and `ChangeColor`. Here are two lines selected from the specification in Program 2.1:

```
TYPE Directions IS (North, East, South, West);
TYPE Colors     IS (Red, Green, Blue, Black, None);
```

These lines introduce *enumeration types,* which we'll cover in more depth in Chapter 4. For now, just understand that each of these types provides a list of values: `Directions` gives the four compass points, and `Colors` gives five possibilities: red, green, blue, white, and no color at all. We come now to two *procedures* defined in the specification:

```
PROCEDURE Face (WhichWay: IN Directions);
-- Pre:  WhichWay has been assigned a value
-- Post: Spider turns to face the given direction.
```

```
PROCEDURE ChangeColor (NewColor: IN Colors);
-- Pre:  NewColor has been assigned a value
-- Post: Spider leaves its tracks in the new color
```

The first, `Face`, must be called by including a *parameter* selected from one of the directions, for example,

```
Spider.Face(WhichWay => Spider.West);
```

which will cause the spider to turn (without moving) to face in a westerly direction (leftward on the screen). The second procedure, `ChangeColor`, must be called with a parameter selected from one of the color values, for example,

```
Spider.ChangeColor(NewColor => Spider.Red);
```

which will cause the spider to leave a red mark on the screen each time it takes a step.

As with all the packages provided by this book, each operation is accompanied by a pair of comments. These, like all comments, are ignored by the compiler but are important parts of the documentation that a human reader needs. The first comment describes the *preconditions* for using the operation. Preconditions are the expectations or assumptions the operation makes about the way it is called. In this case the precondition warns us that the operations must be called with well-defined direction and color values. The second comment gives the *postconditions,* that is, the results after the operation has completed its work.

The combination of preconditions and postconditions serve as a kind of contract between the writer of an operation and its user; if the user promises to meet the preconditions, the writer promises that the operation will deliver the postconditions.

Now let's use these two operations. In Program 2.5 the spider walks around the same kind of square as in Program 2.4, but this time it "draws" each side in a different "color." We've put "color" in quotation marks because the spider package does not require a color monitor to operate properly. As you can see from the sample run, the spider uses the letters R, G, B, and K to simulate the actual colors red, green, blue, and black. Also, a dot simulates the no-color ("invisible") case; it does not show up on the screen because a new dot is displayed over the one in the room grid. You've probably guessed by now that the spider starts up leaving its tracks in the "none" color, that is, leaving no tracks.

Now is a good time to mention the small status box in the upper-left corner of the screen, which displays the spider's current direction and color.

Program 2.5 The Spider Draws a Box

```
WITH Spider;
PROCEDURE Draw_Box IS
-------------------------------------------------------------
--| Draw 4 x 4 box with spider, changing colors as we go
--| Author: M. B. Feldman, The George Washington University
--| Last Modified: July 1998
-------------------------------------------------------------

BEGIN -- Draw_Box

   Spider.Start;
```

```
          Spider.Face(WhichWay => Spider.West);

          Spider.ChangeColor(NewColor => Spider.Green);
          Spider.Step;
          Spider.Step;
          Spider.Step;
          Spider.TurnRight;

          Spider.ChangeColor(NewColor => Spider.Black);
          Spider.Step;
          Spider.Step;
          Spider.Step;
          Spider.TurnRight;

          Spider.ChangeColor(NewColor => Spider.Red);
          Spider.Step;
          Spider.Step;
          Spider.Step;
          Spider.TurnRight;

          Spider.ChangeColor(NewColor => Spider.Blue);
          Spider.Step;
          Spider.Step;
          Spider.Step;
          Spider.TurnRight;

          Spider.Quit;

     END Draw_Box;
```

Sample Run of Program 2.5

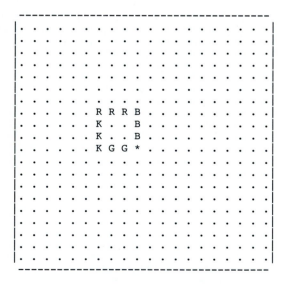

EXERCISES FOR SECTION 2.2

1.   Write a spider program that requests the spider to draw two of your initials on the screen. For example,

```
X     X  XXXXX              XXXXX      X
XX   XX  X                  X          X
XXX XXX  XXX        or      XXX        X
X  X  X  X                  X     X    X
X     X  X                  XXXXX XXXXX
```

2.3   Algorithms with Single Loops

Program 2.5 contains four sequences of almost identical statements. Leaving aside color changes for a moment, Program 2.5 contains sequences of the form

```
Spider.Step;
Spider.Step;
Spider.Step;
Spider.TurnRight;
```

This sequence appears four times in this straight-line program.

Algorithms quite frequently involve repetitive sequences of steps. Indeed, we could write the basic box-drawing algorithm as a *repetition:*

Algorithm for drawing a box:
1.   Repeat steps 1.1 and 1.2 four times.

    1.1   Take three steps forward.

    1.2   Turn right.

In programming, a repetition is generally called a *loop*. We can translate this algorithm into a program that uses an Ada control structure called the FOR construct. Program 2.6 contains just such a structure. The phrases

```
FOR Side IN 1..4 LOOP
```

and

```
END LOOP;
```

instruct the spider to repeat, four times, whichever statement or sequence of statements appears between them. These two phrases are said to *bracket* the intervening statements; the intervening statements themselves are called the *loop body*. The FOR construct in this case starts a *counter*, called Side here, with the value 1, and carries out the loop body for each value of the counter from 1 to 4 inclusive (that is what 1..4 means).

Program 2.6 The Spider Draws a Box Using a Loop Control Structure

```
WITH Spider;
PROCEDURE Draw_Box_with_1_Loop IS
----------------------------------------------------------------
--| Draw 4 x 4 box with spider - use loop
--| Author: M. B. Feldman, The George Washington University
--| Last Modified: July 1998
----------------------------------------------------------------

BEGIN -- Draw_Box_with_1_Loop

  Spider.Start;
  Spider.ChangeColor(NewColor => Spider.Red);

  FOR Side IN 1..4 LOOP
    Spider.Step;
    Spider.Step;
    Spider.Step;
    Spider.TurnRight;
  END LOOP;

  Spider.Quit;

END Draw_Box_with_1_Loop;
```

Sample Run of Program 2.6

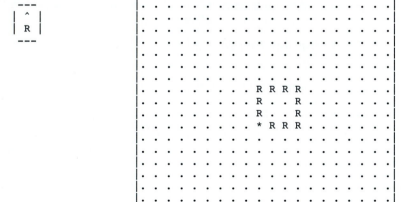

Random Directions and Colors

The box drawn by the spider in Program 2.6 is exactly the same every time the program is run: always in the same location, always red. Let's make the program more interesting by causing the spider to start walking in a randomly selected direction, and to change the color of each side by a random color selection. We can get random colors and directions from these two spider operations:

```
FUNCTION RandomDirection RETURN Directions;
-- Pre:  None
-- Post: Returns a random direction

FUNCTION RandomColor RETURN Colors;
-- Pre:  None
-- Post: Returns a random color
```

These have obvious meanings, made more so by the postconditions. Program 2.7 makes use of these operations to draw a box that will look different each time the program is one. The sample run shows just one execution; try running the program a number of times to observe its behavior.

Program 2.7 Drawing a Box Using Random Colors and Starting Direction

```
PROCEDURE Draw_Box_with_1_Loop_2 IS
-----------------------------------------------------------------
--| Draw 4 x 4 box with spider - use loop
--| Colors and starting direction are selected randomly
--| Author: M. B. Feldman, The George Washington University
--| Last Modified: July 1998
-----------------------------------------------------------------

BEGIN -- Draw_Box_with_1_Loop_2

  Spider.Start;
  Spider.Face(WhichWay => Spider.RandomDirection);

  FOR Side IN 1..4 LOOP
    Spider.ChangeColor(NewColor => Spider.RandomColor);
    Spider.Step;
    Spider.Step;
    Spider.Step;
    Spider.TurnRight;
  END LOOP;

  Spider.Quit;

END Draw_Box_with_1_Loop_2;
```

Sample Run of Program 2.7

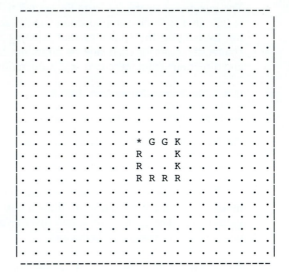

EXERCISES FOR SECTION 2.3

1. Write and test a program that instructs the spider to draw a pattern in the shape of a highway "yield" sign, that is,

    ```
    RRRRRR
     R    R
      R R
       R
    ```

    Hints: Start the spider facing west, draw the top line, and so on. Also note that you can get the spider to draw a "blank" by changing its color to None.

2.4   Algorithms with Nested Loops

Programs 2.6 and 2.7 both contain a sequence of statements

```
Spider.Step;
Spider.Step;
Spider.Step;
```

which is, itself, a repetition. Let's take this into account by rewriting the box-drawing algorithm, adding the color change as we go:

Algorithm for drawing a box:

1.   Repeat steps 1.1 through 1.3 four times.

    1.1   Choose a color.

    1.2   Repeat step 1.2.1 three times.

        1.2.1   Take one step forward.

    1.3   Turn right.

This algorithm is saying that *each of the four times* we reach step 1.2, we execute step 1.2.1 three times. The real power in algorithms is that we can combine straight-line sequences with repetitions (and conditional executions, as we shall see shortly) in almost unlimited ways.

How can we represent this new algorithm in a program? We can combine control structures, to reflect the algorithm steps. In this case we can include an entire FOR construct inside another one. To put it another way, a statement in a loop body can be another entire loop construct. This is called *nesting* control structures. Program 2.8 shows this: The *inner* loop construct

```
FOR Count IN 1..5 LOOP
  Spider.Step;
END LOOP;
```

is nested inside the *outer* one; for variety we changed the number of steps to 5. We use indentation in the program to highlight the nesting, as we use indentation in algorithms and other outlining methods. The indentation is not required by the compiler, but it certainly makes a difference in the clarity of the program! The behavior of this program is very similar to that of Program 2.7, so we have omitted the sample run. Try running it yourself several times to observe the randomness again.

Program 2.8 The Spider Draws a Box Using Nested Loop Control Structures

```
WITH Spider;
PROCEDURE Draw_Box_with_2_Loops IS
----------------------------------------------------------------
--| Draw 4 x 4 box with spider - use nested loops
--| Author: M. B. Feldman, The George Washington University
--| Last Modified: July 1998
----------------------------------------------------------------
BEGIN -- Draw_Box_with_2_Loops

  Spider.Start;
  Spider.Face(WhichWay => Spider.RandomDirection);

  FOR Side IN 1..4 LOOP
    Spider.ChangeColor(NewColor => Spider.RandomColor);
    FOR Count IN 1..5 LOOP
      Spider.Step;
    END LOOP;
    Spider.TurnRight;
```

```
      END LOOP;

   Spider.Quit;

END Draw_Box_with_2_Loops;
```

Spiral Patterns

So far, our loop constructs have used literals to represent the *bounds* (starting and ending values) of the counters. This is not required; loop bounds can vary. To see this, consider the loop structure of Program 2.9:

```
FOR Line IN 1..10 LOOP
   Spider.ChangeColor(NewColor => Spider.RandomColor);

   -- inner loop takes its bound from outer count
   FOR Count IN 1..Line LOOP
      Spider.Step;
   END LOOP;

   Spider.TurnRight;
END LOOP;
```

As the comment indicates, the inner loop takes its high bound from the current value of the outer loop's counter. When the first line is being drawn (Line is 1), the inner loop counter ranges from 1 to 1, so the spider takes one step. When the second line is drawn (Line is 2), the spider takes two steps, and so on until the spider takes ten steps to draw the tenth line. This results in the spiral pattern shown in the sample run; make sure you understand how this happens.

Program 2.9 The Spider Draws a Spiral Pattern

```
WITH Spider;
PROCEDURE Spiral IS
-----------------------------------------------------------------
--| Draw spiral pattern with spider - use nested loops
--| Author: M. B. Feldman, The George Washington University
--| Last Modified: July 1998
-----------------------------------------------------------------
BEGIN -- Spiral

   Spider.Start;
   Spider.Face(WhichWay => Spider.RandomDirection);

   -- draw ten lines, starting in a random direction
   FOR Line IN 1..10 LOOP
      Spider.ChangeColor(NewColor => Spider.RandomColor);

      -- inner loop takes its bound from outer count
      FOR Count IN 1..Line LOOP
         Spider.Step;
      END LOOP;

      Spider.TurnRight;
   END LOOP;
```

```
    Spider.Quit;
END Spiral;
```

Sample Run of Program 2.9

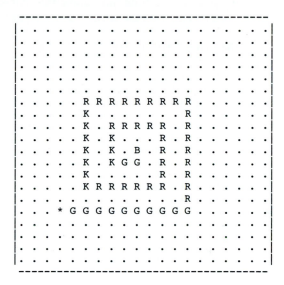

EXERCISES FOR SECTION 2.4

1. Write and test a program that instructs the spider to draw a pattern in the shape of a solid triangle, that is,

   ```
   B
   BB
   BBB
   BBBB
   BBBBB
   BBBBBB
   ```

2. Write a spider program to draw a checkerboard pattern, that is,

   ```
   G G G G
    G G G G
   G G G G
    G G G G
   ```

2.5   Algorithms with Conditional Execution

Another important algorithmic structure is *conditional execution*. To introduce the need for this, consider Program 2.10, which commands the spider to take 12 steps forward. As you can see from the sample run, this program terminates with the raising of an *exception*, in this case `Spider.Hit_the_Wall`.

Program 2.10 The Spider Crashes into a Wall

```
WITH Spider;
PROCEDURE Spider_Crash IS
------------------------------------------------------------
--| This program demonstrates an Ada 95 runtime error.
--| Spider tries to take 12 steps from center of room;
--|   it hits the wall and an exception is raised.
--| Author: M. B. Feldman, The George Washington University
--| Last Modified: July 1998
------------------------------------------------------------
BEGIN -- Spider_Crash

  Spider.Start;
  Spider.ChangeColor(NewColor => Spider.Red);

  FOR Count IN 1..12 LOOP
    Spider.Step;
  END LOOP;

  Spider.Quit;

END Spider_Crash;
```

Because the spider started out in the middle of its room, it could not take more than ten steps forward in the same direction; its crashing into the wall is simulated in the spider package by this exception. The traceback—whose form, like that of a listing file, depends on the compiler—shows the line number in `Spider_Crash` in which the exception was raised, in this case line 16, or the `Spider.Step` statement. The traceback also shows where the exception originated, back in the `Spider` package body, but we are not studying that body yet.

The exception is Ada's mechanism for signaling an error condition in a program. A raised exception can be *handled* by the subprogram in which it raised, or by the one that called that subprogram, or, eventually, by the main program. The Ada standard prescribes that when an exception is raised in some called subprogram and is not handled there, it is *propagated* (passed back to) to the calling subprogram. If no subprogram handles the exception, it eventually comes back to the main program. If it is not handled in the main program either, the main program terminates, with or without a compiler-dependent traceback.

Sample Run of Program 2.10

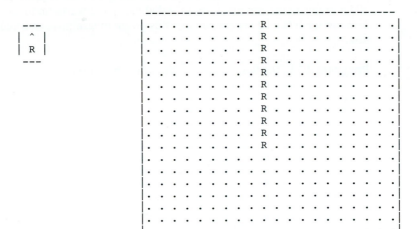

```
raised SPIDER.HIT_THE_WALL
Traceback Information
     Program Name      File Name               Line
     ------------      ---------               ----
     spider.step       spider.adb              264
     spider_crash      spider_crash.adb        16
```

Using Conditional Execution to Prevent Run-Time Exceptions

We will take up exception *handling* in detail in Chapter 7. Meanwhile, it is important to consider how to *prevent* the exception from being raised. In this case the spider program can check to see whether the spider will step into a wall, using a conditional execution. The spider package provides a condition-testing, or *Boolean* operation

```
FUNCTION AtWall RETURN Boolean;
-- Pre:  None
-- Post: Returns True if the spider is standing next to a wall
```

which will be true if, and only if, the spider will hit the wall on its next step.

Now in Program 2.11 the lines

```
IF Spider.AtWall THEN
   EXIT;
END IF;
```

test the condition `spider.AtWall`. If the condition is true, the EXIT statement causes the program to exit the repetition early, continuing execution just below END LOOP. The effect of this in the current program is that the spider walks up to, but not into, the wall. You can see from the sample run that this program terminates normally, with no exception.

Program 2.11 The Spider Goes to the Wall and Stops

```
WITH Spider;
PROCEDURE Go_to_Wall IS
----------------------------------------------------------------
--| Spider steps up to the first wall it meets, then stops
--| Author: M. B. Feldman, The George Washington University
--| Last Modified: July 1998
----------------------------------------------------------------

BEGIN -- Go_to_Wall

  Spider.Start;
  Spider.ChangeColor(NewColor => Spider.Blue);

  FOR Count IN 1..12 LOOP
    IF Spider.AtWall THEN
      EXIT;
    END IF;
    Spider.Step;
  END LOOP;

  Spider.Quit;

END Go_to_Wall;
```

The General Loop Structure

In Program 2.11 the spider tries to count to 12 but never gets there because it reaches the wall and stops. In fact, it is unnecessary to count at all. We can use a *general loop construct* for this, as Program 2.12 shows.

Program 2.12 The Spider Goes to the Wall, Using a General Loop Structure

```
WITH Spider;
PROCEDURE Go_to_Wall_2 IS
----------------------------------------------------------------
--| Spider steps up to the first wall it meets, then stops
--| This version uses a general loop instead of a counting loop
--| Author: M. B. Feldman, The George Washington University
--| Last Modified: July 1998
----------------------------------------------------------------

BEGIN -- Go_to_Wall_2

  Spider.Start;
  Spider.ChangeColor(NewColor => Spider.Blue);

  LOOP
```

```
      IF Spider.AtWall THEN
         EXIT;
      END IF;
      Spider.Step;
   END LOOP;

   Spider.Quit;

END Go_to_Wall_2;
```

A general loop structure looks like a FOR structure without a FOR phrase. In the statements

```
LOOP
   IF Spider.AtWall THEN
      EXIT;
   END IF;
   Spider.Step;
END LOOP;
```

each time the program reaches the end of the loop body—in this case, after it has executed `Spider.Step`—it returns to the top of the loop body and executes the body again. Since the first statement of the loop body is our condition-testing construct, the program has the desired effect: it keeps looping until the spider reaches the wall, then stops.

General loops like this must be used with care. What if the condition never becomes true? (This will not happen in this program, of course, but might happen in some other program.) The program will keep looping indefinitely. Programs (especially embedded ones) are sometimes written to loop indefinitely, and we will see one shortly, but a program that *unintentionally* loops without stopping is a program with a bug in it!

Program 2.13 builds on the previous one by commanding the spider to take a walk around the edges of its room. The first section of the program repeats the general loop of Program 2.12; the second section consists of a four-repetition counting loop, inside of which is nested another general loop as above.

Program 2.13 The Spider Tours Its Room

```
WITH Spider;
PROCEDURE Tour_Room IS
-----------------------------------------------------------------
--| Spider takes a tour around the edges of its room.
--| Author: M. B. Feldman, The George Washington University
--| Last Modified: July 1998
-----------------------------------------------------------------

BEGIN -- Tour_Room

   Spider.Start;
   Spider.ChangeColor(NewColor => Spider.Blue);

   -- first get to a wall
   LOOP
      IF Spider.AtWall THEN
         EXIT;
      END IF;
```

```
      Spider.Step;
END LOOP;

-- now turn and tour the four walls
FOR Wall IN 1..4 LOOP
  Spider.TurnRight;

  -- walk the length of this wall
  LOOP
    IF Spider.AtWall THEN
       EXIT;
    END IF;
    Spider.Step;
  END LOOP;
END LOOP;

Spider.Quit;

END Tour_Room;
```

Sample Run of Program 2.13

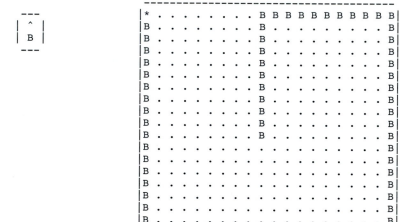

Using EXIT WHEN instead of IF for Conditional Loop Execution

Program 2.14 is very similar to Program 2.13, with identical screen behavior (and, therefore, no sample run).

Program 2.14 The Spider Tours Its Room, Using EXIT WHEN

```
WITH Spider;
PROCEDURE Tour_Room_2 IS
------------------------------------------------------------
--| Spider takes a tour around the edges of its room.
--| This version uses EXIT WHEN instead of IF.
--| Author: M. B. Feldman, The George Washington University
--| Last Modified: July 1998
------------------------------------------------------------

BEGIN -- Tour_Room_2

  Spider.Start;
  Spider.ChangeColor(NewColor => Spider.Blue);

  -- first get to a wall
  LOOP
    EXIT WHEN Spider.AtWall;
    Spider.Step;
  END LOOP;

  -- now turn and tour the four walls
  FOR Wall IN 1..4 LOOP
    Spider.TurnRight;

    -- walk the length of this wall
    LOOP
      EXIT WHEN Spider.AtWall;
      Spider.Step;
    END LOOP;
  END LOOP;

  Spider.Quit;

END Tour_Room_2;
```

The difference is that the two conditional statements

```
IF Spider.AtWall THEN
  EXIT;
END IF;
```

are replaced with a more concise Ada equivalent,

```
EXIT WHEN Spider.AtWall;
```

which gives the indefinite loop construct

```
LOOP
  EXIT WHEN Spider.AtWall;
  Spider.Step;
END LOOP;
```

EXERCISE FOR SECTION 2.5

1. Modify Program 2.14 so that the spider covers the four walls completely but does not visit any parts of the walls a second time. *Hint:* Count the number of steps the spider takes while touring the first wall and the number of steps in touring the third (parallel) wall.

2.6 Putting It All Together: The Drunken Spider

Finally, we develop a spider program that puts together everything we've learned here. Imagine that the spider discovers a large glass of beer in its room and drinks enough beer to become inebriated (a fancy word for "drunk"). The spider tries to tour its room but is too drunk to do this properly. Instead, the spider tries to take a random number of steps. If it does so without reaching a wall, it turns right, selects another random number, and resumes walking. If the spider reaches a wall, it turns around and walks in the opposite direction, completing its count in the new direction. You can probably understand this program, Program 2.15, without further explanation.

Program 2.15 The Drunken Spider

```
WITH Spider;
PROCEDURE Drunken_Spider IS
-----------------------------------------------------------
--| Spider tries to tour its room but has drunk too much, so
--| takes a random number of steps and may hit the wall. If the
--| spider hits the wall, it turns around and keeps going.
--| Author: M. B. Feldman, The George Washington University
--| Last Modified: July 1998
-----------------------------------------------------------

BEGIN -- Drunken_Spider

  Spider.Start;

  LOOP                           -- keep going forever

    Spider.Face(WhichWay => Spider.RandomDirection);
    Spider.ChangeColor(NewColor => Spider.RandomColor);

    -- Spider will count steps correctly
    -- but might change direction
    FOR Count IN 1..Spider.RandomStep LOOP

      IF Spider.AtWall THEN
        Spider.TurnRight;
        Spider.TurnRight;
      END IF;

      Spider.Step;
```

```
    END LOOP;

    Spider.TurnRight;

  END LOOP;

END Drunken_Spider;
```

Sample Run of Program 2.15

```
 ---      ------------------------------------------
| > |    |. . . . . . . . . . . . . . . . ^ . . . .|
| B |    |. . . . . . . . . . . . G G G G G . . . . .|
 ---     |. . . . . . . . . . R . . . . . . . . .|
         |. . . . . . . . . . R . . . . . . . . .|
         |. . . . . . . . . . R B . . . . . . . .|
         |. . . . . . . . . . R B . . . . . . . .|
         |. . . K K K K K K K K K K K K . . . . .|
         |. . . K . . . . . . R B . . . . . . . .|
         |. . . K . . . . . . R B . . . . . . . .|
         |K K K K K K K K K K R B . . . . . . . .|
         |. . . K . . . . . . R B . . . . . . . .|
         |. . . K . . . . . . R B . . . . . . . .|
         |. . . K . . . . . . R B . . . . . . . .|
         |. . . K . . . . . . R B . . . . . . . .|
         |. . . B . . . . . . . R G G G G G G G G G|
         |. . . B . . . . . . . . . . . . . . . .|
         |. . . B . . . . . . . . . . . . . . . .|
         |. . . B B B B B B B B B B *^C . . . .|
         |. . . B . . . . . . . . . . . . . . . .|
          ------------------------------------------
```

The main loop in this program is a general loop without a count or EXIT condition to terminate it. It is therefore a program that will loop indefinitely. This is similar to the program in an automatic teller machine or similar embedded program, which terminates only when the equipment itself is shut off. In our case, we need not shut off the computer. Rather, in most computers, pressing the CONTROL and c keys simultaneously (usually referred to as ctrl-c) will terminate your currently executing program. In the sample run of Drunken_Spider, we pressed ctrl-c to stop the program; most terminals will display this on the screen as ^c, and you can see this here at the end of the bottom row of BS.

CHAPTER REVIEW

The goal of this chapter has been to get you started with developing algorithms and implementing them as programs using control structures. We introduced straight-line algorithms, as well as those with single and nested repetitive loops and with conditional execution. The spider has served as an easy-to-understand mechanism for introducing these structures; the patterns drawn by the spider gave you obvious feedback on the behavior of the spider programs.

Each structure and technique that we discuss here is covered in full detail, with many more applications, in the chapters to come: straight-line programming in Chapters 3 and 4, conditional execution in Chapter 5, counting loops in Chapter 6, general loops and exception handling in Chapter 7.

In this chapter—and most of the book—all the programs are in standard, platform-independent Ada, assuming only that your computer has a simple monochrome screen with 24 rows and 80 columns. In case you are wondering how to do high-resolution or color graphics with Ada, Appendix A shows how to do just this and even provides a high-resolution color spider package. High-resolution color graphics is always dependent upon a particular "platform" (computer plus operating system) and the kind of monitor you have.

CHAPTER 3

Introduction to Straight-Line Programs

Programming is a problem-solving activity. If you are a good problem solver, you have the potential to become a good programmer. One goal of this book is to help you improve your problem-solving ability. It is beneficial to approach each programming problem in a systematic and consistent way. In this chapter we show you how to apply the software development method that we introduced in Chapter 1.

A *straight-line program* is one in which the execution flows in a straight line from the beginning to the end. There is no repetition of statements already executed; there is no opportunity for the program to take alternative paths depending on conditions in its data. This chapter and the next one focus on developing straight-line programs; Chapter 5 introduces alternative paths and Chapter 6 introduces repetition.

Historically, straight-line programs have been called *sequential* programs. More recently, "sequential program" has been used in contrast to "parallel program" or "concurrent program." The two meanings of "sequential" can be confusing. For clarity, therefore, we use "straight-line program" here.

3.1 The General Structure of Ada Programs

Let us start our systematic study of programming by building on the simple Ada program introduced as Program 1.1.

■ Example 3.1

Program 3.1 is similar to Program 1.1 but with the important difference that instead of just displaying a greeting, this program asks the user (the person running the program) to enter his or her initials, then greets the user with these initials. In general we will not show the programs with numbered lines, but we do so here for extra clarity.

Program 3.1 Displaying Initials

```
 1. WITH Ada.Text_IO;
 2. PROCEDURE Hello_Initials IS
 3. -----------------------------------------------------------------
 4. --| Requests, then displays, user's first and last initials.
 5. --| Author: Michael Feldman, The George Washington University
 6. --| Last Modified: June 1998
 7. -----------------------------------------------------------------
 8.
 9.    Initial1 : Character;  -- objects that hold initials
10.    Initial2 : Character;
11.
12. BEGIN -- Hello_Initials
13.
14.    -- Prompt for (request user to enter) user's initials
15.    Ada.Text_IO.Put(Item => "Enter your two initials> ");
16.    Ada.Text_IO.Get(Item => Initial1);
17.    Ada.Text_IO.Get(Item => Initial2);
18.
19.    -- Display user's initials, with a greeting
20.    Ada.Text_IO.Put(Item => "Hello ");
21.    Ada.Text_IO.Put(Item => Initial1);
22.    Ada.Text_IO.Put(Item => Initial2);
23.    Ada.Text_IO.Put(Item => ". Enjoy studying Ada!");
24.    Ada.Text_IO.New_Line;
25.
26. END Hello_Initials;
```

Sample Run

```
Enter your two initials> MF
Hello MF. Enjoy studying Ada!
```

Lines 9 and 10 identify the names of two *variable objects* (Initial1 and Initial2)—memory cells that will be used to store the initials. A comment is used at the end of line 9 to indicate the purpose of these variable objects. The section of the program between the reserved word IS (line 2) and the reserved word BEGIN (line 12) is called the *declarative section,* or sometimes just the *declarations.* Generally, this section describes *objects* (such as our two variable objects here) and *types* (more on this later) to the compiler.

As in Program 1.1 and all the other programs in this book, the first few lines of this program—in this case, lines 3 through 7—constitute a *banner comment* identifying the author, date, and purpose of the program. Comments also appear in lines 14 and 19; each comment serves as a brief description of the following program section. Comments are ignored by the compiler but make up an important part of the program documentation.

The statements in lines 15 through 17 are all calls to input/output procedures. As before, each statement containing `Ada.Text_IO.Put` causes some information to be displayed on the video screen during program execution. The statement

```
Ada.Text_IO.Put(Item => "Enter your two initials> ");
```

asks the program user to enter two letters. The statements

```
Ada.Text_IO.Get(Item => Initial1);
Ada.Text_IO.Get(Item => Initial2);
```

cause the program to wait until two letters are entered on the keyboard by the program user. These letters are "read" (stored) into the two memory cells listed, one letter per cell. The last output line of the program is displayed by the `Ada.Text_IO.Put` statements in lines 20 through 24. These statements display the string `"Hello "`, the two letters just read, and finally the longer greeting message. The symbol `=>` is known as "arrow," and it is proper to pronounce a phrase like `Item => Initial1` as "Item arrow Initial1" ∎

∎ Example 3.2

Program 3.2 is similar to Program 3.1 except that it reads a person's name instead of just that person's initials. The declaration of `FirstName` describes a variable object that is able to hold a sequence of *exactly* ten characters (letters, digits, etc.). That is why the prompt lines request an entry of exactly that many letters.

Program 3.2 Displaying the User's Name

```
WITH Ada.Text_IO;
PROCEDURE Hello_Name IS
------------------------------------------------------------------------
--| Requests, then displays, user's name
--| Author: Michael Feldman, The George Washington University
--| Last Modified: June 1998
------------------------------------------------------------------------

   FirstName: String(1..10); -- object to hold user's name

BEGIN  -- Hello_Name

  -- Prompt for (request user to enter) user's name
  Ada.Text_IO.Put
    (Item => "Enter your first name, exactly 10 letters.");
  Ada.Text_IO.New_Line;
  Ada.Text_IO.Put
    (Item => "Add spaces at the end if it's shorter.> ");
  Ada.Text_IO.Get(Item => FirstName);
```

```
-- Display the entered name, with a greeting
Ada.Text_IO.Put(Item => "Hello ");
Ada.Text_IO.Put(Item => FirstName);
Ada.Text_IO.Put(Item => ". Enjoy studying Ada!");
Ada.Text_IO.New_Line;

END Hello_Name;
```

Sample Run

```
Enter your first name, exactly 10 letters.
Add spaces at the end if it's shorter.> Michael
Hello Michael   . Enjoy studying Ada!
```

Note that in the prompting section of this program, two of the statements are spread over two lines. It is perfectly acceptable, and often desirable, to break up a statement in this fashion, especially if it serves to fit the statements more esthetically onto displayed or printed lines. We can split an Ada statement anywhere except in the middle of a word or in the middle of a quoted string. Also, if a comment is split over two or more lines, each line must begin with --. ■

Reserved Words and Identifiers

All of the lines in the preceding programs satisfy the syntax rules for the Ada language. The programs contain several different elements: *reserved words (keywords), predefined identifiers, special symbols,* and names for memory cells. Let's look at the first three categories. The reserved words all appear in this book in uppercase; they have special meanings in Ada and cannot be used for other purposes. The reserved words in Programs 1.1, 3.1, and 3.2 are (in order of appearance)

```
WITH  PROCEDURE  IS  BEGIN  END
```

The predefined identifiers also have special meanings, but they can be used by the programmer for other purposes (however, we don't recommend this practice). The predefined identifiers in Programs 1.1, 3.1, and 3.2 are (in order of appearance)

```
Ada.Text_IO  Put  New_Line  Character  Get  String
```

There are also some symbols (e.g., =, *, >=) that have special meanings in Ada. Appendix B contains a complete list of reserved words and special symbols; Appendix C summarizes the predefined identifiers.

What is the difference between reserved words and predefined identifiers? You cannot use a reserved word as the name of a memory cell, but in certain cases you can use a predefined identifier. Exactly how Ada would treat such a "reused" predefined identifier depends on just which identifier is involved. In any case the result would be very confusing to the reader of the program. Therefore we strongly recommend that you treat predefined identifiers as though they were reserved words and refrain from reusing them.

The other identifiers that appear in the three sample programs are described in more detail in the next sections.

**PROGRAM
STYLE**

Use of Uppercase and Lowercase

Throughout the text, issues of good programming style are discussed in displays like this one. Programming style displays provide guidelines for improving the appearance and the readability of your programs.

Most programs are examined, studied, and used by someone other than the original author. A program that follows consistent style conventions is easier to read and understand than one that is sloppy or inconsistent. These conventions have no effect whatsoever on the computer; they just make it much easier for humans to understand programs.

In this text, reserved words always appear in uppercase. This is because the reserved words determine the structure and organization of the program. Writing them in uppercase, combined with a consistent indentation style, makes the structure and organization of the program immediately visible to the human eye.

Identifiers are in mixed uppercase and lowercase. The first letter of each identifier is capitalized. If an identifier consists of two or more words (such as New_Line), each word is usually capitalized, and the words are sometimes separated by an underscore character.

The compiler does not differentiate between uppercase and lowercase in reading your program. You could write the reserved word BEGIN as begin and the predefined identifier Character as CHARACTER or even ChArAcTeR. The compiler doesn't care, but we do, as humans striving for clarity and consistency. The compiler does, however, treat the underscore as a character, so Two_Words is different from TwoWords.

Your instructor may prefer a different convention; if so, it is prudent to follow it. In the end, what matters most is using a well-thought-out and consistent programming style.

Programs and Packages

Ada is a language that is designed for writing real-world programs that can be very large, sometimes numbering hundreds of thousands of statements. Because a single program file of that length would be completely unmanageable for humans and computers alike, Ada is built around the idea of libraries and packages. Using these, sets of commonly used operations can be tested once and then put in a library for others to use. Ada comes with many standard, predefined packages; one that you will use very often is Ada.Text_IO. All the predefined Ada libraries begin with the form Ada. Later in the book you will learn how to use other predefined packages and to write packages of your own. For now, keep in mind that almost every Ada program is preceded by at least one WITH clause (formally called a *context clause)* of the form

```
WITH Package_Name;
```

WITH clauses inform the compiler to which packages it must refer in order to understand the operations you are using. Preceding a program by the context clause

```
WITH Ada.Text_IO;
```

informs the compiler that the program will be using this package to read input data from the keyboard and display output data on the monitor. Omitting the context clause would cause one or more compilation errors.

3.2   System Structures: Numerical Input and Output

So far, our program examples have used only character and string quantities. Computers are commonly used to work with numbers, so it is time for a numerical example or two. Computer programs use two general kinds of numerical values: *integer* values, such as 0, 2, and −1048, which are "whole numbers" with no fractional part, and *floating-point* values, such as 0.0, 3.14159 and −185.7, which are numbers with fractional parts. *Ada requires us, generally, to keep integer numbers and floating-point numbers separate and not to mix them in the same calculation.*

In Ada, reading numerical values from the keyboard or a file, and writing or displaying these, are done by using two important components of the standard Ada libraries, called `Ada.Integer_Text_IO` and `Ada.Float_Text_IO`. You now know of three input/output packages. If your program reads or displays ordinary characters and strings or uses `Ada.Text_IO.New_Line`, precede your program with a context clause:

```
WITH Ada.Text_IO;
```

If your program reads and displays integer quantities, precede it by

```
WITH Ada.Integer_Text_IO;
```

If your program reads and displays floating-point quantities, precede it by

```
WITH Ada.Float_Text_IO;
```

It is permissible to have two, or even all three, context clauses, if necessary.

■ Example 3.3

Program 3.3 converts inches to centimeters.

Program 3.3 Converting Inches to Centimeters

```
WITH Ada.Text_IO;
WITH Ada.Float_Text_IO;
PROCEDURE Inch_to_CM IS
-----------------------------------------------------------------------
--| Converts inches to centimeters
--| Author: Michael B. Feldman, The George Washington University
--| Last Modified: June 1998
-----------------------------------------------------------------------

  CMPerInch   : CONSTANT Float := 2.54;
  Inches      : Float;
  Centimeters : Float;
```

```
BEGIN -- Inch_to_CM

   -- Prompt user for value in inches
   Ada.Text_IO.Put (Item => "Enter a length in inches> ");
   Ada.Float_Text_IO.Get (Item => Inches);

   -- Compute equivalent value in centimeters
   Centimeters := CMPerInch * Inches;

   -- Display result
   Ada.Text_IO.Put (Item => "That equals ");
   Ada.Float_Text_IO.Put (Item => Centimeters);
   Ada.Text_IO.Put (Item => " centimeters");
   Ada.Text_IO.New_Line;

END Inch_to_CM;
```

Sample Run

```
Enter a length in inches> 30.5
That equals  7.74700E+01 centimeters
```

The number of inches to be converted is read into the variable object `Inches` by the statement

```
Ada.Float_Text_IO.Get (Item => Inches);
```

The `Get` statement looks similar to the one in the earlier examples. There are many different `Get` statements in the input/output libraries; they have in common the fact that each is able to accept keyboard input and store it in a single data element. As before, we write the prefix `Ada.Float_Text_IO` to indicate that we are interested in the `Get` supplied by the floating-point input/output package.

The statement

```
Centimeters := CMPerInch * Inches;
```

computes the equivalent length in centimeters by multiplying the length in inches by the floating-point constant 2.54 (the number of centimeters per inch); the product is stored in memory cell `Centimeters`. The symbol `:=` is called the *assignment symbol*.

The statement

```
Ada.Float_Text_IO.Put (Item => Centimeters);
```

displays the value of `Centimeters` as the floating-point number 7.74700E+01 in scientific notation. The value printed is equivalent to 7.747×10, or 77.47, as will be explained later.

Suppose the user enters a negative number of inches at the keyboard (say, -1.45). The program will compute a negative number of centimeters. Whether this is appropriate or not depends on the use we are making of the program. Throughout this book we will be introducing better and better ways of ensuring that user input is appropriate before proceeding to a calculation that may not make sense. At this stage we can only identify the problem; we do not yet have the tools to solve it. ∎

■ Example 3.4

Program 3.4 computes the distance of an automobile trip by asking the user to enter the estimated trip time in hours and the average speed in miles per hour.

Program 3.4 Finding Distance Traveled

```
WITH Ada.Text_IO;
WITH Ada.Integer_Text_IO;
PROCEDURE Distance IS
-------------------------------------------------------------------
--| Finds distance traveled, given travel time and average speed
--| Author: Michael B. Feldman, The George Washington University
--| Last Modified: June 1998
-------------------------------------------------------------------
  HowLong : Natural;
  HowFast : Natural;
  HowFar  : Natural;

BEGIN -- Distance

  -- prompt user for hours and average speed
  Ada.Text_IO.Put
    (Item => "How many hours will you be driving (integer) ? ");
  Ada.Integer_Text_IO.Get (Item => HowLong);
  Ada.Text_IO.Put
    (Item=>"At what average speed (miles per hour, integer) ? ");
  Ada.Integer_Text_IO.Get (Item => HowFast);

  -- compute distance driven
  HowFar := HowFast * HowLong;

  -- display results
  Ada.Text_IO.Put (Item => "You will travel about ");
  Ada.Integer_Text_IO.Put (Item => HowFar);
  Ada.Text_IO.Put (Item => " miles");
  Ada.Text_IO.New_Line;

END Distance;
```

Sample Run

```
How many hours will you be driving (integer) ? 3
At what average speed (miles per hour, integer) ? 55
You will travel about        165 miles
```

The numbers are nonnegative integer values (type Natural, which includes zero). Nonnegative integers are still integers, so we can make use of the integer input/output package Ada.Integer_Text_IO, calling the Get and Put operations there.

In Programs 3.3 and 3.4 there are two context clauses (WITH clauses) preceding the program. Why do we need both? Because we are displaying prompts to request user input as well as titles to make the output meaningful, we need to use the character-string part of Ada.Text_IO to do this, in addition to the appropriate numerical input/output package. Ada requires us to supply context clauses for all packages we are using.

In testing this program, we entered positive numbers for the trip time and speed. You might find it interesting to execute the program yourself and enter a negative number. An exception will be raised. This will be discussed in Section 3.11. ■

3.3   Data Structures: Declaring Constant and Variable Objects

Every program begins with one or more context clauses, followed by a program heading such as

```
PROCEDURE Distance IS
```

We tell the Ada compiler the names of memory cells used in a program through object (constant and variable) declarations. The programs seen so far contained declarations for constants and variables. The *constant declaration*

```
CMPerInch: CONSTANT Float := 3.54;
```

in Program 3.3 specifies that the identifier `CMPerInch` will be used as the name of the constant value 2.54. Identifiers that are declared in a constant declaration are called *constants*. Data values that will not change (for example, the number of centimeters per inch is always 2.54) should be associated with an identifier that is a constant. Any Ada statement (other than the declaration) that attempts to change the value of a constant will give rise to a compilation error. A good reason for using constants in a program is that accidental attempts to change constant values will be caught by the compiler.

The *variable object declarations*

```
Initial1: Character;
Initial2: Character;
```

in Program 3.1 give the names of two identifiers that will be used to reference data items that are individual characters as denoted by the predefined identifier `Character`. The variable declarations

```
Inches     : Float;
Centimeters: Float;
```

in Program 3.3 give the names of two identifiers that will be used to reference data items that are floating-point values (for example, 30.0 and 563.57) as denoted by the predefined identifier `Float`. The variable declarations in Program 3.4

```
HowLong: Natural;
HowFast: Natural;
HowFar : Natural;
```

give the names of three identifers whose values will be nonnegative integers, using Ada's predefined integer type `Natural`. We wish these numbers to be nonnegative because negative time and negative speed do not make good physical sense. We will come back frequently to the question of defining sensible ranges of values for our variables.

An identifier given in a variable declaration statement to the left of the : (colon) symbol is called a *variable object,* or usually just *variable*. Variables are used in a program for storing input data items and computational results. The identifier appearing to the right of the : symbol (for example, Integer, Float, Character, String) tells the Ada compiler the *data type* (for example, an integer value, a floating-point value, a single character, or a sequence of characters) of the data that will be stored in the variable. Data types will be considered in more detail in Section 3.9.

You have quite a bit of freedom in selecting the identifiers, or names of variables and constants, that you use in a program. Some valid and invalid identifiers are the following:

Valid identifiers: INITIAL1, initial1, Inches, Centimeters, CM_Per_Inch, hello

Invalid identifiers: 1LETTER, CONSTANT, BEGIN, Two*Four, Joe's, CM__Per__Inch

The syntax rules for identifiers are as follows:

1. An identifier must always begin with a letter; 1LETTER is invalid.

2. An identifier must consist only of letters, digits, and underscores.

3. You cannot use two or more underscore characters in succession; the first character cannot be an underscore. CM__Per__Inch is invalid (two underscores in succession).

4. You cannot use an Ada reserved word as an identifier; BEGIN is invalid.

Note again that both uppercase and lowercase may be used, but remember the style recommendations from Section 3.1. The syntactic rules do not place a limit on the length of an identifier, except that an identifier may not be split over more than one line. Ada requires a declaration for every identifier you create and use in your program (no declaration is required or desirable for predefined identifiers). Identifiers that you create and use are called *user-defined identifiers*.

The names of variables, constants, procedures, packages, package instances, and so on are all identifiers; therefore all follow the syntactic rules just given.

The reserved words and identifiers used thus far are summarized here under their appropriate categories:

Program names: Hello Hello_Initials Hello_Name Inch_To_CM Distance

Predefined packages: Ada.Text_IO Ada.Text_IO.Integer_IO Ada.Text_IO.Float_IO

Operations in predefined packages: Put New_Line Get

Variable objects: Initial1 Initial2 FirstName Inches Centimeters HowLong HowFast HowFar

Constant objects: CMPerInch

Predefined types: Character String Integer Float

In this section we introduced the context clause, program heading, constant declaration, and variable declaration. The syntactic form of each of these Ada language constructs is summarized in the following syntax displays. Each display describes the syntactic form of a construct and provides an example.

SYNTAX DISPLAY

Context Clause

Form:

```
WITH list of package names ;
```

Example:

```
WITH Ada.Text_IO;
WITH Ada.Integer_Text_IO;
```

Interpretation:

A context clause informs the compiler that the named package(s) is (are) being used by this program. The compiler will check all references to resources (e.g., procedures) provided by the package(s), making certain that the program is using them correctly.

Note:

Context clauses can appear only at the very beginning of a source file. Generally, we will give only one package name per context clause; this makes it easier to add or delete context clauses.

SYNTAX DISPLAY

Program Heading

Form:

```
PROCEDURE program name IS
```

Example:

```
PROCEDURE Distance IS
```

Interpretation:

A program heading is used to signal the start of a program.

SYNTAX DISPLAY

Comment

Form:

```
-- comment
```

Example:

```
-- This is a comment
```

Interpretation:
A double hyphen indicates the start of a comment; the comment ends at the end of the line. Comments are listed with the program but are otherwise ignored by the Ada compiler. Note that if you write a program statement *following* a comment on the same line, it will be treated by the compiler as part of the comment and therefore it will be ignored!

SYNTAX
DISPLAY

Constant Object Declaration

Form:

Some_constant : CONSTANT *type* := *value*;

Example:

```
Pi : CONSTANT Float := 3.14159;
```

Interpretation:
The specified *value* is associated with the identifier *Some_constant*. The value of *Some_constant* cannot be changed by any subsequent program statements.

SYNTAX
DISPLAY

Variable Object Declaration

Form:

variable list : *type* ;

Example:

```
Initial1, Initial2: Character;
```

Interpretation:
A memory cell is allocated for each *variable* (an identifier) in the *variable list*. The *type* of data (Character in this case) to be stored in each variable is specified between the colon and the semicolon. Commas are used to separate the identifiers in the variable list.

   To make it easier to add and delete variable declarations, we generally will write each declaration on its own line and give only one variable per declaration.

PROGRAM STYLE

> ## Choosing Identifier Names
>
> It is very important to pick meaningful names for identifiers; they will be easier to understand when used in a program. For example, the identifier `salary` would be a good name for a variable used to store a person's salary; the identifiers s and `Bagel` would be bad choices.
>
> There is no restriction on the length of an identifier. However, it is difficult to form meaningful names using fewer than three letters. On the other hand, typing errors become more likely when identifiers are too long. A reasonable rule of thumb is to use names that are between three and ten characters in length.
>
> If you mistype an identifier, the compiler will usually detect this as a syntax error and display an *undefined identifier* message during program translation. Sometimes, mistyped identifiers resemble other identifiers, so avoid picking names that are similar to each other.
>
> Make sure that you do not choose two names that are identical except for their use of case; the compiler will not be able to distinguish between them.
>
> Some Ada experts advocate using underscores to break up multiword identifiers, writing `CM_Per_Inch`, for example, instead of our `CMPerInch`. In this book we generally use underscores in program names (it's easier for some operating systems) but avoid them in variable and constant names (it makes the names a bit shorter). Of course, consistency is important, and also, if your instructor prefers underscores in your variable names, use them!

PROGRAM STYLE

> ## Form of Declarations and Context Clauses
>
> From the syntax displays, you can see that Ada permits several package names to appear in a single context clause and several variable names to appear in a declaration. Declarations are often changed during the development of a program as variables are added and removed.
>
> It is therefore much easier to develop a program (and to read it as well) if each variable and constant is declared in a separate declaration on its own line. All programs in this book follow this style convention, and we recommend that you follow it too.
>
> The same recommendation applies to context clauses: Because any number of context clauses can precede a program, we recommend that each context clause name only a single package and appear on its own line.

**PROGRAM
STYLE**

> ### Banner Comments
>
> Each program in this book contains a *banner comment*, sometimes called a *block comment* or *header comment,* giving a brief description of the program, with author and date information. An example is
>
> ```
> ----------------------------------------------------------------
> --| Finds distance traveled,
> --| given travel time and average speed
> --| Author: M. B. Feldman, The George Washington University
> --| Last Modified: June 1998
> ----------------------------------------------------------------
> ```
>
> Like all comments, banner comments are ignored by the compiler and are inserted purely for documentation purposes. The use of banner comments is strongly recommended in programs in any programming language, even though neither Ada nor any other language requires them.

EXERCISES FOR SECTION 3.3

Self-Check

1. Should the value of π (3.14159) be stored in a constant or a variable? Why?

2. Which of these are valid Ada identifiers?

   ```
   MyProgram  prog2  prog#2  2NDone  procedure  "MaxScores"
   ```

3. Indicate which of the following identifiers are Ada reserved words, predefined identifiers, identifiers, and invalid identifiers.

END	Put	BILL	PROCEDURE	SUE'S
Rate	OPERATE	START	BEGIN	CONSTANT
XYZ123	123XYZ	This_Is_A_Long_One	Y=Z	

3.4 System Structures: General Form of an Ada Program

To summarize what we have learned so far, the programs shown earlier all have the general form described in Figure 3.1:

- Each program begins with one or more context clauses followed by a program heading.

- The last line of each program begins with the reserved word END.

- The program heading is followed by declarations, if any, which may appear in any order.

- The reserved word BEGIN signals the start of the *sequence of executable statements* part of the program. The *sequence of executable statements* consists of the program statements that are translated into machine language and executed. The program statements that we have seen so far consist of those that perform computations and input/output operations. These are described in the next section.

- The last line in a program has the form

```
END pname;
```

where *pname* is the name of the program.

- Each declaration and statement in an Ada program ends with a semicolon.

- An Ada statement can extend over more than one line; such a statement cannot be split in the middle of an identifier, a reserved word, a number, or a string. Also, we can write more than one statement on a line, although we will not do so in this book and do not recommend it. Each line of a comment must be preceded by --.

Figure 3.1 General Form of an Ada Program

```
WITH package1;
WITH package2;
  ...
WITH packageN;
PROCEDURE pname IS

  declarations (variables, constants, etc.)

BEGIN

  program statement;
  ...
  program statement;

END pname
```

One of the main functions of a computer is to perform arithmetic computations and display the results of computations. Such operations are specified by the sequence of executable statements that appear in the program body following the reserved word BEGIN. Each statement is translated by the Ada compiler into one or more instructions in machine language, which are copied to the object file and later executed. Declarations, on the other hand, describe to the compiler the meaning and purpose of each user-defined identifier. They result in the allocation of some memory space to hold the data values.

PROGRAM
STYLE

Use of Blank Space

The consistent and careful use of blank spaces can significantly enhance the style of a program. A blank space is required between words in a program line (e.g., between PROCEDURE and Distance in Program 3.4).

Because extra blanks between words and symbols are ignored by the compiler, you may insert them as desired to improve the style and appearance of a program.

Always leave a blank space after a comma and before and after operators such as *, –, and =. Indent by two or more spaces all lines except for the first and last lines of the program and the line BEGIN.

Finally, use blank lines between sections of the program.

All of these measures are taken for the sole purpose of improving the style and hence the clarity of the program. They have no effect whatever on the meaning of the program as far as the computer is concerned; however, they make it easier for people to read and understand the program.

Be careful not to insert blank spaces where they do not belong. For example, there cannot be a space between the characters : and = that make up the assignment symbol :=. Also, you cannot put a blank in the middle of an identifier.

3.5   Problem Solving: Software Development Illustrated

In this textbook we will provide solutions to a number of case studies of programming problems. We obtain the solutions by following the software development method outlined in Section 1.5. Let's go through a case study, step by step.

CASE
STUDY

CONVERTING UNITS OF MEASUREMENT

Problem Specification
You work in a store in the United States that imports fabric. Most of the fabric you receive is measured in square meters; however, the store's customers want to know the equivalent amount in square yards. You need to write a program that performs this conversion.

Analysis
The first step in understanding this problem is to determine what you are being asked to do. It should be clear that you must convert from one system of measurement to another, but are you supposed to convert from square meters to square yards or vice versa? The problem states that you receive fabric measured in square meters, so the problem input is *fabric size in square meters.* Your customers want to know the *equivalent amount in square yards,* which must be your problem output.

To solve this problem, *with or without a computer,* we need to know the relationship between square meters and square yards. By examining a metric table, we find that 1 square meter equals 1.196 square yards.

We summarize the data requirements and relevant formulas below. As shown below, we will use the name `SquareMeters` to identify the memory cell that will contain the problem input and the name `SquareYards` to identify the memory cell that will contain the program result, or the problem output.

Data Requirements and Formulas

Problem Inputs:

`SquareMeters` — the fabric dimensions in square meters

Problem Outputs:

`SquareYards` — the fabric dimensions in square yards

Formulas or Relations:

1 square meter equals 1.196 square yards

Design

Next, we try to formulate the algorithm that we must follow to solve the problem. We begin by listing the three major steps, or subproblems, of the algorithm.

Initial Algorithm

1. Read the fabric size in square meters.

2. Convert the fabric size to square yards.

3. Display the fabric size in square yards.

In using the term *read,* we mean: "Find out the value of this quantity from the user of the program"; because this quantity will change from run to run, we need to ask the user for its value each time. Generally, this is done by instructing the computer to ask the user to enter the value on the computer keyboard; sometimes it is done by reading it from an external disk file (secondary storage). Similarly, in using the term *display,* we usually mean "instruct the computer to show the value on the computer monitor."

Next, we decide whether any steps of the algorithm need further refinement or whether they are perfectly clear as stated. Step 1 (reading data) and step 3 (displaying a value) are basic steps and require no further refinement. Step 2 is fairly straightforward, but it might help to add some detail. The refinement of step 2 follows.

Step 2 Refinement

2.1 Multiply the fabric size in square meters by 1.196; the result is the fabric size in square yards.

The complete algorithm with refinements is shown below. The algorithm resembles an outline for a paper. The refinement of step 2, numbered as step 2.1, is indented under step 2. We list the complete algorithm with refinements below to show you how it all fits together.

Algorithm with Refinements

1. Read the fabric size in square meters.

2. Convert the fabric size to square yards.

2.1 Multiply the fabric size in square meters by 1.196; the result is the fabric size in square yards.

3. Display the fabric size in square yards.

Test Plan

We need to test three cases: a normal case of a positive floating-point value, a zero value, and a negative value. In the last case the program will compute a negative number of square yards. Since this doesn't make physical sense, we will need a way of ensuring that it does not happen. Section 3.9 will offer some first solutions to this.

Implementation

To implement the solution, we must write the algorithm as an Ada program that is acceptable to the compiler. Ada's syntax or grammatical rules require that we first list the problem data requirements—that is, what memory cell names we are using and what kind of data will be stored in each memory cell. Next, we convert each algorithm step into one or more Ada statements. If an algorithm step has been refined, we convert its refinements into Ada statements. You will be able to do this yourself as you learn more about Ada.

Program 3.5 shows the program along with a sample execution (the last two lines of the figure). We show the test run for a normal positive value; we leave it to you to run the program for the other test cases.

Program 3.5 Converting Square Meters to Square Yards

```
WITH Ada.Text_IO;
WITH Ada.Float_Text_IO;
PROCEDURE Metric_Conversion IS
-----------------------------------------------------------------
--| Converts square meters to square yards
--| Author: Michael B. Feldman, The George Washington University
--| Last Modified: June 1998
-----------------------------------------------------------------

   MetersToYards : CONSTANT Float := 1.196; -- conversion constant
   SquareMeters  : Float;                   -- input - metric size
   SquareYards   : Float;                   -- output - US size

BEGIN -- Metric_Conversion

   -- Read the fabric size in square meters
   Ada.Text_IO.Put (Item => "Enter the fabric size in square meters > ");
   Ada.Float_Text_IO.Get(Item => SquareMeters);

   -- Convert the fabric size to square yards
   SquareYards := MetersToYards * SquareMeters;

   -- Display the fabric size in square yards
   Ada.Text_IO.Put(Item => "The fabric size in square yards is ");
   Ada.Float_Text_IO.Put(Item => SquareYards);
   Ada.Text_IO.New_Line;

END Metric_Conversion;
```

Sample Run

```
Enter the fabric size in square meters > 45.00
The fabric size in square yards is  5.38200E+01
```

The program consists, as before, of two parts: the declaration part and the program body. The declaration part is based on the data requirements identified in the problem analysis and tells the compiler what memory cells are needed in the program. Memory cells are needed for storing the variables `SquareMeters` and `SquareYards` and for storing the conversion constant `MetersToYards` (whose value is 1.196).

The program body begins, as always, with the line

```
BEGIN
```

and contains the Ada statements that are translated into machine language and later executed. In the program body we find the statements that express the algorithm steps as Ada statements. The statement

```
Ada.Float_Text_IO.Get (Item => SquareMeters);
```

reads the data value typed by the program user (in this case, 45.00) into the memory cell named `SquareMeters`. The statement

```
SquareYards := MetersToYards * SquareMeters;
```

computes the equivalent fabric size in square yards by multiplying the size in square meters by 1.196; the product is stored in memory cell `SquareYards`.

Finally, the `Put` statements display a message string, the value of `SquareYards`, and a second message string. The instruction displays the value of `SquareYards` as a real number in Ada scientific notation (5.38200E+01). The value printed is equivalent to 5.382×10^1, or 53.82, as will be explained later.

Testing

The sample run shows the result for a positive input. As was discussed in the test plan section, you should run the program for zero and negative input values.

3.6   Control Structures: Assignment Statements

The *assignment statement* is used in Ada to perform computations. The assignment statement

```
SquareYards := MetersToYards * SquareMeters;
```

in Program 3.5 assigns a value to the variable `SquareYards`, in this case the result of the multiplication of the constant `MetersToYards` by the variable `SquareMeters`. Valid information must be stored in both `MetersToYards` and `SquareMeters` before the

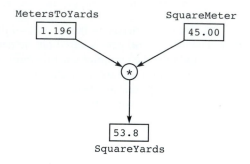

Figure 3.2 Effect of `SquareYards := MetersToYards * SquareYards;`

assignment statement is executed. As shown in Fig. 3.2, only the value of `SquareYards` is affected by the assignment statement; `MetersToYards` and `SquareMeters` retain their original values.

The symbol `:=` is the *assignment symbol* in Ada and should be pronounced "becomes" or "takes the value of" rather than "equals." The `:` and `=` must be adjacent characters with no intervening space. The general form of the assignment statement is shown in the next display.

SYNTAX DISPLAY

Assignment Statement (Arithmetic)

Form:

```
result := expression ;
```

Example:

```
X := Y + Z + 2.0;
```

Interpretation:

The variable specified by *result* is assigned the value of *expression*. The previous value of *result* is destroyed. The expression can be a single variable or a single constant, or it can involve variables, constants, and arithmetic operators, some of which are listed in Table 3.1. The variable specified by *result* must be of the same data type as the expression.

Table 3.1 Some Arithmetic Operators

Operator	Meaning
+	addition
−	subtraction

Table 3.1 Some Arithmetic Operators

Operator	*Meaning*
*	multiplication
/	division
**	exponentiation

It is permissible to write assignment statements of the form

```
Sum := Sum + Item;
```

where the variable Sum is used on both sides of the assignment operator. This is obviously not an algebraic equation, but it illustrates something that is often done in programming. This statement instructs the computer to add the current value of the variable Sum to the value of Item; the result is saved temporarily and then stored back into Sum. The previous value of Sum is destroyed in the process as illustrated in Fig. 3.3; however, the value of Item is unchanged.

Assignment statements can also be written with an expression part that consists of a single variable or value. The statement

```
NewX := X;
```

instructs the computer to copy the value of x into NewX. The statement

```
NewX := −X;
```

instructs the computer to get the value of x, *negate* this value, and store the result in NewX (e.g., If x is 3.5, NewX is −3.5; if X is −17.4, NewX is 17.4). Neither of the assignment statements above changes the value of x.

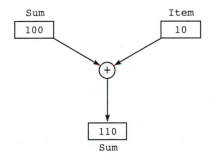

Figure 3.3 Effect of Sum := Sum + Item;

EXERCISES FOR SECTION 3.6

Self-Check

1. Which of the following are valid Ada assignment statements? Why?

   ```
   X = Y;
   A := B - C;
   P + Q := R;
   G := G;
   H := 3 + 4;
   H := 3 + K;
   T := S * T;
   ```

3.7 Control Structures: Input/Output Statements

Information cannot be manipulated by a computer unless it is first stored in main memory. There are three ways to place a data value in memory: Associate it with a constant, assign it to a variable, or read it into a variable from the terminal or a file. The first two approaches can be followed only when the value to be stored will be the same every time the program is run. If we wish to be able to store different information each time, it must be read in as the program is executing (an *input operation*).

As it executes, a program performs computations and assigns new values to variables. The results of a program's execution can be displayed to the program user by an *output operation*.

Input/output operations in Ada are performed by *procedures* that are included in a set of *library packages* supplied with each Ada compiler. We will use procedures from `Ada.Text_IO`, `Ada.Integer_Text_IO`, and `Ada.Float_Text_IO`; later we will use other parts of the input/output libraries. The specific procedure used to read or display a value is determined by the *type* of that value. For the time being, we will manipulate values of four different types: character, string, floating-point number, and integer. As you write each program, you should be aware of the input/output operations that need to be performed and give the required context clauses. Input/output operations in Ada are done using procedure calls, so we now present a syntax display that shows the form of a call.

SYNTAX
DISPLAY

Procedure Call Statement (Simple)

Form:

```
pname (list of parameters);
```

Example:

```
Ada.Text_IO.Put(Item => "Hello.");
Ada.Text_IO.New_Line;
```

Interpretation:

The list of parameters is enclosed in parentheses; each actual parameter value is preceded by the name of that formal parameter.

Note:

In the case of input/output operations, the most important parameter—the value to be output or the variable receiving the input—is always called `Item`. There is no special Ada rule that requires this; it is just the name chosen by the designers of `Ada.Text_IO`.

   As the second example shows, it is possible for a procedure to require no parameters at all. The number, order, and type of parameters are, of course, determined by the writer of the procedure, not by its user.

Performing Input Operations

A *procedure call* statement is used to call an input/output procedure. In Program 3.3, the procedure call statement

```
Ada.Float_Text_IO.Get (Item => Inches);
```

reads a *floating-point value* (a number with a decimal point) into the variable `Inches`. This statement causes the number entered at the keyboard to be stored in the variable `Inches`, as illustrated in Fig. 3.4. After typing a number, the program user should press the ENTER key or the space bar.

   Now recall that in Program 3.1, a user's initials were read. Because each person using the program probably will have different initials, the statements

```
Ada.Text_IO.Get (Item => Initial1);
Ada.Text_IO.Get (Item => Initial2);
```

are used to read in two letters. These statements cause the next two characters entered at the terminal to be stored in the variables `Initial1` and `Initial2` (type `Character`), one character per variable. Figure 3.5 shows the effect of these statements when the letters EK are entered.

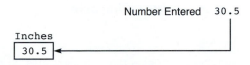

Figure 3.4 Effect of `Ada.Float_Text_IO.Get(Item=>Inches);`

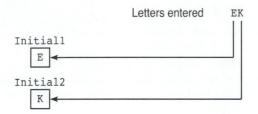

Figure 3.5 Effect of Input of Character Values

It may be necessary to press the ENTER key after typing in the data characters. Some systems will read in these characters as they are typed; most will not begin to read them until after the ENTER key is pressed.

The procedure `Ada.Integer_Text_IO.Get` is used to read an *integer* (a number without a decimal point). This number may or may not be preceded by a sign. The variable into which this number is stored must be of type `Integer`.

The number of characters read by an input operation depends on the type of the variable into which the data are placed. Only one character is read for a variable of type `Character`. In the case of integer and floating-point values, the computer skips over any leading blanks and then continues to read characters until a character that cannot be part of a number is reached (e.g., a blank or a letter) or the ENTER key is pressed.

How does a program user know when to enter the input data and what data to enter? Your program should print a *prompting message* (as explained later in this section and as the examples have shown) to inform the program user what data to enter and when. The cursor indicates the current position on the video screen. As each character is entered, the cursor advances to the next screen position.

Input Tokens

It is interesting to note that the four input characters in Program 3.3 make up a single data value, the number 30.5, which is stored in the variable `Inches` (type `Float`). In Program 3.1, each input character represents a separate data value and is stored in a different variable. And in Program 3.2, where a user's name is read, the sequence of exactly ten characters represents a single value. A sequence of one or more characters representing a single input value is commonly called a *token*. The input sequence `30.5` is a floating-point token, the sequence `Jane Smith` is a string token, and the initials `JS` represent two single-character tokens

SYNTAX
DISPLAY

Get Procedure (Character)

Form:

```
Ada.Text_IO.Get (Item => variable );
```

Example:

```
Ada.Text_IO.Get (Item => Initial1);
```

Interpretation:

The next character pressed on the keyboard is read into *variable* (type `Charac-ter`). A blank counts as a character; an `ENTER` does not.

SYNTAX
DISPLAY

Get Procedure (String)

Form:

```
Ada.Text_IO.Get (Item => variable );
```

Example:

```
Ada.Text_IO.Get (Item => First_Name);
```

Interpretation:

Variable must be a variable of type `string` (`low..high`), where $1 \leq low \leq high$. Exactly high – low + 1 characters are read from the keyboard. An `ENTER` does not count as a character; the computer will wait until exactly the right number of keys, excluding `ENTERS`, are pressed.

SYNTAX
DISPLAY

Get Procedure (Integer)

Form:

```
Ada.Integer_Text_IO.Get (Item => variable );
```

Example:

```
Ada.Integer_Text_IO.Get (Item => How_Long);
```

Interpretation:

The next string of numeric characters entered at the keyboard is read. The numeric string is converted into an integer value and stored in *variable* (type `Integer`). Any leading blank characters or `ENTERS` are ignored. The first nonblank character may be a sign (+ or –) or a digit. The data string is terminated when a nonnumeric character is entered or the space bar or `ENTER` key is pressed.

SYNTAX
DISPLAY

Get Procedure (Floating Point)

Form:

```
Ada.Float_Text_IO.Get (Item => variable );
```

Example:

```
Ada.Float_Text_IO.Get (Item => Inches);
```

Interpretation:

The next string of numeric and other characters entered at the keyboard is read. The characters in this string are converted into a floating-point value and stored in *variable* (type Float). Any leading blank characters or ENTERS are ignored.

The first nonblank character may be a sign (+ or –) or a digit; the remaining characters must be an integer token (if the value is a whole number) or a single decimal point surrounded by numeric characters. Scientific notation (e.g., 123.45E+02) is also permitted.

The data string is terminated when a character is entered that cannot be part of one of the above tokens, or the space bar or ENTER key is pressed.

Performing Output Operations

To see the results of a program execution, we must have some way of displaying the values of selected variables. In Program 3.3 the statements

```
Ada.Text_IO.Put (Item => "That equals ");
Ada.Float_Text_IO.Put (Item => Centimeters);
Ada.Text_IO.Put (Item => " centimeters.");
Ada.Text_IO.New_Line;
```

display the output line

```
That equals 7.74700E+01 centimeters.
```

The procedure Ada.Text_IO.Put is called twice, first to display the string "That equals" and next to display the string " centimeters.". A string must be enclosed in double quotes. When the Ada.Text_IO.Put statement is executed, the characters enclosed in the quotes are printed, but the quotes are not.

The procedure Ada.Float_Text_IO.Put displays the value of variable Centimeters (type Float) between two strings. The number displayed is 77.47 expressed in *scientific notation*. In normal scientific notation, 7.747×10^1 means multiply 7.747 by 10, or move the decimal point right one digit. Because superscripts cannot be entered or displayed at the terminal, the capital letter E is used in computers to indicate scientific notation.

Formatting Character and String Output Values

In Program 3.1 the statements

```
Ada.Text_IO.Put (Item => Initial1);
Ada.Text_IO.Put (Item => Initial2);
```

display the characters stored in the two variables Initial1 and Initial2 (type Character). Each statement causes a single character to be displayed at the current cursor position.

If the variable given to `Ada.Text_IO.Put` is of type `String(low..high)` as in Program 3.2,

```
Ada.Text_IO.Put (Item => First_Name);
```

exactly high – low + 1 characters are displayed.

The procedure `Ada.Integer_Text_IO.Put` is used to display integer values. Whenever an output operation is performed, the characters to be displayed appear at the current cursor position.

The procedure `Ada.Text_IO.New_Line` is used to segment our program output into lines. Each time `Ada.Text_IO.New_Line` is executed, the cursor is advanced to the first position of the next line on the screen.

SYNTAX DISPLAY

Put Procedure (Character)

Form:

```
Ada.Text_IO.Put (Item => variable );
```

Example:

```
Ada.Text_IO.Put (Item => Initial1);
```

Interpretation:
The value of *variable* (type `Character`) is displayed on the screen, and the cursor is advanced to the next position.

SYNTAX DISPLAY

Put Procedure (String)

Form:

```
Ada.Text_IO.Put (Item => variable );
```

Example:

```
Ada.Text_IO.Put (Item => First_Name);
```

Interpretation:
Variable must be a variable of type `String (low..high)`, where 1 _ low _ high. Exactly high – low + 1 characters are displayed on the screen, and the cursor is advanced to the first position after the end of the string.

SYNTAX DISPLAY

New_Line Procedure

Form:

```
Ada.Text_IO.New_Line (Spacing => positive number );
```

Example:

```
Ada.Text_IO.New_Line ( Spacing => 3 );
```

Interpretation:

If `Spacing` is 1, the cursor is moved to the first position of the next line of the display. If `Spacing` is greater than 1, this action is performed `Spacing` times. If `Spacing` is omitted, 1 is used as the default.

PROGRAM
STYLE

Using Prompting Messages to Request Data from the User

The statements

```
Ada.Text_IO.Put (Item => "Enter your two initials >");
```

and

```
Ada.Text_IO.Put (Item => "Enter a length in inches >");
```

are both used to display *prompts* or *prompting messages* in Programs 3.1 and 3.3, respectively.

A prompting message is a string that is displayed just before an input operation is performed. Its purpose is to request that the program user enter data; it may also describe the format of the data expected. It is very important to precede each input operation with a prompting message; otherwise, the program user may have no idea that the program is waiting for data entry or what data to enter.

Formatting Numerical Output Values

Program output is usually designed to be read by humans from a screen display or a printed report. It is therefore important that the output be *formatted* or organized in a way that makes it most easily understood. For example, the decimal value 77.47 is much more obvious to most people than the scientific-notation form of the same value, 7.74700E+01. Also, displays and reports should be organized in nice neat columns so that the information in them is easily digested by the human reader.

Programming languages facilitate production of useful reports by providing ways of precisely controlling both the form and the width of output values, especially numerical ones. In the case of Ada, the integer and floating-point `Put` procedures provide additional *parameters* for output formatting. These are values that are supplied in the procedure call statement.

Integer Output Values

The procedure `Ada.Integer_Text_IO.Put` is used to display integer values. Whenever an output operation is performed, the characters to be displayed appear at the current cursor position.

The integer `Put` procedure allows one additional parameter called `Width`, which indicates the number of print positions to be used for the output value. The statement

```
Ada.Integer_Text_IO.Put (Item => HowFar, Width => 4);
```

will *right-justify* the displayed value of HowFar to four positions. This means that if HowFar is 327, when the value is displayed, it will be preceded by one blank. If HowFar is 19, it will be preceded by two blanks; if HowFar is 1024, it will be preceded by no blanks at all.

Now suppose that HowFar is 12000, which would be a very long trip! In that case the field in the display would be extended to five positions so that no important information would be lost.

In Program 3.4 the output statement supplied no value for Width at all. Ada permits the omission of procedure parameters, but only if the author of the procedure has supplied a *default* value, which will be used instead. The integer Put comes with a default value for Width, but this value can vary from compiler to compiler. This is why in the remaining programs in this book, a value for Width will usually be supplied in the procedure call. We recommend that you follow this practice as well because it makes your programs more portable (independent of a particular compiler).

SYNTAX DISPLAY

Put Procedure (Integer)

Form:

```
Ada.Integer_Text_IO.Put
   (Item => variable, Width => field width);
```

Example:

```
Ada.Integer_Text_IO.Put (Item => How_Long, Width => 5);
```

Interpretation:

The value of *variable* (type Integer) is displayed, using the next Width positions on the screen. If the value (including sign) occupies less than Width positions, it will be preceded by the appropriate number of blanks.

If the value occupies more than Width positions, the actual number of positions is used. If Width is omitted, a compiler-dependent width is used by default.

Table 3.2 shows some examples of formatted integer values.

Table 3.2 Formatted Integer Values

Value	Width	*Displayed Output*
234	4	☐234
234	5	☐☐234
234	6	☐☐☐234
−234	4	−234
−234	6	☐☐−234
234	Len	☐☐☐234 (if Len is 6)
234	1	234
234	0	234

Floating-Point Output Values

The procedure `Ada.Float_Text_IO.Put` is used to display floating-point values. Whenever an output operation is performed, the characters to be displayed appear at the current cursor position. This procedure provides for three formatting parameters:

- `Fore`, which indicates the number of positions before the decimal point,

- `Aft`, which indicates the number of positions after the decimal point, and

- `Exp`, which indicates the number of positions desired following the E. If `Exp` is 0, no exponent will appear at all; this produces a decimal value, rather than a scientific-notation one.

Look again at Program 3.3. If we change the output statement from

```
Ada.Float_Text_IO.Put (Item=>Centimeters);
```

to

```
Ada.Float_Text_IO.Put (Item=>Centimeters, Fore=>5, Aft=>2, Exp=>0);
```

this will produce the value 77.47 preceded by three blanks, instead of 7.74700E+01. Table 3.3 shows some examples of formatted floating-point values.

Table 3.3 Formatted Floating-Point Values

Value	Fore	Aft	Exp	*Displayed Value*
3.14159	2	2	0	□3.14
3.14159	1	2	0	3.14
3.14159	3	1	0	□□3.1
3.14159	1	3	0	3.142
3.14159	2	5	0	□3.14159
3.14159	1	3	2	3.142E+00
0.1234	1	2	0	0.12
−0.006	1	2	0	-0.01
−0.006	1	2	2	−6.00E−3
−0.006	1	5	0	−0.00600
−0.006	4	3	0	□□−0.006

It is very important to realize that these are just different ways of *formatting* output values, that is, controlling the visible form of these values on the screen. Nothing in these output statements alters the actual value stored in memory.

**SYNTAX
DISPLAY**

Put Procedure (Floating Point)

Form:

```
Ada.Float_Text_IO.Put
    (Item => variable , Fore => width before point ,
    Aft => width after point , Exp => width of exponent );
```

Example:

```
Ada.Float_Text_IO.Put
    (Item => Inches, Fore => 5, Aft => 2, Exp => 0);
```

Interpretation:
The value of *variable* is displayed on the screen. Fore gives the desired number of positions in the integer part (to the left of the decimal point); Aft gives the exact number of positions in the fractional part (to the right of the decimal point); Exp gives the exact number of positions in the exponent (after the E).

　　If the integer part of the value, including sign, occupies fewer than Fore positions, blanks are added on the left. If Exp is 0, no exponent is displayed.

EXERCISES FOR SECTION 3.7

Self-Check

1. Correct the syntax errors in the program below and rewrite it so that it follows our style conventions. What does each statement of your corrected program do? What is printed?

    ```
    PROCEDURE SMALL;
       X: Float;
       Y: Foat;
       x: Float;
    BEGIN;
       15.0 = Y;
       Z =-Y + 3.5;
    Y + z = x;
       Put(x, Y, z)
    end small;
    ```

2. Provide the statements needed to display the line below. Display the value of X using ten characters in the space provided.

    ```
    The value of X is ---------- pounds.
    ```

3.8 Data Structures: Introduction to Data Types and Expressions

First, let's clarify exactly what is meant by a data type in a programming language. A *data type* is a set of values and a set of operations on those values. The data type of the object stored in a particular memory cell determines how the bit pattern in that cell is interpreted. For example, the same bit pattern can represent a type `Integer` object, a type `Character` object, a type `Float` object, or even a program instruction. A *predefined data type* is a data type that is predefined in the programming language (for example, `Integer`, `Float`, and `Character`). Besides the standard data types, programmers can define their own data types in Ada. Indeed, defining our own types will be an important part of our study, to be started in Chapter 4.

It is important to understand that in Ada, every variable or constant object has a type, that is, every object has a *known set of values* we can assign it, and a *set of operations* that we can validly perform on it. In the terminology of object-oriented programming, every object has a set of *states* (values) and a set of *methods* (operations). Taken together, the methods characterize the object's *behavior*.

Character Data Type

Our first predefined type is `Character`. We have already seen (Program 3.1) that `Character` variables can be used to store any single-character value. A `Character` value mentioned in a program—a literal—must be enclosed in single quotes (for example, `'A'`); however, quotes are not used when character data are entered as tokens. When the `Ada.Text_IO.Get` procedure is used to read character data into a `Character` variable, the next character entered at the terminal is stored in that variable. The blank character is entered by pressing the space bar; it is written in a program as the literal `' '`.

■ Example 3.5

Program 3.6 first reads and echos three characters entered at the keyboard. Next, it prints them in reverse order enclosed in asterisks. Each character is stored in a variable object of type `Character`; the character value `'*'` is associated with the constant object `Border`. The lines

```
Ada.Text_IO.Put (Item=>Third);
Ada.Text_IO.Put (Item=>Second);
Ada.Text_IO.Put (Item=>First);
```

display the three characters in reverse order. As shown in the program output, each character value is printed in a single print position. ■

Program 3.6 Reversing Three Letters

```
WITH Ada.Text_IO;
PROCEDURE Reverse_Letters IS
-----------------------------------------------------------------
```

```
--| Reverses the order of three input letters
--| Author: Michael B. Feldman, The George Washington University
--| Last Modified: June 1998
-----------------------------------------------------------
   Border : CONSTANT Character := '*';
   First, Second, Third : Character;   -- input - three characters

BEGIN -- Reverse_Letters

   -- Prompt for three characters
   Ada.Text_IO.Put(Item => "Enter 3 characters> ");
   Ada.Text_IO.Get(Item => First);
   Ada.Text_IO.Get(Item => Second);
   Ada.Text_IO.Get(Item => Third);
   Ada.Text_IO.New_Line;

   -- Display these characters in reverse order
   Ada.Text_IO.Put(Item => Border);
   Ada.Text_IO.Put(Item => Third);
   Ada.Text_IO.Put(Item => Second);
   Ada.Text_IO.Put(Item => First);
   Ada.Text_IO.Put(Item => Border);
   Ada.Text_IO.New_Line;

END Reverse_Letters;
```

Sample Run

```
Enter 3 characters> FBI

*IBF*
```

Several operations are defined for character values; the most obvious one is *assignment*. An assignment statement can be used to store a literal value into a character constant or variable or to copy the value of one character variable into another. *Comparison* operations on character values will be introduced in Chapter 5.

Float Data Type

The standard data types in Ada represent familiar objects. For example, the data type Float is that subset of real numbers (in the mathematical sense) that can be represented on the computer. Every Float value in Ada is a real number; however, not all real numbers can be represented in Ada or in any programming language. Some real numbers are too large or too small or cannot be represented precisely owing to the finite size of a memory cell (more on this in Chapter 7). The normal arithmetic operations for real numbers (+, −, *, /) and the assignment operation (:=) can be performed on Float objects in Ada. The metric conversion problem discussed in Section 3.5 is an example of the use of objects of type Float.

Integer Data Type

The other predefined data types that represent numbers are `Integer`, `Natural`, and `Positive`. `Integer` values in Ada correspond to the mathematical integers (e.g., –77, 0, 999, +999). However, because of the finite size of a memory cell, not all integers can be represented in Ada, and every Ada compiler has predefined positive and negative limits on type `Integer` values. These limits are not specified in the standard and are most commonly either –32768 and +32767. (16-bit arithmetic) or –2147483648 and +2147483647 (32-bit arithmetic). `Natural` values correspond to the nonnegative integers (including 0); `Positive` values correspond to the positive integers (excluding 0).

Actually, the types `Natural` and `Positive` are *subtypes* of `Integer`: Every positive integer is also an integer. We will introduce a discussion of subtypes in Chapter 4 and revisit the subject frequently.

The basic distinction between type `Float` and the three integer data types is that a number with a decimal point and fractional part can be stored in a `Float` object, but only whole numbers can be stored in type `Integer`, `Natural`, and `Positive` objects. We often use these to represent a count of items because a count must always be a nonnegative whole number.

What are the operations on integer values? The operations +, –, and * have obvious meanings of sum, difference, and product, respectively. What about division? Dividing one integer by another always gives an integer result, which is the "whole number," or quotient, part of the division. Thus 3/2 gives a result of 1, 14/4 gives a result of 3, and 2/3 gives a result of 0. The fractional part, or remainder, is lost in the division operation.

Because the remainder is lost in an integer division, Ada provides an operation REM that can be applied to two integers. REM gives the remainder in the division operation, as you would compute it in a "long division." Here are some examples:

3 REM 2 is 1 (dividing 3 by 2 gives a quotient of 1 and a remainder of 1).

14 REM 4 is 2 (dividing 14 by 4 gives a quotient of 3 and a remainder of 2).

2 REM 3 is 2 (dividing 2 by 3 gives a quotient of 0 and a remainder of 2).

One last operator merits discussion here: The operator ** is used to represent *exponentiation,* or raising a value to a given power. Given a variable x whose current value is 3,

X ** 2 is 9 (multiply 3 by 3).

X ** 3 is 27 (multiply 3 by 3 by 3).

X ** 4 is 81 (multiply 3 by 3 by 3 by 3).

and so on.

Exponentiation is also defined to raise a floating-point value to a given power. *The power must be an integer, however.* If Y is a floating-point variable with value 1.2, then

Y ** 2 is 1.44 (multiply 1.2 by 1.2).

Y ** 3 is 1.728 (multiply 1.2 by 1.2 times 1.2).

Y ** 1.5 is not allowed, and will result in a compilation error.

Literals and Tokens

Objects of a data type can be variables, constants, or literals. A *literal* is a value that appears directly in a program. For example, a `Float` literal is a number that begins with a digit and contains a decimal point (e.g., 0.112, 456.0, 123.456). A `Float` literal may have a *scale factor*, which is the capital letter E followed by an optional sign and an integer (e.g., `0.112E3`, `456.0E-2`). The scale factor means "multiply the preceding real number by 10 raised to the power appearing after the letter `E` (e.g., `0.112E3` is `112.0`, `456.0E-2` is `4.56`). A `Float` literal may be preceded by a + or − sign when it appears in a program. Examples of valid and invalid `Float` literals are shown in Table 3.4.

Table 3.4 Some Valid and Invalid `Float` Literals

Valid `Float` *Literals*	*Invalid* `Float` *Literals*
`3.14159`	`150` (no decimal point)
`0.005`	`.12345` (no digit before `.`)
`12345.0`	`12345.` (no digit after `.`)
`15.0E-04` (value is `0.0015`)	`15E-03` (`15` invalid `Float`)
`2.345E2` (value is `234.5`)	`12.5E.3` (`.3` invalid exponent)
`-1.2E+6` (value is `-1200000`)	`-.123E3` (`-.123` invalid `Float`)
`1.15E-3` (value is `0.00115`)	

The last valid literal in Table 3.4, `1.15E-3`, has the same value as 1.15×10^{-3} in normal scientific notation where the exponent −3 causes the decimal point to be moved left three digits. A positive exponent causes the decimal point to be moved to the right; the + sign may be omitted when the exponent is positive.

The preceding example has concentrated on `Float` literals; `Integer`, `Character`, `String`, and enumeration literals (next chapter) are also commonly used.

You might be wondering what the difference is between the terms *literal* and *token*. Conventionally, a sequence of characters representing a value is called a literal when it appears within the text of a program, and such a sequence is called a token when it is read from an input device or displayed on an output device.

Expressions with Several Operators

Ada allows us to write expressions with many variables, constants, literals, and operators; in fact, there is no formal limit at all on the complexity of an expression. We must therefore know the order in which the various parts of an expression are evaluated. We'll take a systematic look at this in Chapter 8. To give you some help in the meantime, suppose `W`, `X`, `Y`, and `Z` are all `Integer` variable objects, and let `X` be `3`, `Y` be `4`, and `Z` be `7`. Here's how Ada will evaluate some assignments to the variable `W`:

```
W := X * Y + Z;
```

will store $(3 \times 4) + 7$, or 19, in `W`. The result of the multiplication is added to `Z`. It is as though the expression were written

```
W := (X * Y) + Z;
```

which is also correct Ada and gets the same result. Now

```
W := Z + X * Y;
```

stores $7 + (3 \times 4)$ in w. Again the result of the multiplication is added to z; this is equivalent to writing

```
W := Z + (X * Y);
```

which, of course, is also correct Ada. Ada follows the basic rule that multiplications and divisions are done before additions and subtractions, but parentheses can be used to override the basic rule. For example,

```
W := X * (Y + Z);
```

causes $3 \times (4 + 7)$, or 33, to be stored in w. The parentheses force the addition to be done first and the result to be multiplied by z. Consider

```
W := X / Y + Z;
```

which stores $(3/4) + 7$, or 7, in w (remember division of integers!), and

```
W := X / (Y + Z);
```

which stores $3/(4 + 7)$, or 0, in w (again, dividing the integers here gives 0).

Now suppose that we have two or more addition or subtraction operators in the same expression. In this case, the operations are done in left-to-right order.

```
W := X - Y + Z;
```

stores $(3 - 4)+7$ or 6 in w; the subtraction is done first. If we had written

```
W := X - (Y + Z);
```

the result in w would be $3 - (4 + 7)$, or –8. Again, the parentheses force the addition to be done first. Make sure you understand why

```
W := X - Y - Z;
```

and

```
W : = X - (Y - Z);
```

store –8 and 6, respectively, in w. A similar left-to-right rule applies to multiplication and division operators. Finally, exponentiation is done even before multiplication or division, so the expression

```
Pi * R ** 2
```

is equivalent to

```
Pi * (R ** 2)
```

and not

(Pi * R) ** 2

PROGRAM STYLE

Using Parentheses to Write Expressions You Can Understand

Ada has many operators; you will study most of them in this book. The compiler follows very systematic rules (known formally as *precedence and association rules*) in evaluating complicated expressions with many operators; these are spelled out in Chapter 8. The compiler "knows exactly what it is doing" and will always get a result that is correct by those rules.

However, a human writer or reader of a program may have trouble sorting out the order of execution of the operations in an expression with more than one or two operators, and the result can sometimes be unpleasantly surprising if the human sorts it out differently than the compiler does. Remembering the precedence and association rules is difficult and also unnecessary.

You should instead use two very simple rules in writing an expression: Keep it as simple as you can, and use a lot of parentheses to indicate both to the compiler and to yourself what the intention of the expression is. Using extra parentheses will save you time in debugging; using too few parentheses to save writing effort is false economy.

Using Integer Objects

The following case study gives an example of manipulating Integer objects in Ada.

CASE STUDY

FINDING THE VALUE OF A COIN COLLECTION

Problem Specification

Your little sister has been saving nickels (U.S. five-cent coins) and pennies (U.S. one-cent coins) for quite a while. Because she is getting tired of lugging her piggy bank with her whenever she goes to the store, she would like to trade in her collection for one-dollar banknotes (a dollar is 100 cents) and some change. To do this, she would like to know the value of her coin collection in dollars and cents.

Analysis

To solve this problem, we must be given the count of nickels and the count of pennies in the collection. The first step is to determine the total value of the collection in cents. Once we have this figure, we can do an integer division using 100 as the divisor to get the dollar value; the remainder of this division will be the loose change that she should receive. In the data requirements below, we list the total value in cents (TotalCents) as a program variable because it is needed as part of the computation process; it is not a required problem output.

Data Requirements and Formulas

Problem Inputs:

Nickels : Natural (the number of nickels)

Pennies : Natural (the number of pennies)

Problem Outputs:

Dollars : Integer (the number of dollars she should receive)
Change : Integer (the loose change she should receive)

Additional Program Variables

TotalCents : Integer (the total number of cents)

Relevant Formulas

One nickel equals five pennies.

Design

The algorithm is straightforward and is displayed next.

Initial Algorithm

1. Read in the count of nickels and pennies.

2. Compute the total value in cents.

3. Find the value in dollars and loose change.

4. Display the value in dollars and loose change.

Steps 2 and 3 need refinement.

Step 2 Refinement

2.1. TotalCents is 5 times Nickels plus Pennies.

Step 3 Refinement:

3.1. Dollars is the integer quotient of TotalCents and 100.

3.2. Change is the integer remainder of TotalCents and 100.

Algorithm with Refinements

1. Read in the count of nickels and pennies.

2. Compute the total value in cents.

    2.1. TotalCents is 5 times Nickels plus Pennies.

3. Find the value in dollars and loose change.

    3.1. Dollars is the integer quotient of TotalCents and 100.

    3.2. Change is the integer remainder of TotalCents and 100.

4. Display the value in dollars and loose change.

Test Plan

In addition to testing some typical values, there are several special cases in our test plan: zero nickels and/or zero pennies, and negative input values. Let's put the test plan in the form of a table, shown as Table 3.5.

Table 3.5   Test Plan for Coin Collection

Test Case	Nickels	Pennies	Reason	Expected Result
1	30	77	typical	$2.27
2	0	59	no nickels	$0.59
3	13	0	no pennies	$0.65
4	0	0	no coins	$0.00
5	13	–5	negative	?
6	xyz	4	bad input	?

The last two cases test for out of range input (a negative number when a natural number is required) and "bad" input (letters instead of digits). The question marks indicate that we won't know the result until we run the test. It is important always to test programs with "bad" as well as "good" input: The programmer cannot control which keys will be pressed by the human user, and a program's behavior must always be *predictable*.

Implementation

Program 3.7 shows the program. The statement

```
TotalCents := 5 * Nickels + Pennies;
```

implements algorithm step 2.1 and the statements

```
Dollars := TotalCents / 100;
Change := TotalCents REM 100;
```

implement algorithm steps 3.1 and 3.2.

Note how a value of 1 for the `width` parameter is used to format the displayed values so that they appear just next to the title text. Can you explain why `width=>1` accomplishes this?

Program 3.7 Finding the Value of a Coin Collection

```
WITH Ada.Text_IO;
WITH Ada.Integer_Text_IO;
PROCEDURE Coin_Collection IS
-------------------------------------------------------------------------
--| Finds the value of a coin collection,
--| given pennies and nickels
--| Author: Michael B. Feldman, The George Washington University
--| Last Modified: June 1998
-------------------------------------------------------------------------
```

```
        Pennies    : Natural;              -- input - number of pennies
        Nickels    : Natural;              -- input - number of nickels
        Dollars    : Natural;              -- output - value in dollars
        Cents      : Natural;              -- output - value in cents
        TotalCents : Natural;

    BEGIN -- Coin_Collection

        -- prompt user for number of nickels and pennies
        Ada.Text_IO.Put (Item => "How many nickels do you have? ");
        Ada.Integer_Text_IO.Get (Item => Nickels);
        Ada.Text_IO.Put (Item => "How many pennies do you have? ");
        Ada.Integer_Text_IO.Get (Item => Pennies);
        Ada.Text_IO.New_Line;

        -- compute total value in cents
        TotalCents := 5 * Nickels + Pennies;

        -- find the value in dollars and change
        Dollars := TotalCents / 100;
        Cents   := TotalCents REM 100;

        -- display the value in dollars and change
        Ada.Text_IO.Put (Item => "Your collection is worth ");
        Ada.Integer_Text_IO.Put (Item => Dollars, Width => 1);
        Ada.Text_IO.Put (Item => " dollars and ");
        Ada.Integer_Text_IO.Put (Item => Cents, Width => 1);
        Ada.Text_IO.Put (" cents.");
        Ada.Text_IO.New_Line;

    END Coin_Collection;
```

Sample Run, Case 1

```
How many nickels do you have? 30
How many pennies do you have? 77

Your collection is worth 2 dollars and 27 cents.
```

Sample Run, Case 2

```
How many nickels do you have? 0
How many pennies do you have? 59

Your collection is worth 0 dollars and 59 cents.
```

Sample Run, Case 3

```
How many nickels do you have? 13
How many pennies do you have? 0

Your collection is worth 0 dollars and 65 cents.
```

Sample Run, Case 4

```
How many nickels do you have? 0
How many pennies do you have? 0
```

```
Your collection is worth 0 dollars and 0 cents.
```

Testing

This test run shows input of test cases 1 through 4 from the test plan. These results agree with the expected results. We defer the two error cases until the next section when we discuss errors in general.

Memory Area for the Coin Collection Program

The left side of Figure 3.6 shows the coin collection program loaded into memory and the program memory area before execution of the program body. The right side of the figure shows the contents after the program has run.

The question mark in memory cells Pennies, Nickels, Dollars, Cents, and TotalCents indicates that these variables are *undefined* (value unknown) before program execution begins. During program execution, the data values 30 and 77 are read into the variables Nickels and Pennies, respectively. After the assignment statements are used to compute values for TotalCents, Dollars, and Cents, all variables are defined (have known values) as shown in the right side of Fig. 3.6.

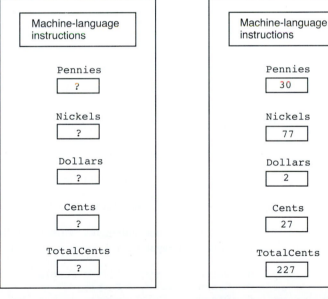

Figure 3.6 Memory for Coin Collection Program

EXERCISES FOR SECTION 3.8

Self-Check

1. Evaluate the following expressions with 7 and 22 as operands:

   ```
   2 / 7        7 / 22        22 REM 7        7 REM 22
   ```

   Repeat this exercise for the pairs of integers:

   ```
   15, 16        3, 23        4, 16
   ```

2. Given the declarations:

   ```
   Pi : CONSTANT Float :=    3.14159;
   MaxI : CONSTANT Integer :=   1000;
   ```

   the `Float` variables x and y, and the `Integer` variables A, B, and I, indicate whether each of the following assignments is valid, and, if so, what its value is. Assume that A is 3, B is 4, and y is −1.0.

   a. `I := A REM B;`
   b. `I := (990 - MaxI) / A;`
   c. `I := A REM Y;`
   d. `X := Pi * Y;`
   e. `I := A / B;`
   f. `X := A / B;`
   g. `X := A REM (A / B);`
   h. `I := B / 0;`
   i. `I := A REM (990 - MaxI);`
   j. `I := (MaxI - 990) / A;`
   k. `X := A / Y;`
   l. `X := Pi ** 2;`
   m. `X := Pi ** Y;`
   n. `X := A / B;`
   o. `I := (MaxI - 990) REM A;`
   p. `I := A REM 0;`
   q. `I := A REM (MaxI - 990);`

3. If we assume that A is 5, B is 2, and y is 2.0, what values are assigned by the valid statements in Exercise 2?

4. Assume that you have the following integer variables:

   ```
   Color, Lime, Straw, Yellow, Red, Orange
   ```

   and the following floating-point variables:

   ```
   Black, White, Green, Blue, Purple, Crayon
   ```

   Evaluate each of the statements below given the following values: Color is 2, Black is 2.5, Crayon is −1.3, Straw is 1, Red is 3, Purple is 0.3E1.

   a. `White := Crayon * 2.5 / Purple;`
   b. `Green := Black / Purple;`
   c. `Orange := Color / Red;`
   d. `Orange := (Color +  Straw) / (2*Straw);`
   e. `Lime := Red / Color + Red REM Color ;`
   f. `Purple := Straw / Red * Color;`

5. Let A, B, C, and X be the names of four Float variables and let I, J, and K be the names of three Integer variables. Each of the following statements contains a violation of the rules for forming arithmetic expressions. Rewrite each statement so that it is consistent with these rules.

    a. X := 4.0 A * C;   d. K := 3(I + J);
    b. A := AC;   e. X := 5A / BC;
    c. I := 2 * -J;   f. I := 5J3;

3.9 Tricks of the Trade: Common Programming Errors

Section 1.10 introduced the three main categories of programming errors: compilation errors, run-time errors, and logic or algorithm errors. In this section we look at some common semantic errors and discuss run-time errors.

Semantic Compilation Errors

Program 3.8 is a modified version of the distance program, Program 3.4. The modified program contains a few intentional errors: We declared How_Fast as Float and also used Ada.Float_Text_IO calls instead of Ada.Integer_Text_IO calls. These are all errors that beginners commonly make.

Program 3.8 Distance Program with Intentional Errors

```
WITH Ada.Text_IO;
WITH Ada.Float_Text_IO;
PROCEDURE Distance_with_Errors IS
-------------------------------------------------------------------
--| Finds distance, given travel time and average speed
--| Author: Michael eldman, The George Washington University
--| Last Modified: June 1998
-------------------------------------------------------------------
  HowLong : Natural;
  HowFast : Float;
  HowFar  : Natural;

BEGIN -- Distance_with_Errors

  -- prompt user for hours and average speed
  Ada.Text_IO.Put
    (Item => "How long will you be driving (integer) ? ");
  Ada.Float_Text_IO.Get (Item => HowLong);
  Ada.Text_IO.Put
    (Item => "At what speed (miles per hour, integer)?");
  Ada.Float_Text_IO.Get (Item => HowFast);

  -- compute distance driven
  HowFast := HowLong * HowFar;

  -- display results
  Ada.Text_IO.Put (Item => "You will travel about ");
```

```
        Ada.Float_Text_IO.Put (Item => HowFar);
        Ada.Text_IO.Put (Item => " miles");
        Ada.Text_IO.New_Line;

END Distance_with_Errors;
```

Figure 3.7 shows a listing from a GNAT compilation of this program.

Figure 3.7   Compilation Listing with Error Messages

```
 1. WITH Ada.Text_IO;
 2. WITH Ada.Float_Text_IO;
 3. PROCEDURE Distance_with_Errors IS
 4. ------------------------------------------------------------
 5. --| Finds distance, given travel time and average speed
 6. --| Author: Michael eldman, The George Washington University
 7. --| Last Modified: June 1998
 8. ------------------------------------------------------------
 9.    HowLong : Natural;
10.    HowFast : Float;
11.    HowFar  : Natural;
12.
13. BEGIN -- Distance_with_Errors
14.
15.    -- prompt user for hours and average speed
16.    Ada.Text_IO.Put
17.       (Item => "How long will you be driving (integer) ?");
18.    Ada.Float_Text_IO.Get (Item => HowLong);
                                 |
       >>> invalid parameter list in call

19.    Ada.Text_IO.Put
20.       (Item => "At what speed (miles per hour, integer) ? ");
21.    Ada.Float_Text_IO.Get (Item => HowFast);
22.
23.    -- compute distance driven
24.    HowFast := HowLong * HowFar;
                              |
       >>> expected type "Standard.Float"
       >>> found type "Standard.Integer"

25.
26.    -- display results
27.    Ada.Text_IO.Put (Item => "You will travel about ");
28.    Ada.Float_Text_IO.Put (Item => HowFar);
                                 |
       >>> invalid parameter list in call
       >>> possible missing instantiation of Text_IO.Integer_IO

29.    Ada.Text_IO.Put (Item => " miles");
30.    Ada.Text_IO.New_Line;
31.
32. END Distance_with_Errors;
```

The first message, at line 18, informs us that the Item parameter to Get is invalid, in this case because we tried to use the floating-point Get to read into an Integer variable. The same message appears at line 28, for the same reason. Finally, the message at line

24 indicates that the multiplication is invalid, because we are trying to multiply a `Float` variable (the incorrectly declared `HowFast`) by a `Natural` one (`HowLong`). Such mixing of integer and floating-point values is not allowed.

Recall from Section 1.10 that compilation errors are of two general kinds: syntax errors and semantic errors. Some Ada compilers distinguish between these in their error messages; others (for example, GNAT) do not. Some compilers try to find both syntactic and semantic errors at the same time; others (like GNAT) generally do it in two stages, first finding the syntax errors, then the semantic ones.

In languages such as Ada with data types, semantic errors occur quite frequently. One of the things you will need to be careful about is making sure that the types of your variables match the expectation of the expression or procedure in which the variables are used. If a procedure expects an `Integer` variable, supplying a `Float` variable won't do; also, you cannot mix `Integer` and `Float` variables in the same expression!

Finally, recall our advice from Section 1.10: There is no need to panic at getting a long list of messages; it happens to all new programmmers and occasionally to experienced ones as well. There are probably only a few actual errors and many extra messages because of propagation, or because you repeated the error in several places, so it's best just to try to correct the first one or two errors, then recompile. You'll be amazed at how quickly the number of messages decreases.

Run-Time Errors

As was discussed above, run-time errors are called *exceptions* in Ada. The most common exceptions encountered by beginners are those relating to the ranges of variables in their programs. A range error occurs when a program tries to save an inappropriate value in a variable. This can happen in one of two ways: Either the program itself computes a result that is out of range for the variable in which it will be saved, or the program user enters an out-of-range value from the keyboard. Ada gives the name `Constraint_Error` to such a range error; Ada uses the term *raising an exception* for reporting the occurrence of such a runtime error.

As an example of the second case, consider case 5 of the test plan for the coin collection program (Program 3.7, Table 3.4). Figure 3.8 shows a sample run in which we enter a negative value for the number of pennies. Recall that the variable `Pennies` was declared to be of type `Natural`, that is, nonnegative.

Figure 3.8 Sample Run of `Coin_Collection`, Negative Input Entered

```
How many nickels do you have? 13
How many pennies do you have? -5

raised Constraint_Error

Traceback Information
    Program Name                File Name                   Line
    ------------                ---------                   ----
    coin_collection             coin_collection.adb         22
```

The form of the exception report and "trace back" to your source program varies from compiler to compiler, but the content is the same: You are told which exception was raised and where.

Figure 3.9 shows the results of test case 6, in which "bad" input is entered, namely, a sequence of characters that cannot be an integer token.

Figure 3.9   Sample Run of `coin_collection`, Noninteger Input Entered

```
How many nickels do you have? xyz

raised unhandled exception

raised ada.text_io.data_error

Traceback Information
    Program Name                 File Name                    Line
    ------------                 ---------                    ----
    coin_collection              coin_collection.adb           22
```

In this case the exception raised is an input/output exception called `Ada.Text_IO.Data_Error`. This exception is raised when a `Get` operation gets a token of the wrong form, in this case a string of letters instead of an integer. The difference between `Constraint_Error` and `Data_Error` is that in the former case the value is formed correctly but is too large or too small, while in the latter case the token is not formed properly.

To summarize, Ada's data types and exception system are designed to help you write programs whose results will make sense. In this book we will pay very careful attention to this matter, because it is important and can be very useful to you.

Debugging a program can be time-consuming. The best approach is to plan your programs carefully and desk check them beforehand to eliminate bugs before they occur. If you are not sure of the syntax for a particular statement, look it up in the syntax displays in the text. Also, take care that your program variables have types that are appropriate and sensible. If you follow this approach, you will save yourself much time and trouble.

CHAPTER REVIEW

In this chapter you have seen how to use the Ada programming language to perform some fundamental operations. You learned how to instruct the computer to read information into memory, perform some simple computations, and display the results of those computations. All of this was done using symbols (punctuation marks, variable names, and special operators such as *, -, and +) that are familiar, easy to remember, and easy to use. You have also learned a bit about data types, a very important concept in developing programs whose results make sense.

In the remainder of this text we introduce more features of the Ada language and provide rules for using these features. You must remember throughout that, unlike the rules of English, the rules of Ada—like those of any computer language—must be followed precisely. The compiler will be unable to translate Ada instructions that violate these rules. Remember to declare every identifier that is used as a variable or constant object and to terminate program statements with semicolons.

New Ada Constructs

Table 3.6 describes the new Ada constructs introduced in this chapter.

Table 3.6 Summary of New Ada Constructs

Construct	Effect
Context Clause	
`WITH Ada.Text_IO;`	indicates that package `Ada.Text_IO` is used by the program
Program Heading	
`PROCEDURE Payroll IS`	identifies `Payroll` as the name of the program
Constant declaration	
`Tax : CONSTANT Float := 25.00;`	associates the constant, `Tax`, with the `Float` value 25.00
`Star :` `  CONSTANT Character := '*';`	associates the constant, `Star`, with the `Character` value `'*'`
Variable declaration	
`X: Float;`	declares a variable object named `x` for storage of `Float` values
`Me : Integer;`	declares a variable object named `Me` for storage of `Integer` values
Assignment Statement	
`Distance := Speed * Time;`	computes the product of `Speed` and `Time` and assigns it to `Distance`.
Input Statements	
`Ada.Text_IO.Get` `  (Item=>Initial);`	enters data into the character variable `Initial`
`Ada.Integer_Text_IO.Get` `  (Item=>HowMany);`	enters data into the integer variable `How-Many`
`Ada.Float_Text_IO.Get` `  (Item=>PayRate);`	enters data into the float variable `PayRate`
Output Statements	
`Ada.Text_IO.Put(Item=>Initial);`	displays the value of the character variable `Initial`

Construct	Effect
`Ada.Integer_Text_IO.Put` `  (Item=>HowMany, Width=>5);`	displays the value of the integer variable `HowMany`, using five columns on the display

`Ada.Float_Text_IO.Put`
`  (Item=>GrossPay, Fore=>4,`
`  Aft=>2, Exp=>0);`
	displays the value of the float variable `PayRate` using four columns before the decimal point and two columns after the decimal point.

Quick-Check Exercises

1. What value is assigned to x by the following statement?

    ```
    X := 25.0 * 3.0 / 2.5;
    ```

2. Given the result from Exercise 1, now what value is assigned to x?

    ```
    X := X - 20.0;
    ```

3. Show the exact form of the output displayed when x is 3.456.

    ```
    Ada.Text_IO.Put(Item => "Three values of X are");
    Ada.Float_Text_IO.Put(Item=>X, Fore=>2, Aft=>1, Exp=>0);
    Ada.Text_IO.Put(Item => '*');
    Ada.Float_Text_IO.Put(Item=>X, Fore=>1, Aft=>2, Exp=>0);
    Ada.Text_IO.Put(Item => '*');
    Ada.Float_Text_IO.Put(Item=>X, Fore=>2, Aft=>3, Exp=>0);
    Ada.Text_IO.New_Line;
    ```

4. Show the exact form of the output displayed when N is 345.

    ```
    Ada.Text_IO.Put(Item => "Three values of N are");
    Ada.Integer_Text_IO.Put(Item => N, Width => 4);
    Ada.Text_IO.Put(Item => '*');
    Ada.Float_Text_IO.Put(Item => N, Width => 5);
    Ada.Text_IO.Put(Item => '*');
    Ada.Float_Text_IO.Put(Item => N, Width => 1);
    Ada.Text_IO.New_Line;
    ```

5. What data type would you use to represent each of the following items: number of children at school, a letter grade on an exam, the average number of school days students are absent each year?

6. Suppose `Ada.Integer_Text_IO.Get` is called twice in succession, for example,

    ```
    Ada.Integer_Text_IO.Get(Item => X);
    Ada.Integer_Text_IO.Get(Item => Y);
    ```

    What character(s) may be typed after the first number is entered? What may be typed after the second number is entered?

7. Suppose `Ada.Text_IO.Get` is called twice in succession, for example,

```
Ada.Text_IO.Get(Item => X);
Ada.Text_IO.Get(Item => Y);
```

What happens if a blank is entered after the first character? What happens if ENTER is pressed after the first character?

8. What kind of errors does a compilation listing show?

Answers to Quick-Check Exercises

1. `30.0`

2. `10.0`

3. `Three values of X are 3.5*3.46* 3.456`

4. `Three values of N are 345*  345*345`

5. `Natural, Character, Float` (or `NonNegFloat`)

6. Any number of blanks and/or ENTERS; same

7. The blank will be read into Y; the ENTER will be skipped, and the next character (if it is not an ENTER) will be read into Y.

8. Compilation errors: syntax and semantic errors

Programming Projects

1. Write a program that reads three data items into variables X, Y, and Z and then finds and displays their product and sum.

2. Write a program that reads in the weight (in pounds) of an object and then computes and displays its weight in kilograms and grams. (*Hint:* One pound is equal to 0.453592 kilogram or 453.59237 grams.)

3. Write a program to convert a temperature in degrees Fahrenheit to degrees Celsius. Use the formula

$$Celsius = (5/9) \times (Fahrenheit - 32)$$

4. Eleven nations in Europe are changing over to a common currency called the *euro*. Foreigners traveling in Europe will need to know how many euros their dollars will buy. On Jan. 1, 1999, the day the euro was introduced, one euro was worth about $1.17 in U.S. currency, but this exchange rate can change at any time. Develop a program that prompts the user for the exchange rate and the number of dollars to be exchanged and then displays the equivalent amount in euros.

5. A track star competes in a 1-mile race. Write a program that reads in the race time in minutes (`Minutes`) and seconds (`Seconds`) for this runner and then computes and displays the speed in feet per second (`FPS`) and in meters per second (`MPS`). (*Hint:* There are 5280 feet in 1 mile, and 1 kilometer equals 3282 feet.) Test your program on each of the following times:

   ```
   minutes   seconds
   3         52.83
   3         59.83
   4         00.03
   4         16.22
   ```

6. A cyclist coasting on a level road slows from a speed of 15 kilometers per hour (km/h) to 5 km/h in 1 minute. Write a computer program that calculates the cyclist's constant rate of acceleration and determines how long it will take the cyclist to come to rest, given an initial speed of 10 miles per hour (*Hint:* Use the equation $a = (v_f - v_i) / t$, where a is acceleration, t is time interval, v_i is the initial velocity, and v_f is the final velocity.)

7. If a human heart beats on the average of once a second for 78 years, how many times does the heart beat in a lifetime? (Use 365.25 for days in a year.) Rerun your program for a heart rate of 75 beats per minute.

8. You have just gotten back from a trip to the beautiful country of LaLa Land. While you were there, you found a great deal on a car, so you brought it back with you. But you have a problem: In your country the distances are measured in miles, but in LaLa Land, the distances are measured in *furlongs*. Each furlong is 1/8 mile (really!). So the odometer (mileage counter) in your beautiful new car tells you how many furlongs you've traveled. Not only that, but speeds are measured in furlongs per fortnight (*fpf*). Each fortnight is two weeks or 14 days (really). Since in LaLa Land, the highway speed limits are, of course, given in these units, your car's digital speedometer gives your car's speed in fpf!

   You love your new car, but don't have money for a new speedometer. Luckily, you're a great programmer, so you can develop a program to convert from fpf to miles per hour (mph). That way, when you look at your speedometer and see, for example, 147840, your program will immediately tell you that you're traveling 55 mph.

   Design and code such a program, testing it with some typical highway speeds. The program will ask for a speed in fpf, and display the result in mph.

9. Different compilers for a given language all follow the same syntax and semantic rules but do not necessarily give the same error messages. In this project you will explore the error messages generated by your Ada compiler. Start with the program `Distance_with_Errors` (Program 3.8). Compile it and compare the error messages with those shown in Figure 3.7. Now correct those errors but introduce some more errors of your own. Recompile the program and observe the messages. Repeat this process several times; try to get as many different messages as possible.

CHAPTER 4

Problem Solving and Using Packages

Programmers who use the software development method seldom tackle each new program as a unique event. Information that is contained in the problem statement and amassed during the analysis and design phases helps the programmer plan and complete the program. Programmers also use segments of earlier program solutions as building blocks to construct new programs. At the very least, they use knowledge gained from previous programs.

The approach followed in the design phase of the method is called *stepwise refinement*. This means that we start with the most abstract formulation of a problem and work down to more detailed subproblems. In this chapter we will show several ways to facilitate and enhance the refinement approach to programming.

In Section 4.1 we introduce *the subtype* as an important concept in data structures. In Sections 4.2 and 4.3 we discuss topics in problem solving. In Section 4.4 we introduce another data structures concept, the *enumeration type,* and in Section 4.5 we present an important concept in system structures, the *package*. You will see how packages are used by working with a standard Ada package, `Ada.Calendar`, which provides date and time services in a way common to all Ada compilers.

You will also see how to use a package that is provided with this book. This package, `Screen`, provides several services for dealing with the terminal screen—namely, clearing the screen, moving the cursor to a specific row–column position, and making the terminal beep.

4.1   Data Structures: Introduction to Subtypes

Recall that a type is a set of values and a set of operations that are appropriate and valid for those values. These two sets define the states and behavior of objects of the type. A *subtype* defines a *subset* of the values associated with the original type, or *base type*; the operations of the subtype are the same as those of the base type.

A *scalar type* is one each of whose values consists of a single component. All the types we have seen so far, except for strings, are in this category. *Composite types,* whose values may consist of several components, are introduced in Chapter 9. In this section we consider how to create subranges of the predefined scalar types `Integer`, `Float`, and `Character`. Subtypes are used both to make a program more readable and to enable detection of an attempt to give a variable a value that is unreasonable in the problem environment.

Subtypes of Predefined Scalar Types

So far in this book we have used two subtypes that are predefined in the Ada language and are thus always available:

```
SUBTYPE Natural IS Integer RANGE 0..Integer'Last;
SUBTYPE Positive IS Integer RANGE 1..Integer'Last;
```

Each of these subtypes defines a subset of the values its base type `Integer`. All the usual `Integer` operations remain available: A positive integer is still an integer.

Ada provides no equivalent predefined subtypes of `Float`. Let us now introduce a programmer-defined subtype,

```
SUBTYPE NonNegFloat IS Float RANGE 0.0 .. Float'Last;
```

which defines the subset of `Float` containing the nonnegative values. We'll be defining and using this subtype in many of the programs in this book.

Subtypes have a common characteristic. An attempt to assign to a variable a value that is not in the defined set of values causes a compilation error or warning if the compiler can detect the attempt. If the compiler cannot detect the attempt—for example, because the out-of-range value is not computed until the program is executed—the compiler builds a check into your program to ensure that `Constraint_Error` is raised if, during execution, the value is indeed out of range.

■ Example 4.1

Subtype declarations begin with the reserved word `SUBTYPE`. Two subtypes are declared below, as well as some variables:

```
SUBTYPE SmallInt IS Integer RANGE -50..50;
SUBTYPE CapitalLetter IS Character RANGE 'A'..'Z';

X, Y, Z : SmallInt;
NextChar : CapitalLetter;
Hours_Worked : NonNegFloat;
```

The first subtype, `SmallInt`, is a subtype with base type `Integer`. The following sequence of assignment statements will cause `Constraint_Error` to be raised at run time:

```
X := 26;
Y := 25;
Z := X + Y;
```

Why is there no compilation error? Remember that the compiler does not actually carry out the computation that you specify; it only produces an object program, which carries out the computation when it is executed. Even though it might be obvious to you that this simple computation will produce an out-of-range result, it is not obvious to the compiler, so the checking can be done, and the exception raised, only at run time.

`CapitalLetter` has the base type `Character`. Any character from `'A'` to `'Z'` inclusive may be stored in a variable of type `CapitalLetter`. `Constraint_Error` will be raised if an attempt is made to store any other character in a variable of type `Capital-Letter`. For example, the assignment statement

```
NextChar := 'a';
```

causes the exception to be raised because the character `'a'` is not included in the subtype `CapitalLetter`. The compiler might notice this attempted out-of-range assignment, but instead of considering this an outright error, it will often give a warning stating that the statement will cause `Constraint_Error` to be raised at run time. ■

SYNTAX DISPLAY

Subtype Declaration

Form:

```
SUBTYPE subtype-name IS
   base-type-name RANGE minvalue .. maxvalue;
```

Example:

```
SUBTYPE Uppercase IS Character RANGE 'A'..'Z';
```

Interpretation:

A new subtype named *subtype-name* is defined. A variable of type *subtype-name* may be assigned a value from *minvalue* through *maxvalue* inclusive. The values *minvalue* and *maxvalue* must belong to the base type, and *minvalue* must be less than *maxvalue*.

Compatibility Rules for Types and Subtypes

Ada does not allow a programmer accidentally to mix the types of operands for an operator. This means that the expression `v1 + v2` leads to a compilation error such as "type incompatible operands" if `v1` is one data type (say `Integer`) and `v2` is another

PROGRAM
STYLE

> ## Motivation for Using Subtypes
>
> You may be wondering why we bother with subtypes. They don't seem to provide any new capabilities. However, they do provide additional opportunity for your program to "bomb" because attempting to store an out-of-range value in a variable causes an exception, usually `Constraint_Error`, to be raised. This should happen only as the result of an error by either the programmer or the program user.
>
> The use of subtypes ensures the immediate detection of an out-of-range value. This contributes to a program's reliability and usefulness because it ensures that variables do not acquire values that are meaningless in the problem being solved (such as a negative number of hours worked in a week).
>
> In this book we use subtypes extensively, especially where it is necessary that a variable be nonnegative.

(say `Float`). However, what if `V1` is type `Integer` and `V2` is type `SmallInt` (a subtype of `Integer`)? In this case the expression is valid because `SmallInt` and `Integer` are considered *compatible types*. Ada has simple compatibility rules: Two values are compatible if they have the same type name or one value's type is a subtype of the other value's type (`Integer` and `SmallInt`, for example) or if their types are subtypes of the same base type (`Positive` and `SmallInt`, for example).

For an interesting example of subtype compatibility, suppose `x` is `Integer` and `y` is `Natural`. No matter what value `y` has, it is still an integer value, so executing the statement

```
X := Y;
```

is always valid and will not raise an exception. On the other hand, consider the statement

```
Y := X;
```

It is legal to write this statement, and it will compile without error, but it is not always valid at execution time, because it depends on the value of x at that moment. If x's value happens to be nonnegative, the execution will go through normally, but if x's value happens to be negative, `Constraint_Error` is raised on the attempt to assign this out-of-range value to `Y`. We observed this behavior in Section 3.8, in testing our coin collection program with a negative number of pennies.

The compatibility relationship between operands determines what operators can be used with the operands. An operator can be used only with operands that are compatible with it and with each other. Assignment of a value to a variable is possible only if the value and the variable are compatible. And an actual parameter that is supplied to a function or procedure must be compatible with the corresponding formal parameter.

These rules ensure, for example, that a `Float` value is not assigned to an `Integer` variable, that an `Integer` value is not assigned to a `Float` variable, and that an `Integer` value is not supplied to `Ada.Text_IO.Put` (which expects a character). On the other hand, a `Positive` value can be supplied to `Ada.Integer_Text_IO.Put` (which expects an `Integer`) because of the subtype relationship.

4.2 Problem Solving: Building Programs from Existing Information

Programmers seldom start off with a blank slate (or empty screen) when they develop a program. Often some—or all—of the solution can be developed from information that already exists or from the solution to another problem.

Carefully following the software development method generates important system documentation before you even begin to code a program. Such documentation, consisting of a description of a problem's data requirements (developed during the analysis phase) and its solution algorithm (developed during the design phase), summarizes your intentions and thought processes.

You can use this documentation as a starting point in coding your program. For example, you can begin by copying the problem data requirements into the program declaration section, then editing those lines to conform to the Ada syntax for constant and variable declarations, thereby completing the declaration section of the program. This approach is especially helpful if the documentation was created with a word processor and is in a file that you can edit.

To develop the program body, first use the initial algorithm and its refinements as program comments. The comments describe each algorithm step and provide program documentation that guides your Ada code. After the comments are in place in the program body, you can begin to write the Ada statements. Place the code for an unrefined step directly under that step. For a refined step, either edit the refinement to convert it from English to Ada or just replace it with Ada code. We illustrate the entire process in the next two case studies.

CASE STUDY

FINDING AREA AND CIRCUMFERENCE OF A CIRCLE

Problem Specification
Read in the radius of a circle and compute and print its area and circumference.

Analysis
Clearly, the problem input is the circle radius. Two outputs are requested: the circle area and circumference. These variables should be type `NonNegFloat` because the inputs and outputs may contain fractional parts but cannot meaningfully be negative. The geometric relationships between a circle's radius and its area and circumference are listed next, along with the data requirements.

Data Requirements and Formulas

Problem Constant
```
Pi : CONSTANT NonNegFloat := 3.14159;
```

Problem Inputs
```
Radius : NonNegFloat --radius of a circle
```

Problem Outputs
```
Area : NonNegFloat --area of a circle
Circum : NonNegFloat --circumference of a circle
```

Relevant Formulas

area of a circle $= \pi \times \text{radius}^2$
circumference of a circle $= 2\pi \times \text{radius}$

Design

Having listed the problem inputs and outputs, we can now list the steps necessary to solve the problem.

Initial Algorithm

1. Read the circle radius.

2. Find the area.

3. Find the circumference.

4. Print the area and circumference.

Pay close attention to the order of the steps. We could interchange steps 2 and 3—it doesn't matter whether we compute the area or the circumference first—but clearly, step 1 must precede the others, because we cannot compute with values we haven't yet read from the user.

Algorithm Refinements

Next, we refine any steps that do not have an obvious solution (steps 2 and 3).

Step 2 Refinement

2.1. Assign Pi * Radius ** 2 to Area.

Step 3 Refinement

3.1. Assign 2.0 * Pi * Radius to Circumference.

Test Plan

The special cases that need to be tested are zero radius and negative radius. A zero radius should give zero area and circumference; a negative radius should raise an exception.

Implementation

Program 4.1 is the Ada program so far. The program body consists of the initial algorithm with its refinements. This outline contains the "framework" consisting of PROCE-DURE, BEGIN, and END, some declarations, and just comments in the program body. Including the statement

```
NULL;
```

just after the BEGIN in fact makes the program syntactically correct Ada even though it has no other statements. It can be compiled just to check whether the basic framework and declarations are correct.

Program 4.1 Framework for Area and Circumference

```
PROCEDURE Area_And_Circum_Frame IS
----------------------------------------------------------------
--| Finds and displays the area and circumference of a circle
--| Author: M. B. Feldman, The George Washington University
--| Last Modified: June 1998
----------------------------------------------------------------
   SUBTYPE NonNegFloat IS Float RANGE 0.0 .. Float'Last;
   Pi : CONSTANT NonNegFloat := 3.14159;

   Radius        : NonNegFloat;  -- input  - radius of a circle
   Area          : NonNegFloat;  -- output - area
   Circumference : NonNegFloat;  -- output - circumference

BEGIN -- Area_And_Circum_Frame
  NULL;

  -- 1. Read the circle radius

  -- 2. Find the area
  -- 2.1 Assign Pi * Radius ** 2 to Area

  -- 3. Find the circumference
  -- 3.1 Assign 2.0 * Pi * Radius to Circumference

  -- 4. Display the Area and Circumference

END Area_And_Circum_Frame;
```

SYNTAX DISPLAY

Null Statement

Form:

```
NULL;
```

Example:

```
PROCEDURE SmallestAdaProcedure IS
BEGIN
   NULL;
END SmallestAdaProcedure;
```

Interpretation:

The null statement is used to indicate an "empty" sequence of statements. NULL is sometimes used to satisfy a syntax rule requiring a sequence of statements, even when the sequence is (intentionally) empty.

To write the final program, we must

- convert the refinements (steps 2.1 and 3.1) to Ada,

- write Ada code for the unrefined steps (steps 1 and 4),

- add the necessary context clauses for input and output,

- delete the NULL statement, and

- delete the step numbers from the comments.

Program 4.2 is the final program.

Program 4.2 Area and Circumference

```
WITH Ada.Text_IO;
WITH Ada.Float_Text_IO;
PROCEDURE Area_And_Circum IS
---------------------------------------------------------------
--| Finds and displays the area and circumference of a circle
--| Author: M. B. Feldman, The George Washington University
--| Last Modified: June 1998
---------------------------------------------------------------

   SUBTYPE NonNegFloat IS Float RANGE 0.0 .. Float'Last;

   Pi : CONSTANT NonNegFloat := 3.14159;

   Radius        : NonNegFloat;  -- input  - radius of a circle
   Area          : NonNegFloat;  -- output - area
   Circumference : NonNegFloat;  -- output - circumference

BEGIN -- Area_And_Circum

   -- Read the circle radius
   Ada.Text_IO.Put (Item => "Enter radius > ");
   Ada.Float_Text_IO.Get (Item => Radius);

   -- Find the area
   Area := Pi * Radius ** 2;

   -- Find the circumference
   Circumference := 2.0 * Pi * Radius;

   -- Display the Area and Circumference
   Ada.Text_IO.Put (Item => "The area is ");
   Ada.Float_Text_IO.Put (Item => Area, Fore => 1, Aft => 2, Exp => 0);
   Ada.Text_IO.New_Line;
   Ada.Text_IO.Put (Item => "The circumference is ");
   Ada.Float_Text_IO.Put
     (Item => Circumference, Fore => 1, Aft => 2, Exp => 0);
   Ada.Text_IO.New_Line;

END Area_And_Circum;
```

Sample Run

```
Enter radius > 5.0
The area is 78.54
The circumference is 31.42
```

Testing

The sample run shows a good test of the solution because it is relatively easy to compute the area and circumference by hand for a radius value of 5.0. The radius squared is 25.0, so the value of the area appears to be correct. The circumference should be 10 times π, which is also an easy number to compute by hand. We leave the other tests in the test plan for you to complete.

EXERCISES FOR SECTION 4.2

Self-Check

1. Describe the problem inputs and outputs and algorithm for computing an employee's gross salary given the hours worked and hourly rate.

2. Describe the problem inputs and outputs and algorithm for the following problem: Read in a pair of numbers and determine the sum and average of the two numbers.

Programming

1. Write a program for Self-Check question 2.

4.3 Problem Solving: Extending a Problem Solution

Another way programmers reuse existing information is by noting that the solution of one problem is often the basis for the solution to another problem. For example, we can easily solve the next problem by building on the solution to the previous problem.

CASE STUDY

UNIT PRICE OF A PIZZA

Problem Specification

You and your college roommates frequently order a late-night pizza snack. There are many pizzerias in the area that deliver to dormitories. Because you are on a tight budget, you would like to know which pizza is the best value.

Analysis

To find which pizza is the best value, we must be able to do a meaningful comparison of pizza costs. One way to do this is to compute the unit price of each pizza. The unit price of an item is obtained by dividing the total price of that item by a measure of its quantity. A good measure of quantity is the pizza weight, but pizzas are not sold by weight—they are sold by size (diameter), measured in inches. Consequently, the best that we can do is to use some meaningful measure of quantity based on the pizza diameter. One such measure is the pizza area. So for our purposes we will define the unit price of a pizza as its price divided by its area.

The data requirements below list the pizza size and price as problem inputs. Although the problem statement does not ask us to display the pizza area, we are listing it as a problem output because the pizza area will give us some idea of how many friends we can invite to share our pizza. The radius (one-half of the diameter) is listed as a program variable because we need it to compute the pizza area, but it is not a problem input or output.

Data Requirements

Problem Constant
```
Pi : CONSTANT Float := 3.14159;
```

Problem Inputs
```
Size : NonNegFloat -- diameter of a pizza
Price : NonNegFloat -- price of a pizza
```

Problem Outputs
```
Area : NonNegFloat -- area of a pizza
UnitPrice : NonNegFloat -- unit price of a pizza
```

Relevant Formulas
area of a circle $= \pi \times \text{radius}^2$
radius of a circle $= \text{diameter}/2$
unit price $= \text{price}/\text{area}$

Design
We mentioned earlier that we are basing the problem solution on the solution to the Case Study in Section 4.2 (finding the area and circumference of a circle). The initial algorithm is similar to the one shown earlier. The step that computes the circle circumference (step 3) has been replaced with one that computes the pizza unit price.

Initial Algorithm
1. Read in the pizza diameter and price.

2. Compute the pizza area.

3. Compute the pizza unit price.

4. Display the unit price and area.

The refinement of step 2 shows that we must compute the pizza radius before we can compute its area.

Step 2 Refinement
2.1 Assign Diameter / 2 to Radius.

2.2. Assign Pi * Radius ** 2 to Area.

Step 3 Refinement

3.1. Assign Price / Area to UnitPrice.

Test Plan

To test this program, run it with a few different pizza sizes. You can verify that the program is working correctly by multiplying the unit price and area. This product should equal the price of the pizza.

Implementation

Program 4.3 shows the framework for the Ada program. We will write this program the same way as before: by editing the data requirements to develop the program declaration part and by using the initial algorithm with refinements as a starting point for the program body.

In Program 4.3, instead of defining our own constant `Pi`, we are using the constant `Pi` provided by an Ada standard library, `Ada.Numerics` (Annex A.5 in the Ada 95 Reference Manual). There, `Pi` is given to 50 decimal places. Note that to use this library, we just write the usual context clause

```
WITH Ada.Numerics;
```

and then get the value of `Pi` as `Ada.Numerics.Pi`.

Program 4.3 Framework for Pizzeria

```
WITH Ada.Numerics;
PROCEDURE Pizzeria_Frame IS
-----------------------------------------------------------
--| Computes and displays the unit price of a pizza
--| Author: M. B. Feldman, The George Washington University
--| Last Modified: July 1998
-----------------------------------------------------------

   SUBTYPE NonNegFloat IS Float RANGE 0.0 .. Float'Last;

   -- Pi : CONSTANT NonNegFloat := 3.14159;
   -- unnecessary; better to get this from the standard library!
   -- we can just refer to Ada.Numerics.Pi

   Diameter  : NonNegFloat;  -- input  - diameter of a pizza
   Price     : NonNegFloat;  -- input  - price of a pizza
   UnitPrice : NonNegFloat;  -- output - unit price of a pizza
   Area      : NonNegFloat;  -- output - area of a pizza
   Radius    : NonNegFloat;  -- radius of a pizza

BEGIN -- Pizzeria_Frame
   NULL;

   -- 1. Read in the pizza diameter and price

   -- 2. Compute the pizza area
   -- 2.1 Assign Diameter/2 to Radius
   -- 2.2 Assign Pi * Radius ** 2 to Area
```

```
    -- 3. Compute the pizza unit price
    -- 3.1 Assign Price / Area to UnitPrice

    -- 4. Display the unit price and area

END Pizzeria_Frame;
```

Program 4.4 gives the final program.

Program 4.4 Unit Price of a Plzza

```
WITH Ada.Text_IO;
WITH Ada.Float_Text_IO;
WITH Ada.Numerics;
PROCEDURE Pizzeria IS
-----------------------------------------------------------------
--| Computes and displays the unit price of a pizza
--| Author: M. B. Feldman, The George Washington University
--| Last Modified: July 1998
-----------------------------------------------------------------

   SUBTYPE NonNegFloat IS Float RANGE 0.0 .. Float'Last;

   Diameter  : NonNegFloat;  -- input  - diameter of a pizza
   Price     : NonNegFloat;  -- input  - price of a pizza
   UnitPrice : NonNegFloat;  -- output - unit price of a pizza
   Area      : NonNegFloat;  -- output - area of a pizza
   Radius    : NonNegFloat;  -- radius of a pizza

BEGIN -- Pizzeria

  -- Read in the pizza diameter and price
  Ada.Text_IO.Put (Item => "Size of pizza in inches > ");
  Ada.Float_Text_IO.Get (Item => Diameter);
  Ada.Text_IO.Put (Item => "Price of pizza $");
  Ada.Float_Text_IO.Get (Item => Price);

  -- Compute the pizza area
  Radius := Diameter/2.0;
  Area := Ada.Numerics.Pi * Radius ** 2;

  -- Compute the pizza unit price
  UnitPrice := Price / Area;

  -- Display the unit price and area
  Ada.Text_IO.New_Line;
  Ada.Text_IO.Put (Item => "The pizza unit price is $");
  Ada.Float_Text_IO.Put
    (Item => UnitPrice, Fore => 1, Aft => 2, Exp => 0);
  Ada.Text_IO.New_Line;
  Ada.Text_IO.Put (Item => "The pizza area is ");
  Ada.Float_Text_IO.Put
    (Item => Area, Fore => 1, Aft => 2, Exp => 0);
  Ada.Text_IO.Put (Item => " square inches.");
  Ada.Text_IO.New_Line;

END Pizzeria;
```

Sample Run

```
Size of pizza in inches > 10
Price of pizza $8.50

The pizza unit price is $0.11
The pizza area is 78.54 square inches.
```

Testing
The sample run gives one test. You can supply others.

PROGRAM
STYLE

Using Comments

Comments make a program more readable by describing the purpose of the program and by describing the use of each identifier. For example, the comment in the declaration

```
Radius: NonNegFloat; -- program input - radius of a circle
```

describes the use of the variable `Radius`.

You should place comments within the program body to describe the purpose of each section of the program. The stepwise refinement method that we use in this book uses comments in the program framework for each step of the algorithm and its refinements. Some of these comments are turned into program statements as these are written; others remain as program documentation.

You may wish to add other comments to a program to make it easier for yourself and others to understand. Make sure a comment within the program body adds useful descriptive information about what the step does rather than simply restate the step in English.

For example, the comment

```
-- Find the area of the circle
Area := Pi * Radius ** 2;
```

is more descriptive than, and therefore preferable to,

```
-- Multiply the Radius by itelf and Pi
Area := Pi * Radius ** 2;
```

PROGRAM
STYLE

More on Banner Comments

Begin each program with a header section, sometimes called a block comment or *banner comment,* that consists of a series of comments specifying the programmer's name, the date of the current version, and a brief description of what the program does. The banner form used in the program examples in this book is usually acceptable. If you write the program for a class assignment, you should also list the class identification and your instructor's name. Your instructor may also require other kinds of comments in your program.

A final word on comments: If a program has too few comments, the reader may have difficulty understanding the program. On the other hand, if there are too many comments, finding the program text among the comments will be difficult. Writing effective comments—knowing just how much to write—is a skill that must be practiced.

Motivation for Conditional and Repetition Control Structures

So far, we have extended the solution to one problem (find a circle radius and circumference) into a second related problem (find the unit price of a pizza). We are not really finished yet because our goal was to be able to do a cost comparison of several pizzas with different prices and sizes in order to determine the best value.

One way to accomplish our larger goal is to run this program several different times, once for each pizza, and record the results. Then we can scan the list of results to determine which pizza has the lowest unit price.

A better solution would be to write a program that repeated the computation steps and also compared unit prices, displaying as its final result the size and price of the pizza with the lowest unit price. Let's write an algorithm that will give us this improved solution.

Initial Algorithm for Improved Solution to Pizza Problem

1. For each size of pizza, read in the pizza size and price and compute unit cost. Compare the unit cost just computed with the previous unit costs and save the size and price of the pizza whose unit cost is the smallest so far.

2. Display the size and price of the pizza with the smallest unit cost.

The purpose of step 1 of the algorithm is to perform the cost computation for each individual pizza and somehow save the size and price of the pizza whose unit cost was the smallest. After all costs are computed, step 2 displays the size and price of the pizza that is the best buy.

Step 1 Refinement

1.1. Repeat the following steps for each size of pizza:

1.2. Read in the next pizza size and price.

1.3. Compute the unit price.

1.4. If the new unit price is the smallest one so far, then save this pizza's size, price, and unit price.

Step 1.1 specifies the *repetition* of a group of steps: step 1.2 (read), step 1.3 (compute), and step 1.4 (compare). We will repeat these steps as many times as necessary until all unit prices are computed. Each time we compute a new unit price, step 1.4 compares it to the others, and the current pizza's size and price are saved if its unit price is smaller than any others computed so far. If the unit price is not the smallest so far, the current pizza's size and price are not saved. Step 1.4 is a *selection* step because it selects between the two possible outcomes: (a) save the pizza's data and (b) do not save the pizza's data.

We will discuss control structures for selection and repetition fully in Chapters 5, 6, and 7.

4.4 Data Structures: Introducing Enumeration Types

So far, most of the data types you have seen have been numerical (Integer, Float). In this section you will be introduced to the important concept of enumeration types. An *enumeration type* is defined by a list of values taking the form of identifiers. These types are called enumeration types because their values are *enumerated,* or given in a list. An enumeration type is useful in representing a *fixed set of values* that are not numerical, such as the days of the week, the months of the year, the years (freshman, sophomore, junior, senior) in a high school or college career, or the expenditure categories in an accounting program. Ada encourages you to use enumeration types by providing a small but useful set of operations on them and also an input/output package that makes it easy to read enumeration values from a keyboard or disk file and display them on the screen.

Defining Enumeration Types

In many programming situations the standard data types and their values are inadequate. For example, in a budget program we might want to distinguish among the following categories of expenditures: entertainment, rent, utilities, food, clothing, automobile, insurance, and miscellaneous. We could always assign an arbitrary code that associates entertainment with a character value of 'e', rent with a character value of 'r', and so on. However, enumeration types allow us to specify the set of values directly. For example, the enumeration type Expenses declared below has eight possible values enclosed in parentheses:

```
TYPE Expenses IS
  (entertainment, rent, utilities, food,
   clothing, automobile, insurance, miscellaneous);

ExpenseKind : Expenses;
```

The variable ExpenseKind (type Expenses) can contain any of the eight values listed after Expenses IS. The values, called *enumeration literals,* associated with an enumeration type are generally identifiers and therefore must conform to the syntax of identifiers. The type declaration must precede any variable declaration that references it.

The enumeration type Days has the values Monday, Tuesday, and so on:

```
TYPE Days IS
  (Monday, Tuesday, Wednesday, Thursday,
   Friday, Saturday, Sunday);
```

It is permissible for the same enumeration literal to appear in several enumeration types, just as it is permissible for the same numerical value to appear in several numerical types. It is, for example, possible to define the three types

```
TYPE Traffic_Light_Colors IS (Red, Yellow, Green);
TYPE Primary_Paint_Colors IS (Red, Yellow, Blue);
TYPE Primary_TV_Colors IS (Red, Blue, Green);
```

in the same program without causing difficulties for the compiler. On the other hand, the compiler treats the Red from `Traffic_Light_Colors` as a different value from the Red from `Primary_TV_Colors`.

Enumeration Type Declaration

Form:

TYPE *enumeration-type* IS (*identifier-list*);

Example:

TYPE Class IS (Freshman, Sophomore, Junior, Senior);

Interpretation:

A new data type named *enumeration-type* is declared. The enumeration literals, or values associated with this type, are specified in the *identifier-list*. The order in which the enumeration literals are given is important, because it defines an ordering of the literals: Freshman is less than Sophomore; Junior is greater than Freshman.

Enumeration Type Attributes and Operations

The order relationship between the values of an enumeration type is fixed when the type is declared. Each literal has a *position* in the type, given as a value of type Natural. For type Days, the first value in its list (Monday) has position 0, the next value (Tuesday) has position 1, and so on.

An assignment statement can be used to define the value of a variable whose type is an enumeration type. The variable

```
Today      : Days;   --current day of the week
Tomorrow   : Days;   --day after Today
```

specifies that Today and Tomorrow are type Days and, therefore, can be assigned any of the values listed in the declaration for type Day. Consequently, the assignment statements

```
Today := Friday;
Tomorrow := Saturday;
```

assign the values Friday to variable Today and Saturday to variable Tomorrow.

An important aspect of Ada's type system is the notion of *attributes*. These are characteristics of a type or variable that can be queried by a program. For the case of enumeration types, six important attributes are:

• First, which gives the first or lowest value in the type;

- `Last`, which gives the last or highest value;

- `Pos`, which given a value in a type, gives its position in the type;

- `Val`, which given a position in a type, gives the value in that position;

- `Pred`, which given a value in a type, gives its *predecessor,* that is, the value that precedes it in the type; and

- `Succ`, which, given a value in a type, gives its *successor,* that is, the value that follows.

Some examples are given below; they assume that `Today` is `Friday` and `Tomorrow` is `Saturday`.

```
Days'First is Monday
Days'Last is Sunday
Days'Pos(Monday) is 0
Days'Val(0) is Monday
Days'Pos(Sunday) is 6
Days'Val(6) is Sunday
Days'Pred(Wednesday) is Tuesday
Days'Pred(Today) is Thursday
Days'Succ(Tuesday) is Wednesday
Days'Succ(Today) is Saturday
```

Because enumeration types are not cyclical (i.e., do not "wrap around"), the queries `Days'Pred(Monday)` and `Day'Succ(Sunday)` are undefined and would cause a run-time exception—namely, the raising of `Constraint_Error`—if attempted. Similarly, if `Tomorrow` had the value `Sunday`, `Days'Succ(Tomorrow)` would cause an exception. Whether the assignment statement

```
Tomorrow := Days'Succ(Today);
```

would cause an exception depends on the value of `Today`; it cannot cause a compilation error because the value of `Today` is usually unknown at compilation time.

SYNTAX DISPLAY

Attribute Query

Form:

type`'`*attribute-name* or *type*`'`*attribute-name(value)*

Example:

```
Traffic_Light_Colors'First
Days'Succ(Wednesday)
Days'Pos(Today)
```

Interpretation:

An attribute query answers a question about certain characteristics of types or variables. For each type, the set of attributes is predefined by the language and cannot normally be changed by the programmer. Note the required presence of the single quote or apostrophe in the attribute query.

Input/Output Operations for Enumeration Types

One of the most convenient Ada features for using enumeration types is a built-in input/output package for reading and displaying enumeration literals. Within `Ada.Text_IO` is a *generic package* called `Enumeration_IO`, which cannot be used immediately. *Instances* must be created; each instance is "tailored" to read and display exactly the literals in a specific enumeration type. For example, in a program in which the type `Days` is defined and the variable declaration `Today:Days` appears, we could write

```
PACKAGE Day_IO IS NEW Ada.Text_IO.Enumeration_IO(Enum=>Days);
```

which would give us the ability to read a value from the keyboard into `Today` or to display the value of `Today` on the screen, using procedure calls like

```
Day_IO.Get(Item => Today);
Day_IO.Put(Item => Today, Width => 10);
```

In the case of `Get`, the exception `Data_Error` is raised if the value entered on the keyboard is not one of the seven literals in `Days`. In this manner the input/output system automatically checks the validity of the value that is entered, making sure that it is a legal value in the enumeration type.

SYNTAX DISPLAY

Get Procedure (Enumeration)

Form:

instance.Get (Item => *variable*);

Example:

Day_IO.Get (Item => Some_Day);

Interpretation:

By *instance* we mean an instance of `Ada.Text_IO.Enumeration_IO` for some enumeration type. The next string of characters that is entered at the keyboard is read into *variable* (of the same enumeration type). Any leading blank characters or RETURNS are ignored. The first nonblank character must be a letter, and the characters must form an identifier. The data string is terminated when a nonidentifier character is entered or the space bar or RETURN key is pressed.

If the identifier that is read is not one of the literals in the enumeration type for which *instance* was created, `Ada.Text_IO.Data_Error` is raised.

SYNTAX
DISPLAY

Put Procedure (Enumeration)

Form:

```
instance.Put
  (Item => variable , Width => field width,
   Set => Text_IO.Upper_Case or Text_IO.Lower_Case);
```

Example:

```
Day_IO.Put
  (Item => Some_Day, Width => 5, Set => Lower_Case);
```

Interpretation:

The value of *variable* (of some enumeration type) is displayed, using the next `Width` positions on the screen. If the value would occupy less than `Width` positions, it is followed by the appropriate number of blanks; if the value would occupy more than `Width` positions, the actual number of positions is used.

If `Width` is omitted, a compiler-dependent width is used by default. The standard values `Text_IO.Upper_Case` and `Text_IO.Lower_Case` are used to determine the form of the displayed value. If `Set` is omitted, the value is displayed in uppercase.

CASE
STUDY

TRANSLATING FROM ENGLISH TO FRENCH COLOR NAMES

Problem Specification

Your roommate comes from France and you are taking a watercolor-painting class together. To make communication with your roommate easier you would like to have the computer give you some help in remembering the French names of the major colors. You'd like to enter an English color name on the keyboard and let the program display the corresponding French name. The English color names are white, black, red, purple, blue, green, yellow, and orange; the French color names are blanc, noir, rouge, violet, bleu, vert, jaune, and orange.

Analysis

The French and English colors can be represented by two enumeration types `French_Colors` and `English_Colors` and can be read and displayed using two instances of `Enumeration_IO`, which we will call `French_Color_IO` and `English_Color_IO`.

Data Requirements

Problem Data Types:

English colors, an enumeration type:
```
TYPE English_Colors IS
  (white, black, red, purple, blue, green, yellow, orange);
```

French colors, also an enumeration type:
```
TYPE French_Colors IS
```

```
(blanc, noir, rouge, violet, bleu, vert, jaune, orange);
```

Problem Inputs:
English color (`Eng_Color : English_Colors`).

Problem Outputs:
French color (`Fr_Color : French_Colors`).

Design
We were careful to list the French and English colors in the same order, so given an English color, the corresponding French color will be in the same position in the French color type. The program depends on this correspondence, which gives us the following algorithm.

Initial Algorithm
1. Prompt the user to enter one of the eight English colors, `Eng_Color`.

2. Find the corresponding French color, `Fr_Color`.

3. Display the French color.

Algorithm Refinements
The only step needing refinement is step 2. We can find the French color corresponding to a given English one by using the `Pos` and `Val` attributes. Since the French and English colors have corresponding positions, we can find the position of the English color in its type, then use that position to find the corresponding value in the French type. To do this, we shall use a program variable `Position` of type `Natural` to store the color position within its type.

Step 2 Refinement

2.1. Save in `Position` the position of `Eng_Color` in its type.

2.2. Save in `Fr_Color` the corresponding value in the French type.

Test Plan
This algorithm depends upon each of the French colors being in the same position in its type as the corresponding English color. Since the number of colors is relatively small, all the cases can be checked to be sure the two color types were given correctly. We also need to test for invalid input, for example, a word or other sequence of characters that is not an English color. If an invalid token is entered, `Ada.Text_IO.Data_Error` should be raised and the program should halt.

Implementation
The complete program is shown in Program 4.5. The program begins with a context clause for `Ada.Text_IO`. Within the program, the two color types are defined and instances of `Ada.Text_IO.Enumeration_IO` are created to read and display values of these types. Finally, the sequence of statements implements the refined algorithm just developed.

Program 4.5 Translating between French and English Colors

```
WITH Ada.Text_IO;
PROCEDURE Colors IS
-----------------------------------------------------------------
--| Displays a French color, given the English color
--| Author: M. B. Feldman, The George Washington University
--| Last Modified: July 1998
-----------------------------------------------------------------

  TYPE English_Colors IS
     (white, black, red, purple, blue, green, yellow, orange);

  TYPE French_Colors IS
     (blanc, noir, rouge, violet, bleu, vert, jaune, orange);

  PACKAGE English_Color_IO IS
     NEW Ada.Text_IO.Enumeration_IO (Enum => English_Colors);

  PACKAGE French_Color_IO IS
     NEW Ada.Text_IO.Enumeration_IO (Enum => French_Colors);

  Eng_Color : English_Colors;
  Fr_Color  : French_Colors;
  Position  : Natural;

BEGIN -- Colors

  Ada.Text_IO.Put (Item => "Please enter an English color > ");
  English_Color_IO.Get (Item => Eng_Color);

  Position := English_Colors'Pos(Eng_Color);
  Fr_Color := French_Colors'Val(Position);

  Ada.Text_IO.Put (Item => "The French color is ");
  French_Color_IO.Put (Item => Fr_Color, Set => Ada.Text_IO.Lower_Case);
  Ada.Text_IO.New_Line;

END Colors;
```

Sample Run

```
Please enter an English color > blue
The French color is bleu
```

Testing

The sample run gives one test. To complete the test plan, run the other tests including one for invalid input.

EXERCISES FOR SECTION 4.4

Self–Check

1. Evaluate each of the following assuming `Today` (type `Day`) is `Thursday` before each operation.

a. `Day'Pos(Monday)`
b. `Day'Pos(Today)`
c. `Day'Val(6)`
d. `Today < Tuesday`

e. `Day'Succ(Sunday)`
f. `Day'Pred(Monday)`
g. `Day'Val(0)`
h. `Today >= Thursday`

4.5 System Structures: The Importance of Packages

Consider the input/output libraries we have been using in this book. Each of the various `Get` and `Put` statements in the earlier examples is really a *procedure call* statement. A procedure is a kind of system building block, a way of putting together a group of program statements and treating them as a unit, causing them to be executed by means of *procedure calls*. In this book you will learn how to write procedures; in this chapter you will continue just to use procedures written by others.

The `Get` and `Put` procedures that we have been using were written by another programmer at another time; they were supplied to us as part of a *package* called `Ada.Text_IO`. Just as a procedure is a kind of subprogram, a way of grouping statements, a package is a way of grouping subprograms (and other program entities that we will introduce later on). It is through the use of packages that procedures can be written and tested for general use (that is, by other programmers) and put in a form in which they can be supplied to others. Ada compilers come with several standard library packages. `Ada.Text_IO` is one of these; in the next section you will see another, called `Ada.Calendar`.

The package concept is one of the most important developments to be found in modern programming languages, such as Ada, Modula-2, Turbo Pascal, C++, Eiffel, and Java. The designers of the different languages have not agreed on what terms to use for this concept: Package, module, unit, and class are commonly used. But it is generally agreed that the package—as it is called in Ada—is the essential programming tool to be used for going beyond the programming of very simple class exercises to what is generally called software engineering, or building real programs of real size for the real world.

It is the package that allows us to develop a set of related operations and other entities, especially types, to test these thoroughly, and then to store them in an Ada program library for our future use or even to distribute them to others. Grouping a set of related entities in a well-defined module, with a clearly specified interface to other programs, is called *encapsulation*. Encapsulation is the way we produce *software components* that are predeveloped and pretested for *reusability* within an organization or distribution in the wider world.

A special kind of package, one that groups a type together with a complete set of operations for that type, is often called an *abstract data type (ADT)* package. `Ada.Calendar` is an excellent example of an ADT package.

You will work with three kinds of packages in this book:

- standard packages—such as `Ada.Text_IO` and `Ada.Numerics`, which you have seen already, and `Ada.Calendar`, introduced in Section 4.6—which are required by the Ada standard and supplied with all compilers;

- packages supplied along with this book, such as the screen-control package introduced in Sections 4.7; and

- packages written as part of your study of this book, such as the packages introduced starting in Chapter 5 and continuing throughout the book.

4.6   System Structures: Using Ada's Calendar Package

In this section you will see how to use another standard Ada library package, `Ada.Calendar`. This important package is specified in the Ada Reference Manual, Section 9.6

In all Ada packages, the resources provided are listed in an Ada source file called the *package specification*. The package specification plays two roles: It describes the package to the compiler, and it serves as a "contract" with the programmer who is using it, telling this human user exactly what resources to expect. Some of the different *kinds* of resources provided by a package are

- types and subtypes,

- procedures, and

- functions.

Ada's calendar package provides a number of useful resources relating to dates and times. Figure 4.1 shows a part of the specification for `Ada.Calendar`; for clarity we have listed only those services needed in this example. Figure 11.3 gives the entire specification for `Ada.Calendar`.

Figure 4.1   Partial Specification of Package Ada.Calendar

```
PACKAGE Ada.Calendar IS

--   standard Ada package, must be supplied with compilers
--   provides useful services for dates and times

--   type definitions

  TYPE Time IS PRIVATE;

  SUBTYPE Year_Number  IS Integer RANGE 1901..2099;
  SUBTYPE Month_Number IS Integer RANGE 1..12;
  SUBTYPE Day_Number   IS Integer RANGE 1..31;
```

```
-- functions to get the current time
-- and return its date components

   FUNCTION Clock RETURN Time;

   FUNCTION Year   (Date : Time) RETURN Year_Number;
   FUNCTION Month  (Date : Time) RETURN Month_Number;
   FUNCTION Day    (Date : Time) RETURN Day_Number;

-- Ada.Calendar provides many other interesting facilities;
-- for clarity, these are omitted from this figure.

END Ada.Calendar;
```

After the first line,

```
PACKAGE Ada.Calendar IS
```

which indicates the beginning of a package specification, four type declaration statements are given. The line

```
TYPE Time IS PRIVATE;
```

specifies `Time` as a `PRIVATE` type, the details of whose values are not known to the package user. We do not know whether a `Time` value is an `Integer` value, or `Float`, or `String`, or something we haven't thought of yet. On the other hand, we are told that this internal value represents a year, calendar day, and time of day in a single bit pattern. We don't really need to know any more about `Time` values, because the package provides all the operations necessary to work with them.

We will discuss `PRIVATE` types in detail later, especially in Chapter 11, where we will develop a few of our own. For now, you need to know that because `Time` is a `PRIVATE` type, the only way you can use `Time` values is to work with them according to the various operations provided by `Ada.Calendar`. There is, for example, no way to display a Time value on the screen. You will see a few `Ada.Calendar` operations in a short while.

Given a program preceded by a context clause

```
WITH Ada.Calendar;
```

the declaration

```
Right_Now : Ada.Calendar.Time;
```

declares a variable capable of holding a time value. The form `Ada.Calendar.Time` is similar to the form `Ada.Text_IO.New_Line` in that the name of the package is used to *qualify* the use of the package resource: `Time` is a resource provided by `Ada.Calendar` just as `New_Line` is a resource provided by `Ada.Text_IO`.

In the specification of `Ada.Calendar` in Fig. 4.1, the next three lines give subtype declarations for years, months, and days:

```
SUBTYPE Year_Number IS Integer RANGE 1901..2099;
SUBTYPE Month_Number IS Integer RANGE 1..12;
SUBTYPE Day_Number IS Integer RANGE 1..31;
```

Recall from Section 4.1 that a type consists of a set of values and a set of operations on these values and that a subtype is a subset of the original set of values together with the full original set of operations. For example, in declaring `Month_Number` to be a subtype of `Integer` and giving its range as `1..12`, we are saying that any variables of type `Month_Number` can hold integer values only in the range 1 through 12, inclusive. Similarly, variables of subtype `Day_Number` can hold integer values in the range 1 through 31, inclusive. All of the operations on integers apply to values of these subtypes, but if an operation attempts to store a value that is outside the declared range, this operation is improper and a `Constraint_Error` exception will be raised at run time.

We reiterate that subtypes are a convenient way to inform the compiler—and the reader of a program—that certain variables have ranges that are restricted according to their intended use. Ada can then help us to avoid and recover from errors by checking that variables store numbers only of appropriate size.

The declarations

```
This_Year   : Ada.Calendar.Year_Number;
This_Month  : Ada.Calendar.Month_Number;
This_Day    : Ada.Calendar.Day_Number;
```

declare variables of the three subtypes provided by `Ada.Calendar`. Again we have used qualified references; this is done to remind both the compiler and the human reader of the package in which the resources are defined.

Next we consider how to determine the current time of day in Ada. Returning to the `Ada.Calendar` specification in Fig. 4.1, the next line

```
FUNCTION Clock RETURN Time;
```

specifies a *function* called `Clock`. Given the declaration

```
Right_Now: Ada.Calendar.Time;
```

then an assignment statement such as

```
Right_Now := Ada.Calendar.Clock;
```

will be compiled into machine instructions that read the computer's internal clock, which delivers the current time of day and stores this time value in the variable `Right_Now`. The expression `Ada.Calendar.Clock` is a *function call;* we will see other function calls shortly.

This value is not very useful to us in this form; for example, we cannot display a time value because its precise form is not available to us. But as the next three lines,

```
FUNCTION Year (Date: Time) RETURN Year_Number;
FUNCTION Month (Date: Time) RETURN Month_Number;
FUNCTION Day (Date: Time) RETURN Day_Number;
```

of the specification show, the package gives us operations to extract the year, month, and day from the internal time value. Each of these operations is a function with a single parameter `Date`, which is of type `Time`. For example, if we declare a variable

```
This_Year : Ada.Calendar.Year_Number;
```

the assignment statement

```
This_Year := Ada.Calendar.Year(Date => Right_Now);
```

will store the current calendar year in `This_Year`. Since `Ada.Calendar.Year_Number` is an ordinary integer subtype, ordinary integer operations can be performed on the value in `This_Year`; specifically, its value can be displayed. This function call is analogous to an `Ada.Text_IO` procedure call such as

```
Ada.Text_IO.Put(Item => FirstInitial);
```

in the sense that a value is being supplied to correspond to the formal parameter. The formal parameter of `Put` is called `Item`; the formal parameter of `Year` is called `Date`.

In using the operations of `Ada.Calendar`, we have no knowledge of the details of *how* they perform. This is of no concern to us; the "contract" embodied in the specification tells us what to expect, and this is all we need to know.

SYNTAX
DISPLAY

Function Call Statement (Simple)

Form:

variable := *fname* (*actual parameters*);

Example:

```
This_Month := Ada.Calendar.Month(Date => Right_Now);
Right_Now := Ada.Calendar.Clock;
```

Interpretation:

The list of parameters (if any) is enclosed in parentheses; each actual parameter value is preceded by the name of that formal parameter. The variable must be of the same type as the return type of the function *fname*. The function *fname* is called, and its returned value is stored in *variable*. During the function execution, the named actual parameters are associated with the corresponding formal parameters.

Note 1:

Multiple parameters are separated by commas. Be careful here: The formal parameters are separated by semicolons, but the actual parameters are separated by commas.

Note 2:

The number of actual and formal parameters must be the same. Each actual parameter that is an expression is evaluated when *fname* is called; this value is assigned to the corresponding formal parameter.

Note 3:

The type of each actual parameter must agree with the type of the corresponding formal parameter. Ada does not allow, for example, an integer-valued actual parameter to be associated with a float-valued formal parameter.

Note 4:

In this book, each actual parameter is listed with the name of the corresponding formal parameter (the two are separated by =>). Therefore, strictly speaking, the *order* of the actual parameters does not have to match that of the formal parameters. It is nevertheless good practice to list the actual parameters in an order corresponding to the order of the formal parameters.

Note that as the second example shows, functions can be defined to have no parameters at all. The number, order, and type of the parameters is, of course, determined by the *writer* of the function, not its *user*.

CASE STUDY

DISPLAYING TODAY'S DATE IN "MM/DD/YYYY" FORM

Let's use the knowledge gained in this chapter to solve the problem of displaying today's date.

Problem Specification

Display today's date in the form mm/dd/yyyy; for example, if today is October 21, 1998, we display 10/21/1998. If today is July 8, 2000, we display 7/8/2000.

Analysis

Today's date can be obtained from the computer's internal clock by using the appropriate Ada calendar facilities to get a time value and then to extract the month, day, and year. These three values can then be formatted to give the desired display.

Data Requirements

Problem Data Types:

We need only the type Time and the subtypes Year_Number, Month_Number, and Day_Number, all provided by the standard package Ada.Calendar.

Problem Inputs:

No inputs need to be entered by the user.

Problem Outputs:

Today's date, in the form mm/dd/yyyy.

Design

Initial Algorithm

1. Get the current time value from the computer's clock.

2. Extract the current month, day, and year from the time value.

3. Format and display the date.

Algorithm Refinements

Step 2 Refinement

2.1. Extract the current month from the time value.

2.2. Extract the current day from the time value.

2.3. Extract the current year from the time value.

We can illustrate the steps in the refinement process with a diagram that shows the algorithm subproblems and their interdependencies. An example of such a diagram, called a *structure chart*, is shown in Fig. 4.2.

As we trace down this diagram, we go from an abstract problem to a more detailed subproblem. The original problem is shown at the top, or level 0, of the structure chart. The major subproblems appear at level 1. The different subproblems resulting from the refinement of each level-1 step are shown at level 2 and are connected to their respective level-1 subproblem. This diagram shows that the subproblem *Extract date values from time value* is dependent on the solutions to the subproblems *Extract month, extract day,* and *extract year*. Because the subproblem *Get current time* is not refined further, there are no level-2 subproblems connected to it.

Structure charts are intended to show the structural relationship between the subproblems. The algorithm (not the structure chart) shows the order in which each step must be carried out to solve the problem.

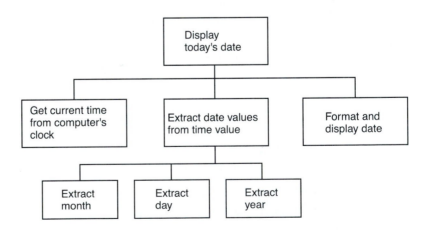

Figure 4.2 Structure Chart for Formatting and Displaying Today's Date

Test Plan

In this case, no user inputs are provided to the program. The only thing to test is the correct extraction and formatting of the month, day, and year. It is easy to check whether the program produced the correct date; just look at an ordinary calendar.

Implementation

Program 4.6 shows the Ada program for this problem.

Program 4.6 Displaying Today's Date

```
WITH Ada.Text_IO;
WITH Ada.Calendar;
WITH Ada.Integer_Text_IO;
PROCEDURE Todays_Date IS
----------------------------------------------------------------
--| Finds and displays today's date in the form mm/dd/yyyy
--| Author: M. B. Feldman, The George Washington University
--| Last Modified: July 1998
----------------------------------------------------------------
   RightNow  : Ada.Calendar.Time;            -- current time
   ThisYear  : Ada.Calendar.Year_Number;     -- current year
   ThisMonth : Ada.Calendar.Month_Number;    -- current month
   ThisDay   : Ada.Calendar.Day_Number;      -- current day

BEGIN -- Todays_Date

   -- Get the current time value from the computer's clock
   RightNow := Ada.Calendar.Clock;

   -- Extract current month, day, and year from the time value
   ThisMonth := Ada.Calendar.Month(Date => RightNow);
   ThisDay   := Ada.Calendar.Day  (Date => RightNow);
   ThisYear  := Ada.Calendar.Year (Date => RightNow);

   -- Format and display the date
   Ada.Text_IO.Put (Item => "Today's date is ");
   Ada.Integer_Text_IO.Put (Item => ThisMonth, Width => 1);
   Ada.Text_IO.Put (Item => '/');
   Ada.Integer_Text_IO.Put (Item => ThisDay, Width => 1);
   Ada.Text_IO.Put (Item => '/');
   Ada.Integer_Text_IO.Put (Item => ThisYear, Width => 1);
   Ada.Text_IO.New_Line;

END Todays_Date;
```

Sample Run

```
Today's date is 7/24/1998
```

The program begins with the appropriate context clauses, including one for `Ada.Calendar`. Variables for the time, month, day, and year are declared.

Finally, the results are formatted and displayed using a sequence of `Put` statements from `Ada.Text_IO` and `Ada.Integer_Text_IO`. Notice how the integer values are displayed using a width of 1 to keep them "up against" the slashes.

Testing
The sample run shows the correct date, correctly formatted.

DISPLAYING TODAY'S DATE IN "MONTH DD, YYYY" FORM

Problem Specification
Display today's date in the form MONTH dd, yyyy.

Analysis
This problem is similar to the previous one. In fact, it can be solved just by modifying the previous algorithm. Package Ada.Calendar gives us only the number of the current month from 1 to 12, so we need to specify the names of the months. We can do this with an enumeration type:

```
TYPE Months IS
   (January, February, March, April, May, June,
    July, August, September, October, November, December);
```

The current month can be displayed by using an instance of Ada.Enumeration_IO, as in the colors program:

```
PACKAGE Month_IO IS
   NEW Ada.Text_IO.Enumeration_IO(Enum => Months);
```

Design
All steps of the algorithm are the same, except for a step 3 refinement.

Step 3 Refinement

3.1 Find the name of the month.

3.2 Format and display the current month, day, and year.

We need to find the name corresponding to the number of the current month. Because the month is given from 1 to 12, and the positions of the names are 0 to 11, subtracting 1 from the month will give us the right position in Months, from which we can find the month name using the Val attribute. If the month name is stored in a variable Month_Name of type Months, we have

```
Month_Name := Months'Val(This_Month - 1);
```

The solution to this problem is shown in Program 4.7.

Program 4.7 Displaying Today's Date in Another Format

```
WITH Ada.Text_IO;
WITH Ada.Integer_Text_IO;
```

```
WITH Ada.Calendar;
PROCEDURE Todays_Date_2 IS
-------------------------------------------------------------------
--| Displays today's date in the form MONTH dd, yyyy
--| An enumeration type is used for months
--| The date is gotten from PACKAGE Ada.Calendar
--| Author: M. B. Feldman, The George Washington University
--| Last Modified: July 1998
-------------------------------------------------------------------

   TYPE Months IS
      (January, February, March, April, May, June,
       July, August, September, October, November, December);

   PACKAGE Months_IO IS
     NEW Ada.Text_IO.Enumeration_IO(Enum => Months);

   RightNow  : Ada.Calendar.Time;            -- current time
   ThisYear  : Ada.Calendar.Year_Number;     -- current year
   ThisMonth : Ada.Calendar.Month_Number;    -- current month
   ThisDay   : Ada.Calendar.Day_Number;      -- current day

   MonthName: Months;

BEGIN -- Todays_Date_2

   -- Get the current time value from the computer's clock
   RightNow := Ada.Calendar.Clock;

   -- Extract current month, day, and year from the time value
   ThisMonth := Ada.Calendar.Month(Date => RightNow);
   ThisDay   := Ada.Calendar.Day  (Date => RightNow);
   ThisYear  := Ada.Calendar.Year (Date => RightNow);

   -- Format and display the date
   MonthName := Months'Val(ThisMonth - 1);

   Ada.Text_IO.Put (Item => "Today's date is ");
   Months_IO.Put (Item => MonthName, Set => Ada.Text_IO.Upper_Case);
   Ada.Text_IO.Put (Item => ' ');
   Ada.Integer_Text_IO.Put (Item => ThisDay, Width => 1);
   Ada.Text_IO.Put (Item => ',');
   Ada.Integer_Text_IO.Put (Item => ThisYear, Width => 5);
   Ada.Text_IO.New_Line;

END Todays_Date_2;
```

Sample Run

```
Today's date is JULY 24, 1998
```

4.7   System Structures: Using a Screen-Control Package

The `Ada.Text_IO` package provides operations for reading from the terminal keyboard and writing to the screen, but it provides no direct operations for controlling the screen in interesting ways, such as moving the cursor to a given row–column position before writing. Doing this requires an additional package that uses `Ada.Text_IO` to send *control characters* to the terminal; the control characters act as instructions to it instead of data it should display. Because this package, which we will call `Screen`, is not part of standard Ada, we provide it with this book. The details of just how this package operates are left until Chapter 8, but it is possible for you to use the package without understanding its innards.

A package consists of two files, the *specification* file and the *body* file. As was discussed in Section 4.6, the specification gives the "contract with the user," or list of promised resources. The body delivers the actual source code for the procedures and functions promised by the specification. Because the input/output and `Ada.Calendar` packages are supplied in precompiled form by all Ada compilers, we have seen only their specifications; the source code for the bodies is not available to us. Other packages may be supplied to you in source-code form, with both the specification and body files provided. `Screen` is one of these packages.

Program 4.8 shows the specification for `Screen`.

Program 4.8 Specification for Screen Package

```
PACKAGE Screen IS
------------------------------------------------------------------
--| Procedures for drawing pictures on ANSI Terminal Screen
--| Author: M. B. Feldman, The George Washington University
--| Last Modified: July 1998
------------------------------------------------------------------

  -- constants; the number of rows and columns on the terminal

  ScreenDepth : CONSTANT Integer := 24;
  ScreenWidth : CONSTANT Integer := 80;

  -- subtypes giving the ranges of acceptable inputs
  -- to the cursor-positioning operation

  SUBTYPE Depth IS Integer RANGE 1..ScreenDepth;
  SUBTYPE Width IS Integer RANGE 1..ScreenWidth;

  PROCEDURE Beep;
  -- Pre:  None
  -- Post: Terminal makes its beep sound once

  PROCEDURE ClearScreen;
  -- Pre:  None
  -- Post: Terminal Screen is cleared

  PROCEDURE MoveCursor (Column : Width; Row : Depth);
  -- Pre:  Column and Row have been assigned values
  -- Post: Cursor is moved to the given spot on the screen

END Screen;
```

This package provides two constants, `ScreenWidth` and `ScreenDepth`, corresponding to the number of columns (usually 80) and rows (usually 24) on the screen. There are also two subtypes, `Width` and `Depth`, giving the ranges for valid cursor positions (`1..ScreenDepth` and `1..ScreenWidth`, respectively).

The package provides three procedures. The first two, `Beep` and `ClearScreen`, take no parameters: A procedure call statement

```
Screen.Beep;
```

causes the terminal to beep; a procedure call statement

```
Screen.ClearScreen;
```

causes the screen to go blank, erasing all previous information from it. The last procedure, `MoveCursor`, takes row and column parameters, so that, for example,

```
Screen.MoveCursor (Row => 10, Column => 22);
Text_IO.Put (Item => '*');
```

has the effect of displaying an asterisk in the location of row 10, column 22. Finally,

```
Screen.MoveCursor (Row => 5, Column => 10);
Text_IO.Put (Item => "-----");
```

displays the string ----- in row 5, columns 10 through 14, inclusive.

Note the style of comments documenting each of these procedures. These are called *preconditions* and *postconditions* and are used to describe each procedure's assumptions and behavior in an informal but structured way. We'll come back to this subject in more detail in Chapter 7; meanwhile, you can get used to reading this style of documenting our packages.

Program 4.9 gives the body of this package. You might not understand exactly how the procedures work. Don't worry about this right now; we'll return to it in Chapter 8.

Program 4.9 Body of Screen Package

```
WITH Ada.Characters.Latin_1;
WITH Ada.Text_IO;
WITH Ada.Integer_Text_IO;
PACKAGE BODY Screen IS
-----------------------------------------------------------------
--| Body of screen-handling package
--| Author: M. B. Feldman, The George Washington University
--| Last Modified: July 1998
-----------------------------------------------------------------

  PROCEDURE Beep IS
  BEGIN
    Ada.Text_IO.Put (Item => Ada.Characters.Latin_1.BEL);
    Ada.Text_IO.Flush;
  END Beep;

  PROCEDURE ClearScreen IS
  BEGIN
    Ada.Text_IO.Put (Item => Ada.Characters.Latin_1.ESC);
    Ada.Text_IO.Put (Item => "[2J");
    Ada.Text_IO.Flush;
  END ClearScreen;

  PROCEDURE MoveCursor (Column : Width; Row : Depth) IS
  BEGIN
```

```
      Ada.Text_IO.Flush;
      Ada.Text_IO.Put (Item => Ada.Characters.Latin_1.ESC);
      Ada.Text_IO.Put ("[");
      Ada.Integer_Text_IO.Put (Item => Row, Width => 1);
      Ada.Text_IO.Put (Item => ';');
      Ada.Integer_Text_IO.Put (Item => Column, Width => 1);
      Ada.Text_IO.Put (Item => 'f');
   END MoveCursor;

END Screen;
```

Using the Screen Package

Ada's standard packages—the ones whose names begin with `Ada.`—come with the Ada compiler and do not need to be compiled. Before any non-standard package can be used by other programs, it must be compiled. The specification must be compiled first, then the body. To use the screen package, you must have a copy of the specification and body files available in your computer's file system. If you do not, you must type them in exactly as shown in Programs 4.8 and 4.9, then compile them both. If you subsequently modify the specification file, you must recompile both it and the body, and all other programs that use the package as well. If you do not modify either file, you will not have to recompile it; your Ada compiler's library system will keep it available for use with any program with the context clause

```
WITH Screen;
```

As an example of the use of the screen package, consider Program 4.10, which first clears the screen, then beeps three times, then draws a "smiley face" in the center of the screen. After each beep, there is a statement

```
DELAY 0.1;
```

which causes the computer to wait 0.1 second before sending the next beep. This is done so that even on a very fast computer you will hear three distinct beeps.

Program 4.10 Smiley: a Program That Uses the Screen Package

```
WITH Ada.Text_IO;
WITH Screen;
PROCEDURE Smiley IS
------------------------------------------------------------------------
--| Draws a "smiley face" in the center of the terminal screen
--| Author: M. B. Feldman, The George Washington University
--| Last Modified: July 1998
------------------------------------------------------------------------

BEGIN -- Smiley

  Screen.ClearScreen;
  Screen.Beep;
  DELAY 0.1;
  Screen.Beep;
  DELAY 0.1;
  Screen.Beep;
```

```
DELAY 0.1;
Screen.MoveCursor (Row => 7, Column => 34);
Ada.Text_IO.Put (Item =>    "HAVE A NICE DAY!");
Screen.MoveCursor (Row => 9, Column => 39);
Ada.Text_IO.Put (Item =>    "_____");
Screen.MoveCursor (Row => 10, Column => 37);
Ada.Text_IO.Put (Item =>   "/        \");
Screen.MoveCursor (Row => 11, Column => 36);
Ada.Text_IO.Put (Item =>   "/          \");
Screen.MoveCursor (Row => 12, Column => 35);
Ada.Text_IO.Put (Item => "|            |");
Screen.MoveCursor (Row => 13, Column => 35);
Ada.Text_IO.Put (Item => "|   O   O   |");
Screen.MoveCursor (Row => 14, Column => 36);
Ada.Text_IO.Put (Item =>   "\     o    /");
Screen.MoveCursor (Row => 15, Column => 37);
Ada.Text_IO.Put (Item =>    "\ \___/ /");
Screen.MoveCursor (Row => 16, Column => 38);
Ada.Text_IO.Put (Item =>     "\      /");
Screen.MoveCursor (Row => 17, Column => 39);
Ada.Text_IO.Put (Item =>      "-----");
Screen.MoveCursor (Row => 24, Column => 1);
```

END Smiley;

Sample Run

HAVE A NICE DAY!

There is one more thing you need to know about `screen`. Even though all Ada compilers support the same Ada language, not all Ada programs can show correct output on all terminals because different kinds of terminals have different characteristics. This package assumes that the terminal you are using responds to ANSI control sequences. Most UNIX and VMS terminals do. So does an IBM-PC or compatible computer running DOS or Windows 95, provided that the ANSI.SYS device driver is listed in the computer's CONFIG.SYS file. If you run `smiley` but your screen does not look like the sample run, see your computer center or teacher or, if you are using your own PC-compatible, check whether ANSI.SYS is properly installed. Some installations of Windows NT cannot handle ANSI.SYS; instead, you can use the alternative package on the CD-ROM.

4.8 Tricks of the Trade: Common Programming Errors

When you define enumeration types, keep in mind that the order is important. For example,

```
TYPE Days IS (Mon, Tue, Wed, Thu, Fri, Sat, Sun);
```

is not the same as

```
TYPE Days IS (Sun, Mon, Tue, Wed, Thu, Fri, Sat);
```

because the positions of the various literals are different in the two types.

An enumeration Get first reads characters until it reads a character that cannot be part of an enumeration literal, then checks whether the literal read is a valid one in the given type. If ABC is a valid literal but not ABC123, entering ABC123 will cause Ada.Text_IO.Data_Error to be raised.

When you work with packages that are not part of the Ada system, remember that they may have to be compiled before you can use them. Compile the specification first, then the body. After the specification is compiled, you can compile any program that uses the package, but you cannot link that program until the body is compiled. Once you have compiled the package, the compiled form remains available in your file system unless you delete it.

CHAPTER REVIEW

In this chapter, we discussed more aspects of problem solving. We reviewed the stepwise-refinement approach to solving problems and showed how to use the documentation created by following the software development method as the outline of the final program. We also showed how we could extend a solution to one problem to form the basis of the solution for another problem. We illustrated how structure charts are used to show relationships between different levels of subproblems or between algorithm steps and their refinements. We discussed the representation of the various steps in an algorithm and illustrated the stepwise refinement of algorithms.

In this chapter enumeration types were introduced, along with Ada's standard input/output library for reading and displaying enumeration values. Enumeration types are useful in allowing the programmer to give meaningful names to values such as days of the week, months of the year, colors of the rainbow, and command sets.

This chapter also continued the use of packages, begun in Chapter 3 with the use of the input/output libraries. We discussed Ada's standard package Ada.Calendar and a package called Screen that is provided with this book.

New Ada Constructs in Chapter 4

Table 4.1 describes the new Ada constructs introduced in this chapter.

Table 4.1   Summary of New Ada Constructs

Construct	Effect
Subtype definition:	
SUBTYPE FDIC_Insured IS Float RANGE 0.0..100000.0;	declares a subtype of Float in the range 0.0–100000.0
Enumeration type definition:	
TYPE CompassPoints IS (North, South, East, West);	defines a type whose values are enumerated as a list of identifiers

Quick-Check Exercises

1. Does a compiler translate comments?

2. Each statement in a program should have a comment. (True or false?)

3. What is a structure chart?

4. Explain how a structure chart differs from an algorithm.

Answers to Quick-Check Exercises

1. No

2. False

3. A structure chart is a diagram that is used to show an algorithm's subproblems and their interdependence.

4. A structure chart shows the relationship between subproblems; an algorithm lists the sequence in which subproblems are performed.

Review Questions for Chapter 4

1. Discuss the strategy of stepwise refinement.

2. Provide guidelines for the use of comments.

3. Briefly describe the steps you would take to derive an algorithm for a given problem.

4. The diagram that shows the algorithm steps and their interdependencies is called a _____.

Programming Projects

1. Write a program that draws two of your initials in the center of the screen. For example,

    ```
    X     X   XXXXX              XXXXX       X
    XX    XX  X                  X           X
    XXX  XXX  XXX      or        XXX         X
    X  X  X   X                  X       X   X
    X     X   X                  XXXXX   XXXXX
    ```

2. Write a program that clears the screen, and then beeps and flashes the word HELP in the center of the screen three times at 1-second intervals. (*Hint:* To "flash" a word, display a word and then display the same number of blank characters in the same spot on the screen.)

3. Write a program that displays today's date in the center of the screen.

4. Find out the names of the days of the week in some other language and write a program that translates from those names to the English ones. Revise your program to do the translation in the other direction.

5. Many different date forms are in current use around the world. Here are a few examples of how September 21, 1998 might appear in different countries:

    21/9/1998 (many countries; the day is written before the month)

    21 September 1998 (Britain)

    21.IX.1998 (Germany; the month is given as in Roman numerals)

    Modify Program 4.6 or Program 4.7 so that one or more of these forms is used. If you are familar with any other date forms, you can use those as well.

6. In shopping for a new house, you must consider several factors. In this problem the initial cost of the house, the estimated annual heating fuel costs, and the annual tax rate are available. Develop a case study for a program that will determine the total cost after a five-year period for each set of house data below. You should be able to inspect your program output to determine the "best buy."

Initial House Cost	Annual Fuel Cost	Tax Rate
$67,000	$2300	0.025
$62,000	$2500	0.025
$75,000	$1850	0.020

    To calculate the house cost, add the fuel cost for five years to the initial cost, then add the taxes for five years. Taxes for one year are computed by multiplying the tax rate by the initial cost.

CHAPTER 5

Decision Statements; Writing Functions and Packages

In this chapter we show you how to represent decisions in algorithms by writing steps with two or more alternative courses of action. You will see how to implement conditional execution in Ada by using Boolean conditions and the Ada IF statement.

This chapter also introduces you to the process of writing simple reusable functions and putting them in packages for later use by yourself and others. As examples of reusable functions, we consider those in the standard Ada math library.

This continues the practice begun in Chapter 4, in which each chapter introduces new material that will help you structure small program units but also shows you immediately how to integrate this new material into larger, system-level units. In this way you will always focus your attention on the two equally important problems of building individual programs and building libraries of programs into systems.

5.1 Control Structures: Boolean Expressions and the IF Statement

All the algorithms that we illustrated in Chapters 3 and 4 are straight-line algorithms—that is, each algorithm step is executed exactly once in the order in which it appears. Often, we are faced with situations in which we must provide alternative steps that may or may not be executed, depending on the input data. To motivate the need for conditional execution, let us start with a case study.

CASE STUDY

GIVEN TODAY, FIND YESTERDAY AND TOMORROW

Problem Specification
Prompt the user for a day of the week from the terminal, and display yesterday and tomorrow.

Analysis
Recall from Chapter 4 that the days of the week are best represented as an enumeration type, so the days can easily be read and displayed by an instance of `Ada.Text_IO.Enumeration_IO`. Yesterday and tomorrow can be found by using the successor and predecessor attributes.

Data Requirements

Problem Data Types
Days of the week, an enumeration type:

```
TYPE Days IS (Monday, Tuesday, Wednesday, Thursday,
              Friday, Saturday, Sunday);
```

Problem Inputs
```
Today : Days
```

Problem Outputs
```
Yesterday: Days
Tomorrow: Days
```

Design

Initial Algorithm
1. Prompt the user for the current day and read it from the keyboard.

2. Find Yesterday and Tomorrow

   2.1. Set Yesterday to the predecessor of Today.

   2.2. Set Tomorrow to the successor of Today.

3. Display the results on the screen.

Algorithm Refinements

This algorithm looks fine, but recall that in Ada the enumeration types do not "wrap around." Suppose the user entered Monday or Saturday. The predecessor of Monday and the successor of Saturday are undefined, and trying to compute either one would raise Constraint_Error. This is a case in which the language type system does not quite agree with the physical world. To account for this, we need to include two special cases in our algorithm, which result in revisions to steps 2.1 and 2.2:

2.1. If today is the first day of the week, then yesterday is the last day of the (previous) week; otherwise, yesterday is the predecessor of today.

2.2. If today is the last day of the week, then tomorrow is the first day of the (following) week; otherwise, tomorrow is the successor of today.

These special cases are, in fact, conditional steps: They include the words *if* and *otherwise*.

Test Plan

In addition to a normal case, we need to test two special cases, namely, those in which today is Sunday (to be sure that tomorrow is Monday) and today is Monday (to be sure that yesterday was Sunday). Also test for invalid input that is not one of the seven day abbreviations.

Implementation

Program 5.1 gives the complete solution to the problem. The statements corresponding to the revised algorithm steps 2.1 and 2.2 are examples of the IF statement:

```
IF Today = Days'First THEN
   Yesterday := Days'Last;
ELSE
   Yesterday := Days'Pred(Today);
END IF;
```

and

```
IF Today = Days'Last THEN
   Tomorrow := Days'First;
ELSE
   Tomorrow := Days'Succ(Today);
END IF;
```

Program 5.1 Finding Yesterday and Tomorrow

```
WITH Ada.Text_IO;
PROCEDURE Three_Days IS
----------------------------------------------------------------
--| Finds yesterday and tomorrow, given today
--| Author: Michael Feldman, The George Washington University
--| Last Modified: June 1998
----------------------------------------------------------------

  TYPE Days IS (Monday, Tuesday, Wednesday,
               Thursday, Friday, Saturday, Sunday);
  PACKAGE Day_IO IS
    NEW Ada.Text_IO.Enumeration_IO (Enum => Days);
```

```
      Yesterday : Days;
      Today     : Days;
      Tomorrow  : Days;

BEGIN -- Three_Days

   -- prompt user to enter a day abbreviation
   Ada.Text_IO.Put (Item => "Enter the name of a day of the week > ");
   Day_IO.Get (Item => Today);

   -- find yesterday
   IF Today = Days'First THEN
     Yesterday := Days'Last;
   ELSE
     Yesterday := Days'Pred(Today);
   END IF;

   Ada.Text_IO.Put (Item => "Yesterday was ");
   Day_IO.Put (Item => Yesterday);
   Ada.Text_IO.New_Line;

   Ada.Text_IO.Put (Item => "Today is ");
   Day_IO.Put (Item => Today);
   Ada.Text_IO.New_Line;

   -- find tomorrow
   IF Today = Days'Last THEN
     Tomorrow := Days'First;
   ELSE
     Tomorrow := Days'Succ(Today);
   END IF;

   Ada.Text_IO.Put (Item => "Tomorrow is ");
   Day_IO.Put (Item => Tomorrow);
   Ada.Text_IO.New_Line;

END Three_Days;
```

Sample Run

```
Enter the name of a day of the week > monday
Yesterday was SUNDAY
Today is MONDAY
Tomorrow is TUESDAY
```

Testing

The sample run shows only one special-case test. To complete the test plan, run the program for the other cases as well.

Boolean Expressions and Conditions

In the statement

```
IF Today = Days'First THEN
  Yesterday := Days'Last;
```

```
ELSE
  Yesterday := Days'Pred(Today);
END IF;
```

the expression

```
Today = Days'First
```

is called a *Boolean expression*. There are only two possible values for a Boolean expression: `True` or `False`. If `Today` is, in fact `Days'First`, the preceding Boolean expression evaluates to `True`; if not, the expression evaluates to `False`. Chapter 8 examines all the operators that can be used on Boolean expressions. For now, we will concentrate on learning how to write and use simple Boolean expressions called *conditions*.

Most conditions that we use will have one of the following forms:

```
variable    relational operator    variable
variable    relational operator    constant
```

Relational operators are the familiar symbols

< (less than)

<= (less than or equal to)

> (greater than)

>= (greater than or equal to)

= (equal to)

/= (not equal to)

All these operators should be familiar to you except the last. Ada uses the symbol pair `/=` to express the condition "not equal to." In mathematics this is usually written ≠, but this symbol does not appear on computer keyboards. Also, be careful that you write `>=` and not `=>` for "greater than or equal to"; the latter symbol is used in Ada for other things, such as

```
Ada.Text_IO.Put(Item => "Hello");
```

and its mistaken use as a relational operator will lead to a compilation error.

The variables in a Boolean condition can be of `Integer`, `Float`, `String`, or enumeration type. In the `Integer` and `Float` cases the relational operators have their familiar meanings: 3 < 4, −17.5 > −30.4. In the case of enumeration types the comparisons are with respect to the order in which the values are defined in the type definition. Given two types

```
TYPE Days IS (Monday, Tuesday, Wednesday, Thursday,
              Friday, Saturday, Sunday);
TYPE Colors  IS (Red, Orange, Yellow, Green, Blue, Purple);
```

these conditions are all true:

```
Monday < Tuesday
Wednesday /= Tuesday
Wednesday = Wednesday
Wednesday >= Tuesday

Purple > Red
Yellow < Green
Green >= Yellow
```

The conditions

```
Purple > Friday
3 <= 4.5
Green > 2
```

would cause compilation errors because the two values in each comparison are associated with different types and therefore cannot be compared. It would be like comparing apples and oranges.

If the `Integer` variable `I` is 5, the `Float` variable `x` is 3.9, and the `Days` variable `Today` is `Wednesday`, these relations are true:

```
I > 0
X <= 3.9
Today > Tuesday
```

Finally, we note that the `character` type is defined as an enumeration type and the relations are with respect to the alphabetic order. It's actually a bit more complicated than this; we'll come back to it in more detail in Chapter 8.

■ Example 5.1

The relational operators and some sample conditions are shown in Table 5.1. Each condition is evaluated according to the following variable values: ■

X	Power	MaxPow	Y	Item	MinItem	MomOrDad	Num	Sentinel
−5	1024	1024	7	1.5	−999.0	'M'	999	999

Table 5.1 Ada Relational Operators and Sample Conditions

Operator	Condition	Meaning	Value
<=	X <= 0	x less than or equal to 0	true
<	Power < MaxPow	Power less than MaxPow	false
>=	X >= Y	x greater than or equal to y	false
>	Item > MinItem	Item greater than MinItem	true
=	MomOrDad = 'M'	MomOrDad equal to 'M'	true
/=	MinItem /= Item	MinItem ≠ Item	true

Operator	Condition	Meaning	Value
/=	Num /= Sentinel	Num ≠ Sentinel	false

The IF Statement

You can use the IF statement to select among several alternatives. An IF statement always contains a Boolean expression. For example, given the Float variables Gross-Pay, NetPay, and Tax, the IF statement

```
IF GrossPay > 100.00 THEN
   NetPay := GrossPay - Tax;
ELSE
   NetPay := GrossPay;
END IF;
```

selects one of the two assignment statements listed. It selects the statement following THEN if the Boolean expression is true (i.e, if GrossPay is greater than 100.00); it selects the statement following ELSE if the Boolean expression is false (i.e., if Gross-Pay is not greater than 100.00).

The preceding IF statement has two alternatives, exactly one of which will be executed for a given value of GrossPay.

Figure 5.1 is a graphic description, called a *flowchart*, of the preceding IF statement. This figure shows that the condition enclosed in the diamond-shaped box (GrossPay > 100.00) is evaluated first. If the condition is true, the arrow labeled True is followed, and the assignment statement in the rectangle on the right is executed. If the condition is false, the arrow labeled False is followed, and the assignment in the rectangle on the left is executed.

Example 5.2 illustrates that an IF statement can also have a single alternative that is executed only when the condition is true.

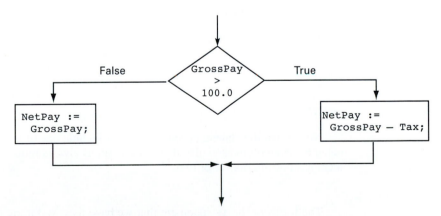

Figure 5.1   Two–Alternative IF Statement

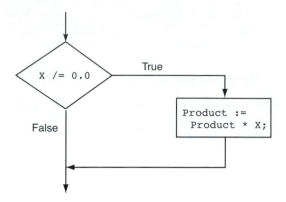

Figure 5.2 Single-Alternative IF Statement

■ Example 5.2

The following IF statement has one alternative, which is executed only when x is not equal to 0. It causes Product to be multiplied by x; the new value is then saved in Product, replacing the old value. If x is equal to 0, the multiplication is not performed. Figure 5.2 is a flowchart of this IF statement.

```
-- Multiply Product by a nonzero X only
IF X /= 0.0 THEN
   Product := Product * X;
END IF;
```
■

■ Example 5.3

The following IF statement has two alternatives. It displays either Hi Mom or Hi Dad depending on the character stored in the variable MomOrDad (type Character). If this variable's value is 'M', "Hi Mom" is displayed. If the variable has any other value at all, "Hi Dad" is displayed.

```
IF MomOrDad = 'M' THEN
   Ada.Text_IO.Put(Item => "Hi Mom");
   Ada.Text_IO.New_Line;
ELSE
   Ada.Text_IO.Put(Item => "Hi Dad");
   Ada.Text_IO.New_line;
END IF;
```

Notice that the statement sequences may include one or more statements, all terminated by semicolons, and also that the END IF; is always required whether the IF statement has one alternative or two.
■

The forms of the IF statement that we have used so far are summarized in the displays that follow.

SYNTAX
DISPLAY

IF Statement (Two Alternatives)

Form:

```
IF condition THEN
  statement sequence T
ELSE
  statement sequence F
END IF;
```

Example:

```
IF X >= 0.0 THEN
  Ada.Text_IO.Put(Item => "Positive");
ELSE
  Ada.Text_IO.Put(Item => "Negative");
END IF;
```

Interpretation:

If the *condition* evaluates to true, then *statement sequence T* is executed and *statement sequence F* is skipped; otherwise, *statement sequence T* is skipped and *statement sequence F* is executed.

Note:

There is no semicolon after THEN or after ELSE. Inserting a semicolon here will cause a compilation error.

SYNTAX
DISPLAY

IF Statement (One Alternative)

Form:

```
IF condition THEN
  statement sequence T
END IF;
```

Example:

```
IF X > 0.0 THEN
  PosProd := PosProd * X;
  CountPos := CountPos + 1;
END IF;
```

Interpretation:

If the *condition* evaluates to true, then *statement sequence T* is executed; otherwise, it is skipped.

PROGRAM STYLE

> ### Formatting the IF statement
>
> In all the IF statement examples, the statement sequences are indented. If the word ELSE appears, it is entered on a separate line and aligned with the words IF and END IF. The format of the IF statement makes its meaning apparent. This is done solely to improve program readability and is highly recommended; the format that is used makes no difference to the compiler.

EXERCISES FOR SECTION 5.1

Self-Check

1. State the types of the values that can appear as operands of the relational operators.

2. Assuming that x is 15.0 and y is 25.0, what are the values of the following conditions?

   ```
   X /= Y      X < X      X >= (Y - X)      X = (Y + X - Y)
   ```

3. For each of the following program fragments, state whether the fragment is legal. If not, why not? If so, what is displayed?

   a.
   ```
   IF 12 < 12 THEN
      Ada.Text_IO.Put(Item => "Never");
   ELSE
      Ada.Text_IO.Put(Item => "Always");
   END IF;
   ```

   b.
   ```
   IF 12 < 15.0 THEN
      Ada.Text_IO.Put(Item => "Never");
   ELSE
      Ada.Text_IO.Put(Item => "Always");
   END IF;
   ```

   c.
   ```
   Var1 := 15.0;
   Var2 := 25.12;
   IF (2*Var1) > Var2 THEN
      Ada.Text_IO.Put(Item => "OK");
   ELSE
      Ada.Text_IO.Put(Item => "Not OK");
   END IF;
   ```

   d.
   ```
   Var1 := 15.0;
   Var2 := 25.12;
   IF (2*Var1) > Var2 THEN
      Ada.Text_IO.Put(Item => "OK");
   END IF;
   Ada.Text_IO.Put(Item => "Not OK");
   ```

5.2 Problem Solving: Decision Steps in Algorithms

Let's continue our study of conditional execution with another case study, this one to find the alphabetically first letter of three letters.

CASE
STUDY

FINDING THE ALPHABETICALLY FIRST LETTER

Problem Specification
Read three letters and find and display the one that comes first in the alphabet.

Analysis
From the previous section we know how to compare two items to see which one is smaller using the relational operator <. We can use this operator to determine whether one letter precedes another in the alphabet. For example, the condition 'A' < 'F' is true because A precedes F in the alphabet. Because we have no direct way to compare three items, our strategy will be to do a sequence of pairwise comparisons. We will start by comparing the first two letters to find the smaller of that pair. The result of the second comparison will be the smallest of the three letters.

Data Requirements

Problem Inputs
Ch1, Ch2, Ch3 : Character

Problem Outputs
AlphaFirst : Character   -- the alphabetically first letter

Design

Initial Algorithm
1. Read three letters into Ch1, Ch2, and Ch3.

2. Save the alphabetically first letter of Ch1, Ch2, and Ch3 in AlphaFirst.

3. Display the alphabetically first letter.

Algorithm Refinements
Step 2 can be performed by first comparing Ch1 and Ch2 and saving the alphabetically first letter in AlphaFirst; this result can then be compared to Ch3. The refinement of step 2 follows.

Step 2 Refinement
2.1. Save the alphabetically first letter of Ch1 and Ch2 in AlphaFirst.

2.2. Save the alphabetically first letter of Ch3 and AlphaFirst in AlphaFirst.

Figure 5.3 shows the structure chart that corresponds to this algorithm.

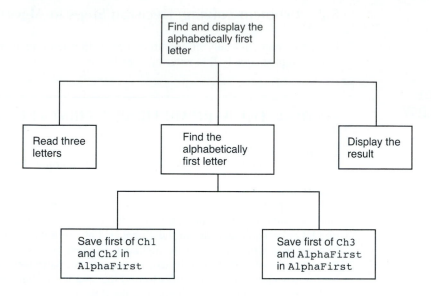

Figure 5.3   Structure Chart for Finding the Alphabetically First Letter

Test Plan

Test this program with different sequences of letters corresponding to the possible orderings of three distinct letters. Also, test it with cases in which at least two of the letters are equal. In this way you are ensuring that all of the paths through the IF statements are tested.

Implementation

Program 5.2 shows the desired program. The IF statement with two alternatives saves either Ch1 or Ch2 in AlphaFirst. The IF statement with one alternative stores Ch3 in AlphaFirst if Ch3 precedes the value already in AlphaFirst. Later you will see that IF statements with more than two alternatives are also possible in Ada.

Program 5.2 Finding the First Letter

```
WITH Ada.Text_IO;
PROCEDURE First_Letter IS
-----------------------------------------------------------------
--| Finds and displays the alphabetically first letter.
--| Author: Michael Feldman, The George Washington University
--| Last Modified: July 1998
-----------------------------------------------------------------

   Ch1, Ch2, Ch3  : Character;    -- input  - three letters
   AlphaFirst     : Character;    -- output - first letter

BEGIN  -- First_Letter

   -- Read three letters
   Ada.Text_IO.Put
```

```
     (Item => "Enter any three letters, then press ENTER > ");
  Ada.Text_IO.Get (Item => Ch1);
  Ada.Text_IO.Get (Item => Ch2);
  Ada.Text_IO.Get (Item => Ch3);

  -- Save the smaller of Ch1 and Ch2 in AlphaFirst
  IF Ch1 < Ch2 THEN
     AlphaFirst := Ch1;      -- Ch1 comes before Ch2
  ELSE
     AlphaFirst := Ch2;      -- Ch2 comes before Ch1
  END IF;

  -- Save the smaller of Ch3 and AlphaFirst in AlphaFirst
  IF Ch3 < AlphaFirst THEN
     AlphaFirst := Ch3;      -- Ch3 comes before AlphaFirst
  END IF;

  -- Display result
  Ada.Text_IO.Put (Item => AlphaFirst);
  Ada.Text_IO.Put (Item => " is the first letter alphabetically");
  Ada.Text_IO.New_Line;

END First_Letter;
```

Sample Run

```
Enter any three letters, then press ENTER > THE
E is the first letter alphabetically
```

Testing

As usual, the sample output shows one of the test cases.

EXERCISES FOR SECTION 5.2

Self-Check

1. What value is assigned to x for each of the following segments when y is 15.0.

    a. ```
        X := 25.0;
        IF Y /= (X - 10.0) THEN
           X := X - 10.0;
        ELSE
           X := X / 2.0;
        END IF;
        ```

    b.  ```
        IF Y < 15.0 THEN
           X := 5 * Y;
        ELSE
           X := 2 * Y;
        END IF;
        ```

Programming

1. Write Ada statements to carry out the following steps.

a. If `Item` is nonzero, multiply `Product` by `Item` and save the result in `Product`; otherwise, skip the multiplication. In either case, display the value of `Product`.

b. Store the absolute difference of `x` and `y` in `z`, where the absolute difference is `(X - Y)` or `(Y - X)`, whichever is positive.

c. If `x` is zero, add 1 to `ZeroCount`. If `x` is negative, add `x` to `MinusSum`. If `x` is greater than zero, add `x` to `PlusSum`.

5.3   Tricks of the Trade: Tracing a Program or Algorithm

A critical step in the design of an algorithm or program is to verify that it is correct before you spend extensive time entering or debugging it. Often, a few extra minutes spent in verifying the correctness of an algorithm will save hours of testing time later.

One important technique, a hand trace or desk check (mentioned in Chapter 1), consists of a careful, step-by-step simulation on paper of how the computer would execute the algorithm or program. The results of this simulation should show the effect of each step's execution using data that are relatively easy to process by hand.

As an example, the completely refined algorithm for the alphabetically first letter problem appears next.

Refined Algorithm

1. Read three letters into `Ch1`, `Ch2`, and `Ch3`.

2. Save the alphabetically first letter of `Ch1`, `Ch2`, and `Ch3` in `AlphaFirst`.

    2.1.   Save the alphabetically first letter of `Ch1` and `Ch2` in `AlphaFirst`.

        2.1.1.   IF `Ch1` precedes `Ch2` THEN

            2.1.2.   `AlphaFirst` gets `Ch1`

        ELSE

            2.1.3   `AlphaFirst` gets `Ch2`

        END IF;

    2.2   Save the alphabetically first letter of `Ch3` and `AlphaFirst` in `AlphaFirst`.

        2.2.1.   IF `Ch3` precedes `AlphaFirst` THEN

            2.2.2.`AlphaFirst` gets `Ch3`

        END IF;

3. Display the alphabetically first letter.

Table 5.2 shows a trace of the algorithm for the data string THE. Each step is listed at the left in order of its execution. The values of variables that are referenced by a step are shown after the step. If a step changes the value of a variable, the table shows the new value. The effect of each step is described at the far right. For example, the table shows that the step

Read three letters into Ch1, Ch2, Ch3

stores the letters T, H, and E in the variables Ch1, Ch2, and Ch3.

Table 5.2 Trace of First Letter Algorithm

Algorithm Step	Ch1	Ch2	Ch3	AlphaFirst	Effect
	?	?	?	?	
1. Read three letters	T	H	E		Reads the data
2.1.1 If Ch1 precedes Ch2					Is 'T' < 'H' ? value is false
2.1.3 AlphaFirst gets Ch2			H		'H' is first so far
2.2.1 If Ch3 precedes AlphaFirst					Is 'E' < 'H' ? value is true
2.2.2 AlphaFirst gets Ch3				E	'E' is first
3. Display AlphaFirst					Displays 'E' is the first letter.

The trace in Table 5.2 clearly shows that the alphabetically first letter, E, of the input string is stored in AlphaFirst and displayed. To verify that the program is correct, it would be necessary to select other data that cause the two conditions to evaluate to different combinations of their values. Because there are two conditions and each has two possible values (true or false), there are 2 × 2, or 4 different combinations that should be tried. (What are they?) An exhaustive (complete) desk check of the program would show that it works for all of these combinations.

Besides testing for the four cases discussed above, you should verify that the program works correctly for unusual data. For example, what would happen if all three letters or a pair of letters were the same? Would the program still provide the correct result? To complete the desk check, it would be necessary to show that the program does indeed handle these special situations properly.

In tracing each case, you must be very careful to execute the program exactly as it would be executed by the computer. A desk check in which you assume that a particular step will be executed a certain way, without explicitly testing each condition and tracing each program step, is of little value.

■ **Example 5.4**

In later chapters you will see that it is useful to be able to order a pair of data values so that the smaller value ends up in one variable (say, x) and the larger value ends up in another (say, Y). To understand the algorithm for doing this, imagine that you have a blue cup filled with orange juice and a red one filled with milk. If you wanted to exchange the contents of the two cups, you'd need to used a third cup, and you'd follow these steps:

1. Pour the contents of the blue cup into the third cup.

2. Pour the contents of the red cup into the blue cup.

3. Pour the contents of the third cup into the red cup.

Now given two values stored in the variables x and Y, the following IF statement rearranges any two values stored in these two variables as just described. If the two numbers are already in the proper order, the statement sequence is not executed.

```
IF X > Y THEN    -- switch X and Y
  Temp := X; -- Store old X in Temp
  X := Y;       -- Store old Y in X
  Y := Temp; -- Store old X in Y
END IF;
```

The variables x, Y, and Temp must, of course, all be the same type. As in the cups analogy, an additional variable, Temp, is needed for storage of a copy of one of the values. The trace in Table 5.3 illustrates the need for Temp, assuming that x and Y have original values of 12.5 and 5.0, respectively. If Temp were not used, one of the values would be lost; be sure you understand why this is so. ■

Table 5.3 Trace of IF Statement to Order X and Y

Statement Part	X	Y	Temp	Effect
	12.5	5.0	?	
IF X > Y THEN				12.5 > 5.0 is true
Temp := X;			12.5	Store old x in Temp
X := Y;	5.0			Store old y in x
Y := Temp;		12.5		Store old x in y

EXERCISES FOR SECTION 5.3

Self-Check

1. Provide sample data and traces for the remaining three cases of the alphabetically first letter problem. Also, test the special cases where two letters are the same and all three letters are the same. What is the value of the conditions in the latter case?

5.4 Problem Solving: Extending a Solution

Often, what appears to be a new problem will turn out to be a variation of one that you have already solved. Consequently, an important skill in problem solving is the ability to recognize that a problem is similar to one that you solved earlier. As you progress through your education, you will start to build up a collection of programs and procedures. Whenever possible, you should try to adapt or reuse parts of a program that have been shown to work correctly. In this section we show a Case Study that solves a simple payroll problem; shortly we will introduce a second payroll problem whose solution is an extension of the first one.

CASE STUDY

PAYROLL PROBLEM

Problem Specification
Develop a program to compute the pay owed in a given week to an employee of a company. The *gross pay* is computed as the number of hours that employee worked times the employee's wage per hour. The *net pay* is the gross pay minus the income tax that is deducted and sent to the government. The tax is 15% of that part of the gross pay that exceeds $100. That is, if the employee earns $250 in a given week, the tax is 15% of $150, or $22.50.

Analysis
We begin by listing the data requirements and the algorithm.

Data Requirements

Problem Constants
maximum salary without a tax deduction (TaxBracket = 100.00)
tax rate (TaxRate = 0.15)

Problem Inputs
hours worked (Hours : NonNegFloat)
hourly rate (Rate : NonNegFloat)

Problem Outputs
gross pay (`GrossPay : NonNegFloat`)
tax (`Tax: NonNegFloat`)
net pay (`NetPay : NonNegFloat`)

Relevant Formulas
gross pay = hourly rate × hours worked
tax = tax rate × (gross − tax bracket)
net pay = gross pay − tax

Unlike problem inputs, whose values may vary, problem constants have the same values for each run of the program. Each constant value is associated with an identifier (`TaxRate` and `TaxBracket` above). The program style display following this problem describes the reason for this association.

Design
The structure chart for this algorithm is given in Fig. 5.4.

Initial Algorithm
1. Display user instructions.

2. Enter hours worked and hourly rate.

3. Compute gross salary.

4. Compute net salary.

5. Display gross salary, tax, and net salary.

Now let's write the refinement of algorithm step 4 as a *decision step*.

Step 4 Refinement
4.1. IF GrossPay > TaxBracket THEN
Deduct a tax of TaxRate × (GrossPay − TaxBracket)
ELSE
Deduct no tax
END IF;

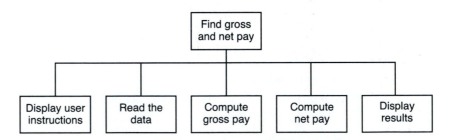

Figure 5.4   Structure Chart for Payroll Program

Test Plan

To test this program, run it with several sets of data. One data set should yield a gross salary greater than $100.00, and the other should yield a gross salary less than $100.00. You should also test the program with a data set that yields a gross salary that is $0.00, one that yields a gross salary of exactly $100.00, and at least one for invalid inputs.

Implementation

The payroll program is shown in Program 5.3.

Program 5.3 Payroll Program

```
WITH Ada.Text_IO;
WITH Ada.Float_Text_IO;
PROCEDURE Weekly_Pay IS
-----------------------------------------------------------------
--| Computes and displays gross pay and net pay given an hourly
--| rate and number of hours worked.  Deducts a tax of 15% of
--| gross salary exceeding $100.
--| Author: Michael Feldman, The George Washington University
--| Last Modified: July 1998
-----------------------------------------------------------------

   SUBTYPE NonNegFloat IS Float RANGE 0.0 .. Float'Last;

   TaxBracket : CONSTANT NonNegFloat := 100.00;
                                 -- maximum salary for no deduction
   TaxRate:      CONSTANT NonNegFloat :=  0.15;   -- tax rate

   Hours:        NonNegFloat; -- inputs - hours worked, hourly rate
   HourlyRate:   NonNegFloat;
   GrossPay:     NonNegFloat; -- outputs - gross pay, net pay
   Tax:          NonNegFloat;
   NetPay:       NonNegFloat;

BEGIN -- Weekly_Pay

   -- Enter Hours and Rate
   Ada.Text_IO.Put (Item => "Hours worked > ");
   Ada.Float_Text_IO.Get (Item => Hours);
   Ada.Text_IO.Put (Item => "Hourly rate $");
   Ada.Float_Text_IO.Get (Item => HourlyRate);
   Ada.Text_IO.New_Line;

   -- Compute gross salary
   GrossPay := Hours * HourlyRate;

   -- Compute tax and net salary
   IF GrossPay > TaxBracket THEN
     Tax := TaxRate * (GrossPay - TaxBracket);
     NetPay := GrossPay - Tax;      -- Deduct a tax amount
   ELSE
     NetPay := GrossPay;            -- Deduct no tax
   END IF;

   -- Display Results
   Ada.Text_IO.Put (Item => "Gross pay is $");
   Ada.Float_Text_IO.Put(Item => GrossPay, Fore => 1, Aft => 2, Exp => 0);
   Ada.Text_IO.New_Line;
   Ada.Text_IO.Put (Item => "TaxDeduction is $");
```

```
Ada.Float_Text_IO.Put (Item => Tax, Fore => 1, Aft => 2, Exp => 0);
Ada.Text_IO.New_Line;
Ada.Text_IO.Put (Item => "Net pay is $");
Ada.Float_Text_IO.Put (Item => NetPay, Fore => 1, Aft => 2, Exp => 0);
Ada.Text_IO.New_Line;

END Weekly_Pay;
```

Sample Run

```
Hours worked > 35
Hourly rate $7.50

Gross pay is $262.50
TaxDeduction is $24.38
Net pay is $238.13
```

Testing
The sample run shows one set of test data from the test plan.

PROGRAM STYLE

Use of Constants

The constants `Tax` and `TaxBracket` appear in the preceding `IF` statement and in Program 5.3. We might have been tempted to insert the constant values (100.00 and 0.15) directly in the `IF` statement, writing

```
IF GrossPay > 100.00 THEN
   Tax := GrossPay - 0.15 * (GrossPay - 100.);
   NetPay := GrossPay - Tax;
ELSE
   NetPay := GrossPay;
END IF;
```

There are two reasons why it is better style to use the constants as we did originally. First, the original `IF` statement is easier to understand because it uses the names `Tax` and `TaxBracket`, which are descriptive, rather than numbers, which have no intrinsic meaning.

Second, a program that is written with constants is much easier to modify than one that is not. If the tax bracket and tax value were to change—and tax-related things always change—we would need to change only the constant declaration. If the constant values were inserted directly in the `IF` statement, as was just shown above, we would have to change them not only in the `IF` statement but also in all the other statements in which they appeared. In a program of realistic length, finding all these occurrences would be a tedious and error-prone process.

For both reasons we recommend that you try to avoid dispersing constant values through your programs; instead, use constants that are declared by name.

Extending the Problem Solution

An experienced programmer usually writes programs that can be easily changed or modified to fit other situations. One reason for this is that programmers (and program users) often wish to make slight improvements to a program after having used it. If the original program is designed carefully from the beginning, the programmer will be able to accommodate changing specifications with a minimum of effort. In the next problem it is possible to insert a new decision step rather than having to rewrite the entire program.

CASE STUDY

COMPUTING OVERTIME PAY

Problem Specification

Develop a payroll program so that employees who work more than 40 hours a week are paid 1.5 times their hourly rate for all overtime hours.

Analysis

This problem is an extension of the payroll problem solved by Program 5.3. Employees who work more than 40 hours should be paid one rate for the first 40 hours and a higher rate for the extra hours over 40. Employees who work 40 hours or less should be paid the same rate for all hours worked. We can solve this problem by replacing step 3 (compute gross pay) in the original algorithm with a decision step that selects either a straight pay computation or a computation with overtime pay.

Data Requirements

Problem Inputs

hours worked (`Hours : NonNegFloat`)
hourly rate (`Rate : NonNegFloat`)

Problem Outputs

gross pay (`Gross : NonNegFloat`)
tax (`Tax: NonNegFloat`)
net pay (`Net : NonNegFloat`)

Problem Constants

maximum salary for no tax deduction (`TaxBracket = 100.00`)
amount of tax deducted (`Tax = 25.00`)
maximum hours without overtime pay (`MaxHours = 40.0`)

Relevant Formulas

gross pay = hourly rate × hours worked
tax = tax rate × (gross − tax bracket)
net pay = gross pay − tax

Design

The critical change to the algorithm involves modifying step 3 of the algorithm. The algorithm is repeated next, followed by a new refinement for step 3.

Initial Agorithm

1. Display user instructions.

2. Enter hours worked and hourly rate.

3. Compute gross pay including any overtime pay.

4. Compute net pay.

5. Display results.

Algorithm Refinements

Step 3 Refinement

3.1. IF no overtime hours were worked THEN

> 3.2.   Compute GrossPay as Hours * HourlyRate
>
> ELSE
>
> 3.3.   Compute GrossPay as (the pay for 40 hours) + (the pay for overtime hours)
>
> END IF;

Implementation

As shown below, we should replace the assignment statement in Program 4.1 that computes gross pay by

```
-- Compute gross pay including any overtime pay
IF Hours <= MaxHours THEN
  GrossPay := Hours * HurlyRate;
ELSE
  GrossPay :=
    (MaxHours * HourlyRate) +
    ((Hours — MaxHours) * (1.5 * HourlyRate));
END IF;
```

If the condition Hours <= MaxHours is true, there is no overtime pay, so gross pay is computed as before; otherwise, GrossPay is computed by using the second assignment statement above. The pay for the first 40 hours is added to the pay earned for the overtime hours (Hours - MaxHours).

Note how we have used parentheses in the overtime calculation to make our intention clear. Modifying Program 5.3 as discussed here is left as an exercise.

EXERCISES FOR SECTION 5.4

Self-Check

1. Trace Program 5.3 when Hours is 30.0 and HourlyRate is 9.00. Perform the trace when Hours is 20.0 and Rate is 6.00.

2. Rewrite the algorithm for the payroll problem so that the computation of gross salary is performed in two steps rather than in one. First compute the base pay for all hours worked. Then add in an extra amount only if overtime hours were worked.

5.5 Control Structures: The Multiple-Alternative IF Statement

Until now, we have used IF statements to implement decisions involving one or two alternatives. In this section you will see how the IF statement can be used to implement decisions involving more than two alternatives.

■ Example 5.5

The following IF statement has three alternatives. It causes one of three variables (Num-Pos, NumNeg, or NumZero) to be increased by 1 depending on whether x is greater than 0, less than 0, or equal to 0, respectively. This statement might be part of a program to keep track of the number of positive, negative, and zero values in a set of values. It assumes that all the variables have been properly initialized. The word ELSIF is an Ada reserved word and is *not* a typographical error.

```
-- Increment NumPos, NumNeg, or NumZero depending on X
IF  X > 0 THEN
  NumPos := NumPos + 1;
ELSIF X < 0 THEN
  NumNeg := NumNeg + 1;
ELSE -- X = 0
  NumZero := NumZero + 1;
END IF;
```

The execution of this IF statement proceeds as follows: The first condition (x > 0) is tested; if it is true, the statement NumPos := NumPos+1 increments NumPos by 1 and the rest of the IF statement is skipped. If the first condition is false, the second condition (x < 0) is tested; if it is true, NumNeg is incremented; otherwise, NumZero is incremented. It is important to realize that the second condition is tested only when the first condition is false. A trace of the IF statement for x = −7 is shown in Table 5.4.

Table 5.4   Trace of IF Statement in Example 5.5 for X = –7

Statement Part	X	Effect
	–7	
`IF X > 0 THEN`		$-7 > 0$ is false
`ELSIF X < 0 THEN`		$-7 < 0$ is true
`NumNeg := NumNeg + 1;`		Add 1 to `NumNeg`

SYNTAX
DISPLAY

IF Statement (Multiple Alternatives)

Form:

```
IF condition₁ THEN
   statement sequence₁
ELSIF condition₂ THEN
   statement sequence₂
   ...
ELSIF conditionₖ THEN
   statement sequenceₖ
ELSE
   statement sequenceₙ
END IF;
```

Example:

```
IF N >= 0 THEN
   Ada.Text_IO.Put(Item=>"Positive");
ELSIF N = 0 THEN
   Ada.Text_IO.Put(Item=>"Zero");
ELSE
   Ada.Text_IO.Put(Item=>"Negative");
END IF;
```

Interpretation:

The conditions in a multiple-alternative IF statement are evaluated from top to bottom until a true value is obtained. The statement sequence following the first true condition is executed and the rest of the IF statement is skipped. If every condition is false, *statement sequenceₙ* (between ELSE and END) is executed.

Notes:

At most, one statement sequence is executed. If ELSE and *statement sequenceₙ* are present, exactly one statement sequence is always executed. If ELSE and *statement sequenceₙ* are omitted, no statement sequence is executed when every expression is false.

Also note the spelling required by Ada: ELSIF is spelled without a second E or space; END IF must have a space between END and IF.

PROGRAM
STYLE

> ### Writing a Multiple-Alternative IF Statement
>
> When writing a multiple-alternative IF statement, align the reserved words IF, ELSE, ELSIF, and END IF and indent each statement sequence consistently. This is done to make the IF statement more readable.

Order of Conditions

Very often, the conditions in a multiple-alternative decision are not mutually exclusive. This means that it may be possible for more than one condition to be true for a given data value. If this is the case, the order of the conditions becomes very important because only the statement sequence following the first true condition is executed.

■ Example 5.6

Table 5.5 describes the assignment of letter grades (as commonly used in the United States) based on the score on a 100-point examination.

Table 5.5   Letter Grades in U.S. Universities

Exam Score	Grade Assigned
90 and above	A (excellent)
80–89	B (very good)
70–79	C (fair)
60–69	D (barely passing)
below 60	F (failing)

The following multiple-alternative IF statement displays the letter grade assigned according to this table. The last three conditions are true for an exam score of 85; however, a grade of B is assigned because the first true condition is Score >= 80.

```
-- correct grade assignment
IF Score >= 90 THEN
   Ada.Text_IO.Put (Item=>'A');
ELSIF Score >= 80 THEN
   Ada.Text_IO.Put (Item=>'B');
ELSIF Score >= 70 THEN
   Ada.Text_IO.Put (Item=>'C');
ELSIF Score >= 60 THEN
   Ada.Text_IO.Put (Item=>'D');
ELSE
   Ada.Text_IO.Put (Item=>'F');
END IF;
```

It would be wrong to write the decision as shown next. All passing exam scores (60 or above) would be incorrectly categorized as a grade of D because the first condition would be true and the rest would be skipped. Writing the IF this way would be a mis-translation of the table into code.

```
-- incorrect grade assignment
IF Score >= 60 THEN
   Ada.Text_IO.Put (Item=>'D');
ELSIF Score >= 70 THEN
   Ada.Text_IO.Put (Item=>'C');
ELSIF Score >= 80 THEN
   Ada.Text_IO.Put (Item=>'B');
ELSIF Score >= 90 THEN
   Ada.Text_IO.Put (Item=>'A');
ELSE
   Ada.Text_IO.Put (Item=>'F');
END IF;
```

■

■ Example 5.7

You can use a multiple-alternative IF statement to implement a *decision table* that describes several alternatives. Let's say that you are an accountant setting up a payroll system for a small firm. Each line of Table 5.6 indicates an employee's salary range and a corresponding base tax amount and tax percentage. Given a salary amount, the tax is calculated by adding the base tax for that salary range and the product of the percentage of excess and the amount of salary over the minimum salary for that range.

Table 5.6   Tax Table for Example 5.7

Bracket	Salary Range	Base Tax	Percentage of Excess
1	0.00 – 1499.99	0.00	15%
2	1500.00 – 2999.99	225.00	16%
3	3000.00 – 4999.99	465.00	18%
4	5000.00 – 7999.99	825.00	20%
5	8000.00 – 14999.99	1425.00	25%

For example, the second line of the table specifies that the tax due on a salary of $2000.00 is $225.00 plus 16% of the excess salary over $1500.00 (i.e., 16% of $500.00). Therefore the total tax due is $225.00 plus $80.00, or $305.00.

The IF statement in Fig. 5.5 implements the tax table. If the value of salary is within the table range (0.00 to 14999.99), exactly one of the statements assigning a value to Tax will be executed. A trace of the IF statement for salary = $2000.00 is shown in Table 5.7. The value assigned to Tax is $305.00, as desired.

Figure 5.5   IF Statement for Tax Table 5.6

```
IF Salary < 0.0 THEN
   Ada.Text_IO.Put (Item=>"Error! Negative salary $");
   Ada.Float.Text_IO.Put (Item=>Salary, Fore=>1, Aft=>2, Exp=0);
   Ada.Text_IO.New_Line;
ELSIF Salary < 1500.00 THEN -- first range
   Tax := 0.15 * Salary;
ELSIF Salary < 3000.00 THEN -- second range
   Tax := (Salary - 1500.00) * 0.16 + 225.00;
ELSIF Salary < 5000.00 THEN -- third range
   Tax := (Salary - 3000.00) * 0.18 + 465.00;
ELSIF Salary < 8000.00 THEN -- fourth range
   Tax := (Salary - 5000.00) * 0.20 + 825.00;
ELSIF Salary < 15000.00 THEN -- fifth range
   Tax := (Salary - 8000.00) * 0.25 + 1425.00;
ELSE
   Ada.Text_IO.Put (Item=>"Error! Too large salary $");
   Ada.Float.Text_IO.Put (Item=>Salary, Fore=>1, Aft=>2, Exp=0);
   Ada.Text_IO.New_Line;
END IF;
```

Table 5.7   Trace of Fig. 5.5 for Salary = $2000.00

Statement Part	Salary	Tax	Effect
	2000.00	?	
IF Salary < 0.0			2000.0 < 0.0 is false
ELSIF Salary < 1500.00			2000.0 < 1500.0 is false
ELSIF Salary < 3000.00			2000.0 < 3000.0 is true
Tax := (Salary - 1500.00)			difference is 500.00
* 0.16			product is 80.00
+ 225.00			sum is 305.00

PROGRAM STYLE

Validating the Value of Variables

It is important to validate the value of a variable before you perform computations using invalid or meaningless data. Instead of computing an incorrect tax amount, the IF statement above displays an error message if the value of Salary is outside the range covered by the table (0.0 to 14999.99). The first condition is used to detect negative salaries, and an error message is displayed if Salary is less than zero. All conditions evaluate to False if Salary is greater than 14999.99, and the alternative following ELSE displays an error message.

Nested IF Statements

The statement sequence inside a control statement can contain another control statement. For example, an IF statement can contain another IF. The second control statement is said to be *nested* inside the first control statement. The inner control statement can itself contain a control statement; in fact, there is no theoretical limit on the depth to which control statements can be nested.

The ability to nest control statements allows us to write very sophisticated programs. In Chapters 5 and 6 we will introduce many examples of IF statements nested inside loops and vice versa. For the time being, consider the following example.

■ Example 5.8

Many U.S. secondary schools and universities use the Grade Point Average (GPA) to summarize each student's achievement. Each subject receives a grade of A through F; then each grade is assigned a numerical weight: A is weighted 4.0, B is 3.0, C is 2.0, D is 1.0, and F is 0.0. Then the GPA is formed by summing all the subject weights and dividing by the number of subjects.

Depending on a student's GPA, the following fragment—which uses *nested IF statements*—displays one of three messages. If the GPA is less than or equal to 1.5, the painful message following the second ELSE is displayed. If GPA is greater than 1.5, the *inner* IF statement is executed, and a more pleasant message is displayed.

```
IF GPA > 1.5 THEN
  IF GPA < 3.0 THEN
    Ada.TextIO.Put(Item => "Progressing satisfactorily");
  ELSE
    Ada.Text_IO.Put
      (Item => "Made the Honors List - send money");
  END IF;
ELSE
  Ada.Text_IO.Put (Item => "Flunked out");
END IF;
```

The following nested statements have the same effect as the ones above. Again, the inner IF statement is executed when GPA exceeds 1.5.

```
IF GPA <= 1.5 THEN
  Ada.Text_IO.Put (Item => "Flunked out");
ELSE
  IF GPA < 3.0 THEN
    Ada.Text_IO.Put (Item => "Progressing satisfactorily");
  ELSE
    Ada.Text_IO.Put
      (Item => "Made the Honors List - send money");
  END IF;
END IF;
```

Nested IF statements can sometimes be confusing to write and to read. Often, a single multiple-alternative IF statement can replace nested IF statements, resulting in a more readable program. Verify for yourself that the following IF statement has the same effect as the earlier nested IF statements.

```
IF GPA <= 1.5 THEN
  Ada.Text_IO.Put (Item => "Flunked out");
ELSIF GPA < 3.0 THEN
  Ada.Text_IO.Put (Item => "Progressing satisfactorily");
ELSE
  Ada.Text_IO.Put (Item => "Made the Honors List - send money");
END IF;
```

PROGRAM STYLE

Indentation Conventions for Nested Control Structures

It is a good idea to develop a consistent indentation style for nested control structures. Note in the preceding examples that the entire nested IF is indented the same amount as the Put following the ELSE.

Developing a consistent indentation style is one way of making your programs clear and easy to read. Many companies have adopted companywide or projectwide programming style standards that include indentation rules. This makes it easy for programmers to read each other's source code. There is no one "best" indentation rule; the most important principle is consistency.

In this book we indent each structure several spaces deeper than the structure within which it is nested. The complete program examples use a consistent indentation of two spaces, and the code fragments in the text are usually indented a bit more for added clarity. We recommend an indentation convention similar to that used in the programs. If your teacher states different rules, follow them consistently.

EXERCISES FOR SECTION 5.5

Self-Check

1. Trace the execution of the IF statement in Fig. 5.7 for salary = 13500.00.

2. What would be the effect of reversing the order of the first two conditions in the IF statement of Fig. 5.7?

Programming

1. Rewrite the IF statement for Example 5.8 using only the relational operator < in all conditions.

2. Implement the following decision table using a multiple-alternative IF statement. Assume that the grade point average is within the range 0.0 – 4.0.

Grade Point Average	Transcript Message
0.0 – 0.99	Failed semester -- registration suspended
1.0 – 1.99	On probation for next semester
2.0 – 2.99	(no message)
3.0 – 3.49	Deans list for semester
3.5 – 4.0	Highest honors for semester

5.6 System Structures: Using Ada's Math Library

We use computers for many kinds of applications, some of which require that we actually write programs to do mathematical computations. It is therefore useful to have available a set of the usual elementary functions such as square root, sine, cosine, and so on. Ada provides such a set of functions in a standard library called Ada.Numerics.Elementary_Functions. The full description of this standard library package is found in Appendix E; Program 5.4 shows how one of the its functions, Sqrt, is used to compute a square root. The name of its Float parameter (and that of the other functions in the library) is x.

Program 5.4 Computing Several Square Roots

```
WITH Ada.Text_IO;
WITH Ada.Float_Text_IO;
WITH Ada.Numerics.Elementary_Functions;
PROCEDURE Square_Roots IS
-----------------------------------------------------------------
--| Illustrates the square root function provided by
--| Author: Michael Feldman, The George Washington University
--| Last Modified: July 1998
-----------------------------------------------------------------

  SUBTYPE NonNegFloat IS Float RANGE 0.0 .. Float'Last;

  First : NonNegFloat;
  Second: NonNegFloat;
  Answer: NonNegFloat;

BEGIN  -- Square_Roots

  Ada.Text_IO.Put (Item => "Please enter first number > ");
  Ada.Float_Text_IO.Get(Item => First);
  Answer := Ada.Numerics.Elementary_Functions.Sqrt(X => First);
  Ada.Text_IO.Put (Item => "The first number's square root is ");
  Ada.Float_Text_IO.Put (Item => Answer, Fore => 1, Aft => 5, Exp => 0);
  Ada.Text_IO.New_Line;
```

```
Ada.Text_IO.Put (Item => "Please enter second number > ");
Ada.Float_Text_IO.Get(Item => Second);
Ada.Text_IO.Put (Item => "The second number's square root is ");
Ada.Float_Text_IO.Put
   (Item => Ada.Numerics.Elementary_Functions.Sqrt (X => Second),
    Fore => 1, Aft => 5, Exp => 0);
Ada.Text_IO.New_Line;

Answer := Ada.Numerics.Elementary_Functions.Sqrt(X => First + Second);
Ada.Text_IO.Put
   (Item => "The square root of the sum of the numbers is ");
Ada.Float_Text_IO.Put (Item => Answer, Fore => 1, Aft => 5, Exp => 0);
Ada.Text_IO.New_Line;

END Square_Roots;
```

Sample Run

```
Please enter first number > 9
The first number's square root is 3.00000
Please enter second number > 16
The second number's square root is 4.00000
The square root of the sum of the numbers is 5.00000
```

As you can see from the sample run, this program prompts the user for two floating-point values and computes the square roots of the two numbers and of their sum. Note in the program that the second call of the square root function is nested in the Put statement and that in the third call, the parameter is the expression First + Second. This is just to illustrate that function calls can be nested in other expressions and that expressions can be nested in function calls.

In Chapter 8 we'll come back to the math library.

5.7   System Structures: Writing Functions

In Chapter 4 you saw how to use some functions in a predefined package, namely, the Month, Day, and Year functions in the standard package Ada.Calendar; in the previous section you saw how to use the square root function from another standard package, Ada.Numerics.Elementary_Functions. This section introduces the very important subject of how to *write* such functions; the next section shows how to put functions in packages for yourself and others to use again later.

Function Specifications

In general, a function is written so as to require the caller to supply some values to it. When called, the function performs its desired computation and then *returns* a result to the calling program. The line indicating the name of the function, the list of expected parameters, and the type of the returned result is called a *function specification* or sometimes *function declaration*. You saw three such specifications in Chapter 4:

```
FUNCTION Year (Date: Time) RETURN Year_Number;
```

```
FUNCTION Month (Date: Time) RETURN Month_Number;
FUNCTION Day (Date: Time) RETURN Day_Number;
```

The specification for `Year` tells the compiler—and the reader—that this function must be called with one value of type `Time` and that it returns a result of type `Year_Number` to the program that calls it. The other two specifications are similar.

Here is a specification for a function to find the larger of two integer values and return it to the calling program:

```
FUNCTION Maximum(Value1, Value2: Integer) RETURN Integer;
```

Notice that between the parentheses is a list of the expected parameters and that after the word RETURN is the type of the returned result. In this case the function is to determine which of the two parameters is larger and return it as the result.

Calling a Function

Recall from Chapter 4 that we were able to extract the year from a system-generated time value by writing

```
ThisYear := Calendar.Year(Date => RightNow);
```

where `This_Year` was declared as a variable of type `Ada.Calendar.Year_Number` and `RightNow` was a variable of type `Ada.Calendar.Time`. Notice that between the parentheses is an association of the name of the *formal* parameter (`Date`) with the variable containing the value of the *actual* parameter (`RightNow`).

How could we use our function `Maximum` in a similar way? Given an integer variable `Larger`, writing

```
Larger := Maximum (Value1 => 24, Value2 => -57);
```

stores the value 24 in the variable `Larger` because that is the larger of the two values. Given two integer variables `Grade1` and `Grade2`, writing

```
Grade1 := -24;
Grade2 := 113;
Larger := Maximum(Value1=>Grade1,Value2=>Grade2);
```

stores in `Larger` the value 113, again because that is the larger value. Notice again how the formal parameters `Value1` and `Value2` are associated with the actual parameters `Grade1` and `Grade2`, and notice that it is improper to write, for example,

```
Larger := Maximum (Grade1 => Value1 ,Grade2 => Value2);
```

because `Value1` is the formal parameter and `Grade1` is the actual. The formal parameter comes first, followed by the actual parameter.

The difference between these two examples is that the function `Year` already exists (in package `Ada.Calendar`) but the function `Maximum` does not. We have a specification indicating the name of the function, how it is to be called, and what it returns, but we do not yet actually have a function that will find the larger number.

Function Bodies

To complete our function `Maximum`, we need to write a *function body,* that is, a small program in Ada in a form that the compiler will recognize as a function. Here is the desired function body:

```
FUNCTION Maximum (Value1, Value2: Integer) RETURN Integer IS
  Result: Integer;
BEGIN
  IF Value1 > Value2 THEN
    Result := Value1;
  ELSE
    Result := Value2;
  END IF;
  RETURN Result;
END Maximum;
```

This function body has the basic form of an Ada program. There is a header line similar to the first line of a program; this line ends with the word IS. Next there is a section of declarations; here we are declaring only a single program variable `Result`. Following the word BEGIN is the statement sequence of the function body, and the function body ends with an END. The IF statement in the function body stores in the variable `Result` the larger of `Value1` and `Value2`. Finally, the value in `Result` is returned to the calling program as the function result. This value can be stored directly in a variable of the calling program, as in the examples above, or used as part of an expression implementing a larger calculation.

The variable `Result` is called a *local variable* of the function. Because it is declared inside the function body, it has no existence outside the function body. It is good practice when writing a function to put the variables that are needed by the function *inside* the function body so that they are the private property of the function and cannot be seen or disturbed by any other program.

To see an example of how a function is declared as part of a larger program, consider Program 5.5, in which the user is prompted to enter two integer values `FirstValue` and `SecondValue`. These values are then passed to the function `Maximum`, which returns the larger value to the main program. The answer is then displayed. The function `Maximum` is declared in the declaration part of the main program.

Program 5.5 Finding the Larger of Two Integer Values with a Function

```
WITH Ada.Text_IO;
WITH Ada.Integer_Text_IO;
PROCEDURE Max_Two IS
-------------------------------------------------------------
--| Finds the larger of two integer values using our
--| Maximum function.
--| Author: Michael Feldman, The George Washington University
--| Last Modified: July 1998
-------------------------------------------------------------

  FirstValue:  Integer; -- input
  SecondValue: Integer; -- input
  Larger:      Integer; -- output

  -- function specification
```

```
      FUNCTION Maximum (Value1, Value2: Integer) RETURN Integer;

      -- function body
      FUNCTION Maximum (Value1, Value2: Integer) RETURN Integer IS
        Result: Integer;
      BEGIN
        IF Value1 > Value2 THEN
          Result := Value1;
        ELSE
          Result := Value2;
        END IF;
        RETURN Result;
      END Maximum;

  BEGIN

      Ada.Text_IO.Put (Item => "Please enter first integer value  > ");
      Ada.Integer_Text_IO.Get (Item => FirstValue);
      Ada.Text_IO.Put (Item => "Please enter second integer value > ");
      Ada.Integer_Text_IO.Get (Item => SecondValue);

      Larger := Maximum(Value1=>FirstValue, Value2=>SecondValue);

      Ada.Text_IO.Put (Item => "The larger number is ");
      Ada.Integer_Text_IO.Put (Item => Larger, Width => 1);
      Ada.Text_IO.New_Line;

  END Max_Two;
```

Sample Run

```
Please enter first integer value  > 374
Please enter second integer value > -158
The larger number is 374
```

**SYNTAX
DISPLAY**

Function Specification

Form:

```
FUNCTION fname ( formal parameters ) RETURN result type ;
```

Example:

```
FUNCTION Square (Num : Integer) RETURN Integer;
```

Interpretation:

The function *fname* is declared. The list of *formal parameters* is enclosed in parentheses. The data type of the function result is indicated by the identifier *result type*.

SYNTAX
DISPLAY

Function Body

Form:

```
FUNCTION fname ( formal parameters ) RETURN result type IS
   local declaration section
BEGIN
   statement sequence
END fname;
```

Example:

```
FUNCTION Square (Num : Integer) RETURN Integer IS
   Result: Integer;
BEGIN
   Result := Num * Num;
   RETURN Result;
END Square;
```

Interpretation:

The function *fname* is declared. The list of *formal parameters* is enclosed in parentheses. The data type of the function result is indicated by the identifier *result type*. Any identifiers that are declared in the *local declaration section* exist only during the execution of the function. The function body describes the data manipulation to be performed by the function. At least one RETURN statement must be executed each time the function is called.

Note 1:

The result type is not restricted in Ada. It may be any type.

Note 2:

If there are no parameters, you should omit the formal parameters and parentheses.

Note 3:

The first line of the function body must agree exactly with the function specification, except that the specification ends with a semicolon and the first line of the body ends with IS. The way the line ends indicates to the compiler whether it should treat the line as a specification or as the first line of a body. It is therefore important not to confuse the two endings, lest you confuse the compiler.

EXERCISES FOR SECTION 5.7

Self-Check

1. In programming, what is a function? Briefly describe why you think functions are useful.

5.8   System Structures: Writing a Package

As you have seen, it is possible to declare a function as part of a program. It is certainly permitted to declare a function like this, and doing so provides an easy way to test the function. However, the real usefulness of functions—and of procedures, for that matter—is achieved when they are collected together as a group of related items and placed in a package. A package is compiled and placed in a library, either your own personal program library or, in a group project, the team's library. Once a package is compiled, it—and all the resources in it—is available for use by means of a simple context clause (WITH statement).

Package Specifications and Package Bodies

Recall from Section 4.7 that a package consists of two files: the *specification* and the *body*. The specification is like a table of contents for the package, listing all the different resources (types, functions and procedures) that are available in the package; the package body contains the actual Ada code for each of these resources.

In the case of the standard packages (Ada.Text_IO and Ada.Calendar, for example) the package body source files are not always supplied with the compiler, since these may be trade secrets of the compiler developer. In this case, the executable (precompiled) version of the package body is supplied. These are usually installed along with the compiler and are usually available to you without further action on your part.

In the case of programmer-defined packages, it is the programmer's responsibility to write both the specification file and the body file. This book shows a number of programmer-defined packages, for which the Ada source code is given.

Ada requires that a package be separated into these two files to provide a mechanism for *encapsulation,* which is defined as separation of specification and implementation. The specification serves as a "contract" between the package and the programs that use the package. Writing this contract in one file, then providing the contract "deliverables" in a second file, *encapsulates* the implementation of the package. Encapsulation is one of the important principles in object-oriented programming (OOP); when you develop packages, you are, in fact, doing one form of OOP.

A Package Containing Minimum and Maximum Functions

Finding the larger or smaller of two numbers is frequently required in programming. The programming task would therefore be made easier if we could write functions once to find the minimum and maximum, then package them up for future use. Our first step is to write a package specification. Remember that the specification is a table of contents for the package. This specification can be compiled as it stands, just to be sure that there are no compilation errors. The package specification is shown as Program 5.6. Note again the use of preconditions and postconditions to document the functions.

Program 5.6 Package Specification for Min_Max

```
PACKAGE Min_Max IS
-----------------------------------------------------------------
--| specifications of functions provided by Min_Max package
```

```
--| Author: Michael Feldman, The George Washington University
--| Last Modified: July 1998
------------------------------------------------------------------

   FUNCTION Minimum (Value1, Value2: Integer) RETURN Integer;
   -- Pre:  Value1 and Value2 have been assigned values
   -- Post: Returns the smaller of the two input values

   FUNCTION Maximum (Value1, Value2: Integer) RETURN Integer;
   -- Pre:  Value1 and Value2 have been assigned values
   -- Post: Returns the larger of the two input values

END Min_Max;
```

We now must write the package body. We can incorporate the `Maximum` function written above. Also, we can write the `Minimum` function very easily: Given the `Maximum` function, writing a `Minimum` function is just a matter of making a change to the inequality in the `IF` statement:

```
IF Value1 < Value2 THEN
  Result := Value1;
ELSE
  Result := Value2;
END IF;
```

Program 5.7 gives the entire package body. Be certain that you understand that the package specification contains the function specifications and the package body contains the function bodies.

Program 5.7 Package Body for Min_Max

```
PACKAGE BODY Min_Max IS
------------------------------------------------------------------
--| bodies of functions provided by Min_Max package
--| Author: Michael Feldman, The George Washington University
--| Last Modified: July 1998
------------------------------------------------------------------

   FUNCTION Minimum (Value1, Value2: Integer) RETURN Integer IS
     Result: Integer;
   BEGIN

     IF Value1 < Value2 THEN
        Result := Value1;
     ELSE
        Result := Value2;
     END IF;
     RETURN Result;

   END Minimum;

   FUNCTION Maximum (Value1, Value2: Integer) RETURN Integer IS
     Result: Integer;
   BEGIN

     IF Value1 > Value2 THEN
        Result := Value1;
     ELSE
```

```
            Result := Value2;
        END IF;
        RETURN Result;

    END Maximum;

END Min_Max;
```

Package Specification

Form:

```
PACKAGE pname IS
  list of specifications of resources
  provided by the package
END pname;
```

Example:

```
PACKAGE Min_Max IS
  FUNCTION Minimum (Value1, Value2: Integer) RETURN Integer;
  FUNCTION Maximum (Value1, Value2: Integer) RETURN Integer;
END Min_Max;
```

Interpretation:

The package specification gives a list or "table of contents" of the resources to be provided by the package. These resources can be procedures, functions, and types (see Section 4.6 for an example of a package providing types). The package specification must be compiled before the corresponding body is compiled.

Package Body

Form:

```
PACKAGE BODY pname IS
  sequence of function and procedure bodies
  implementing the resources listed in the
  package specification for pname
END pname;
```

Example:

Program 5.7 serves as an example. For brevity we will not repeat it here.

Interpretation:

The resources (functions and procedures) that are promised in the specification must be delivered in the corresponding package body. If any are missing, a compilation error will result.

Note:

The function and procedure specifications in the package specification must agree *exactly* with the corresponding function and procedure headers in the package body. Specifically, the names, types, and order of parameters must agree exactly. A formal parameter named `value1` in the specification cannot, for example, be called `val1` in the body. Ada compilers are *very* fussy about this. Care taken here will avoid compilation errors.

CASE STUDY

FINDING THE LARGEST AND SMALLEST OF THREE NUMBERS

Problem Specification

Find the largest and smallest of three numbers to be provided by the user.

Analysis

We cannot directly compare the three numbers, so, as in Program 5.2, we will compare them pairwise.

Data Requirements

Problem Inputs

the three numbers (`Num1, Num2, Num3: Integer`)

Problem Outputs

the largest and smallest numbers (`Largest,Smallest: Integer`)

Design

Instead of doing the comparisons directly, we can use the package `Min_Max` to find the larger and smaller of pairs of numbers. Given the three numbers, we can find the smaller of the first two numbers, then find the smaller of this result and the third number. We can apply the same approach to finding the largest number.

Initial Algorithm

1. Prompt the user for the three numbers.

2. Find the largest of the three numbers.

3. Find the smallest of the three numbers.

4. Display the results.

Algorithm Refinements

Step 2 Refinement:

2.1. Let `Largest` temporarily be the larger of `Num1` and `Num2`.

2.2. Now let `Largest` be the larger of itself and `Num3`.

Step 3 Refinement:

3.1. Let `Smallest` temporarily be the smaller of `Num1` and `Num2`.

3.2. Now let `Smallest` be the smaller of itself and `Num3`.

Test Plan

Test with different orderings of three integers to be certain that the maximum and minimum are always selected regardless of the original ordering.

Implementation

The coding is straightforward because our minimum and maximum functions already exist in the package. Assuming that the specification and body for `Min_Max` have both been successfully compiled, Program 5.8 solves the problem. Note the context clause

```
WITH Min_Max;
```

at the beginning of the program, along with the other context clauses for the input/output packages.

Program 5.8 Find the Minimum and Maximum of Three Integers

```
WITH Ada.Text_IO;
WITH Ada.Integer_Text_IO;
WITH Min_Max;
PROCEDURE Min_Max_Three IS
------------------------------------------------------------
--| Finds the largest and smallest of three integer values
--| using the Minimum and Maximum functions from package Min_Max
--| Author: Michael Feldman, The George Washington University
--| Last Modified: July 1998
------------------------------------------------------------

   Num1:     Integer;    -- program inputs
   Num2:     Integer;
   Num3:     Integer;
   Largest:  Integer;    -- program outputs
   Smallest: Integer;

BEGIN -- Min_Max_Three

   -- prompt user for inputs
   Ada.Text_IO.Put (Item => "Please enter first integer value  > ");
   Ada.Integer_Text_IO.Get (Item => Num1);
   Ada.Text_IO.Put (Item => "Please enter second integer value > ");
   Ada.Integer_Text_IO.Get (Item => Num2);
   Ada.Text_IO.Put (Item => "Please enter third integer value  > ");
   Ada.Integer_Text_IO.Get (Item => Num3);
```

```
-- find largest of the three inputs
Largest := Min_Max.Maximum(Value1=>Num1, Value2=>Num2);
Largest := Min_Max.Maximum(Value1=>Largest, Value2=>Num3);

-- find smallest of the three inputs
Smallest := Min_Max.Minimum(Value1=>Num1, Value2=>Num2);
Smallest := Min_Max.Minimum(Value1=>Smallest, Value2=>Num3);

-- display results
Ada.Text_IO.Put (Item => "The smallest number is ");
Ada.Integer_Text_IO.Put (Item => Smallest, Width => 1);
Ada.Text_IO.Put (Item => " and the largest number is ");
Ada.Integer_Text_IO.Put (Item => Largest, Width => 1);
Ada.Text_IO.New_Line;

END Min_Max_Three;
```

Sample Run

```
Please enter first integer value  > -29
Please enter second integer value > 574
Please enter third integer value  > 0
The smallest number is -29 and the largest number is 574
```

Testing

Once again, the sample run shows just one test case.

EXERCISES FOR SECTION 5.8

Self-Check

1. What is the difference between a package specification and a package body? Why do we require both?

5.9 Tricks of the Trade: Common Programming Errors

When writing IF statements, remember not to put a semicolon after THEN or ELSE and always to put semicolons after the other statements. Also do not forget the required END IF; at the end of the entire structure. Also remember that the end of an IF statement is always written END IF (two words), while the alternatives of a multiple-alternative IF are written ELSIF (one word, only one E).

When writing multiple-alternative IF statements, be careful to put the alternatives in an order that is correct for the problem being solved.

When writing a package, be sure that everything you promise in the specification is delivered in the body and that the parameter list for each function or procedure in the specification matches *exactly* the corresponding procedure or function header in the body. Remember that you must compile the package specification without compilation errors before you can attempt to compile the package body.

If the *body* of a package is changed but not the *specification*, do not recompile the specification; just recompile the body and repeat the link step. If you recompile the specification, all programs that use the package will have to be recompiled.

CHAPTER REVIEW

This chapter introduced you to an important control structure, the IF statement, for building decision steps into programs. IF statements are of three types: single-alternative, two-alternative, and multiple-alternative. IF statements provide a way to build decision making into a program.

You also learned how to write simple user-defined functions and how to structure a package you are writing. A package consists of a specification file and a body file. The specification gives a "contract with the user," telling both the reader and the compiler what to expect in a package. The body then provides all the things promised by the specification.

New Ada Constructs in Chapter 5

The new Ada constructs that were introduced in this chapter are described in Table 5.8.

Table 5.8   Summary of New Ada Constructs

Construct	*Effect*
IF Statement	
One Alternative	

`IF X /= 0.0 THEN`
`   Product := Product * X;`
`END IF;`
	Multiplies `Product` by `X` only if `X` is nonzero.

Two Alternatives	

`IF X >= 0 THEN`
`  Ada.Integer.Text_IO.Put(Item=>X);`
`  Ada.Text_IO.Put(" is positive");`
`ELSE`
`  Ada.Integer.Text_IO.Put(Item=>X);`
`  Ada.Text_IO.Put(" is positive");`
`END IF;`
	If `X` is greater than or equal to 0, the message `" is positive"` is displayed. Otherwise, the message `" is negative"` is displayed.

Several Alternatives	

Construct	Effect
| ```
IF  X  <  0.0  THEN
   Ada.Text_IO.Put(Item=>"negative");
   AbsX  :=  −X;
ELSIF  X  =  0.0  THEN
   Ada.Text_IO.Put(Item=>"zero");
   AbsX  :=  X;ELSE
   Ada.Text_IO.Put(Item=>"positive");
END  IF;
``` | One of three messages is displayed depending on whether x is negative, positive, or zero. `AbsX` is set to represent the absolute value or magnitude of x. |

Function Specification

```
FUNCTION Sign (X :Float) RETURN Character;
```
specifies a function

Function Body

| ```
FUNCTION Sign (X :Float) RETURN Character IS
   Temp: Character;
BEGIN -- Sign
   IF  X  >=  0  THEN
      Temp  :=  '+';
   ELSE
      Temp  :=  '-';
   END  IF;
   RETURN  Temp;
END  Sign;
``` | Returns a character value that indicates the sign (`'+'` or `'-'`) of its type `Float` argument. |

Quick-Check Exercises

1. An IF statement implements _____ execution.

2. What is pseudocode?

3. What values can a Boolean expression have?

4. The relational operator /= means _____.

5. A _____ is used to verify that an algorithm is correct.

6. When `Speed` is 75, what value is assigned to `Fee` by the IF statement on the left? By the IF statement on the right? Which IF statement is correct?

```
IF Speed > 35 THEN          IF Speed > 75 THEN
   Fee := 20.00;               Fee := 60.0;
ELSIF Speed > 50 THEN       ELSIF Speed > 50 THEN
   Fee := 40.00;               Fee := 40.00;
ELSIF Speed > 75 THEN       ELSIF Speed > 35 THEN
   Fee := 60.00;               Fee := 20.00;
END IF;                     END IF;
```

7. Explain the difference between the statements on the left and the statements on the right below. For each of them, what is the final value of x if the initial value of x is 1?

```
IF  X  >=  0  THEN              IF  X  >=  0  THEN
    X  :=  X  +  1;                 X  :=  X  +  1;
ELSIF  X  >=  1  THEN           END  IF;
    X  :=  X  +  2;             IF  X  >=  1  THEN
END  IF;                           X  :=  X  +  2;
                               END  IF;
```

Answers to Quick-Check Exercises

1. Conditional

2. A mixture of English and Ada used to describe algorithm steps

3. `True` and `False`

4. Not equal

5. Hand trace

6. left: 20.00, first condition is met; right: 40.00. The one on the right is correct.

7. A multiple-alternative `IF` statement is on the left; a sequence of `IF` statements is on the right. x becomes 2 on the left; x becomes 4 on the right.

Review Questions for Chapter 5

1. A decision in Ada is actually an evaluation of a(n) _____ expression.

2. List the six relational operators discussed in this chapter.

3. What should the programmer do after writing the algorithm but before entering the program?

4. Trace the following program fragment and indicate what will be displayed if a data value of 27.34 is entered.

    ```
    Ada.Text_IO.Put(Item => "Enter a temperature> ");
    Ada.Float.Text_IO.Get (Temp);
    IF Temp > 32.0 THEN
       Ada.Text_IO.Put(Item => "Not Freezing");
    ELSE
       Ada.Text_IO.Put(Item => "Ice Forming");
    END IF;
    ```

5. Write the appropriate `IF` statement to compute `GrossPay` given that the hourly rate is stored in the variable `Rate` and the total hours worked is stored in the variable `Hours`. Pay time and a half for more than 40 hours worked.

6. Explain the difference between a package specification and a package body.

Programming Projects

1. Modify the structure chart and program for the first letter problem (Section 5.2) to find the alphabetically first of *four* letters.

2. Modify the structure chart and program for the first letter problem to find the alphabetically *last* of three letters.

3. Develop and test the program—a modification of Program 5.3—for the over-time pay problem described in Section 5.4.

4. Develop and test a payroll program based on Program 5.3 that computes the tax withheld according to the tax rates given in Table 5.6 and Figure 5.5.

5. Write a program that reads in a room number, its capacity, and the size of the class enrolled so far and displays an output line showing the classroom number, capacity, number of seats filled and available, and a message indicating whether the class is filled or not. Display the following heading before the output line.

```
Room    Capacity    Enrollment    Empty seats    Filled/Not Filled
```

Display each part of the output line under the appropriate column heading. Test your program with the following classroom data:

Room	Capacity	Enrollment
426	25	25
327	18	14
420	20	15
317	100	90

6. Write a program that will determine the additional state tax owed by an employee. The state charges a 4% tax on net income. Determine net income by subtracting a $500 allowance for each dependent from gross income. Your program will read gross income, number of dependents, and tax amount already deducted. It will then compute the actual tax owed and display the difference between tax owed and tax deducted followed by the message `"Taxpayer owes"` or `"Refund to taxpayer"`, depending on whether this difference is positive or negative.

7. The Ring-a-Ding-Ding Telephone Company has the following rate structure for long-distance calls:

   a. Any call started after 6:00 P.M. (1800 hours) but before 8:00 A.M. (0800 hours) is discounted 50%.

   b. Any call started after 8:00 A.M. (0800 hours) but before 6:00 P.M. (1800 hours) is charged full price.

   c. All calls are subject to a 4% federal tax.

   d. The regular rate for a call is $0.25 per minute.

e. Any call longer than 60 minutes receives a 15% discount on its cost (after any other discount is subtracted but before tax is added).

Write a program that reads the start time for a call based on a 24-hour clock and the length of the call. The gross cost (before any discounts or tax) should be displayed, followed by the net cost (after discounts are deducted and tax is added).

8. Write a program that uses package Min_Max to find the smallest and largest of four integers read from the terminal.

9. Create and test a second version of package Min_Max. Copy the specification and body of Min_Max, change the name in both files to Min_Max_Float, and modify the functions so that Float parameters are used instead of Integer. Write a program that tests *both* packages together. (*Hint:* You will need two context clauses.)

10. In trying to determine the best maximum speed limit on a highway, the traffic police would like to collect statistical data on the actual speeds of cars under the new laws; they have hired you to develop a computer program to help them. As a first step, develop and test a package, Speeds, that provides a function to classify a speed into one of the following classifications:

Class 1: $0 <$ speed $<= 45$ miles per hour (m.p.h.)
Class 2: $45 <$ speed $<= 55$
Class 3: $55 <$ speed $<= 65$
Class 4: $65 <$ speed $<= 75$
Class 5: $75 <$ speed

The specification will contain an enumeration type to define the classes:

```
TYPE SpeedClasses IS (Class1, Class2, Class3, Class4, Class5);
```

a subtype to specify the realistic range of speeds on the highway:

```
SUBTYPE SpeedRange IS Natural RANGE 0..130;
```

and a function specification:

```
FUNCTION Classify (Speed: SpeedRange) RETURN SpeedClasses;
```

The package body will contain the function body for Classify

The main program should test the function according to a test plan that you design. For each test, prompt the user for a speed, call the function to classify it, and display the speed classification using an instance of Ada.Text_IO. Enumeration_IO.

CHAPTER 6

Counting Loops; Subtypes

The preceding chapters introduced you to two control structures: *sequence,* in which statements are simply written one after the other, and conditional execution or *selection,* embodied in the IF statement, which allows one of a set of paths to be taken.

The third category of control structure in structured programming is *repetition,* or *iteration,* which allows a section of a program to be repeated, the number of repetitions being determined by some condition. In this chapter you will see how to specify the repetition of a group of statements (called a *counting loop*) using the FOR statement. You will study how to design counting loops in Ada programs. Two other repetition constructs are introduced in Chapter 7.

Also in this chapter, the important concept of *subtypes* is extended, and you will see how using subtypes of scalar data types—integer, float, character, and enumeration—makes reading and writing programs easier and makes the programs more reliable.

Finally, two important system-structuring ideas are introduced: *overloading* and *exception handling*. Overloading permits several operations with similar behavior to be given the same name, and exception handling provides a method for keeping control when an error arises, instead of returning control automatically to the run-time system.

6.1 Control Structures: Counting Loops and the FOR Statement

Just as the ability to make decisions is a very important programming tool, so is the ability to specify that a group of operations is to be repeated. For example, a company with seven employees will want to repeat the gross pay and net pay computations in its payroll program seven times: once for each employee.

The repetition of steps in a program is called a *loop*. The *loop body* contains the steps to be repeated. Ada provides three control statements for specifying repetition. This chapter examines the FOR statement; the general and WHILE statements are examined in Chapter 7.

The FOR Statement

The FOR statement can be used to specify some forms of repetition quite easily, as shown in the next examples.

■ Example 6.1

The statements

```
Ada.Text_IO.Put(Item => "Hello there. ";
Ada.Text_IO.Put(Item => "Hello there. ";
Ada.Text_IO.Put(Item => "Hello there. ";
Ada.Text_IO.Put(Item => "Hello there. ";
Ada.Text_IO.Put(Item => "Hello there. ";
```

can be written more concisely as

```
FOR Count IN 1..5 LOOP
  Ada.Text_IO.Put(Item => "Hello there. ";
END LOOP;
```

The preceding FOR statement causes the Put operation to be performed five times. The FOR statement is used to implement *counting loops,* which are loops where the exact number of loop repetitions can be specified as a variable or constant value. Here, the number of repetitions required was five. The reserved words END LOOP terminate the FOR statement.

The FOR statement specifies that the variable Count should take on each of the values in the range 1 to 5 during successive loop repetitions. This means that the value of Count is 1 during the first loop repetition, 2 during the second loop repetition, and 5 during the last loop repetition. ■

Count is called a *loop counter* because its value controls the loop repetition. In our example the loop counter is intialized to 1 when the FOR statement is first reached; after each execution of the loop body, the loop counter is incremented by 1 and tested to see whether loop repetition should continue.

Unlike other variables, a FOR loop counter is not declared. A loop counter may also be referenced in the loop body, but its value cannot be changed by statements in the loop body. Example 6.3 shows a FOR statement whose loop counter is referenced in the loop body.

■ Example 6.2

The following FOR loop displays a sequence of HowMany asterisks. If HowMany has a value of 5, five asterisks in a row will be displayed; if HowMany has a value of 27, 27 asterisks will be displayed, and so on.

```
FOR Count IN 1 .. HowMany LOOP
  Ada.Text_IO.Put(Item => '*');
END LOOP;
```
■

■ Example 6.3

Program 6.1 uses a FOR loop to print a list of integer values and their squares. During each repetition of the loop body, the statement NumSquared := Num**2; computes the square of the loop counter Num; then the values of Num and NumSquared are displayed. A trace of this program is shown in Table 6.1.

Program 6.1 Squares

```
WITH Ada.Text_IO;
WITH Ada.Integer_Text_IO;
PROCEDURE Squares IS
------------------------------------------------------------------
--| Displays a list of integer values and their squares.
--| Author: M. B. Feldman, The George Washington University
--| Last Modified: August 1998
------------------------------------------------------------------

  MaxNum : CONSTANT Natural := 4;
  NumSquared : Natural;    -- output - square of Num

BEGIN -- Squares

  Ada.Text_IO.Put(Item => "         Num     Num ** 2 ");
  Ada.Text_IO.New_Line;
  Ada.Text_IO.Put(Item => "         ---     ---------");
  Ada.Text_IO.New_Line;

  FOR Num IN 1..MaxNum LOOP
    NumSquared := Num ** 2;
    Ada.Integer_Text_IO.Put (Item => Num, Width => 10);
    Ada.Integer_Text_IO.Put (Item => NumSquared, Width => 10);
    Ada.Text_IO.New_Line;
  END LOOP;

END Squares;
```

Sample Run

```
Num       Num ** 2
---       ---------
 1            1
 2            4
 3            9
 4           16
```

The trace in Table 6.1 shows that the loop counter Num is initialized to 1 when the FOR loop is reached. After each loop repetition, Num is incremented by 1 and tested to see whether its value is still less than or equal to MaxNum (4). If the test result is true, the loop body is executed again, and the next values of Num and NumSquared are displayed. If the test result is false, the loop is exited. Num is equal to MaxNum during the last loop repetition. After this repetition the value of Num becomes undefined (indicated by the question mark in the last table line), and the loop is exited. The counter Num ceases to exist and cannot be referenced again unless the loop is entered again, in which case the counter is given a new existence. ∎

Table 6.1 Trace of Program 6.1

Statement	Num	NumSquared	*Effect*
	?	?	
FOR Num IN 1..MaxNum LOOP	1		Initialize Num
NumSquared := Num**2;		1	NumSquared gets 1 * 1
Ada.Integer_Text_IO.Put (Item=>Num,Width=>10);			Display 1
Ada.Integer_Text_IO.Put (Item=>NumSquared,Width=>10);			Display 1
Increment and test Num	2		2 <= 4 is true
Square := Num**2;		4	NumSquared gets 2 * 2
Ada.Integer_Text_IO.Put (Item=>NumSquared,Width=>10);			Display 2
Ada.Integer_Text_IO.Put (Item=>NumSquared,Width=>10);			Display 4
Increment and test Num	3		3 <= 4 is true
NumSquared := Num**2;		9	NumSquared gets 3 * 3
Ada.Integer_Text_IO.Put (Item=>Num,Width=>10);			Display 3
Ada.Integer_Text_IO.Put (Item=>NumSquared,Width=>10);			Display 9
Increment and test Num	4		4 <= 4 is true
NumSquared := Num**2;		16	NumSquared gets 4 * 4
Ada.Integer_Text_IO.Put (Item=>Num,Width=>10);			Display 4

Statement	Num	NumSquared	*Effect*
`Ada.Integer_Text_IO.Put` `(Item=>NumSquared,Width=>10);`			Display 16
Increment and test `Num`	?		Exit loop

It is also possible to count backward in a FOR loop. Writing IN REVERSE instead of IN causes the loop counter to start at its maximum value and be decremented by 1, instead of incremented, in each loop iteration. Finally, it is not necessary for the minimum counter value—generally called the *lower bound* of the loop—to be 1. These aspects of counting loops are illustrated in the next example.

■ Example 6.4

Program 6.2 is a modification of Program 6.1. This time the smallest and largest numbers `MinNum` and `MaxNum` are read from the terminal, and the squares are printed from low to high and then from high to low. There are two loops in this program!   ■

Program 6.2 Finding the Squares in Forward and Reverse Order

```
WITH Ada.Text_IO;
WITH Ada.Integer_Text_IO;
PROCEDURE Squares_Up_and_Down IS
-------------------------------------------------------------
--| Displays a list of integer values and their squares,
--| in forward, then in reverse order
--| Author: M. B. Feldman, The George Washington University
--| Last Modified: August 1998
-------------------------------------------------------------

   MinNum :      Positive;   -- input - smallest value to square
   MaxNum :      Positive;   -- input - largest value to square
   NumSquared : Natural;     -- output - square of Num

BEGIN -- Squares_Up_and_Down

   Ada.Text_IO.Put
     (Item => "Enter the smallest positive you wish to square > ");
   Ada.Integer_Text_IO.Get(Item => MinNum);
   Ada.Text_IO.Put
     (Item => "Enter the largest positive you wish to square > ");
   Ada.Integer_Text_IO.Get(Item => MaxNum);

   Ada.Text_IO.Put(Item => "       Num     Num ** 2 ");
   Ada.Text_IO.New_Line;
   Ada.Text_IO.Put(Item => "       ---     --------- ");
   Ada.Text_IO.New_Line;

   FOR Num IN MinNum..MaxNum LOOP
      NumSquared := Num ** 2;
      Ada.Integer_Text_IO.Put (Item => Num, Width => 10);
      Ada.Integer_Text_IO.Put (Item => NumSquared, Width => 10);
      Ada.Text_IO.New_Line;
```

```
      END LOOP;
      Ada.Text_IO.New_Line;
      FOR Num IN REVERSE MinNum..MaxNum LOOP
        NumSquared := Num ** 2;
        Ada.Integer_Text_IO.Put (Item => Num, Width => 10);
        Ada.Integer_Text_IO.Put (Item => NumSquared, Width => 10);
        Ada.Text_IO.New_Line;
      END LOOP;

   END Squares_Up_and_Down;
```

Sample Run

```
Enter the smallest positive you wish to square > 3
Enter the largest positive you wish to square > 7
         Num     Num ** 2
         ---    ----------
          3          9
          4         16
          5         25
          6         36
          7         49

          7         49
          6         36
          5         25
          4         16
          3          9
```

SYNTAX
DISPLAY

> ## FOR Statement (Counting Loop, Simple Form)
>
> **Forms:**
>
> ```
> FOR counter IN lowbound .. highbound LOOP
>    statement sequence
> END LOOP;
>
> FOR counter IN REVERSE lowbound .. highbound LOOP
>    statement sequence
> END LOOP;
> ```
>
> **Example:**
>
> ```
> FOR I IN Min .. Max LOOP
>    Ada.Integer_Text_IO.Put (Item => I, Width => 5);
>    Ada.Text_IO.New_Line;
> END LOOP;
> ```
>
> **Interpretation:**
>
> The number of times *statement sequence* is executed is determined by the values of *lowbound* and *highbound*. The value of the loop counter *counter* is set to *lowbound* before the first execution of *statement sequence; counter* is incremented by 1 after each execution of *statement sequence. Lowbound* and *highbound* must be expressions, constants, or variables with integer or enumeration values.

> If REVERSE is present, as in the second form above, *counter* is initialized to *repetitions* before the first execution of *statement sequence,* then decremented by 1 after each execution of *statement sequence.*
>
> **Note:**
>
> If the value of *highbound* is less than that of *lowbound, statement sequence* is not executed. No statement within *statement sequence* can change the value of *counter.* The variable *counter* is not declared separately and has no existence outside the loop.

Accumulating a Sum

We can use a counting loop to accumulate the sum of a collection of data values as shown in the next problem.

CASE STUDY

SUM OF INTEGERS

Problem Specification
Write a program that finds the sum of all integers from 1 to N.

Analysis
To solve this problem, it will be necessary to find some way to form the sum of the first N positive integers.

Data Requirements

Problem Inputs

the last integer in the sum (N : Positive)

Problem Outputs

the sum of integers from 1 to N (Sum : Natural)

Design

Initial Algorithm

1. Prompt the user for the last integer (N).

2. Find the sum (Sum) of all the integers from 1 to N inclusive.

3. Display the sum.

Algorithm Refinements

Step 2 Refinement

2.0. Set Sum to zero

2.1. Add 1 to sum

2.2. Add 2 to sum

2.3. Add 3 to sum

. . .

2.N. Add N to sum

For a large value of N it would be rather time-consuming to write this list of steps. We would also have to know the value of N before writing this list; consequently, the program would not be general, since it would work for only one value of N.

Because steps 2.1 through 2.N are all quite similar, we can represent each of them with the general step

2.i. Add i to sum

This general step must be executed for all values of i from 1 to N, inclusive. This suggests the use of a counting loop with i as the loop counter.

Program Variables:
loop counter—represents each integer from 1 to N (i : Positive).

The variable i will take on the successive values 1, 2, 3, ...,N. Each time the loop is repeated, the current value of i must be added to sum. We now have a new refinement of step 2.

Step 2 Refinement
2.1. FOR each integer i from 1 to N LOOP
    Add i to Sum
    END LOOP;

Test Plan
What should happen if a zero is entered for N? A negative number? You should predict the results and test to find out whether your predictions were correct.

Implementation
The complete program is shown in Program 6.3. The statements

```
Sum := 0; -- Initialize Sum to zero
FOR I IN 1 .. N LOOP
  Sum := Sum + I ; -- Add the next integer to Sum
END LOOP;
```

are used to perform step 2. To ensure that the final sum is correct, the value of sum must be initialized to zero (algorithm step 2.0) before the first addition operation. The FOR statement causes the assignment statement sum := sum + I; to be repeated N times. Each time, the current value of I is added to the sum being accumulated and the result is saved back in sum. Note that sum must be of type Natural, rather than Positive, to initialize it to zero.

Program 6.3 Sum of Integers from 1 to N

```
WITH Ada.Text_IO;
WITH Ada.Integer_Text_IO;
PROCEDURE Sum_Integers IS
-----------------------------------------------------------------
--| Finds and displays the sum of all integers from 1 to N.
--| Author: M. B. Feldman, The George Washington University
--| Last Modified: August 1998
-----------------------------------------------------------------

   N   : Positive;              -- input  - last integer added
   Sum : Natural;               -- output - sum being accumulated

BEGIN -- Sum_Integers

   -- Read the last integer, N
   Ada.Text_IO.Put (Item => "Enter the last integer in the sum > ");
   Ada.Integer_Text_IO.Get (Item => N);

   -- Find the sum (Sum) of all integers from 1 to N
   Sum := 0;                 -- Initialize Sum to 0
   FOR I IN 1 .. N LOOP
      Sum := Sum + I;        -- Add the next integer to Sum
   END LOOP;

   -- Display the sum
   Ada.Text_IO.Put (Item => "The sum of the integers from 1 to ");
   Ada.Integer_Text_IO.Put (Item => N, Width => 1);
   Ada.Text_IO.Put (Item => " is ");
   Ada.Integer_Text_IO.Put (Item => Sum, Width => 1);
   Ada.Text_IO.New_Line;

END Sum_Integers;
```

Sample Run

```
Enter the last integer in the sum > 25
The sum of the integers from 1 to 25 is 325
```

A trace of the program for a data value of 3 is shown in Table 6.2. The trace verifies that the program performs as desired because the final value stored in Sum is 6 (1+2+3). The loop counter I ceases to exist after it reaches the value of N (3 in this case). As shown in the table, the statement Sum := Sum + I; is executed exactly three times.

Testing
Did the test results agree with your predictions?

Table 6.2 Trace of Program 6.3

Statement	i	N	Sum	Effect
`Ada.Text_IO.Put(Item=>"Enter...");`	?	?	?	Display prompt
`Ada.Integer_Text_IO.Get(Item=>N)`		3		Read 3 into N
`Sum := 0;`			0	Initialize Sum
`FOR I IN 1..N LOOP`	1	3	0	Initialize I
`Sum := Sum + 1`			1	Add 1 to Sum
Increment and test I	2	3		2 <= 3 is true
`Sum := Sum + 1`			3	Add 2 to Sum
Increment and test I	3	3		3 <= 3 is true
`Sum := Sum + 1;`			6	Add 3 to Sum
Increment and test I	?	3		Exit loop
`Ada.Text_IO.Put` `  (Item=>"The Sum is");`				Display message
`Ada.Integer_Text_IO.Put` `  (Item =>Sum, Width=>1);`			6	Display 6

EXERCISES FOR SECTION 6.1

Self-Check

1. For each of the following programs, state whether the program is legal. If so, what does it display? If not, why not?

a.
```
WITH Ada.Integer_Text_IO;
PROCEDURE LoopTest IS
BEGIN
  FOR Count IN 1..10 LOOP
    Ada.Integer_Text_IO.Put(Item => Count);
  END LOOP;
  Ada.Text_IO.New_Line;
  Ada.Integer_Text_IO.Put(Item => Count);
  Ada.Text_IO.New_Line;
END LoopTest;
```

b.
```
WITH Ada.Integer_Text_IO;
PROCEDURE LoopTest IS
  Count: Positive;
BEGIN
  Count := 537;
  FOR Count IN 1..10 LOOP
```

```
        Ada.Integer_Text_IO.Put(Item => Count);
      END LOOP;
      Ada.Text_IO.New_Line;
      Ada.Integer_Text_IO.Put(Item => Count);
      Ada.Text_IO.New_Line;
    END LoopTest;
```

Programming

1. Write a program fragment that will compute the sum of the squares of the integers from 1 to 10, inclusive.

2. Write a FOR loop that will display the line

   ```
   10 9 8 7 6 5 4 3 2 1
   ```

   a. using REVERSE in the loop statement

   b. without using REVERSE in the loop statement

6.2 Problem Solving: Generalizing a Solution

After you finish a program, someone will often ask a "What if?" question. The person asking the question usually wants to know whether the program would still work if some of the restrictions implied by the problem statement were removed. If the answer is "No," you might have to modify the program to make it work. Try to anticipate these questions in advance and make your programs as general as possible right from the start. Sometimes this can be as easy as changing a program constant to a problem input.

One question that comes to mind for the last problem is: What if we wanted to find the sum and average of a list of any numbers, not just the sum of the first N integers. Would the program still work? Clearly, the answer to this question is "No." However, it would not be too difficult to modify the program to solve this more general problem.

**CASE
STUDY**

GENERAL SUM PROBLEM

Problem Specification
Write a program that finds and displays the sum of a list of numbers.

Analysis
To add any list of numbers, a new variable (CurrentValue) would be needed to store each value to be summed. The numbers must be provided as input data. Because the numbers are not necessarily positive, we will make CurrentValue and Sum type Integer.

Data Requirements

Problem Inputs

number of items to be summed (NumValues : Natural)
temporary storage for each data value to be summed (CurrentValue: Integer)

Problem Outputs:

sum of the NumValues data values (Sum: Integer)

Design

Initial Algorithm

1. Prompt the user for the number (NumValues) of values to be summed.

2. Prompt the user for each data value and add it to the sum.

3. Display the sum.

This algorithm is very similar to the earlier one. Step 2 is modified slightly and is refined below.

Algorithm Refinements

Step 2 Refinement

2.1. Initialize Sum to 0.

2.2. FOR each data value LOOP
    Read the data value into CurrentValue and add CurrentValue to Sum.
    END LOOP;

In this refinement the variable CurrentValue is used to store each number to be summed. After each number is read into CurrentValue, it is added to Sum. If there are more data items, the loop body is repeated, and the next data item replaces the last one in CurrentValue. The number of data values to be summed is read into NumValue before the loop is reached. NumValues determines the number of loop repetitions that are required. A loop counter is needed to count the data items as they are processed and to ensure that all data are summed.

Program Variables

loop counter—the number of data items added so far (Count : Positive)

Implementation

The program is very similar to Program 6.3. We leave it, as well as the test plan and testing, as an exercise.

We can further generalize this solution to find the minimum, maximum, and average of a list of data values—for example, the results of a class examination. The average is computed by finding the sum of all the values, then dividing by the number of values. From the previous example we know how to find the sum. The minimum and maximum can be found at the same time, using our package Min_Max.

CASE
STUDY

MINIMUM, MAXIMUM, AND AVERAGE OF A LIST OF NUMBERS

Problem Specification

Write a program that finds and displays the minimum, maximum, and average of a list of integers.

Analysis

This is quite similar to the previous two problems. We can use the variables `CurrentValue` and `Sum` as above. As each value is read, it must be added into the sum and also compared against the current minimum, `Smallest`, and the current maximum, `Largest`. The comparisons can be handled by the `Minimum` and `Maximum` functions already provided in the `Min_Max` package.

Because each new value, *including the first,* needs to be compared to `Smallest` and `Largest`, what initial values should these two variables have? It might be tempting to simply initialize them to zero, like the sum. This would be a mistake: Suppose that all the values to be read happened to be positive? The program would give incorrect results, since it would report that the smallest value was zero instead of the really smallest value (which in this case would be greater than zero).

One way to solve this problem is to initialize `Smallest` to the *largest* possible integer value that we will accept from the user. For now, we will just let this be the largest possible value of the type `Integer`. This way, any value that the user could enter would automatically be no larger than this initial value. Luckily, Ada gives us an easy way to discover the largest possible value of `Integer`: It is the attribute `Integer'Last`. This value is a large number whose actual value depends upon the compiler you are using. Because we also need to find the largest number, we should initialize `Largest` to the *smallest* possible `Integer` value, namely, `Integer'First`.

Data Requirements

Problem Inputs

number of items to be averaged (`NumValues : Positive`)
temporary storage for each data value (`CurrentValue: Integer`)

Problem Outputs

minimum of the `NumValues` data values (`Smallest: Integer`)
largest of the `NumValues` data values (`Largest: Integer`)
average of the `NumValues` data values (`Average: Integer`)

Initial Algorithm

1. Prompt the user for the number (`NumValues`) of values to be summed.

2. Prompt the user for each data value; add it to the sum, determine whether it is a new minimum, and determine whether it is a new maximum.

3. Divide the sum by the number of numbers to produce the average.

4. Display the minimum, maximum, and average.

This algorithm is very similar to the earlier one. Step 2 is modified and is refined below; there is a new step 3.

Algorithm Refinements

Step 2 Refinement

2.1. Initialize Sum to 0, Smallest to Integer'Last, and Largest to Integer'First.

2.2. FOR each data value LOOP
Read the data value into CurrentValue and add CurrentValue to Sum
Determine whether the data value is a new minimum or maximum
END LOOP;

In this refinement the variable CurrentValue is used to store each number to be summed. After each number is read into CurrentValue, it is added to Sum. If there are more data items, the loop body is repeated and the next data item replaces the last one in CurrentValue. The number of data values to be summed is read into NumValues before the loop is reached. NumValues determines the number of loop repetitions that are required. A loop counter is needed to count the data items as they are processed and ensure that all data are summed.
We need a further refinement of step 2.2:

Step 2.2 Refinement:

2.2 FOR each data value LOOP

2.2.1 Read the data value into CurrentValue and add CurrentValue to Sum

2.2.2 Replace Smallest with the smaller of itself and CurrentValue

2.2.3 Replace Largest with the larger of itself and CurrentValue

END LOOP;

Program Variables

loop counter—the number of data items added so far (Count : Natural)

Implementation

Program 6.4 shows the entire program. Note that this program finds the average as an integer value by dividing Sum by NumValues. This is because all the numbers are integers and the division throws away the fractional part of the quotient. In Chapter 8 we will examine how to convert between integer and floating-point values. This will allow us to calculate the average of a set of integers as a floating-point value.

Averages are generally stated as fractional values, but this can sometimes be confusing if the data values are inherently whole numbers. For example, it was reported some years ago that the average American family had 2.5 children. While this was true mathematically, many thought it was a bit strange: What does it mean to have half a child? In this situation, saying "the average is about 3" might have been more effective, especially in comparison with earlier years in which the average number of children was about 4. The important fact was that families were getting smaller!

Program 6.4   Finding Minimum, Maximum, and Average Values

```ada
WITH Ada.Text_IO;
WITH Ada.Integer_Text_IO;
WITH Min_Max;
PROCEDURE Min_Max_Average IS
-----------------------------------------------------------
--| Finds and displays the minimum, maximum, and average
--| of a list of data items.
--| Author: M. B. Feldman, The George Washington University
--| Last Modified: August 1998
-----------------------------------------------------------

  NumValues:     Positive; -- input - number of items averaged
  CurrentValue: Integer;  -- the next data item to be added

  Sum:           Integer;  -- program variable - accumulated sum

  Smallest:      Integer;  -- output - minimum of the data values
  Largest:       Integer;  -- output - maximum of the data values
  Average:       Integer;  -- output - average of the data values

BEGIN   -- Min_Max_Average

  -- Read the number of items to be averaged
  Ada.Text_IO.Put(Item =>
    "Enter number (at least 1) of integers to be averaged > ");
  Ada.Integer_Text_IO.Get(Item => NumValues);
  Ada.Text_IO.New_Line;

  -- Initialize program variables
  Smallest := Integer'Last;
  Largest := Integer'First;
  Sum := 0;

  -- Read each data item, add it to Sum,
  -- and check if it is a new minimum or maximum
  FOR Count IN 1 .. NumValues LOOP
    Ada.Text_IO.Put(Item => "Integer item no. ");
    Ada.Integer_Text_IO.Put(Item => Count, Width => 1);
    Ada.Text_IO.Put(Item => " > ");
    Ada.Integer_Text_IO.Get(Item => CurrentValue);

    Sum := Sum + CurrentValue;
    Smallest := Min_Max.Minimum
        (Value1 => Smallest, Value2 => CurrentValue);
    Largest   := Min_Max.Maximum
        (Value1 => Largest,  Value2 => CurrentValue);
  END LOOP;

  -- compute the average; since Sum and NumValues are integers,
  -- the average is truncated; that is, the fractional part
  -- is discarded

  Average := Sum / NumValues;

  -- Display the results
  Ada.Text_IO.Put(Item => "The Smallest is ");
  Ada.Integer_Text_IO.Put(Item => Smallest, Width => 1);
  Ada.Text_IO.New_Line;
```

```
Ada.Text_IO.Put(Item => "The Largest is ");
Ada.Integer_Text_IO.Put(Item => Largest, Width => 1);
Ada.Text_IO.New_Line;
Ada.Text_IO.Put(Item => "The Average is ");
Ada.Integer_Text_IO.Put(Item => Average, Width => 1);
Ada.Text_IO.New_Line;

END Min_Max_Average;
```

Sample Run

```
Enter number (at least 1) of integers to be averaged > 7

Integer item no.  1 > -5
Integer item no.  2 > 2
Integer item no.  3 > 29
Integer item no.  4 > 16
Integer item no.  5 > 0
Integer item no.  6 > -17
Integer item no.  7 > 4
The Smallest is -17
The Largest is 29
The Average is 4
```

EXERCISES FOR SECTION 6.2

Self-Check

1. In Program 6.4, explain how and why we choose the initial values of the variables `Smallest` and `Largest`.

6.3 Problem Solving: Using an External File for Input Data

A modification of Program 6.4 could use an external (disk) file for the input data. In fact, most real-world computer programs make heavy use of external files. The user prepares a file of data using an editor, then uses it later as input to the program. If the program is being developed and debugged, requiring several test runs, preparing the data this way saves having to enter them interactively each time the program is tested. We shall cover this topic more systematically in Chapters 9 and 10; for now, let's just consider how Program 6.4 would be changed to allow an external file for input.

The `Get` operations that we have been working with all assume that input is coming interactively from the keyboard. In fact, each `Get` (for characters, strings, integers, floating-point quantities, and enumeration literals) has a second form requiring an additional parameter that names a disk file. For example, the input operation to read an integer value from a disk file called, say, `TestScores`, would be

```
Ada.Integer_Text_IO.Get (File => TestScores, Item => CurrentValue);
```

In general these operations look just like the interactive ones except for the file name. `TestScores` is an Ada variable, which must be declared as

```
TestScores: Ada.Text_IO.File_Type;
```

The type `File_Type` is provided by `Ada.Text_IO`.

Now suppose that the user prepared the input data with an editor and stored them in a disk file called `scores.dat`. The program needs a way to associate the name of the file in the program (`TestScores` in this case) with the name of the file as it is known to the operating system (`scores.dat` in this case). This is done by means of an operation called `Ada.Text_IO.Open`. In this case the operation would look like this:

```
Ada.Text_IO.Open
  (File => TestScores, Mode => Ada.Text_IO.In_File,
   Name => "scores.dat");
```

The parameter `Mode` indicates whether we are reading from the file (`Ada.Text_IO.In_File`, as in this example) or writing to it (`Ada.Text_IO.Out_File`). Notice also that the operating system file name must appear in quotes.

It is important to type the name of the file *exactly* as it is listed in the directory you get from the operating system. Many operating systems use *case-sensitive* file names, which means that if the operating system file name is lowercase (e.g., `scores.dat`), your parameter in the `Open` statement must also be uppercase (as in our example); if the operating system file name is in lowercase, your parameter must be also. If you supply to `Open` a file name that does not exist in your current directory, the Ada exception `Name_Error` will be raised.

Program 6.5 shows this modified program. There are no prompts, because there is no interactive user entering the data. The file `scores.dat`, created with an editor, contains first the number of values to be read, then the actual values, one value per line. The program opens the file, then enters a loop that "logs," or displays on the terminal, the values as they are read from the file and processed; finally, the results are displayed as before. The sample run shows the results for the following file contents:

```
8
57
22
100
42
37
70
81
100
```

Program 6.5 Finding Minimum, Maximum, and Average of Values from a File

```
WITH Ada.Text_IO;
WITH Ada.Integer_Text_IO;
WITH Min_Max;
PROCEDURE Min_Max_Average_File IS
----------------------------------------------------------------------
--| Finds and displays the minimum, maximum, and average
--| of a list of data items; the data items are read from a file.
```

```
--| Author: Michael B. Feldman, The George Washington University
--| Last Modified: September 1998
--------------------------------------------------------------------------

   NumValues:    Positive;   -- input - the number of items to be averaged
   CurrentValue: Integer;    -- input - the next data item to be added

   Smallest:     Integer;    -- output - minimum of the data values
   Largest:      Integer;    -- output - maximum of the data values
   Average:      Integer;    -- output - average of the data values

   Sum:          Integer;    -- program variable - sum being accumulated
   TestScores:   Ada.Text_IO.File_Type;
                             -- program variable - names the input file

BEGIN  -- Min_Max_Average_File

  -- Open the file and associate it with the file variable name
  Ada.Text_IO.Open
    (File => TestScores, Mode => Ada.Text_IO.In_File,
     Name => "scores.dat");

  -- Read from the file the number of items to be averaged
  Ada.Integer_Text_IO.Get(File => TestScores, Item => NumValues);
  Ada.Text_IO.Put("The number of scores to be averaged is ");
  Ada.Integer_Text_IO.Put(Item => NumValues, Width => 1);
  Ada.Text_IO.New_Line;

  -- Initialize program variables
  Smallest := Integer'Last;
  Largest := Integer'First;
  Sum := 0;

  -- Read each data item, log to the screen, add it to Sum,
  -- and check if it is a new minimum or maximum
  FOR Count IN 1 .. NumValues LOOP
    Ada.Integer_Text_IO.Get(File => TestScores, Item => CurrentValue);
    Ada.Text_IO.Put("Score number ");
    Ada.Integer_Text_IO.Put(Item => Count, Width => 1);
    Ada.Text_IO.Put(" is ");
    Ada.Integer_Text_IO.Put(Item => CurrentValue, Width => 1);
    Ada.Text_IO.New_Line;

    Sum := Sum + CurrentValue;
    Smallest :=
      Min_Max.Minimum(Value1 => Smallest, Value2 => CurrentValue);
    Largest  :=
      Min_Max.Maximum(Value1 => Largest,  Value2 => CurrentValue);
  END LOOP;

  -- compute the average; since Sum and NumValues are integers,
  -- the fractional part of the average is discarded

  Average := Sum / NumValues;

  -- display the results
  Ada.Text_IO.Put(Item => "The Smallest is ");
  Ada.Integer_Text_IO.Put(Item => Smallest, Width => 1);
  Ada.Text_IO.New_Line;
  Ada.Text_IO.Put(Item => "The Largest is ");
```

```
     Ada.Integer_Text_IO.Put(Item => Largest, Width => 1);
     Ada.Text_IO.New_Line;
     Ada.Text_IO.Put(Item => "The Average is ");
     Ada.Integer_Text_IO.Put(Item => Average, Width => 1);
     Ada.Text_IO.New_Line;

END Min_Max_Average_File;
```

Sample Run

```
The number of scores to be averaged is 8
Score number 1 is 57
Score number 2 is 22
Score number 3 is 100
Score number 4 is 42
Score number 5 is 37
Score number 6 is 70
Score number 7 is 81
Score number 8 is 100
The Smallest is 22
The Largest is 100
The Average is 63
```

6.4 Problem Solving: Repeating a Program Body

In the discussion of repetition in programs we mentioned that we would like to be able to execute the payroll program for several employees in a single run. We will see how to do this next.

CASE
STUDY

MULTIPLE-EMPLOYEE PAYROLL PROBLEM

Problem Specification
Modify the payroll program from Section 5.4 (Program 5.3) to compute gross pay and net pay for a group of employees.

Analysis
The number of employees must be provided as input data along with the hourly rate and hours worked by each employee. The same set of variables will be used to hold the data and computational results for each employee. The computations will be performed in the same way as before.

Data Requirements

Problem Constants
maximum salary for no tax deduction (TaxBracket = 100.0)
tax rate (TaxRate = 25.00)

Problem Inputs

number of employees (`NumEmp : Positive`)
hours worked by each employee (`Hours : NonNegFloat`)
hourly rate for each employee (`Rate : NonNegFloat`)

Problem Outputs

gross pay (`Gross : NonNegFloat`)
net pay (`Net : NonNegFloat`)

Design

Algorithm

1. Prompt for the number of employees (`NumEmp`).

2. `FOR` each employee `LOOP`
   Enter payroll data and compute and print gross and net pay.
   `END LOOP;`

An additional variable is needed to count the number of employees processed and to control the `FOR` loop in step 2.

Program Variable

loop counter—counts the employees that are processed: (`CountEmp : Positive`)

The structure chart is shown in Fig. 6.1. (The structure chart for the subproblem "find gross and net pay" was shown in Fig. 5.4.)

Implementation:

Program 6.6 gives the entire program. Notice how the code is very similar to that in the original program, with the addition of a few more declarations and the loop construct. Sample output is given for three employees.

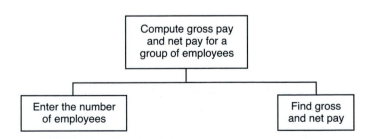

Figure 6.1 Structure Chart for Multiemployee Payroll Program

Program 6.6 Multiemployee Payroll Program

```
WITH Ada.Text_IO;
WITH Ada.Integer_Text_IO;
WITH Ada.Float_Text_IO;
PROCEDURE Multi_Payroll IS
-----------------------------------------------------------------
--| Computes and displays gross pay and net pay for a number
--| of employees, given each employee's hourly rate and
--| hours worked.
--| Author: M. B. Feldman, The George Washington University
--| Last Modified: August 1998
-----------------------------------------------------------------

   SUBTYPE NonNegFloat IS Float RANGE 0.0 .. Float'Last;

   TaxBracket : CONSTANT NonNegFloat := 100.00;
                                     -- maximum salary for no tax
   TaxRate :    CONSTANT NonNegFloat :=  0.15;   -- tax rate

   NumEmp    : Positive;          -- inputs - number of employees
   Hours :       NonNegFloat;     -- hours worked, hourly rate
   HourlyRate: NonNegFloat;

   GrossPay:  NonNegFloat;        -- outputs - gross pay, net pay
   Tax:       NonNegFloat;
   NetPay:    NonNegFloat;

BEGIN -- Multi_Payroll

   Ada.Text_IO.Put ("Please enter number of employees > ");
   Ada.Integer_Text_IO.Get (Item => NumEmp);

   FOR CountEmp IN 1 .. NumEmp LOOP

      -- Enter Hours and HourlyRate
      Ada.Text_IO.Put (Item => "Employee number ");
      Ada.Integer_Text_IO.Put (Item => CountEmp, Width => 1);
      Ada.Text_IO. New_Line;
      Ada.Text_IO.Put (Item => "  Hours worked > ");
      Ada.Float_Text_IO.Get (Item => Hours);
      Ada.Text_IO.Put (Item => "  Hourly rate $");
      Ada.Float_Text_IO.Get (Item => HourlyRate);

      -- Compute gross salary
      GrossPay := Hours * HourlyRate;

      -- Compute net salary
      IF GrossPay > TaxBracket THEN
        Tax := TaxRate * (GrossPay - TaxBracket);
        NetPay := GrossPay - Tax;      -- Deduct a tax amount
      ELSE
        Tax := 0.0;
        NetPay := GrossPay;            -- Deduct no tax
      END IF;

      -- Display Results
      Ada.Text_IO.Put (Item => "  Gross pay is $");
      Ada.Float_Text_IO.Put
        (Item => GrossPay, Fore => 1, Aft => 2, Exp => 0);
```

```
            Ada.Text_IO.New_Line;
            Ada.Text_IO.Put (Item => "   Tax deduction is $");
            Ada.Float_Text_IO.Put
               (Item => Tax, Fore => 1, Aft => 2, Exp => 0);
            Ada.Text_IO.New_Line;
            Ada.Text_IO.Put (Item => "   Net pay is $");
            Ada.Float_Text_IO.Put
               (Item => NetPay, Fore => 1, Aft => 2, Exp => 0);
            Ada.Text_IO.New_Line;

      END LOOP;

   END Multi_Payroll;
```

Sample Run

```
Please enter number of employees > 3
Employee number 1
   Hours worked > 35
   Hourly rate $7.50
   Gross pay is $262.50
   Tax deduction is $24.38
   Net pay is $238.13
Employee number 2
   Hours worked > 37.5
   Hourly rate $11.25
   Gross pay is $421.88
   Tax deduction is $48.28
   Net pay is $373.59
Employee number 3
   Hours worked > 3
   Hourly rate $6.50
   Gross pay is $19.50
   Tax deduction is $0.00
   Net pay is $19.50
```

6.5   Control Structures: Nested Loops

In this section we examine *nested loops*. Nested loops consist of an outer loop with one or more inner loops. Each time the outer loop is repeated, the inner loops are reentered, their loop control parameters are reevaluated, and all required iterations are performed.

■ Example 6.5

Program 6.7 shows a program with two nested FOR loops. The outer loop is repeated three times (for OuterCounter equals 1, 2, and 3). Each time the outer loop is repeated, the statements

```
Ada.Text_IO.Put (Item => "OUTER");
Ada.Integer_Text_IO.Put (Item => OuterCounter, Width => 7);
Ada.Text_IO.New_Line;
```

display the string "OUTER" and the value of OuterCounter (the outer loop counter). Next, the inner loop is entered, and its loop counter InnerCounter is reset to 1. The number of times the inner loop is repeated depends on the current value of Outer-Counter. Each time the inner loop is repeated, the statements

```
Ada.Text_IO.Put (Item => "INNER");
Ada.Integer_Text_IO.Put (Item => InnerCounter, Width => 10);
Ada.Text_IO.New_Line;
```

display the string "INNER" and the value of InnerCounter (the inner loop counter). ■

Program 6.7 Nested FOR Loops

```
WITH Ada.Text_IO;
WITH Ada.Integer_Text_IO;
PROCEDURE Nested_Loops IS
------------------------------------------------------------
--| Illustrates a pair of nested FOR loops.
--| Author: M. B. Feldman, The George Washington University
--| Last Modified: August 1998
------------------------------------------------------------

BEGIN -- Nested_Loops

  Ada.Text_IO.Put (Item => "         OuterCounter  InnerCounter");
  Ada.Text_IO.New_Line;

  FOR OuterCounter IN 1 .. 3 LOOP

    Ada.Text_IO.Put(Item => "OUTER");
    Ada.Integer_Text_IO.Put (Item => OuterCounter, Width => 10);
    Ada.Text_IO.New_Line;

    FOR InnerCounter IN 1 .. OuterCounter LOOP
      Ada.Text_IO.Put(Item => "  INNER");
      Ada.Integer_Text_IO.Put (Item => InnerCounter, Width => 22);
      Ada.Text_IO.New_Line;
    END LOOP;

  END LOOP;

END Nested_Loops;
```

Sample Run

```
        OuterCounter  InnerCounter
OUTER        1
   INNER                    1
OUTER        2
   INNER                    1
   INNER                    2
OUTER        3
   INNER                    1
   INNER                    2
   INNER                    3
```

In Program 6.7 the outer loop counter OuterCounter is used as the upper bound that determines the number of repetitions of the inner loop. This is perfectly valid. It is also valid to use the same variable name as the loop counter of both an outer and an inner FOR loop in the same nest. This is strongly discouraged, however, because it causes the compiler to create two "nested" variables with the same name. Although this is not a problem for the compiler, it certainly is a source of confusion for the human reader of the program!

■ Example 6.6

Program 6.8 prints an isosceles triangle. The program contains an outer loop (loop counter Row) and two inner loops. Each time the outer loop is repeated, two inner loops are executed. The first inner loop prints the leading blank spaces; the second inner loop prints one or more asterisks.

The outer loop is repeated five times; the number of repetitions performed by the inner loops is based on the value of Row. Table 6.3 lists the inner loop control parameters for each value of Row. Four blanks and one asterisk are printed when Row is 1, three blanks and three asterisks are printed when Row is 2, and so on. When Row is 5, the first inner loop is skipped and nine $(2 \times 5 - 1)$ asterisks are printed. ■

Program 6.8 Triangle

```
WITH Ada.Text_IO;
PROCEDURE Triangle IS
-----------------------------------------------------------------
--| Draws an isosceles triangle
--| Author: M. B. Feldman, The George Washington University
--| Last Modified: August 1998
-----------------------------------------------------------------

   NumLines: CONSTANT Integer := 5;
   Blank   : CONSTANT Character := ' ';
   Star    : CONSTANT Character := '*';

BEGIN -- Triangle

   FOR Row IN 1 .. NumLines LOOP         -- draw each row

     FOR LeadBlanks IN REVERSE 1 .. NumLines - Row LOOP
       Ada.Text_IO.Put(Item => Blank);  -- leading blanks
     END LOOP;

     FOR CountStars IN 1 .. (2*Row) - 1 LOOP
       Ada.Text_IO.Put(Item => Star);   -- display asterisks
     END LOOP;

     Ada.Text_IO.New_Line;              -- terminate row

   END LOOP;

END Triangle;
```

Sample Run

```
        *
       ***
      *****
     *******
    *********
```

Table 6.3 Trace of Inner Loop Parameters in Triangle

Row	LeadBlanks	CountStars	*Effect*
1	REVERSE 1..4	1..1	Displays 4 blanks and 1 asterisk
2	REVERSE 1..3	1..3	Displays 3 blanks and 3 asterisks
3	REVERSE 1..2	1..5	Displays 2 blanks and 5 asterisks
4	REVERSE 1..1	1..7	Displays 1 blank and 7 asterisks
5	REVERSE 1..0	1..9	Displays 0 blanks and 9 asterisks

EXERCISES FOR SECTION 6.5

Self-Check

1. What is displayed by the following program segments, assuming that M is 3 and N is 5?

   a.
   ```
   FOR I IN 1..N LOOP
       FOR J IN 1..I LOOP
           Ada.Text_IO.Put(Item => '*');
       END LOOP;
       Ada.Text_IO.New_Line;
   END LOOP;
   ```

   b.
   ```
   FOR I IN 1..N LOOP
       FOR J IN 1..M LOOP
           Ada.Text_IO.Put(Item => '*');
       END LOOP;
       Ada.Text_IO.New_Line;
   END LOOP;
   ```

2. Show the output displayed by the following nested loops.

   ```
   FOR I IN 1..2 LOOP
       Ada.Text_IO.Put(Item=>"Outer");
       Ada.Integer_Text_IO.Put(Item=>I, Width=>5);
       FOR J IN 1..3 LOOP
           Ada.Text_IO.Put(Item=>"Inner   ");
           Ada.Integer_Text_IO.Put(Item=>I, Width=>3);
           Ada.Integer_Text_IO.Put(Item=>J, Width=>3);
       END LOOP;
       FOR K IN REVERSE 1..2 LOOP
   ```

```
        Ada.Text_IO.Put(Item=>"Inner   ");
        Ada.Integer_Text_IO.Put(Item=>I, Width=>3);
        Ada.Integer_Text_IO.Put(Item=>K, Width=>3);
     END LOOP;
  END LOOP;
```

Programming

1. Write a nest of loops that causes the following output to be displayed.

```
1
1 2
1 2 3
1 2 3 4
1 2 3
1 2
1
```

6.6   Data Structures: More on Subtypes

In this section we continue our study of subtypes. We begin with enumeration subtypes.

Subtypes of Enumeration Types

Subtypes of programmer-defined types can be defined just as easily as subtypes of pre-defined types. As an example, consider the month-name type introduced in Section 4.6:

```
TYPE Months IS
   (January, February, March, April, May, June,
    July, August, September, October, November, December);
```

Now we can define subtypes for three seasons as follows:

```
SUBTYPE Spring IS Months RANGE March .. May;
SUBTYPE Summer IS Months RANGE June .. August;
SUBTYPE Autumn IS Months RANGE September .. November;
```

We cannot easily define a subtype Winter (the months December, January, and February) because, unfortunately, Ada requires that the values of a subtype be specified in the form of a range and therefore *contiguous*, that is, adjacent in the base type definition. Sometimes a way can be found to work around this, as in the case of the day-names type introduced in Section 5.1:

```
TYPE Days IS
   (Monday, Tuesday, Wednesday, Thursday,
    Friday, Saturday, Sunday);
```

Since Monday through Friday are contiguous and Saturday and Sunday are contiguous, we can define subtypes for weekdays and weekend days:

```
SUBTYPE Weekdays IS Days RANGE Monday .. Friday;
SUBTYPE Weekend  IS Days RANGE Satday .. Sunday;
```

However, this work-around requires the Days type to look different from the "normal" American calendar in which the week starts on Sunday.

Type Membership: The Operator IN

An important operator that applies to almost all types in Ada is IN. It can be used to determine whether a given value is a member of a given type's set of values.

■ Example 6.7

Suppose that Today is of type Days and that we have defined the two subtypes Weekdays and Weekend as above. The following IF statement serves as an example of the use of IN:

```
IF Today IN Weekdays THEN
   Ada.Text_IO.Put(Item => "Another day, another dollar...");
ELSE
   Ada.Text_IO.Put(Item => "We've worked hard, let's play hard!");
END IF;
```

Program 6.9 can be used to determine whether we need to go to work tomorrow. It is based on Program 5.1. Notice the use of the IF statement shown above. ■

Program 6.9 Do We Have to Work Tomorrow?

```
WITH Ada.Text_IO;
PROCEDURE Work_Days IS
-------------------------------------------------------------
--| Demonstrates the use of enumeration subtypes:
--| prompts user for a day of the week and determines whether
--| the following day is a weekday or weekend day.
--| Author: M. B. Feldman, The George Washington University
--| Last Modified: August 1998
-------------------------------------------------------------

   TYPE Days IS (Monday, Tuesday, Wednesday, Thursday,
                 Friday, Saturday, Sunday);
   SUBTYPE WeekDays IS Days RANGE Monday .. Friday;
   SUBTYPE WeekEnd  IS Days RANGE Saturday .. Sunday;
   PACKAGE Day_IO IS NEW Ada.Text_IO.Enumeration_IO (Enum => Days);

   Today    : Days;   -- input - day of the week
   Tomorrow : Days;   -- output - next day

BEGIN -- Work_Days

   -- prompt user to enter a day name
   Ada.Text_IO.Put (Item => "Enter a day of the week > ");
   Day_IO.Get (Item => Today);
```

```
-- find tomorrow
IF Today = Days'Last THEN
   Tomorrow := Days'First;
ELSE
   Tomorrow := Days'Succ(Today);
END IF;

Ada.Text_IO.Put (Item => "Tomorrow is ");
Day_IO.Put (Item => Tomorrow);
Ada.Text_IO.New_Line;

-- Is Tomorrow a week day or a weekend day?
IF Tomorrow IN Weekdays THEN
   Ada.Text_IO.Put (Item => "Another day, another dollar...");
   Ada.Text_IO.New_Line;
ELSE
   Ada.Text_IO.Put (Item => "We've worked hard, let's play hard!");
   Ada.Text_IO.New_Line;
END IF;

Ada.Text_IO.Put (Item => "Have a good day tomorrow.");
Ada.Text_IO.New_Line;

END Work_Days;
```

Sample Run

```
Enter a day of the week > Saturday
Tomorrow is SUNDAY
We've worked hard, let's play hard!
Have a good day tomorrow.
```

As you have seen in this chapter, another use for IN is in counting loops. So far, you have seen only loops whose range is 1..repetitions. Another useful form of the counting loops is to give the name of a type or subtype as the range of the loop. Suppose that SmallInt is defined with a range -50..50:

```
SUBTYPE SmallInt IS Integer RANGE -50 .. 50;
```

then the loop

```
FOR Counter IN SmallInt LOOP
  Ada.Integer_Text_IO.Put(Item => Counter);
  Ada.Text_IO.New_Line;
END LOOP;
```

displays all the values in the type SmallInt (−50, −49, −48, ...), one at a time.

■ Example 6.8

Program 6.10 displays the addition table for integer values between 0 and 9 (type SmallNat). For example, the table line beginning with the digit 9 shows the result of adding to 9 each of the digits 0 through 9. The initial FOR loop prints the table heading, which is the operator + and the list of digits from 0 through 9.

The nested FOR loops are used to print the table body. The outer FOR loop (loop counter Left) first prints the current value of Left. In the inner FOR loop, each value of Right (0 through 9) is added to Left and the individual sums are printed. Each time the outer loop is repeated, 10 additions are performed; a total of 100 sums are printed. ■

Program 6.10 Addition Table

```ada
WITH Ada.Text_IO;
WITH Ada.Integer_Text_IO;
PROCEDURE Addition_Table IS
-----------------------------------------------------------------
--| Displays an addition table.
--| Author: M. B. Feldman, The George Washington University
--| Last Modified: August 1998
-----------------------------------------------------------------

  MaxDigit : CONSTANT Natural := 9;
  SUBTYPE SmallNatural IS Natural RANGE 0 .. MaxDigit;

BEGIN  -- Addition_Table

  -- Display the table heading.
  Ada.Text_IO.Put(Item => "+");
  FOR Right IN SmallNatural LOOP      -- Display heading
    Ada.Integer_Text_IO.Put(Item => Right, Width => 3);
  END LOOP;
  Ada.Text_IO.New_Line;              -- Terminate heading

  -- Display the table body.
  FOR Left IN SmallNatural LOOP

    -- Display each row of the table
    Ada.Integer_Text_IO.Put(Item => Left, Width => 1);

    FOR Right IN SmallNatural LOOP
      Ada.Integer_Text_IO.Put (Item => Left + Right, Width => 3);
    END LOOP;

    Ada.Text_IO.New_Line;            -- Terminate table row

  END LOOP;

END Addition_Table;
```

Sample Run

```
+  0  1  2  3  4  5  6  7  8  9
0  0  1  2  3  4  5  6  7  8  9
1  1  2  3  4  5  6  7  8  9 10
2  2  3  4  5  6  7  8  9 10 11
3  3  4  5  6  7  8  9 10 11 12
4  4  5  6  7  8  9 10 11 12 13
5  5  6  7  8  9 10 11 12 13 14
6  6  7  8  9 10 11 12 13 14 15
7  7  8  9 10 11 12 13 14 15 16
8  8  9 10 11 12 13 14 15 16 17
9  9 10 11 12 13 14 15 16 17 18
```

■ Example 6.9

Program 6.11 shows how this structure can be used to display all the days, weekdays, and weekend days in the week. This program uses three FOR loops, one for the base type Days and one for each of the two subtypes. To make it interesting, we display the days in reverse order. ■

Program 6.11 Using Enumeration Subtypes

```
WITH Ada.Text_IO;
PROCEDURE Reverse_Display_Days IS
-----------------------------------------------------------
--| Display the days of the week, weekdays, weekend days;
--| demonstrate enumeration subtypes and how they can be used
--| to control a loop running in reverse.
--| Author: M. B. Feldman, The George Washington University
--| Last Modified: August 1998
-----------------------------------------------------------

  TYPE Days IS (Mon, Tue, Wed, Thu, Fri, Sat, Sun);
  SUBTYPE WeekDays IS Days RANGE Mon .. Fri;
  SUBTYPE WeekEnd  IS Days RANGE Sat .. Sun;
  PACKAGE Day_IO IS NEW Ada.Text_IO.Enumeration_IO (Enum => Days);

BEGIN -- Reverse_Display_Days

  Ada.Text_IO.Put (Item => "The days of the week are ");
  FOR Day IN REVERSE Days LOOP
    Day_IO.Put (Item => Day, Width => 4);
  END LOOP;
  Ada.Text_IO.New_Line;

  Ada.Text_IO.Put (Item => "The weekdays are ");
  FOR Day IN REVERSE WeekDays LOOP
    Day_IO.Put (Item => Day, Width => 4);
  END LOOP;
  Ada.Text_IO.New_Line;

  Ada.Text_IO.Put (Item => "The weekend days are ");
  FOR Day IN REVERSE WeekEnd LOOP
    Day_IO.Put (Item => Day, Width => 4);
  END LOOP;
  Ada.Text_IO.New_Line;

END Reverse_Display_Days;
```

Sample Run

```
The days of the week are SUN SAT FRI THU WED TUE MON
The weekdays are FRI THU WED TUE MON
The weekend days are SUN SAT
```

■ Example 6.10

Program 6.12 uses the `Screen` package from Chapter 4 to draw vertical and horizontal lines on the screen, dividing the screen into four quadrants. We repeat the subtype and constant declarations from `Screen` here, just to remind you:

```
ScreenDepth : CONSTANT Integer := 24;
ScreenWidth : CONSTANT Integer := 80;

SUBTYPE Depth IS Integer RANGE 1..ScreenDepth;
SUBTYPE Width IS Integer RANGE 1..ScreenWidth;
```

The loop

```
FOR Count IN Screen.Width LOOP
   Screen.MoveCursor (Row => 12, Column => Count);
   Ada.Text_IO.Put (Item => '-');
   Screen.MoveCursor
     (Row => 13, Column => (Screen.Screen_Width - Count) +
   Ada.Text_IO.Put (Item => '-');
END LOOP;
```

draws the horizontal separator consisting of two lines of hyphen characters on rows 12 and 13 of the screen. The parameters to the first call of `Screen.MoveCursor` move the cursor one position to the right in each loop iteration; just to make the program more interesting, the second call moves the cursor one position to the left each time. ■

Program 6.12 Dividing the Screen into Four Quadrants

```
WITH Ada.Text_IO;
WITH Screen;
PROCEDURE Four_Pieces IS
-----------------------------------------------------------------
--| This program divides the screen into four pieces
--| by drawing horizontal and vertical lines. The Screen
--| package is used to position the cursor.
--| Author: M. B. Feldman, The George Washington University
--| Last Modified: August 1998
-----------------------------------------------------------------

BEGIN -- Four_Pieces

  Screen.ClearScreen;

  FOR Count IN Screen.Depth LOOP
    Screen.MoveCursor (Row => Count, Column => 41);
    Ada.Text_IO.Put (Item => '|');
    Screen.MoveCursor
      (Row => (Screen.Screen_Depth - Count) + 1, Column => 42);
    Ada.Text_IO.Put (Item => '|');
  END LOOP;

  FOR Count IN Screen.Width LOOP
    Screen.MoveCursor (Row => 12, Column => Count);
    Ada.Text_IO.Put (Item => '-');
    Screen.MoveCursor
```

```
        (Row => 13, Column => (Screen.Screen_Width - Count) + 1);
      Ada.Text_IO.Put (Item => '-');
    END LOOP;

    Screen.MoveCursor (Row => 24, Column => 1);

END Four_Pieces;
```

SYNTAX
DISPLAY

FOR Statement (Counting Loop, Type-Name Form)

Forms:

```
FOR counter IN type-name LOOP
  statement sequence
END LOOP;
FOR counter IN REVERSE type-name LOOP
  statement sequence
END LOOP;
```

Example:

```
FOR WhichDay IN Weekdays LOOP
  Day_IO.Put (Item => WhichDay; Ada.Text_IO.New_Line;
END LOOP;
```

Interpretation:

The number of times *statement sequence* is executed is determined by the number of values in the type given by *type-name*, which must be the name of an integer or enumeration type or subtype.

The value of the loop counter *counter* is set to *type-name*'First before the first execution of *statement sequence; counter* is incremented to its successor value after each execution of *statement sequence;* the last execution of *statement sequence* occurs when *counter* is equal to *type-name*'Last.

The value of *counter* must not be changed within *statement sequence*. The variable *counter* is not declared separately and has no existence outside the loop.

If REVERSE is present, *counter* is initialized to *type-name*'Last and the iteration is done backward, decrementing *counter* to its predecessor value after each execution of *statement sequence*.

Limitations of the FOR Statement

The FOR statement is very powerful and useful, but it has one important limitation: The loop counter is *always* either incremented (by taking the successor) or decremented (by taking the predecessor). The FOR statement can therefore be used only to loop through *all* the values of a given range. There is no way to count by 2s, for example.

Ada provides two other loop statements, which can be used with arbitrary loop control conditions, not just counting straight through the values of a range. Specifically, we can use either the general loop or the WHILE loop structure, both of which we present in Chapter 7.

EXERCISES FOR SECTION 6.6

Self-Check

1. Explain why it is a good idea to use the name of a subtype, instead of literals, in a loop statement, wherever it is possible to do so.

6.7 Tricks of the Trade: Debugging and Regression Testing

Chapters 1 and 3 described the general categories of error messages that you are likely to see: compilation errors and run-time errors, or exceptions. It is also possible for a program to execute without generating any error messages but still produce incorrect results. Sometimes the cause of an exception, or the origin of incorrect results, is apparent and the error can be fixed easily. Often, however, the error is not obvious and may require considerable effort to locate.

The first step in attempting to find a logic error is to try to determine what part of the program is generating incorrect results. Then insert extra output statements in your program to provide a trace of its execution. For example, if the averaging loop in Program 6.4 is not computing the correct sum, you might want to insert extra diagnostic output statements, such as the last five lines in the following loop:

```
FOR Count IN 1 .. NumItems LOOP
   Ada.Text_IO.Put(Item => "Integer item no. ");
   Ada.Integer_Text_IO.Put(Item => Count, Width => 1);
   Ada.Text_IO.Put(Item => " > ");
   Ada.Float_Text_IO.Get (Item => CurrentValue);
   Sum := Sum + CurrentValue;

   -- diagnostic statements
   Ada.Text_IO.Put (Item => "*****Sum = ");
   Ada.Integer_Text_IO.Put (Item => Sum);
   Ada.Text_IO.Put (Item => "*****Count = ");
   Ada.Integer_Text_IO.Put (Item => Count);
   Ada.Text_IO.New_Line;
END LOOP;
```

The diagnostic Put statements will display each partial sum that is accumulated and the current value of Count. Each of these statements displays a string of asterisks at the beginning of its output line. This makes it easier to identify diagnostic output in the debugging runs and makes it easier to locate the diagnostic Put statements in the source program.

Once it appears that you have located an error, you will want to take out the extra diagnostic statements. As a temporary measure, it is sometimes advisable to make these diagnostic statements comments by preceding them with comment marks (--). This is called *commenting out* code. If errors crop up again in later testing, it is easier to remove the comment marks than to retype the diagnostic statements.

Using Debugger Programs

Many compilation systems have *debugger programs* available to help you debug an Ada program. The debugger program lets you execute your program one statement at a time (single-step execution) so that you can see the effect of each statement. You can select several variables whose values will be automatically displayed after each statement executes. This allows you to trace the program's execution. Besides printing a diagnostic when a run-time error occurs, the debugger indicates the statement that caused the error and displays the values of the variables you selected.

You can also separate your program into segments by setting *breakpoints* at selected statements. A breakpoint is like a fence between two segments of a program. You can request the debugger to execute all statements from the last breakpoint up to the next breakpoint. When the program stops at a breakpoint, you can select variables to examine, in this way determining whether the program segment executed correctly. If a program segment executes correctly, you will want to execute through to the next breakpoint. If it does not, you might want to set more breakpoints in that segment or perhaps perform single-step execution through that segment.

The debugger is generally a feature of the compilation system, not part of the programming language. Therefore we cannot give any further details, because they depend on the system that you are working on. You should try to find out from your teacher or computer center whether an Ada debugger is available and, if so, how to use it. Debuggers are helpful and can save you a lot of time in debugging a complicated program.

Regression-Testing a Program

After all compilation errors have been corrected and the program appears to execute as expected, the program should be tested thoroughly to make sure that it works. Go back to your test plan and run all the tests again, not just the one that exposed the logic error. This principle is called *regression testing* and is designed to help you be sure that fixing one logic error did not accidentally introduce another one!

6.8   System Structures: Overloading and the Useful Functions Package

In Section 5.8 we showed how to write a simple package, `Min_Max`, containing functions to find the minimum and maximum of two integer values. Let us rework that package to include two more useful mathematical functions: the sum of integers from 1 to *N* and the product of integers from 1 to *N*. The latter function is called *factorial*.

First, we shall rewrite the package specification to name the package `Useful_Functions` and include specifications for the two new functions. Note in the specification that the sum and factorial functions require parameters of type `Positive` and return `Positive` results. Program 6.13 shows the package specification.

Program 6.13 Specification for Package Useful_Functions

```
PACKAGE Useful_Functions IS
-------------------------------------------------------------
--| Specifications of functions provided
--| by Useful_Functions package
--| Author: M. B. Feldman, The George Washington University
--| Last Modified: August 1998
-------------------------------------------------------------

   FUNCTION Minimum (Value1, Value2: Integer) RETURN Integer;
   FUNCTION Minimum (Value1, Value2: Float)   RETURN Float;
   -- Pre:  Value1 and Value2 have been assigned values
   -- Post: Returns the smaller of the two input values

   FUNCTION Maximum (Value1, Value2: Integer) RETURN Integer;
   FUNCTION Maximum (Value1, Value2: Float)   RETURN Float;
   -- Pre:  Value1 and Value2 have been assigned values
   -- Post: Returns the larger of the two input values

   FUNCTION Sum (N: Positive) RETURN Positive;
   -- Pre:  N has been assigned a value
   -- Post: Returns the sum of integers from 1 to N

   FUNCTION Factorial (N: Positive) RETURN Positive;
   -- Pre:  N has been assigned a value
   -- Post: Returns the product of integers from 1 to N

END Useful_Functions;
```

The Overloading Principle

There is something else noteworthy about the specification in Program 6.13. Function specifications appear for *two* functions called Minimum and *two* functions called Maximum. Looking at the two Minimum functions,

```
FUNCTION Minimum (Value1, Value2: Integer) RETURN Integer;
FUNCTION Minimum (Value1, Value2: Float)   RETURN Float;
```

we see that they have the same names but different *parameter profiles;* that is, their input parameters and return types are different. This is an example of *overloading,* which in Ada allows two or more different operations to have the same name, as long as there is enough difference in their parameter profiles that the compiler can distinguish them.

The advantage of overloading is that operations with similar behavior or functionality can be given similar names. This makes programs easier to write and to read because the programmer is not forced to invent names like MinimumInteger and MinimumFloat merely because the language requires all subprograms to have distinct names.

Actually, you've been using overloading all along when you've used the standard input/output libraries. Each package in these libraries has several Gets and several Puts, all with the same name but different parameter profiles.

When the compiler reaches a procedure or function call, it selects the appropriate procedure to include in the executable program by examining the parameter profile. If the profile matches one of the procedures made available by context clauses, all is well. If there is no match, a compilation error results. It could be that there are *two* matches; this case also results in a compilation error.

Another example of overloading comes from the arithmetic operations that we have been doing. An assignment statement such as

```
Result := Result + Count;
```

uses a *different* + depending on whether its operands are Integer or Float. Indeed, the machine instructions generated by the compiler are quite different for the two numeric types. We could write specifications for the integer and float versions of + that look just like function specifications:

```
FUNCTION "+" (Left: Integer; Right: Integer) RETURN Integer;
FUNCTION "+" (Left: Float;   Right: Float  ) RETURN Float;
```

Mathematically, an arithmetic operation is just a special kind of function; writing an operator specification this way just reflects that mathematical fact. There is no problem in naming both of the operations + (the quotes are required in this form for syntactic reasons): They have different parameter profiles, so the compiler can distinguish between them.

Specifications of *all* the predefined types and operators in Ada appear in the Language Reference Manual in a section called PACKAGE Standard; a version of this very useful description appears in Appendix C. PACKAGE Standard is automatically available to all Ada programs; no context clause is necessary. When the compiler reaches a statement such as

```
Result := Result + Count;
```

it examines the types of Result and Count to discover whether a matching + is available. If Result is an integer and Count is a float, for example, there is no matching + in PACKAGE Standard, so a compilation error arises.

PROGRAM
STYLE

Using Overloading Wisely

Used carefully, overloading can be a very helpful concept in writing Ada programs, because it allows operations to be given meaningful names, and all operations with similar functionality can be given the same name.

Clearly, overloading can be abused by using it too much or by using it to name functions and procedures that do not have similar behavior. This would mislead and confuse the reader of a program and so should be avoided.

Writing the Body of Useful_Functions

The next step is to provide the package body of Useful_Functions, which consists of function bodies for the six functions. The body of sum is adapted from Program 6.3; the body of Factorial can be readily adapted from the body of sum. (Note, however, that Result is initialized to 1, not 0). The complete package body appears in Program 6.14.

Program 6.14 Body of Useful_Functions

```
PACKAGE BODY Useful_Functions IS
-----------------------------------------------------------------
--| Body of Useful_Functions package
--| Author: M. B. Feldman, The George Washington University
--| Last Modified: August 1998
-----------------------------------------------------------------

   -- minimum of two Integer values
   FUNCTION Minimum (Value1, Value2: Integer) RETURN Integer IS
     Result: Integer;
   BEGIN -- Minimum
     IF Value1 < Value2 THEN
        Result := Value1;
     ELSE
        Result := Value2;
     END IF;
     RETURN Result;
   END Minimum;

   -- minimum of two Float values
   FUNCTION Minimum (Value1, Value2: Float) RETURN Float IS
     Result: Float;
   BEGIN -- Minimum
     IF Value1 < Value2 THEN
        Result := Value1;
     ELSE
        Result := Value2;
     END IF;
     RETURN Result;
   END Minimum;

   -- maximum of two Integer values
   FUNCTION Maximum (Value1, Value2: Integer) RETURN Integer IS
     Result: Integer;
   BEGIN -- Maximum
     IF Value1 > Value2 THEN
        Result := Value1;
     ELSE
        Result := Value2;
     END IF;
     RETURN Result;
   END Maximum;

   -- maximum of two Float values
   FUNCTION Maximum (Value1, Value2: Float) RETURN Float IS
     Result: Float;
   BEGIN -- Maximum
     IF Value1 > Value2 THEN
        Result := Value1;
     ELSE
```

```
        Result := Value2;
      END IF;
    RETURN Result;
  END Maximum;

  -- sum of integers from 1 to N
  FUNCTION Sum (N: Positive) RETURN Positive IS
    Result: Natural;
  BEGIN -- Sum
    Result := 0;
    FOR Count IN 1..N LOOP
      Result := Result + Count;
    END LOOP;
    RETURN Result;
  END Sum;

  -- factorial, or product of integers from 1 to N
  FUNCTION Factorial (N: Positive) RETURN Positive IS
    Result: Positive;
  BEGIN -- Factorial
    Result := 1;
    FOR Count IN 1..N LOOP
      Result := Result * Count;
    END LOOP;
    RETURN Result;
  END Factorial;

END Useful_Functions;
```

Program 6.15 illustrates the overloading principle in action by finding the maximum of two integers and the maximum of two floats. Notice in this program that `Useful_Functions.Maximum` appears to be called twice. In fact, *different* functions are being called, as you can see from the different parameter profiles: In the first call integers are supplied; in the second call, floats are supplied.

Program 6.15 Illustrating the Overloading Principle

```
WITH Ada.Text_IO;
WITH Ada.Integer_Text_IO;
WITH Ada.Float_Text_IO;
WITH Useful_Functions;
PROCEDURE Max_Int_Flt IS
-----------------------------------------------------------
--| Illustrates the overloading principle using the Maximum
--| functions for both integer and float quantities
--| Author: M. B. Feldman, The George Washington University
--| Last Modified: August 1998
-----------------------------------------------------------

  Int1 :       Integer; -- inputs
  Int2 :       Integer;
  LargerInt : Integer; -- output

  Flt1 :       Float;   -- inputs
  Flt2 :       Float;
  LargerFlt : Float;    -- output

BEGIN -- Max_Int_Flt
```

```
Ada.Text_IO.Put (Item => "Please enter first integer value  > ");
Ada.Integer_Text_IO.Get (Item => Int1);
Ada.Text_IO.Put (Item => "Please enter second integer value > ");
Ada.Integer_Text_IO.Get (Item => Int2);

LargerInt := Useful_Functions.Maximum(Value1=>Int1, Value2=>Int2);

Ada.Text_IO.Put (Item => "The larger integer is ");
Ada.Integer_Text_IO.Put (Item => LargerInt, Width => 1);
Ada.Text_IO.New_Line;

Ada.Text_IO.Put (Item => "Please enter first float value  > ");
Ada.Float_Text_IO.Get (Item => Flt1);
Ada.Text_IO.Put (Item => "Please enter second float value > ");
Ada.Float_Text_IO.Get (Item => Flt2);

LargerFlt := Useful_Functions.Maximum(Value1=>Flt1, Value2=>Flt2);

Ada.Text_IO.Put (Item => "The larger float is ");
Ada.Float_Text_IO.Put
   (Item => LargerFlt, Fore => 1, Aft => 2, Exp => 0);
Ada.Text_IO.New_Line;

END Max_Int_Flt;
```

Sample Run

```
Please enter first integer value  > -27
Please enter second integer value > 34
The larger integer is 34
Please enter first float value  > 29.77
Please enter second float value > 15.09
The larger float is 29.77
```

Finally, Program 6.16 gives a program that prompts the user for an integer between 1 and 10, then displays a table of the sum and factorial of each of the integers from 1 to the number entered.

Program 6.16 A Program That Uses Useful_Functions

```
WITH Ada.Text_IO;
WITH Ada.Integer_Text_IO;
WITH Useful_Functions;
PROCEDURE Sum_and_Factorial IS
-----------------------------------------------------------------
--| Prompts the user for an integer N from 1 to 10
--| and displays the sum and factorial of all integers from
--| 1 to N. Sum and Factorial are gotten from the
--| Useful_Functions package.
--| Author: M. B. Feldman, The George Washington University
--| Last Modified: August 1998
-----------------------------------------------------------------

SUBTYPE OneToTen IS Positive RANGE 1..10;

MaxNum:     OneToTen;   -- input - a value from one to ten
SumToCount: Positive;   -- output - sum and product of
```

```
            ProdToCount:  Positive;    --    integers from one to Count

    BEGIN -- Sum_and_Factorial

        Ada.Text_IO.Put (Item => "Please enter an integer from 1 to 10 > ");
        Ada.Integer_Text_IO.Get (Item => MaxNum);
        Ada.Text_IO.New_Line;

        Ada.Text_IO.Put(Item => "  N    Sum    Factorial");
        Ada.Text_IO.New_Line;
        Ada.Text_IO.Put(Item => " ----------------------");
        Ada.Text_IO.New_Line;

        FOR Count IN 1..MaxNum LOOP
           SumToCount   := Useful_Functions.Sum (N => Count);
           ProdToCount  := Useful_Functions.Factorial (N => Count);

           Ada.Integer_Text_IO.Put (Item => Count, Width => 3);
           Ada.Integer_Text_IO.Put (Item => SumToCount, Width => 7);
           Ada.Integer_Text_IO.Put (Item => ProdToCount, Width => 9);
           Ada.Text_IO.New_Line;
        END LOOP;

    END Sum_and_Factorial;
```

Sample Run

```
Please enter an integer from 1 to 10 > 9

 N    Sum    Factorial
----------------------------
 1     1        1
 2     3        2
 3     6        6
 4    10       24
 5    15      120
 6    21      720
 7    28     5040
 8    36    40320
 9    45   362880
```

PROGRAM STYLE

> ### Displaying a Table
>
> Program 6.16 displays a table of output values. The table heading is displayed, before the loop is reached, by the statements
>
> ```
> Ada.Text_IO.Put (Item => "  N    Sum    Factorial");
> Ada.Text_IO.New_Line;
> Ada.Text_IO.Put (Item => " ----------------------");
> Ada.Text_IO.New_Line;
> ```
>
> The spaces in the first string are used to align the column headings over their respective table values. We have left enough spaces to center the column titles of the respective values. The second string is used to "draw a line" between the column titles and the values. Within the FOR loop, the four statements

```
Ada.Integer_Text_IO.Put (Item => Count, Width => 3);
Ada.Integer_Text_IO.Put (Item => SumToCount, Width => 7);
Ada.Integer_Text_IO.Put (Item => ProdToCount, Width => 9);
Ada.Text_IO.New_Line;
```

display three output values on each line of the table, using 19 columns per line.

6.9 System Structures: Introduction to Exception Handling

It is useful to take a close look at Program 6.16 and make a list of the things that could go wrong with its execution:

- The user could enter a value that is a perfectly good integer value but is out of range for the variable MaxNum (for example, the user could enter a 0, a negative number, or a number greater than 10). In this case the program would terminate with a Constraint_Error, Ada's usual exception for out-of-range conditions.

- The user could enter a value that begins with a nonnumeric character, such as ABC or A1. In this case the program would terminate with Ada.Text_IO.Data_Error, because the input/output system would complain about bad data.

- The user could enter a value that, when passed to Factorial, could produce a result that is simply too large. Factorials grow quite large very quickly, and it does not take a very large input value to cause the factorial to be larger than Integer'Last.

As written, Program 6.16 will terminate if any of these conditions arises, and the Ada "run-time system" will display a message. Generally the name of the exception will be displayed, but otherwise the form of the message depends upon the compiler.

Ada provides a useful mechanism called *exception handling,* which allows the programmer to "catch" the exception before it goes to the Ada run-time system. The programmer can supply, at the bottom of the program, procedure, or function, a set of statements, called *exception handlers,* indicating what is to be done in case an exception is raised. Later chapters, beginning with Chapter 7, will introduce exception handling systematically; for now, Program 6.17 shows you the general idea.

Program 6.17 Sum and Factorial with Exception Handling

```
WITH Ada.Text_IO;
WITH Ada.Integer_Text_IO;
WITH Useful_Functions;
PROCEDURE Robust_Sum_Fact IS
-------------------------------------------------------------
--| Prompts the user for an integer N from 1 to 50
--| and displays the sum and factorial of all integers from
--| 1 to N. Sum and Factorial are gotten from the package
--| Useful_Functions.
--| This version incorporates an exception handler part.
--| Author: M. B. Feldman, The George Washington University
```

```
--| Last Modified: August 1998
   -------------------------------------------------------------

   SUBTYPE OneToFifty IS Positive RANGE 1..50;

   MaxNum:       OneToFifty;  -- input - a value from one to ten
   SumToCount:   Positive;    -- outputs - sum and product of
   ProdToCount:  Positive;    --   integers from one to Count

BEGIN -- Robust_Sum_Fact

   Ada.Text_IO.Put (Item => "Please enter an integer from 1 to 50 > ");
   Ada.Integer_Text_IO.Get (Item => MaxNum);
   Ada.Text_IO.New_Line;

   Ada.Text_IO.Put(Item => "  N     Sum     Factorial");
   Ada.Text_IO.New_Line;
   Ada.Text_IO.Put(Item => "  ---------------------");
   Ada.Text_IO.New_Line;

   FOR Count IN 1..MaxNum LOOP
      SumToCount    := Useful_Functions.Sum (N => Count);
      ProdToCount   := Useful_Functions.Factorial (N => Count);

      Ada.Integer_Text_IO.Put (Item => Count, Width => 3);
      Ada.Integer_Text_IO.Put (Item => SumToCount, Width => 7);
      Ada.Integer_Text_IO.Put (Item => ProdToCount, Width => 9);
      Ada.Text_IO.New_Line;
   END LOOP;

EXCEPTION

   WHEN Constraint_Error =>
      Ada.Text_IO.Put
        (Item => "The input value or result is out of range.");
      Ada.Text_IO.New_Line;
   WHEN Ada.Text_IO.Data_Error =>
      Ada.Text_IO.Put (Item => "The input value is not well formed.");
      Ada.Text_IO.New_Line;

END Robust_Sum_Fact;
```

Sample Run

```
Please enter an integer from 1 to 50 > 100
The input value or result is out of range.
```

Notice that at the bottom of the program, there is a section:

```
EXCEPTION

   WHEN Constraint_Error =>
      Ada.Text_IO.Put
        (Item => "The input value or result is out of range.");
      Ada.Text_IO.New_Line;
   WHEN Ada.Text_IO.Data_Error =>
      Ada.Text_IO.Put (Item => "The input value is not well formed.");
      Ada.Text_IO.New_Line;
```

```
END Robust_Sum_Fact;
```

Each group of statements beginning with WHEN is called an *exception handler*. If the program executes normally, execution stops at the "normal" last statement (the last line before the word EXCEPTION); it is as though the exception-handling section were not there. However, if an exception is raised anywhere in the program, execution of the statement causing the exception is halted, and control is passed immediately to the appropriate exception handler. Once the handler's statements have been executed (in this case, displaying a message), the program terminates normally. No message is displayed by the run-time system; because the program handled its own exception, the run-time system has no need to do so. Try running this program with various good and bad inputs to observe how it behaves.

How useful is this? We will see in Chapter 7 how exception handling can make programs much less prone to terminate with error messages from the run-time system and also how exception handling can be used to ensure the validity of user input. In the simple case considered here, the usefulness of exception handling is that it allows the programmer to control the form of the message displayed when the program terminates. This is better than leaving it to the run-time system, the form of whose messages depends on the compiler.

6.10 Tricks of the Trade: Common Programming Errors

Remember that the counter variable in a FOR loop has no existence outside the loop. If you need to remember the value of the counter variable, copy it into a different variable.

CHAPTER REVIEW

We showed how to implement repetition in Ada using the counting loop or FOR statement.

Algorithm and program traces are used to verify that an algorithm or program is correct. Errors in logic can be discovered by carefully tracing an algorithm or program. Tracing an algorithm or program before entering the program in the computer will save you time in the long run.

We also introduced the important concept of subtypes. Subtypes are used both to improve program readability and to enable the detection of out-of-range values. The operators that can be used with a subtype are the same as for its base type.

We also discussed the issue of type compatiblity. A subtype is compatible with its base type and with all other subtypes of the same base type. This means that an operator can have one operand whose type is the subtype and one operand whose type is the base type, or indeed another subtype.

Another important concept that was introduced in this chapter was overloading, which in Ada permits several functions or procedures to be given the same name, as long as they have different parameter profiles. This is convenient for giving names to operations like `Minimum`, which have similar function regardless of the type on which they operate.

Finally, exception handling was discussed. Exception handling is Ada's way of allowing a program to keep control even in the event of an error.

New Ada Constructs in Chapter 6

The new Ada constructs introduced in this chapter are described in Table 6.4.

Table 6.4 Summary of New Ada Constructs

Construct	Effect
FOR statement:	
```FOR CurMonth IN MarchJuly LOOP Ada.Float_Text_IO.Get (Item=>MonthSales); YearSales := YearSales+MonthSales; END LOOP;```	The loop body is repeated for each value of `CurMonth` from `March` through `July`, inclusive. For each month, the value of `MonthSales` is read and added to `YearSales`.

Quick-Check Exercises

For each of the following program fragments, indicate how many times each output statement is executed and the last value displayed.

1.
```
FOR I IN 1..10 LOOP
    FOR J IN 1..5 LOOP
       Ada.Integer_Text_IO.Put(Item => I * J, Width => 5);
    END LOOP;
    Ada.Text_IO.New_Line;
END LOOP;
```

2.
```
FOR I IN 1..10 LOOP
    FOR J IN 1..I LOOP
       Ada.Integer_Text_IO.Put(Item => I * J, Width => 5);
    END LOOP;
    Ada.Text_IO.New_Line;
END LOOP;
```

3.
```
FOR Counter IN 1..5 LOOP
    Ada.Integer_Text_IO.Put(Item => Counter, Width => 5);
END LOOP;
Ada.Integer_Text_IO.Put(Item => Counter, Width => 5);
```

Answers to Quick-Check Exercises

1. The Put statement executes 50 times; the New_Line executes 10 times; the last value displayed is 50.

2. The Put statement executes $1 + 2 + 3 + ... + 9 + 10$, or 55, times; the New_Line executes 10 times; the last value displayed is 100.

3. No result is displayed, because the program has a compilation error. The variable Counter cannot be accessed outside of the loop.

Review Questions

1. Write a FOR statement that runs from 'z' to 'A' and displays only the consonants. (*Hint:* Test each character against the vowels.)

2. Write a nested loop that displays the first six letters of the alphabet on a line, the next five letters on the next line, the next four letters on the next line, and so on, down to and including one letter (the letter U) on the last line. Use either uppercase or lowercase letters.

3. Explain the overloading principle. What examples have you seen of its use?

Programming Projects

1. Modify Programming Project 11 of Chapter 5 so that ten speeds are handled in a single run. Also, print a count of the number of speeding automobiles.

2. Compute and display a table showing the first 15 powers of 2, starting with 2^0.

3. Develop a program that reads in 20 values and displays the number of values that are positive (greater than or equal to 0) and the number that are negative. Also display "more positive" or "more negative" on the basis of the result.

4. Section 4.3 presented a case study to determine the best value of several pizzas in a pizzeria. Program 4.4 implemented part of the solution by computing the price per unit area of a pizza. In this project you can complete the solution by extending Program 4.4 so that the user is prompted for the number of pizzas to be compared, then for the size and price of each pizza. The program will then compute the best value. Find out the sizes and prices of the pizzas in a pizzeria near you and use those data to test your program.

5. Develop a program that prompts the user for a starting month and year and an ending month and year and then writes, into an output file, one line for each day in the period between the starting and ending dates. Each line should show the month, the day, and the year.

6. Develop a program that prints the multiplication table for the integers 0 through 9.

7. Modify the group payroll program (Program 6.6) so that the input is taken from a file, the tax is computed using the rates of Fig. 5.5 and Table 5.6, and, at the end of the run, a summary is given of the total amount of gross pay for the company and the total amount of tax withheld.

8. When the euro, the new common European currency, was introduced on Jan. 1, 1999, its exchange rates against 11 existing European currencies were fixed. For example, one euro is worth exactly 13.56 Austrian schillings. The exchange rates against other currencies will vary. In this project you will develop a case study and a program that produces a table of currency values. The program will prompt the user for the exchange rates for the U.S. dollar and the British pound. Each row of the table will represent one of the 13 noneuro currencies; the columns will be labeled 1, 50, 100, 200, and 500. In each cell of the table, display the number of euros a traveler could purchase for the given number of other currency units. For example, fill in the franc row to show the number of euros for 1, 50, 100, 200, and 500 francs, respectively. The fixed exchange rates follow; you can check a bank or newspaper for the dollar and pound rates.

Austrian schillings	13.56	Irish punts	0.79
Belgian francs	40.34	Italian lire	1,936.27
Dutch guilders	2.20	Luxembourg francs	40.34
Finnish markkas	5.95	Portuguese escudos	200.48
French francs	6.56	Spanish pesetas	166.39
German marks	1.96		

9. (Thanks to Chet Lund!) The Bunny Hop is a party dance that was popular in the 1940s and 1950s. All the party guests stand in a line around the room; each guest faces the back of the previous one and holds his or her waist loosely. The music starts and the dancers follow these steps:

> Step sideways with the right foot.
> Bring the right foot back.
> Step sideways with the right foot.
> Bring the right foot back.
> Step sideways with the left foot.
> Bring the left foot back.
> Step sideways with the right foot.
> Bring the right foot back.
> Step sideways with the right foot.
> Bring the right foot back.
> Step sideways with the right foot.
> Bring the right foot back.
> Hop forward one step on both feet.
> Hop forward one step on both feet.
> Hop forward one step on both feet.

The pattern repeats until the music stops or everyone is tired. Develop a program that prompts the user for a number of repetitions and then uses nested loops to display that number of repetitions of the pattern. Ask your instructor if you and the other students in your class can demonstrate the dance.

CHAPTER 7

Other Loop Forms; Procedures; Exception Handling

7.1   Control Structures: The General LOOP and EXIT Statements

In all the loops we have used so far, the exact number of loop repetitions required could be determined before the start of loop execution. We used the FOR statement to implement these counting loops.

Ada's FOR loop is limited in that counting can proceed only over a range that is *discrete* (i.e., of an integer or enumeration type). Furthermore, the counter variable is updated by taking its successor (or predecessor if REVERSE is used)— either adding 1 (subtracting 1) if it is an integer counter or taking the Succ (Pred) attribute if it is an enumeration counter. This means that counting cannot proceed, for example, by 2s.

There are three kinds of looping problems for which the Ada FOR statement is inappropriate:

- when the loop does not step through all the values of a discrete type in forward or reverse order (e.g., only every third value is of interest);

- when the most natural type for the loop control variable is not discrete (e.g., if it is Float); and

- when the number of iterations depends on conditions arising during the execution of the loop.

The first two cases are called *counter-controlled loops;* they are still controlled by counters even though a FOR statement cannot be used. The third case is often called an *event-controlled loop,* because some arriving event, in the input data or some user inter-action, triggers the end of the loop. In cases like these we can use the general LOOP/EXIT and WHILE loop to implement conditional loops. The general LOOP statement is discussed next; the WHILE statement is introduced later in the chapter.

■ Example 7.1

Program 7.1 displays the odd numbers from 1 to 39, inclusive. Because the step size is not 1, we cannot use a FOR loop for this. A general loop structure is used instead. A variable OddNumber is declared and used to control the loop. OddNumber is initialized to 1; then the structure

```
LOOP
  EXIT WHEN OddNumber > 39;
...
END LOOP;
```

controls the loop. Inside the loop body, OddNumber is incremented:

```
OddNumber := OddNumber + 2;
```

The loop ends when the EXIT condition becomes true. This is tested each time the EXIT statement is reached.   ■

Program 7.1 Looping When the Increment Is Not 1

```
WITH Ada.Text_IO;
WITH Ada.Integer_Text_IO;
PROCEDURE Odd_Numbers IS
-------------------------------------------------------------
--| Displays odd numbers from 1 to 39 inclusive
--| Author: M. B. Feldman, The George Washington University
--| Last Modified: August 1998
-------------------------------------------------------------

  OddNumber : Integer;

BEGIN -- Odd_Numbers

  OddNumber := 1;                       -- initialize loop
  LOOP
    EXIT WHEN OddNumber > 39;          -- test for exit
    Ada.Integer_Text_IO.Put(Item => Oddnumber, Width => 3);
    OddNumber := Oddnumber + 2;        -- update
  END LOOP;

  Ada.Text_IO.New_Line;
```

```
END Odd_Numbers;
```

Sample Run

```
 1   3   5   7   9  11  13  15  17  19  21  23  25  27  29  31  33  35  37  39
```

■ Example 7.2

Program 7.2 displays a table of Celsius and equivalent Fahrenheit temperatures for the range of temperatures from 100 degrees Celsius to –20 degrees Celsius in steps of –10 degrees. The assignment statement

```
Fahrenheit := (1.8 * Celsius) + 32.0;
```

converts each Celsius value in this range to a real Fahrenheit value. You can check this formula by knowing the freezing points (0 and 32 degrees) and boiling points (100 and 212 degrees) in the two systems. Because an integer can't be multiplied by 1.8 and the step size is not 1, a general loop is used instead of a FOR.

Three Float constants are declared in the program. CStart is the starting value of the Float loop control variable Celsius, CLimit is the limit value, and CStep is the step value. The loop is executed for values of Celsius in the sequence 100.0, 90.0, 80.0, ... , 0.0, –10.0, –20.0.   ■

Program 7.2 Looping When the Increment Is Not an Integer

```
WITH Ada.Text_IO;
WITH Ada.Float_Text_IO;
PROCEDURE Temperature_Table IS
----------------------------------------------------------------
--| Displays a table of Fahrenheit and
--| equivalent Celsius temperatures.
--| Author: M. B. Feldman, The George Washington University
--| Last Modified: August 1998
----------------------------------------------------------------

   CStart : CONSTANT Float := 100.0; -- initial Celsius temp
   CStep :  CONSTANT Float := -10.0; -- change in Celsius temp
   CLimit : CONSTANT Float := -20.0; -- final Celsius temp

   Celsius :         Float;          -- Celsius temp
   Fahrenheit :      Float;          -- Fahrenheit temp

BEGIN -- Temperature_Table

   Ada.Text_IO.Put(Item => "Celsius     Fahrenheit");
   Ada.Text_IO.New_Line (Spacing => 2);

   Celsius := CStart;                    -- initialize
   LOOP
     EXIT WHEN Celsius < CLimit;         -- test for exit

     Fahrenheit := 1.8 * Celsius + 32.0;
     Ada.Float_Text_IO.Put
```

```
                (Item => Celsius, Fore => 4, Aft => 0, Exp => 0);
            Ada.Text_IO.Put(Item => "          ");
            Ada.Float_Text_IO.Put
                (Item => Fahrenheit, Fore => 3, Aft => 1, Exp => 0);
            Ada.Text_IO.New_Line;

            Celsius := Celsius + CStep;      -- update
        END LOOP;

END Temperature_Table;
```

Sample Run

```
Celsius      Fahrenheit

 100.0          212.0
  90.0          194.0
  80.0          176.0
  70.0          158.0
  60.0          140.0
  50.0          122.0
  40.0          104.0
  30.0           86.0
  20.0           68.0
  10.0           50.0
   0.0           32.0
 -10.0           14.0
 -20.0           -4.0
```

■ Example 7.3

Program 7.3 traces the progress of a hungry worm approaching an apple. Each time it
moves, the worm cuts the distance between itself and the apple by its own body length
until the worm is close enough to enter the apple. A general loop is the correct looping
structure to use because we have no idea beforehand how many moves are required.

Program 7.3 Looping Controlled by an Event

```
WITH Ada.Text_IO;
WITH Ada.Float_Text_IO;
PROCEDURE Worm_and_Apple IS
---------------------------------------------------------------
--| Displays distances between a worm and an apple.  The worm
--| keeps reducing the distance by its body length until it is
--| close enough to bite the apple.
--| Author: M. B. Feldman, The George Washington University
--| Last Modified: August 1998
---------------------------------------------------------------

  SUBTYPE NonNegFloat IS Float RANGE 0.0 .. Float'Last;

  WormLength: CONSTANT NonNegFloat := 8.5;
                           -- worm body length in CM

  InitialDist: NonNegFloat;  -- input - starting distance
                           --    of worm from apple
```

```
   Distance:     NonNegFloat;   -- output - diminishing distance
                                 --    between worm and apple

BEGIN -- Worm_and_Apple

   Ada.Text_IO.Put (Item => "Initial distance (CM) away from apple > ");
   Ada.Float_Text_IO.Get(Item => InitialDist);
   Ada.Text_IO.New_Line;

   -- Cut the distance between the worm and the apple by
   -- the worm's body length until the worm is close enough
   -- to bite the apple

   Distance := InitialDist;              -- initialize
   LOOP
      EXIT WHEN Distance <= WormLength;  -- test for exit

      Ada.Text_IO.Put(Item => "The distance is ");
      Ada.Float_Text_IO.Put
        (Item => Distance, Fore => 4, Aft => 2, Exp => 0);
      Ada.Text_IO.New_Line;

      Distance := Distance - WormLength; -- update
   END LOOP;

   -- Display final distance before entering the apple.
   Ada.Text_IO.New_Line;
   Ada.Text_IO.Put (Item => "Final distance between worm and apple is ");
   Ada.Float_Text_IO.Put(Item => Distance, Fore => 4, Aft => 2, Exp => 0);
   Ada.Text_IO.New_Line;
   Ada.Text_IO.Put(Item => "The worm bites the apple.");
   Ada.Text_IO.New_Line;

END Worm_and_Apple;
```

Sample Run

```
Initial distance (CM) away from apple > 27

The distance is    27.00
The distance is    18.50
The distance is    10.00

Final distance between worm and apple is    1.50
The worm bites the apple.
```

The assignment statement just before the loop initializes the variable Distance to the starting distance, InitialDist, which the user entered as 27. Next, the loop header is reached and the loop exit condition

```
Distance <= WormLength
```

is evaluated. Because this condition is not yet true, the loop body (through END LOOP) is executed. The loop body displays the value of Distance, and the statement

```
Distance := Distance - WormLength;
```

reduces the value of Distance, thereby bringing the worm closer to the apple. The loop exit condition is tested again with the new value of Distance (18.50); because 18.50 <= 8.5 is still not true, the loop body displays Distance again, and Distance becomes 10.00. The loop exit condition is tested a third time, the loop body displays Distance again, and Distance becomes 1.50. The loop exit condition is tested again; because 1.50 <= 8.5 is true, loop exit occurs, and the statements following the loop end are executed.

It is important to realize that the loop is not exited at the exact instant that Distance becomes 1.50. If more statements appeared in the loop body after the assignment to Distance, they would be executed. Loop exit does not occur until the loop exit condition is retested at the top of the loop and found to be true. ∎

Every loop must contain *initialization*, *test*, and *update* steps. Unlike a FOR, which has a very strict syntax, in a general loop the initialization and update steps can be arbitrary statements. Therefore the compiler cannot check to ensure that you have included them, so you must be careful. In Program 7.3, if the initialization statement is missing, the initial value of Distance will be meaningless. The last step ensures that we make progress toward the exit condition (Distance <= WormLength) during each repetition of the loop. If the last step is missing, the value of Distance cannot change, so the loop will execute "forever" (an infinite loop).

SYNTAX DISPLAY

LOOP Statement (General)

Form:

```
LOOP
   statement sequence₁
   EXIT WHEN condition;
   statement sequence₂
END LOOP;
```

Example:

```
PowerOf2 := 1;
LOOP
   EXIT WHEN PowerOf2 > 10000;
   Ada.Integer_Text_IO.Put (Item => PowerOf2);
   PowerOf2 := PowerOf2 * 2;
END LOOP;
```

Interpretation:

Statement sequence₁ is executed and *condition* (a Boolean expression) is tested. If *condition* is found to be true, the loop is exited and the next program statement after END LOOP is executed. If *condition* is found to be false, *statement sequence₂* is executed and the loop is repeated.

Notes:

EXIT transfers out of the innermost loop in which it appears; that is, if EXIT appears inside a nested loop, only the inner loop is exited.

So far, we have seen only loops in which the EXIT statement is the first one in the loop body, that is, *statement sequence₁* is empty. Later we will look at other cases.

■ Example 7.4

It is instructive to compare the two loop forms that we currently know how to write: the FOR loop and the general loop. We can always get the effect of a FOR loop using a general loop, but we cannot always get the effect of a general loop using a FOR loop. The following loops behave identically:

```
FOR i IN 1..5 LOOP
   Square := i * i;
   Ada.Integer_Text_IO.Put (Item => i, Width => 1);
   Ada.Integer_Text_IO.Put (Item => Square, Width => 1);
   Ada.Text_IO.New_Line;
END LOOP;

i := 1;
LOOP
   EXIT WHEN i > 5;
   Square := i * i;
   Ada.Integer_Text_IO.Put (Item => i, Width => 1);
   Ada.Integer_Text_IO.Put (Item => Square, Width => 1);
   Ada.Text_IO.New_Line;
   i := i + 1;
END LOOP;
```

We can make the following observations about the two loop forms just shown:

1. The statement i := 1; in the general loop is our initialization statement; in the FOR loop, this is handled implicitly as part of the FOR statement.

2. The statement i := i+1; in the general loop body increments i by 1. This step is implicit in the FOR loop.

3. Unlike the FOR statement, in which the counter variable is declared implicitly and has no existence outside the loop body, the loop variable in the general loop is a "normal" variable: It must be declared, and it is known outside the loop body just like any other variable.

Now that we've seen examples of the three cases in which a general loop is appropriate, let's go on to a case study.

CASE
STUDY

THE WATER BALLOON DROP

You and your friends are celebrating the end of final exams and are thinking of interesting things to do. You think it might be fun to drop water-filled rubber balloons from the tops of various high buildings onto the street below. On the other hand, you realize that the people on the ground might react unfavorably to this sport, so you decide instead to use your programming knowledge to develop a computer simulation. The simulation will, given the height of the building, track the balloon's progress on its way to the ground. The desired time interval is an input to the program. The time interval and building height are inputs; at each interval the program will display the elapsed seconds and the distance remaining.

The distance traveled in t seconds by a object dropped from an initial height is represented by the formula distance $= 1/2 \times gt^2$, where g is the gravitational constant 9.80665.

Analysis

Data Requirements and Formulas

Problem Inputs:
Height of the building in meters (`BuildingHeight: NonNegFloat`)
Desired time interval in seconds (`DeltaT: NonNegFloat`)

Problem Outputs:
Elapsed time (`ElapsedTime: NonNegFloat`)
Current height (`Height: Float`)

Formulas:
distance traveled $= 1/2 \times g \times (\text{elapsedtime})^2$

Design
The initial algorithm follows.

Algorithm
1. Read inputs from user

2. Initialize `Height` to `BuildingHeight`

3. `LOOP`

3.1. `EXIT WHEN Height <= 0.0`

    3.2   Increment elapsed time by time interval

    3.3   Height is the initial height minus the distance traveled

    3.4   Display current height and current elapsed time

```
      END LOOP
```

Test Plan
We leave the test plan as an exercise.

Implementation
Program 7.4 shows the resulting program.

Testing
The sample output shows the result of dropping an object from a building approximately the height of the Washington Monument (150 meters). The balloon drops to the ground quite rapidly, doesn't it?

Program 7.4 Simulating an End-of-Exams Prank

```ada
WITH Ada.Text_IO;
WITH Ada.Float_Text_IO;
PROCEDURE Balloon_Drop IS
-----------------------------------------------------------
--| Simulates the travel of a water balloon from the top of
--| a building.
--| Author: M. B. Feldman, The George Washington University
--| Last Modified: August 1998
-----------------------------------------------------------

  SUBTYPE NonNegFloat IS Float RANGE 0.0 .. Float'Last;

  g : CONSTANT NonNegFloat := 9.80665;
                                -- gravitational constant

  BuildingHeight:  NonNegFloat;  -- input - height of building
  DeltaT: NonNegFloat;           -- input - time interval

  Height: Float;                 -- output - height of balloon
  ElapsedTime: NonNegFloat;      -- output - elapsed time

BEGIN -- Balloon_Drop

  -- Enter building height and time interval.
  Ada.Text_IO.Put(Item => "Building height in meters > ");
  Ada.Float_Text_IO.Get(Item => BuildingHeight);
  Ada.Text_IO.Put (Item => "Time in seconds between table lines > ");
  Ada.Float_Text_IO.Get(Item => DeltaT);
  Ada.Text_IO.New_Line(Spacing => 2);

  -- Display balloon height until it hits the ground.
  Ada.Text_IO.Put(Item => "      Time      Height");
  Ada.Text_IO.New_Line;

  ElapsedTime := 0.0;
  Height := BuildingHeight;      -- initialize

  LOOP
    EXIT WHEN Height <= 0.0;
    Ada.Float_Text_IO.Put
      (Item => ElapsedTime, Fore => 8, Aft => 3, Exp => 0);
    Ada.Float_Text_IO.Put
```

```
        (Item => Height, Fore => 8, Aft => 3, Exp => 0);
    Ada.Text_IO.New_Line;
    ElapsedTime := ElapsedTime + DeltaT;
    Height := BuildingHeight - 0.5 * g * (ElapsedTime ** 2);
END LOOP;

-- Balloon hits the ground.
Ada.Text_IO.New_Line;
Ada.Text_IO.Put(Item => "SPLATT!!!");
Ada.Text_IO.New_Line;

END Balloon_Drop;
```

Sample Run

```
Building height in meters > 150
Time in seconds between table lines > 0.5


        Time        Height
        0.000      150.000
        0.500      148.774
        1.000      145.097
        1.500      138.968
        2.000      130.387
        2.500      119.354
        3.000      105.870
        3.500       89.934
        4.000       71.547
        4.500       50.708
        5.000       27.417
        5.500        1.674

SPLATT!!!
```

EXERCISES FOR SECTION 7.1

Self-Check

1. What values would be printed if the order of the statements in the loop body of Progam 7.1 were reversed?

2. What is the least number of times that the body of a general loop may be executed?

3. How would you modify the loop in Program 7.3 so that it also determines the number of moves (CountMoves) made by the worm before biting the apple? Which is the loop control variable, Distance or CountMoves?

4. How many times is the following loop body repeated? What is printed during each repetition of the loop body?

```
X := 3;
Count := 0;
LOOP
   EXIT WHEN Count >= 3;
   X := X * X;
   Ada.Integer_Text_IO.Put(Item => X);
   Count := Count + 1;
END LOOP;
```

5. Answer Self-Check Exercise 4 if the last statement in the loop is

    ```
    Count := Count + 2;
    ```

6. Answer Self-Check Exercise 4 if the last statement in the loop body is omitted.

Programming

1. There are 9870 people in a town whose population increases by 10% each year. Write a loop that determines how many years (CountYears) it takes for the population to go over 30,000.

2. Write a loop that prints a table showing n and 2^n while 2^n is less than 10,000.

7.2   Problem Solving: Loop Design

It is one thing to be able to analyze the operation of loops like those in Programs 7.1 through 7.4; it is another to design our own loops. We will attack this problem in two ways. One approach is to analyze the requirements for a new loop to determine what initialization, test, and update of the loop control variable are needed. A second approach is to develop *templates* for loop forms that frequently recur and to use a template as the basis for a new loop. We will discuss loop templates later in this section.

To gain some insight into the design of the loop that is needed for the worm and apple problem, we should study the comment in Program 7.3 that summarizes the goal of this loop:

```
-- Cut the distance between the worm and the apple by
-- the worm's body length until the worm is close enough
-- to bite the apple
```

To accomplish this goal, we must concern ourselves with loop control and loop processing. Loop control involves making sure that loop exit occurs when it is supposed to; loop processing involves making sure the loop body performs the required operations.

To help us formulate the necessary loop control and loop processing steps, it is useful to list what we know about the loop. In this example, if Distance is the distance of the worm from the apple, we can make the following observations:

1. Just before the loop begins, `Distance` must be equal to `InitialDist`.

2. During pass *i*, `Distance` must be less than the value of `Distance` during pass *i* − 1 by the length of the worm (for *i* > 1).

3. Just after loop exit, `Distance` must be between 0 and the worm's body length.

Statement 1 simply indicates that `InitialDist` is the starting distance of the worm from the apple. Statement 2 says that the distance of the worm from the apple must be cut by the worm's body length during each iteration. Statement 3 derives from the fact that the worm enters the apple when `Distance <= WormLength`. `Distance` cannot be less than `WormLength` after loop exit; if it were, loop exit should have occurred at the end of an earlier pass.

Statement 1 by itself tells us what initialization must be performed. Statement 2 tells us how to process `Distance` within the loop body (i.e., reduce it by the worm's length). Finally, statement 3 tells us when to exit the loop. Because `Distance` is decreasing, loop exit should occur when `Distance <= WormLength` is true. These considerations give us the following outline, which is the basis for the loop shown in Program 7.3.

1. Initialize `Distance` to `InitialDist`

2. LOOP

    EXIT WHEN `Distance <= WormLength`

    3. Display Distance

    4. Reduce `Distance` by `WormLength`

    END LOOP;

Working Backward to Determine Loop Initialization

It is not always so easy to come up with the initialization steps for a loop. In some cases we must work backward from the results that we know are required in the first pass to determine what initial values will produce these results.

■ Example 7.5

Your little cousin is learning the binary number system and has asked you to write a program that displays all powers of 2 that are less than a certain value (say 10,000). Assuming that each power of 2 is stored in the variable `Power`, we can make the following observations about the loop:

1. `Power` during pass *i* is 2 times `Power` during pass *i* − 1 (for *i* > 1) .

2. `Power` must be between 10,000 and 20,000 just after loop exit.

Statement 1 derives from the fact that the powers of a number 2 are all multiples of 2. Statement 2 derives from the fact that only powers less than 10,000 are displayed. From statement 1 we know that `Power` must be multiplied by 2 in the loop body. From statement 2 we know that the loop exit condition is `Power >= 10000`, so the loop repetition condition is `Power < 10000`. These considerations lead us to the following outline:

1. Initialize `Power` to ____

2. `LOOP`

    `EXIT WHEN Power >= 10000`

    3. Display `Power`

    4. Multiply `Power` by 2

    `END LOOP;`

One way to complete step 1 is to ask what value should be displayed during the first loop repetition. The value of `N` raised to the power 0 is 1 for any number `N`; specifically, 2^0 is 1. Therefore, if we initialize `Power` to 1, the value displayed during the first loop repetition will be correct. ■

General Loops with Zero Iterations

The body of a general loop is not executed if the loop repetition test fails (evaluates to false) when it is first reached. To verify that you have the initialization steps correct, you should make sure that a program still generates the correct results for zero iterations of the loop body. If `WormLength` is greater than or equal to the value read into `InitialDist` (say, 2.5), the loop body in Program 7.3 would not execute, and the following lines would be correctly displayed:

```
Initial distance (CM) away from apple > 2.5


Final distance between worm and apple is    2.50
The worm bites the apple.
```

Entering an Unspecified Number of Values

Very often, we do not know exactly how many data items will be entered before a program begins execution. This may be because there are too many data items to count them beforehand (e.g., a stack of exam scores for a very large class) or because the number of data items provided may depend on how the computation proceeds.

There are two ways to handle this situation using a general loop. One approach is to ask whether there are any more data before each data item is read. The user should enter Y (for yes) or N (for no), and the program would either read the next item (Y) or terminate data entry (N). The Y/N variable is sometimes known as a *flag*. The other way is to terminate data entry when a particular *value* occurs in the data. This value is often called a *sentinel:* It comes at the end of the data.

Flag-Controlled Loop

■ **Example 7.6**

Let us use this approach to design a loop that accumulates the sum (in `Sum`) of a collection of exam scores. The statements below are true assuming that `MoreData` always contains the value `'Y'` or `'N'`.

1.   `Sum` is the sum of all scores read so far.

2.   `MoreData` is `'N'` just after loop exit.

From statement 1 we know that we must add each score to `Sum` in the loop body and that `Sum` must initially be 0 for its final value to be correct. From statement 2 we know that loop exit must occur when `MoreData` is `'N'`, so the loop repetition condition is `MoreData = 'Y'`. These considerations lead us to the following loop form:

1.   Initialize `Sum` to 0

2.   Initialize `MoreData` to ____

3.   LOOP

    EXIT WHEN MoreData = 'N';

   4.   Read the next score into `Score`

   5.   Add `Score` to `Sum`

   6.   Read the next value of `MoreData`

    END LOOP;

The loop exit condition, `MoreData = 'N'`, derives from the fact that `MoreData` is either `'Y'` or `'N'`, and loop exit occurs when `MoreData` is `'N'`. To ensure that at least one pass is performed, step 2 should be

2.   Initialize `MoreData` to `'Y'`

In the following loop, the value of the type `Character` variable `MoreData` controls loop repetition. It must be initialized to `'Y'` before the loop is reached. A new character value (`'Y'` or `'N'`) is read into `MoreData` at the end of each loop repetition. The loop processing consists of reading each exam score (into `Score`) and adding it to `Sum`. Loop exit occurs when the value read into `MoreData` is not equal to `'Y'`.

```
Sum := 0;
MoreData := 'Y';
LOOP
  EXIT WHEN MoreData = 'N'
  Ada.Text_IO. Put (Item => "Enter the next score > ");
  Ada.Integer_Text_IO.Get (Item => Score);
  Ada.Text_IO.New_Line;
  Sum := Sum + Score;
```

```
Ada.Text_IO.Put
   (Item => "Any more data? Enter Y (Yes) or N (No) > ");
Ada.Text_IO.Get (Item => MoreData);
END LOOP;
```

The following sample dialogue would be used to enter the scores 33, 55, and 77. The problem with this approach is that the program user must enter an extra character value, Y, before each actual data item is entered.

```
Enter the next score > 33
Any more data? Enter Y (Yes) or N (No) > Y
Enter next data item > 55
Any more data? Enter Y (Yes) or N (No) > Y
Enter next data item: 77
Any more data? Enter Y (Yes) or N (No) > N
```
■

Template for Flag-Controlled Loop

The general form of the loop just seen can be used to write other loops as the need arises. This general form is

1. Initialize flag variable to its affirmative value

2. LOOP

    EXIT WHEN flag variable is no longer true

    ...

    Read new value of flag variable

    END LOOP;

Sentinel-Controlled Loops and Priming Reads

A second approach to solving the problem addressed in the preceding section is to instruct the user to enter a unique data value, or *sentinel value,* when done. The program would test each data item and terminate when this sentinel value is read. The sentinel value should be carefully chosen and must be a value that could not normally occur as data. This approach is more convenient because the program user enters only the required data.

■ Example 7.7

The following statements must be true for a sentinel-controlled loop that accumulates the sum of a collection of exam scores.

1. Sum is the sum of all scores read so far.

2. Score contains the sentinel value just after loop exit.

Statement 2 derives from the fact that loop exit occurs after the sentinel is read into score. These statements lead to the following trial loop form:

Incorrect Sentinel-Controlled Loop

1. Initialize Sum to 0

2. Initialize Score to _____

3. LOOP

   EXIT WHEN Score is the sentinel

   4.   Read the next score into Score

   5.   Add Score to Sum

   END LOOP;

Because Score has not been given an initial value, the loop exit condition in step 3 cannot be evaluated when it is first reached. One way around this would be to initialize Score to any value other than the sentinel (in step 2) and then read in the first score at step 3. A preferred solution is to read in the first score as the initial value of Score before the loop is reached and then switch the order of the read and add steps in the loop body. The outline for this solution is shown below.

Correct Sentinel-Controlled Loop

1. Initialize Sum to 0

2. Read the first score into Score

3. LOOP

   EXIT WHEN Score is the sentinel

   4.   Add Score to Sum

   5.   Read the next score into Score

   END LOOP;

Step 2 reads in the first score, and step 4 adds this score to 0 (initial value of Sum). Step 5 reads all remaining scores, including the sentinel. Step 4 adds all scores except the sentinel to Sum. The initial read (step 2) is often called the *priming read*, to draw an analogy with an old hand-operated water pump that must be primed by pouring a cup of water into it before it can begin to pump water out of a well. The following Ada implementation uses −1 (value of Sentinel) as the sentinel because all normal exam scores will be nonnegative:

```
Sum := 0;
Ada.Text_IO.Put (Item => "When done, enter -1 to stop.");
Ada.Text_IO.New_Line;
Ada.Text_IO.Put (Item => "Enter the first score > ");
```

```
Ada.Integer_Text_IO.Get (Item => Score);
Ada.Text_IO.New_Line;
LOOP
   EXIT WHEN Score = Sentinel
   Sum := Sum + Score;
   Ada.Text_IO.Put (Item => "Enter the next score > ");
   Ada.Integer_Text_IO.Get (Item => Score);
   Ada.Text_IO.New_Line;
END LOOP;
```

Although it might look strange at first to see the statement

```
Ada.Integer_Text_IO.Get (Item => Score);
```

at two different points in the program, this is a perfectly good programming practice and causes no problems. Note that `Score` must be `Integer`, not `Natural`, because the sentinel value is negative. The following sample dialogue would be used to enter the scores 33, 55, and 77. Compare this with the dialogue shown in Example 7.6.

```
When done, enter -1 to stop.
Enter the first score > 33
Enter the next score > 55
Enter the next score > 77
Enter the next score >  -1
The sum of the scores is 165.
```

It is usually instructive (and often necessary) to question what happens when there are no data items to process. In this case the sentinel value should be entered as the "first score," and loop exit would occur right after the first (and only) test of the loop repetition condition, so the loop body would not be executed (i.e., a loop with zero iterations). `Sum` would retain its initial value of 0, which would be correct. ■

Template for a Sentinel-Controlled Loop with a Priming Read

1. Read the first value of input variable

2. LOOP

   EXIT WHEN input variable is equal to the sentinel

   . . .

   Read the next value of input variable

   END LOOP;

The sentinel value must be a value that would not be entered as a normal data item. For program readability we usually store the sentinel value in a constant.

Remembering the Previous Data Value in a Loop

In some situations it is necessary to remember the data value that was processed during the previous iteration of a loop. For example, some keyboards are "bouncy" and cause multiple occurrences of the same character to be sent when a single key is pressed. Some faculty members are forgetful and may enter the same exam score twice in succession. An IF statement nested inside a loop can be used to check whether or not the current data value is the same as the last data value.

■ Example 7.8

Program 7.5 finds the product of a collection of data values. If there are multiple consecutive occurrences of the same data value, only the first occurrence is included in the product. For example, the product of the numbers 10, 5, 5, 5, and 10 is $10 \times 5 \times 10$, or 500. Assuming that a new data value is read into NextNum during each loop iteration, we can make the following observations.

1. Product in pass i is the same as Product in pass $i - 1$ if NextNum in pass i is NextNum in pass $i - 1$; otherwise, Product during pass i is NextNum times Product in pass $i - 1$ (for $i > 1$).

2. NextNum is the sentinel just after loop exit.

Statement 1 requires the loop to "remember" the value that was read into NextNum during the previous iteration. We will introduce a new program variable, PreviousNum, for this purpose. The current value of NextNum should be incorporated in the product only if it is different from the previous value of NextNum (saved in PreviousNum). A trial loop form follows.

Initial Loop Form

1. Initialize Product to _____

2. Initialize PreviousNum to _____

3. Read the first number into NextNum

4. LOOP

   EXIT WHEN NextNum is the sentinel

   5.   IF NextNum is not equal to PreviousNum THEN

         6.   Multiply Product by NextNum

         END IF;

   7.   Set PreviousNum to NextNum

   8.   Read the next number into NextNum

   END LOOP;

For `Product` to be correct during the first pass, it must be initialized to 1 (step 1). We must also initialize `PreviousNum` so that the condition in step 4 can be evaluated. To ensure that the first number read into `NextNum` is incorporated in the product, we must pick a value for `PreviousNum` that is different from the initial data value. The safest thing to do is to initialize `PreviousNum` to the sentinel. (Why?) These considerations lead to the following revised loop form.

Revised Loop Form

1. Initialize `Product` to 1

2. Initialize `PreviousNum` to the sentinel

3. Read the first number into `NextNum`

4. `LOOP`

    `EXIT WHEN NextNum` is the sentinel

    5. `IF NextNum` is not equal to `PreviousNum THEN`

        6.   Multiply Product by `NextNum`

        `END IF;`

    7. Set `PreviousNum` to `NextNum`

    8. Read the next number into `NextNum`

    `END LOOP;`

Within the loop, steps 7 and 8 prepare for the next iteration by saving the previous value of `NextNum` in `PreviousNum` before reading the next data value. (What would happen if the order of these two steps were reversed?) ∎

Program 7.5 illustrates the proper form of a sentinel-controlled loop. The constant `Sentinel` has the value 0 because it is meaningless to include 0 in a collection of numbers being multiplied. To determine whether or not to execute the loop, each value that is read into `NextNum` must be compared to `Sentinel`. For this test to make sense in the beginning, the first data value must be read before the loop is reached. The next value must be read at the end of the loop so that it can be tested before starting another iteration.

Program 7.5 Product of a Series of Integers

```
WITH Ada.Text_IO;
WITH Ada.Integer_Text_IO;
PROCEDURE Multiply_Integers IS
----------------------------------------------------------------
--| Finds the product of a collection of non-zero integers.
--| If there are multiple consecutive occurrences of the same
--| value, only the first value is included in the product.
--| Author: M. B. Feldman, The George Washington University
```

```
--| Last Modified: August 1998
------------------------------------------------------------

   Sentinel : CONSTANT Natural := 0;   -- sentinel value

   NextNum :        Integer;        -- input - new data item
   PreviousNum : Integer;           -- save previous data item
   Product :        Integer;        -- output - product of data

BEGIN -- Multiply_Integers

   Product := 1;
   PreviousNum := Sentinel;
   Ada.Text_IO.Put (Item => "Enter 0 to stop.");
   Ada.Text_IO.New_Line;
   Ada.Text_IO.Put (Item => "Enter first number > ");
   Ada.Integer_Text_IO.Get (Item => NextNum); -- priming read

   LOOP
      EXIT WHEN NextNum = Sentinel;

      IF NextNum /= PreviousNum THEN
         Product := Product * NextNum; -- compute next product
      END IF;
      PreviousNum := NextNum;          -- remember previous item
      Ada.Text_IO.Put (Item => "Enter next  number  > ");
      Ada.Integer_Text_IO.Get (Item => NextNum);
   END LOOP;

   Ada.Text_IO.Put (Item => "The product is ");
   Ada.Integer_Text_IO.Put(Item => Product, Width => 1);
   Ada.Text_IO.New_Line;

END Multiply_Integers;
```

Sample Run

```
Enter 0 to stop.
Enter first number > 10
Enter next  number  > 5
Enter next  number  > 5
Enter next  number  > 5
Enter next  number  > 10
Enter next  number  > 0
The product is 500
```

Remember, in a sentinel-controlled loop, the read operation appears twice: before the loop header (the priming read) and at the end of the loop body.

PROGRAM
STYLE

A Problem with Sentinel-Controlled Loops

Sentinel-controlled loops are popular, but they do have a disadvantage. We have been stressing the importance of defining subtypes that reflect the range of data that will normally appear. A sentinel, on the other hand, makes sense only if it is a value that does *not* normally appear in the data. Therefore the range of data values must be extended beyond the normal range to accommodate the sentinel, as we extended the range of Score to be Integer rather than Natural.

The difficulty that arises in extending the range is that the Get call might not catch an *incorrectly* entered data value. One solution is to use an extra variable of the extended range just to read the input data. If a value is entered into it that is not the sentinel, that value is copied into the other variable, whose range is that of the normally occurring data. Copying the value will raise Constraint_Error if the value is out of range.

EXERCISES FOR SECTION 7.2

Self-Check

1. What output values are displayed by the following loop for a data value of 5?

```
Ada.Text_IO.Put(Item => "Enter an integer> ");
Ada.Integer_Text_IO.Get(Item => X);
Product := X;
Count := 0;
LOOP
   EXIT WHEN Count >= 4;
   Ada.Integer_Text_IO.Put(Item => Product, Width => 1);
   Product := Product * X;
   Count := Count + 1;
END LOOP;
```

2. What values are displayed if the call to Ada.Integer_Text_IO.Put comes at the end of the loop instead of at the beginning?

3. Discuss the difference between flag-controlled and sentinel-controlled loops.

Programming

1. Write a program segment that computes $1 + 2 + 3 + ... + (N - 1) + N$, where N is a data value. Follow the loop body with an IF statement that compare this value to $(N \times (N + 1)) / 2$ and displays a message indicating whether the values are the same or different. What message do you think will be displayed?

7.3   Control Structures: The WHILE Statement

Ada has another kind of loop statement that is also present in other languages: the WHILE statement. This statement always tests the loop exit condition at the *top* of the loop.

Here are a WHILE statement and a general LOOP statement that both accomplish the same purpose, which is to compute and display all powers of 2 less than 10,000:

```
Power := 1;
WHILE Power < 10000 LOOP
   Ada.Integer_Text_IO.Put (Item => Power, Width => 5);
   Power := Power * 2;
END LOOP;

Power := 1;
LOOP
   EXIT WHEN Power >= 10000;
   Ada.Integer_Text_IO.Put (Item => Power, Width => 5);
   Power := Power * 2;
END LOOP;
```

The test in the WHILE loop (Power < 10000) is the *complement,* or opposite, of the test that is used in the general loop. The loop body is repeated *as long as* the value of Power is less than 10,000. Loop repetition stops when the condition is false, whereas in the general loop, repetition stops when the condition is true. The condition in a WHILE is thus a loop *continuation* condition, whereas that in the general loop is a loop *exit* condition. The test in a WHILE is always done at the top; in a general loop it can be placed wherever the programmer finds it to be suitable.

SYNTAX DISPLAY

WHILE Statement

Form:

```
WHILE expression LOOP
   statement sequence
END LOOP;
```

Example:

```
PowerOf2 := 1;
WHILE PowerOf2 < 10000 LOOP
   Ada.Integer_Text_IO.Put (Item => PowerOf2);
   PowerOf2 := PowerOf2 * 2;
END LOOP;
```

Interpretation:

The expression (a condition) is tested, and if it is true, the statement sequence is executed and the expression is retested. The statement sequence is repeated as long as (WHILE) the expression is true. When the expression is tested and found to be false, the WHILE loop is exited and the next program statement after END LOOP is executed. *Note:* If the expression evaluates to false the first time it is tested, the statement sequence will not be executed.

To summarize our study of loop constructs: This book uses all three loop forms, but we prefer the general loop over the WHILE loop for two reasons. First, the general loop is more flexible, because we can place an EXIT WHEN statement at the top of the loop body, or at the bottom, or in the middle, as the algorithm dictates. Second, the "positive logic" of the general loop—the loop terminates upon a true condition—is usually clearer and more intuitive than the "negative logic" of the WHILE—the loop terminates upon a false condition.

EXERCISES FOR SECTION 7.3

Self-Check

1. Discuss the differences between the general and WHILE loop statements.

Programming

1. In Programs 7.1 through 7.5, rewrite the general loops as WHILE loops. Make sure you translate the loop exit conditions properly!

7.4 System Structures: Robust Exception Handling

A good program should be written to anticipate likely input errors and behave accordingly, retaining control instead of "crashing" or just returning control to the operating system. Such a program is called a *robust* program; the property of *robustness* is advantageous in a program. A robust Ada program is one that retains control and behaves predictably even when exceptions are raised.

Program 6.17 was written with an exception-handling section at the end so that it would display an appropriate message if an input value was out of range or badly formed or if a result would overflow the computer's arithmetic system. This is only a partial solution, because the program terminates without giving the user another chance to enter an acceptable value. There are many techniques for completing the solution; the one that we consider here is the use of Ada exception handlers.

We will get user input by entering a loop that exits only when the input value is acceptable. We will detect out-of-range or badly formed input values using an exception handler form similar to that in Program 6.17. It is necessary to associate the exception handler with the input statement rather than with the entire program. A pseudocode description of the process follows.

Template for a Robust Input Loop, Initial Version

```
LOOP
      Prompt the user for an input value

      Get the input value from the user

      EXIT the loop if and only if no exception was raised on input

      If an exception was raised, notify the user

END LOOP;
```

The first two lines in the loop body should present no problem to you at this point. The last line is coded using an exception-handler section like that in Program 6.17.

As is clear from the following syntax displays, Ada's rules require that an exception handler be associated with a *block* or *frame*, that is, a sequence of statements between a BEGIN and an END. A procedure or function has a block as part of its body; the exception handler in Program 6.17 is associated with that block. Luckily, we can build a smaller block wherever we need one within a program, just by enclosing a group of statements between BEGIN and END.

SYNTAX
DISPLAY

Exception Handler

Form:

```
WHEN exception name =>
   sequence of statements
```

Example:

```
WHEN Constraint_Error =>
   Ada.Text_IO.Put(Item => "Input number is out of range");
   Ada.Text_IO.New_Line;
   Ada.Text_IO.Put(Item => "Please try entering it again.");
   Ada.Text_IO.New_Line;
```

Interpretation:

This structure is valid only in the exception-handler part of a BEGIN/END block. If *exception name* was raised in the block, *sequence of statements* is executed, after which control passes to the next statement after the block's END.

Note:

Exception name can be a predefined exception or a programmer-defined exception. In Chapter 11 we will show how to define your own exceptions. The predefined exceptions that are most commonly used follow:

- Constraint_Error—an attempt is made to store a value in a variable that is out of range for that variable, that is, out of the range of the variable's type or subtype
- Ada.Text_IO.Data_Error—an attempt is made to read a value which is invalid for the variable being read

SYNTAX DISPLAY

Exception Handler Block

Form:
```
BEGIN
  normal sequence of statements
EXCEPTION
WHEN exception-name₁ =>
  sequence-of-statements₁
WHEN exception-name₂ =>
  sequence-of-statements₂...
WHEN exception-name_N =>
  sequence-of-statements_N
END;
```

Example:
An example is given in Program 7.6.

Interpretation:
The only code permitted between EXCEPTION and END is a sequence of one or more exception handlers.

If an exception is raised by any statement in *normal-sequence-of-statements*, execution of the statement causing the exception is immediately halted, and control passes to the appropriate exception handler. If the block has no exception-handler part or no exception handler is appropriate (i.e., the exception that was raised is not named in any of the handlers), control passes out of the block to the statement following the END, and the exception is reraised at that point.

Note:
The last sentence means that if an exception is raised in executing the statements of a function or procedure and that function or procedure has no exception-handler part, the exception is *propagated*, or "passed back," to the program that called the function or procedure, and an attempt is made to find an appropriate handler *there*. If the procedure was the main program, the program ends and control passes to the Ada run-time system, which reports the exception to the user.

In the following pseudocode (a refinement of the pseudocode on page 268) the entire loop body is made into a block by enclosing it between BEGIN and END. The structure beginning EXCEPTION is associated with this block.

Template for a Robust Input Loop, Refined Version

```
LOOP
    BEGIN

            Prompt the user for an input value
            Get the input value from the user
        EXIT;            -- valid data

    EXCEPTION               -- invalid data
```

Determine which exception was raised and notify the user

```
      END;

END LOOP;
```

If control reaches the EXIT—that is, if the input is correct—loop exit occurs. Control passes to the exception handler if the input is incorrect; after execution of the exception handler, control flows to the END LOOP, which of course causes the loop to be repeated. This gives the user another chance to enter correct input.

SYNTAX
DISPLAY

EXIT Statement

Form:

```
EXIT;
```

Example:
An example was just given in the robust input loop pseudocode.

Interpretation:
EXIT is a meaningful statement only within a loop structure. EXIT transfers control to the next statement after the nearest END LOOP.

■ Example 7.9

Program 7.6 shows a robust input handler. The purpose of the program is to add five integers in the range –10 through 10. A subtype SmallInt is declared with this range, then Ada.Integer_Text_IO.Get is used to get input in this range, storing the value in the variable InputValue of type SmallInt. If the value that is entered is out of range, the attempt to store it in InputValue raises Constraint_Error. The exception handler for Constraint_Error notifies the user that the input is out of range.

Program 7.6 An Example of Robust Numeric Input

```
WITH Ada.Text_IO;
WITH Ada.Integer_Text_IO;
PROCEDURE Exception_Loop IS
-----------------------------------------------------------------
--| Illustrates how to write a robust input loop that
--| prompts user to re-enter invalid input and
--| refuses to continue until input is good.
--| Author: M. B. Feldman, The George Washington University
--| Last Modified: August 1998
-----------------------------------------------------------------

  MinVal : CONSTANT Integer := -10;
  MaxVal : CONSTANT Integer :=  10;
  SUBTYPE SmallInt  IS Integer RANGE MinVal .. MaxVal;
```

```
      InputValue: SmallInt;
      Sum:        Integer;

BEGIN -- Exception_Loop

   Sum := 0;

   FOR Count IN 1..5 LOOP

      LOOP       -- inner loop just to control robust input
        BEGIN    -- block for exception handler

           Ada.Text_IO.Put(Item => "Enter an integer between ");
           Ada.Integer_Text_IO.Put (Item => SmallInt'First, Width => 0);
           Ada.Text_IO.Put(Item => " and ");
           Ada.Integer_Text_IO.Put (Item => SmallInt'Last, Width => 0);
           Ada.Text_IO.Put(Item => " > ");
           Ada.Integer_Text_IO.Get(Item => InputValue);

           EXIT; -- leave the loop only upon correct input

        EXCEPTION
          WHEN Constraint_Error =>
            Ada.Text_IO.Put ("Value is out of range. Please try again.");
            Ada.Text_IO.New_Line;
          WHEN Ada.Text_IO.Data_Error =>
            Ada.Text_IO.Put ("Value is not an integer. Please try again.");
            Ada.Text_IO.New_Line;
            Ada.Text_IO.Skip_Line;

        END;      -- block for exception handler
      END LOOP;

      Sum := Sum + InputValue; -- add new value into Sum
   END LOOP;

   Ada.Text_IO.Put (Item => "The sum is ");
   Ada.Integer_Text_IO. Put (Item => Sum, Width => 1);
   Ada.Text_IO.New_Line;

END Exception_Loop;
```

Sample Run

```
Enter an integer between -10 and 10 > 20
Value is out of range. Please try again.
Enter an integer between -10 and 10 > -11
Value is out of range. Please try again.
Enter an integer between -10 and 10 > x
Value is not an integer. Please try again.
Enter an integer between -10 and 10 > 0
Enter an integer between -10 and 10 > -5
Enter an integer between -10 and 10 > y
Value is not an integer. Please try again.
Enter an integer between -10 and 10 > 3
Enter an integer between -10 and 10 > 4
Enter an integer between -10 and 10 > -7
The sum is -5
```

Suppose that the input entered is not an integer; for example, suppose that it is a letter. In this case, `Ada.Text_IO.Data_Error` is raised. In this situation the letter is *not* consumed from the input stream. If the program just loops around, it will try to read the same letter again and again and again, causing an infinite loop. To prevent this unpleasant occurrence, the handler for `Ada.Text_IO.Data_Error` contains a statement,

```
Ada.Text_IO.Skip_Line;
```

that causes the bad input to be skipped, creating a fresh line for input. Actually, `Ada.Text_IO.Skip_Line` causes all input, up to and including the carriage return with which you end a line, to be skipped.

Suppose a floating-point value—say, 345.67—is entered when an integer is called for. An odd consequence of the design of `Ada.Text_IO` is that the 345 will be accepted as a valid integer, and the decimal point will raise `Ada.Text_IO. Data_Error` if you try to read another integer. When your program is reading an integer token with `Ada.Integer_Text_IO.Get`, input stops whenever a character is reached that is not part of an integer token. In this case the decimal point stops input. This is one reason for including the `Ada.Text_IO.Skip_Line` statement in the exception handler. ■

CASE STUDY

ROBUST MENU-DRIVEN COMMAND INTERPRETER

Problem Specification
A very important and common computer application is a command interpreter, which accepts and processes commands from the keyboard. Your development group is starting work on a package to perform various statistical operations—averaging, finding the median, and plotting—on data sets. Your part of the project is to develop a menu-driven command interpreter, leaving the details of the statistical operations to your colleagues. The command interpreter must behave properly, no matter what the input from the keyboard.

Analysis
The best way to represent this fixed set of commands is with an enumeration type. Input of enumeration values is then provided by an instance of `Ada.Text_IO. Enumeration_IO`, which allows the user to enter commands in either uppercase or lowercase and validates the input by raising `Ada.Text_IO.Data_Error` if the input is not a valid command.

Data Requirements

Problem Types:
the valid commands (`TYPE Commands IS (A, M, P, Q);`)

Problem Inputs:
a user command (`MenuSelection: Commands`)

Problem Outputs:

No actual computations are done in this stage of development; the only outputs are status messages from the command interpreter.

Design

Initial Algorithm

The basic algorithm for a command handler is a loop that is not exited until the user enters a "quit" command.

1. LOOP

    2.   Prompt the user to enter a command

    3.   EXIT WHEN the command is to quit

    4.   The command was not quit, so process it

END LOOP;

Algorithm Refinements

The program cannot proceed if the user enters an invalid command. This leads to a refinement of Step 2:

2.1 LOOP

    2.1   Prompt the user to enter a command

    2.2   EXIT if and only if the command is valid

END LOOP;

and so the refined algorithm is a pair of nested general loops:

1. LOOP

    2.1   LOOP

        2.2   Prompt the user to enter a command

        2.3   EXIT if and only if the command is valid

    END LOOP;

    3.   EXIT WHEN the command is to quit

    4.   The command was not quit, so process it

END LOOP;

Test Plan

Since it is very important that the program behave properly for all input cases, it is necessary to test the behavior for each one of the valid commands and for representative samples of invalid input.

Implementation

Program 7.7 shows an implementation of this algorithm using Ada exception handling to catch invalid input. This program uses `Screen.MoveCursor` to control the positioning of the cursor and `DELAY` to cause execution to be delayed for a brief period before clearing the screen and prompting the user again. Correct input results in the program exiting from the inner loop, then selecting and performing the desired command. The program leaves the outer loop and terminates when the command entered is `Q` or `q`, which in this program represents "quit." For the other valid commands, the program displays a "stub" message, indicating that a computation would be performed at that point, if the code for the computation were present.

Program 7.7 Framework for a Menu-Driven Command Interpreter

```
WITH Ada.Text_IO;
WITH Ada.Integer_Text_IO;
WITH Screen;
PROCEDURE Menu_Handler IS
-------------------------------------------------------------
--| Framework for a menu-driven command interpreter
--| Author: M. B. Feldman, The George Washington University
--| Last Modified: August 1998
-------------------------------------------------------------

  TYPE Commands IS (A, M, P, Q);
  PACKAGE Command_IO IS
    NEW Ada.Text_IO.Enumeration_IO (Enum => Commands);

  MenuSelection : Commands;  -- input - a commands

BEGIN -- Menu_Handler

  LOOP    -- this is the outer loop that keeps the program
          -- running until a "quit" command is entered.

    LOOP -- inner loop continues until valid input is entered
      BEGIN -- exception handler block

        Screen.ClearScreen;
        Screen.MoveCursor (Row => 5, Column => 20);
        Ada.Text_IO.Put (Item => "Main Command Menu");
        Screen.MoveCursor (Row => 7, Column => 20);
        Ada.Text_IO.Put (Item => "A - Compute Average");
        Screen.MoveCursor (Row => 8, Column => 20);
        Ada.Text_IO.Put (Item => "M - Compute Median");
        Screen.MoveCursor (Row => 9, Column => 20);
        Ada.Text_IO.Put (Item => "P - Plot the data");
        Screen.MoveCursor (Row => 10, Column => 20);
        Ada.Text_IO.Put (Item => "Q - Quit the program");

        Screen.MoveCursor (Row => 14, Column => 20);
        Ada.Text_IO.Put ("Enter a command, please > ");

        -- this statement will raise Data_Error if input
        -- is not one of the valid commands
        Command_IO.Get (Item => MenuSelection);

        -- these statements are executed if command is valid
```

```
            -- otherwise, control passes to exception handler
            Screen.MoveCursor (Row => 17, Column => 20);
            Ada.Text_IO.Put ("Thank you for correct input.");
            EXIT;       -- valid command; go process it

         EXCEPTION      -- invalid command

            WHEN Ada.Text_IO.Data_Error =>
               Screen.MoveCursor (Row => 17, Column => 20);
               Screen.Beep;
               Ada.Text_IO.Put
                 (Item => "Invalid command; please re-enter");
               Ada.Text_IO.Skip_Line;
               Ada.Text_IO.New_Line;
               DELAY 2.0;

         END;           -- of exception handler block
      END LOOP;

      -- We come here if command was valid
      Screen.MoveCursor (Row =>20, Column => 20);

      EXIT WHEN MenuSelection = Q;

      IF MenuSelection = A THEN
        Ada.Text_IO.Put
          (Item => "Here we would do the average. ");
        Ada.Text_IO.New_Line;
      ELSIF MenuSelection = M THEN
        Ada.Text_IO.Put
          (Item => "Here we would do the median.  ");
        Ada.Text_IO.New_Line;
      ELSIF MenuSelection = P THEN
        Ada.Text_IO.Put
          (Item => "Here we would do the plotting.");
        Ada.Text_IO.New_Line;
      END IF;

      DELAY 2.0;

   END LOOP;

   Ada.Text_IO.Put (Item => "Goodbye for today.  ");
   Ada.Text_IO.New_Line;

END Menu_Handler;
```

Sample Run

```
Main Command Menu

A - Compute Average
M - Compute Median
P - Plot the data
Q - Quit the program


Enter a command, please > m
```

```
Thank you for correct input.

Here we would do the median.
```

Testing
The sample run shows the state of the screen after input of a correct command.

PROGRAM
STYLE

> ### Stubs in Programs
>
> The command interpreter of Program 7.6 contains several *stubs*, which are just statements indicating that a part of the program is still under development. A well-designed stub is legal code so that the program can be compiled and tested even without being fully developed.
>
> It is quite common to use stubs in program development; it is a useful technique in writing and testing programs incrementally. Such incremental development allows you to run a partially completed program so that you are not overwhelmed by having to develop the program all at once.

EXERCISES FOR SECTION 7.4

Self-Check

1. How would Program 7.7 be different if Ada did not provide exception handling?

2. In programming, what are stubs and how are they used?

Programming

1. Modify Program 7.7 so that the user is given three attempts (instead of an unlimited number of attempts) to enter a given value correctly.

7.5 System Structures: Writing Procedures

In this book you have been using calls to procedures provided by the standard input/output libraries and another package called screen. In this section you will learn how to write procedures.

Writing Procedures

Procedures and functions are both subprograms, but they differ in two important ways. First, a procedure is called with a procedure call statement, as in

```
Ada.Float_Text_IO.Put (Item => X, Fore => 3, Aft => 2, Exp => 0);
```

whereas a function is used in an expression, for example,

```
Temp := UsefulFunctions.Minimum (Value1 => X, Value2 => Y) + 45;
```

A function returns a result so that the result can be used in an expression; a procedure does not return a result.

The second important difference is that a function is permitted to have parameters that are passed only *into* the function, whereas a procedure is allowed to have parameters of three kinds, or *modes:*

- *Mode IN parameters*—These are passed *into* the procedure and, inside the procedure, are treated as constants and may not be changed (e.g., they may not appear on the left side of an assignment statement).

- *Mode OUT parameters*—These are computed in the procedure and passed *out* to the caller.

- *Mode IN OUT parameters*—These are passed *into* the procedure, possibly *changed* by it, and passed back *out* again.

The determination of a particular parameter's mode is based on the direction of the data flow between the procedure and its calling programs. If the parameter is used to transmit data *to* the procedure, its mode should be IN; if the parameter receives data *from* the procedure, its mode should be OUT.

Mode IN parameters are similar to the parameters of a function and are used to transmit values that will not be changed by the procedure, only used by it. For example, the parameters to the various Put procedures provided by Ada.Text_IO are IN parameters, because the data and formatting values are transmitted from the caller to the procedure.

Mode OUT parameters are commonly used in input routines like the Get operations in Ada.Text_IO. It might seem strange that an *input* routine should have an OUT parameter, but the input routine receives a value from the terminal or a file and passes it *out* to the program that calls it. The caller receives the input value from the procedure.

Mode IN OUT parameters are used when a procedure will modify its parameters. An example follows.

■ Example 7.10

Here is a procedure specification for a procedure order, which orders the values in the two variables whose names are supplied to it as actual parameters, placing the smaller of the two values in x and the larger in y:

```
PROCEDURE Order (X: IN OUT Float; Y: IN OUT Float);
```

A procedure call statement

```
Order (X => Num1, Y => Num2);
```

is intended to order the values in the two floating-point variables Num1 and Num2. Suppose, for example, that Num1 is 3.0 and Num2 is –5.0. After the above call we want Num1 to be –5.0 and Num2 to be 3.0. Ordering pairs of values is a very common operation in programming, especially in sorting applications. Here is the body of procedure Order:

```
PROCEDURE Order (X: IN OUT Float; Y: IN OUT Float) IS
-- Pre: X and Y are assigned values
-- Post: X has the smaller value and Y has the larger value

  Temp: Float;

BEGIN

  IF X > Y THEN
    -- interchange the values of X and Y
    Temp := X;
    X := Y;
    Y := Temp;
  END IF;

END Order;
```

The variable Temp is a local variable of the procedure, necessary to carry out the interchange. Temp is created when the procedure is called; it is destroyed when the procedure returns to its caller. x and y must be IN OUT parameters because their values are changed by the procedure. The effect of calling procedure Order is shown in Program 7.8, which carries out a very simple sort of three numbers Num1, Num2, and Num3 by calling Order three times:

```
Order (X => Num1, Y => Num2);
Order (X => Num1, Y => Num3);
Order (X => Num2, Y => Num3);
```

Because each statement contains a different association of *actual parameters* with the *formal parameters* x and y, a different pair of variables is ordered each time the procedure is called. Figure 7.1 shows a structure chart for this program. ∎

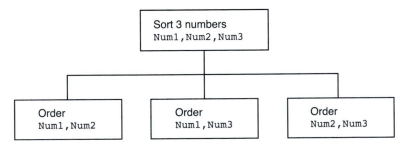

Figure 7.1. Structure Chart for Simple Sort Program

Program 7.8 A Very Simple Sorting Program

```ada
WITH Ada.Text_IO;
WITH Ada.Float_Text_IO;
PROCEDURE Sort_3_Numbers IS
-----------------------------------------------------------------
--| Reads three numbers and sorts them
--| so that they are in increasing order.
--| Author: M. B. Feldman, The George Washington University
--| Last Modified: August 1998
-----------------------------------------------------------------

  Num1 : Float;               -- a list of three cells
  Num2 : Float;
  Num3 : Float;

  -- procedure specification
  PROCEDURE Order (X: IN OUT Float; Y: IN OUT Float);

  -- procedure body
  PROCEDURE Order (X: IN OUT Float; Y: IN OUT Float) IS
  -- Pre:  X and Y are assigned values.
  -- Post: X has the smaller value and Y has the larger value.

    Temp : Float;             -- copy of number originally in X

  BEGIN  -- Order

    IF X > Y THEN
      -- interchange the values of X and Y
      Temp := X;             -- Store old X in Temp
      X := Y;                -- Store old Y in X
      Y := Temp;             -- Store old X in Y
    END IF;

  END Order;


BEGIN  -- Sort_3_Numbers

  Ada.Text_IO.Put (Item => "Enter 3 float values to be sorted>");
  Ada.Text_IO.New_Line;
  Ada.Float_Text_IO.Get(Item => Num1);
  Ada.Float_Text_IO.Get(Item => Num2);
  Ada.Float_Text_IO.Get(Item => Num3);

  -- Sort the numbers
  Order (X => Num1, Y => Num2);
  Order (X => Num1, Y => Num3);
  Order (X => Num2, Y => Num3);

  -- Display the results.
  Ada.Text_IO.Put(Item => "The three numbers in order are: ");
  Ada.Float_Text_IO.Put (Item => Num1, Fore => 5, Aft => 2, Exp => 0);
  Ada.Float_Text_IO.Put (Item => Num2, Fore => 5, Aft => 2, Exp => 0);
  Ada.Float_Text_IO.Put (Item => Num3, Fore => 5, Aft => 2, Exp => 0);
  Ada.Text_IO.New_Line;

END Sort_3_Numbers;
```

Sample Run

```
Enter 3 float values to be sorted>
23.7 -99.4 1.78
The three numbers in order are:    -99.40    1.78    23.70
```

To show the importance of the choice of parameter mode for procedure order, Figure 7.2 gives a compilation listing for a modification of the procedure, with the parameter modes changed from IN OUT to IN. Notice that the Ada compiler has marked as errors the lines in which attempts are made to change the IN parameters.

Figure 7.2   Procedure Order with Compilation Errors

```
 1. PROCEDURE Order (X: IN Float; Y: IN Float) IS
 2.
 3.    Temp : Float;   -- copy of number originally in X
 4.
 5. BEGIN   -- Order
 6.
 7.    IF X > Y THEN
 8.      -- interchange the values of X and Y
 9.      Temp := X;-- Store old X in Temp
10.      X := Y;   -- Store old Y in X
           |
        >>> assignment to "IN" mode parameter not allowed

11.      Y := Temp;-- Store old X in Y
           |
        >>> assignment to "IN" mode parameter not allowed

12.    END IF;
13.
14. END Order;
```

Rules for Parameter List Correspondence

1. The correspondence between actual and formal parameters is determined by their position in their respective parameter lists unless named association is used. These lists must be of the same size. The names of corresponding actual and formal parameters may be, and often are, different.

2. The type of each actual parameter must be compatible with the type of the corresponding formal parameter, that is, either of the same type or of a related subtype.

3. For mode OUT and IN OUT parameters, an actual parameter must be a variable. For mode IN parameters, an actual parameter may be a variable, constant, or expression.

The Procedure Data Area

Each time a procedure call statement is executed, an area of memory is allocated for storage of that procedure's data. Included in the procedure data area are storage cells for any formal parameters, local variables or constants that may be declared in the procedure. The procedure data area is always erased when the procedure terminates, and it is recreated (with all nonconstant cells undefined) when the procedure is called again.

Memory cells are allocated in the procedure data area for each formal parameter. These cells are used in different ways for parameters of the three modes:

- For a mode IN parameter, the value of the corresponding actual parameter is copied into this cell when the procedure is called. The compiler will not permit a statement within the procedure to change the value in this cell.

- For a mode OUT parameter, the local cell is initially undefined; the procedure computes a value and saves it in this memory cell. After the procedure completes its work, just before it returns to its calling program, the value in the local cell is copied back into the actual parameter in the calling program.

- For a mode IN OUT parameter, the behavior is a combination of the other two. The actual value is copied into the local cell when the procedure is called. Statements of the procedure may change the value in the local cell. Just before the procedure returns to its caller, the value in the local cell is copied back into the actual parameter in the calling program.

We note that these rules apply to parameters of *scalar* type, which are the only kind we have studied so far. Beginning in Chapter 9, you will see that parameter-passing behavior may differ somewhat for parameters of *structured* type. Also, parameters are passed to a function's data area, just as they are to a procedure's; recall, though, that function parameters in Ada can have mode IN parameters only; mode OUT and IN OUT parameters are not permitted.

Executing a Procedure with Parameters

In executing Program 7.8, suppose that the user enters 8.0, 10.0, and 6.0, for Num1, Num2, and Num3, respectively. Figure 7.3 shows the data areas for the main program and procedure Order immediately after the statement

```
Order(X => Num1, Y => Num2);
```

calls the procedure but before its first executable statement. This diagram shows the data values read into Num1, Num2, and Num3. The double-headed arrows symbolize the copying of main program variables Num1 and Num2 into formal parameters X and Y, respectively. It also shows that the local variable Temp is undefined initially.

The execution of the procedure is traced in Table 7.1. The actual and formal parameters are shown at the top of the table. Because the value of Num1 is less than that of Num2, the True alternative is skipped and the variable values are unchanged.

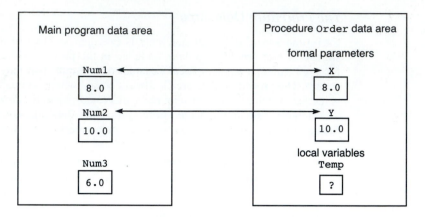

Figure 7.3 Parameter Correspondence for Order (Num1, Num2) (after Order has been called but before its statements have been executed)

Table 7.1 Trace of Procedure Execution for Order (Num1, Num2)

Statement in Order	Num1	X	Num2	Y	Temp	*Effect*
	8.0	8.0	10.0	10.0	?	
IF X > Y THEN						8.0 > 10.0 is false; do nothing
Just before procedure returns	8.0	8.0	10.0	10.0		Copy parameter values back to actuals

The parameter correspondence specified by the procedure call statement

```
Order (X => Num1, X => Num3);
```

is pictured in Fig. 7.4. This time parameter x corresponds to variable Num1 and parameter y corresponds to variable Num3, and the values are copied accordingly.

This second execution of the procedure is traced in Table 7.2. The actual and formal parameters are shown at the top of the table. The procedure execution switches the values stored in main program variables Num1 and Num3, as desired.

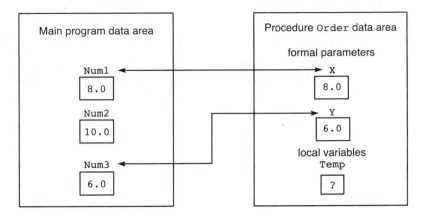

Figure 7.4 Parameter Correspondence for Order (Num1, Num3) (after Order has been called but before its statements have been executed)

Table 7.2 Trace of Procedure Execution for Order (Num1, Num3)

Statement in Order	Num1	X	Num2	Y	Temp	*Effect*
	8.0	8.0	6.0	8.0	?	
IF X > Y THEN						8.0 > 6.0 is true
Temp := X;					8.0	save old x in Temp;
X := Y;		6.0				save old y in x;
Y := Temp;				8.0	8.0	save Temp in y.
Just before procedure returns	6.0	6.0	8.0	8.0		copy parameter values back to actuals

Syntax Rules for Parameter Lists

This section presents the syntax rules for procedure declarations and procedure call statements with parameters. The displays that follow summarize these rules.

Procedure Specification (Procedure with Parameters)

Form:

```
PROCEDURE pname (formal-parameters);
```

Example:

```
PROCEDURE Double (X: IN Integer; Y: OUT Integer);
```

Interpretation:

The procedure *pname* is declared. The *formal parameters* are enclosed in parentheses and separated by semicolons.

SYNTAX
DISPLAY

Procedure Body (Procedure with Parameters)

Form:

```
PROCEDURE pname (formal-parameters) IS
  local declaration-section
BEGIN
  statement sequence
END pname;
```

Example:

```
PROCEDURE Double (X: IN Integer; Y: OUT Integer) IS
BEGIN
  Y := 2 * X;
END Double;
```

Interpretation:

The procedure *pname* is declared. The *formal parameters* are enclosed in parentheses and separated by semicolons. Any identifiers that are declared in the *declaration-section* are defined only during the execution of the procedure.

The *statement sequence* describes the data manipulation to be performed by the procedure. The formal parameter names are used in this description.

SYNTAX
DISPLAY

Procedure Call Statement (Procedure with Parameters)

Form:

```
pname (actual-parameters)
```

Example:

```
Double (Y => Q, X => P);
```

Interpretation:

The *actual-parameters* are enclosed in parentheses and separated by commas; each actual parameter is preceded by the name of the corresponding formal parameter. When procedure *pname* is called into execution, each actual parameter is associated with the corresponding formal parameter.

The formal parameter list determines the form of any actual parameter list that may be used to call the procedure. This form is determined during the translation of the program when the compiler processes the procedure declaration.

Later, when a procedure call statement is reached, the compiler checks the actual parameter list for consistency with the formal parameter list. An actual parameter list may be a list of expressions, variables, or constants separated by commas. The actual parameter list must satisfy the rules shown in the following box.

PROGRAM STYLE

Named Association in Actual Parameter Lists

In this book, *named association* is used to associate each formal parameter with an actual parameter (the two are separated by =>). This naming is optional in Ada; if it is used, the *order* of the actual parameters does not have to match the order of the formal parameters. The previous example `Double` shows this; the actual/formal pairs occur out of order.

It is, however, good practice to use named association and also to list the actual parameters in an order corresponding to the order of the formal parameters. In this way, no confusion arises for the reader of the program as to which actual parameter matches which formal parameter.

EXERCISES FOR SECTION 7.5

Self-Check

1. It is tempting to programmers to avoid the problem of deciding whether parameters should be IN, OUT, or IN OUT by simply assigning the same mode to all parameters. If you were to do this, which mode would you use? Why? Do you think choosing a single mode is a good idea?

7.6 System Structures: A Package for Robust Input

The ability to request and read numeric input robustly is a very common requirement in programs. It therefore makes sense to consider how we can package robust input so that it can just be used, instead of rewritten, for each program that needs to do it.

We will do this by analogy with the `Ada.Integer_Text_IO` and `Ada.Float_Text_IO` packages that we have been using all along in this book. These standard packages read input values by calls to procedures that are called `Get` (recall that because of overloading, these procedures can all have the same name provided that they have different parameter profiles). We shall write a package, `Robust_Input`, that provides the necessary robust `Get` operations for integer and floating-point values. `Robust_Input` is a good example of how we can encapsulate commonly needed operations in a package with an easy-to-understand interface.

Program 7.9 gives the package specification for `Robust_Input`. There are two procedures, both called `Get` (this is permitted because of the overloading principle). Here is the one for integer input:

```
PROCEDURE Get (Item : OUT Integer;
               MinVal : IN Integer
               MaxVal : IN Integer);
```

This procedure will read an integer value from the keyboard and return it to the caller in the actual parameter corresponding to `Item`. The other two parameters specify the range of acceptable input. The procedure `Get` for floating-point values is analogous.

Program 7.9 Specification for Package Robust_Input

```
PACKAGE Robust_Input IS
-----------------------------------------------------------------
--| Package for getting numeric input robustly.
--| Author: M. B. Feldman, The George Washington University
--| Last Modified: August 1998
-----------------------------------------------------------------

  PROCEDURE Get (Item : OUT Integer;
                 MinVal : IN Integer;
                 MaxVal : IN Integer);
  -- Gets an integer value in the range MinVal..MaxVal
  -- Pre: MinVal and MaxVal are defined
  -- Post: MinVal <= Item <= MaxVal


  PROCEDURE Get (Item : OUT Float;
                 MinVal : IN Float;
                 MaxVal : IN Float);
  -- Gets a float value in the range MinVal..MaxVal
  -- Pre: MinVal and MaxVal are defined
  -- Post: MinVal <= Item <= MaxVal

END Robust_Input;
```

Program 7.10 gives the package body for `Robust_Input`. It consists of the bodies of the two procedures promised in the procedure specification. Note that in the body for the integer `Get`, a subtype is declared corresponding to the range parameters and a corresponding variable:

```
SUBTYPE TempType IS Integer RANGE MinVal..MaxVal;
TempItem : TempType;        -- temporary copy of Item
```

The statement sequence of this procedure is very similar to that of Program 7.7; a loop is used to retain control if an exception is raised. The subtype `TempType` and variable `TempItem` are necessary so that if `Ada.Integer_Text_IO.Get` produces a value that is out of range, `Constraint_Error` will be raised.

Program 7.10 Body of Package Robust_Input

```
WITH Ada.Text_IO;
WITH Ada.Integer_Text_IO;
WITH Ada.Float_Text_IO;
PACKAGE BODY Robust_Input IS
-----------------------------------------------------------------
--| Body of package for robust numeric input handling
--| Author: M. B. Feldman, The George Washington University
--| Last Modified: August 1998
-----------------------------------------------------------------

   PROCEDURE Get (Item : OUT Integer;
                  MinVal : IN Integer;
                  MaxVal : IN Integer) IS

     SUBTYPE TempType IS Integer RANGE MinVal..MaxVal;
     TempItem : TempType;      -- temporary copy of Item

   BEGIN -- Get

     LOOP
       BEGIN       -- exception handler block
         Ada.Text_IO.Put(Item => "Enter an integer between ");
         Ada.Integer_Text_IO.Put(Item => MinVal, Width => 0);
         Ada.Text_IO.Put(Item => " and ");
         Ada.Integer_Text_IO.Put(Item => MaxVal, Width => 0);
         Ada.Text_IO.Put(Item => " > ");
         Ada.Integer_Text_IO.Get(Item => TempItem);
         Item := TempItem;
         EXIT;     -- valid data
       EXCEPTION   -- invalid data
         WHEN Constraint_Error =>
           Ada.Text_IO.Put (Item =>
             "Value is out of range. Please try again.");
           Ada.Text_IO.New_Line;
           Ada.Text_IO.Skip_Line;
         WHEN Ada.Text_IO.Data_Error =>
           Ada.Text_IO.Put (Item =>
             "Value is not an integer. Please try again.");
           Ada.Text_IO.New_Line;
           Ada.Text_IO.Skip_Line;
       END;         -- exception handler block
     END LOOP;

   END Get;

   PROCEDURE Get (Item : OUT Float;
                  MinVal : IN Float;
                  MaxVal : IN Float) IS

     SUBTYPE TempType IS Float RANGE MinVal..MaxVal;
     TempItem : TempType;      -- temporary copy of Item

   BEGIN -- Get

     LOOP
       BEGIN          -- exception handler block
         Ada.Text_IO.Put
           (Item => "Enter a floating-point value between ");
```

```
                    Ada.Float_Text_IO.Put
                       (Item => MinVal, Fore=> 1, Aft => 2, Exp => 0);
                    Ada.Text_IO.Put(Item => " and ");
                    Ada.Float_Text_IO.Put
                       (Item => MaxVal, Fore=> 1, Aft => 2, Exp => 0);
                    Ada.Text_IO.Put(Item => " > ");
                    Ada.Float_Text_IO.Get(Item => TempItem);
                    Item := TempItem;
                    EXIT;        -- valid data
                 EXCEPTION    -- invalid data
                    WHEN Constraint_Error =>
                       Ada.Text_IO.Put (Item =>
                          "Value is out of range. Please try again.");
                       Ada.Text_IO.New_Line;
                       Ada.Text_IO.Skip_Line;
                    WHEN Ada.Text_IO.Data_Error =>
                       Ada.Text_IO.Put (Item =>
                          "Value is not floating point. Please try again.");
                       Ada.Text_IO.New_Line;
                       Ada.Text_IO.Skip_Line;
                 END;             -- exception handler block
              END LOOP;

           END Get;

    END Robust_Input;
```

Finally, Program 7.11 serves to test the package operations. Two integer and two floating-point subtypes are declared; the `Robust_Input` operations are called. This is an example of a "test driver" program, whose purpose is just to test the operations provided by a package.

Program 7.11 A Program That Uses Robust_Input

```
WITH Robust_Input;
PROCEDURE Test_Robust_Input IS
----------------------------------------------------------------
--| Demonstrates Robust_Input package
--| Author: M. B. Feldman, The George Washington University
--| Last Modified: August 1998
----------------------------------------------------------------

   SUBTYPE SmallInt  IS Integer RANGE -10 ..10;
   SUBTYPE LargerInt IS Integer RANGE -100..100;
   SUBTYPE SmallFloat  IS Float RANGE -10.0 ..10.0;
   SUBTYPE LargerFloat IS Float RANGE -100.0..100.0;

   Small   : SmallInt;
   SmallF  : SmallFloat;
   Larger  : LargerInt;
   LargerF : LargerFloat;

BEGIN -- Test_Robust_Input

   Robust_Input.Get(Small,SmallInt'First,SmallInt'Last);
   Robust_Input.Get(Larger,LargerInt'First,LargerInt'Last);
   Robust_Input.Get(SmallF,SmallFloat'First,SmallFloat'Last);
   Robust_Input.Get(LargerF,LargerFloat'First,LargerFloat'Last);
```

```
END Test_Robust_Input;
```

Sample Run

```
Enter an integer between -10 and 10 > 11
Value is out of range. Please try again.
Enter an integer between -10 and 10 > -11
Value is out of range. Please try again.
Enter an integer between -10 and 10 > 10
Enter an integer between -100 and 100 > 101
Value is out of range. Please try again.
Enter an integer between -100 and 100 > 99
Enter a floating-point value between -10.00 and 10.00 > 10.001
Value is out of range. Please try again.
Enter a floating-point value between -10.00 and 10.00 > -12
Value is out of range. Please try again.
Enter a floating-point value between -10.00 and 10.00 > x
Value is not floating point. Please try again.
Enter a floating-point value between -10.00 and 10.00 > 0
Enter a floating-point value between -100.00 and 100.00 > 5.0003
```

EXERCISES FOR SECTION 7.6

Self-Check

1. The following procedure is like the ones in Program 7.10 but does not have a
    loop or special block for the exception handlers; the handlers are just written to
    go with the procedure's BEGIN and END. Is this correct as far as the Ada compil-
    er is concerned? If so, describe the difference in behavior from the original.

```
PROCEDURE Get (Item   : OUT Integer;
               MinVal : IN Integer;
               MaxVal : IN Integer) IS

   SUBTYPE TempType IS Integer RANGE MinVal..MaxVal;
   TempItem : TempType;        -- temporary copy of MinVal

BEGIN -- Get

   Ada.Text_IO.Put(Item => "Enter an integer between ");
   Ada.Integer_Text_IO.Put(Item => MinVal, Width => 0);
   Ada.Text_IO.Put(Item => " and ");
   Ada.Integer_Text_IO.Put(Item => MaxVal, Width => 0);
   Ada.Text_IO.Put(Item => " > ");
   Ada.Integer_Text_IO.Get(Item => TempItem);
   Item := TempItem;

EXCEPTION   -- invalid data
   WHEN Constraint_Error =>
      Ada.Text_IO.Put
         ("Value entered out of range. Try again.");
      Ada.Text_IO.New_Line;
      Ada.Text_IO.Skip_Line;
```

```
        WHEN Ada.Text_IO.Data_Error =>
          Ada.Text_IO.Put
            ("Value entered not an integer. Try again.");
          Ada.Text_IO.New_Line;
          Ada.Text_IO.Skip_Line;

    END Get;
```

Programming

1. Write a procedure similar to those in `Robust_Input` (Programs 7.9 and 7.10) that reads a month name robustly.

7.7   Tricks of the Trade: Testing with Exception Handling

Ada's exception handling provides a powerful tool for designing programs whose behavior is predictable even if its inputs are badly formed or out of range. If exception handling were not available, it would be the programmer's responsibility to validate all incoming data—for example, by checking its range with an `IF` statement. Indeed, Ada programs can certainly be written this way—with no use of exception handling—but the result would not take advantage of this built-in power.

Even if exception handling is used to advantage, however, the programmer still has several important responsibilities in this area:

- Analyze your program so that you know the places where exceptions may be raised, and be sure to place exception handlers in appropriate blocks in your program. This will ensure that exceptions are not unexpectedly passed back to the calling program or to the run-time system.

- When you test your program, be sure to test it with badly formed or out-of-range data so that your exception-handling flow is tested. When you are finished testing, you should be confident that you know exactly what your program will do under each set of input conditions. The test data that are supplied to Program 7.11 show an example of how this is done.

In summary, Ada's exception handling provides a useful way to take account of unusual circumstances in your program but does not relieve you of the responsibility to design and test carefully so that your program's behavior will always be predictable.

7.8   Tricks of the Trade: Programs That Never Halt

This chapter has covered general and `WHILE` loops in which the programmer must supply an explicit test for loop exit, and explicit statements that modify the conditions that the loop test will examine. What happens if you make an error in writing the exit test or loop-incrementation statements? There is a risk that the exit test will never become true, so the loop will never exit at all! The result will be a nonhalting program.

Sometimes it is easy to see that your program is in such an *infinite loop*. If the loop body displays some output in every cycle, you will see a continuous stream of output on the screen. On the other hand, if the loop body just does a computation and no output is displayed until after loop exit, the program will appear to have "hung," with nothing apparently happening. In either case it is up to you to interrupt the program from the keyboard. This kind of external interrupt is not part of the programming language, but rather a function of the operating system. In most systems, pressing control-c will interrupt the program, but this is not always the case. If you are on a single-user computer, sometimes you have no alternative but to reboot it or even switch it off altogether.

We are discussing this topic here and not as a common error, because a nonhalting program is not always an incorrect one. Programs that never halt are actually quite common in embedded systems. For example, an automatic teller machine has a program in it that starts when power is switched on and stops only when power is switched off. There is probably no halting code in the program itself. A nonhalting program is undesirable only if you did not intend to write it!

7.9 Tricks of the Trade: Common Programming Errors

Beginners sometimes confuse IF and loop statements because both statements contain a condition. Make sure that you use an IF statement to implement a decision step and a loop statement to implement a conditional loop. Remember to terminate each control structure with an END IF or END LOOP. The compiler will detect a syntax error if an END IF or END LOOP is missing.

Be careful when using tests for equality and inequality to control the repetition of a WHILE or general loop. The following loop is intended to process all transactions for a bank account while the balance is positive:

```
LOOP
   EXIT WHEN Balance = 0.0
   Update (Balance);
END LOOP;
```

If the bank balance goes from a positive to a negative amount without being exactly 0.0, the loop will not terminate (an infinite loop). The following loop would be safer:

```
LOOP
   EXIT WHEN Balance <= 0.0
   Update (Balance);
END LOOP;
```

Verify that the loop exit condition for a loop will eventually become true. If you use a sentinel-controlled loop, remember to provide a prompt that tells the program user what value to enter as the sentinel. Make sure that the sentinel value cannot be entered as a normal data item.

Keep in mind that exception handlers have to be associated with BEGIN-END blocks, and remember that once a program transfers to an exception handler, control does not automatically return to the statement that caused the exception. If you need to return to that statement (as in the robust input loop), you need to use a LOOP-END LOOP structure to do so.

7.10 Continuing Saga: A Child Package for the Spider

Let's pay another visit to the spider. You've seen so far how to command the spider to move around and draw shapes on the screen. Now that you know how to write procedures, let's consider how to add our own commands to the set of commands the spider can obey. Look again at the specification, Program 2.1. Specifically, we note the absence of two useful commands:

- Left (the spider can already turn right) and

- Step(HowMany: Positive), that is, step forward a given number of steps, not just a single step.

Suppose we were just writing a spider program. How could we get the effect of the Left command? There are several ways, as we show in these code fragments. First, we can turn left by turning right:

```
Spider.Right;
Spider.Right;
Spider.Right;
```

This works, but it is not very realistic—would *you* turn left that way? Another approach is to ask in which direction the spider is facing and then tell it to face in another direction:

```
IF Spider.IsFacing = North THEN
   Spider.Face(WhichWay => West);
ELSIF Spider.IsFacing = East THEN
   Spider.Face(WhichWay => North);
ELSIF Spider.IsFacing = South THEN
   Spider.Face(WhichWay => East);
ELSE -- Spider must be facing West
   Spider.Face(WhichWay => South);
END IF;
```

This will work, but we have to be very careful in writing it that all the directions are covered and that the Face command has the right parameter. We note that Spider.Directions is an enumeration type,

```
TYPE Directions IS (North, East, South, West);
```

and that a left turn can be implemented very easily as the predecessor of the current direction. We've seen a similar problem before, in Program 5.1, in which given a representation of today, we needed to find yesterday and tomorrow. We must be a bit careful in taking the predecessor: If the current direction is North, just taking the predecessor will fail on Constraint_Error because the enumeration doesn't "wrap around." The statement that we need is, in fact,

```
IF Spider.IsFacing = Spider.North THEN
   Spider.Face(Spider.West);
ELSE
   Spider.Face(Spider.Directions'Pred(Spider.IsFacing));
END IF;
```

or, to write it in more general terms (in case some day the directions are given in French),

```
IF Spider.IsFacing = Spider.Directions'First THEN
  Spider.Face(Spider.Directions'Last);
ELSE
  Spider.Face(Spider.Directions'Pred(Spider.IsFacing));
END IF;
```

Implementing the new `Step` is much easier: It's just a counting loop with `Spider.Step` as the loop body.

Putting the New Commands in a Child Package

It is now time to implement the new commands as a set of procedures. Because these are commonly used commands, it is best to put them in a package. Since this new package is not just using the original spider package but is, in fact, closely related to it, we can define this relationship in an Ada *child package*.

We have seen child packages before; indeed, all the standard packages that we've used are children of Ada. The specification for our child package, `Spider.My_Stuff`, appears as Program 7.12 and just codes the procedure specifications that we've discussed here.

Program 7.12 Specification for Child Package Spider.My_Stuff

```
PACKAGE Spider.My_Stuff IS
------------------------------------------------------------
--| Additional Spider Commands; this is a child package.
--| Author: M. B. Feldman, The George Washington University
--| Last Modified: August 1998
------------------------------------------------------------

  PROCEDURE Left;
  -- Pre:  None
  -- Post: Spider turns 90 degrees to the left.

  PROCEDURE Step(HowMany: IN Positive);
  -- Pre:  None
  -- Post: Spider takes HowMany steps forward
  --    in the direction it is facing.
  -- Raises: Hit_the_Wall is if spider tries to step into a wall.

END Spider.My_Stuff;
```

The body of `Spider.My_Stuff` appears as Program 7.13. The procedure bodies incorporate the statements that we just discussed; note, however, that no qualifications are necessary on the various calls. That is, we can write `IsFacing` instead of `Spider.IsFacing`, and so on. This tells us that the body of the child package can automatically "see" everything in its parent package's specification. (It cannot see into its parent package's body, though.)

Program 7.13 Body of Child Package Spider.My_Stuff

```
PACKAGE BODY Spider.My_Stuff IS
-------------------------------------------------------------
--| Child Package Body for Additional Spider Commands
--| Author: M. B. Feldman, The George Washington University
--| Last Modified: August 1998
-------------------------------------------------------------

  PROCEDURE Left IS
  BEGIN
    IF IsFacing = Directions'First THEN
      Face(Directions'Last);
    ELSE
      Face(Directions'Pred(IsFacing));
    END IF;
  END Left;

  PROCEDURE Step(HowMany: IN Positive) IS
  BEGIN
    FOR Count IN 1..HowMany LOOP
      Step;
    END LOOP;
  END Step;

END Spider.My_Stuff;
```

SYNTAX
DISPLAY

Child Package

Syntactically, a child package is exactly like any other, except for its name, which is of the form `Parent.Child`. The parent package must exist already to permit compilation of the child package. Under normal circumstances, one is not permitted to compile new children of the package `Ada`, since this parent package is reserved for standard (language-defined) packages.

Writing Applications of the Spider Packages, Parent and Child

Program 7.14 shows how to use the packages `Spider` and `Spider.My_Stuff`. Note that because this program uses both packages, it must have context clauses (WITHs) for both. The spider draws a box, turning left at the corners instead of right. This program is simpler than Program 2.8 because we can take advantage of the multiple-step command in the child package. We omit the sample run because it is very similar to the output of the box programs of Section 2.4.

Program 7.14 The Spider Draws a Counterclockwise Box

```
WITH Spider;
WITH Spider.My_Stuff;
PROCEDURE Draw_Box_with_Loops_Left IS
-------------------------------------------------------------
--| Draw 4 x 4 box with spider, turning left as it goes
--| Author: M. B. Feldman, The George Washington University
```

```
--| Last Modified: August 1998
-------------------------------------------------------------

BEGIN -- Draw_Box_with_Loops_Left

  Spider.Start;

  FOR Side IN 1..4 LOOP
    Spider.My_Stuff.Step(HowMany => 5);
    Spider.My_Stuff.Left;
  END LOOP;

  Spider.Quit;

END Draw_Box_with_Loops_Left;
```

CHAPTER REVIEW

This chapter introduced the general LOOP and EXIT statements and the WHILE statement. These are used to implement loops whose repetition is controlled by a condition, especially when the exact number of repetitions required is not known before the loop begins. In designing a general or WHILE loop, we must consider both the loop control and loop processing operations that must be performed. Separate program statements are needed for initializing and updating variables that appear in the loop repetition condition.

One common technique for controlling the repetition of a loop is using a special sentinel value to indicate that all required data have been processed. In this case, an input variable must appear in the loop repetition condition. This variable is initialized when the first data value is read (priming read), and it is updated at the end of the loop when the next data value is read. Loop repetition terminates when the sentinel value is read.

Writing procedures is an important part of programming, and this technique was also introduced in this chapter. Finally, we considered exception handling in some detail, and a package providing robust numeric input operations was developed.

New Ada Constructs in Chapter 7

The new Ada statements introduced in this chapter are described in Table 7.3.

Table 7.3 Summary of New Ada Constructs

Construct	Effect

General loop statement

```
Sum := 0;
LOOP
   EXIT WHEN Sum > MaxSum;
   Ada.Text_IO.Put
      (Item=>"Next integer > ");
   Ada.Integer_Text_IO.Get
      (Item=>Next);
   Sum := Sum + Next;
END LOOP;
```

A series of data items is read; their sum is accumulated in Sum. This process stops when the accumulated sum exceeds MaxSum.

WHILE Statement

```
Sum := 0;
WHILE Sum <= MaxSum LOOP
   Ada.Text_IO.Put
      (Item=>"Next integer > ");
   Ada.Integer_Text_IO.Get
      (Item=>Next);
   Sum := Sum + Next;
END LOOP;
```

A series of data items is read; their sum is accumulated in Sum. This process stops when the accumulated sum exceeds MaxSum.

Procedure with Parameters

```
PROCEDURE A (X : IN Float;
   Op : IN Character;
   XTo3 : IN OUT Float) IS

BEGIN --A
   IF Op = '*' THEN
      XTo3 := X * X * X;
   ELSIF Op = '+' THEN
      XTo3 := X + X + X;
   ELSE
      Ada.Text_IO.Put
         (Item => "Invalid");
   END IF;
END A;
```

Procedure A has two IN parameters and one IN OUT parameter

If Op is '*', then the value returned is x * x * x; otherwise, if Op is '+', then the value returned is x + x + x; otherwise, an error message is displayed. A result is returned by assigning a new value to the actual parameter (a variable) that corresponds to parameter XTo3.

Procedure Call Statement

```
A (X=>5.5, Op=>'+', XTo3=>Y);
```

Calls procedure A. 5.5 is passed into x, '+' is passed into Op, and the value 16.5 is stored in Y.

Exception-Handler Block

```
BEGIN
   X := Y + Z;
   Y := A / G;
EXCEPTION
   WHEN Constraint_Error =>
      Ada.Text_IO.Put
         (Item=>"Out of Range");
END;
```

If Y + Z is out of range for X, "Out of Range" is displayed. If G is 0, A cannot be divided by G and "Out of Range" is displayed.
Control passes to the statement following END.

Quick-Check Exercises

1. A WHILE loop is called a _____ loop.

2. A WHILE loop is always used for counting. (True or false?)

3. The priming step for a WHILE loop is what kind of statement? When is it used?

4. The sentinel value is always the last value added to a sum being accumulated in a sentinel-controlled loop. (True or false?)

5. It is an error if a WHILE loop body never executes. (True or false?)

Answers to Quick-Check Exercises

1. Conditional

2. False

3. An input operation, used in a sentinel-controlled loop

4. False, the sentinel should not be processed.

5. False

Review Questions for Chapter 6

1. Define a sentinel value.

2. For a sentinel value to be used properly when reading in data, where should the input statements appear?

3. Write a program called sum to sum and display a collection of integer amounts entered at the standard input device until a sentinel value of −1 is entered. Use a WHILE statement.

4. Write a procedure called LetterGrade that has one input parameter called Grade and that will display the corresponding letter grade using a straight scale (90−100 is an A, 80−89 is a B, etc.).

5. Explain the difference between IN parameters, OUT parameters, and IN OUT parameters.

6. Explain the allocation of memory cells when a procedure is called.

7. Explain the purpose of a robust input loop.

8. Hand trace the program below given the following data:

    4.0, 2.0, 8.0, 4.0

    1.0, 4.0, 2.0, 1.0

    9.0, 3.0, 3.0, 1.0

-22.0, 10.0, 8.0, 2.0

```
WITH Ada.Text_IO;
WITH Ada.Float_Text_IO;
PROCEDURE Slope IS

   Sentinel CONSTANT Float := 0.0;
   Slope, y2, y1, x2, x1 : Float;

BEGIN -- Slope
   Ada.Text_IO.Put(Item => "Enter four real numbers > ");
   Ada.Text_IO.New_Line;
   Ada.Float_Text_IO.Get(Item => y2);
   Ada.Float_Text_IO.Get(Item => y1);
   Ada.Float_Text_IO.Get(Item => x2);
   Ada.Float_Text_IO.Get(Item => x1);
   Slope := (y2 - y1) / (x2 - x1);
   WHILE Slope /= Sentinel LOOP
      Ada.Text_IO.Put(Item => "Slope is ");
      Ada.Float_Text_IO.Put(Item => Slope, Fore=>1, Aft=>2,Exp=>0);
      Ada.Text_IO.New_Line;
      Ada.Text_IO.Put(Item => "Enter four real numbers > ");
      Ada.Text_IO.New_Line;
      Ada.Float_Text_IO.Get(Item => y2);
      Ada.Float_Text_IO.Get(Item => y1);
      Ada.Float_Text_IO.Get(Item => x2);
      Ada.Float_Text_IO.Get(Item => x1);
      Slope := (y2 - y1) / (x2 - x1);
   END LOOP;
END Slope;
```

Programming Projects

1. Write a program that will find the product of a collection of data values. Your program should terminate when a zero value is read.

2. Write a program to read in an integer *N* and compute $slow = 1 + 2 + 3 + ... + N$ (the sum of all integers from 1 to *N*). Then compute $Fast = (N \times (N + 1)) / 2$ and compare Fast and slow. Your program should print both Fast and slow and indicate whether or not they are equal. (You will need a loop to compute slow.) Which computation method is preferable?

3. Write a program to read a list of integer data items and find and print the index of the first and the last occurrences of the number 12. Your program should print index values of 0 if the number 12 is not found. The index is the sequence number of the data item 12. For example, if the eighth data item is the only 12, the index value 8 should be printed for the first and last occurrence.

4. Write a program to read in a collection of exam scores ranging in value from 1 to 100. Your program should count and display the number of outstanding scores (90–100), the number of satisfactory scores (60–89), and the number of unsatisfactory scores (1–59). Test your program on the following data:

   63 75 72 72 78 67 80 63 75 90 89 43 59 99 82 12 100

In addition, display each exam score and its category, and the average exam score for the collection.

5. Write a program to process weekly employee time cards for all employees of an organization. Each employee will have three data items indicating an identification number, the hourly wage rate, and the number of hours worked during a given week. Each employee is to be paid time and a half for all hours worked over 40. A tax amount of 3.625 percent of gross salary will be deducted. The program output should show the employee's number and net pay. Use `Robust_Input` and some local procedures.

6. In Program 7.7 the command interpreter will loop indefinitely, refusing to exit until the input is correct. It is not always desirable to give a user an unlimited number of attempts to enter correct input. For example, if the input loop is requesting a user identification code or password, repeated incorrect entries may indicate that the user is unauthorized and is trying to guess the authorization sequence. Modify Program 7.7 so that the user is given five attempts to enter a given command properly. At the end of five unsuccessful attempts, the program will terminate with an appropriate message.

7. Redesign the body of `Robust_Input` (Programs 7.10) so that the range of the input data is checked explicitly with an `IF` statement instead of including a handler for `Constraint_Error`. Could you eliminate exception handling altogether? (*Hint*: How would you deal with the case of an alphabetic character being entered instead of an integer?)

8. Suppose you own a soft-drink distributorship that sells Coke (ID number 1), Pepsi (ID number 2), Canada Dry (ID number 3), and Dr. Pepper (ID number 4) by the case. Develop a case study and a program to

   a. read in the case inventory for each brand for the start of the week;

   b. process all weekly sales and purchase records for each brand; and

   c. display the final inventory. Each transaction will consist of two data items. The first item will be the brand identification number (an integer). The second will be the amount purchased (a positive integer value) or the amount sold (a negative integer value). The weekly inventory for each brand (for the start of the week) will also consist of two items: the identification and initial inventory for that brand. For now, you may assume that you always have sufficient foresight to prevent depletion of your inventory for any brand. Use `Robust_Input` (Programs 7.9 and 7.10) to handle the interactive numerical input. (*Hint*: Your data entry should begin with eight values representing the case inventory. These should be followed by the transaction values.)

9. Modify your results from Project 8 so that the program is menu-driven. Modify the menu handler of Program 7.7 to handle these selections:

```
E       Enter inventory
P       Purchase soda
S       Sell soda
D       Display inventory
Q       Quit program
```

10. Modify your results from Project 9 so that the inventory is read from an external file instead of entered interactively. The program should also write the new inventory out to an external file before quitting. Make sure that the output file has the same format as the input file, so that each run of the program can use the inventory file generated by the previous run.

11. The square root of a number N can be approximated by repeated calculation using the formula

```
NG = .5(LG + (N / LG))
```

where NG stands for next guess and LG stands for last guess. Write a function that implements this process where the first parameter will be a positive float number, the second will be an initial guess of the square root, and the third will be the computed result.

The initial guess will be the starting value of LG. The procedure will compute a value for NG using the formula above. The difference between NG and LG is checked to see whether these two guesses are almost identical. If so, the procedure is exited and NG is the square root; otherwise, the new guess (NG) becomes the last guess (LG) and the process is repeated (i.e., another value is computed for NG, the difference is checked, etc.).

For this program the loop should be repeated until the difference is less than 0.005 (Delta). Use an initial guess of 1.0 and test the program for the numbers 4.0, 120.5, 88.0, 36.01, and 10000.0.

12. Add and test a command NECorner to Spider.My_Stuff (Programs 7.13 and 7.14) that causes the spider to move to the northeast corner of its room. Now add and test three more commands: SECorner, SWCorner, and NWCorner, which cause the spider to move to the other corners.

13. Develop and test a program to read a calendar date, in the familiar MMM DD YYYY form, robustly. Use an enumeration type for the month names. To get the day and year values, you can just use the Robust_Input.Get procedure. There is more to this than just getting the month, day, and year separately. The user could enter Feb 30 1998, for example. The month, day, and year are all valid individually, but the date is invalid. The program must therefore validate the entire date as well as its individual components. (*Hint:* Investigate the possibilities in Ada.Calendar. See the full specification in Figure 11.3.)

CHAPTER 8

Scalar Data Types; the CASE Statement

So far in our programming, we have used six predefined data types: `Integer`, `Natural`, `Positive`, `Float`, `Boolean`, and `Character`. In this chapter we take a closer look at these data types and discuss the various operations that can be performed on them. All the data types in this chapter are *scalar* data types; that is, only one value can be stored in a single variable. In Chapter 9 we will begin a study of *composite* data types, that is, data types that can be used to store multiple values in a single variable.

In Sections 8.2 and 8.3 we revisit some of the facilities in `Ada.Numerics`, showing how to plot a sine curve and generate random numbers.

Section 8.6 introduces one more control structure, namely, the `CASE` statement. This statement is a convenient alternative to the multiple-alternative `IF` structure in many programs.

Finally, Section 8.7 opens up the body of the spider package. By now you have learned enough material to understand this package in its entirety.

8.1   Data Structures: Numeric Data Types

The predefined data types `Integer`, `Natural`, `Positive`, and `Float` are used to represent numeric information. `Integer` variables are used to represent data that are inherently whole numbers; `Float` variables are used to represent numeric data that may have a fractional part. The subtypes `Natural` and `Positive` are used to represent integer values that cannot sensibly be negative; a `Natural` value is allowed to be zero; a `Positive` value is not.

Differences between Numeric Types

You may be wondering why it is necessary to have so many numeric types. Because a whole number is a special case of one with a fractional part (i.e., the fractional part is zero), the data type `Float` could, in theory, be used for all numerical values. There are two important reasons why, in practice, we do not do this.

First, it is always best to use the most appropriate type for representing the values in a program. This not only makes the program easier for the reader to understand but also makes it possible for the compiler to ensure that the values that are assigned to a variable are appropriate values and that the operations that are performed on them are appropriate operations.

Another reason for not using `Float` values exclusively is that on many computers, operations involving integers are faster and less storage space is needed to store integers. Also, operations with integers are always precise, whereas there may be some loss of accuracy when dealing with floating-point values.

These differences result from the way floating-point numbers and integers are represented internally in memory. All data are represented in memory as *binary sequences,* sequences of 0s and 1s. However, the binary sequence that is stored for the `Integer` value 13 is not the same as the binary sequence that is stored for the `Float` value 13.0. The actual internal representation that is used is computer-dependent, but it will normally have the format shown in Fig. 8.1. In some computers, floating-point format uses more bits than integer format.

As Fig. 8.1 shows, integers are represented by standard binary integer values. If you are familiar with the binary number system, you know that, for example, the integer 13 is represented as the binary number 01101.

Floating-point format is analogous to scientific notation. The storage area occupied by a floating-point number is divided into two parts: the *mantissa* and the *exponent*. The mantissa is a binary fraction between 0.5 and 1.0 (–0.5 and –1.0 for a negative number). The exponent is a power of 2. The mantissa and exponent are chosen so that the formula

$$\textit{floating-point-number} = \textit{mantissa} \times 2^{\textit{exponent}}$$

is correct.

Besides the capability of storing fractions, floating-point format can represent a range of numbers considerably larger than can integer format. For example, Program 8.1 shows how to use attributes to find the characteristics of the integer and floating-point types provided by your Ada compiler.

Figure 8.1   Integer and Floating–Point Formats

Program 8.1 Retrieving Some Characteristics of Numeric Types

```
WITH Ada.Integer_Text_IO;
WITH Ada.Float_Text_IO;
WITH Ada.Text_IO;
PROCEDURE Attributes IS
-------------------------------------------------------------
--| Displays various integer and float attributes
--| Author: M. B. Feldman, The George Washington University
--| Last Modified: August 1998
-------------------------------------------------------------

BEGIN -- Attributes

   Ada.Text_IO.Put(Item => "Smallest integer is ");
   Ada.Integer_Text_IO.Put(Item => Integer'First);
   Ada.Text_IO.New_Line;
   Ada.Text_IO.Put(Item => "Largest integer is ");
   Ada.Integer_Text_IO.Put(Item => Integer'Last);
   Ada.Text_IO.New_Line;
   Ada.Text_IO.Put(Item => "Bits in an integer ");
   Ada.Integer_Text_IO.Put(Item => Integer'Size, Width => 1);
   Ada.Text_IO.New_Line;

   Ada.Text_IO.Put(Item => "Smallest float is ");
   Ada.Float_Text_IO.Put(Item => Float'First);
   Ada.Text_IO.New_Line;
   Ada.Text_IO.Put(Item => "Largest float is ");
   Ada.Float_Text_IO.Put(Item => Float'Last);
   Ada.Text_IO.New_Line;
   Ada.Text_IO.Put(Item => "Bits in a float ");
   Ada.Integer_Text_IO.Put(Item => Float'Size, Width => 1);
   Ada.Text_IO.New_Line;
   Ada.Text_IO.Put(Item => "Bits in a mantissa ");
   Ada.Integer_Text_IO.Put(Item => Float'Mantissa, Width => 1);
   Ada.Text_IO.New_Line;

END Attributes;
```

Sample Run

```
Smallest integer is -2147483648
Largest integer is  2147483647
Bits in an integer 32
Smallest float is -3.40282E+38
Largest float is  3.40282E+38
Bits in a float 32
Bits in a mantissa 21
```

The sample run, under GNAT on the Apple Macintosh, shows 32 bits for both `Integer` and `Float`; this is typical of current computers and compilers. Note that for the same number of bits (32), the range of floating-point numbers is approximately the huge range -10^{38} to $+10^{38}$, while the range of integers is only about $-10^9..+10^9$.

Numeric Literals

A constant value that appears in an expression is called a *literal*. In Ada a `Float` literal must have a decimal point in it and at least one digit on either side of the point. A literal may also have a decimal *scale factor*. For example, in the literal `2.998E+5` the scale factor is 10^5; in the literal `3E4` the scale factor is 10^4 (this is another way to write the value 30,000). It is also possible in Ada to use underscores—not commas—to separate groups of digits, so `30_000` is a valid `Integer` literal.

It is also possible to write literals in nondecimal number system bases. The decimal literal `29` can also be represented as `2#11101#` $(16 + 8 + 4 + 1)$ in base 2 (binary), `8#35#` $(24+5)$ in base 8 (octal), and `16#1D#` $(16 + 13)$ in base 16 (hexadecimal). Bases 2–16 are provided in Ada. The same base syntax is also legal for input tokens!

Type of an Expression

The type of an expression is determined by the type of its operands, and all operands of an expression must be the same type. For example, in the expression

```
X + 3.5
```

the variable `x` must be the same type (`Float`) as the literal 3.5; the expression is type `Float`. If `I` is an `Integer` variable, the expression

```
10 - I
```

is type `Integer`. If `I` is a `Float` variable, this expression is incorrect and will lead to a compilation error.

Numeric Operators

There are two kinds of arithmetic operators: *monadic* and *dyadic*. A monadic operator takes a single operand; a dyadic operator takes two operands. In Ada, the three monadic operators are +, −, and `ABS`. If `x` has an integer or float value, `+x` returns the same value (essentially it has no effect), `−x` negates the value (e.g., `−(−x)` = `x`), and `ABS x` returns the absolute value (e.g., `ABS 3 = ABS (-3) = 3`).

The four dyadic arithmetic operators +, −, *, and / can be used with integer or floating-point operands. The operands must both be `Float` (or subtypes of `Float`) or both be `Integer` (or subtypes of `Integer`). The division operator / deserves special consideration. If the operands of a division operation are floating-point values, the full result is kept and is also floating point. If the operands of division are integer values, the result is an integer equal to the truncated quotient of `M` divided by `N` (i.e., the integer part of the quotient). For example, if `M` is 7 and `N` is 2, the value of `M/N` is the truncated quotient of 7 divided by 2 or 3. On the other hand, if `x` is 7.0 and `y` is 2.0, then `x/y` is 3.5.

Ada provides one more dyadic operator, exponentiation, represented by `**`. An expression `x**M` means "raise x to the Mth power," that is, multiply x by itself M times. The left operand of `**` can be an integer or floating-point value; the right operand must be an integer value. Further, if the left operand is an integer, the right operand must not be negative because then the result would not be an integer value.

■ Example 8.1

Table 8.1 shows some examples of valid and invalid expressions involving the integer and floating-point division operators. For integer division, the result is always 0 when the magnitude of the first operand is less than the magnitude of the second operand. ■

Table 8.1   The Division Operators

3 / 15 = 0	3 / -15 = 0	3.0 / 15.0 = 0.2
15 / 3 = 5	15 / -3 = -5	15 / 3.0 is invalid (mixed types)
16 / 3 = 5	16 / -3 = -5	16.0 / 3.0 = 5.333...
17 / 3 = 5	-17 / 3 = -5	-17.0 / 3.0 = -5.667...
18 / 3 = 6	-18 / -3 = 6	18.0 / 3.0 = 6.0

The remainder operator, REM, can also be used with integer operands. The expression A REM B is equal to the remainder of A divided by B, if A and B are both positive. The following relations are satisfied by the REM operator:

```
A   REM (-B) =    A REM B
(-A) REM   B  = -(A REM B)
```

Table 8.2 shows some typical results for the integer division and REM operators.

Table 8.2   Results of Integer Division and REM Operators

A	B	A/B	A REM B	A	B	A/B	A REM B
10	5	2	0	-10	5	-2	0
11	5	2	1	-11	5	-2	-1
12	5	2	2	-12	5	-2	-2
13	5	2	3	-13	5	-2	-3
14	5	2	4	-14	5	-2	-4
10	-5	-2	0	-10	-5	2	0
11	-5	-2	1	-11	-5	2	-1
12	-5	-2	2	-12	-5	2	-2
13	-5	-2	3	-13	-5	2	-3
14	-5	-2	4	-14	-5	2	-4

ABS and REM are reserved words that represent operators and not function names. Therefore the expression ABS x is correct without parentheses. In the expression ABS(-3) the parentheses denote that the operator ABS is applied after the operator -.

■ Example 8.2

Program 8.2 displays each digit of its input value `Decimal` in reverse order (e.g., if `Decimal` is 738, the digits that are printed are 8, 3, 7). This is accomplished by displaying each remainder (0 through 9) of `Decimal` divided by 10; the integer quotient of `Decimal` divided by 10 becomes the new value of `Decimal`.   ■

Program 8.2 Displaying Digits in Reverse Order

```
WITH Ada.Text_IO;
WITH Robust_Input;
WITH Ada.Integer_Text_IO;
PROCEDURE Display_Digits IS
------------------------------------------------------------
--| Displays digits of a nonnegative integer in reverse order.
--| Author: M. B. Feldman, The George Washington University
--| Last Modified: August 1998
------------------------------------------------------------

   Base : CONSTANT Natural := 10;      -- number system base
   Decimal : Natural;                  -- original number
   Digit :    Natural;                 -- each digit

BEGIN  -- Display_Digits

   Robust_Input.Get (Item=>Decimal, MinVal=>0, MaxVal => Natural'Last);

   -- Find and display remainders of Decimal divided by 10
   Ada.Text_IO.Put(Item=> "The digits in reverse order are ");
   LOOP
     EXIT WHEN Decimal = 0;

     Digit := Decimal REM Base;     -- Get next remainder
     Ada.Integer_Text_IO.Put(Item => Digit, Width => 2);
     Decimal := Decimal / Base;     -- Get next quotient

   END LOOP;

   Ada.Text_IO.New_Line;

END Display_Digits;
```

Sample Run

```
Enter an integer between 0 and 2147483647 > 9752013
The digits in reverse order are  3 1 0 2 5 7 9
```

The input value `Decimal` is used as the loop control variable. Within the loop, the REM operator is used to assign to `Digit` the rightmost digit of `Decimal`, and integer division is used to assign the rest of the number to `Decimal`. The loop is exited when `Decimal` becomes 0. Trace this program as an exercise.

Multiple-Operator Expressions Revisited

Often, a problem requires writing an expression that contains more than one operator, as discussed in Section 3.8. In such a case, it is always wise to use parentheses to show exactly which operations apply to which operands. However, to make the result of an expression predictable even if the programmer omits the parentheses, programming languages, including Ada, provide rules for the order of execution of operations. These are called *precedence* and *associativity* rules. For example, in the expression A + B * C, is * performed before + or after? Is the expression X / Y * Z evaluated as (X / Y) * Z or X / (Y * Z)? Understanding these rules will help you to understand expressions better.

Some expressions with multiple operators are

```
1.8 * Celsius + 32.0
(Salary - 5000.00) * 0.20 + 1425.00
```

where `Celsius` and `Salary` are `Float` variables. In both of these cases the algebraic rule that multiplication is performed before addition is applicable. The use of parentheses in the second expression ensures that subtraction is done first. The following Ada rules for expression evaluation are based on standard algebraic rules.

Rules for Expression Evaluation

a. All parenthesized subexpressions are evaluated first. Nested parenthesized subexpressions are evaluated inside out, with the innermost subexpression evaluated first.

b. *Operator precedence*—Arithmetic operators in the same subexpression are evaluated in the following order:

`**`,ABS	first
`*`, `/`, REM	next
`+`, `−` (monadic)	next
`+`, `−` (dyadic)	last

c. *Left associative*—Operators in the same subexpression and at the same precedence level (such as + and −, or * and /) are evaluated left to right.

Note that in Ada, certain combinations of operators *require* parentheses. For example, A**B**C is a compilation error according to Ada syntax rules; you must write either A**(B**C) or (A**B)**C. ■

■ Example 8.3

The formula for the area of a circle

$$a = \pi \times r^2$$

can be written in Ada as

```
Area :=  Pi * Radius ** 2 ;
```

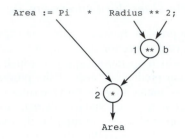

Figure 8.2   Evaluation Tree for Area := Pi * Radius ** 2

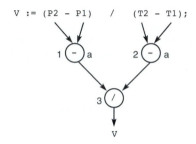

Figure 8.3   Evaluation Tree for Average Velocity

where `Pi` is the constant we have seen before. The *evaluation tree* for this formula is shown in Fig. 8.2. In this tree the arrows connect each operand with its operator. The order of operator evaluation is shown by the number to the left of each operator; the rules that apply are shown to the right.   ∎

∎ Example 8.4

The formula for the average velocity, *v*, of a particle traveling on a line between points p_1 and p_2 in time t_1 to t_2 is

$$v = \frac{P_2 - P_1}{T_2 - T_1}$$

This formula can be written in Ada as

```
V := (P2 - P1) / (T2 - T1);
```

It is evaluated as shown in Fig. 8.3.   ∎

∎ Example 8.5

Consider the expression

```
Z - (A + B / 2) + W * Y
```

which contains `Integer` variables only. The parenthesized subexpression (A + B / 2) is evaluated first (rule a) beginning with B / 2 (rule b). Once the value of B / 2 is determined, it can be added to A to obtain the value of (A + B / 2). Next the multiplication operation is performed (rule b) and the value for W * Y is determined. Then the value of (A + B / 2) is subtracted from Z (rule c), and finally this result is added to W * Y. Figure 8.4 gives an evaluation tree. ■

Writing Mathematical Formulas in Ada

There are two problem areas in writing a mathematical formula in Ada; one concerns multiplication and the other concerns division. In everyday algebra, multiplication is often implied in a mathematical formula by writing the two items to be multiplied next to each other, for example, $a = bc$. In Ada, however, the * operator must always be used to indicate multiplication, as in

```
A :=   B * C
```

The other difficulty arises in formulas involving division. We normally write the numerator and denominator on separate lines:

$$m = \frac{y - b}{x - a}$$

In Ada, all assignment statements must be written in a linear form; consequently, parentheses are often needed to enclose the numerator and the denominator and to clearly indicate the order of evaluation of the operators in the expression. The formula above would be written as

```
M :=  (Y - B) / (X - A);
```

■ Example 8.6

Table 8.3 illustrates how several mathematical formulas can be written in Ada. Assume that all variables except *j* are `Float`. ■

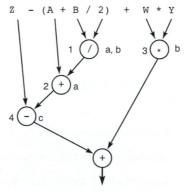

Figure 8.4   Evaluation Tree for Z − (A + B / 2) + W * Y

Table 8.3 Mathematical Formulas and Ada Expressions

	Mathematical Formula	Ada Expression
1.	$b^2 - 4ac$	B ** 2 - 4.0 * A * C
2.	$a + b - c$	A + B - C
3.	$\dfrac{a+b}{c+d}$	(A + B) / (C + D)
4.	$\dfrac{1}{1+a^2}$	1.0 / (1.0 + A ** 2)
5.	$a \times -(b + c)$	A * (-(B + C))
6.	x^j	X ** J

The points illustrated in Table 8.3 are summarized as follows:

- Always specify multiplication explicitly by using the operator * where needed (1).

- Use parentheses to control the order of operator evaluation (3, 4).

- Never write two arithmetic operators in succession; they must be separated by an operand or parentheses (5).

- Never mix operand types in an expression (1, 4; note the floating-point constants there). The only exception is the exponentiation operator **, whose right operand must be Integer even if its left operand is Float. Thus the exponentiation in (1), (4), and (6) is correct.

■ Example 8.7

This example shows the use of the monadic operator ABS, which computes the absolute value of its operand. If the value of x is –3.5, the statement

```
Y := 5.7 + ABS(X + 0.5)
```

assigns a value of 8.7 to the Float variable Y. The execution of this statement is traced as follows:

1. The expression argument (x + 0.5) is evaluated as –3.0.

2. The ABS operator returns the absolute value of its operand (3.0).

3. The sum of 5.7 and the function result (3.0) is assigned to Y (8.7).

Assignment Compatibility

An expression involving floating-point operands can be assigned to a variable only of type `Float` (or a subtype thereof). An expression involving integer operands can be assigned to a variable of type `Integer` (or a subtype thereof). As was discussed in Section 6.9, an attempt to assign a value of the wrong type to a variable will result in a compilation error; an attempt to assign an out-of-range value to a variable (e.g., a negative expression result to a `Positive` variable) will result in `Constraint_Error` being raised.

Conversions among Numeric Types

Ada does not allow mixing types in an expression (except in the case of exponentiation, as discussed above). However, Ada does provide a means for performing *explicit conversion* of a value of one type into a value of another. Specifically, Ada allows explicit conversion of float values to integer values and vice versa. This is done by using a function-call syntax, where the name of the new type is used as the function. The result of this "function call" is of the new type, unless the result is out of range, in which case `Constraint_Error` is raised as usual.

An integer value always has an exact equivalent in floating-point form, but a floating-point value does not always have an exact integer equivalent. Ada therefore *rounds* such a conversion to the nearest integer value, rounding away from zero if the float quantity is exactly halfway between two integers.

Suppose we have the following declarations:

```
F: Float;
N: NonNegFloat;
I: Integer;
P: Positive;
T: Natural;
```

Here are some conversions that can be done:

```
F := Float(I);          -- always possible
N := Float(P);          -- always possible
I := Integer(F);        -- always possible; result is rounded
I := Integer(N);        -- always possible, result is rounded

N := NonNegFloat(I);    -- raises Constraint_Error if I is negative
T := Natural(F);        -- raises Constraint_Error if F is negative

I := Integer(5.49);     -- result is 5
I := Integer(5.51);     -- result is 6
I := Integer(5.5);      -- result is 6

I := Integer(-5.3);     -- result is -5
I := Integer(-5.6);     -- result is -6
I := Integer(-5.5);     -- result is -6
```

Conversion between two subtypes of `Integer` or two subtypes of `Float` is always possible and will succeed if the result is in range. If `I` happens to be –57, for example, then

```
T := Natural(I);
```

will raise `Constraint_Error`.   ∎

∎ Example 8.8

In the very common problem of calculating the average of a set of floating-point numbers, the sum of the numbers—`SumOfItems`, say—is `Float` (or a subtype thereof) but the *number* of numbers—`NumOfItems`, say—is `Positive` (or a subtype thereof). It is a compilation error to write the expression

```
SumOfItems / NumOfItems
```

because the types do not agree; instead, we can write the expression

```
SumOfItems / Float(NumOfItems)
```

which divides the value of `SumOfItems` by the floating-point equivalent of `NumOfItems`. This expression is used in the assignment statement below to store the "average value" in `Average`:

```
Average := SumOfItems / Float(NumOfItems);
```
                                                                        ∎

PROGRAM STYLE

> ### Explicit Type Conversion
>
> We now know that Ada allows type conversion to be done explicitly so that floating-point and integer values can be combined in an expression. It is advisable to do this only when it is really necessary. Overuse of such conversions—in the most extreme case, to do all arithmetic in floating point—makes a program much more difficult to understand and also robs you of the assistance you get from Ada in ensuring that appropriate values and operations are used. An occasional explicit conversion is beneficial, but as in so many other things, moderation is a virtue.

Fixed-Point Types: The Duration Type

In addition to the integer and floating-point types that we use so much, Ada provides a third kind of numeric type: the *fixed-point type*. Type `Duration` is a fixed-point predefined type and is used by package `Ada.Calendar`. Whereas `Ada.Calendar.Time` represents *time of day* ("what time is it now?"), `Duration` represents *elapsed time* ("how long before the train leaves?"). A duration value of 1.0 represents the passage of exactly one second; a value of 0.1 represents the passage of a tenth of a second. Package `Ada.Calendar` provides a subtype of `Duration` called `Day_Duration` as follows:

```
SUBTYPE Day_Duration IS Duration RANGE 0.0 .. 86_400.0;
```

whose range is chosen to span exactly one day, because 86,400 is the number of seconds in 24 hours. `Ada.Calendar` also provides a function to retrieve, from a value of type `Ada.Calendar.Time`, the number of seconds since midnight on the given day:

```
FUNCTION Seconds (T: Time) RETURN Day_Duration;
```

This function goes along with the `Year`, `Month`, and `Day` functions that we used in Section 4.6. All you need to know about `Duration` and `Day_Duration` values is that they are much easier to work with if they are first converted to type `Float`.

■ Example 8.9

Program 8.3 displays the time of day in `hh:mm:ss` form, using European or military 24-hour time.

Program 8.3 Time of Day

```
WITH Ada.Text_IO;
WITH Ada.Integer_Text_IO;
WITH Ada.Calendar;
PROCEDURE Time_of_Day IS
-----------------------------------------------------------------
--| Displays the current time in hh:mm:ss form, 24-hour clock
--| Author: M. B. Feldman, The George Washington University
--| Last Modified: August 1998
-----------------------------------------------------------------

   CurrentTime      : Ada.Calendar.Time;
   SecsPastMidnight : Natural;
   MinsPastMidnight : Natural;
   Secs             : Natural;
   Mins             : Natural;
   Hrs              : Natural;

BEGIN -- Time_of_Day

   CurrentTime := Ada.Calendar.Clock;

   SecsPastMidnight := Natural(Ada.Calendar.Seconds(CurrentTime));
   MinsPastMidnight := SecsPastMidnight/60;
   Secs             := SecsPastMidnight REM 60;
   Mins             := MinsPastMidnight REM 60;
   Hrs              := MinsPastMidnight / 60;

   Ada.Text_IO.Put(Item => "The current time is ");
   Ada.Integer_Text_IO.Put (Item => Hrs, Width => 1);
   Ada.Text_IO.Put (Item => ':');

   IF Mins < 10 THEN
     Ada.Text_IO.Put (Item => '0');
   END IF;
   Ada.Integer_Text_IO.Put (Item => Mins, Width => 1);
   Ada.Text_IO.Put (Item => ':');

   IF Secs < 10 THEN
     Ada.Text_IO.Put (Item => '0');
```

```
        END IF;
        Ada.Integer_Text_IO.Put (Item => Secs, Width => 1);

END Time_of_Day;
```

Sample Run

```
The current time is 16:05:44
```

This program uses the package `Ada.Calendar` to find the time of day. Recall that `Ada.Calendar.Clock` returns a value of type `Ada.Calendar.Time`. The statement

```
CurrentTime := Ada.Calendar.Clock;
```

finds the value of current date/time; the function call

```
.. := Ada.Calendar.Seconds(CurrentTime);
```

returns the value of seconds since midnight as a `Duration` value. Since Ada does not provide many arithmetic operations to deal with `Duration` values, it is easier to convert this value to integer form. Declaring

```
SecsPastMidnight: DayInteger;
```

we can proceed to write

```
SecsPastMidnight := Natural(Ada.Calendar.Seconds(CurrentTime));
```

Note how we converted the `Duration` value. A fixed-point type can be fractional; since we are not interested in fractions of seconds, the rounding doesn't hurt us.

Finding the hours, minutes, and seconds in the current time is straightforward:

```
MinsPastMidnight := SecsPastMidnight / 60;
Secs             := SecsPastMidnight REM 60;
Mins             := MinsPastMidnight REM 60;
Hrs              := MinsPastMidnight / 60;
```

As an example of these calculations, suppose that the current time is 11:55:20 P.M. Knowing that an hour has 3600 seconds and a minute 60, we can easily calculate the value that `Ada.Calendar.Seconds` returns the number of seconds past midnight, as

$$(3600 \times 23) + (60 \times 55) + 20 = 82800 + 3300 + 20 = 86120$$

We now have to go back the other way, extracting hours, minutes, and seconds. The number of minutes past midnight is 86120/60, or 1435 (integer division!); the number of seconds is 86120 REM 60, or 20, and so on. ∎

Fixed-Point Types: Decimal Types

Because a floating-point representation system uses a fixed number of bits in its mantissa, and therefore provides a fixed maximum number of significant digits, it is only a rough approximation of the real numbers, and many values cannot be represented exactly.

We will discuss this problem further in Section 8.2. For now, consider that there are business applications, especially those using monetary quantities, in which exact representation is essential. Ada 95 has a solution for this. The Ada 95 standard contains, in addition to the base language, a number of *annexes,* or appendices. Most of the standard libraries we use in this book appear in Annex A, which all compiler developers are required to implement. Other annexes are optional. One optional annex is Annex F, Information Systems. This annex provides for *decimal types,* that is, fixed-point types whose machine representation of fractional decimal quantities is exact. We will not consider decimal types in depth in this book.

EXERCISES FOR SECTION 8.1

Self-Check

1. Suppose we have the following declarations:

   ```
   F: Float;
   N: NonNegFloat;
   I: Integer;
   T: Natural;
   ```

   and that F is –3.7, and I is –5. Describe the result of each of the following assignment statements:

   ```
   F := Float(I);
   I := Integer(F);
   I := Integer(N);

   N := NonNegFloat(I);
   T := Natural(F);

   I := Integer(6.2);
   I := Integer(100.88);
   I := Integer(9.5);
   ```

2. Some older Ada compilers used to use 16 bits for `Integer`, so `Integer'Last` was 32767. Suppose we called `Ada.Calendar.Clock` and converted the result to `Integer`. At what time of day would it make a difference whether `Integer'Last` is 32767 or something larger?

8.2 System Structures: More on Ada.Numerics; the USE Clause

As we saw in Section 5.6, Ada provides a standard library of elementary mathematical functions, called `Ada.Numerics.Elementary_Functions`. The full specification is given in Appendix E; Table 8.4 shows some of the functions that are provided:

Table 8.4 Some Functions in `Ada.Numerics.Elementary_Functions`

Function	Purpose
`Arctan(X)`	Returns the angle y in radians satisfying $X = \tan(y)$, where $-\pi/2 <= y <= \pi/2$
`Cos(X)`	Returns the cosine of angle X (in radians)
`Exp(X)`	Returns e^X where $e = 2.71828...$
`Log(X)`	Returns the natural logarithm of X for $X > 0.0$
`Sin(X)`	Returns the sine of angle X (in radians)
`Sqrt(X)`	Returns the square root of X for $X >= 0.0$

All functions take arguments of type `Float` (or a subtype thereof) and return a value of type `Float`. The arguments for `sin` and `Cos` must be expressed in radians, not degrees. The arguments for `Log` and `Sqrt` must be nonnegative; a negative argument will cause the exception `Ada.Numerics.Argument_Error` to be raised.

■ Example 8.10

The predefined exponentiation operator in Ada does not apply to floating-point exponents. This means that it is not possible to write x^y directly when x and y are type `Float`. Some, but not all, math packages provide such an exponentiation operation. However, from the study of logarithms we know that

$$\ln(x^y) = y \times \ln(x)$$

and

$$z = e^{\ln(z)}$$

where e is 2.71828... So we can derive that

$$x^y = e^{(y \times \ln(x))}$$

This formula can be implemented in Ada as

```
XToPowerY := Ada.Numerics.Elementary_Functions.Exp
   (y * Ada.Numerics.Elementary_Functions.Ln(x))
```
■

Writing Terse Code: The USE Clause

In this book we have been faithful to the convention that all calls to package-provided procedures and functions be prefixed with the name of the package, as in

```
Ada.Text_IO.New_Line;
Ada.Integer_Text_IO.Get (Item => Next_Num);
Y := Ada.Numerics.Elementary_Functions.Sqrt (X);
```

Prefixing the name of the package is called *qualification*. There are two main advantages to doing this. First, the reader can tell at a glance exactly which package has provided a given operation. Even in a class project a program may have "WITH-ed" several packages, including standard Ada packages, compiler-provided packages like `Ada.Numerics.Elementary_Functions`, and packages that you write yourself or that are supplied by your teacher. Qualification makes it easy to see, for debugging purposes or for enhancing your program at a later date, just which operations came from which packages. We will discuss the second advantage in a moment.

Ada provides a method for avoiding the need to qualify all references to package-provided operations. This is called the USE clause; it looks just like a context clause, and (in this book) is written at the top of a program unit along with the context clause. For example,

```
WITH Ada.Numerics.Elementary_Functions;
USE Ada.Numerics.Elementary_Functions;
```

might appear at the top of a program. If a USE clause is present, qualifying the package references is no longer required, although it is certainly still permitted. Given a USE clause, the two statements

```
Y := Ada.Numerics.Elementary_Functions.Sqrt(X);
Y := Sqrt(X);
```

are both permitted and have the same meaning. An advantage of the USE clause is that expressions can be somewhat more tersely written, but of course the information about just which package provided the `sqrt` operation is lost to the reader.

This direct information about which package provides which operation is also lost to the compiler if a USE clause is present. This means that the compiler, in translating an unqualified reference to a package operation, must search its tables for *all* the packages mentioned by USE clauses, and this is a somewhat time-consuming task for the compiler. This is the second advantage of qualified reference: It makes the compiler's job a bit easier.

PROGRAM STYLE

> ## The Proper Use of USE Clauses
>
> As we have seen, a USE clause has certain advantages, but qualification of all references also has advantages. Many experienced Ada professionals believe that the advantages of qualification outweigh those of USE clauses, and we tend to agree. Generally, we will avoid USE clauses, continuing in the style with which we began the book.
>
> There are certain circumstances, such as the math library, in which the names of the operations are so obvious, and relate so closely to everyday mathematics, that the more compact expression notation is desirable; in such cases we will write a USE clause. Some authors and developers also write USE clauses for the standard input/output libraries; we choose not to do this.
>
> As in the case of type conversions, moderation is a virtue in the use of USE clauses, and we advocate careful, case-by-case consideration of whether the USE or the qualified reference is more advantageous.

■ Example 8.11

The function sqrt (square root) can be used to compute the roots of a quadratic equation in x of the form

$$aX^2 + bX + c = 0$$

where a, b, and c are type Float. The two roots are expressed in algebraic form as

$$Root_1 = \frac{-b + \sqrt{b^2 - 4ac}}{2a}, Root_1 = \frac{-b - \sqrt{b^2 - 4ac}}{2a}$$

The Ada implementation is

```
IF Disc > 0.0 THEN
  Root1 := (-b + Sqrt(Disc)) / (2.0 * a);
  Root2 := (-b - Sqrt(Disc)) / (2.0 * a);
END IF;
```

where the variable Disc represents the *discriminant* $(b^2 - 4ac)$ of the equation. ■

■ Example 8.12

Program 8.4 draws a sine curve. It uses the Ada function sin, provided by the math package Ada.Numerics.Elementary_Functions, which returns the trigonometric sine of its parameter, an angle expressed in radians.

Program 8.4 Plotting a Sine Curve Using the Math Package

```
WITH Ada.Text_IO;
WITH Ada.Float_Text_IO;
WITH Ada.Numerics;
USE  Ada.Numerics;
WITH Ada.Numerics.Elementary_Functions;
USE  Ada.Numerics.Elementary_Functions;
PROCEDURE Sine_Curve IS
-----------------------------------------------------------------------
--| Plots a sine curve.
--| Author: M. B. Feldman, The George Washington University
--| Last Modified: August 1998
-----------------------------------------------------------------------

  RadPerDegree : CONSTANT Float    := Pi / 180.0; -- radians per degree
                                                  -- Pi in Ada.Numerics
  MinAngle :   CONSTANT Float    := 0.0;          -- smallest angle
  MaxAngle :   CONSTANT Float    := 360.0;        -- largest angle
  PlotWidth : CONSTANT Integer := 40;             -- width of plot
  PlotHeight :CONSTANT Integer := 20;             -- height of plot
  StepAngle : CONSTANT Float :=                   -- change in angle
    (MaxAngle-MinAngle) / Float(PlotHeight);
  Star :       CONSTANT Character := '*';         -- plotting symbol
  Blank:       CONSTANT Character := ' ';         -- to "pad" the '*'

  SUBTYPE ColumnRange IS Integer RANGE 0..PlotWidth;
```

```
Angle   :        Float;                          -- angle in degrees
Radian :        Float;                           -- angle in radians
Scale :         Float;                           -- scale factor
Pad :           ColumnRange;                      -- blank padding size

BEGIN  -- Sine_Curve

  Ada.Text_IO.Put(Item => "                       Sine curve plot");
  Ada.Text_IO.New_Line(2);
  Scale := Float(PlotWidth / 2);
  Angle := MinAngle;

  LOOP
    EXIT WHEN Angle > MaxAngle;

    Radian := Angle * RadPerDegree;
    Pad := Natural(Scale * (1.0 + Sin(Radian)));

    Ada.Float_Text_IO.Put
      (Item =>Angle, Fore => 4, Aft => 0, Exp => 0);

    -- Display blank padding
    Ada.Text_IO.Put(Item => Blank);
    FOR BlankCount IN 1 .. Pad LOOP
      Ada.Text_IO.Put(Item => Blank);
    END LOOP;

    Ada.Text_IO.Put(Item => Star);  -- Plot * in next column
    Ada.Float_Text_IO.Put
      (Item =>Sin(Radian), Fore => 6, Aft => 6, Exp => 0);
    Ada.Text_IO.New_Line;
    Angle := Angle + StepAngle;

  END LOOP;

END Sine_Curve;
```

Sample Run

```
                    Sine curve plot

    0.0                        *       0.000000
   18.0                        *          0.309017
   36.0                         *          0.587785
   54.0                          *          0.809017
   72.0                           *          0.951057
   90.0                            *          1.000000
  108.0                           *          0.951057
  126.0                          *          0.809017
  144.0                         *          0.587785
  162.0                        *          0.309017
  180.0                       *       -0.000000
  198.0                   *       -0.309017
  216.0            *       -0.587785
  234.0        *       -0.809017
  252.0    *       -0.951056
  270.0 *       -1.000000
  288.0    *       -0.951056
  306.0       *       -0.809017
  324.0          *       -0.587785
```

```
342.0              *      -0.309017
360.0                *      0.000000
```

Because degrees are a more intuitive way to represent angles, the outer FOR loop is executed for values of Angle equal to 0, 18, 36, ..., 360 degrees. This requires a conversion to radians to give sin a sensible parameter value. We need a conversion constant, RadPerDegree, which is the value π/180.0. We use the value of Pi provided by Ada.Numerics.

Now let us see how to plot the curve. For each Angle, the first of the assignment statements

```
Radian := Angle * RadPerDegree;
Pad := Natural(Scale * (1.0 + Sin(Radian)));
```

computes the number of radians corresponding to Angle. Then the variable Pad is assigned a value based on Sin(Radian). This value increases from 0 when Sin(Radian) is −1.0 to twice the value of Scale when Sin(Radian) is 1.0. Pad, the limit variable in the inner FOR loop, determines how many blanks precede each character * displayed on the screen. In this way the position of each * displayed represents the sine of the current angle. The angle is displayed at the left end of each line; the sine value is also displayed as a floating-point number after each *. ∎

PROGRAM
STYLE

Checking Boundary Values

Example 8.12 states that the value of Pad ranges from 0 to twice Scale as the sine value goes from −1.0 to 1.0. It is always a good idea to check the accuracy of these assumptions; this can usually be done by checking the boundaries of the range as shown below.

```
Sin(Radian) is -1.0, Pad is Natural(Scale * (1.0 + (-1.0)))
Pad is Natural(20.0 * 0.0)
Pad is Natural(0.0) = 0


Sin(Radian) is +1.0, Pad is Natural(Scale * (1.0 + 1.0))
Pad is Natural(20.0 * 2.0)
Pad is Natural(40.0) = 40
```

It is also a good idea to check the boundary values for all loop control variables to see that they make sense. For example, the outer loop control variable, Angle, has an initial value of MinAngle (0.0) and a final value of MaxAngle (360.0). The inner loop control variable, BlankCount, has an initial value of 1 and a final value of Pad.

**CASE
STUDY**

APPROXIMATING THE VALUE OF *e*

Problem Specification
Computing a value by approximation is a frequent problem in engineering and scientific computation. Here we give an example of this. The math constant *e* (whose value is the nonterminating decimal 2.71828...) is the base of the natural logarithms. This value is provided by Ada as `Ada.Numerics.E`. Suppose we did not have the numerics package; develop a program that will compute the value of *e*. The user will supply the desired number of decimal places of accuracy.

Analysis
There are a number of mathematical quantities that can be represented using a series approximation, where a series is represented by a summation of an infinite number of terms. For example, *e* can be determined by evaluating the expression

$$1 + 1/1! + 1/2! + 1/3! + ... + 1/n! + ...$$

where *n*! is the factorial of *n*, defined as follows:

$$0! = 1$$
$$n! = n \times (n-1)! \text{ (for } n >= 1)$$

Notice that this is just a different, equivalent, way of defining the same `Factorial` that we defined in Section 6.7. Instead of calculating the factorial for each term in the series, we shall use a different method as outlined below.

We can get an approximation to the value of *e* by summing the series for a finite value of *n*. Obviously, the larger the value of *n* we use, the more accurate will be the computed result. This expression can be represented by using *summation notation* as

$$\sum_{i=0}^{n} \frac{1}{i!}$$

where the first term is obtained by substituting 0 for *i* (1/0! is 1/1), the second term is obtained by substituting 1 for *i* (1/1!), etc.

To get an approximation to the desired accuracy, we use a *successive approximations* method. Suppose that the number of decimal places is given by `Places`. Start with a single term, then add terms until two successive approximations differ by no more than $1/10^{Places}$. This last quantity is usually called *epsilon,* which in mathematics is used to mean a very small interval. For example, if we desire six decimal places, epsilon is $0.000001 = 1/10^6$.

Design
A general loop can be used to implement the preceding formula easily. The data requirements and algorithm follow.

Data Requirements

Problem Inputs:
the number of decimal places (`Places : Positive`)

Problem Outputs:
the approximate value of *e* (e: Float)

Program Variables:
i, to produce the *i*th term (i: Natural)
the *i*th term of the series (ithTerm : Float)
the previously computed estimate of *e* (eOld: Float)
the desired accuracy (Epsilon: Float)

Design
The algorithm for this case study follows.

Algorithm
1. Prompt user for the value of Places

2. Set Epsilon to $1.0/10.0^{\text{Places}}$

3. Initialize e to 1.0

4. Initialize the *i*th term to 1.0

5. LOOP

    6. Save previous e in eOld

    7 Increment *i*

    8. Compute the *i*th term in the series

    9. Add the *i*th term to e

    10. EXIT WHEN e and eOld differ by no more than Epsilon

    END LOOP;

11. Display the approximate value of e

Implementation
Program 8.5 implements this algorithm.

Program 8.5 Estimating e by Successive Approximations

```
WITH Ada.Text_IO;
WITH Ada.Integer_Text_IO;
WITH Ada.Float_Text_IO;
PROCEDURE Estimate_e IS
----------------------------------------------------------------------------
--| Computes the value of e by a series approximation.
--| Number of places of accuracy is specified by user input.
--| Author: M. B. Feldman, The George Washington University
--| Last Modified: August 1998
----------------------------------------------------------------------------

   Places  : Positive;   -- Input - decimal places of accuracy
   e       : Float;      -- Output - the value being approximated
```

```
eOld      : Float;        -- the value being approximated
i         : Natural;      -- to produce the i-th term
ithTerm   : Float;        -- ith term in series
Epsilon   : Float;        -- desired difference between successive tries

BEGIN -- Estimate_e

  Ada.Text_IO.Put (Item => "Enter desired number of decimal places > ");
  Ada.Integer_Text_IO.Get(Item => Places);

  Epsilon := 1.0 / (10.0 ** Places);

  Ada.Text_IO.Put (Item => "Number of Terms  Approximate Value of e");
  Ada.Text_IO.New_Line;
  Ada.Text_IO.Put (Item => "---------------  ----------------------");
  Ada.Text_IO.New_Line;

  -- Compute each term and add it to the accumulating sum.
  e := 1.0;                   -- initial sum
  ithTerm := 1.0;             -- first term
  i := 0;
  LOOP -- and quit when desired accuracy is achieved

    eOld := e;                 -- save previous approximation

    i := i + 1;
    ithTerm := ithTerm / Float(i);

    e := e + ithTerm;     -- find new value

    Ada.Integer_Text_IO.Put(Item => i, Width => 9);
    Ada.Float_Text_IO.Put
      (Item => e, Fore => 10, Aft => Places+2, Exp => 0);
    Ada.Text_IO.New_Line;

    EXIT WHEN ABS (e - eOld) <= Epsilon;

  END LOOP;

END Estimate_e;
```

Sample Run

```
Enter desired number of decimal places > 10
Number of Terms  Approximate Value of e
---------------  ----------------------
        1        2.000000000000
        2        2.500000000000
        3        2.666666746140
        4        2.708333492279
        5        2.716666936874
        6        2.718055725098
        7        2.718254089355
        8        2.718278884888
        9        2.718281745911
       10        2.718281984329
       11        2.718281984329
```

Inside the loop, the statement

```
ithTerm := ithTerm / Float(i);
```

computes the value of the ith term in the series by dividing the previous term by the type `Float` representation of the variable `i`. The formula

$$(1 / (i - 1)!) / i = 1 / (i \times (i - 1)!) = 1 / i!$$

shows that this division does indeed produce the next term in the series. Because 0! is 1, `ithTerm` must be intialized to 1.0. The statement

```
e = e + ithTerm;
```

adds the new value of `ithTerm` to the sum being accumulated in `e`. Trace the execution of this loop to satisfy yourself that `ithTerm` takes on the values 1/1!, 1/2!, 1/3!, and so on, during successive loop iterations.

Numerical Inaccuracies

One of the problems in processing floating-point numbers is that there is sometimes an error in representing floating-point data. Just as there are certain numbers that cannot be represented exactly in the decimal number system (e.g., the fraction 1/3 is 0.333333...), so there are numbers that cannot be represented exactly in floating-point form. The *representational error* will depend on the number of binary digits (bits) that are used in the mantissa: The more bits there are, the smaller the error.

The number 0.1 is an example of a real number that has a representational error. The effect of a small error is often magnified through repeated computations. Therefore the result of adding 0.1 ten times is not exactly 1.0, so the following loop might fail to terminate on some computers:

```
Trial := 0.0;
LOOP
  EXIT WHEN Trial = 0.0;
  ...
  Trial := Trial + 0.1;
END LOOP;
```

If the loop repetition test is changed to `Trial < 1.0`, the loop may execute ten times on one computer and eleven times on another. For this reason, it is best to use integer values—which are always exact—whenever possible in loop repetition tests.

Other problems occur when manipulating very large and very small real numbers. In adding a large number and a small number, the larger number may "cancel out" the smaller number (a *cancellation error*). If x is much larger than y, x + y and x may have the same value (e.g., 1000.0 + 0.0001234 is equal to 1000.0 on some computers).

For this reason, you can sometimes obtain more accurate results by carefully selecting the order in which computations are performed. For example, in computing the value of `e` in the preceding case study, the terms of the series

$$1 + 1/1! + 1/2! + ... + 1/n!$$

were generated in left-to-right order and added to a sum being accumulated in e. When *n* is large, the value of $1/n!$ is very small, so the effect of adding a very small term to a sum that is larger than 2.0 may be lost. If the terms were generated and summed in right-to left-order instead, the computation result might be more accurate.

If two very small numbers are multiplied, the result may be too small to be represented accurately and will become zero. This is called *arithmetic underflow*. Similarly, if two very large numbers are multiplied, the result may be too large to be represented. This is called *arithmetic overflow* and, in Ada, causes Constraint_Error to be raised. Arithmetic underflow and overflow can also occur in processing very large and small integer values.

EXERCISES FOR SECTION 8.2

Self-Check

1. Rewrite the following mathematical expressions using Ada math functions.

   a. $\sqrt{(U + V)} \times W^2$

   b. $\log_n (X^Y)$

   c. $\sqrt{(X - Y)^2}$

   d. $|XY - W/Z|$

2. Evaluate the following expression:

   ```
   Sqrt(ABS(Integer(-15.8)))
   ```

Programming

1. We know that *e* is in fact provided by Ada as Ada.Numerics.E. Look up this value and check the results of Program 8.5 against it for several different numbers of decimal places of accuracy.

2. Write a function that computes, for float numbers *a* and *b*, $e^{a \times \ln(b)}$. Call this function with several different values of *a* and *b*, and display the results. Verify for yourself that the results are correct.

3. Using type conversion, write an Ada statement to round any float value x to the nearest two decimal places. (*Hint*: You have to multiply by 100.0 before rounding.)

8.3 System Structures: More on Ada.Numerics: Random Numbers

It is common in simulation and other applications to use *random* or *pseudorandom* numbers. A random number has a completely unpredictable value (e.g., the Seconds part of a call to Ada.Calendar.Clock) that depends on the precise time it was called. Running the program at a different time of day will most likely give a different number. A pseudorandom sequence, on the other hand, is a sequence of numbers within a given range. The numbers are produced by some mathematical formula such that the numbers appear to have been chosen randomly, but the sequence can be repeated the next time the program is run.

Pseudorandom Numbers in Ada.Numerics

It is beyond the scope of this book to discuss the mathematics of pseudorandom numbers, but it is useful to know that Ada provides random number generators in Ada.Numerics. Figure 8.5 shows part of the specification of a *discrete* random number generator.

Figure 8.5   Partial Specification for Ada.Numerics.Discrete_Random

```
GENERIC
  TYPE Result_Subtype IS (<>);
PACKAGE Ada.Numerics.Discrete_Random IS

  -- Basic facilities

  TYPE Generator IS LIMITED PRIVATE;

  FUNCTION Random (Gen : Generator) RETURN Result_Subtype;

  PROCEDURE Reset (Gen  : IN Generator);

PRIVATE

  ... -- as in Ada.Calendar.Time, we do not know the form of this

END Ada.Numerics.Discrete_Random;
```

This package is generic, like Ada.Text_IO.Enumeration_IO. Before it can be used, it must be instantiated or "tailored." You will learn more about writing and using generics in Chapter 12; for now, you need to know that the line

```
TYPE Result_Subtype IS (<>);
```

means that the package can be instantiated for any integer or enumeration type or subtype and that the resulting instance will produce pseudorandom values in the range of that type or subtype. For example, to produce a generator of random integers in the range 1 to 50, we would write

```
SUBTYPE Fifty IS Integer RANGE 1..50;
PACKAGE Random50 IS
```

```
NEW Ada.Numerics.Discrete_Random (Result_Subtype => Fifty);
```

The line

```
TYPE Generator IS LIMITED PRIVATE;
```

indicates a type whose values have no operations available. Contrast this with `Ada.Calendar.Time`, a merely `PRIVATE` type whose values we can assign and test for equality. It is beyond our scope to explain why this type is necessary; to use the random number generator, you must declare a variable of this type (say, `G`) and simply pass it to the operations `Random` and `Reset` each time you call them. For example, given a variable `Number` of type `Fifty`, the statement

```
Number := Random50.Random (Gen => G);
```

stores in `Number` a pseudorandom value in the range 1 to 50.

The random number generator produces a *sequence* of numbers. The generator starts itself with the same value (unknown to us) each time the program is run. Therefore, if we just make a sequence of calls as above, we will get the same sequence of values tomorrow as we did yesterday. The procedure `Reset` can be used to prevent this repetition of the sequence; for example, the call

```
Random50.Reset(Gen => G);
```

causes the generator to be set from the time-of-day clock, so each run of the program produces a different sequence.

■ Example 8.13

Program 8.6 generates a sequence of 120 pseudorandom integers in the range 1 to 50. The nested loops provide for displaying these numbers in rows of 12. Try compiling this program and running it several times. Do you get the same sequence each time? Try commenting out the line that resets the generator and then recompiling the program and running it several times. Do you get the same sequence each time now?   ■

Program 8.6 Generating a Pseudorandom Sequence

```
WITH Ada.Text_IO;
WITH Ada.Integer_Text_IO;
WITH Ada.Numerics.Discrete_Random;
PROCEDURE Random_Numbers IS
------------------------------------------------------------------
--| Generates 120 random integers in the range 1..50
--| Uses the random number generator from Ada.Numerics
--| Author: M. B. Feldman, The George Washington University
--| Last Modified: August 1998
------------------------------------------------------------------

  SUBTYPE RandomRange IS Positive RANGE 1..50;
  PACKAGE Random_50 IS NEW Ada.Numerics.Discrete_Random
    (Result_Subtype => RandomRange);
```

```
          G: Random_50.Generator;        -- LIMITED PRIVATE variable;
                                          -- we must keep passing it to Random,
                                          -- but can't use it.

       BEGIN -- Random_Numbers

          Random_50.Reset (Gen => G);   -- starts G from time of day clock

          FOR Row IN 1..10 LOOP          -- displays 10 rows of 12 numbers
             FOR Num IN 1..12 LOOP
                Ada.Integer_Text_IO.Put
                   (Item => Random_50.Random(Gen => G), Width => 4);
             END LOOP;
             Ada.Text_IO.New_Line;
          END LOOP;

       END Random_Numbers;
```

Sample Run

```
14   36   11    6   17    6   31   39   15   31   46   27
35   43   12   35   43   44   39    1   35   33   21   46
47   41   25   40   20   37   32   37    5   48   26   46
50   30    2   30   13   30   39   25   13   11    7   45
41   10    9   14   11    6   41   47   32   24   33   25
15   15   27   26   32   36    5   34   47   30   22   21
 8   14   29   17   41   34   17   25   46   15   38   33
43    5   31   13   23    1   30    3   46   14    8   10
 3   47    6   44   29   33   33   11   48   33    2    6
42   14   45    5   38   29   34   43   38    9   32   23
```

EXERCISES FOR SECTION 8.3

Programming

1. The discrete random number generator can be instantiated for enumeration types. Declare

   ```
   TYPE Coin IS (Tails, Heads);
   ```

   and write a program similar to Program 8.6 that generates and displays a large number of coin flips and counts the number of heads and tails. Instantiate `Ada.Text_IO.Enumeration_IO` to display the flips. Is the number of heads roughly the same as the number of tails? Do the heads and tails alternate, or are there runs of heads and runs of tails?

8.4 Data Structures: The Boolean Type

We introduced the `Boolean` data type in Chapter 5. We have used `Boolean` expressions (expressions that evaluate to `True` or `False`) to control loop repetition and to select one of the alternatives in an `IF` statement. Some examples of `Boolean` expressions are the following:

```
GrossPay > TaxBracket
Item /= Sentinel
TranType = 'C'
```

`Boolean` is one of Ada's predefined types; in fact, it is an enumeration type, defined as

```
TYPE Boolean IS (False, True);
```

The simplest `Boolean` expression is a `Boolean` variable or constant. A `Boolean` variable or constant can be set to either of the `Boolean` values, `False` or `True`. The statement

```
Debug : CONSTANT Boolean := True;
```

specifies that the `Boolean` constant `Debug` has the value `True`; the declarations

```
Switch : Boolean;
Flag : Boolean;
```

declare `Switch` and `Flag` to be `Boolean` variables, that is, variables that can be assigned only the values `True` and `False`.

Boolean Operators

A `Boolean` variable or constant is the simplest form of a `Boolean` expression (e.g., `Switch`). We have used the relational operators (=, <, >, etc.) with numeric data to form conditions or `Boolean` expressions (e.g., `Salary < Minsal`).

There are four `Boolean` operators: `AND`, `OR`, `XOR`, and `NOT`. These operators are used with operands that are `Boolean` expressions:

```
(Salary < MinSal) OR (NumDepend > 5)
(Temp > 90.0) AND (Humidity > 0.90)
Athlete AND (NOT Failing)
Married XOR CollegeGraduate
```

The first expression can be used to determine whether an employee pays income tax. It evaluates to `True` if either condition in parentheses is true. The second expression can be used to describe an unbearable summer day: temperature and humidity both above 90. The expression evaluates to `True` only when both conditions are true. The third expression has two `Boolean` variables (`Athlete` and `Failing`) as its operands. Any individual for whom this expression is true is eligible for intercollegiate sports. The fourth expression evaluates to `True` if the individual is *either* married *or* a college graduate but *not both*. It might be useful to a public opinion pollster.

The Boolean operators can be used with Boolean expressions only. The Boolean operators are summarized in Table 8.5, which shows that the AND operator yields a true result only when both its operands are true, that the OR operator yields a false result only when both its operands are false, and that the XOR operator yields a true result only when exactly one of its operands is true. The NOT operator has a single operand and yields the *logical complement*, or negation, of its operand.

Table 8.5 Boolean Operators

op1	op2	NOT op1	op1 AND op2	op1 OR op2	op1 XOR op2
false	false	true	false	false	false
false	true	true	false	true	true
true	false	false	false	true	true
true	true	false	true	true	false

Operator Precedence

The precedence of an operator determines its order of evaluation. Table 8.6 shows the precedence of all operators that can occur in an Ada expression.

Table 8.6 Operator Precedence

Operator	*Precedence*
**, NOT, ABS	highest (evaluated first)
*, /, REM	multiplying operators
+, -	monadic adding operators
+, -, &	dyadic adding operators (& is concatenation, coming in Chapter 10)
<, <=, =, /=, >=, >	relational operators
AND, OR, XOR	dyadic logical operators (evaluated last)

■ Example 8.14

The expression

```
X < Y + Z
```

involving the float variables X, Y, and Z is interpreted as

```
X < (Y + Z)
```

because + has higher precedence than <. The expression

```
X < Y OR Z < Y
```

is interpreted as

```
(X < Y) OR (Z < Y)
```

because OR has lower precedence than <. The expression

```
NOT Sunny OR Warm
```

is interpreted as

```
(NOT Sunny) OR Warm
```

because NOT has higher precedence than OR.

As is clear from Table 8.6 and Example 8.14, Ada has many operators, and their relative precedences are often difficult to remember. It is therefore advisable to keep expressions relatively simple and to use parentheses to make clear what you mean. ■

■ Example 8.15

Table 8.7 gives legal Boolean expressions if x, y, and z are Float and Flag is type Boolean. The value of each expression is shown in brackets assuming that x is 3.0, y is 4.0, z is 2.0, and Flag is True.

Table 8.7 Some Boolean Expressions

	Expression	*Value*
1.	(X > Z) AND (Y > Z)	True
2.	(X + Y / Z) <= 3.5	False
3.	(Y > X) XOR (Y > Z)	False
4.	NOT Flag	False
5.	(X = 1.0) OR (X = 3.0)	True
6.	(0.0 < X) AND (X < 3.5)	True
7.	(X <= Y) AND (Y <= Z)	False
8.	NOT Flag OR ((Y + Z) >= (X - Z))	True
9.	NOT (Flag OR ((Y + Z) >= (X - Z)))	False

Expression 1 gives the Ada form of the relationship "X and Y are greater than Z." It is often tempting to write this as

```
X AND Y > Z
```

However, this is an illegal Boolean expression because the float variable x cannot be an operand of the Boolean operator AND. Similarly, expression 5 shows the correct way to express the relationship "X is equal to 1.0 or to 3.0."

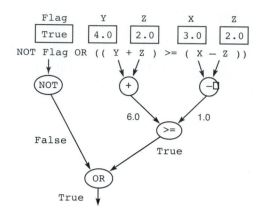

Figure 8.6 Evaluation Tree for a Boolean Expression

Expression 6 is the Ada form of the relationship $0.0 < X < 3.5$ (i.e., "X is in the range 0.0 to 3.5"). Similarly, expression 7 shows the Ada form of the relationship $X <= Y <= Z$, that is, "Y is in the range X to Z, inclusive."

Finally, expression 8 is evaluated in Fig. 8.6; the values given at the beginning of this example are shown above the expression. The expression in Fig. 8.6 is rewritten below with parentheses enclosing the term NOT Flag. Although these parentheses are not required, they do clarify the meaning of the expression, and we recommend their use:

```
(NOT Flag) OR ((Y + Z) >= (X - Z))
```
■

Short-Circuit Boolean Operators

When evaluating Boolean expressions, Ada evaluates both sides of the expression but in an order that is not defined by the language. This is not usually a problem; generally, we are interested only in the final result of the evaluation. Circumstances do arise, however, when it is desirable to evaluate the right side of an AND only if the left side is true, or the right side of an OR only if the left side is false. Ada provides for this purpose two additional operators: AND THEN and OR ELSE. These are called *short-circuit* operators: The evaluation of the right operand is skipped if evaluating the left operand determines the result of the expression.

■ Example 8.16

Both sides are always evaluated in the expression

```
NOT Flag OR ((Y + Z) /= (X - Z))
```

but in the expression

```
NOT Flag OR ELSE ((Y + Z) /= (X - Z))
```

if `Flag` is `True`, then `NOT Flag` is `False`, so the expression must evaluate to `True` regardless of the value of the parenthesized expression following `OR` (i.e., `True OR ...` must always be `True`). Consequently, the parenthesized expression following `OR ELSE` is not evaluated when `Flag` is `True`.

Short-circuit evaluation has important applications. Sometimes it is necessary to omit evaluation of the right operand, lest a run-time error arise. ∎

∎ Example 8.17

If x is 0, the expression

```
(X /= 0.0) AND (Y / X > 5.0)
```

is `False` because `(X /= 0.0)` is `False` and `False AND ...` must always be `False`. Not only is there no need to evaluate the subexpression `(Y / X > 5.0)` when x is zero, it is an error to do so: `Constraint_Error` would be raised because the divisor x is zero. An expression like this must be written

```
(X /= 0.0) AND THEN (Y / X > 5.0)
```

to prevent the right side from being evaluated whenever x is zero. ∎

Boolean Assignment Statements

We can write assignment statements that assign a `Boolean` value to a `Boolean` variable. The statement

```
Same := X = Y;
```

assigns `True` to the `Boolean` variable `Same` when x and y are equal; otherwise, `False` is assigned. The assignment above has the same effect as the `IF` statement

```
IF X = Y THEN
   Same := True;
ELSE
   Same := False;
END IF;
```

∎ Example 8.18

The following assignment statement assigns the value `True` to `Even` if and only if `N` is an even number:

```
Even := (N REM 2) = 0;
```

This statement assigns `True` to `Even` when the remainder of `N` divided by 2 is 0. (All even numbers are divisible by 2.) ∎

Using Boolean Variables as Program Flags

Boolean variables are sometimes used as *program flags* to signal whether or not a special event occurs in a program. The fact that such an event occurs is important to the future execution of the program. A Boolean variable used as a program flag is initialized to one of its two possible values (True or False) and reset to the other as soon as the event being monitored occurs.

■ Example 8.19

In Section 7.6 we developed, for package Robust_Input, a procedure for reading an integer value Item between the values MinVal and MaxVal. That procedure used Ada exception handling to determine whether the input value was in range. Suppose Ada did not have an exception-handling capability. (Some languages don't.) Here is a loop for reading input within range that has similar behavior but does not use exception handling:

```
-- Keep reading until a valid number is read.
Between := False;    -- Assume a valid number is not read
WHILE NOT Between LOOP

   Ada.Text_IO.Put(Item => "Enter an integer between ");
   Ada.Integer_Text_IO.Put(Item => MinVal, Width => 0);
   Ada.Text_IO.Put(Item => " and ");
   Ada.Integer_Text_IO.Put(Item => MaxVal, Width => 0);
   Ada.Text_IO.Put(Item => " > ");
   Ada.Integer_Text_IO.Get(Item => Item);
   Between := (Item >= MinVal) AND (Item <= MaxVal);

END LOOP;
```

This loop continues to read integer values until a value between its two input parameters, MinVal and MaxVal, is entered. The first data value within range is returned as the procedure result. The Boolean variable Between is used as a program flag to signal whether or not the event "data entry of an integer between MinVal and MaxVal" has occurred. The variable Between is initialized to False before the WHILE loop. Inside the WHILE loop, the assignment statement

```
Between := (Item >= MinVal) AND (Item <= MaxVal)
```

resets Between to True when a value between MinVal and MaxVal is read into N. The loop is repeated as long as Between is still False. Finally, we could write the last statement equally well as

```
Between := Item IN MinVal .. MaxVal;
```

■

Reading and Displaying Boolean Values

It is easy to read and display `Boolean` values in Ada because `Boolean` is an enumeration type. All that is necessary is to instantiate `Ada.Text_IO.Enumeration_IO` to handle the job. Because `Boolean` is a commonly used predefined type, this instance can be created once and for all in your Ada program library. Putting the lines

```
WITH Ada.Text_IO;
PACKAGE Boolean_IO IS NEW Ada.Text_IO.Enumeration_IO (Enum => Boolean);
```

in file and compiling that file are all it takes. You can then supply a context clause

```
WITH Boolean_IO;
```

to use the `Get` and `Put` operations for `Boolean` values.

■ Example 8.20

Two well-known laws of logic are called De Morgan's laws after their discoverer. These two laws state that for two `Boolean` variables x and y, for any combination of values of x and y,

```
NOT(X OR Y)  = (NOT X) AND (NOT Y)
NOT(X AND Y) = (NOT X) OR  (NOT Y)
```

Program 8.7 illustrates the validity of these laws, the use of a `Boolean` flag to control an input loop, and also the use of `Boolean_IO`. ■

Program 8.7 Demonstration of De Morgan's Laws and Boolean_IO

```
WITH Ada.Text_IO;
WITH Boolean_IO;
PROCEDURE Show_DeMorgan IS
-----------------------------------------------------------------
--| Demonstrates the validity of De Morgan's Laws,
--| and also Boolean_IO
--| a Boolean flag is also used to control the input loop
--| Author: M. B. Feldman, The George Washington University
--| Last Modified: August 1998
-----------------------------------------------------------------

  X         : Boolean;
  Y         : Boolean;
  MoreInput : Boolean;

BEGIN -- Show_DeMorgan

  MoreInput := True;
  WHILE MoreInput LOOP

    Ada.Text_IO.Put (Item => "Please enter True or False value for X >");
    Boolean_IO.Get (Item => X);
    Ada.Text_IO.Put (Item => "Please enter True or False value for Y >");
```

```
          Boolean_IO.Get (Item => Y);

          Ada.Text_IO.Put("NOT(X OR Y)         = ");
          Boolean_IO.Put(Item => NOT(X OR Y), Width => 1);
          Ada.Text_IO.New_Line;

          Ada.Text_IO.Put("(NOT X) AND (NOT Y) = ");
          Boolean_IO.Put(Item => (NOT X) AND (NOT Y), Width => 1);
          Ada.Text_IO.New_Line;
          Ada.Text_IO.New_Line;

          Ada.Text_IO.Put("NOT(X AND Y)        = ");
          Boolean_IO.Put(Item => NOT(X AND Y), Width => 1);
          Ada.Text_IO.New_Line;

          Ada.Text_IO.Put("(NOT X) OR (NOT Y)  = ");
          Boolean_IO.Put(Item => (NOT X) OR (NOT Y), Width => 1);
          Ada.Text_IO.New_Line;
          Ada.Text_IO.New_Line;

          Ada.Text_IO.Put
            (Item=>"Another combination (enter True or False)? ");
          Boolean_IO.Get (Item => MoreInput);

      END LOOP;

  END Show_DeMorgan;
```

Sample Run

```
Please enter True or False value for X > false
Please enter True or False value for Y > false
NOT(X OR Y)         = TRUE
(NOT X) AND (NOT Y) = TRUE

NOT(X AND Y)        = TRUE
(NOT X) OR (NOT Y)  = TRUE

Do you wish to try another combination (True/False)? true
Please enter True or False value for X > false
Please enter True or False value for Y > true
NOT(X OR Y)         = FALSE
(NOT X) AND (NOT Y) = FALSE

NOT(X AND Y)        = TRUE
(NOT X) OR (NOT Y)  = TRUE

Do you wish to try another combination (True/False)? false
```

The program prompts the user for values for Boolean variables x and y. These values must be entered as any enumeration values would, as True or False. (The case of the letters does not matter.) The sample run shows, by evaluating the four Boolean expressions above, that De Morgan's laws are true for the two cases shown. You can try the remaining two cases yourself.

This case study involves the manipulation of type Natural data. It also illustrates the use of Boolean variables as program flags.

**PROGRAM
STYLE**

Using a Global Boolean Constant for Debugging

We mentioned earlier that the programmer should plan for debugging by including diagnostic print statements in the original code. One way to prevent the diagnostic print statements from executing during production runs is to declare a global `Boolean` constant (say, `Debugging`) whose value is `True` during debugging and `False` during production runs. The declaration part of the main program will contain the constant declaration

```
Debugging : CONSTANT Boolean := True; -- turn diagnostics on
```

during debugging runs and the constant declaration

```
Debugging : CONSTANT Boolean := False; -- turn diagnostics off
```

during production runs.

The diagnostic print statements below will be executed only when `Debugging` is `True` (i.e., during debugging runs):

```
IF Debugging THEN
   Ada.Text_IO.Put (Item => "Procedure ProcessGoods entered");
   Ada.Text_IO.New_Line;
   Ada.Text_IO.Put (Item => "Input parameter Salary is ");
   Ada.Float_Text_IO.Put
     (Item => Salary, Fore => 6, Aft => 2, Exp => 0);
   Ada.Text_IO.New_Line;
END IF;
```

**CASE
STUDY**

TESTING WHETHER A NUMBER IS PRIME

Problem Specification
Write a program that tests a positive integer to determine whether or not it is a prime number. A *prime number* is an integer that has no divisors other than 1 and itself. Examples of prime numbers are the integers 2, 3, 5, 7, and 11.

Analysis
Our program will either display a message indicating that its data value is a prime number or display the smallest divisor of the number if it is not prime.

Data Requirements

Problem Inputs
the number to be tested for a prime number (`N : Positive`)

Problem Outputs
the smallest divisor if `N` is not prime (`FirstDiv : Positive`)

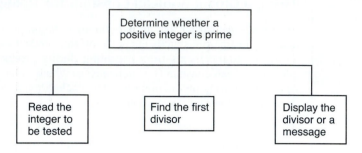

Figure 8.7 Structure Chart for Prime-Testing Program

Design

Initial Algorithm
1.   Read in the number to be tested for a prime number.

2.   Find the smallest divisor > 1 or determine that the number is prime.

3.   Display a message that the number is prime or print its smallest divisor.

We will use the `Boolean` variable `Prime` as a program flag to indicate the result of step 2 as described below. A structure chart is shown in Fig. 8.7.

Additional Program Variables
program flag that will be set to `True` if `N` is prime, `False` otherwise
(`Prime : Boolean`)

Step 3 Refinement
3.1. `IF` `N` is prime `THEN`

Display a message that `N` is prime

`ELSE`

Display the first divisor of `N`

`END IF;`

Let us consider step 2. Define a subtype `SmallPos` to include the positive numbers from 2 to `MaxN` (1000). Variable `FirstDiv` (the first divisor) is type `SmallPos`, and we need to compute the values of `FirstDiv` and `Prime` by determining whether or not `N` has any divisors other than 1 and itself.

If `N` is an *even* integer, it is divisible by 2. Therefore, 2 is the only even integer that can be prime, and 2 is the smallest divisor of all other even integers.

If `N` is an *odd* integer, its only possible divisors are the odd integers less than `N`. In fact, it can be proved that a number is prime if it is not divisible by any odd integer less than or equal to its square root. These considerations form the basis for the algorithm shown next.

Step 2 Refinement

2.1. `IF N = 2 THEN`

    2.2.   `N` is a prime number

`ELSIF N is even then`

    2.3.   2 is the smallest divisor and `N` is not prime

`ELSE`

    2.4.   Test each odd integer between 3 and `N` to see whether it is a divisor of `N`

`END IF;`

Step 2.4 must test each odd integer as a possible divisor of `N` until a divisor is found.

Step 2.4 Refinement

2.4.1. Assume that `N` is a prime number (i.e., set `Prime` to `True`)

2.4.2. Initialize `FirstDiv` to 3

2.4.3. `LOOP`

    `EXIT WHEN Prime is False OR FirstDiv >= ` $\sqrt{N}$ ` LOOP`

        2.4.4. `IF FirstDiv is a divisor of N THEN`

        2.4.5. Set `Prime` to `False` (`N` is not prime)

            `ELSE`

        2.4.6. Set `FirstDiv` to the next odd number

           `END IF;`

    `END LOOP;`

Implementation

The implementation and testing are left as an exercise. When you develop this program, be sure to test it with some relatively small numbers. It is very CPU-intensive, and testing it with large numbers on a time-sharing computer will be discourteous to other users!

EXERCISES FOR SECTION 8.4

Self-Check

1. Draw the evaluation tree for expression 9 of Example 8.15.

2. Evaluate the following statements.

    a. `Boolean'Pos(True)`
    b. `Boolean'Pred(True)`
    c. `Boolean'Succ(False)`
    d. `Boolean'Pos(True)` - `Boolean'Pos(False)`

3. Write the following `Boolean` assignment statements.

    a. Assign a value of `True` to `Between` if the value of `N` lies between `-K` and `+K`, inclusive; otherwise, assign a value of `False`.

    b. Assign a value of `True` to `UpCase` if `Ch` is an uppercase letter; otherwise, assign a value of `False`.

    c. Assign a value of `True` to `Divisor` if `M` is a divisor of `N`; otherwise, assign a value of `False`.

Programming

1. Write a function that returns a `Boolean` value indicating whether or not its first parameter is divisible by its second parameter.

8.5   Data Structures: The Character Type

Character variables are declared by using the data type `Character`. A character literal consists of a single printable character (letter, digit, punctuation mark, etc.) enclosed in single quotes. A character value may be assigned to a character variable or associated with a constant identifier as follows:

```
Star : CONSTANT Character := '*';
NextLetter : Character;
. . .
NextLetter := 'A';
```

The character variable `NextLetter` is assigned the character value `'A'` by the assignment statement above. A single character variable or literal can appear on the right-hand side of a character assignment statement. Character values can also be compared, read, and displayed. Each character has its own unique numeric code; the binary form of this code is stored in a memory cell that has a character value.

The Ada 95 standard (Reference Manual, Section A.3) uses the 256-character ISO 8859-1 (Latin-1) character set. This character set, an extension of the older 128-character ASCII set, includes the usual letters a–z and A–Z but also a number of additional characters to provide for the additional letters used in non-English languages. For example, French uses accented letters such as é and à; German has letters using the umlaut such as ü; the Scandinavian languages have dipthongs such as æ; and so forth. For the purposes of this book we use just the 26 uppercase and lowercase letters of English.

Figure 8.8, which is adapted from the Reference Manual, Annex A, Section A.1, gives the first 128 characters of the character set; these are the most commonly used ones. The position of each character is equal to that character's internal code. For example, `Character'Pos('A')` is 65.

Figure 8.8 The First 128 Characters of the Ada Character Type

```
TYPE Character IS

    (nul,  soh,  stx,  etx,      eot,  enq,  ack,  bel,     -- 0..7
     bs,   ht,   lf,   vt,       ff,   cr,   so,   si,      -- 8..15

     dle,  dc1,  dc2,  dc3,      dc4,  nak,  syn,  etb,     -- 16..23
     can,  em,   sub,  esc,      fs,   gs,   rs,   us,      -- 24..31

     ' ',  '!',  '"',  '#',      '$',  '%',  '&',  ''',     -- 32..39
     '(',  ')',  '*',  '+',      ',',  '-',  '.',  '/',     -- 40..47

     '0',  '1',  '2',  '3',      '4',  '5',  '6',  '7',     -- 48..55
     '8',  '9',  ':',  ';',      '<',  '=',  '>',  '?',     -- 56..63

     '@',  'A',  'B',  'C',      'D',  'E',  'F',  'G',     -- 64..71
     'H',  'I',  'J',  'K',      'L',  'M',  'N',  'O',     -- 72..79

     'P',  'Q',  'R',  'S',      'T',  'U',  'V',  'W',     -- 80..87
     'X',  'Y',  'Z',  '[',      '\',  ']',  '^',  '_',     -- 88..95

     '`',  'a',  'b',  'c',      'd',  'e',  'f',  'g',     -- 96..103
     'h',  'i',  'j',  'k',      'l',  'm',  'n',  'o',     -- 104..111

     'p',  'q',  'r',  's',      't',  'u',  'v',  'w',     -- 112..119
     'x',  'y',  'z',  '{',      '|',  '}',  '~',  del,     -- 120..127

     . . . );
```

The ordinary printable characters have codes from 32 (code for blank or space) to 126 (code for symbol ~); the additional European characters have codes from 160 to 255. The other codes represent nonprintable control characters. Sending a control character to an output device causes the device to perform a special operation such as returning the cursor to column 1, advancing the cursor to the next line, ringing a bell, and so on.

■ **Example 8.21**

Program 8.8 reads a sentence ending in a period and counts the number of blanks in the sentence. Each character that is entered after the prompting message is read into the variable `Next` and tested to see whether it is a blank.

The statement

```
Ada.Text_IO.Get (Item => Next);
```

appears once to prime the loop and a second time within the loop body and is used to read one character at a time from the data line because `Next` is type `Character`. The loop is exited when the last character that is read is a period. ■

Program 8.8 Counting the Number of Blanks in a Sentence

```
WITH Ada.Text_IO;
WITH Ada.Integer_Text_IO;
PROCEDURE Blank_Count IS
------------------------------------------------------------
--| Counts the number of blanks in a sentence.
--| Author: M. B. Feldman, The George Washington University
--| Last Modified: August 1998
------------------------------------------------------------

   Blank :     CONSTANT Character :=  ' ';
   Sentinel : CONSTANT Character :=  '.';  -- sentinel char

   Next  : Character;              -- next character in sentence
   Count : Natural;               -- number of blank characters

BEGIN  -- Blank_Count

   Count :=  0;                   -- Initialize Count
   Ada.Text_IO.Put (Item => "Enter a sentence ending with a period.");
   Ada.Text_IO.New_Line;

   -- Process each input character up to the period
   Ada.Text_IO.Get(Item => Next);       -- Priming read
   Ada.Text_IO.Put(Item => Next);

   LOOP
     EXIT WHEN Next = Sentinel;
     IF Next = Blank THEN
       Count := Count + 1;              -- Increment blank count
     END IF;
     Ada.Text_IO.Get(Item => Next); -- Get next char
     Ada.Text_IO.Put(Item => Next);
   END LOOP;

   Ada.Text_IO.New_Line;
   Ada.Text_IO.Put(Item => "The number of blanks is ");
   Ada.Integer_Text_IO.Put(Item => Count, Width => 1);
   Ada.Text_IO.New_Line;

END Blank_Count;
```

Sample Run

```
Enter a sentence ending with a period.
The  q uick    brown fox   jumped over th  e lazy dogs.
The  q uick    brown fox   jumped over th  e lazy dogs.
The number of blanks is 16
```

Using Relational Operators with Characters

In Program 8.8, the Boolean expressions

```
Next = Blank
Next = Sentinel
```

are used to determine whether two character variables have the same or different values. Order comparisons can also be performed on character variables by using the relational operators < , <= , > , and >= .

To understand the result of an order comparison, we must know something about the way characters are represented internally. These binary numbers are compared by the relational operators in the normal way. Looking at Figure 8.8, you can see some features of the "ordinary" part of the code:

- The digits are an increasing sequence of consecutive characters:

    `'0'<'1'<'2'<'3'<'4'<'5'<'6'<'7'<'8'<'9'`

- The uppercase letters are an increasing sequence of consecutive characters:

    `'A'<'B'<'C'< ... <'X'<'Y'<'Z'`

- The lowercase letters are an increasing sequence of consecutive characters:

    `'a'<'b'<'c'< ... <'x'<'y'<'z'`

- The digit characters precede the uppercase letters; the uppercase letters precede the lowercase letters:

    `'0' < '9' < 'A' < 'Z' < 'a' < 'z'`

■ Example 8.22

Let us write a function specified by

```
FUNCTION Capitalize (InChar : Character) RETURN Character;
```

If `InChar` is a lowercase letter, `Capitalize(InChar)` returns the corresponding uppercase letter; otherwise, `Capitalize(InChar)` just returns `InChar` unchanged. The function body makes use of the `Pos` (position) and `Val` (value) attribute functions as well as the fact that all the uppercase letters are "together" in the type `Character`, as are all the lowercase letters. If `InChar` is lowercase, its position relative to `'a'` is used to find the value of the corresponding uppercase letter. As an example, if `InChar` is `'g'`, its position relative to `'a'` is 6 (remember, the positions start with 0). The corresponding uppercase value is the value at the same position relative to `'A'`, namely, `'G'`.

```
FUNCTION Capitalize (InChar : Character) RETURN Character IS
   Temp : Character;
BEGIN
   IF InChar >= 'a' AND InChar <= 'z' THEN
     Temp := Character'Val(Character'Pos(Inchar)
        - Character'Pos('a') + Character'Pos('A'));
   ELSE
     Temp := InChar;
   END IF;
   RETURN Temp;
END Capitalize;
```

In the IF condition, instead of using explicit comparison operators, we can use Ada's IN operator to test for subtype membership.

```
FUNCTION Capitalize (InChar : Character) RETURN Character IS
  Temp : Character;
BEGIN
  IF InChar IN 'a' .. 'z' THEN
    Temp := Character'Val(Character'Pos(Inchar)
      - Character'Pos('a') + Character'Pos('A'));
  ELSE
    Temp := InChar;
  END IF;
  RETURN Temp;
END Capitalize;
```

As it happens, the package Ada.Characters.Handling (see below) provides a function To_Upper that provides this behavior; it is instructive to see here how you would write it if it were not in the standard library. ∎

Representing Control Characters

The character set includes a number of "nonprintable" characters that are used for controlling input and output devices. These control characters cannot be represented in programs in the usual way (i.e., by enclosing them in quotes). A control character can be specified in Ada using its position in the Character type (see Figure 8.8). For example, Character'Val(10) is the line feed character, and Character'Val(7) is the bell character. The statements

```
Ada.Text_IO.Put(Item => Character'Val(10));
Ada.Text_IO.Put(Item => Character'Val(7));
Ada.Text_IO.Put(Item => Character'Val(7));
```

will cause the output device to perform a line feed and then ring its bell twice.

Ada also has a more intuitive way of representing the control characters; the Character type gives them all names. The statements

```
Ada.Text_IO.Put(Item => Character.LF);
Ada.Text_IO.Put(Item => Character.Bel);
Ada.Text_IO.Put(Item => Character.Bel);
```

give the same effect as the statements above, but use the names of the characters instead of their numerical values. A program that uses the Ada.Characters.Latin_1 package must of course be preceded by a context clause

```
WITH Ada.Characters.Latin_1;
```

∎ Example 8.23

A *collating sequence* is a sequence of characters arranged in the order in which they appear in a character set. The Character type is really an enumeration type; each character's position in this type corresponds to its Latin-1 value. Given the declarations

```
MinPos : CONSTANT Positive := 32;
MaxPos : CONSTANT Positive := 90;
```

the loop

```
FOR NextPos IN MinPos .. MaxPos LOOP
  Ada.Text_IO.Put(Item => Character'Val(NextPos));
END LOOP;
```

displays part of the Latin-1 collating sequence. It lists the characters with values 32 through 90, inclusive. The first character—in position 32—is a blank, as follows:

```
 !"#$%&'()*+,-./0123456789:;<=>?@ABCDEFGHIJKLMNOPQRSTUVWXYZ
```

■ Example 8.24

In Section 4.7 we introduced the package `Screen` (Programs 4.8 and 4.9), which we have used several times since. In Section 4.7 we advised you not to worry about the details of the package body; now, having studied the `Character` type systematically, you are ready to understand those details. In Program 4.9 the procedure `Beep` contains a statement

```
Ada.Text_IO.Put (Item => Ada.Characters.Latin_1.BEL);
```

which sends the bell character to the terminal. Instead of displaying this character, the terminal will beep. Procedure `ClearScreen` contains the statements

```
Ada.Text_IO.Put (Item => Ada.Characters.Latin_1.ESC);
Ada.Text_IO.Put (Item => "[2J");
```

which send four characters to the terminal. According to standard American National Standards Institute (ANSI) terminal control commands, this sequence will cause the screen to be erased. Finally, the procedure `MoveCursor` contains these lines:

```
Ada.Text_IO.Put (Item => Ada.Characters.Latin_1.ESC);
Ada.Text_IO.Put (Item => '[');
Ada.Integer_Text_IO.Put (Item => Row, Width => 1);
Ada.Text_IO.Put (Item => ';');
Ada.Integer_Text_IO.Put (Item => Column, Width => 1);
Ada.Text_IO.Put (Item => 'f');
```

The sequence of characters sent to the terminal by these statements will cause the cursor to be moved to the given row/column position. Suppose `Row` is 15. Under these circumstances, sending the integer value `Row` does not cause the terminal to display the characters 15; rather, because these characters are sent in the middle of a control command (preceded by `Ada.Characters.Latin_1.ESC` and `'['`), the terminal obeys the command and moves the cursor to row 15. The command must end with `'f'`. It might seem strange to you, but that is what the ANSI terminal control standard specifies. As you saw in the examples using the screen package, these commands really do cause the terminal to carry out the desired actions. ■

The Package Ada.Characters.Handling

Ada provides a package Ada.Characters.Handling, which contains a set of functions to do useful operations on characters. Figure 8.9 gives a partial specification for this package; the full specification is in the Reference Manual, Annex A, Section A.3.

Figure 8.9   Partial Specification of Ada.Characters.Handling

```
PACKAGE Ada.Characters.Handling IS

  -- Character classification functions

  FUNCTION Is_Control        (Item : IN Character) RETURN Boolean;
  FUNCTION Is_Graphic        (Item : IN Character) RETURN Boolean;
  FUNCTION Is_Letter         (Item : IN Character) RETURN Boolean;
  FUNCTION Is_Lower          (Item : IN Character) RETURN Boolean;
  FUNCTION Is_Upper          (Item : IN Character) RETURN Boolean;
  FUNCTION Is_Digit          (Item : IN Character) RETURN Boolean;
  FUNCTION Is_Alphanumeric   (Item : IN Character) RETURN Boolean;
  FUNCTION Is_Special        (Item : IN Character) RETURN Boolean;

  -- Conversion functions for Character and String

  FUNCTION To_Lower (Item : IN Character) RETURN Character;
  FUNCTION To_Upper (Item : IN Character) RETURN Character;

  FUNCTION To_Lower (Item : IN String) RETURN String;
  FUNCTION To_Upper (Item : IN String) RETURN String;

  . . .

END Ada.Characters.Handling;
```

The functions Is_Letter, Is_Lower, Is_Upper, and Is_Digit return True if their input character is in the given category; Is_Alphanumeric returns True if the character is a letter or a digit; Is_Control returns True if the input character has position 0..31; Is_Graphic returns true if the input character has position 32..126.

To_Upper, like the function Capitalize in Example 8.23, returns an uppercase letter; To_Lower produces a lowercase letter. There are corresponding functions for strings: the second To_Upper converts all letters in the string to uppercase.

EXERCISES FOR SECTION 8.5

Self-Check

1.   Evaluate the following. Assume that the letters are consecutive characters.

   a. Character'Pos('D') - Character'Pos('A')
   b. Character'Pos('d') - Character'Pos('a')
   c. Character'Succ(Character'Pred('a'))
   d. Character'Val(Character'Pos('C'))

e. `Character'Val(Character'Pos('C') -`
   `Character'Pos('A')+Character'Pos('a'))`
f. `Character'Pos('7') - Character'Pos('6')`
g. `Character'Pos('9') - Character'Pos('0')`
h. `Character'Succ(Character'Succ(Character'Succ('d')))`
i. `Character'Val(Character'Pos('A') + 5)`

8.6   Control Structures: The CASE Statement

The CASE statement is used in Ada to select one of several alternatives. It is especially useful when the selection is based on the value of a single variable or a simple expression. The type of this variable or expression must be discrete; that is, it must be an integer or enumeration type or subtype.

■ Example 8.25

The CASE statement

```
CASE MomOrDad IS
   WHEN 'M' =>
      Ada.Text_IO.Put (Item => "Hello Mom - Happy Mother's Day");
   WHEN 'D' =>
      Ada.Text_IO.Put (Item => "Hello Dad - Happy Father's Day");
   WHEN OTHERS =>
      Ada.Text_IO.Put (Item => "invalid character ");
      Ada.Text_IO.Put (Item => MomOrDad);
END CASE;
```

has the same behavior as the following IF statement:

```
IF MomOrDad = 'M' THEN
   Ada.Text_IO.Put (Item => "Hello Mom - Happy Mother's Day");
ELSIF MomOrDad = 'D' THEN
   Ada.Text_IO.Put (Item => "Hello Dad - Happy Father's Day");
ELSE
   Ada.Text_IO.Put (Item => "invalid character ");
   Ada.Text_IO.Put (Item => MomOrDad);
END IF;
```

The message displayed by the CASE statement depends on the value of the CASE selector MomOrDad. If the CASE selector matches the first CASE choice, 'M', the first message is displayed. If the CASE selector matches the second CASE choice, 'D', the second message is displayed. Otherwise, the WHEN OTHERS clause is executed.

The WHEN OTHERS choice is necessary whenever the other choices of the CASE statement do not exhaust all possible values of the selector; if it were not present in this case (assuming MomOrDad is type Character), a compilation error would arise.   ■

■ Example 8.26

Given the enumeration type Days,

```
TYPE Days IS (Mon, Tue, Wed, Thu, Fri, Sat, Sun);
```

if Today is of type Days, the following CASE statement displays the full name of a day of the week:

```
CASE Today IS
  WHEN Mon =>
    Ada.Text_IO.Put (Item => "Monday");
  WHEN Tue =>
    Ada.Text_IO.Put (Item => "Tuesday");
  WHEN Wed =>
    Ada.Text_IO.Put (Item => "Wednesday");
  WHEN Thu =>
    Ada.Text_IO.Put (Item => "Thursday");
  WHEN Fri =>
    Ada.Text_IO.Put (Item => "Friday");
  WHEN Sat =>
    Ada.Text_IO.Put (Item => "Saturday");
  WHEN Sun =>
    Ada.Text_IO.Put (Item => "Sunday");
END CASE;
```

Seven different choices are shown in this program; the value of Today (type Day) is used to select one of these for execution. The seven possible values of Today are listed in CASE choices; the task for that CASE choices, a sequence of statements, follows the => ("arrow") symbol. Because all seven values of Today are listed in CASE choices, no WHEN OTHERS is necessary. After the appropriate Ada.Text_IO.Put statement is executed, the CASE statement and procedure are exited.

We might use such a statement instead of an Enumeration_IO instance because the enumeration Put displays a value either in uppercase or in lowercase, with no option to display a value with initial uppercase only. ■

■ Example 8.27

A CASE statement can be used in a student transcript program that computes a student's grade point average (GPA), as is the custom in most United States universities. For each case shown, the total points (Points) earned toward the GPA increase by an amount based on the letter grade (Grade); the total credits earned toward graduation (Grad-Credits) increase by 1 if the course is passed. The expression

```
Character'Pos('A') - Character'Pos(Grade) + 4
```

evaluates to 4 when the Grade is 'A', 3 when Grade is 'B', and so on. In the following CASE statement, note the two "short cuts" that we have used: the range 'A'..'D' and the sequence 'F' | 'I' | 'W', where the vertical bars mean "or."

```
CASE Grade IS
  WHEN 'A'..'D'  =>
    Points := Points+Character'Pos('A')-Character'Pos(Grade)+4;
```

```
      GradCredits := GradCredits + 1;
   WHEN 'P' =>
      GradCredits := GradCredits + 1;
   WHEN 'F'| 'I' | 'W' =>
      Ada.Text_IO.Put (Item => "No points to GPA or graduation");
      Ada.Text_IO.New_Line;
   WHEN OTHERS =>
      Ada.Text_IO.Put (Item => "Illegal grade ");
      Ada.Text_IO.Put (Item =>grade);
      Ada.Text_IO.New_Line;
END CASE;
```

A grade of A through D earns a variable number of points (4 for an A, 3 for a B, etc.) and one graduation credit; a grade of P earns one graduation credit; and a grade of F, I, or W earns neither graduation credits nor points. The WHEN OTHERS clause displays an error message if the program user enters a grade that is not listed in a CASE choice. ■

■ Example 8.28

Given an enumeration type

```
TYPE Months IS
      (Jan, Feb, Mar, Apr, May, Jun, Jul, Aug, Sep, Oct, Nov, Dec);
```

and variables ThisYear in the range 1901..2099 (the range of Year_Number in Ada.Calendar), DaysInMonth of type Positive, and ThisMonth of type Months, this CASE statement saves in DaysInMonth the number of days in ThisMonth:

```
CASE ThisMonth IS
   WHEN Feb =>
      IF (ThisYear MOD 4 = 0) AND
         ((ThisYear MOD 100 /= 0) OR (ThisYear MOD 400 = 0)) THEN
         NumberOfDays := 29;                -- leap year
      ELSE
         NumberOfDays := 28;
      END  IF;
   WHEN Apr | Jun | Sep | Nov =>
      NumberOfDays := 30;
   WHEN Jan | Mar | May | Jul | Aug | Oct | Dec =>
      NumberOfDays := 31;
END CASE;
```

All values of ThisMonth are covered in the choices; no WHEN OTHERS is needed. ■

SYNTAX
DISPLAY

CASE Statement

Form:

```
CASE selector IS
  WHEN choice₁ =>
    statement sequence₁
  WHEN choice₂ =>
    statement sequence₂
  ...
  WHEN choiceₙ  =>
    statement sequenceₙ
  WHEN OTHERS =>
    statement sequenceₒ
END CASE;
```

Example:

```
CASE N IS
  WHEN 1 | 2 =>
    Ada.Text_IO.Put (Item => "Buckle my shoe");
  WHEN 3 | 4 =>
    Ada.Text_IO.Put (Item => "Shut the door");
  WHEN 5 | 6 =>
    Ada.Text_IO.Put (Item => "Pick up sticks");
  WHEN OTHERS =>
    Ada.Text_IO.Put (Item => "Forget it...");
END CASE;
CASE Month IS
  WHEN December | January .. February =>
    Ada.Text_IO.Put (Item => "Winter months");
  WHEN March .. May =>
    Ada.Text_IO.Put (Item => "Spring months");
  WHEN June .. August =>
    Ada.Text_IO.Put (Item => "Summer months");
  WHEN September .. November =>
    Ada.Text_IO.Put (Item => "Autumn months");
ND CASE;
```

Interpretation:

The *selector* expression is evaluated and compared to each of the CASE *choices*. Each *choice* is a list of one or more possible values for the selector. Only one *statement sequence* will be executed; if the selector value is listed in $choice_i$, statement $sequence_i$ is executed. If the selector value is not listed in any $choice_i$, statement $sequence_o$ is executed. Control is next passed to the first statement following the END CASE.

Notes:

- A WHEN OTHERS alternative must be present if the other choices do not cover all possible values in the type of *selector*.
- Each possible *selector* value may appear in, at most, one $choice_i$.
- The type of each value listed in $choice_i$ must correspond to the type of the selector expression.
- Any discrete (integer or enumeration) data type is permitted as the selector type.

PROGRAM
STYLE

> ## Comparison of the IF and the CASE Statements
>
> You can use an IF-THEN-ELSIF statement, which is more general than the CASE statement, to implement a multiple-alternative decision. The CASE statement, however, is more readable and should be used whenever practical. It is also more reliable, because the compiler checks to ensure that all values of the selector variable are covered in the choices.

EXERCISES FOR SECTION 8.6

Self–Check

1. Write an IF statement that corresponds to the following CASE statement:

```
CASE X > Y IS
   WHEN True  =>
      Ada.Text_IO.Put(Item => "X greater");
   WHEN False =>
      Ada.Text_IO.Put(Item => "Y greater or equal");
END CASE;
```

Programming

1. Rewrite the CASE statement in Example 8.28 as an IF structure.

2. If type Color is defined as the enumeration type (Red, Green, Blue, Brown, Yellow), write a CASE statement that assigns a value to Eyes (type Color), given that the first two letters of the color name are stored in Letter1 and Letter2.

3. Write a CASE statement that displays a message indicating whether NextCh (type Character) is an operator symbol (+, -, *, =, <, >, /), a punctuation symbol (comma, semicolon, parenthesis, brace, bracket), or a digit. Your statement should display the category selected. Write the equivalent IF statement.

8.7 Continuing Saga: Inside the Spider Package

You have seen a number of examples of how to use the spider package, whose specification was given as Program 2.1. You have not yet looked inside the body of the package; you now have enough background to understand the body. This package uses much of the material that was discussed in this chapter, including numeric subtypes, Boolean expressions, CASE statements, and the screen package. Program 8.9 shows the body of the spider package. It quite long, but we can examine it in sections.

Program 8.9 Body of the Spider Package

```
WITH Ada.Text_IO;
WITH Ada.Numerics.Discrete_Random;
WITH Screen;
PACKAGE BODY Spider IS
-------------------------------------------------------------------
--| This package provides procedures to emulate "Spider"
--| commands. The spider can move around the screen drawing
--| simple patterns. This version is for a 24 x 80 screen.
--| Original Author: John Dalbey, Cal Poly San Luis Obispo, 1992
--| Adapted by: Michael B. Feldman, The George Washington University
--| Last Modified: August 1998
-------------------------------------------------------------------

   -- Spider's View of her Room - rows and cols both numbered 1..20
   SUBTYPE Rows IS Positive RANGE 1..20;
   SUBTYPE Cols IS Positive RANGE 1..20;
   RowsInRoom   : CONSTANT Positive := Rows'Last;
   ColsInRoom   : CONSTANT Positive := Cols'Last;

   -- Screen Description Constants: for 24 x 80 screen,
   -- 1 spider row = 1 screen row, 1 spider col = 2 screen cols
   RowLow       : CONSTANT Screen.Depth := 2;  -- room row bounds
   RowHigh      : CONSTANT Screen.Depth := RowLow + Rows'Last;
   ColLow       : CONSTANT Screen.Width := 21; -- lower column bound

   -- Spider Current State Information
   Spidersym    : CONSTANT character := '*';
   CurrentColumn: Cols;                    -- spider's position
   CurrentRow   : Rows;                    --    in the room.
   Heading      : Directions;              -- spider's direction
   Ink          : Colors;                  -- spider's color

   -- internal procedures and functions, not in specification
   -- and therefore not available to client program

   FUNCTION ColorSymbols (Color: Colors) RETURN Character IS
   -- Pre:  Color is defined
   -- Post: Returns the drawing character corresponding to Color
   BEGIN
     CASE Color IS
       WHEN Red   => RETURN 'R';
       WHEN Blue  => RETURN 'B';
       WHEN Green => RETURN 'G';
       WHEN Black => RETURN 'K';
       WHEN None  => RETURN '.';
     END CASE;
   END ColorSymbols;

   FUNCTION Compass (Direction: Directions) RETURN Character IS
   -- Pre:  Direction is defined
   -- Post: Returns drawing character corresponding to Direction
   BEGIN
     CASE Direction IS
```

```
      WHEN North => RETURN '^';
      WHEN East  => RETURN '>';
      WHEN South => RETURN 'v';
      WHEN West  => RETURN '<';
   END CASE;
END Compass;

PROCEDURE DrawSymbol (Which: Character) IS
-- Pre:  Which is defined
-- Post: Which appears in its proper position on the screen
BEGIN
   Screen.MoveCursor (Row => (RowLow - 1) + CurrentRow,
                      Column => (ColLow - 2) + (2 * CurrentColumn));
   Ada.Text_IO.Put (Item => Which);
   Ada.Text_IO.Flush;
END DrawSymbol;

PROCEDURE DrawStatus IS
-- Pre:  None
-- Post: Status Box appears on the screen
BEGIN
   Screen.MoveCursor (Row => 2, Column => 1);
   Ada.Text_IO.Put (" --- ");
   Screen.MoveCursor (Row => 3, Column => 1);
   Ada.Text_IO.Put ("|   |");
   Screen.MoveCursor (Row => 4, Column => 1);
   Ada.Text_IO.Put ("|   |");
   Screen.MoveCursor (Row => 5, Column => 1);
   Ada.Text_IO.Put (" --- ");
END DrawStatus;

PROCEDURE DrawRoom  IS
-- Pre:  None
-- Post: Room appears on the screen
BEGIN
   Screen.ClearScreen;
   Screen.MoveCursor (Row => 1, Column => 1);
   -- Top Bar
   Ada.Text_IO.Put ("                      ");
   Ada.Text_IO.Put (" ------------------------------------- ");
   Ada.Text_IO.New_Line;
   FOR I in 1..20 LOOP
   Ada.Text_IO.Put ("                      ");
   Ada.Text_IO.Put ("|. . . . . . . . . . . . . . . . . . .|");
   Ada.Text_IO.New_Line;
   END LOOP;
   Ada.Text_IO.Put ("                      ");
   Ada.Text_IO.Put (" ------------------------------------- ");
   DrawStatus;
END DrawRoom;

PROCEDURE ChangeColor (NewColor : Colors) IS
-- Pre:  NewColor is defined
-- Post: Ink is changed to NewColor and displayed in status box
BEGIN
   Ink := NewColor;
   Screen.MoveCursor ( Row => 4, Column => 3);
   Ada.Text_IO.Put (ColorSymbols(Ink));
END ChangeColor;
```

```
PROCEDURE ShowDirection IS
-- Pre:  None
-- Post: Heading is displayed in the status box
BEGIN
  Screen.MoveCursor(Row => 3,Column => 3);
  Ada.Text_IO.Put (Compass(Heading));
END ShowDirection;

PROCEDURE ShowSpider IS
-- Pre:  None
-- Post: The spider symbol appears in its current position
BEGIN
  DrawSymbol (SpiderSym);
END ShowSpider;

-- Random number generators; instances of the generic one
PACKAGE RandomSteps IS NEW Ada.Numerics.Discrete_Random
  (Result_Subtype => Steps);
GSteps: RandomSteps.Generator;

PACKAGE RandomColors IS NEW Ada.Numerics.Discrete_Random
  (Result_Subtype => Colors);
GColors : RandomColors.Generator;

PACKAGE RandomDirections IS NEW Ada.Numerics.Discrete_Random
  (Result_Subtype => Directions);
GDirections : RandomDirections.Generator;

-- These procedures are in the package specification
-- and implement the "official" spider commands

PROCEDURE Start IS
BEGIN
  DrawRoom;
  CurrentColumn := 10; -- these are in the spider's view
  CurrentRow := 11;
  Heading := North;
  ChangeColor(NewColor => Green);
  ShowSpider;
  ShowDirection;
  RandomSteps.Reset(Gen => GSteps);
  RandomColors.Reset(Gen => GColors);
  RandomDirections.Reset(Gen => GDirections);
END Start;

PROCEDURE TurnRight IS
BEGIN
  IF Heading = Directions'Last THEN
    Heading := Directions'First;
  ELSE
    Heading := Directions'Succ (Heading);
  END IF;
  ShowDirection;
END TurnRight;

PROCEDURE Face (WhichWay: IN Directions) IS
BEGIN
  Heading := WhichWay;
  ShowDirection;
END Face;
```

```
FUNCTION IsPainting RETURN Colors IS
BEGIN
  RETURN Ink;
END IsPainting;

FUNCTION IsFacing RETURN Directions IS
BEGIN
  RETURN Heading;
END IsFacing;

FUNCTION AtWall RETURN Boolean IS
BEGIN
  -- Check for out of bounds (in the spider's view)
  CASE Heading IS
    WHEN North =>
      RETURN CurrentRow <= Rows'First;
    WHEN East  =>
      RETURN CurrentColumn >= Cols'Last;
    WHEN South =>
      RETURN CurrentRow >= Rows'Last;
    WHEN West  =>
      RETURN CurrentColumn <= Cols'First;
  END CASE;
END AtWall;

FUNCTION RandomStep RETURN Steps IS
BEGIN
  RETURN RandomSteps.Random(GSteps);
END RandomStep;

FUNCTION RandomColor RETURN Colors IS
BEGIN
  RETURN RandomColors.Random(GColors);
END RandomColor;

FUNCTION RandomDirection RETURN Directions IS
BEGIN
  RETURN RandomDirections.Random(GDirections);
END RandomDirection;

PROCEDURE Step IS
BEGIN

  -- leave a track where spider is standing
  DrawSymbol (ColorSymbols (Ink) );

  -- If out of bounds raise exception.
  IF AtWall THEN
    Screen.Beep;
    RAISE Hit_the_Wall;
  END IF;

  -- change the spider's location
  CASE Heading IS
    WHEN North =>
      CurrentRow := CurrentRow - 1;
    WHEN East  =>
      CurrentColumn := CurrentColumn + 1;
    WHEN South =>
```

```
              CurrentRow := CurrentRow + 1;
         WHEN West   =>
              CurrentColumn := CurrentColumn - 1;
      END CASE;

      -- draw the spider in her new location
      DrawSymbol (SpiderSym);

      -- if debug mode, wait for user to press RETURN
      IF Debugging = On THEN
        Ada.Text_IO.Skip_Line;
      ELSE
        DELAY 0.2;
      END IF;
   END Step;

   PROCEDURE Quit IS
   -- Quit command.
   BEGIN
      Screen.MoveCursor(Row => 23,Column => 1);
   END Quit;

   DebugFlag    : Boolean := False;       -- Is single stepping on?

   PROCEDURE Debug (Setting: Switch) is
   -- Toggle debugging mode
   BEGIN
      IF Setting = ON THEN
        DebugFlag := true;
        Screen.MoveCursor (Row => 10,Column => 1);
        Ada.Text_IO.Put ("-- DEBUG ON -- ");
        Ada.Text_IO.New_Line;
        Ada.Text_IO.Put ("  Press Enter");
      ELSE
        DebugFlag := false;
        Screen.MoveCursor (Row => 10,Column => 1);
        Ada.Text_IO.Put ("               ");
        Ada.Text_IO.New_Line;
        Ada.Text_IO.Put ("               ");
      END IF;
   END Debug;

   FUNCTION Debugging RETURN Switch IS
   BEGIN
      IF DebugFlag THEN
        RETURN On;
      ELSE
        RETURN Off;
      END IF;
   END Debugging;

END Spider;
```

State Variables and Coordinate Transformations

First we describe the spider's view of its environment. The spider's room has 20 rows (RowsInRoom) and 20 columns (ColsInRoom), defined in terms of the positive subtypes Rows and Cols:

```
-- Spider's View of her Room - rows and cols both numbered 1..20
SUBTYPE Rows IS Positive RANGE 1..20;
SUBTYPE Cols IS Positive RANGE 1..20;
RowsInRoom   : CONSTANT Positive := Rows'Last;
ColsInRoom   : CONSTANT Positive := Cols'Last;
```

Recalling that `Directions` and `Colors` were defined in the package specification as

```
TYPE Directions IS (North, East, South, West);
TYPE Colors     IS (Red, Green, Blue, Black, None);
```

now in the body we declare the spider's own symbol, an asterisk ('*'), and four variables that describe the current location, direction, and color of the spider. These variables together compose the spider's state, that is, all its characteristics that can change during the life of the program. The variables are therefore called *state variables*.

```
-- Spider Current State Information
Spidersym     : CONSTANT character := '*';
CurrentColumn: Cols;                       -- spider's position
CurrentRow    : Rows;                       --    in the room.
Heading       : Directions;                 -- spider's direction
Ink           : Colors;                     -- spider's color
```

We now must consider that the spider's room is "painted" on a terminal screen that is defined in the package `Screen` (Program 4.8). The screen has 24 rows (the subtype `Screen.Depth`) and 80 columns (the subtype `Screen.Width`). We therefore describe the location and size of the actual room picture on the screen as follows:

```
-- Screen Description Constants for 24 x 80 screen,
-- 1 spider row = 1 screen row, 1 spider col = 2 screen cols
RowLow     : CONSTANT Screen.Depth := 2;    -- lower row bound
RowHigh    : CONSTANT Screen.Depth
               := RowLow + Rows'Last;        -- upper row bound
ColLow     : CONSTANT Screen.Width := 21;    -- lower col bound
ColHigh    : CONSTANT Screen.Width
               := ColLow + 2 * Cols'Last;    -- upper col bound
```

The upper left corner of the room is at row = 2, column = 21. This corresponds to the spider's row = 1, column = 1. The spider's row = 20, column = 20, corresponds to the screen coordinates row = 22 (2 + 20), column 61 (21 + 2*20). Why are we multiplying the columns by 2? Each screen column is about half as wide as each screen row is high, so to make the room look square, we use alternating screen columns. In graphics terminology: the terminal screen has rectangular *pixels* (picture elements).

We are dealing with two sets of coordinates, the spider's coordinates (a row/column pair as viewed by the spider) and the room's physical coordinates on the screen (a different row/column pair as seen on the screen). The procedure `DrawSymbol` has the responsibility to convert between the coordinate systems. This is a simple example of *coordinate transformation*, a concept that is often used in computer graphics and other engineering applications.

```
PROCEDURE DrawSymbol (Which: Character) IS
  -- Pre:  Which is defined
  -- Post: Which appears in its proper position on the screen
BEGIN
  Screen.MoveCursor (Row => (RowLow - 1) + CurrentRow,
```

```
                              Column => (ColLow - 2) + (2 * CurrentColumn));
       Ada.Text_IO.Put (Item => Which);
       Ada.Text_IO.Flush;
    END DrawSymbol;
```

Note how the parameters to `Screen.MoveCursor` are computed. For example, the spider's row 1 is the screen's row 2; the spider's column 10 is the screen's column 39 (19 + 2*10). The call to `Ada.Text_IO.Flush` is present because in many operating systems output is buffered, that is, nothing is actually displayed on the screen until a line is complete. Including the `Flush` call therefore indicates a complete line to the operating system, and the character is displayed immediately.

You have noticed that the spider's color is displayed as a specific character and its direction is displayed by an "arrow" pointing in the correct direction. The next two functions, `ColorSymbols` and `Compass`, take care of the necessary transformations, each function using a CASE statement to determine the appropriate character.

```
FUNCTION ColorSymbols (Color: Colors) RETURN Character IS
-- Pre:  Color is defined
-- Post: Returns the drawing character corresponding to Color
BEGIN
  CASE Color IS
    WHEN Red   => RETURN 'R';
    WHEN Blue  => RETURN 'B';
    WHEN Green => RETURN 'G';
    WHEN Black => RETURN 'K';
    WHEN None  => RETURN '.';
  END CASE;
END ColorSymbols;


FUNCTION Compass (Direction: Directions) RETURN Character IS
-- Pre:  Direction is defined
-- Post: Returns drawing character corresponding to Direction
BEGIN
  CASE Direction IS
    WHEN North => RETURN '^';
    WHEN East  => RETURN '>';
    WHEN South => RETURN 'v';
    WHEN West  => RETURN '<';
  END CASE;
END Compass;
```

The Spider's User Commands

The declarations and subprograms above are all included in the spider package body but *not* in the package specification. These, and several other "service subprograms," are not intended to be called by a spider program. Omitting them from the specification guarantees that they cannot be called by an external program; they are reserved for internal use only.

Let's look at one of the spider's user commands, that is, the subprograms that are indeed listed in the specification. `AtWall` returns a `Boolean` value; each of the CASE choices returns the result of computing a `Boolean` expression.

```
FUNCTION AtWall RETURN Boolean IS
BEGIN
```

```
  -- Check for out of bounds (in the spider's view)
  CASE Heading IS
    WHEN North =>
      RETURN CurrentRow <= Rows'First;
    WHEN East  =>
      RETURN CurrentColumn >= Cols'Last;
    WHEN South =>
      RETURN CurrentRow >= Rows'Last;
    WHEN West  =>
      RETURN CurrentColumn <= Cols'First;
  END CASE;
END AtWall;
```

Finally, we examine the following IF statement contained in the procedure step:

```
-- If out of bounds raise exception.
IF AtWall THEN
  Screen.Beep;
  RAISE Hit_the_Wall;
END IF; The next statement,
```

The statement

```
RAISE Hit_the_Wall;
```

is the first time we have seen RAISE used; in this case it causes Hit_the_Wall to be raised immediately. Because there is no exception handler in step, the procedure halts and returns to its caller, where the exception is raised again. This is what caused the program Spider_Crash (Program 2.10) to terminate with an exception. In the other spider programs we used IF statements to prevent "crashes"; instead, we could have used exception handlers, and we invite you to do this as an exercise.

In this brief trip through the spider package you have seen that this package pulls together many of the concepts that were introduced in this chapter and earlier ones. The spider package is an easily understood example of a computer graphics application. You might be curious about whether computer graphics can be done using Ada. Of course it can; we just did! We used a very simple, monochrome, 24 × 80 screen but used a number of important graphics principles to do so. Appendix A shows examples of high-resolution color graphics with Ada.

8.8 Tricks of the Trade: Common Programming Errors

A good deal of care is required in working with complicated expressions. It is easy to omit parentheses or operators inadvertently. If an operator or a single parenthesis is omitted, a syntax error will be detected. If a pair of parentheses is omitted, the expression, although syntactically correct, may compute the wrong value.

Sometimes it is beneficial to break a complicated expression into subexpressions that are separately assigned to *temporary variables* and then to manipulate these temporary variables. For example, it is easier to write correctly the three assignment statements

```
Temp1 := Sqrt(X + Y);
```

```
Temp2 := 1 + Temp1;
Z := Temp1 / Temp2;
```

than the single assignment statement

```
Z := Sqrt(X + Y) / (1 + Sqrt(X + Y));
```

which has the same effect. Using three assignment statements also happens to be more efficient in this case because the square root operation is performed only once; it is performed twice in the previous single assignment statement.

Be careful to use the correct type of operands with each operator. The arithmetic operators can be used only with operands of type `Integer` or `Float` or subtypes of these. The relational operators can be used with any scalar data type. The `Boolean` operators can be used only with type `Boolean` operands.

Make sure that an operator does not have incompatible type operands. The `Boolean` expression

```
3 /= '3'
```

is invalid because it compares an integer to a character value. All operators require compatible operands; make sure that you supply the right type operand to mathematical functions. An example is `sqrt`, whose argument must be `Float` and nonnegative.

Remember that in a CASE statement there must be enough CASE choices to exhaust every possible value of the CASE selector variable or expression. If there are not, a WHEN OTHERS choice must be provided; otherwise, a compilation error will result. If you find that you are writing a large number of WHEN OTHERS choices, your case selector variable may be of an inappropriate type (e.g., `Integer` instead of a subtype or enumeration type).

CHAPTER REVIEW

This chapter described how to write arithmetic expressions involving several operators and introduced a package of mathematical functions called `Ada.Numerics.Elementary_Functions`. Also introduced was the idea of an *explicit type conversion*. Type conversion makes it possible to mix integer and floating-point values in one expression by explicitly converting floats to integers and vice versa.

This chapter also discussed the manipulation of other scalar data types, including the standard types, `Boolean` and `Character`, and presented more detail on programmer-defined subtypes. Several new operators were introduced, including the integer operator REM and the Boolean operators AND, OR, XOR, and NOT. Attention was paid to certain attributes of scalar types, such as the `First` and `Last` attributes of subtypes and the `Pos` and `Val` attributes of integer and, especially, enumeration values.

The concept of pseudorandom numbers was introduced in this chapter, along with a description of some of Ada's random-number facilities.

The CASE statement was introduced, along with a number of examples of its use. A package was shown that provided facilities for printing the value of numbers in words.

New Ada Constructs in Chapter 8

The new Ada constructs introduced in this chapter are described in Table 8.8.

Table 8.8. Summary of New Ada Constructs

Statement	Effect
Arithmetic Assignment `I := J / K + (L + 5) REM N;`	Adds the result (an integer) of `J/K` to the result (an integer) of `(L + 5) REM N`. `J`, `K`, `L`, and `N` must all be type `Integer` or an integer subtype.
Character Assignment `NextCh := 'A';`	Assigns the character value `'A'` to `NextCh`.
Boolean assignment `Even := (N REM 2 = 0);`	If `N` is an even number, assigns the value `True` to `Even`; otherwise, assigns the value `False` to `Even`.

Case Statement
 	
`CASE NextCh IS`
`  WHEN 'A'|'a' =>`
`    Ada.Text_IO.Put(Item=>"Excellent");`
`  WHEN 'B'|'b' =>`
`    Ada.Text_IO.Put(Item=>"Good");`
`  WHEN 'C'|'c' =>`
`    Ada.Text_IO.Put(Item=>"OK");`
`  WHEN 'D'|'d'|'F'|'f' =>`
`    Ada.Text_IO.Put(Item=>"Poor");`
`    Probation(WhichStudent => IDNum);`
`  WHEN OTHERS =>`
`    Ada.Text_IO.Put`
`      (Item => "Grade out of Range!");`
`END CASE;`
	Displays one of four messages based on the value of `NextCh` If `NextCh` is `'D'`,`'d'`,`'F'`,`'f'`, procedure `Probation` is also called with `IDNum` as an actual parameter.

Quick-Check Exercises

1. The operator ____ means floating-point division, the operator ____ means integer division, and the operator ____ yields the remainder of _____ division.

2. Write a `Boolean` condition that is `True` if `N` divides `M`.

3. Evaluate the `Boolean` expression

   `True AND ((30 REM 10) = 0)`

4. Evaluate the Boolean expression

   ```
   False AND (((30 REM 10) / 0) = 0)
   ```

   What occurs when Ada evaluates this expression? Suppose the AND were replaced by AND THEN?

5. In the Latin-1 character set, give the values of these expressions:

   ```
   Character'Val(Character'Pos('a'))
   Character'Val(Character'Pos('a') + 3)
   Character'Val(Character'Pos('z') - 26)
   Character'Val(Character'Pos('z') - 32)
   ```

6. If two variables are type-compatible, can one always be assigned to the other?

7. Under what condition can one variable be assigned to another when they are
   not type-compatible?

8. A CASE statement is often used instead of _____.

9. Which of the following can appear in a CASE selector?

   a range of integers, a list of integers, a Float value, a Boolean value, a Character value, a string value, an enumeration literal

Answers to Quick-Check Exercises

1. / (float operands), / (integer operands), REM, integer

2. (M REM N) = 0

3. True

4. Constraint_Error is raised; the error won't be detected because in short-circuit evaluation the right side won't be evaluated.

5. 'a', 'd', 'a', 'z'

6. Yes, if they are the same type or the one getting a new value is the base type
   and the other is a subtype of that base type. If the one getting a new value is a
   subtype, the value of the variable being assigned must be in range.

7. A variable of one numeric type can be converted to the other type.

8. A multiple-alternative IF construct

9. All but Float and string

Review Questions

1. Compare and contrast integer types and floating-point types. What are the advantages and disadvantages of each?

2. What is the result of each of the following operations?

```
11 REM 2   _____      11 / 2   _____
12 REM -3  _____      12 / -3  _____
27 REM 4   _____     -25 / 4   _____
18 REM 6   _____     -18 / -5  _____
```

3. What is the result of the expression `(3 + 4 / 2) + 8 - 15 REM 4`?

4. Write an assignment statement that rounds a floating-point variable `Num1` to two digits after the decimal point, leaving the result in `Num1`.

5. Write a procedure called `Change` that has one `IN` parameter `C`, type `NonNeg-Float`, and four `OUT` parameters `Q`, `D`, `N`, and `P`, type `Natural`. The procedure returns the number of quarters ($0.25 coins) in `Q`, the number of dimes ($0.10 coins) in `D`, the number of nickels ($0.05 coins) in `N`, and the number of pennies ($0.01) in `P` to make change with the minimum number of coins. `c` (the change amount) is less than $1.00. (*Hint*: Use the integer division and `REM` operators.)

6. List and explain three computational errors that can occur in type `Float` expressions.

7. Write an `IF` statement that displays `True` or `False` according to the following conditions: Either `Flag` is `True` or `Color` is `Red`, or both `Money` is `Plenty` and `Time` is `Up`.

8. Write the statement to assign a value of `True` to the `Boolean` variable `OverTime` only if a worker's weekly `Hours` are greater than 40.

9. Write a `Boolean` expression using the `Character'Pos` attribute that determines whether the position of `'a'` in Latin-1 is greater than that of `'z'`. What is the value of this expression?

10. When should an `IF` statement be used instead of a `CASE` statement?

11. Write a `CASE` statement to select an operation based on `Inventory`. Increment `TotalPaper` by `PaperOrder` if `Inventory` is `'B'` or `'C'`; increment `TotalRibbon` by `RibbonOrder` if `Inventory` is `'L'`, `'T'`, or `'D'`; increment `TotalLabel` by `LabelOrder` if `Inventory` is `'A'` or `'X'`. Do not take any action if `Inventory` is `'M'`.

12. Write the `FOR` statement that displays the character values of the positive numbers 32 through 126, inclusive. Use `OrdNum` as the loop control variable. What is the value of `OrdNum` after completion of the loop?

Programming Projects

1. Write a program to read in a collection of integers and determine whether each is a prime number. Test your program with the four integers 7, 17, 35, and 96. All numbers should be processed in one run.

2. Let n be a positive integer consisting of up to ten digits, $d_{10}d_9...d_1$. Write a program to list in one column each of the digits in the number n. The rightmost digit, d_1, should be listed at the top of the column. (*Hint*: As computed according to the formula

    ```
    digit = n REM 10
    ```

    what is the value of `digit` if $n = 3704$?)

    Test your program for values of n equal to 6, 3704, and 170498.

3. An integer N is divisible by 9 if the sum of its digits is divisible by 9. Use the algorithm developed for Programming Project 2 to determine whether the following numbers are divisible by 9.

    ```
    N =   154368
    N =   621594
    N =   123456
    ```

4. Redo Programming Project 3 by reading each digit of the number to be tested into the character variable `Digit`. Form the sum of the numeric values of the digits. (*Hint*: The numeric value of `Digit` (type `Character`) is

    ```
    Character'Pos(Digit) - Character'Pos('0').)
    ```

5. The value of e^x is represented by the series

    $$1 + x + x^2/2! + x^3/3! + ... + x^n/n! + ...$$

    Write a program to compute and print the value of this series for any x and any n. Compare the result to `Exp(x)` (available in the Ada math library) and print a message `O.K.` or `Not O.K.`, depending on whether the difference between these results exceeds 0.001. How many terms—that is, what value of n—seem to provide good results without making the computation take too many steps?

6. The interest paid on a savings account is compounded daily. This means that if you start with *StartBal* dollars in the bank, at the end of the first day you will have a balance of

    $$StartBal \times (1 + rate/365)$$

    dollars, where *rate* is the annual interest rate (0.10 if the annual rate is 10 percent). At the end of the second day you will have

    $$StartBal \times (1 + rate/365) \times (1 + rate/365)$$

    dollars, and at the end of N days you will have

    $$StartBal \times (1 + rate/365)^N$$

    dollars. Write a program that processes a set of data records, each of which contains values for *StartBal*, *rate*, and N and computes the final account balance.

7. Compute the monthly payment and the total payment for a bank loan, given:

a. the amount of the loan,

b. the duration of the loan in months, and

c. the interest rate for the loan.

Your program should read in one loan at a time, perform the required computation, and display the values of the monthly payment and the total payment. Test your program with at least the following data (and more if you want):

Loan	Months	Rate
16000	300	12.50
24000	360	13.50
30000	300	15.50
42000	360	14.50
22000	300	15.50
300000	240	15.25

(*Hints*: The formula for computing monthly payment is

$$monthpay = \frac{ratem \times exm^{months} \times loan}{exm - 1.0}$$

where

$$ratem = rate / 1200.0$$

$$exm = (1.0 + ratem)$$

The formula for computing the total payment is

$$total = monthpay \times months.)$$

8. Refer to Chapter 5, Programming Project 11, which called for the development of a classification package for automobile speeds. In this project you will develop a simulator for a speed survey, in the form of a main program that collects and summarizes the speeds for 500 passing cars. Use an instance of `Ada.Numerics.Discrete_Random` to generate random speeds of passing cars; choose an appropriate range for these speeds, based on your experience on the highways. Keep track of the number of cars in each of the five categories, and at the end of the run, display your results numerically and in the form of a horizontal bar graph. A line in the bar graph will look like this, say, for 153 Class 3 cars:

```
Class 3   153 ****************
```

Note that there are 16 asterisks; each asterisk represents ten speeds. If the number of cars is not an exact multiple of ten, include one asterisk for the "extra" cars. For example, eight cars in a given class will be represented by a single asterisk, and eighteen cars will be represented by two asterisks.

9. A company has ten employees, many of whom work overtime (more than 40 hours) each week. The company accountant wants a payroll program that reads each employee's name, hourly rate (rate), and hours worked (hours). The program must compute the gross salary and net pay as follows:

$$gross = \begin{cases} hours \times rate & (hours \leq 40) \\ 1.5 \times rate \times (hours - 40) + 40 \times rate & (hours > 40) \end{cases}$$

$$net = \begin{cases} gross & (gross \leq 65) \\ gross - (15 + 0.45 \times gross) & (gross > 65) \end{cases}$$

The program should print each employee's gross salary and net pay. The total amount of the payroll, which can be computed by adding the gross salaries for all employees, should be displayed at the end. Test your program on the following data:

Name	Rate	Hours
Ivory Hunter	6.50	35
Track Star	4.50	10
Smokey Bear	3.25	80
Oscar Grouch	6.00	10
Jane Jezebel	4.65	25
Fat Eddie	8.00	40
Pumpkin Pie	9.65	35
Sara Lee	5.00	40
Human Eraser	6.25	52

10. If you've studied the body of the spider package, you can try modifying it. Here are some possibilities:

a. Move the spider's room-coordinate declarations (Cols, Rows, etc.) to the specification, then add to the package a procedure Jump with row and column parameters. This allows a spider program to cause the spider to jump to an arbitrary location in its room. Now write a spider program that causes the spider to jump to a *random* location.

b. (Difficult) Modify the package and procedure Start so that a spider program can specify the size of the room using parameters to the Start procedure. This will require a great deal of thought and redesign of the package!

CHAPTER 9

Composite Types: Records and Arrays

In the programs written so far, each variable was associated with a single memory loca-tion. These variables are called *scalar* variables, and their data types are scalar or unstructured types. In this chapter we will begin the study of *composite types*. A com-posite type is one that defines a collection of related data values. The items in a variable of a composite type can be processed individually, although some operations may be performed on the structure as a whole.

Ada provides *type constructors,* which can be used to form composite types from simpler types. The type constructors RECORD and ARRAY are introduced in this chapter, and some simple cases are explored. More complex and interesting uses of arrays and records are taken up beginning in Chapter 11.

A *record* is a data structure containing a group of related data items; the individual components, or *fields,* of a record can contain data of different types. An *array* is a data structure that is used for storage of a collection of data items that are all of the same type. An array has *elements;* each element has a position within the array, known as its *index* or *subscript.*

Think of a single record as being analogous to a 3 × 5 file card containing, for example, the name, address, birthday, and phone number of one of your friends. Each card has the same structure: a collection of fields, each field having its own type. A record type declaration, then, is a way to describe this record structure. Each data item is stored in a separate record field; we can reference each data item stored in a record through its field name. For example, `Person.Name` references the field `Name` of the record `Person`.

Think of an array as being analogous to the box in which you keep your set of cards. An array type declaration describes the structure of the array. If the array is called `Friends`, then one of the friend records might be referenced as `Friends(37)`, the card in the thirty-seventh position of the array. Each array element can hold a value of any type, whether it be a simple integer or character or a complex user-defined record type. An array element can even hold another array.

Records and arrays make it easier to organize and represent information in Ada and other modern programming languages, and these composite types are an important contributor to the power of these languages to enable us to write complex programs.

9.1 Data Structures: Record Types

As described in the introduction, a record is a structure containing several fields, each field having its own type; this structure is described by a *record type declaration*. As is always the case with types, the record type declaration does not create any records; it is only a template or recipe for creating records.

Record Type Declaration

Before a record can be created or saved, the record format must be specified by means of a record type declaration.

■ Example 9.1

The staff of our small software firm is growing rapidly. To keep our records more accessible and organized, we decide to store relevant data, such as the descriptive information shown below, in an employee data base:

```
ID  : 1234
Name:  Caryn Jackson
Gender : Female
Number of Dependents: 3
Hourly Rate: 7.50
```

Noting that the number of dependents should be of type `Natural` and the hourly rate and taxable salary should both be of type `NonNegFloat`, let us give an appropriate type declaration for each piece of information in the first three lines above:

```
NameSize :CONSTANT Positive := 20;
```

```
SUBTYPE IDType IS Positive RANGE 1111..9999;
SUBTYPE NameType IS String(1..NameSize);
TYPE GenderType IS (Female,Male);
```

We next declare a record type `EmployeeBasic` to store this basic information. We must specify the name of each field and the type of information stored in each field. We choose the field names in the same way as we choose all other identifiers: The names describe the nature of the information represented.

```
TYPE EmployeeBasic IS RECORD
   ID : IDType;
   Name : NameType;
   Gender : GenderType;
   NumDepend : Natural;
   Rate : NonNegFloat;
END RECORD;
```

The record type is a template that describes the format of each record and the name of each individual data element. A variable declaration is required to allocate storage space for a record. The record variables `Clerk` and `Janitor` are declared next.

```
Clerk : EmployeeBasic;
Janitor : EmployeeBasic;
```

The record variables `Clerk` and `Janitor` both have the structure specified in the declaration for record type `EmployeeBasic`. Thus the memory allocated for each consists of storage space for five distinct values. Figure 9.1 shows the record variable `Clerk`, assuming that the values shown earlier are stored in memory. ∎

As illustrated in the type declaration for `EmployeeBasic`, each of the fields of a record can be a predefined or user-defined type. There are no limitations on the type of a field, except that the type specification must be the name of a type that has already been declared. The record type declaration is described in the next display.

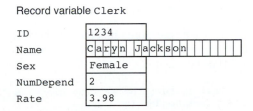

Figure 9.1 Record Variable Clerk

SYNTAX
DISPLAY

Record Type Declaration

Form:

```
TYPE rec-type IS RECORD
  F₁ : type₁;
  F₂ : type₂;
      .    .    .
  Fₙ : typeₙ;
END RECORD;
```

Example:

```
TYPE Fraction IS RECORD
  Numerator: Integer;
  Denominator: Positive;
END RECORD;
```

Interpretation:

The identifier *rec-type* is the name of the record structure being described. Each identifier F_i is a field name; the data type of each field F_i is specified by $type_i$.

Note:

$type_i$ may be any predefined or user-defined type. Also, the field names must be unique: No two fields may have the same field name.

Manipulating Individual Fields of a Record

We can reference a record field by using a *field selector,* which consists of the record variable name followed by the field name. A period separates the field name and record name.

■ Example 9.2

The data shown in Fig. 9.1 could have been stored in `clerk` through this sequence of assignment statements:

```
Clerk.ID := 1234;
Clerk.Name := "Caryn Jackson          ";
Clerk.Gender := Female;
Clerk.NumDepend := 3;
Clerk.Rate := 7.50;
```

Once data are stored in a record, they can be manipulated in the same way as other data in memory.

The statements

```
Ada.Text_IO.Put(Item => "The clerk is ");
CASE Clerk.Gender IS
  WHEN Female =>
    Ada.Text_IO.Put (Item => "Ms. ");
  WHEN Male =>
    Ada.Text_IO.Put (Item => "Mr. ");
END CASE;
```

```
Ada.Text_IO.Put (Item => Clerk.Name);
```

display the clerk's name after an appropriate title (`Ms.` or `Mr.`). For the data above, the output would be

```
The clerk is Ms. Caryn Jackson
```
■

■ Example 9.3

Program 9.1 computes the distance from an arbitrary point on the *x-y* plane to the origin (intersection of the *x*- and *y*-axes). The values of the *x*-coordinate and the *y*-coordinate are entered as data and stored in the fields `x` and `y` of the record variable `Point1`. The formula distance, *d*, from the origin to an arbitrary point (X, Y) is computed by the following formula:

$$d = \sqrt{X^2 + Y^2}$$

Each coordinate of the record variable `Point1` is read separately. `Ada.Text_IO` does not provide operations to read an entire record; we will write our own operations to read records later in this chapter. ■

Program 9.1 Distance from Point to Origin

```
WITH Ada.Text_IO;
WITH Ada.Float_Text_IO;
WITH Ada.Numerics.Elementary_Functions;
USE  Ada.Numerics.Elementary_Functions;
PROCEDURE Distance_to_Origin IS
-----------------------------------------------------------------------
--| Finds the distance from a point to the origin.
--| Author: Michael B. Feldman, The George Washington University
--| Last Modified: September 1998
-----------------------------------------------------------------------

  TYPE Point IS RECORD
    X : Float;
    Y : Float;
  END RECORD;

  Point1 : Point;             -- the data point
  Distance : Float;           -- its distance to the origin

BEGIN -- Distance_to_Origin

  Ada.Text_IO.Put(Item => "Enter X coordinate (floating point) > ");
  Ada.Float_Text_IO.Get(Item => Point1.X);
  Ada.Text_IO.Put(Item => "Enter Y coordinate (floating point) > ");
  Ada.Float_Text_IO.Get(Item => Point1.Y);
  Distance := Sqrt(Point1.X ** 2 + Point1.Y ** 2);
  Ada.Text_IO.Put(Item => "Distance to origin is ");
  Ada.Float_Text_IO.Put(Item => Distance, Fore=>1,Aft=>2,Exp=>0);
  Ada.Text_IO.New_Line;

END Distance_to_Origin;
```

Sample Run

```
Enter X coordinate (floating point) > 3
Enter Y coordinate (floating point) > 4
Distance to origin is 5.00
```

Operations on Records

A type is always a set of values and a set of operations on those values. Now that we know how to declare record types, let us summarize the operations that are available for record values.

Four basic operations act on a record: *store, retrieve, assignment,* and *equality test.*

- *Store:* The store operation inserts a value into the record field. If R1 is a record with a field named F1 and E is an expression that is compatible with field F1, the statement

  ```
  R1.F1 := E;
  ```

  stores the result of evaluating E in field F1 of record R1.

- *Retrieve:* If the field R1.F1 is compatible with variable C (that is, if they have the same type), the statement

  ```
  C := R1.F1;
  ```

  retrieves the value in field F1 of record R1 and copies it into C. Note that it is always permissible, given two record variables R1 and R2 of the same type, to write

  ```
  R1.F1 := R2.F1;
  ```

- *Assignment:* An assignment statement can also be used to copy the entire contents of one record to another of the same type. If R1 and R2 are record variables of the same type, the statement

  ```
  R1 := R2;
  ```

  copies all fields of record R2 to record R1.

- *Equality test:* Finally, Boolean expressions such as

  ```
  R1 = R2
  ```

  are permitted; this expression is true if and only if each field of R1 is equal to its corresponding field in R2. Further, the result of the Boolean expression

  ```
  R1 /= R2
  ```

  is true if and only if at least one of the fields of R1 is not equal to its corresponding field in R2.

If Clerk and Janitor are both record variables of type Employee, the statement

```
Clerk := Janitor; --copy Janitor to Clerk
```

copies each field of Janitor into the corresponding field of clerk. It is also permissible to determine in a single statement whether two records R1 and R2 of the same record type are equal, that is, whether each field of R1 is equal to the corresponding field of R2. For example,

```
IF R1 = R2 THEN
   DoSomething;
ELSE
   DoSomethingElse;
END IF;
```

executes DoSomething if R1 and R2 both contain the same field values, field by field, and executes DoSomethingElse otherwise.

Because arithmetic and logical operations—except for equality and inequality—can be performed only on individual memory cells, record variables cannot be used as the operands of *predefined* arithmetic and relational operators. These operators can be used only with individual fields of a record. However, we shall see in Chapter 11 that it is possible for a programmer to *define* arithmetic and relational operators on records.

EXERCISES FOR SECTION 9.1

Self-Check

1. Each part in an inventory is represented by its part number, a descriptive name, the quantity on hand, and price. Define a record type Part.

2. A catalog listing for a textbook consists of the author's name, title, publisher, and year of publication. Declare a record type CatalogEntry and variable Book and write assignment statements that store the relevant data for this textbook in Book.

9.2 Control Structures: Records as Subprogram Parameters

A record can be passed as a parameter to a function or procedure, provided that the actual parameter is of the same type as its corresponding formal parameter. The use of records as parameters can shorten parameter lists considerably because one parameter (the record variable) can be passed instead of several related parameters.

Reading a Record

Ada normally uses procedures to read data from the terminal or a file. The Get procedures that are available in the input/output packages are defined only for individual values, not for records. To read a record, we can use a call of the appropriate Get to read each field. It is common to read an entire record at once, so it makes sense to define a procedure for doing this; the body of the procedure will contain the individual Get calls for each record field.

■ Example 9.4

Program 9.2 contains a procedure GetPoint to read a point in the *x-y* plane and a function Distance, which calculates the distance between two points $P_1 = (X_1, Y_1)$ and $P_2 = (X_2, Y_2)$. The formula that is used to calculate the distance d is

$$d = \sqrt{(X_2 - X_1)^2 + (Y_2 - Y_1)^2}$$

The main program requests the coordinates of two points from the user, then calculates and displays the distance between them. Notice how straightforward it is to write and call subprograms with record parameters. ■

Program 9.2 Distance between Two Points

```
WITH Ada.Text_IO;
WITH Ada.Float_Text_IO;
WITH Ada.Numerics.Elementary_Functions;
USE  Ada.Numerics.Elementary_Functions;
PROCEDURE Distance_between_Points IS
-------------------------------------------------------------------------
--| Finds the distance between two points on the x-y plane.
--| Author: Michael B. Feldman, The George Washington University
--| Last Modified: September 1998
-------------------------------------------------------------------------

  TYPE Point IS RECORD
    X : Float;
    Y : Float;
  END RECORD;

  Point1 : Point;                  -- one data point
  Point2 : Point;                  -- the other data point

  PROCEDURE GetPoint(Item: OUT Point) IS
  -- Pre: none
  -- Post: the point, Item, is defined with values from the user

  BEGIN

    Ada.Text_IO.Put(Item => "Enter X coordinate (floating point) > ");
    Ada.Float_Text_IO.Get(Item => Item.X);
    Ada.Text_IO.Put(Item => "Enter Y coordinate (floating point) > ");
    Ada.Float_Text_IO.Get(Item => Item.Y);

  END GetPoint;
```

```
FUNCTION Distance(P1 : Point; P2 : Point) RETURN Float IS
-- Pre: P1 and P2 are defined
-- Post: returns the Cartesian distance between the points

BEGIN

  RETURN Sqrt((P2.X-P1.X) ** 2 + (P2.Y-P1.Y) ** 2);

END Distance;

BEGIN -- Distance_between_Points

  Ada.Text_IO.Put(Item => "First Point");
  Ada.Text_IO.New_Line;
  GetPoint(Item => Point1);
  Ada.Text_IO.Put(Item => "Second Point");
  Ada.Text_IO.New_Line;
  GetPoint(Item => Point2);
  Ada.Text_IO.Put(Item => "Distance between points is ");
  Ada.Float_Text_IO.Put
    (Item => Distance(Point1, Point2), Fore=>1,Aft=>2,Exp=>0);
  Ada.Text_IO.New_Line;

END Distance_between_Points;
```

Sample Run

```
First Point
Enter X coordinate (floating point) > 3
Enter Y coordinate (floating point) > 4
Second Point
Enter X coordinate (floating point) > 9
Enter Y coordinate (floating point) > 12
Distance between points is 10.00
```

Record Aggregate Assignment

When an entire record must be assigned at one time, it is unnecessary to assign each field in a separate assignment statement. Instead, you can use an *aggregate*. An aggregate is just a list of all the field values in the record, separated by commas and enclosed in parentheses. An aggregate looks like a parameter list in a procedure call: The values can just be listed in sequence (positional association) or given with their names (named association). Generally, we will use the latter form because it is clearer and easier to understand.

A record `Clerk` of type `Employee`, as used above, could be filled in with an aggregate assignment as follows:

```
Clerk :=
  (ID => 1234,
  Name => "Caryn Jackson          ",
  Gender => Female,
  NumDepend => 2,
  Rate => 7.50);
```

We have listed the fields in the order in which they were declared in the type definition, but in fact we could have put them in any order because the field names help the compiler (and the human reader) make the association.

It is permissible to write an aggregate assignment without specifying the field names, for example,

```
Clerk := (1234,"Caryn Jackson        ", Female, 2, 7.50);
```

However, this form, called *positional association,* is not nearly as clear and also requires that the fields be listed exactly in the order in which they appear in the type definition. We will generally use the first, or *named association,* form of record aggregate assignment.

EXERCISES FOR SECTION 9.2

Self-Check

1. For the record type `Part` in Self-Check Exercise 1, Section 9.1, provide the following program segments for a record variable `P: Part`:

    a. Assign a value to each record field using an individual assignment statement

    b. Assign a value to `P` using an aggregate with named association

    c. Same as (b), but use positional association

9.3 System Structures: A Package for Calendar Dates

In Chapters 4 and 8 we discussed some of the uses of Ada's predefined package `Ada.Calendar`. This package provides many facilities for working with dates and times, but it does not provide a way to represent calendar dates that is suitable for reading and displaying. In this section we develop a specification for a simple package to give us a nicer form for dates, including procedures to read and display dates. In Chapter 11 we will refine this package to make it more capable and robust.

Specification for the Simple Dates Package

The package specification is found in Program 9.3.

Program 9.3 Specification of Simple Dates Package

```
WITH Ada.Calendar;
PACKAGE Simple_Dates IS
```

```
--|------------------------------------------------------------------
--| Specification for package to represent calendar dates
--| in a form convenient for reading and displaying.
--| Author: Michael B. Feldman, The George Washington University
--| Last Modified: September 1998
--|------------------------------------------------------------------

  TYPE Months IS
    (Jan, Feb, Mar, Apr, May, Jun, Jul, Aug, Sep, Oct, Nov, Dec);

  TYPE Date IS RECORD
    Month: Months;
    Day:   Ada.Calendar.Day_Number;
    Year:  Ada.Calendar.Year_Number;
  END RECORD;

  PROCEDURE Get(Item: OUT Date);
  -- Pre:  None
  -- Post: Reads a date in mmm dd yyyy form, returning it in Item

  PROCEDURE Put(Item: IN Date);
  -- Pre:  Item is defined
  -- Post: Displays a date in mmm dd yyyy form

  FUNCTION Today RETURN Date;
  -- Pre:  None
  -- Post: Returns today's date

END Simple_Dates;
```

We want the `Simple_Dates` package to provide a standard representation for the months of the year. We do this by giving an enumeration type `Months` representing the abbreviated names of the months:

```
TYPE Months IS
  (Jan, Feb, Mar, Apr, May, Jun, Jul, Aug, Sep, Oct, Nov, Dec);
```

We can now make use of this type and the day and year types provided by `Ada.Calendar` to define a record type for a date, using the month abbreviation for the month field, as follows:

```
TYPE Date IS RECORD
  Month: Months;
  Day: Ada.Calendar.Day_Number;
  Year: Ada.Calendar.Year_Number;
END RECORD;
```

We could have defined our own year and month number types, but we chose instead to use types that were already available to us in a predefined Ada package (instead of "reinventing the wheel"). The input program `Get` will read a date in the form

```
OCT 31 1998
```

and the output program `Put` will display dates in this form as well.

One more operation is included: a function `Today` that returns a date record that is initialized with the date the program is being run. In other words, given a declaration

```
D: Simple_Dates.Date;
```

the statement

```
D := Simple_Dates.Today;
```

sets the fields of D to today's month, day, and year, respectively. Two things are note-worthy about this function. First, it is an example of a *parameterless* function; like Ada.Calendar.Clock, it requires no parameters. Second, the return type of the function is a record, namely, one of type Date.

Body of the Dates Package

Program 9.4 shows the body of package Simple_Dates.

Program 9.4 Body of Simple Dates Package

```
WITH Ada.Calendar;
WITH Ada.Text_IO;
WITH Ada.Integer_Text_IO;
PACKAGE BODY Simple_Dates IS
------------------------------------------------------------------
--| Body for package to represent calendar dates
--| in a form convenient for reading and displaying.
--| Author: Michael B. Feldman, The George Washington University
--| Last Modified: September 1998
------------------------------------------------------------------

  PACKAGE Month_IO IS
    NEW Ada.Text_IO.Enumeration_IO(Enum => Months);


  PROCEDURE Get(Item: OUT Date) IS

  BEGIN -- Get

    Month_IO.Get(Item => Item.Month);
    Ada.Integer_Text_IO.Get(Item => Item.Day);
    Ada.Integer_Text_IO.Get(Item => Item.Year);

  END Get;


  PROCEDURE Put(Item: IN Date) IS

  BEGIN -- Put

    Month_IO.Put (Item => Item.Month, Width=>1);
    Ada.Text_IO.Put(Item => ' ');
    Ada.Integer_Text_IO.Put(Item => Item.Day, Width => 1);
    Ada.Text_IO.Put(Item => ' ');
    Ada.Integer_Text_IO.Put(Item => Item.Year, Width => 4);

  END Put;

  FUNCTION Today RETURN Date IS
```

```
       Right_Now  : Ada.Calendar.Time;      -- holds internal clock value
       Result     : Date;

   BEGIN -- Today

       -- Get the current time value from the computer's clock
       Right_Now := Ada.Calendar.Clock;

       -- Extract the current month, day, and year from the time value
       Result.Month := Months'Val(Ada.Calendar.Month(Right_Now)- 1);
       Result.Day := Ada.Calendar.Day  (Right_Now);
       Result.Year := Ada.Calendar.Year (Date => Right_Now);

       RETURN Result;

   END Today;

END Simple_Dates;
```

There are just two procedures: `Get` and `Put`. `Simple_Dates.Get` expects its input to be in the form given above. It is not a robust procedure like the ones in `Robust_Input` (Section 7.6) that prompt the user until correct input is entered; it is more like the predefined `Get` routines in `Ada.Text_IO`: If anything is wrong with the input, `Get` simply allows the exception to be passed back to the calling routine.

What can go wrong? The month, day, or year that the user enters can be badly formed or out of range, or the combination of month, day, and year can form a nonexistent date such as `Feb 30 1999`. A badly formed month, day, or year will result in `Ada.Text_IO.Data_Error` being raised by `Months_IO`; an out-of-range month or year will result in `Constraint_Error` being raised. This routine does not discover the case of a nonexistent date; a revised version of the package, to be developed in Chapter 11, will correct this shortcoming and add the desired robustness.

The procedure `Simple_Dates.Put` displays a date in the `MMM DD YYYY` form. Also note how the function `Today` uses the package `Ada.Calendar` to produce today's date and return it to the caller. Program 9.5 shows a test of the `Simple_Dates` package. Because the package is not robust, we include an exception-handling loop in the test program.

Program 9.5 Test of Simple Dates Package

```
WITH Ada.Text_IO;
WITH Simple_Dates;
PROCEDURE Test_Simple_Dates IS
-------------------------------------------------------------------------
--| Program to test the Simple_Dates package
--| Author: Michael B. Feldman, The George Washington University
--| Last Modified: September 1998
-------------------------------------------------------------------------

   D: Simple_Dates.Date;

BEGIN -- Test_Simple_Dates

   D := Simple_Dates.Today;
   Ada.Text_IO.Put(Item => "Today is ");
   Simple_Dates.Put(Item => D);
```

```
            Ada.Text_IO.New_Line;

            LOOP

              BEGIN -- block for exception handler
                Ada.Text_IO.Put("Please enter a date in MMM DD YYYY form > ");
                Simple_Dates.Get(Item => D);
                EXIT; -- only if no exception is raised
              EXCEPTION
                WHEN Constraint_Error =>
                  Ada.Text_IO.Skip_Line;
                  Ada.Text_IO.Put(Item => "Invalid date; try again, please.");
                  Ada.Text_IO.New_Line;
                WHEN Ada.Text_IO.Data_Error =>
                  Ada.Text_IO.Skip_Line;
                  Ada.Text_IO.Put(Item => "Invalid date; try again, please.");
                  Ada.Text_IO.New_Line;
              END;

            END LOOP;

            Ada.Text_IO.Put(Item => "You entered ");
            Simple_Dates.Put(Item => D);
            Ada.Text_IO.New_Line;

          END Test_Simple_Dates;
```

Sample Run

```
Today is SEP 4 1998
Please enter a date in MMM DD YYYY form > mmm dd yyyy
Invalid date; try again, please.
Please enter a date in MMM DD YYYY form > Dec 15 1944
You entered DEC 15 1944
```

EXERCISES FOR SECTION 9.3

Self-Check

1. Can a client program that uses `simple_Dates` change the day field of a `Date` variable? For example, suppose the variable represents November 30, 1998. Can the client program change the 30 to a 31?

9.4   Data Structures: Hierarchical Records

In solving any programming problem, we must select data structures that enable us to represent a variety of different kinds of information efficiently in the computer. The selection of data structures is a very important part of the problem-solving process. The data structures that are used can have a profound effect on the efficiency and simplicity of the completed program.

The data structuring facilities in Ada are quite powerful and general. In the previous examples, all record fields were scalar types or strings. It is possible to declare a record type with fields that are other structured types. We will call a record type with one or more fields that are record types a *hierarchical record*.

We began our study of records by introducing a record type `Employee`. In this section we will modify that record by adding new fields for storage of the employee's address, starting date, and date of birth. We repeat for convenience the declarations for `EmployeeBasic`:

```
NameSize :CONSTANT Positive := 20;

SUBTYPE IDType IS Positive RANGE 1111..9999;
SUBTYPE NameType IS String(1..NameSize);
TYPE GenderType IS (Female,Male);
TYPE EmployeeBasic IS RECORD
  ID : IDType;
  Name : NameType;
  Gender : GenderType;
  NumDepend : Natural;
  Rate : NonNegFloat;
END RECORD;
```

and add some constants and subtypes:

```
ZipCodeSize : CONSTANT Positive := 5;
AddressSize : CONSTANT Positive := 20;

SUBTYPE AddressString IS String(1..NameSize);
SUBTYPE ZipString IS String(1..ZipCodeLength);
```

Next we define an additional record type: `Address`.

```
TYPE Address IS RECORD
  Street : AddressString;
  City :   AddressString;
  State :  AddressString;
  ZipCode : ZipString;
END RECORD;
```

Finally, here is the declaration of the hierarchical record for an employee and a declaration of an employee variable. Notice how simple the employee record is, given the component record types; notice also how we have used the `Date` type provided by the package `Simple_Dates` developed in the previous section:

```
TYPE Employee IS RECORD
  PayData : EmployeeBasic;
  Home :    Address;
```

```
   StartDate : Simple_Dates.Date;
   BirthDate : Simple_Dates.Date;
END RECORD;

Programmer: Employee;
```

If `Programmer` is a record variable of type `Employee`, the hierarchical structure of `Programmer` can be sketched as shown in Fig. 9.2. This diagram provides a graphic display of the record form. It shows that `Programmer` is a record with fields `PayData`, `Home`, `StartDate`, and `BirthDate`. Each of these fields is itself a record (called a *subrecord* of `Programmer`). The fields of each subrecord are indicated under it.

To reference a field in this diagram, we must trace a complete path to it starting from the top of the diagram. For example, the field selector

```
Programmer.StartDate
```

references the subrecord `StartDate` (type `Simple_Dates.Date`) of the variable `Programmer`. The field selector

```
Programmer.StartDate.Year
```

references the `Year` field of the subrecord `Programmer.StartDate`. The field selector

```
Programmer.Year
```

is incomplete (which `Year` field?) and would cause a compilation error.

The record copy statement

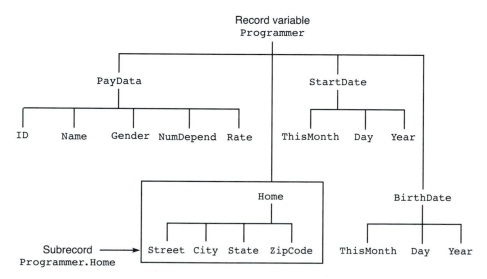

Figure 9.2 Record Variable Programmer

```
Programmer.StartDate :=   DayOfYear;
```

is legal if DayOfYear is a record variable of type Date. This statement copies each field of DayOfYear into the corresponding field of the subrecord Programmer.StartDate.
    The statements

```
Ada.Text_IO.Put(Item => "Year started: ");
Ada.Integer_Text_IO.Put(Item => Programmer.StartDate.Year, Width=>4);
Ada.Text_IO.Put(Item => "Month started: ");
Ada.Integer_Text_IO.Put(Item => Programmer.StartDate.Month, Width=>4);
```

display two fields of the subrecord Programmer.StartDate. The statements

```
Ada.Text_IO.Put(Item => Programmer.PayData.Name);
Ada.Text_IO.Put(Item => "started work in ");
Ada.Integer_Text_IO.Put(Item => Programmer.StartDate.Year, Width=>4);
```

display the line

```
Caryn Jackson        started work in 1985
```

Procedure ReadEmployeeBasic in Program 9.6 can be used to read in a record of type EmployeeBasic.

Program 9.6 Procedure ReadEmployeeBasic

```
PROCEDURE ReadEmployeeBasic (Item : OUT EmployeeBasic) IS
-- Reads one basic employee record into Item.
-- Pre : None
-- Post: Data are read into record Item.

BEGIN -- ReadEmployeeBasic

  Ada.Text_IO.Put(Item => "ID > ");
  Ada.Integer_Text_IO.Get(Item => Item.ID);
  Ada.Text_IO.Put(Item => "Name > ");
  Ada.Text_IO.Get(Item => Item.Name);
  Ada.Text_IO.Put(Item => "Gender (Female or Male) > ");
  GenderType_IO.Get(Item => Item.Gender);
  Ada.Text_IO.Put(Item => "Number of dependents > ");
  Ada.Integer_Text_IO.Get(Item => Item.NumDepend);
  Ada.Text_IO.Put(Item => "Hourly rate > ");
  Ada.Float_Text_IO.Get(Item => Item.Rate);

END ReadEmployeeBasic;
```

Program 9.7 calls this procedure, Simple_Dates.Get, and ReadAddress (see Programming Exercise 1 below).

Program 9.7 Procedure ReadEmployee

```
PROCEDURE ReadEmployee (Item : OUT Employee) IS
-- Reads a record into record variable Item.
-- Pre : None
-- Post: Reads data into all fields of record Employee.
```

```
BEGIN -- ReadEmployee

   ReadEmployeeBasic (Item => Item.PayData);
   ReadAddress (Item => Item.Home);
   Simple_Dates.Get (Item => Item.StartDate);
   Simple_Dates.Get (Item => Item.BirthDate)

END ReadEmployee;
```

The procedure call statement

```
ReadEmployee (Clerk)
```

causes the data read to be stored in record variable `Clerk`. This procedure uses `GenderType_IO` to read the gender of the employee; `GenderType_IO` would need to be defined as an instance of `Ada.Text_IO.Enumeration_IO`.

This example has shown that even though the standard text input/output packages provide for reading and displaying only a single value at a time, it is easy to construct an input or display procedure for a simple record type (e.g., `Simple_Dates.Get`) and to write one for an entire hierarchical record by calling the simpler ones.

EXERCISES FOR SECTION 9.4

Self-Check

1. What must be the type of `NewAddress` if the following statement is correct?

   ```
   Programmer.Home := NewAddress;
   ```

2. Write the field selector needed to reference each of the following fields:

   a. the programmer's salary

   b. the programmer's street address

   c. the programmer's month of birth

   d. the month the programmer started working

Programming

1. Write the procedure `ReadAddress` suggested above.

9.5 Data Structures: Array Types

A record contains fields, each of which is potentially of a different type; such a composite type is often called *heterogeneous*. An array, on the other hand, contains elements all of which are of the *same* type; such a type is often called *homogeneous*. As with record types, we first declare an *array type*, which provides a template, or recipe, for creating arrays. Then we actually create an array—cause the compiler to allocate storage for it—with an array variable declaration.

Array Type Declaration

The array type `FloatArray` is declared below followed by the declaration of array x of type `FloatArray`:

```
TYPE FloatArray IS ARRAY (1..8) OF Float;
X : FloatArray;
```

The type declaration indicates our desire that each array be a collection of eight memory cells. The variable declaration causes a specific collection of eight cells to be associated with the name x; these memory cells are usually adjacent to each other in memory. Each element of array x can contain a single `Float` value, so a total of eight `Float` values can be stored and referenced using the array name x.

Referencing Elements of an Array

To process the data stored in an array, we must be able to reference each individual element. The *array subscript* (sometimes called *array index*) is used to differentiate between elements of the same array. For example, if x is the array with eight elements declared above, we refer to the elements of the array x as shown in Fig. 9.3.

The *subscripted variable* x(1) (read as "x sub 1") may be used to reference the first element of the array x; x(2), the second element; and x(8), the eighth element. The number enclosed in brackets is the array subscript. As we will see later, the subscript does not have to be a constant.

■ Example 9.5

Let x be the array shown in Fig. 9.3. Some statements that manipulate this array are shown in Table 9.1.

X(1)	X(2)	X(3)	X(4)	X(5)	X(6)	X(7)	X(8)
16.0	12.0	6.0	8.0	2.5	12.0	14.0	−54.5

Figure 9.3 The Eight Elements of the Array X

Table 9.1   Statements that Manipulate Array X

Statement	Explanation
`Ada.Float_Text_IO.Put(X(1));`	Displays value of `X(1)`, or 16.0.
`X(4) := 25.0;`	Stores value 25.0 in `X(4)`.
`Sum := X(1) + X(2);`	Stores sum of `X(1)` and `X(2)`, or 28.0, in `Sum`.
`Sum := Sum + X(3);`	Adds `X(3)` to `Sum`. The new `Sum` is 34.0.
`X(4) := X(4) + 1.0;`	Adds 1.0 to `X(4)`. The new `X(4)` is 26.0.
`X(3) := X(1) + X(2);`	Stores sum of `X(1)` and `X(2)`, or 28.0, in `X(3)`.

The contents of array x are shown in Fig. 9.4 after execution of these statements. Only x(3) and x(4) are changed. ∎

∎ Example 9.6

Some declarations for a manufacturing plant operations program are shown below. The type declarations declare two scalar subtypes, EmpRange and HoursRange; an enumeration type, Days; and two array types, EmpArray and DayArray. Two array variables, Vacation and PlantHours, are declared in the variable declaration section:

```
NumEmp : CONSTANT Positive := 10;  -- Number of employees
SUBTYPE EmpRange IS Positive RANGE 1..NumEmp; -- subscript range
SUBTYPE HoursRange IS Float RANGE 0.0..24.0;  -- hours in a day
TYPE Days IS
   (Monday, Tuesday, Wednesday, Thursday, Friday, Saturday, Sunday);

TYPE EmpArray IS ARRAY(EmpRange) OF Boolean;
TYPE DayArray IS ARRAY(Days) OF HoursRange;

Vacation : EmpArray;
PlantHours : DayArray;
```

The array Vacation has ten elements (subscripts 1 through NumEmp); each element of array Vacation can store a Boolean value. The contents of this array could indicate which employees were on vacation (Vacation(i) is True if employee i is on vacation). If employees 1, 3, 5, 7, and 9 were on vacation, the array would have the values shown in Fig. 9.5.

The array PlantHours has seven elements (subscripts Monday through Sunday). The array element PlantHours(Sunday) could indicate how many hours the plant was operating during Sunday of the past week. The array shown in Fig. 9.6 indicates that the plant was closed on the weekend, operating single shifts on Monday and Thursday, double shifts on Tuesday and Friday, and a triple shift on Wednesday. ∎

X(1)	X(2)	X(3)	X(4)	X(5)	X(6)	X(7)	X(8)
16.0	12.0	28.0	26.0	2.5	12.0	14.0	−54.5

Figure 9.4   The Array X After Modification

Vacation(1)	True
Vacation(2)	False
Vacation(3)	True
Vacation(4)	False
Vacation(5)	True
Vacation(6)	False
Vacation(7)	True
Vacation(8)	False
Vacation(9)	True
Vacation(10)	False

Figure 9.5 Array Vacation

PlantHours(Sunday)	0.0
PlantHours(Monday)	8.0
PlantHours(Tuesday)	16.0
PlantHours(Wednesday)	24.0
PlantHours(Thursday)	8.0
PlantHours(Friday)	16.0
PlantHours(Saturday)	0.0

Figure 9.6 Array PlantHours

SYNTAX DISPLAY

Array Type Declaration

Form:

TYPE *array-type* IS ARRAY (*subscript-type*) OF *element-type*;

Example:

```
SUBTYPE WordWidth IS Positive RANGE 1..32;
TYPE BitVector IS ARRAY (WordWidth) OF Boolean;
```

Interpretation:

The identifier *array-type* describes a collection of array elements; each element can store an item of type *element-type*. The *subscript-type* can be any discrete type, that is, any predefined or user-defined integer or enumeration type or subtype. There is one array element corresponding to each value in the *subscript-type*. All elements of an array are of the same *element-type*.

Notes:

1. The element-type can be any predefined or user-defined scalar or composite type.

2. A floating-point type cannot be a subscript-type because it is not discrete, as it represents a continuous range of values.

3. It is unwise to use as a *subscript-type* a predefined type with a large range of values (e.g., Integer) because doing so would result in arrays with a gigantic number of elements. Generally, our subscript types will be either user-defined subtypes of Integer with fairly small ranges or user-defined enumeration types.

It is important to realize that an array type declaration does not cause allocation of storage space in memory. The array type describes the structure of an array only. Only variables actually store information and require storage. Storage space is not allocated until a variable of this type is declared.

Operations on Arrays

Two basic operations act on elements of an array: store and retrieve; also, as in records, assignment and equality test are available for array variables.

- *Store:* The store operation inserts a value into the array. If A is an array, c is an expression that is compatible with the element type of A, and i is an expression that is compatible with the subscript type, the statement

  ```
  A(i) := C;
  ```

  stores the contents of c in element i of array A.

- *Retrieve:* If c is a variable that is assignment compatible with the element type of A, the statement

  ```
  C := A(i);
  ```

  retrieves element i of array A and copies its value into c. For both of these statements the value of subscript i must be in the range of the array subscript type; otherwise, Constraint_Error will be raised.

- *Assignment:* The assignment operator can also be used to copy the contents of one array to another if the arrays are compatible (of the same array type). If A and B are compatible arrays, the statement

  ```
  A := B;
  ```

  copies all values associated with array B to array A.

- *Equality test:* The equality and inequality operators can also be used to compare two arrays if they are compatible (of the same array type). If A and B are compatible arrays, the Boolean expression

  ```
  A = B;
  ```

evaluates to `True` if and only if each element of A is equal to the corresponding element of B, and the Boolean expression

```
A /= B;
```

evaluates to `True` if and only if any elements of A are not equal to the corresponding elements of B.

The discussion above summarizes all the information that we need to know to use an array. We do not need to know how Ada stores the elements of an array in memory or how it implements the *retrieve* and *store* operators above.

Aggregate Array Assignment

As in the case of records, an entire array can be filled with values by three methods:

- assignment to each element with an individual assignment statement, either randomly or sequentially;

- copying one entire array to another with an array assignment statement, as discussed just above; and

- storing values in an entire array using an aggregate, similar to that used in records.

It is the last method that concerns us now. Given an array A of type `TestArray`, the 100 `Float` values could, if they were all known in advance, be stored in A with a single statement such as

```
A := (1.0, 27.0, 35.0, -4.0, 15.0, ...);
```

where the ellipsis must be replaced completely with the other 95 values. This is surely tedious, but it is better than writing 100 separate assignment statements. As in the case of records, named association can also be used:

```
A := (1 => 1.0, 2 => 27.0, ...);
```

where the remaining 98 values also need to be supplied. Whereas in record aggregates we prefer named association, in array aggregates it can be cumbersome because an array can have a large number of elements. In using array aggregates we will generally use positional association unless there is a good reason not to do so.

A common and useful application of array aggregates is to initialize most or all elements of an array with the *same* value. Suppose that our array A were to be "cleared" so that all values were 0. This could be done in a loop:

```
FOR I IN 1..MaxSize LOOP
   A(I) := 0.0;
END LOOP;
```

or with a single aggregate assignment:

```
A := (1..MaxSize => 0.0);
```

The aggregate assignment is certainly more concise, expresses the will of the programmer clearly, and may possibly execute faster. Suppose now that A were to be initialized such that its first 5 elements were as above but the other 95 were to be 0. The assignment

```
A := (1.0, 27.0, 35.0, -4.0, 15.0, OTHERS => 0.0);
```

does the trick. The OTHERS clause informs the compiler to store 0s in all those elements not expressly listed in the aggregate. If, say, only the first, third, and fifth elements were nonzero, named association could be used:

```
A := (1 => 1.0, 3 => 27.0, 5 => 35.0, OTHERS => 0.0);
```

Finally, the assignment

```
A := (OTHERS => 0.0);
```

fills the entire array with 0s even more concisely: Because no other elements were explicitly filled, the OTHERS applies to all elements.

It is important to remember in using an aggregate that *all* elements of the array must be initialized by the aggregate; otherwise, a compilation error results. OTHERS initializes all elements that are not otherwise given.

EXERCISES FOR SECTION 9.5

Self-Check

1. What is the difference between the expressions x3 and x(3)?

2. For the following declarations, how many memory cells are reserved for data and what type of data can be stored there?

   ```
   TYPE AnArray IS ARRAY(1..5) OF Character;
   Grades : AnArray;
   ```

   When is the memory allocated: after the type declaration or after the variable declaration?

3. Write the variable and type declarations for all of the following valid arrays:

   a. Subscript type Boolean, element type Float

   b. Subscript type 'A'..'F', element type Integer

   c. Subscript type Character, element type Boolean

   d. Subscript type Integer, element type Float

   e. Subscript type Character, element type Float

   f. Subscript type Float, element type Character

g. Subscript type Day (enumeration type), element type Float

9.6 Problem Solving: Selecting Array Elements for Processing

Using a Subscript as an Index to an Array

As indicated in the preceding section, the subscript type of an array may be any discrete type or subtype. In the next few sections, most of the examples will deal with arrays whose subscript type is a subtype of type Positive. We are doing this because it is expedient; you should keep in mind that the features described carry over to other subscript types as well. We will discuss arrays with nonnumeric subscripts in Section 9.9.

Each array reference includes the array name and a parenthesized subscript. The subscript (sometimes called an *index*) that is used to reference an array element must be an expression that is compatible with the declared subscript type. Very often, the subscript type is a subtype with a minimum value of 1 (e.g., (1..MaxSize)). Because the minimum subscript value is positive, it must be an expression whose value is in the range specified by the subscript type. For the array Vacation declared in Example 9.6, the allowable subscript values are the positive integers from 1 through 50.

■ Example 9.7

Table 9.2 shows some sample statements involving the array x shown in Fig. 9.3. I is assumed to be a Positive variable with value 6. Make sure you understand each statement.

Table 9.2 Some Sample Statements for Array X

Statement	*Effect*
`Ada.Float_Text_IO.Put(X(4));`	Displays 8.0 (value of X(4)).
`Ada.Float_Text_IO.Put(X(I));`	Displays 12.0 (value of X(6)).
`Ada.Float_Text_IO.Put(X(I)+1.0);`	Displays 13.0 (value of 12.0 + 1.0).
`Ada.Float_Text_IO.Put(X(I+1));`	Displays 14.0 (value of X(7)).
`Ada.Float_Text_IO.Put(X(2*I));`	Constraint_Error: there is no X(12).
`Ada.Float_Text_IO.Put(X(2*I-4));`	Displays –54.5 (value of X(8)).
`Ada.Float_Text_IO.Put` `  (X(Positive(X(4))));`	Displays –54.5 (value of X(8)).
`X(I)  := X(I+1);`	Assigns 14.0 (value of X(7)) to X(6).
`X(I-1) := X(I);`	Assigns 14.0 (new value of X(6)) to X(5).
`X(I) - 1 := X(I);`	Syntax error: Illegal assignment statement

The last Put statement uses Positive(X(4)) as a subscript expression. Because this evaluates to 8, the value of X(8) (and not X(4)) is displayed. If the value of Positive(X(4)) were outside the range 1 through 8, Constraint_Error would be raised at execution time.

Two different subscripts are used in the last three assignment statements in the table. The first assignment copies the value of x(7) into x(6) (subscripts I+1 and I); the second assignment statement copies the value of x(6) into x(5) (subscripts I and I-1). The last assignment statement causes a syntax error, because there is an expression to the left of the assignment symbol, :=.

In Table 9.2 there is an attempt to display element x(12), which is not in the array. This attempt will result in Constraint_Error being raised. ∎

SYNTAX DISPLAY

Array Reference

Form:

name (subscript)

Example:

X(3*I - 2)

Interpretation:

The *subscript* must be an expression that is compatible with the *subscript-type* specified in the declaration for the array name. If the expression is of the wrong data type, a "type mismatch" compilation error will be detected; if the value expression depends on values not known at compile time, Constraint_Error will be raised at execution time if the expression value is out of the subscript range.

Using FOR Loops with Arrays

Often we wish to process the elements of an array in sequence, starting with the first. An example would be entering data into the array or displaying its contents. This can be accomplished by using a FOR loop whose loop control variable (e.g., I) is also used as the array subscript (e.g., x(I)). Increasing the value of the loop control variable by 1 causes the next array element to be processed.

∎ Example 9.8

The array Cubes declared below can be used to store the cubes of the first ten integers (e.g., Cubes(1) is 1, Cubes(10) is 1000).

```
Size : CONSTANT Positive := 10;
SUBTYPE Index IS Positive RANGE 1..Size;
TYPE IntArray IS ARRAY (Index) OF INTEGER;
Cubes : IntArray;                    -- array of cubes
```

The FOR statement

```
FOR I IN 1 .. Size LOOP
  Cubes(I) := I * I * I;
END LOOP;
```

(1)	(2)	(3)	(4)	(5)	(6)	(7)	(8)	(9)	(10)
1	8	27	64	125	216	343	512	729	1000

Figure 9.7 Array Cubes

initializes this array as shown in Fig. 9.7.

A better way to write the FOR loop is

```
FOR I IN Index LOOP
  Cubes(I) := I * I * I;
END LOOP;
```

The behavior of this loop is the same as that of the previous loop: Each element of the array is accessed in sequence. The advantage of writing the loop this way is that, assuming that Index is the subscript type of the array, if the bounds of Index are ever changed and the program is recompiled, no other statements will have to change. In cases in which an entire array is being referenced in sequence, we will usually use this form of loop control. ■

■ Example 9.9

Program 9.8 reads an array of values from the terminal, calculates the average of the values, and displays a table of differences, each showing the given value's difference from the average.

Program 9.8 Table of Differences

```
WITH Ada.Text_IO;
WITH Ada.Integer_Text_IO;
WITH Ada.Float_Text_IO;
PROCEDURE Show_Differences IS
-------------------------------------------------------------------
--| Computes the average value of an array of data and
--| prints the difference between each value and the average.
--| Author: Michael B. Feldman, The George Washington University
--| Last Modified: September 1998
-------------------------------------------------------------------

  MaxItems : CONSTANT Positive := 8;     -- number of data items

  SUBTYPE Index IS Positive RANGE 1..MaxItems;
  TYPE FloatArray IS ARRAY (Index) OF Float;

  X        : FloatArray;                  -- array of data
  Average  : Float;                       -- average value of data
  Sum      : Float;                       -- sum of the data

BEGIN -- Show_Differences

  -- Enter the data.
  Ada.Text_IO.Put(Item => "Please enter ");
  Ada.Integer_Text_IO.Put(Item => MaxItems, Width=>0);
  Ada.Text_IO.Put(Item => " floating-point numbers > ");
```

```
                 Ada.Text_IO.New_Line;

                 FOR I IN Index LOOP
                    Ada.Float_Text_IO.Get(Item => X(I));
                 END LOOP;
                 Ada.Text_IO.New_Line;

                 -- Compute the average value.
                 Sum := 0.0;                          -- Initialize SUM
                 FOR I IN Index LOOP
                    Sum := Sum + X(I);                -- Add each element to Sum
                 END LOOP;

                 Average := Sum / Float(MaxItems);   -- Find average value
                 Ada.Text_IO.Put(Item => "Average value is ");
                 Ada.Float_Text_IO.Put(Item=>Average, Fore=>5, Aft=>2, Exp=>0);
                 Ada.Text_IO.New_Line;

                 -- Display the difference between each item and the average.
                 Ada.Text_IO.Put
                    (Item => "Table of differences between X(I) and average");
                 Ada.Text_IO.New_Line;
                 Ada.Text_IO.Put(Item => "    I        X(I)      Difference");
                 Ada.Text_IO.New_Line;

                 FOR I IN Index LOOP
                    Ada.Integer_Text_IO.Put(Item => I, Width=>4);
                    Ada.Text_IO.Put(Item => "     ");
                    Ada.Float_Text_IO.Put(Item=>X(I), Fore=>5, Aft=>2, Exp=>0);
                    Ada.Text_IO.Put(Item => "     ");
                    Ada.Float_Text_IO.Put
                       (Item=>X(I)-Average, Fore=>5, Aft=>2, Exp=>0);
                    Ada.Text_IO.New_Line;
                 END LOOP;

              END Show_Differences;
```

Sample Run

```
Please enter 8 floating-point numbers >
16 12 6 8 2.5 12 14 -54.5

Average value is      2.00
Table of differences between X(I) and average
    I        X(I)      Difference
    1        16.00        14.00
    2        12.00        10.00
    3         6.00         4.00
    4         8.00         6.00
    5         2.50         0.50
    6        12.00        10.00
    7        14.00        12.00
    8       -54.50       -56.50
```

In this program the declarations

```
MaxItems : CONSTANT Positive := 8;                  -- number of data items

SUBTYPE Index IS Positive RANGE 1..MaxItems;
```

```
TYPE FloatArray IS ARRAY (Index) OF Float;

X : FloatArray;                          -- array of Float numbers
```

declare an array type and allocate storage for an array object x with subscripts in the range 1–8. The program uses three FOR loops to process the array x. The loop control variable I is also used as the array subscript in each loop.

The first FOR loop

```
FOR I IN Index LOOP
  Ada.Float_Text_IO.Get(Item => X(I));
END LOOP;
```

is used to read one data value into each array element (the first item is stored in x(1), the second item in x(2), etc.). The Get procedure is called once for each value of I in the range of Index, that is, from 1 to 8; each call causes a new data value to be read and stored in x(I). The subscript I determines which array element receives the next data value. The sample run causes the array to acquire the values shown in Fig. 9.3.

The second FOR loop is used to accumulate (in Sum) the sum of all values stored in the array; this loop will be traced later. The last FOR loop,

```
FOR I IN Index LOOP
  Ada.Integer_Text_IO.Put(Item => I, Width=>4);
  Ada.Text_IO.Put(Item => "    ");
  Ada.Float_Text_IO.Put(Item => X(I), Fore=>5, Aft=>2, Exp=>0);
  Ada.Text_IO.Put(Item => "    ");
  Ada.Float_Text_IO.Put(Item => X(I)-Average, Fore=>5, Aft=>2, Exp=>0);
  Ada.Text_IO.New_Line;
END LOOP;
```

is used to display a table showing each array element, x(I), and the difference between that element and the average value, x(I) - Average.

The program fragment

```
Sum := 0.0;                          -- Initialize SUM
FOR I IN Index LOOP
  Sum := Sum + X(I);                 -- Add each element to SUM
END LOOP;
```

accumulates the sum of all eight elements of array x in the variable Sum. Each time the FOR loop is repeated, the next element of array x is added to Sum. The execution of this program fragment is traced in Table 9.3 for the first three repetitions of the loop.

Table 9.3   Partial Trace of FOR Loop of Program 9.8

Statement Part	I	X(I)	Sum	Effect
Sum:= 0;			0	Initializes Sum
FOR I IN Index LOOP	1	16.0		Initializes I to 1
Sum := Sum + X(I)			16.0	Add x(1) to Sum
increment and test I	2	12.0		2 <= 8 is true

Statement Part	I	X(I)	Sum	Effect
Sum := Sum + X(I)			28.0	Add x(2) to Sum
increment and test I	3	6.0		3 <= 8 is true
Sum := Sum + X(I)			34.0	Add x(3) to Sum

In Program 9.8 the subscripted variable x(I) is an actual parameter for the floating-point Get and Put procedures. It is always necessary to read data into an array one element at a time as shown in this example. In most instances it is also necessary to display one array element at a time.

PROGRAM
STYLE

Designing Arrays for Expansion and Reuse

The constant MaxItems and subtype Index are used throughout Program 9.8 to represent the subscript range of the array. This enables us to extend the program easily to handle more items by just changing the constant value and recompiling the program. Nothing else in the program needs to be changed.

EXERCISES FOR SECTION 9.6

Self-Check

1. Describe the effect of each statement in Table 9.2, assuming that I is 5.

2. If an array is declared to have ten elements, must the program use all ten of them?

3. The following sequence of statements changes the initial contents of array x displayed in Fig. 9.3. Describe what each statement does to the array and show the final contents of array x after all statements execute.

```
I := 3;

X(I) := X(I) + 10.0;

X(I - 1) := X(2 * I - 1);

X(I + 1) := X(2 * I) + X(2 * I + 1);

FOR I IN 5 .. 7 LOOP
   X(I) := X(I + 1);
END LOOP;

FOR I IN REVERSE 1..3 LOOP
   X(I + 1) := X(I);
END LOOP;
```

4. Write program statements that will do the following to array x shown in Fig. 9.3.

   a. Replace the third element with 7.0.

   b. Copy the element in the fifth location into the first one.

   c. Subtract the first element from the fourth and store the result in the fifth one.

   d. Increase the sixth element by 2.

   e. Find the sum of the first five elements.

   f. Multiply each of the first six elements by 2 and place each product in an element of the array `AnswerArray`.

   g. Display all even-numbered elements on one line.

9.7 Problem Solving: Using Arrays

Sequential Versus Random Access to Arrays

The same array can be processed in *sequential order* and in *random order*. Often, we need to manipulate all elements of an array in some uniform manner (as in Program 9.8). In situations like this it makes sense to process the array elements in sequence (sequential access), starting with the first and ending with the last. This is usually accomplished by using a FOR loop whose loop control variable is also the array subscript.

Suppose the program represented the total sales of each of eight different products. In that case, in a second part of the program we might want to modify a specific value to account for additional sales. We might prompt the user for a product number (1–8 in this case) and an amount, then select just that array element for processing. This is called *random access* because the order is not predictable beforehand.

Copying and Comparing Arrays

A third way of manipulating an array—accessing the entire array at once—is provided by the assignment (:=), equality (=), and inequality (/=) operations. As in the case of records, it is possible to assign the entire contents of one array to another array provided that the arrays are compatible. Arrays follow the same compatibility rules as scalars and records do: Two arrays are compatible if their type names are identical or they are subtypes of the same type. Given the declarations

```
MaxSize : CONSTANT Positive := 100;
SUBTYPE Index IS Positive RANGE 1..MaxSize;
TYPE TestArray IS ARRAY (Index) OF Float;
W : TestArray;
X : TestArray;
Y : TestArray;
```

the assignment statement

```
X := Y;
```

copies each value in array Y to the corresponding element of array X (i.e., Y(1) is copied to X(1), Y(2) to X(2), etc.). Furthermore, the use of = and /= in the fragment

```
IF X = Y THEN
  Ada.Text_IO.Put(Item => "Arrays X and Y are equal");
ELSIF W /= Y THEN
  Ada.Text_IO.Put(Item => "Arrays W and Y are unequal");
END IF;
```

is quite correct. The additional declaration

```
Z : ARRAY (Index) OF Float;
```

happens to be correct Ada, although we recommend against its use. z is declared directly as an array instead of as a variable of an array *type* as x and y were. The Ada compiler, which tries to establish the type name of every variable, will give z an internal type name, which our program cannot know. The assignment statements

```
Z := Y;                   -- invalid array copy
X := Z;                   -- invalid array copy
```

and the IF fragment

```
IF Z = X THEN ...
```

are illegal and result in compilation errors. Even though array z has the same structure as arrays x and y, the type of array z is *anonymous* and is not compatible with the type of arrays x and y (type TestArray). Note that the *elements* of z are compatible with the *elements* of x and y (they are all Float), and therefore assignments such as

```
Z(3) := Y(5);
X(9) := Z(1);
```

and comparisons such as

```
IF X(9) = Z(1) THEN...
IF Y(3) /= Z(5) THEN ...
```

are legal.

PROGRAM STYLE

Avoiding Anonymous Array Types

Because using anonymous (unnamed) array types causes difficulties with array assignment and comparison, the use of anonymous (unnamed) types should be avoided, and we avoid it in this book.

Arrays as Parameters

The rules for manipulating array parameters in a procedure are similar to those for manipulating scalar parameters: IN parameters may not be altered by the procedure.

The next two examples illustrate the use of arrays as parameters assuming the following declarations:

```
MaxSize : CONSTANT Positive := 5;
SUBTYPE Index IS Positive RANGE 1..MaxSize;
TYPE TestArray IS ARRAY (Index) OF Float;
X, Y, Z : TestArray;
```

■ Example 9.10

Although it is possible to use a single assignment statement to copy one array to another, no arithmetic on entire arrays is defined in Ada. For example, the assignment statement

```
Z := X + Y;              -- illegal addition of arrays
```

is invalid because Ada has no predefined operator + that acts on array operands. Procedure AddArray in Program 9.9 can be used to add two arrays of type TestArray.

Program 9.9 Procedure AddArray

```
PROCEDURE AddArray (A, B  : IN TestArray; C : OUT TestArray) IS
   -- Pre:  A(I) and B(I) (I in range Index) are assigned values
   -- Post: C(I) := A(I) + B(I) (I in range Index).

BEGIN   -- AddArray

   -- Add corresponding elements of each array
   FOR I IN Index LOOP
     C(I) := A(I) + B(I);
   END  LOOP;

END AddArray;
```

The parameter correspondence established by the procedure call statement

```
AddArray (A => X, B => Y, C => Z);
```

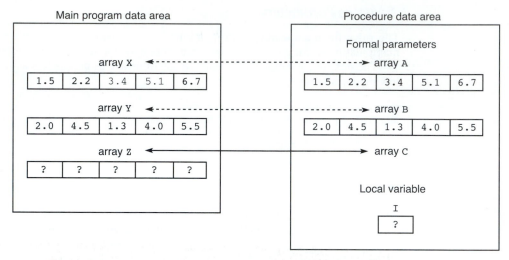

Figure 9.8 Parameter Correspondence for AddArray(X, Y, Z)

is shown in Fig. 9.8.

Formal parameter arrays A and B in the procedure correspond to actual arrays X and Y; formal parameter array C corresponds to actual array Z. The procedure results are stored in array Z. After execution of the procedure, Z(1) will contain the sum of X(1) and Y(1), or 3.5; Z(2) will contain 6.7, and so on. Arrays X and Y will be unchanged. ∎

More on the Rules of Parameter Passing

Recall from Section 7.5 that the values of actual scalar IN OUT parameters are always copied into the corresponding formal parameters in the procedure's data area and that all the OUT and IN OUT results are copied back into the calling program just before the procedure terminates normally and returns to the caller. The rules for structured parameters are somewhat different. The Ada standard allows structured parameters to be copied, as for scalars, but also allows them to be passed more efficiently, simply by copying the *address* of the actual parameter into the location of the corresponding formal parameter in the subprogram's data area. The Ada compiler writer can choose which method to use.

If the latter method (usually called *call by reference*) is used, a modification to an IN OUT parameter will be effective immediately in the calling program, instead of waiting until the procedure returns to its caller. This is because in the latter method, the formal parameter and the actual parameter refer to exactly the same set of locations. Why are the rules different for the scalar and structured cases?

Suppose that an exception is raised in the execution of the procedure and is not handled by an exception handler in that procedure. Ada requires that the procedure terminate abnormally and that the exception be *propagated* (passed back) to the calling program, which could then handle it with its own handler. In this case the scalar OUT or IN OUT parameters will not be copied back, because the procedure didn't terminate normally. This is usually a good thing: The program writer is sure that the original parameter values, not the new ones, remain in the calling program if the procedure does not run to normal completion.

Why not do the same thing with array and record parameters? Arrays and records can be large, and so copying them to and from subprograms could take a large amount of time and space. Ada therefore gives the compiler the option of just passing the address of a structured parameter. Most Ada compilers pass structured parameters by reference; some compilers pass *small* ones by copying and *large* ones by reference to try to get the best of both worlds. Although in theory a user does not know which method is being used, it is reasonably safe to assume that a compiler will use reference passing for large structured parameters, and therefore:

- There is no large time or space penalty in using arrays or records as parameters.

- It is wise to assume that, if a subprogram propagates an exception back to the caller, some of the actual parameters may have new values but others may not. It is certain, however, that by the time a procedure returns normally—no exception is raised, or at least it is successfully handled within the procedure—all the parameters will have acquired their new values.

■ Example 9.11

Procedure `Exchange` in Program 9.10 exchanges the values of its two type `Float` parameters.

Program 9.10 Procedure Exchange

```
PROCEDURE Exchange (P, Q : IN OUT Float) IS
   -- Exchanges the values of P and Q.
   -- Pre:  P and Q are assigned values.
   -- Post: P has the value passed into Q and vice-versa.

   Temp : Float;        -- temporary variable for the exchange

BEGIN   -- Exchange

  Temp := P;
  P  := Q;
  Q  := Temp;

END Exchange;
```

The procedure call statement

```
Exchange (X(1), X(2));
```

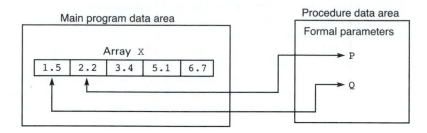

Figure 9.9 Parameter Correspondence for Exchange(X(1),X(2))

uses this procedure to exchange the contents of the first two elements (type `Float`) of array x. The actual parameter x(1) corresponds to formal parameter P; the actual parameter x(2) corresponds to formal parameter Q. This correspondence is shown in Fig. 9.9 for the array x.

It is not permitted to use a subscripted variable as a formal parameter. For example, the procedure declaration

```
PROCEDURE Exchange ( X(i), X(j) : IN OUT Float);
```

would cause a compilation error.   ∎

PROGRAM STYLE

Choosing the Best Parameter Mode

It is very important to keep in mind that all Ada compilers pass *all* scalar parameters by copying, and most compilers pass structured parameters by reference, *regardless of their mode*. This is quite different from the rules of other languages, especially Pascal.

In Pascal, programmers often pass arrays by reference (VAR parameters) to save time and space, even if the array is not going to be modified and is used as a read-only parameter. Therefore programmers who have Pascal experience often think that they should pass all Ada arrays as IN OUT to be sure they are passed by reference. This is a misunderstanding that leads to poor design. In Ada, arrays are (almost always) passed by reference even if they are IN parameters, and scalars are never passed by reference even if they are IN OUT.

Because of this rule, there is absolutely no efficiency gain in passing an array as an IN OUT parameter when its use is as an IN parameter. It is therefore best to choose the parameter mode that best describes the *use* of the parameter, not the method by which it is passed.

EXERCISES FOR SECTION 9.7

Self-Check

1. When is it better to pass an entire array of data to a procedure rather than individual elements?

2. When is a copy of an entire array made for an array that is a function procedure parameter? What happens to the copy after the procedure executes?

3. Is it acceptable to modify, within a function, an element of an array that is passed as a parameter to that function? What about a procedure?

4. Given the following declarations:

```
A: ARRAY(1..5) OF Integer;
B: ARRAY(1..5) OF Integer;
C, D: ARRAY(1..5) OF Integer;

TYPE List IS ARRAY (1..5) OF Integer;

E: List;
F: List;
G, H: List;
```

Explain why each of the following statements is valid or invalid:

```
A := B;
C := D;
E := F;
G := H;
```

Programming

1. Write a procedure that assigns a value of `True` to element I of the output array if element I of one input array has the same value as element I of the other input array; otherwise, assign a value of `False`. If the input arrays have subscript type `IndexType`, the output array should have the following type:

```
TYPE BoolArray IS ARRAY(IndexType) OF Boolean;
```

9.8   Problem Solving: Reading Part of an Array

Usually, we don't know exactly how many elements there will be in an array. For example, if we are processing exam scores, there might be 150 students in one class, 200 in the next, and so on. In this situation we can declare an array that will accommodate the largest class. Only part of this array will actually be processed for a smaller class.

■ Example 9.12

The array `scores` declared below can accommodate a class of up to 250 students. Each array element can contain an integer value between 0 and 100.

```
MaxSize : CONSTANT Positive := 250;
MaxScore : CONSTANT Positive := 100;
SUBTYPE ClassIndex  IS Positive RANGE 1..MaxSize;
SUBTYPE ClassRange  IS Natural RANGE 0..MaxSize;
SUBTYPE ScoreRange  IS Natural RANGE 0..MaxScore;
TYPE ScoreArray IS ARRAY (ClassIndex) OF ScoreRange;

Scores : ScoreArray;
ClassSize : ClassRange;
```

Procedure `ReadScores` in Program 9.11 reads up to 250 exam scores. It displays a warning message when the array is filled. The actual number of scores read is returned as the value of `ClassSize`.

Program 9.11 Procedure ReadScores

```
PROCEDURE ReadScores (Scores : OUT ScoreArray;
                         ClassSize : OUT ClassRange) IS
-- Reads an array of exam scores (Scores)
-- for a class of up to MaxSize students.
-- Pre : None
-- Post: The data values are stored in array Scores.
--       The number of values read is stored in ClassSize.

   Sentinel : CONSTANT Integer := -1;  -- Sentinel value
   TempScore : Integer;                -- Temporary storage for a score

BEGIN

  Ada.Text_IO.Put
    (Item => "Enter next score after the prompt or -1 to stop.");
  Ada.Text_IO.New_Line;

  ClassSize := 0;                         -- initial class size
  -- Read each array element until done.
  LOOP

    Robust_Input.Get(Item => TempScore,
                     MinVal => Sentinel,
                     MaxVal => ScoreRange'Last);

    EXIT WHEN (TempScore = Sentinel) OR (ClassSize = MaxSize);
```

```
     ClassSize := ClassSize + 1;
     Scores(ClassSize) := TempScore;        -- Save the score

  END LOOP;

  IF ClassSize = MaxSize THEN
     Ada.Text_IO.Put(Item => "Array is filled.");
     Ada.Text_IO.New_Line;
  END IF;

END ReadScores;
```

In any subsequent processing of array `Scores`, the variable `ClassSize` should be used to limit the number of array elements processed. Only the subarray with subscripts `1..ClassSize` is defined. All array elements with subscripts larger than `ClassSize` are still undefined and should not be manipulated. `ClassSize` should be passed as a parameter to any procedure that processes the partially filled array. ∎

EXERCISES FOR SECTION 9.8

Self-Check

1. In procedure `ReadScores`, what prevents the user from entering more than `MaxSize` scores?

2. What is the range of data values that can be entered? What is the range of data values that can be stored in the array?

3. Why can't we use a FOR loop instead of a general loop in procedure `Read-Scores`?

9.9 Data Structures: Interesting Array Examples

As we have seen, in Ada the subscript type of an array can be any discrete type or subtype. A number of different array types are described in Table 9.4.

Table 9.4   Some Array Types and Applications

Application

Storing a person's name, up to ten letters

Declarations
```
SUBTYPE NameLength IS Positive RANGE 1..10;
TYPE NameArray IS ARRAY(NameLength) OF Character;
```

```
Name : NameArray;
```

Example
```
Name(1) := 'A';
```

Application

Storing Fahrenheit temperatures corresponding to −10 through 10 degrees Celsius

Declarations
```
SUBTYPE CelsiusRange IS Integer RANGE -10..10;
TYPE TemperatureArray IS ARRAY(CelsiusRange) OF Float;
Fahrenheit : TemperatureArray;
```

Example
```
Fahrenheit(-10) := 14.0;
```

Application

Storing the number of times each capital letter occurs

Declarations
```
SUBTYPE UpperCase IS Character RANGE 'A'..'Z';
TYPE LetterCountArray IS ARRAY(UpperCase) OF Natural;
LetterCount : LetterCountArray;
```

Example
```
LetterCount('A') := 0;
```

Application

Storing a set of flags indicating which letters occurred and which did not

Declarations
```
SUBTYPE UpperCase IS Character RANGE 'A'..'Z';
TYPE LetterFoundArray IS ARRAY(UpperCase) OF Boolean;
LetterFound : LetterFoundArray;
```

Example
```
LetterCount('X') := False;
```

Application

Storing the number of `True` answers and `False` answers to a quiz

Declarations
```
TYPE AnswerArray IS ARRAY(Boolean) OF Natural;
Answers : AnswerArray;
```

Example
```
Answers(True) := 15;
```

The array Name has 10 elements and can be used to store the letters of a person's name. The array Fahrenheit has 21 elements and can be used to store the Fahrenheit temperature corresponding to each Celsius temperature in the range −10 though 10 degrees Celsius. For example, Fahrenheit(0) would be the Fahrenheit temperature, 32.0, corresponding to 0 degrees Celsius. Arrays LetterCount and LetterFound have the same subscript type (i.e., the uppercase letters) and will be discussed in Example 9.14. The array Answers has only two elements with subscript values False and True.

■ Example 9.13

The array MonthSales, declared below, could be used to keep track of the amount of sales in each month. The subscript type is Simple_Dates.Months, so the subscript values are the constants Jan to Dec.

```
TYPE SalesArray IS ARRAY (Simple_Dates.Months) OF Float;
CurrentMonth   : Simple_Dates.Months;
MonthSales : SalesArray;
CurrentSales : Float;
```

The element type of SalesArray is given as Float, which can be negative. This is appropriate because in an unusually bad month, the value of returned goods can exceed that of newly sold goods, so the net sales can be negative. The aggregate assignment

```
MonthSales := (OTHERS => 0.0);
```

initializes this array to all zeros. The statement

```
MonthSales(CurrentMonth) := MonthSales(CurrentMonth) + CurrentSales;
```

adds the value of CurrentSales to the element of MonthSales selected by the subscript CurrentMonth. ■

■ Example 9.14

The arrays LetterCount and LetterFound described in Table 9.4 have the subscript type UpperCase. Hence there is an array element for each uppercase letter. Letter-Count('A') could be used to count the number of occurrences of the letter A in a line; LetterFound('A') could be used to indicate whether or not the letter A occurs. If the letter A occurs, LetterFound('A') would be True; otherwise, LetterFound('A') would be False.

Program 9.12 uses the arrays LetterCount and LetterFound described above to display the number of occurrences of each letter in a line of text. The case of the letter is ignored (e.g., 't' and 'T' are considered the same letter). Only counts greater than 0 are printed.

Program 9.12 Concordance Program

```ada
WITH Ada.Text_IO;
WITH Ada.Integer_Text_IO;
WITH Ada.Characters.Handling;
PROCEDURE Concordance IS
-------------------------------------------------------------------
--| Finds and displays the number of occurrences of each letter.
--| The case of each letter is immaterial.  Letters with counts
--| of zero are not displayed.
--| Author: Michael B. Feldman, The George Washington University
--| Last Modified: September 1998
-------------------------------------------------------------------

   Sentinel : CONSTANT Character := '.';

   SUBTYPE UpperCase IS Character RANGE 'A'..'Z';
   SUBTYPE LowerCase IS Character RANGE 'a'..'z';
   TYPE LetterCountArray IS ARRAY (UpperCase) OF Natural;
   TYPE LetterFlags      IS ARRAY (UpperCase) OF Boolean;

   LetterCount : LetterCountArray; -- array of counts
   LetterFound : LetterFlags;      -- array of flags
   NextChar : Character;                       -- each input character

BEGIN -- Concordance

  -- Initialize LetterCount
  LetterCount := (OTHERS => 0);              -- Initialize counts
  LetterFound := (OTHERS => False);          -- Initialize flags

  -- Read and process each data character.
  Ada.Text_IO.Put(Item => "Enter a line of text ending with a period.");
  Ada.Text_IO.New_Line;

  LOOP
    Ada.Text_IO.Get(Item => NextChar);

    -- Increment the count for this character, if it is a letter
    IF NextChar IN UpperCase THEN
      LetterCount(NextChar) := LetterCount(NextChar) + 1;
      LetterFound(NextChar) := True;
    ELSIF NextChar IN LowerCase THEN
      NextChar := Ada.Characters.Handling.To_Upper(NextChar);
      LetterCount(NextChar) := LetterCount(NextChar) + 1;
      LetterFound(NextChar) := True;
    END IF;
    EXIT WHEN NextChar = Sentinel;
  END LOOP;

  -- Display counts of letters that are in the line.
  Ada.Text_IO.New_Line;
  Ada.Text_IO.New_Line;
  Ada.Text_IO.Put(Item => "Letter      Occurrences");
  Ada.Text_IO.New_Line;
  FOR WhichChar IN UpperCase LOOP
    IF LetterFound(WhichChar) THEN
      Ada.Text_IO.Put(Item => "      ");
      Ada.Text_IO.Put(Item => WhichChar);
      Ada.Integer_Text_IO.Put
```

```
            (Item => LetterCount(WhichChar), Width => 16);
        Ada.Text_IO.New_Line;
      END IF;
   END LOOP;

END Concordance;
```

Sample Run

```
Enter a line of text ending with a period.
This is a test of the concordance program.
```

Letter	Occurrences
A	3
C	3
D	1
E	3
F	1
G	1
H	2
I	2
M	1
N	2
O	4
P	1
R	3
S	3
T	4

In Program 9.12 the array `LetterFound` is not really needed and was included in the example mainly to show an application of an array of Booleans. The condition

```
LetterFound(NextChar)
```

could be written just as easily as

```
LetterCount(NextChar) > 0
```

Writing the condition in this way would eliminate the need for the second array. ∎

EXERCISES FOR SECTION 9.9

Self-Check

1. Describe the following array types, assuming that `IndexType` is a subtype of `Integer` with range −5−5:

   a. `ARRAY (1..20) OF Character;`

   b. `ARRAY ('0'..'9') OF Boolean;`

   c. `ARRAY (IndexType) OF Float;`

    d. ARRAY (Boolean) OF Character;

    e. ARRAY (Character) OF Boolean;

2. Provide array type definitions for representing the following:

    a. The areas associated with each room in a group of rooms (living room, dining room, kitchen, etc.).

    b. The number of students in each grade of an elementary school.

    c. A letter associated with each color in a collection of colors. This letter will be the first letter of the color name.

9.10 Problem Solving: Searching and Sorting an Array

In this section we will discuss two common problems in processing arrays: searching an array to determine the location of a desired value and sorting an array to rearrange the array elements in sequence. As an example of an array search, we might wish to search the array of exam scores read in by procedure ReadScores (see Section 9.8, Program 9.11) to determine which student, if any, got a particular score. An example of an array sort would be rearranging the array elements so that they are in increasing (or decreasing) order by score.

Searching an Array

We repeat the type definitions used in Section 9.8 for convenience here:

```
MaxSize : CONSTANT Positive := 250;
MaxScore : CONSTANT Positive := 100;
SUBTYPE ClassIndex  IS Positive RANGE 1..MaxSize;
SUBTYPE ClassRange  IS Natural RANGE 0..MaxSize;
SUBTYPE ScoreRange  IS Natural RANGE 0..MaxScore;
TYPE ScoreArray IS ARRAY (ClassIndex) OF ScoreRange;

Scores : ScoreArray;
ClassSize : ClassRange;
```

We can search an array for a particular score (called the search target) by examining each array element and testing to see whether it matches the target score. If a match occurs, we have found the target and can return its subscript as the search result. If a match does not occur, we should continue searching until either we get a match or we test all array elements. The input data requirements for a search function are as follows:

```
Scores : ScoreArray       -- the array to be searched
ClassSize : ClassRange    -- the number of elements in Scores
Target : ScoreRange       -- the score being searched for
```

The function result is the subscript of the first element containing Target, or zero if Target was not found. The algorithm for searching the array is:

Algorithm for Search

1. Start with the first array element.

2. LOOP

   EXIT WHEN the current element is the last element

   OR the current element matches the target

   3. Advance to the next element.

   END LOOP;

4. IF the current element matches the target THEN

   5. Return its subscript.

   ELSE

   6. Return zero.

   END IF;

The loop in step 2 compares each array element to the target. Loop exit occurs if there is a match or if the element being tested is the last element. After loop exit, the IF statement defines the function result by repeating the last comparison. Program 9.13 shows function Search. The function uses a local variable CurrentScore to control the loop. This variable must be able to go temporarily "out of range" to ClassSize+1 if the array is full and the target is not present. To avoid a constraint error in this situation, CurrentScore is of type Integer.

Program 9.13 Function Search

```
FUNCTION Search (Scores: ScoreArray; ClassSize: ClassRange;
                 Target: ScoreRange) RETURN ClassRange IS

   -- Searches for Target in array Scores
   -- Pre : ClassSize and subarray Scores(1..ClassSize) are defined
   -- Post: Returns the subscript of Target if found;
   --       otherwise, returns 0

   CurrentScore: Integer;           -- array subscript

BEGIN  -- Search

  -- Compare each value in Scores to Target until done
  CurrentScore := 1;               -- Start with the first record
  LOOP
    EXIT WHEN (CurrentScore > ClassSize)
    OR ELSE (Scores(CurrentScore) = Target)
      CurrentScore := CurrentScore + 1; -- advance to next score
  END LOOP;

  -- Define the function result.
  IF CurrentScore <= ClassSize
    AND THEN Scores(CurrentScore) = Target THEN
    RETURN CurrentScore;
  ELSE
```

```
        RETURN 0;
    END IF;

END Search;
```

The loop condition compares the array element selected by `CurrentScore` to the target. If they are equal, loop exit occurs. If they are unequal and the last element has not been reached, `CurrentScore` advances to the next array element.

Loop exit occurs when the last element is reached or the target is found. Note that if the array is full and the target is not present, `CurrentScore` will be `ClassSize+1`. We must ensure that no attempt is made in this case to reference an array element, and therefore the loop and `IF` tests are written as short-circuit tests. After loop exit, the `IF` statement returns the subscript (`CurrentScore`) of the current element if `Target` was found; otherwise, it returns zero.

Sorting an Array

In Section 7.5 we discussed a simple sort operation involving three numbers. We performed the sort by examining pairs of numbers and exchanging them if they were out of order. There are many times when we would like to sort the elements in an array, for example, to display a grade report in alphabetical order or in order by score. Let's assume that we are interested in *upward* sorting, that is, the first element of the sorted array contains the smallest value.

This section discusses a fairly intuitive (but not very fast) algorithm called the *selection sort*. To perform a selection sort of an array with N elements (subscripts `1..N`), we locate the smallest element in the subarray with subscripts `2..N` and then switch this smallest element with the element at subscript 1, thereby placing the smallest element at position 1. Then we locate the smallest element remaining in the subarray with subscripts `3..N`, and switch it with the element at subscript 2, thereby placing the second smallest element at position 2. Then we locate the smallest element remaining in subarray `4..N` and switch it with the element at subscript 3, and so on.

Figure 9.10 traces the operation of the selection sort algorithm. The diagram on the left shows the original array. Each subsequent diagram shows the array after the next largest element is moved to its final position in the array. The subarray in the darker color represents the portion of the array that is sorted after each exchange occurs. Note that it will require, at most, N-1 exchanges to place the smallest element of an array with N elements. The algorithm follows.

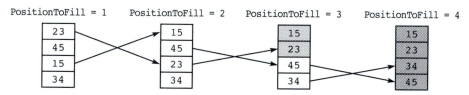

Figure 9.10 Trace of Selection Sort

Selection Sort Algorithm

1. `FOR PositionToFill IN 1..N-1 LOOP`

    2.   Find the smallest element in subarray `PositionToFill+1..N`.

    3.   IF the smallest element is not at subscript `PositionToFill` THEN

          Switch the largest element with the one at subscript `PositionToFill`.

          `END IF;`

    `END LOOP;`

The refinement of step 2 also contains a FOR loop and is shown next.

Step 2 Refinement

2.1. Save `PositionToFill` as the position of the smallest so far in the subarray

2.2. `FOR ItemToCompare IN PositionToFill+1..N LOOP`

    2.3.   IF the element at `ItemToCompare` is smaller than smallest so far THEN

            Save `ItemToCompare` as the position of the smallest so far.

            `END IF;`

    `END LOOP;`

Continuing with our use of the `ScoreArraytype`, procedure `SelectSort` in Program 9.14 implements the selection sort algorithm.

Program 9.14 Selection Sort Procedure

```
PROCEDURE SelectSort
  (Scores: IN OUT ScoreArray; ClassSize: IN ClassRange) IS
-- Pre:  Scores and ClassSize are defined
-- Post: The first ClassSize elements of Scores
--    are sorted in ascending order

  IndexOfMin: ClassRange;

BEGIN

  FOR PositionToFill IN 1..ClassSize - 1 LOOP

    -- Find the element in subarray PositionToFill..ClassSize
    -- with largest Score
    IndexOfMin := PositionToFill;
    FOR ItemToCompare IN PositionToFill + 1 .. ClassSize LOOP
      IF Scores(ItemToCompare) < Scores(IndexOfMax) THEN
        IndexOfMin := ItemToCompare;
      END IF;
    END LOOP;

    IF IndexOfMin /= PositionToFill THEN
      Exchange(Scores(PositionToFill),Scores(IndexOfMin));
    END IF;
```

```
    END LOOP;

END SelectSort;
```

Local variable `IndexOfMin` holds the location of the smallest exam score found so far in the current subarray. After each execution of the inner `FOR` loop, procedure `Exchange` is called to exchange the elements with subscripts `IndexOfMin` and `PositionToFill`, provided that the element at `PositionToFill` is not the smallest element. After the execution of `SelectSort`, the elements of the array `Scores` are in increasing order.

Analysis of Search and Sort: Big-O Notation

There are many algorithms for searching and sorting arrays. Because arrays can have a very large number of elements, the time that is required to process all the elements of an array can become significant, so it is important to have some idea of the relative efficiency of different algorithms. It is difficult to get a precise measure of the performance of an algorithm or program. For this reason we normally try to approximate the effect on an algorithm of a change in the number of items, N, that it processes. In this way, we can see how an algorithm's execution time increases with N, so we can compare two algorithms by examining their growth rates.

For example, if we determine that the expression

$$2N^2 + N - 5$$

expresses the relationship between processing time and N, we say that the algorithm is an $O(N^2)$ algorithm where O is an abbreviation for *Order of Magnitude*. (This notation is called *Big-O Notation*.) The reason that this is an $O(N^2)$ algorithm instead of an $O(2N^2)$ algorithm or an $O(N^2 + N - 5)$ is that we are interested in only the fastest-growing term (the one with the largest exponent) and we ignore constants.

To search an array of N elements for a target, we have to examine all N elements when the target is not present in the array. If the target is in the array, we only have to search until we find it. However, it could be anywhere in the array, and it is equally likely to be at the beginning of the array as at the end. So on average, we have to examine $N/2$ array elements to locate a target value that is in an array. This means that an array search is an $O(N)$ process, so the growth rate is *linear*.

To determine the growth rate of a sorting algorithm, we normally focus on the number of array element comparisons that it requires. To perform a selection sort on an array with N elements requires $N - 1$ comparisons during the first pass through the array, $N - 2$ comparisons during the second pass, and so on. Therefore the total number of comparisons is represented by the series

$$1 + 2 + 3 + \dots + (N - 2) + (N - 1)$$

The value of this series is expressed in closed form as

$$\frac{(N \times N - 1)}{2} = \frac{N^2}{2} - \frac{N}{2}$$

Therefore selection sort is an $O(N^2)$ process and the growth rate is *quadratic* (proportional to the square of the number of elements).

What difference does it make whether an algorithm is an $O(N)$ process or an $O(N^2)$ process? Table 9.5 evaluates N and N^2 for different values of N. A doubling of N causes N^2 to increase by a factor of 4. Since N increases much more slowly with N, the performance of an $O(N)$ algorithm is not as adversely affected by an increase in N as is an $O(N^2)$ algorithm.

Table 9.5   Table of Values of N and N^2

N	N^2
2	4
4	16
8	64
16	256
32	1024
64	4096
128	16384
256	65536
512	262144

In this book we will be using relatively small arrays in our programming, so algorithm performance is not a major concern. However, analyzing the performance of algorithms is an important subject about which you will study a great deal as you progress in your education, because knowing how to compute the expected Big O of an algorithm can, for large arrays and other data structures, make the difference between writing a program whose running time is acceptable and one that may run for weeks or months.

CASE
STUDY

SORTING AN ARRAY OF RECORDS

Our study of arrays began with a statement that the element type of an array can be any type, including a structured type like a record. In this section we consider how to sort an array of records.

Declaring an Array of Records

We begin with a set of declarations similar to the ones in the previous section. The new declarations define a subtype `StudentName` as a string of (exactly) 20 characters, a type `ScoreRecord` as a record containing a student's name and a test score, and a type `ScoreArray` as an array of these records.

```
MaxSize  : CONSTANT Positive := 250;
MaxScore : CONSTANT Positive := 100;

SUBTYPE StudentName IS String(1..20);
SUBTYPE ClassIndex  IS Positive RANGE 1..MaxSize;
SUBTYPE ClassRange  IS Natural RANGE 0..MaxSize;
```

```
SUBTYPE ScoreRange  IS Natural RANGE 0..MaxScore;

TYPE ScoreRecord IS RECORD
  Name:   StudentName;
  Score: ScoreRange;
END RECORD;

TYPE ScoreArray IS ARRAY (ClassIndex) OF ScoreRecord;

Scores : ScoreArray;
ClassSize : ClassRange;
```

These declarations mean that each element of `Scores` is a record with two fields. We can store values in an element of the array by combining subscripting with field selection:

```
Scores(27).Name   := "Jones, Mary          ";
Scores(27).Score := 79;
```

Note that the string representing the name must be *exactly* 20 characters long, and therefore we have included the extra blanks as required. Figure 9.11 shows a diagram of this array structure, with the first three records occupied.

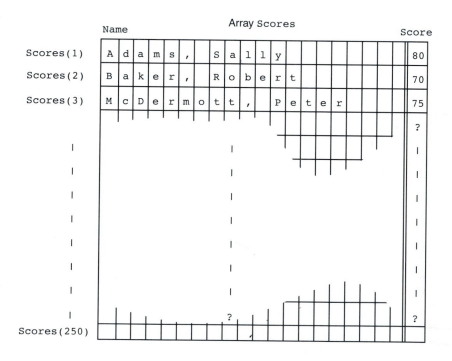

Figure 9.11 An Array of Records

Reading Records from a File

In fact, arrays of records are more often filled by reading fields from an external file. Program 9.15 uses modified versions of Programs 9.10 and 9.14. The procedure `GetRecords` assumes that a data file has been created, either by another Ada program or by a human using a text editor. In this file, each line consists of a student name and a score. In creating such a file, one must be careful to provide exactly 20 characters in the student name. Assuming that the person who created this file was careful and that all the data in the file are valid, the two fields in each student record are read from the file by

```
Ada.Text_IO.Get(File => F, Item => Scores(WhichStudent).Name);
Ada.Integer_Text_IO.Get(File => F, Item => Scores(WhichStudent).Score);
```

Sorting the File of Records

Given the `SelectSort` procedure from Program 9.14, sorting the file of records is easy. Instead of using the "whole" array element as the key, or basis of comparison, the score field of each array element is used. In the sort procedure itself, only a single line needs to be modified: the line which compares two array elements needs to be changed to

```
IF Scores(ItemToCompare).Score < Scores(IndexOfMax).Score THEN
```

After the execution of procedure `SelectSort`, the student records will be ordered by exam score (record with smallest score first).

The revised version of `SelectSort` appears as a procedure in Program 9.15, with the necessary changes made to accommodate the fact that we are using a file of score *records* instead of an array of scores.

Program 9.15 Sorting a File of Test Score Records

```
WITH Ada.Text_IO;
WITH Ada.Integer_Text_IO;
WITH Simple_Dates;
PROCEDURE Sort_Score_File IS
-------------------------------------------------------------------
--| Sorts and displays an array of test score records
--| The records are read from a file scorfile.dat
--| Author: Michael B. Feldman, The George Washington University
--| Last Modified: September 1998
-------------------------------------------------------------------

  MaxSize : CONSTANT Positive := 250;
  MaxScore : CONSTANT Positive := 100;

  SUBTYPE StudentName IS String(1..20);
  SUBTYPE ClassIndex IS Positive RANGE 1..MaxSize;
  SUBTYPE ClassRange IS Natural  RANGE 0..MaxSize;
  SUBTYPE ScoreRange IS Natural  RANGE 0..MaxScore;

  TYPE ScoreRecord IS RECORD
     Name:  StudentName;
     Score: ScoreRange;
  END RECORD;
```

```
TYPE ScoreArray IS ARRAY (ClassIndex) OF ScoreRecord;

Scores : ScoreArray;
ClassSize : ClassRange;

PROCEDURE GetRecords
  (Scores: OUT ScoreArray; ClassSize: OUT ClassRange) IS
-- Pre:  None
-- Post: Scores contains records read from file; ClassSize
--    indicates the number of records read

  TestScores: Ada.Text_IO.File_Type;
  TempSize:   ClassRange;
  TempRecord: ScoreRecord;

BEGIN  -- GetRecords

  -- Open the file and associate it with the file variable name
  Ada.Text_IO.Open
    (File => TestScores, Mode => Ada.Text_IO.In_File,
     Name => "scorfile.dat");

  -- Read each data item
  -- and store it in the appropriate element of Scores

  TempSize := 0;                          -- initial class size
  -- Read each array element until done.
  LOOP
    EXIT WHEN Ada.Text_IO.End_Of_File(TestScores) OR
              TempSize = MaxSize;

    Ada.Text_IO.Get(File => TestScores, Item => TempRecord.Name);
    Ada.Integer_Text_IO.Get
      (File => TestScores, Item => TempRecord.Score);

    TempSize := TempSize + 1;
    Scores(TempSize) := TempRecord;       -- Save the score

  END LOOP;

  IF TempSize = MaxSize THEN
    Ada.Text_IO.Put(Item => "Array is filled.");
    Ada.Text_IO.New_Line;
  END IF;

  ClassSize := TempSize;

END GetRecords;


PROCEDURE Exchange(Student1, Student2: IN OUT ScoreRecord) IS
-- Pre:  Student1 and Student2 are defined
-- Post: Student1 and Student2 are interchanged

  TempRecord: ScoreRecord;

BEGIN

  TempRecord := Student1;
```

```
        Student1 :=    Student2;
        Student2 :=    TempRecord;

   END Exchange;

   PROCEDURE SelectSort
     (Scores: IN OUT ScoreArray; ClassSize: IN ClassRange) IS
   -- Pre:  Scores and ClassSize are defined
   -- Post: The records in the first ClassSize elements of Scores
   --   are sorted in ascending order by score

      IndexOfMin: ClassRange;

   BEGIN

      FOR PositionToFill IN 1..ClassSize - 1 LOOP

        -- Find the element in subarray 1..PositionToFill
        -- with largest Score
        IndexOfMin := PositionToFill;
        FOR ItemToCompare IN PositionToFill + 1 .. ClassSize LOOP
          IF Scores(ItemToCompare).Score < Scores(IndexOfMin).Score THEN
            IndexOfMin := ItemToCompare;
          END IF;
        END LOOP;

        IF IndexOfMin /= PositionToFill THEN
          Exchange(Scores(PositionToFill),Scores(IndexOfMin));
        END IF;

      END LOOP;

   END SelectSort;

   PROCEDURE DisplayScores
     (Scores: IN ScoreArray; ClassSize: IN ClassRange) IS
   -- Pre:  Scores and ClassSize are defined
   -- Post: dislays the first ClassSize records in Scores

   BEGIN

      FOR I IN 1..ClassSize LOOP
        Ada.Integer_Text_IO.Put(Item => I, Width => 3);
        Ada.Text_IO.Put(Item => "  ");
        Ada.Text_IO.Put(Item => Scores(I).Name);
        Ada.Integer_Text_IO.Put(Item => Scores(I).Score, Width => 4);
        Ada.Text_IO.New_Line;
      END LOOP;

   END DisplayScores;


BEGIN -- Sort_Score_File

  Ada.Text_IO.Put(Item => "Today is ");
  Simple_Dates.Put(Item => Simple_Dates.Today);
  Ada.Text_IO.New_Line;

  GetRecords(Scores => Scores, ClassSize => ClassSize);
  Ada.Text_IO.Put(Item => "Original Test File:");
```

```
            Ada.Text_IO.New_Line;
            Ada.Text_IO.New_Line;
            DisplayScores(Scores => Scores, ClassSize => ClassSize);

            SelectSort(Scores => Scores, ClassSize => ClassSize);
            Ada.Text_IO.New_Line;
            Ada.Text_IO.Put(Item => "Sorted Test File:");
            Ada.Text_IO.New_Line;
            Ada.Text_IO.New_Line;
            DisplayScores(Scores => Scores, ClassSize => ClassSize);
            Ada.Text_IO.New_Line;

END Sort_Score_File;
```

Sample Run

```
Today is SEP 6 1998
Original Test File:

      1   Jones, Mary            75
      2   Hubbard, Kathy         99
      3   Andersen, Lars         80
      4   Gribben, George        21
      5   Rogers, Roy            34
      6   Evans, Dale            76
      7   VanDoren, Charles     100

Sorted Test File:

      1   Gribben, George        21
      2   Rogers, Roy            34
      3   Jones, Mary            75
      4   Evans, Dale            76
      5   Andersen, Lars         80
      6   Hubbard, Kathy         99
      7   VanDoren, Charles     100
```

EXERCISES FOR SECTION 9.10

Self-Check

1. Another technique for searching an array is to introduce a program flag, say, Found, that is initially False and is set to True inside a search loop if the target value is found. Loop repetition continues as long as Found is still False and all elements have not been tested. After loop exit, the value of Found determines whether the current subscript or zero is returned as the function result. Write the procedure body.

2. Trace the execution of the selection sort on the list below. Show the array after each exchange occurs. How many exchanges are required? How many comparisons?

```
10 55 34 56 76 5
```

3. How could you get the scores in descending order (largest score first)? What changes would be needed to sort the array `class` by student name instead of score?

Programming

1. Write a procedure to count the number of students with a passing grade on the exam (60 or higher).

2. Another method of performing the selection sort is to place the smallest value in position 1, the next smallest in position 2, and so on. Write this version.

3. Modify Program 9.15 so that the array is sorted by the students' names instead of by the test scores.

4. Combine procedures `SelectSort` and `ReadScores`, and function `Search`, into a program to read a set of scores from a file, sort the array, and then determine whether any student got a score of 75 on the test.

9.11 Tricks of the Trade: Common Programming Errors

When programmers use records, their most common compilation error is incorrectly specifying the record field to be manipulated. The full field selector (record variable and field name) must be used unless the entire record is to be manipulated. Copying one record to another or comparison of two records can be done only if the two records are of the same type. Passing a record as a parameter to a procedure or function can be done only if the actual parameter has the same type as the formal one. When records are read, or written at the terminal, each field must be processed separately.

Similarly, in using arrays the most common compilation errors come from type inconsistencies. Remember that two arrays must have the same type name to be assigned or compared and that an array passed as an actual parameter must have the same type as the formal parameter.

The most common run-time error when arrays are used is a `Constraint_Error`, which is raised when the subscript value is outside the allowable range for the array being processed. Most often, this error is caused by an incorrect subscript expression, a loop parameter error, or a nonterminating loop. Before you spend considerable time debugging, you should carefully check all suspect subscript calculations for out-of-range errors. You can check most easily by inserting diagnostic output statements in your program to print subscript values that might be out of range.

If an out-of-range subscript occurs inside a loop, you should make sure that the loop is terminating properly. If the loop control variable is not being updated as expected, the loop may be repeated more often than required. This could happen, for example, if the update step came after the loop end statement or if the loop begin and end were erroneously omitted.

You should also doublecheck the subscript values at the loop boundaries. If these values are in range, it is likely that all other subscript references in the loop will be in range as well. Using the form

```
FOR SubscriptVariable IN IndexType LOOP
```

instead of writing the bounds explicitly helps to ensure that the subscript variable stays in bounds, because the loop body cannot modify it.

As with all Ada data types, make sure that there are no type inconsistencies. The subscript type and element type used in all array references must correspond to the types specified in the array declaration.

CHAPTER REVIEW

Summary

In this chapter we studied the record data structure. Records were shown to be useful for organizing a collection of related data items of different types. We were able to create some very general data structures to model our "real-world" data organization through the use of hierarchical records.

In processing records, we learned how to reference each individual component through the use of a field selector consisting of the record variable name and field name separated by a period.

Each individual component of a record must be manipulated separately in an input or output operation or in an arithmetic expression. However, it is permissible to assign one record variable to another record variable of the same type (record copy statement), to compare two records of the same type for equality or inequality, and to pass a record as a parameter to a procedure or function.

This chapter also introduced a data structure called an array, a convenient facility for naming and referencing a collection of like items. We discussed how to declare an array type and how to reference an individual array element by placing a subscript in parentheses, following the array name.

The FOR statement enables us to reference easily the elements of an array in sequence. We used FOR statements to initialize arrays, to read and print arrays, and to control the manipulation of individual array elements in sequence.

New Ada Constructs in Chapter 8

The new Ada constructs that were introduced in this chapter are described in Table 9.6.

Table 9.6   Summary of New Ada Constructs

Statement	Effect
Record Declaration	
| ```
SUBTYPE PartID IS
  Positive RANGE 1111..9999;
TYPE Part IS RECORD
  ID : PartID;
  Quantity : Integer;
  Price : Float;
END RECORD;

Nuts, Bolts : Part;
``` | A record type `Part` is declared with fields that can store two integers and a float number. `Nuts` and `Bolts` are record variables of type `Part`. |
Record Reference	
`TotalCost := Nuts.Quantity * Nuts.Price;`	Multiplies two fields of `Nuts`.
`Ada.Integer_Text_IO.Put(Item=>Bolts.ID);`	Displays ID field of `Bolts`.
Record Copy	
`Bolts := Nuts;`	Copies record `Nuts` to `Bolts`.
Record Aggregate Assignment	
| ```
Bolts :=
  (ID=>2234, Quantity=>53, Price=>0.09);
``` | Assigns values to all fields of `Bolts`. |
Record Compare	
`IF Nuts = Bolts THEN`	Compares `Nuts` to `Bolts`.
Array Declaration	
| ```
TYPE IntArray IS
  ARRAY (1..10) OF Integer;
``` | The data type describes an array with 10 type Integer elements. |
`Cube, Count : IntArray`	`Cube` and `Count` are arrays with this structure.
`SUBTYPE Index IS Integer RANGE 0..10;`	The data type Index is a range used as a subscript type
`Name: ARRAY (Index) OF Character;`	`Name` is an array of characters.
Array Reference	
| ```
FOR I IN 1 .. 10 LOOP
  Cube(I) := I * I * I;
END LOOP;
``` | Saves $I^3$ in the Ith element of array `Cube`. |
| `IF Cube(5) > 100 THEN` | Compares `Cube(5)` to 100. |
| ```
Ada.Integer_Text_IO.Put
  (Item=>Cube(1),Width=>5);
Ada.Integer_Text_IO.Put
  (Item=>Cube(2),Width=>5);
``` | Displays the first two cubes. |
```

Statement	Effect
Array Aggregate Assignment	
`Count := (3=>29,5=>17,OTHERS => 1);`	Sets all elements of `Count` to 1 except `Count(3)` and `Count(5)`.
Array Copy	
`Count := Cube;`	Copies contents of array `Cube` to array `Count`.
Array Comparison	
`IF Count /= Cube THEN`	Compares each element of `Count` to the corresponding element of `Cube`.

Quick-Check Exercises

1. What is the primary difference between a record and an array? Which would you use to store the catalog description of a course? Which would you use to store the names of students in the course?

2. What is a field selector?

3. When can you use the assignment operator with record operands? When can you use the equality operator?

4. If `AStudent` is a variable whose type is the record type declared below, provide a program segment that displays the initials of `AStudent`.

    ```
    TYPE Student  IS RECORD
       First: String(1..20);
       Last : String(1..20);
       Age: Natural;
       Score: Natural;
       Grade : Character;
    END RECORD;
    ```

5. How many fields are there in a record of type `student`?

6. If an `Integer` uses four bytes of storage and a character uses one byte, how many bytes of storage are occupied by a variable of type `student`?

7. Write a procedure that displays a variable of type `student`.

8. What is a composite structure?

9. Which predefined types cannot be array subscript types? Array element types?

10. Can values of different types be stored in an array?

11. If an array is declared to have ten elements, must the program use all ten?

12. When can the assignment operator be used with an array as its operands? Answer the same question for the equality operator.

13. The two methods of array access are _____ and _____.

14. The _____ loop allows us to access the elements of an array in _____ order.

Answers to Quick-Check Exercises

1. The values stored in an array must all be the same type; the values stored in a record do not have to be the same type. Record for catalog item; array for list of names.

2. Used to select a particular record field for processing.

3. When the records are the same type; when the records are the same type.

4. `Ada.Text_IO.Put (Item=>AStudent.First(1));`

   `Ada.Text_IO.Put (Item=>AStudent.Last(1));`

5. 5

6. 49

7.

```
PROCEDURE WriteStudent (OneStu : Student) IS
BEGIN
   Ada.Text_IO.Put (Item=>"Student is ");
   Ada.Text_IO.Put (Item=>OneStu.First);
   Ada.Text_IO.Put (Item=>' ');
   Ada.Text_IO.Put (Item=>OneStu.Last);
   Ada.Text_IO.Put (Item=>"; age is ");
   Ada.Integer_Text_IO.Put (Item => OneStu.Age, Width=>1);
   Ada.Text_IO.Put (Item=>"; score is ");
   Ada.Integer_Text_IO.Put (Item => OneStu.Score, Width=>1);
   Ada.Text_IO.Put (Item=>"; grade is ");
   Ada.Text_IO.Put (Item=>OneStu.Grade);
   Ada.Text_IO.New_Line;
END WriteStudent;
```

8. A composite structure is a grouping of related values in main memory.

9. Float; all can be element types.

10. No.

11. No.

12. If the arrays are the same type.

13. Direct, and sequential

14. FOR, sequential.

Review Questions for Chapter 8

1. Declare a newspaper subscriber record called `Subscriber`, which contains the fields `Name`, `StreetAddress`, `MonthlyBill` (how much the subscriber owes), and which paper the subscriber receives (`Weekday`, `Sunday`, or `Both`).

2. Write an Ada program to enter and then display the data in record `Competition` declared below:

```
StringSize: CONSTANT Positive := 20;

TYPE OlympicEvent IS RECORD
   Event: String(1..StringSize);
   Entrant: String(1..StringSize);
   Country : String(1..StringSize);
   Place : Integer
END RECORD;

Competition: OlympicEvent;
```

3. Declare the proper data structure to store the following student data: Grade Point Average, Major, Address (consisting of StreetAddress, City, State, and ZipCode) and ClassSchedule (consisting of up to six class records, each of which has Description, Time, and Days fields). Use whatever data types are most appropriate for each field.

4. Declare an array of floats called `Week` that can be referenced by using any day of the week as a subscript, where `Sunday` is the first subscript.

5. What are two common ways of selecting array elements for processing?

6. Write an Ada program segment to print out the index of the smallest and the largest numbers in an array x of 20 integers with values from 0 to 100. Assume array x already has values assigned to each element.

7. The parameters for a procedure are two arrays (type `FloatArray`) and an integer representing the length of the arrays. The procedure copies the first array in the parameter list to the other array in reverse order using a loop structure. Write the procedure.

Programming Projects

1. A number expressed in scientific notation is represented by its mantissa (a fraction) and its exponent. Write a procedure that reads two character strings representing numbers in Ada scientific notation and stores each number in a record with two fields. Write a procedure that displays the contents of each record as a floating-point value. Also write a procedure that computes the sum, product, difference, and quotient of the two numbers. (*Hint*: The string literal `"-0.1234E20"` represents a number in scientific notation. The fraction –0.1234 is the mantissa and the number 20 is the exponent.)

2. Write a program to read N data items into two arrays x and y of size 20. Store the product of corresponding elements of x and y in a third array z, also of size 20. Display a three-column table showing the arrays x, Y, and z. Then compute and display the square root of the sum of the items in Z. Make up your own data, with N less than 20.

3. Assume for the moment that your computer has the very limited capability of being able to read and display only single decimal digits at a time and to add together two integers consisting of one decimal digit each. Write a program to read in two integers of up to ten digits each, add these numbers together, and display the result. Test your program on the following numbers:

    ```
    X =    1487625
    Y =      12783

    X =   60705202
    Y =   30760832

    X =   1234567890
    Y =   9876543210
    ```

    (*Hints*: Store the numbers x and y in two arrays x and y of size 10, one decimal digit per element (type Character). If the number is less than 10 digits in length, enter enough leading zeros (to the left of the number) to make the number 10 digits long.

    ```
                         array X
    [1] [2] [3] [4] [5] [6] [7] [8] [9] [10]
     0   0   0   1   4   8   7   6   2   5

                         array Y
    [1] [2] [3] [4] [5] [6] [7] [8] [9] [10]
     0   0   0   0   0   1   2   7   8   3
    ```

    You will need a loop to add together the digits in corresponding array elements, starting with the element with subscript 10. Don't forget to handle the carry if there is one! Use a Boolean variable carry to indicate whether or not the sum of the last pair of digits is greater than 9.)

4. Write a program for the following problem: You are given a collection of scores for the last exam in your computer course. You are to compute the average of these scores and then assign grades to each student according to the following rule. If a student's score is within 10 points (above or below) of the average, assign the student a grade of Satisfactory. If the score is more than 10 points higher than the average, assign the student a grade of Outstanding. If the score is more than 10 points below the average, assign the student a grade of Unsatisfactory. (*Hint*: The output from your program should consist of a labeled three-column list containing the name, exam score, and grade of each student.)

5. It can be shown that a number is prime if there is no smaller prime number that divides it. Consequently, to determine whether N is prime, it is sufficient to check only the prime numbers less than N as possible divisors. Use this information to write a program that stores the first 100 prime numbers in an array. Have your program display the array after it is done.

6. The results of a survey of the households in your township have been made available. Each record contains data for one household, including a four-digit integer identification number, the annual income for the household, and the number of members of the household. Write a program to read the survey results into three arrays and perform the following analyses.

    a. Count the number of households included in the survey and print a three-column table displaying the data read in. (You may assume that no more than 25 households were surveyed.)

    b. Calculate the average household income, and list the identification number and income of each household that exceeds the average.

    c. Determine the percentage of households having incomes below the poverty level. The poverty level income can be computed using the formula

    $$p = \$6500.00 + \$750.00 \ (m - 2)$$

    where m is the number of members of each household. This formula shows that the poverty level depends on the number of family members, m, and that the poverty level increases as m gets larger.

Test your program on the following data:

Identification number	Annual income	Household members
1041	$12,180	4
1062	13,240	3
1327	19,800	2
1483	22,458	8
1900	17,000	2
2112	18,125	7
2345	15,623	2
3210	3,200	6
3600	6,500	5
3601	11,970	2
4725	8,900	3
6217	10,000	2
9280	6,200	1

CHAPTER 10

Strings and Files

This chapter contains two main topics—strings and text files—and shows how they are used, as well as several ways in which they are related.

In this chapter you will see that a string is just an array of characters and that Ada provides a number of special operations, such as slicing and concatenation, to deal with strings. There are also some standard Ada 95 libraries to deal with character and string translations and variable-length strings.

You will also see more examples of how to use files of data with your programs. You will learn to enter program data from data files and to save program results on output files. Using data files frees you from having to reenter test data continually while debugging a program. Using output files enables you to save output on disk rather than to simply view it on the screen. Input and output redirection allows you to specify, on the command line, the names of disk files to be used instead of the keyboard and the screen.

Finally, you will learn about the Ada 95 command line package, which provides a standard way to get input arguments from the operating system command line.

10.1 Data Structures: The String Data Type

Until now, we have used strings in Ada in a very intuitive way, without much systematic consideration. In this section we will take a somewhat more systematic look at the character string, an important data structure in many applications. Ada provides a predefined type `string`, which is a certain kind of array of characters. The basic ideas are as follows:

429

- A string value is an array of characters, with a subscript range that must be a subtype of `Positive`.

- It is possible to assign or refer to a part, or *slice*, of a string.

- String values can be compared and assigned like other Ada variables, but their lengths must match exactly.

- Strings can be concatenated, or "pasted together," to form longer ones.

Declaring a String Variable

The declarations

```
NameSize : CONSTANT Positive := 11;
SUBTYPE NameType IS String(1..NameSize);
```

provide for string values containing exactly 11 characters. Now the declarations

```
FirstName : NameType;
LastName  : NameType;
```

allocate storage for two string variables.

Referencing Individual Characters in a String

We can manipulate individual characters in a string variable in the same way that we manipulate individual elements of an array.

■ Example 10.1

The following program fragment reads 11 characters into string variable `FirstName` and displays all characters stored in the string:

```
Ada.Text_IO.Put(Item => "Enter your first name and an initial,");
Ada.Text_IO.Put(Item => " exactly 11 characters > ");

FOR I IN 1..NameSize LOOP
  Ada.Text_IO.Get (Item => FirstName(I));
END LOOP;

Ada.Text_IO.Put (Item => "Hello ");
FOR I IN 1..NameSize LOOP
  Ada.Text_IO.Put (Item => FirstName(I));
END LOOP;

Ada.Text_IO.Put(Item => '!');
Ada.Text_IO.New_Line;
```

A sample run of this program segment is as follows:

```
Enter your first name and an initial, exactly 11 characters > Jonathon B.
```

```
Hello Jonathon B.!
```

Eleven data characters are read into string variable `FirstName` after the prompt in the first line is displayed. The string variable `FirstName` is

(1)	(2)	(3)	(4)	(5)	(6)	(7)	(8)	(9)	(10)	(11)
J	o	n	a	t	h	o	n		B	.

The statements

```
FirstName(9)  := ''';
FirstName(10) := 's';
```

replace the contents of `FirstName(9)` (the blank character) and `FirstName(10)` (capital B) with the two characters shown above (an apostrophe and the letter s). The IF statement

```
IF FirstName(I) = ''' THEN
  Ada.Text_IO.Put (Item => "possessive form");
END IF;
```

displays the message `possessive form` when the value of `I` is 9. ■

A Character Is Not Compatible with a One-Character String

■ **Example 10.2**

String variable `OneString`, declared below, is a string of length 1.

```
OneString : String(1..1);
NextCh : Character;
```

The assignment statements

```
OneString(1) := NextCh;
NextCh := OneString(1);
```

are valid; they store a copy of `NextCh` in string `OneString`. However, the assignment statements

```
OneString := NextCh;
NextCh := OneString;
```

are invalid; they cause a "type compatibility" compilation error. A string that happens to be only one character long is still of a different type than a character! ■

Assigning, Comparing, and Displaying Strings

Besides manipulating individual characters in a string variable, we can manipulate the string as a unit.

■ Example 10.3

The assignment statement

```
LastName := "Appleseed";
```

appears to store the string value `Appleseed` in the string variable `LastName` declared earlier. This is not true, however: String assignment is correct only if the lengths of the strings on both sides are exactly the same. Because `Appleseed` has only nine letters, the assignment above might cause a warning at compilation time but would always cause `Constraint_Error` to be raised at execution time. If we add two blanks, the assignment will go through as desired:

```
LastName := "Appleseed  ";
```

The contents of `LastName` is

(1)	(2)	(3)	(4)	(5)	(6)	(7)	(8)	(9)	(10)	(11)
A	p	p	l	e	s	e	e	d	#	#

where the # characters are used here only to give a visible picture of the blank.
The statements

```
Ada.Text_IO.Put(Item => LastName);
Ada.Text_IO.Put (Item => ', ');
Ada.Text_IO. (Item => FirstName);
Ada.Text_IO.New_Line;
```

display the output line

```
Appleseed  , Jonathon B.
```

Note the two blanks following the last name!
As with other array types, we can copy the contents of one string variable to another of the same length, and we can compare two strings of the same length. ■

■ Example 10.4

The statement

```
FirstName := LastName;
```

copies the string value stored in `LastName` to `FirstName`; the `Boolean` condition

```
FirstName = LastName
```

is `True` after the assignment but would have been `False` before. ■

Reading Strings

Ada provides several `Get` procedures in `Ada.Text_IO` for entering a string value.

■ Example 10.5

The statement

```
Ada.Text_IO.Get(FirstName);
```

reads *exactly* 11 characters (including blanks, punctuation, and so on) into the string variable FirstName. The data entry operation is *not* terminated by pressing the ENTER key; if only five characters are entered before the ENTER is pressed, the computer simply waits for the additional six characters! This is a common error made by many Ada beginners, who think that their program is stuck when nothing seems to happen after ENTER is pressed. In fact, the program is doing just what it was told: Read *exactly* 11 characters. It is not possible to read more than 11 characters into FirstName; the additional characters just stay in the file waiting for the next Get call.

This is an unsatisfying way to read strings, since it provides no way to read a string that is shorter than the maximum length of the string variable. A better way is to use the Get_Line procedure in Ada.Text_IO. ■

■ Example 10.6

Given a variable

```
NameLength : Natural;
```

the statement

```
Ada.Text_IO.Get_Line (Item => LastName, Last => NameLength);
```

tries to read 11 characters as before, but if ENTER is pressed before 11 characters are read, reading stops. NameLength is used as an OUT parameter corresponding to Get_Line's formal parameter Last, and after the Get operation, NameLength contains the actual number of characters read. If fewer characters are read than the string can accommodate, the remaining characters in the string are *undefined*. ■

■ Example 10.7

Given the declarations

```
FirstNameLength : Natural;
LastNameLength  : Natural;
```

the statements

```
Ada.Text_IO.Put(Item => "Enter your first name followed by CR > ");
Ada.Text_IO.Get_Line(Item => FirstName, Last => FirstNameLength);
Ada.Text_IO.Put(Item => "Enter your last name followed by CR > ");
Ada.Text_IO.Get_Line(Item => LastName, Last => LastNameLength);
```

can be used to enter string values into the string variables `FirstName` and `LastName`. Up to 11 characters can be stored in `FirstName` and `LastName`. If the data characters `Johnny` are entered after the first prompt and the data characters `Appleseed` are entered after the second prompt, string `FirstName` contains

(1)	(2)	(3)	(4)	(5)	(6)	(7)	(8)	(9)	(10)	(11)
J	o	h	n	n	y	?	?	?	?	?

and string `LastName` contains

(1)	(2)	(3)	(4)	(5)	(6)	(7)	(8)	(9)	(10)	(11)
A	p	p	l	e	s	e	e	d	?	?

The variables `FirstNameLength` and `LastNameLength` contain 5 and 9, respectively. The statement

```
Ada.Text_IO.Put(Item => FirstName);
```

will display `Johnny` followed by five blanks. ■

The first two syntax displays below appeared originally in Section 3.8; they are repeated here for completeness. The third display specifies the `Get_Line` procedure.

SYNTAX
DISPLAY

Get Procedure (Character)

Form:

```
Ada.Text_IO.Get (Item => variable );
```

Example:

```
Ada.Text_IO.Get (Item => Initial1);
```

Interpretation:
The next character pressed on the keyboard is read into *variable* (type `Charac-ter`). A blank counts as a character; ENTER does not.

SYNTAX
DISPLAY

Get Procedure (String)

Form:

```
Ada.Text_IO.Get (Item => variable );
```

Example:

```
Ada.Text_IO.Get (Item => First_Name);
```

Interpretation:
Variable must be a variable of type String (low..high), where 1 ≤ low ≥ high. Exactly high – low + 1 characters are read from the keyboard. ENTER does not count as a character; the computer will wait until exactly the specified number of characters are entered.

SYNTAX DISPLAY

Get_Line Procedure

Form:

```
Ada.Text_IO.Get_Line (Item => variable1 , Last => variable2);
```

Example:

```
Ada.Text_IO.Get_Line
   (Item => First_Name, Last => NameLength);
```

Interpretation:
Variable1 must be a variable of type String(low..high), where 1 ≤ low ≥ high. Get_Line attempts to read high – low + 1 characters. Reading stops if ENTER is pressed. After the Get_Line operation, *variable2* contains the actual number of characters read. If the string variable is only partially filled by the operation, the remaining characters are undefined.

String Slicing

The flexibility of string handling in Ada is enhanced by using *string slicing*. This is the ability to store into, or extract, a *slice*, or section, of a string variable just by specifying the bounds of the desired section.

■ Example 10.8

Given the string variables FirstName and LastName as above, the slices

```
FirstName(1..4)
LastName (5..11)
```

refer to the first through fourth characters of FirstName and the fifth through eleventh characters of LastName, respectively. The statement

```
Ada.Text_IO.Put(Item => FirstName(1..FirstNameLength));
```

displays the string Johnny with no extra blanks. Given declarations

```
WholeNameLength : Natural;
```

```
WholeName : String(1..24);
```

the statements

```
WholeNameLength := FirstNameLength + LastNameLength + 2;
WholeName(1..LastNameLength) := LastName(1..LastNameLength);
WholeName(LastNameLength+1..LastNameLength+2) := ", ";
WholeName(LastNameLength+3..WholeNameLength) :=
  FirstName(1..FirstNameLength);
Ada.Text_IO.Put(Item => WholeName(1..WholeNameLength));
```

will store in `WholeName`, and display

```
Appleseed, Johnny
```                                                          ■

String Concatenation

One more string operation merits consideration here. The *string concatenation* operator
`&`, applied to two strings `s1` and `s2`, concatenates, or "pastes together," its two arguments.

■ Example 10.9

The statement

```
S3 := S1 & S2;
```

stores in `s3` the concatenation of `s1` and `s2`. For the assignment to be valid, the length of
`s3` still must match the sum of the lengths of `s1` and `s2`; if it does not,
`Constraint_Error` will be raised, as usual. Continuing with the name example above,
`WholeName` can be created more simply by using concatenation:

```
WholeNameLength := FirstNameLength + LastNameLength + 2;
WholeName(1..WholeNameLength) :=
  LastName(1..LastNameLength) & ", " & FirstName(1..FirstNameLength);
```

Concatenation is an operation on strings that returns a string, so the result of a concatenation can also be passed directly as a parameter, for example to `Ada.Text_IO.Put`:

```
Ada.Text_IO.Put(Item =>
  LastName(1..LastNameLength) & ", " & FirstName(1..FirstNameLength)); ■
```

**CASE
STUDY**

GENERATING CRYPTOGRAMS

Problem Specification

A *cryptogram* is a coded message that is formed by substituting a code character for
each letter of an original message, usually called the *plain text*. The substitution is performed uniformly though the original message, that is, all A's might be replaced by Z,

all B's by Y, and so on. We will assume that all other characters, including numbers, punctuation, and blanks between words, remain unchanged.

Analysis

The program must examine each character in the message and replace each character that is a letter by its code symbol. We will store the code symbols in an array Code with subscript range ('A'..'Z') and element type Character. The character stored in Code('A') will be the code symbol for the letter 'A'. This will enable us simply to look up the code symbol for a letter by using that letter as an index to the array Code.

Data Requirements

Problem Types

```
SUBTYPE UpperCase IS Character RANGE 'A'..'Z';
```

Problem Inputs

the array of code symbols (Code : ARRAY (UpperCase) OF Character)
the plain text message

Problem Outputs

the encrypted message or cryptogram

Design

The initial algorithm follows.

Initial Algorithm

1. Read in the code symbol for each letter.

2. Read the plain text message.

3. Encode the message.

4. Display the cryptogram.

Step 1 Refinement

1.1 Display the alphabet.

1.2. FOR each uppercase letter LOOP

Read in the code symbol and store it in string Code.

```
END LOOP;
```

Step 3 Refinement

3.1 FOR each character in the message LOOP

    3.2   IF it is a letter THEN

    3.3   Convert to the corresponding code symbol.

```
    END IF;

END LOOP;
```

Test Plan
We leave the test plan as an exercise.

Implementation
Program 10.1 shows the implementation of the cryptogram generator.

Program 10.1 Cryptogram Generator

```
WITH Ada.Text_IO;
PROCEDURE Cryptogram IS
-------------------------------------------------------------------------
--| Program to generate a cryptogram
--| Author: Michael B. Feldman, The George Washington University
--| Last Modified: September 1998
-------------------------------------------------------------------------

  SUBTYPE Letter IS Character RANGE 'A'..'Z';
  TYPE CodeArray IS ARRAY (Letter) OF Character;

  SUBTYPE Message IS String(1..60);

  Code       : CodeArray;         -- input - array of code symbols
  PlainText : Message;            -- input - plain text message
  CodedText : Message;            -- output - coded message

  HowLong    : Natural;

  FUNCTION Cap (InChar : Character) RETURN Character IS
  -- Pre: InChar is defined
  -- Post: if InChar is a lower-case letter, returns its upper-case
  --    equivalent; otherwise, returns InChar unmodified

  BEGIN -- Cap

    IF InChar IN 'a'..'z' THEN
      RETURN Character'Val(Character'Pos(InChar)
            - Character'Pos('a') + Character'Pos('A'));
    ELSE
      RETURN InChar;
    END IF;

  END Cap;

BEGIN -- Cryptogram

  Ada.Text_IO.Put(Item => "Enter a code symbol under each letter.");
  Ada.Text_IO.New_Line;
  Ada.Text_IO.Put(Item => "ABCDEFGHIJKLMNOPQRSTUVWXYZ");
  Ada.Text_IO.New_Line;

  -- Read each code symbol into array Code.
  FOR NextLetter IN Letter LOOP
    Ada.Text_IO.Get(Item => Code(NextLetter));
  END LOOP;
  Ada.Text_IO.Skip_Line;

  -- Read plain text message
  Ada.Text_IO.Put(Item => "Enter each character of your message.");
  Ada.Text_IO.New_Line;
```

```
Ada.Text_IO.Put(Item => "No more than 60 characters, please.");
Ada.Text_IO.New_Line;
Ada.Text_IO.Put(Item => "Press RETURN after your message.");
Ada.Text_IO.New_Line;

-- Display scale so user knows how many characters
Ada.Text_IO.Put(Item => "         1         2         3" &
                "         4         5         6");
Ada.Text_IO.New_Line;
Ada.Text_IO.Put(Item => "123456789012345678901234567890" &
                "123456789012345678901234567890");
Ada.Text_IO.New_Line;

Ada.Text_IO.Get_Line (Item => PlainText, Last => HowLong);

-- Encode message by table lookup
FOR WhichChar IN 1..HowLong LOOP
  IF Cap(PlainText(WhichChar)) IN Letter THEN
    CodedText(WhichChar) := Code(Cap(PlainText(WhichChar)));
  ELSE
    CodedText(WhichChar) := PlainText(WhichChar);
  END IF;
END LOOP;

-- Display coded message
Ada.Text_IO.Put (Item => CodedText(1..HowLong));
Ada.Text_IO.New_Line;

END Cryptogram;
```

Sample Run

```
Enter a code symbol under each letter.
ABCDEFGHIJKLMNOPQRSTUVWXYZ
zyxwvutsrqponmlkjihgfedcba
Enter each character of your message.
No more than 60 characters, please.
Press ENTER after your message.
         1         2         3         4         5         6
123456789012345678901234567890123456789012345678901234567890
The quick brown fox jumped over the lazy dogs
gsv jfrxp yildm ulc qfnkvw levi gsv ozab wlth
```

In the sample run, the code symbol for each letter is entered directly beneath that letter. Since a message is limited to 60 characters in length, the program displays a scale, and each letter of the plain text message is entered below its position number.

Testing
The sample run gives one test; we leave the rest as an exercise.

EXERCISES FOR SECTION 10.1

Self-Check

1. Suppose that s1 is `'ABCDE'`, s2 is `'FGHI'`, and s3 is declared as `String(1..8)` and has a value `'pqrstuvw'`. Explain what will happen as a result of each of these assignments:

   ```
   S3 := S1 & S2;
   S3 := S1(2..4) & S2;
   S3(1..5) := S3(4..8);
   ```

2. Why is a space or a comma not encoded in program `Cryptogram`?

Programming

1. Make changes to the cryptogram program to encode the blank character and the punctuation symbols `,`, `;`, `:`, `?`, `!`, and `.`.

2. Write a procedure that stores the reverse of an input string parameter in its output parameter (for example, if the input string is `'happy    '`, the output string should be `'yppah    '`.) The actual length of the string being reversed should also be an input parameter.

3. Write a program that uses the procedure in Programming Exercise 2 to determine whether or not a string is a palindrome. (A palindrome is a string that reads the same way from left to right as it does from right to left—for instance, `'Level'` is a palindrome.)

10.2 System Structures: Ada 95 Character and String Packages

Ada 95 provides several standard packages for dealing with characters and variable-length strings; these offer a rich collection of operations for text processing.

To cover the Ada 95 string packages here in much detail would go beyond our available space. Instead, we give a summary of the capabilities, referring the reader to Section A.4 of the Ada 95 Reference Manual.

Type Character

In Ada 83 the type `character` is defined in terms of the 128-character ASCII code. In Ada95, `character` is given a more international flavor; this type is defined in terms of the Latin-1 character set, which has 256 values and allows for the additional letters used in non-English languages, such as the French à, the German ü, and the Scandinavian Æ. Since the first 128 characters are the same as in the familiar ASCII, the change causes few problems for most work in English. This was discussed in Section 8.5, along with the package `Ada.Characters.Handling`.

Ada.Strings, Ada.Strings.Maps, and Ada.Strings.Fixed

`Ada.Strings` provides a number of interesting child packages for dealing with text processing and encoding. We show only a very small selection here.

`Ada.Strings.Maps` provides a set of types and functions used for creating sets of characters and translating between them. For example, if `M` is of type `Ada.Strings.Maps.Character_Mapping` and `C` is of type `Character`,

```
M := Ada.Strings.Maps.To_Mapping(From => "ABCD", To => "PQRS");
```

returns in `M` a mapping that maps `'A'` into `'P'`, `'B'` into `'Q'`, `'C'` into `'R'`, and `'D'` into `'S'`. All other characters—the ones not named in the mapping—are mapped into themselves. The statement

```
C := Ada.Strings.Maps.Value(M, 'D');
```

returns `'S'` to the variable `C`; the statement

```
C := Ada.Strings.Maps.Value(M, 'G');
```

returns `'G'` to the variable `C`, that is, it makes no change.

`Ada.Strings.Fixed` provides a large number of search, delete, replace, trim, and other operations on normal Ada fixed-length strings such as we have been studying here.

One useful function, `Translate`, translates an entire string into another string using the character mappings from `Ada.Strings.Maps`. For example, if `S1` is a ten-character string containing `"ABC 123 DD"`, and `S2` is a ten-character string, the statement

```
S2 := Ada.Strings.Fixed.Translate(Source => S1, Mapping => M);
```

returns `"PQR 123 SS"` to `S2`.

These functions make it easy to develop translators such as the cryptogram program. As an example, Program 10.2 shows a modified cryptogram program that uses many of the facilities described in this section.

Program 10.2 Cryptogram Using Ada 95 Facilities

```
WITH Ada.Text_IO;
WITH Ada.Characters.Handling;
WITH Ada.Strings.Maps;
WITH Ada.Strings.Fixed;
PROCEDURE Cryptogram_2 IS
-----------------------------------------------------------------------
--| Program to generate a cryptogram, using Ada 95 facilities
--| Author: Michael B. Feldman, The George Washington University
--| Last Modified: September 1998
-----------------------------------------------------------------------
```

```
      SUBTYPE Message IS String(1..60);

      Code        : String(1..26);      -- input - string of code symbols
      PlainText : Message;              -- input - plain text message

      CodedText : Message;              -- output - coded message

      CodeMap   : Ada.Strings.Maps.Character_Mapping;
      HowLong   : Natural;

  BEGIN -- Cryptogram_2

      Ada.Text_IO.Put(Item => "Enter a code symbol under each letter.");
      Ada.Text_IO.New_Line;
      Ada.Text_IO.Put(Item => "ABCDEFGHIJKLMNOPQRSTUVWXYZ");
      Ada.Text_IO.New_Line;

      -- Read code string from terminal, convert to mapping
      Ada.Text_IO.Get(Item => Code);
      Ada.Text_IO.Skip_Line;
      CodeMap := Ada.Strings.Maps.To_Mapping
        (From => "ABCDEFGHIJKLMNOPQRSTUVWXYZ", To => Code);

      -- Read plain text message
      Ada.Text_IO.Put(Item => "Enter each character of your message.");
      Ada.Text_IO.New_Line;
      Ada.Text_IO.Put(Item => "No more than 60 characters, please.");
      Ada.Text_IO.New_Line;
      Ada.Text_IO.Put(Item => "Press RETURN after your message.");
      Ada.Text_IO.New_Line;

      -- Display scale so user knows how many characters
      Ada.Text_IO.Put(Item => "         1         2         3" &
                     "         4         5         6");
      Ada.Text_IO.New_Line;
      Ada.Text_IO.Put(Item => "12345678901234567890123456789" &
                     "12345678901234567890123456789");
      Ada.Text_IO.New_Line;

      Ada.Text_IO.Get_Line (Item => PlainText, Last => HowLong);

      -- Encode message using Translate function
      CodedText(1..HowLong) :=
        Ada.Strings.Fixed.Translate
        (Source =>
           Ada.Characters.Handling.To_Upper
             (Item => PlainText(1..HowLong)),
         Mapping => CodeMap);

      -- Display coded message
      Ada.Text_IO.Put (Item => CodedText(1..HowLong));
      Ada.Text_IO.New_Line;

  END Cryptogram_2;
```

Ada.Strings.Bounded and Ada.Strings.Unbounded

`Ada.Strings.Bounded` is a generic package that provides a similar set of operations on bounded strings, which are strings with a given maximum length whose actual length can vary. The package is generic, with a single parameter `Max` to give the maximum length of all strings created by a given instance of the package. For example,

```
MaxName: CONSTANT Positive := 30;
PACKAGE Names IS
  NEW Ada.Strings.Bounded.Generic_Bounded_Length(Max => MaxName);
```

provides an instance so that a string variable, say,

```
Name: Names.Bounded_String;
```

can be at most 30 characters long. The package keeps track of the actual length.

Finally, `Ada.Strings.Unbounded` provides similar operations for unbounded strings, that is, strings for which no maximum length is given. The actual length of a string object such as

```
VeryLongString: Ada.Strings.Unbounded.Unbounded_String;
```

can range from 0 to `Positive'Last`.

10.3 System Structures: A Systematic View of Text Files

Up to this point, we have written most programs as interactive programs; in other words, each program reads all input data from the keyboard and displays all outputs on the screen. This mode of operation is fine for small programs. However, as you begin to write larger programs, you will see that there are many advantages to using disk files for program input and output.

You can create a data file using a text editor in the same way that you create a program file. Once the data file is entered in computer memory, you can carefully check and edit each line before you save it as a disk file. When you enter data interactively, you do not have the opportunity to examine and edit the data.

After the data file is saved on disk, you can instruct your program to read data from the data file rather than from the keyboard. This mode of program execution is called *batch mode*. Because the program data are supplied before execution begins, prompting messages are not required in batch programs. Instead, batch programs must contain display statements that echo print data values, thereby providing a record of the data that are read and processed in a particular run.

Besides giving you the opportunity to check for errors in your data, using data files has another advantage. Because a data file can be read many times, during debugging you can rerun the program as often as you need to without retyping the test data each time.

You can also instruct your program to write its output to a disk file rather than display it on the screen. When output is written to the screen, it disappears after it scrolls off the screen and cannot be retrieved. However, if program output is written to a disk file, you can use an operating system command such as TYPE *filename* (VAX/VMS and MS-DOS) or cat *filename* (UNIX) to list file *filename* as often as you wish or look at it with your editor. You can also get a hard copy of a disk file by sending it to the printer.

Finally, you can use the output file generated by one program as a data file for another program. For example, a payroll program may compute employee salaries and write each employee's name and salary to an output file. A second program that prints employee checks could use the output of the payroll program as its data file.

Ada's Package Specification for Text Files

You know already that in Ada, input and output are done with packages; Ada.Text_IO is the one we are using in this book. An excerpt of the Ada.Text_IO specification dealing with files appears as Fig. 10.1.

Figure 10.1. Section of Ada.Text_IO Dealing with Text Files

```
WITH IO_Exceptions;
PACKAGE Text_IO IS

  TYPE File_Type IS LIMITED PRIVATE;

  TYPE File_Mode IS (In_File, Out_File);

  ...

  -- File Management

  PROCEDURE Create(File : IN OUT File_Type;
                   Mode : IN File_Mode := Out_File;
                   Name : IN String := "";
                   Form : IN String := "");

  PROCEDURE Open(File : IN OUT File_Type;
                 Mode : IN File_Mode; Name : IN String;
                 Form : IN String := "");

  PROCEDURE Close(File : IN OUT File_Type);
  PROCEDURE Delete(File : IN OUT File_Type);
  PROCEDURE Reset(File : IN OUT File_Type; Mode : IN File_Mode);
  PROCEDURE Reset(File : IN OUT File_Type);

  FUNCTION Mode(File : IN File_Type) RETURN File_Mode;
  FUNCTION Name(File : IN File_Type) RETURN String;
  FUNCTION Form(File : IN File_Type) RETURN String;

  FUNCTION Is_Open(File : IN File_Type) RETURN Boolean;

  -- Control of default Input and output Files

  PROCEDURE Set_Input(File : IN File_Type);
  PROCEDURE Set_Output(File : IN File_Type);

  FUNCTION Standard_Input RETURN File_Type;
  FUNCTION Standard_Output RETURN File_Type;
```

```
FUNCTION Current_Input RETURN File_Type;
FUNCTION Current_Output RETURN File_Type;

-- Specification of Line and Page lengths

PROCEDURE Set_Line_Length(File : IN File_Type; To : IN Count);
PROCEDURE Set_Line_Length(To : IN Count);

PROCEDURE Set_Page_Length(File : IN File_Type; To : IN Count);
PROCEDURE Set_Page_Length(To : IN Count);

FUNCTION Line_Length(File : IN File_Type) RETURN Count;
FUNCTION Line_Length RETURN Count;

FUNCTION Page_Length(File : IN File_Type) RETURN Count;
FUNCTION Page_Length RETURN Count;

-- Column, Line, and Page Control

PROCEDURE New_Line
   (File : IN File_Type; Spacing : IN Positive_Count := 1);
PROCEDURE New_Line(Spacing : IN Positive_Count := 1);

PROCEDURE Skip_Line
   (File : IN File_Type; Spacing : IN Positive_Count := 1);
PROCEDURE Skip_Line(Spacing : IN Positive_Count := 1);

FUNCTION End_of_Line(File : IN File_Type) RETURN Boolean;
FUNCTION End_of_Line RETURN Boolean;

PROCEDURE New_Page(File : IN File_Type);
PROCEDURE New_Page;

PROCEDURE Skip_Page(File : IN File_Type);
PROCEDURE Skip_Page;

FUNCTION End_of_Page(File : IN File_Type) RETURN Boolean;
FUNCTION End_of_Page RETURN Boolean;

FUNCTION End_of_File(File : IN File_Type) RETURN Boolean;
FUNCTION End_of_File RETURN Boolean;

PROCEDURE Set_Col(File : IN File_Type; To : IN Positive_Count);
PROCEDURE Set_Col(To : IN Positive_Count);

PROCEDURE Set_Line(File : IN File_Type; To : IN Positive_Count);
PROCEDURE Set_Line(To : IN Positive_Count);

FUNCTION Col(File : IN File_Type) RETURN Positive_Count;
FUNCTION Col RETURN Positive_Count;

FUNCTION Line(File : IN File_Type) RETURN Positive_Count;
FUNCTION Line RETURN Positive_Count;

FUNCTION Page(File : IN File_Type) RETURN Positive_Count;
FUNCTION Page RETURN Positive_Count;

-- Character Input-Output

PROCEDURE Get(File : IN File_Type; Item : OUT Character);
```

```
PROCEDURE Get(Item : OUT Character);
PROCEDURE Put(File : IN File_Type; Item : IN Character);
PROCEDURE Put(Item : IN Character);

-- String Input-Output

PROCEDURE Get(File : IN File_Type; Item : OUT String);
PROCEDURE Get(Item : OUT String);
PROCEDURE Put(File : IN File_Type; Item : IN String);
PROCEDURE Put(Item : IN String);

PROCEDURE Get_Line(File : IN File_Type;
                   Item : OUT String; Last : OUT natural);
PROCEDURE Get_Line(Item : OUT String; Last : OUT natural);
PROCEDURE Put_Line(File : IN File_Type; Item : IN String);
PROCEDURE Put_Line(Item : IN String);

...

END Text_IO;
```

A file is defined as a type:

```
TYPE File_Type IS LIMITED PRIVATE;
```

We have seen PRIVATE before, but not LIMITED PRIVATE. The latter term is used to designate a type that behaves like a PRIVATE type—the client program cannot directly access details of objects of that type—but is even more restricted: The assignment and equality-checking operations are taken away. A type of this kind has *no* predefined operations; all client-accessible operations must be defined in the package specification.

Refer to this partial specification as you read the remainder of this section. Many more operations are defined in the specification than we will ever be using in this book, but it is helpful to know that the Ada standard defines all the operations in such a clear fashion as a package specification. The full specification for Ada.Text_IO, which runs for a number of pages, appears in Appendix D.

Reading and Writing Files with Ada.Text_IO

Several previous examples have used files for their input and output. This section gives a systematic explanation of how to get an Ada program to read from a data file and to write program results to an output file with Ada.Text_IO. *At any given time, a text file can be available for either input or output, but not both simultaneously.*

A *text file* is a collection of characters stored under the same name in secondary memory (that is, on a disk). A text file has no fixed size. To mark the end of a text file, the computer places a special character, called the *end-of-file* character (denoted as <eof>), following the last character in a text file. The Ada literature usually refers to this marker as the *file terminator*. Its exact form depends on the operating system.

As you create a text file using an editor program, you press the ENTER key to separate the file into lines. Each time you press ENTER, another special character, called the *end-of-line* character (denoted as <eol>), or *line terminator*, is placed in the file.

Here are the contents of a text file that consists of three lines of letters, blank characters, and punctuation. Each line ends with `<eol>`, and `<eof>` follows the last `<eol>` in the file. For convenience in scanning the file's contents, we have listed each line of the file as a separate line. In the actual file stored on disk the characters are stored in consecutive storage locations, each character occupying a single storage location. The first character of the second line (the letter `I`) occupies the next storage location following the first `<eol>`.

```
This is a text file!<eol>
It has two lines.<eol><eof>
```

A text file can also contain numeric data or mixed numeric and character data. Here is a text file that consists of numeric data and blank characters. Each number is stored on disk as a sequence of digit characters; blank characters separate numbers on the same line.

```
1234  345<eol>
999  -17<eol><eof>
```

The Keyboard and the Screen as Text Files

In interactive programming, Ada treats data entered at the keyboard as if they were read from the predefined file called `Ada.Text_IO.Standard_Input`. Pressing the ENTER key enters the `<eol>` in this file. In interactive mode we normally use a sentinel value to indicate the end of data rather than attempt to enter `<eof>` in the system file `Ada.Text_IO.Standard_Input`. We could use `<eof>`, however. Its keyboard representation depends on the operating system; `control-D` and `control-Z` are often used.

Similarly, displaying characters on the screen is equivalent to writing characters to system file `Ada.Text_IO.Standard_Output`. The `New_Line` procedure places the `<eol>` in this file, resulting in the cursor moving to the start of the next line of the screen. Both `Standard_Input` and `Standard_Output` are text files because their individual components are characters.

The End_of_Line and End_of_File Functions

Both `<eol>` and `<eof>` are different from the other characters in a text file because they are not data characters; in fact, the Ada standard doesn't even specify what they should be because their form depends on the operating system. Many of the Ada `Get` operations skip over the line terminators. However, if an Ada program attempts to read `<eof>`, the exception `Ada.Text_IO.End_Error` is raised.

If we can't read or write these characters in the normal way, how do we process them? `Ada.Text_IO` provides two functions that enable us to determine whether the next character is `<eol>` or `<eof>`. The function `Ada.Text_IO.End_of_Line` returns a value of `True` if the next character is `<eol>`; the function `Ada.Text_IO.End_of_File` returns a value of `True` if the next character is `<eof>`. The algorithm that follows uses the `End_of_Line` and `End_of_File` functions to control the processing of a data file.

Algorithm Skeleton for Processing a Text File, Character by Character

```
LOOP
  EXIT WHEN Ada.Text_IO.End_of_File (data file);
  LOOP
    EXIT WHEN Ada.Text_IO.End_of_Line (data file);
    -- process each character in the current line
  END LOOP;
END LOOP;
```

If the data file is not empty, the initial call to `End_of_File` returns a value of `False`, and the computer executes the inner loop. This loop processes each character in a line up to (but not including) the `<eol>`. For the two-line character data file shown above, the first execution of the loop processes the first line of characters:

```
This is a text file!
```

When the next character is `<eol>`, the `End_of_Line` function returns `True`, so the inner loop is exited. The `<eol>` is processed immediately after loop exit, and the outer loop is repeated.

Each repetition of the outer loop begins with a call to the `End_of_File` function to test whether the next character is the `<eof>` character. If it is, the `End_of_File` function returns `True`, so the outer loop is exited. If the next character is not `<eof>`, the `End_of_File` function returns `False`, so the inner loop executes again and processes the next line of data up to `<eol>`. For the file above, the second execution of the inner loop processes the second line of characters:

```
It has two lines.
```

After the second `<eol>` is processed, the next character is `<eof>`, so the `End_of_File` function returns `True`, and the outer loop is exited. We use this algorithm later in a program that duplicates a file by copying all its characters to another file.

SYNTAX DISPLAY

End_of_Line Function (for Text Files)

Form:

`Ada.Text_IO.End_of_Line(`*filename*`)`

Interpretation:

The function result is `True` if the next character in file *filename* is `<eol>`; otherwise, the function result is `False`.

Note:

If *filename* is omitted, the file is assumed to be `Ada.Text_IO.Standard_Input` (usually the terminal keyboard).

SYNTAX
DISPLAY

> ## End_of_File Function (for Text Files)
>
> **Form:**
>
> ```
> Ada.Text_IO.End_of_File(filename)
> ```
>
> **Interpretation:**
>
> The function result is `True` if the next character in file *filename* is <eof>; otherwise, the function result is `False`.
>
> **Note:**
>
> If *filename* is omitted, the file is again assumed to be `Ada.Text_IO.Standard_Input`. If a read operation is attempted when `End_of_File(filename)` is `True`, an attempt to read past the end of the input file error occurs and the program stops.

Declaring a Text File

Before we can reference a text file in a program, we must declare it just like any other data object, as in

```
InData  : Ada.Text_IO.File_Type;
OutData : Ada.Text_IO.File_Type;
```

Directory Names for Files

To read or write a text file with an Ada program, we must know the file's *directory name,* or *external name,* which is the name used to identify it in the disk's directory. A disk's directory lists the names of all files stored on the disk. A file's directory name must follow the conventions that apply on your particular computer system. For example, some systems (MS-DOS, for example) limit you to a file name that consists of eight characters, a period, and a three-letter extension. Many programmers use the extension `.dat` or `.txt` to designate a text file.

Preparing a File for Input or Output

Before a program can use a file, the file must be prepared for input or output. If a file is being used for input, its components can be read as data. As we said above, a file cannot be read and written simultaneously. If a file is being used for output, new components can be written to the file.

The procedure call statement

```
Ada.Text_IO.Open
  (File => InData, Mode => Ada.Text_IO.In_File, Name => "scores.dat");
```

prepares file `InData` for input by associating it with the disk file `scores.dat` and moving its file position pointer to the beginning of the file. The *file position pointer* selects the next character to be processed in the file. The file `scores.dat` must have been previously created and located in the current disk directory; if it is not available, the exception `Ada.Text_IO.Name_Error` is raised.

The procedure call statement

```
Ada.Text_IO.Create
  (File=>OutData, Mode=>Ada.Text_IO.Out_File, Name=>"test.out");
```

prepares file `OutData` for output. If no file `test.out` exists on disk, a file that is initially empty (that is, `test.out` has no characters) is created. If a file `test.out` already exists on disk, it is deleted and a new one is created.

To read and process a file a second time in the same program run, first close it by performing an operation such as

```
Ada.Text_IO.Close(File => OutData);
```

and then reopen it for input. A program can read and echo print (to the screen) an output file it creates by calling the `Close` procedure with the newly created file as its parameter. An `Open` operation prepares this file for input, and your program can then read data from that file.

It is important to keep in mind that although names in Ada are not case-sensitive, file names in directories usually are (though this depends a bit on the operating system). So `TEST.DAT` is not the same file as `test.dat`. Using a name in the `Open` procedure whose case is inconsistent with that of the actual file name is a common cause of `Name_Error`.

Generally, your program expects the file to be in the *current directory,* the same directory as the program itself. If you want to use a file from a different directory, you must give the full path in the `Create` or `Open`. The path format varies from system to system, but will often resemble `c:\myfiles\test.dat` (DOS, Windows) or `/usr/student/mary/myfiles/test.dat` (UNIX).

Finally, a file name doesn't have to be coded explicitly into your program. A file name is nothing but a string, so the program can prompt the user for it. This will be shown in the next program example.

Reading and Writing a Text File

You've learned how to declare a text file and how to prepare one for processing. All that remains is to find out how to instruct the computer to read data from an input file or to write program results to an output file.

If `NextCh` is a type `Character` variable, we know that the procedure call statement

```
Ada.Text_IO.Get (Item => NextCh);
```

reads the next data character typed at the keyboard into `NextCh`. This is really an abbreviation for the procedure call statement

```
Ada.Text_IO.Get (File => Ada.Text_IO.Standard_Input, Item => NextCh);
```

which has the same effect. The statement

```
Ada.Text_IO.Get (File => InData, Item => NextCh);
```

reads the next character from file InData into NextCh, where the next character is the one selected by the file position pointer. The computer automatically advances the file position pointer after each read operation. Remember to open InData for input before the first read operation.

In a similar manner the procedure call statements

```
Ada.Text_IO.Put (Item => NextCh);
Ada.Text_IO.Put (File => Ada.Text_IO.Standard_Output, Item => NextCh);
```

display the value of ch on the screen. The statement

```
Ada.Text_IO.Put (File => OutData, Item => NextCh);
```

writes the value of ch to the end of file OutData. Remember to open OutData for output before the first call to procedure Put.

■ Example 10.10

It is a good idea to have a backup or duplicate copy of a file in case the original file data are lost. Program 10.3 is an Ada program that copies one file to another; it prompts the user for the names of the input and output files.

Program 10.3 File Copy Program

```
WITH Ada.Text_IO;
PROCEDURE Copy_File IS
-----------------------------------------------------------------------
--| Program copies its input file into its output file
--| then closes the output file, re-opens it for input,
--| and displays its contents on the screen.
--| Author: Michael B. Feldman, The George Washington University
--| Last Modified: September 1998
-----------------------------------------------------------------------

  MaxName       : CONSTANT Positive := 80;
  SUBTYPE NameRange IS Positive RANGE 1..MaxName;

  InFileName   : String(NameRange):= (OTHERS => '#');
  OutFileName  : String(NameRange):= (OTHERS => '#');
  InNameLength : NameRange;
  OutNameLength: NameRange;
  InData       : Ada.Text_IO.File_Type;
  OutData      : Ada.Text_IO.File_Type;

  NextCh       : Character;

BEGIN -- Copy_File

  -- get input file name and open it
  Ada.Text_IO.Put(Item => "Please enter name of file to copy >");
  Ada.Text_IO.Get_Line(Item => InFileName, Last => InNameLength);
```

```
Ada.Text_IO.Open   (File=>InData, Mode=>Ada.Text_IO.In_File,
                     Name=>InFileName(1..InNameLength));

-- get output file name and create it
Ada.Text_IO.Put(Item => "Please enter name of the new file >");
Ada.Text_IO.Get_Line(Item => OutFileName, Last => OutNameLength);
Ada.Text_IO.Create(File=>OutData, Mode=>Ada.Text_IO.Out_File,
                   Name=>OutFileName(1..OutNameLength));

-- copy input file to output file, character by character
LOOP
  EXIT WHEN Ada.Text_IO.End_of_File(File => InData);
  LOOP
    EXIT WHEN Ada.Text_IO.End_of_Line(File => InData);

    Ada.Text_IO.Get(File => InData, Item => NextCh);
    Ada.Text_IO.Put(File => OutData, Item => NextCh);

  END LOOP;

  Ada.Text_IO.Skip_Line(File => InData);
  Ada.Text_IO.New_Line(File => OutData);
END LOOP;

Ada.Text_IO.Close(File => InData);
Ada.Text_IO.Close(File => OutData);

-- reopen the new file and display it on the screen
Ada.Text_IO.Open(File=>InData, Mode=>Ada.Text_IO.In_File,
                 Name=>OutFileName(1..OutNameLength));

WHILE NOT Ada.Text_IO.End_of_File(File => InData) LOOP
  WHILE NOT Ada.Text_IO.End_of_Line(File => InData) LOOP

    Ada.Text_IO.Get(File => InData, Item => NextCh);
    Ada.Text_IO.Put(Item => NextCh);

  END LOOP;

  Ada.Text_IO.Skip_Line(File => InData);
  Ada.Text_IO.New_Line;
END LOOP;

Ada.Text_IO.Close(File => InData);

EXCEPTION

  WHEN Ada.Text_IO.Name_Error =>
    Ada.Text_IO.Put
      (Item => "File to copy doesn't exist in this directory!");
    Ada.Text_IO.New_Line;

END Copy_File;
```

The first set of nested loops in Program 10.3 implement the algorithm first shown above. The data file, InData, is the argument in the calls to functions End_of_Line and End_of_File. As long as the next character is not <eol>, the statements

```
Ada.Text_IO.Get (File => InData, Item => NextCh);
```

```
Ada.Text_IO.Put (File => OutData, Item => NextCh);
```

read the next character of InData into NextCh, and then write that character to file Out-Data.

If the next character is <eol>, the inner loop is exited and the statements

```
Ada.Text_IO.Skip_Line (File => InData);
Ada.Text_IO.New_Line (File => OutData);
```

are executed. The Ada.Text_IO.Skip_Line procedure does not read any data but simply advances the file position pointer for InData past the <eol> to the first character of the next line. The second statement writes the <eol> to file OutData. After the <eol> is processed, function End_of_File is called again to test whether there are more data characters left to be copied.

It is interesting to contemplate the effect of omitting either the Skip_Line or the New_Line statement. If the New_Line is omitted, the <eol> will not be written to file OutData whenever the end of a line is reached in file InData. Consequently, OutData will contain all the characters in InData on one (possibly very long) line. If the Skip_Line is omitted, the file position pointer will not be advanced and the <eol> will still be the next character. Consequently, End_of_Line(InData) will remain True, the inner loop is exited immediately, and another <eol> is written to file OutData. This continues "forever" or until the program is terminated by its user or until its time limit is exceeded.

After copying the file, the program closes test.out, reopens it for input, and displays its contents on the screen; the algorithm in the second part of the program is nearly identical to that in the first part. We have used WHILE instead of general loops just to show another way to code the same algorithm.

A common source of error is forgetting to use a file name with End_of_Line or End_of_File. In this case the system uses Ada.Text_IO.Standard_Input. A similar error is forgetting to use a file name with Get or Put. Normally, no error diagnostic is displayed, because there is nothing illegal about this; the computer simply assumes that the keyboard or screen is intended instead of the disk file. The cause of the incorrect behavior of the program is therefore not obvious. ■

Behaviors of the Various Get Operations in Ada.Text_IO

Learning to write input operations correctly is one of the most difficult tasks for a beginner in any programming language, including Ada. It is important to realize that Ada.Text_IO provides many different Get operations. We most frequently use four types: Get for a single character, Get and Get_Line for strings (as we used in section 10.1), and Get for numeric and enumeration values. Each of these behaves slightly differently with respect to blanks and line terminators in a file (including Standard_Input). Here is a summary of their behaviors; we have used the "short form" for reading from the terminal, but the behavior is identical if a file is used.

- Get(Item : OUT Character) first skips any line terminators, then reads *one* character from the input file. A blank counts as a character.

- `Get(Item : OUT String)` first determines the length of the string and attempts to perform *exactly* that number of character `Get` operations. It follows that line terminators are skipped. In fact, even if each character in the input is immediately followed by a line terminator (i.e., all the lines are one character long), all the characters are read and all the line terminators are skipped.

- `Get_Line (Item : OUT String; Last : OUT Natural)` reads characters (including blanks) up to the length of the string. Reading stops if the string's length is longer than the current line (i.e., if a line terminator is encountered). The line terminator is then skipped, that is, the equivalent of a `Skip_Line` is executed. If the input line is longer than the string, the remaining characters in the line remain available for the next input operation.

- `Get (Item : numeric or enumeration type)` skips over any leading blanks, tab characters, and line terminators, then reads characters as long as they continue to meet the syntax of a literal of the desired type. The character that causes reading to stop remains available for the next input operation.

This operation can cause trouble if you are not careful: Suppose that you are trying to read an integer value and accidentally type a few numeric digits followed by a letter or punctuation character. This last character will cause reading to stop *but remain available*; the already-read numeric digits make up a valid integer literal, so the typing error will not be discovered until the *next* input operation, which will probably not expect that character and raise `Ada.Text_IO.Data_Error`. Be careful!

Now is the time to take another look at the procedures in the package `Robust_Input` (Section 7.6) to be certain that you understand exactly how they work to prevent such a situation from arising.

10.4 Problem Solving: Operating System Redirection of Standard Files

Many popular operating systems, including UNIX and MS-DOS, have a feature that allows the standard input and output files—normally the keyboard and screen, respectively—to be "redirected" or temporarily reassigned to disk files. This feature, which is independent of Ada or any other programming language, allows you, for example, to tell a program that normally gets its input interactively to get it instead from a given file. Similarly, a program that normally writes its output to the screen can be told to put all that output in a file instead. In UNIX or MS-DOS, if you have an Ada program called `MyProg`, say, which uses keyboard `Get` calls, executing the operating system-level command

```
MyProg < FileOne.dat
```

causes `MyProg` to take all its standard input from `FileOne.dat` instead of the keyboard. (This assumes that `FileOne.dat` has been created and filled with data.) Executing the command

```
MyProg < FileOne.dat > FileTwo.dat
```

causes the program, without any change in its source code, to read its input from `File-One.dat` and write its output to `FileTwo.dat`. This is a handy technique, used in writing many operating system commands. It doesn't work well if the program is highly interactive, with a lot of prompting, because the prompts go to the output file while the input comes from the input file, untouched by human hands! The next case study will show a program that does not prompt but uses keyboard `Get` calls; its input data can be entered either from the keyboard or by redirection.

CASE STUDY

A HISTOGRAM-PLOTTING PROGRAM

Researchers in linguistics or cryptography (the study of secret codes) are often interested in the frequency of occurrence of the various letters in a section of text. A particularly useful way to summarize the number of occurrences is the *histogram* or *bar graph*, in which a bar is drawn for each letter, the length of the bar corresponding to the relative frequency of occurrence.

Problem Specification
Write a program that draws a histogram for the frequency of occurrence of the letters of the alphabet. Uppercase and lowercase letters are to be counted separately; nonletter characters can be ignored.

Analysis
This program is a variation of the concordance program, Program 9.13, developed in Section 9.9. Instead of getting input as a single line from the terminal, this program will read a text file by using input redirection, compute the number of occurrences of each of the 52 (lowercase and uppercase) letters, and draw an appropriately tall vertical bar on the screen for each of the 52 letters. A sample screen dump, produced by running the program with its own source file used as input, is shown in Fig. 10.2.

Design

Algorithm
The initial algorithm for this program is as follows:

1. Initialize all letter counters to 0.

2. Read the input file character by character. For each character that is a letter, increment the appropriate letter counter.

3. Plot the results on the screen.

   We leave it to the student to fill in the algorithm refinements and to develop a test plan.

Implementation
Program 10.4 gives the program for this case study.

Figure 10.2 Output from Histogram Program for Its Own Source File

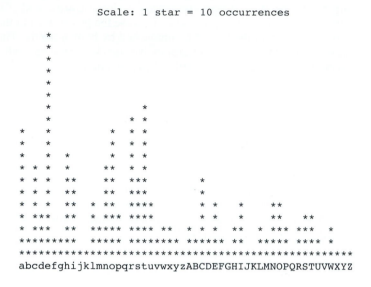

```
                   Scale: 1 star = 10 occurrences


            *
            *
            *
            *
            *
            *
            *
            *                   *
            *                 *  *
    *       *           *    *  *
    *       *           *    *  *
    *   *   *           **   *  *
    *   *   *           **   *  *
    *   *   **       **  ***       *
    *   *   **       **  ***       *
    *   *   **  *  ** ****     * *    *      **
    *  ***  **  *  *** ****    * *    *     **    **
    *  ***  **  ***** **** **  * *  ** * *** ***  *
    *********  ***** ******** ****** ** ***** **** *
    **************************************************
    abcdefghijklmnopqrstuvwxyzABCDEFGHIJKLMNOPQRSTUVWXYZ
```

Program 10.4 Histogram-Plotting Program

```
WITH Ada.Text_IO;
WITH Ada.Integer_Text_IO;
WITH Screen;
PROCEDURE Histogram IS
------------------------------------------------------------------------
--| Plots a histogram on the screen consisting of vertical bars.
--| Each bar represents the frequency of occurrence of a given
--| alphabet letter in the input file.
--| The input file is assumed to be Standard_Input;
--| use input redirection if you wish to use a disk file instead.
--| Author: Michael B. Feldman, The George Washington University
--| Last Modified: September 1998
------------------------------------------------------------------------

  SUBTYPE UpperCase IS Character RANGE 'A'..'Z';
  SUBTYPE LowerCase IS Character RANGE 'a'..'z';
  TYPE Occurrences IS ARRAY(Character RANGE <>) OF integer;
  Uppers   : Occurrences(UpperCase);
  Lowers   : Occurrences(LowerCase);

  NextCh   : Character;
  Scale    : Natural;
  MaxCount : Natural := 0;
  WhichCol : Screen.Width;


  PROCEDURE Plot(WhichCol  : Screen.Width;
                 BottomRow : Screen.Depth;
                 HowMany   : Screen.Depth;
```

```
               WhichChar : Character) IS

   -- draws one vertical bar on the screen
   -- Pre: WhichCol, BottomRow, HowMany, and WhichChar are defined
   -- Post: draws a bar in column WhichCol, using character WhichChar
   --        to do the plotting. The bottom of the bar is given by
   --        BottomRow; the bar contains HowMany characters.

   BEGIN -- Plot

     FOR Count IN 0 .. Howmany - 1 LOOP

        Screen.MoveCursor(Column => WhichCol, Row => BottomRow - Count);
        Ada.Text_IO.Put(Item => WhichChar);

     END LOOP;

   END Plot;

BEGIN -- Histogram

   -- initialize letter-counter arrays
   Uppers := (OTHERS => 0);
   Lowers := (OTHERS => 0);

   -- read each character in the file; update letter counters
   LOOP
     EXIT WHEN Ada.Text_IO.End_Of_File;
     LOOP
       EXIT WHEN Ada.Text_IO.End_Of_Line;

       Ada.Text_IO.Get(NextCh);
       CASE NextCh IS
         WHEN UpperCase =>
           Uppers(NextCh) := Uppers(NextCh) + 1;
           IF Uppers(NextCh) > MaxCount THEN
             MaxCount := Uppers(NextCh);
           END IF;
         WHEN LowerCase =>
           Lowers(NextCh) := Lowers(NextCh) + 1;
           IF Lowers(NextCh) > MaxCount THEN
             MaxCount := Lowers(NextCh);
           END IF;
         WHEN OTHERS =>
           NULL;
       END CASE;

     END LOOP;
     Ada.Text_IO.Skip_Line;
   END LOOP;

   Scale := MaxCount / 20 + 1;

   Screen.ClearScreen;
   Screen.MoveCursor(Row => 1, Column => 15);
   Ada.Text_IO.Put(Item => "Scale: 1 star = ");
   Ada.Integer_Text_IO.Put(Item => Scale, Width => 1);
   Ada.Text_IO.Put(Item => " occurrences");
   Screen.MoveCursor(Row => 22, Column => 4);
   Ada.Text_IO.Put
```

```
      (Item => "abcdefghijklmnopqrstuvwxyzABCDEFGHIJKLMNOPQRSTUVWXYZ");
WhichCol := 4;

FOR C IN LowerCase LOOP

   IF Lowers(C) /= 0 THEN
      Plot(WhichCol, 21, Lowers(C) / scale + 1, '*');
   END IF;
   WhichCol := WhichCol + 1;

END LOOP;

FOR C IN UpperCase LOOP

   IF Uppers(C) /= 0 THEN
      Plot(WhichCol, 21, Uppers(C) / scale + 1, '*');
   END IF;
   WhichCol := WhichCol + 1;

END LOOP;

Screen.MoveCursor(Row => 24, Column => 1);

END Histogram;
```

Procedure `Plot` takes care of plotting the vertical bars on the screen, from bottom to top. Its parameters are the column in which the bar is desired, the bottom row of the column, the height of the column, and the character to be used for plotting the bar. `Screen.MoveCursor` is used to move the cursor from the bottom of the column to the top, plotting a character at each point.

The main program counts the occurrences of each letter as was done in the concordance program (Program 9.12), with one essential difference: A record must be kept of the maximum number of occurrences. This is done because a column can be no more than 20 rows high, so the height of the columns must be scaled to the maximum. For example, if no letter occurs more than 60 times in the file, a 20-row column corresponds to approximately 60 occurrences. Each dot in the column then corresponds roughly to three occurrences of that letter; the number of occurrences of each letter, then, is divided by three to get the height of the column; 1 is added so that if there are any occurrences at all of a given letter, that column will be at least one row tall.

EXERCISES FOR SECTION 10.4

Programming

1. Rewrite `Copy_File` (Program 10.3) so that redirection is used to get the names of the input and output files.

10.5 Problem Solving: Getting Input Values from a String

`Ada.Text_IO` provides `Get` and `Put` operations that do not use files at all. Each of the `Get` operations takes its input from a *string* instead of either `Standard_Input` or a named file. For example, suppose we have

```
Line          : String(1..80);
LineLength    : Natural;

IntegerVariable: Integer;
IntLast       : Natural;

FloatVariable : Float;
FloatLast     : Natural;
```

We can read an entire line (of 80 characters or less) into `Line` and then read individual values from that string. Suppose we know that the first value in the line is supposed to be an integer value and that the second value is supposed to be a float value. We can write

```
Ada.Text_IO.Get_Line (Item => Line, Last => LineLength);
```

and then read from the string `Line` into the integer variable

```
Ada.Integer_Text_IO.Get
  (From => Line, Item => IntegerVariable, Last => IntLast);
```

which reads the first token from `Line`, converts it to integer form, and stores it in `IntegerVariable`. The behavior of this `Get` is identical to the other integer `Gets`—for example, raising `Ada.Text_IO.Data_Error` if the first token is not a string representing an integer value—except that input comes from a string instead of a file. The variable `IntLast` contains the index (in `Line`) of the last character read.

Now we can read the second token as a float value, by writing

```
Ada.Float_Text_IO.Get
  (From => Line(IntLast+1..Line'Last),
   Item => FloatVariable,
   Last => FloatLast);
```

Note that as with the `From` parameter, we must specify the slice of `Line` that follows the first (integer) value.

This input style is used in writing "industrial-strength" robust input procedures. For example, such a procedure could handle a `Data_Error` exception by rereading the token using a different `Get`.

To reiterate: All the `Gets`—character, string, integer, float, and enumeration—have three forms:

- Input comes from standard input.

- Input comes from an external named text file.

- Input comes from a string.

EXERCISES FOR SECTION 10.5

Self-Check

1. Suppose that the name of a text file given as a parameter to `Ada.Text_IO.Open` is not a valid file name or that the file cannot be found in the current directory. What happens? When does it happen?

Programming

1. "Hard-wiring" the name of a file into a program is usually considered to be poor programming style, because it limits the flexibility of the program. Rewrite `Copy_File` (Program 10.3) so that the names of the input and output files are read as strings from the keyboard. (*Hint:* Use `Get_Line`.)

10.6 Problem Solving: Reading Command Parameters

It is common that a program must be "configured" with certain values before it begins to do its work. A popular method for passing such parameters into the program is to use *command line parameters* (sometimes called *command line flags* or *command line options*). Ada provides this capability in the package `Ada.Command_Line`, which allows a program to retrieve the flags or parameters entered on the operating system command line when the program is invoked. The specification for this package is shown in Fig. 10.3.

Figure 10.3 Ada 95 Command Line Package

```
PACKAGE Ada.Command_Line IS

  FUNCTION Argument_Count RETURN Natural;

  FUNCTION Argument (Number : IN Positive) RETURN String;

  FUNCTION Command_Name RETURN String;

  TYPE Status IS RANGE implementation-defined;

  Success : CONSTANT Status;
  Failure : CONSTANT Status;

  PROCEDURE Set_Status (Code : IN Status);

END Ada.Command_Line;
```

Program 10.5 illustrates the use of the first two functions.

Program 10.5 Illustration of Ada.Command_Line

```
WITH Ada.Text_IO;
WITH Ada.Command_Line;
PROCEDURE Command_Arguments IS
-------------------------------------------------------------------
--| Demonstrate Ada 95 command-line parameters
--| Author: Michael B. Feldman, The George Washington University
--| Last Modified: September 1998
-------------------------------------------------------------------

  HowMany: Natural;  -- how many command-line arguments were there?

BEGIN -- Command_Arguments

  Ada.Text_IO.Put(Item => Ada.Command_Line.Command_Name);

  HowMany := Ada.Command_Line.Argument_Count;

  IF HowMany = 0 THEN
    Ada.Text_IO.Put_Line(Item => ": No command-line arguments today.");
  ELSE
    Ada.Text_IO.Put_Line(Item => ": The command-line arguments are: ");

    FOR Count IN 1..HowMany LOOP
      Ada.Text_IO.Put
        (Item => Ada.Command_Line.Argument(Number => Count));
      Ada.Text_IO.New_Line;
    END LOOP;
  END IF;

END Command_Arguments;
```

Sample Run

```
command_arguments: The command-line arguments are:
abc
123
3xy
```

Note that Argument always returns a string; if the program requires an integer, float, or enumeration value, the appropriate string-input Get procedure (see Section 10.5) can be used to convert the string.

The sample run illustrates the result of typing, on the UNIX command line (for example),

```
command_arguments abc 123 3xy
```

Some operating systems allow a program, invoked by the command line, to return a value, usually a small nonnegative integer, to the command shell. The procedure Set_Status can be used to set this value if the operating system allows it. Furthermore, the function Command_Name allows the program to find out its own name as known to the operating system, that is, the name by which it is invoked on the command line.

LENGTHS OF LINES IN A TEXT FILE

In preparing this book for production at the publisher, the authors were faced with meeting a page layout requirement that no line of program source code exceed 72 characters in length. This requirement led to the present case study; the author actually used the resulting program to assist in meeting the layout requirement.

Problem Specification

Develop a program that, given the name of a text file and a specified limit on line length, reads each line of the file and displays it, together with its line number, if and only if it exceeds the given limit. At the end, display the maximum line length found in the file. The program is to have two input arguments: the maximum desired length and the name of the file being checked.

Analysis

The program can use command line parameters to get its input arguments. The full data requirements are as follows.

Data Requirements

Program Inputs

desired maximum length (MaxLength: Natural)
text file to be checked (InputText: Ada.Text_IO.File_Type)

Program Outputs

line number of each long line (LineNumber: Natural)
each excessively long line (Line: String(1..120))

Design

Algorithm

1. Get command arguments and open the input file.

2. Read each line of the file and display it with its line number if and only if its length exceeds the desired maximum.

3. Display the length of the longest line found.

We leave the straightforward refinements and test plan to the student as an exercise.

Implementation

Program 10.6 implements the algorithm. The first command argument is an integer, so it is read from that argument (as string) using the string-input Ada.Integer_Text_IO.Get procedure. The second argument is a file name and so can be passed directly from the command argument to the Ada.Text_IO.Open operation.

Program 10.6 Find the Lengths of the Lines in a Text File

```
WITH Ada.Text_IO;
WITH Ada.Integer_Text_IO;
```

```
WITH Ada.Command_Line;
PROCEDURE Line_Length IS
----------------------------------------------------------------------
--| Compute maximum line length in a file
--| First command line parameter gives the desired max number
--| of characters; second parameter gives input file.
--| Program displays lines longer than the desired max,
--| and finds the length of the longest line in the file.
--| Author: Michael B. Feldman, The George Washington University
--| Last Modified: September 1998
----------------------------------------------------------------------

   DesiredMax: Natural;          -- input  - desired maximum length
   MaxLength : Natural;          -- output - maximum line length

   LineNumber: Natural;          -- counts the lines in the file
   Line      : String(1..120);   -- holder for input line read from file
   Length    : Natural;          -- holds length of current line

   InputText : Ada.Text_IO.File_Type;

BEGIN -- Line_Length;

  -- Get command parameters and open input file
  Ada.Integer_Text_IO.Get (From => Ada.Command_Line.Argument(1),
                           Item => DesiredMax,
                           Last => Length);

  Ada.Text_IO.Put
    (Item => "Reading from " & Ada.Command_Line.Argument(2));
  Ada.Text_IO.New_Line;

  Ada.Text_IO.Open (File => InputText, Mode => Ada.Text_IO.In_File,
                    Name => Ada.Command_Line.Argument(2));

  -- loop through file reading lines
  MaxLength := 0;
  LineNumber := 0;

  LOOP
    EXIT WHEN Ada.Text_IO.End_of_File (File => InputText);

    Ada.Text_IO.Get_Line
      (File => InputText, Item => Line, Last => Length);

    -- keep track of number of lines in the file
    LineNumber := LineNumber + 1;

    -- is line too long?
    IF Length > DesiredMax THEN
      Ada.Integer_Text_IO.Put(Item => LineNumber, Width => 3);
      Ada.Text_IO.Put(Item => " " & Line(1..Length));
      Ada.Text_IO.New_Line;
    END IF;

    -- is line longer than longest so far?
    IF Length > MaxLength THEN
      MaxLength := Length;
    END IF;
```

```
      END LOOP;

      -- display results
      Ada.Text_IO.Put(Item => "The longest line length in " &
                              Ada.Command_Line.Argument(2) & " is ");
      Ada.Integer_Text_IO.Put(Item => MaxLength, Width => 1);
      Ada.Text_IO.New_Line;

END Line_Length;
```

Testing

The sample run shows the results of running the program on its own source file, that is, of typing, on the command line,

```
line_length 71 line_length.adb
```

Sample Run

```
Reading from line_length.adb
   5
---------------------------------------------------------------------------
   13
---------------------------------------------------------------------------
The longest line length in line_length.adb is 72
```

10.7 Tricks of the Trade: Common Programming Errors

A variable of type `String(1..N)` is a string variable of length N (a constant). A string variable of length N can be assigned a string value consisting of exactly N characters. If a string value that is too short or too long is assigned to a string variable, `Constraint_Error` is generally raised at run time; the error may not have been detected by the compiler. If one string variable is assigned to another, they must both be the same length. You can use string slicing to ensure that the lengths agree. Also keep in mind that if s is a string of length 1, then

```
S := 'A';
```

is not valid because s is a string and `'A'` is a character.

When reading a string, do not forget that the `Ada.Text_IO.Get` procedure for strings reads exactly the number of characters called for by the string length. If you enter fewer characters, even if you press ENTER, the program will wait for you to enter the remaining characters.

File processing in any programming language can be difficult to master; Ada is no exception. The name, which will be used as a file variable in the program, will usually differ from the actual directory name of the associated disk file. All file names must be declared as variables (type `Ada.Text_IO.File_Type`) and associated with the corresponding disk file by using a `Ada.Text_IO.Create` or `Ada.Text_IO.Open` procedure call statement.

The `Ada.Text_IO.Get` procedures can be used only after a file (other than standard input) has been opened for input. Similarly, the `Ada.Text_IO.Put` procedure can be used only after a file (other than standard output) has been created for output. Be sure to specify the file name as the first `Get` or `Put` parameter; otherwise, standard input (keyboard) or standard output (screen) is assumed. `Ada.Text_IO.End_Error` is raised if a `Get` operation is performed when the file position pointer for a file has passed the last file component. Also, when you use `Ada.Text_IO.End_Of_Line` or `Ada.Text_IO.End_Of_File` to control data entry, don't forget to include the name of the data file as the function argument.

CHAPTER REVIEW

In this chapter you studied the use of Ada strings, which are arrays of characters. A number of useful operations are provided for strings, and several standard packages as well.

You also learned how to instruct a program to read its data from a data file rather than from the keyboard and how to save the output generated by a program as a file on disk. Both techniques make it easier to debug large programs because test data can be prepared in advance and read repeatedly by a program in successive test runs, instead of needing to be entered each time the program is restarted.

New Ada Constructs in Chapter 10

The new Ada constructs that were introduced in this chapter are listed in Table 10.1.

Table 10.1 New Ada Constructs

Construct	Effect
String Declaration	
`Name : String(1..11);`	Declares a string variable `Name` of length 11.
String Assignment	
`Name := "Daffy Duck"`	Saves `"Daffy Duck"` in array `Name`.
String Concatenation	
`Name := "Jane" & " " & "Jones"`	Saves `"Jane Jones"` in array `Name`.
String Slicing	
`IF Count(1..5) = Cube(6..10)`	Compares slices of `Count` and `Cube`.
String Input	
`Ada.Text_IO.Get_Line` `  (Item=>Name,Last=>L);`	Reads a string into `Name`. Stops if all characters of `Name` are filled or if the end of the input line is reached. The number of characters read is returned in L.

Construct	Effect
File Declaration, Open and Close	
`MyInput: Ada.Text_IO.File_Type;` `MyOutput: Ada.Text_IO.File_Type;`	Declares two files.

`Ada.Text_IO.Open`
`  (File=>MyInput,`
`  Mode=>Ada.Text_IO.In_File,`
`  Name=>"mydata.dat");`
	Attempts to open a data file for input.

`Ada.Text_IO.Open`
`  (File=>MyOutput,`
`  Mode=>Ada.Text_IO.Out_File,`
`  Name=>"testoutput.dat");`
	Attempts to open a data file for output.

`Ada.Text_IO.Close(File=>MyInput);`	Closes the file.
End of File and End of Line Functions	
`IF Ada.Text_IO.End_Of_File` `  (File=>MyInput) THEN`	True if we are at the end of the file.
`IF Ada.Text_IO.End_Of_Line` `  (File=>MyInput) THEN`	True if we are at the end of the current line in the file.

Quick-Check Exercises

1. The _____ operation prepares a file for input, and the _____ operation prepares it for output.

2. A _____ separates a _____ file into lines, and the _____ appears at the end of a file.

3. What happens if a program attempts to read past the file terminator in a file?

4. What happens if a given file on disk cannot be found by a program?

5. What happens if a program attempts to write to a file that is open for input (or read from a file that is open for output)?

Answers to Quick-Check Exercises

1. `Open`, `Create`

2. Line terminator or `<eol>`, text, file terminator or `<eof>`

3. `Ada.Text_IO.End_Error` is raised.

4. `Ada.Text_IO.Name_Error` is raised.

5. `Ada.Text_IO.Mode_Error` is raised.

Review Questions for Chapter 10

1. List three advantages to using files for input and output instead of the standard input and output you have used thus far in this course.

2. Where are files stored?

3. There are at least four different ways to provide the names of external files to a program. One is operating system redirection. What are the others?

4. Write a loop that reads up to ten integer values from a data file and displays them on the screen. If there are not ten integers in the file, the message `That's all, folks` should be displayed after the last number.

Programming Projects

1. The results of a true–false exam have been coded for input to a program. Each student's information consists of a student identification number and that student's answers to ten true–false questions. The available data are as follows:

   ```
   Student ID          Answer string

      0080                FTTFTFTTFT
      0340                FTFTFTTTFF
      0341                FTTFTTTTTT
      0401                TTFFTFFTTT
      0462                TTFTTTFFTF
      0463                TTTTTTTTTT
      0464                FTFFTFFTFT
      0512                TFTFTFTFTF
      0618                TTTFFTTFTF
      0619                FFFFFFFFFF
      0687                TFTTFTTFTF
      0700                FTFFTTFFFT
      0712                FTFTFTFTFT
      0837                TFTFTTFTFT
   ```

   Develop and test a program that first reads in the answer string representing the ten correct answers (use `FTFFTFFTFT` as data), then reads the student responses into an array and, for each student, computes the number of correct responses. The program then determines the best score, `Best`, and display a three-column table displaying the ID number, score, and grade for each student. The grades are A if the score is equal to `Best` or `Best` − 1, C if it is `Best` − 2 or `Best` − 3, and F otherwise.

2. Assume that a set of sentences is to be processed. Each sentence consists of a sequence of words, separated by one or more blank spaces. Write a program that will read these sentences and count the number of words that have one letter, two letters, and so on, up to ten letters.

3. Write an interactive program that plays the game of Hangman. Read the word to be guessed into the string Word. The player must guess the letters belonging to Word. The program should terminate when either all letters have been guessed correctly (player wins) or a specified number of incorrect guesses have been made (computer wins). (*Hint:* Use a string Solution to keep track of the solution so far. Initialize Solution to a string of symbols '*'. Each time a letter in Word is guessed, replace the corresponding '*' in Solution with that letter.)

4. Write a program that reads several lines from a data file and writes each word of the file on a separate line of an output file, followed by a count of the number of letters in that word. After all lines are processed, the program should display the number of words processed and data lines read. Assume that words are separated by one or more blanks. Include a procedure, SkipBlanks, that skips over a sequence of blanks between words.

5. Whatsamatta U. offers a service to its faculty for computing grades at the end of each semester. A program processes three weighted test scores and calculates a student's average and letter grade (an A is 90–100, a B is 80–89, and so on). The program reads the student data from a file and writes each student's name, test score, average, and grade to an output file.

   Write a program to provide this valuable service. The data will consist first of the three test weights, then a series of student records, each of which consists of the student's name, ID number (four digits), and the three test scores. Calculate the weighted average for each student and the corresponding grade. This information should be printed along with the initial three test scores. The weighted average for each student is equal to

   ```
   weight1 * grade1 + weight2 * grade2 + weight3 * grade3
   ```

   For summary statistics, print the highest average, the lowest average, the average of the averages, the median average, and the total number of students processed. The median is that average obtained by the "middle" student when the file is sorted by weighted average. To find this, it will be necessary to read the file into an array and store each student's average in a field of the memory record. In this way the array can be sorted. Some sample data follow:

   ```
   0.35  0.25  0.40
   Mouse, Minnie 1014 100 76 88
   Duck, Donald 2234 90 85 65
   ```

6. Develop a case study and menu-driven program to maintain records for your bank savings account. The program will take its initial input from a file, each line of which represents a transaction. Each transaction will have a date, a transaction type (deposit, withdrawal, or interest), and an amount of money. The transactions will be stored in an array of capacity 200. Once the array is initialized from the file, the user will be able to enter more transactions interactively, and, at user option, display the entire set of transactions and a running account balance after each transaction. Finally, the program will write the set of transactions back to the file.

CHAPTER 11

Programming with Objects: Abstract Data Types

Many of the programs in this book so far have focused on developing a single program for a single application. In this chapter we consider the question of building reusable software components, or software building blocks that can be used by many programs. These fall into several categories; the one we take up here is called *abstract data types*.

An abstract data type (ADT) is a package whose specification provides a type and a set of operations on that type. ADTs are an important form of *encapsulation,* which is, in turn, one of the key concepts in object-oriented programming (OOP). Encapsulation is the process of locating, in a single module, a data structure and all its operations. ADT packages are quite similar to the *classes* that are used in other object-oriented languages.

In this chapter you will see how package Ada.Calendar is a good example of an ADT, and you will use a number of its operations for the first time.

Also in this chapter you will learn to write ADTs, and you will see the details of three useful reusable components: calendar dates, currency or monetary quantities, and employee records. Finally, we return to the spider, presenting an ADT to support multiple spiders in one room.

11.1 System Structures: Abstract Data Types (ADTs)

Data abstraction is a powerful programming tool. It is the conceptual approach of combining a data type with a set of operations on that data type. Furthermore, data abstraction is the philosophy that we can use such data types without knowing the details of their representation in the underlying computer system.

Data abstraction enables us to consider the data objects needed and the operations that must be performed on those objects without being concerned with unnecessary details. Indeed, data abstraction is an important part of object-oriented programming.

You have already practiced data abstraction—you have used the Float data type to represent decimal numbers without knowing much about the internal representation of that data type on a computer. In fact, floating-point representations vary considerably from one computer to another. In some cases there are no hardware instructions for floating-point arithmetic; it is all done with calls to subprograms. The point is that you have used floating-point literals, variables, and operations with confidence, without knowing or even caring how they are represented.

The most important thing in data abstraction is the familiar definition of *type:* a set of values and a set of operations that are appropriate for those values. Each one of the types you have used so far, whether predefined or user-defined, has not only values but also operations. In Ada the compiler ensures that all operations that are applied to a value are appropriate for that value. Ada provides powerful facilities for defining your own types—your own data abstraction—and with careful design, you can guarantee that all operations applied to values of your own types are appropriate for those values.

Ada's Specification for Predefined Types: Package Standard

Ada has a convenient way of specifying all the predefined types— Integer, Float, Boolean, Character, and so on—and their operations. Because Ada programmers learn very quickly to understand package specifications, the designers of the language chose to specify these things with a package specification called standard. Figure 11.1 shows the section of standard that describes Float. Notice that the arithmetic and relational operators are specified as functions. For example,

```
FUNCTION "+"  (Left, Right : Float) RETURN Float;
```

tells us concisely that "+" takes two Float operands and returns a result of type Float. Mathematically, an operator is really just a certain kind of function, so this notation is appropriate. You will see later in this chapter that Ada also gives *you* the ability to specify new operators in this manner.

Figure 11.1 Section of Package Standard Describing Float

```
PACKAGE Standard IS

   ...

 -- Section of package Standard that defines the type Float and its
 -- operations. Excerpted and reformatted from the Ada 95 RM Sect. A.1.

  TYPE Float IS DIGITS Implementation_Defined;
```

```
      -- "Implementation_Defined" means that the Standard does not
      -- specify the details, because they depend on the computer's
      -- arithmetic system.

-- The predefined operators for this type are as follows:

   FUNCTION "="  (Left, Right : Float) RETURN Boolean;
   FUNCTION "/=" (Left, Right : Float) RETURN Boolean;
   FUNCTION "<"  (Left, Right : Float) RETURN Boolean;
   FUNCTION "<=" (Left, Right : Float) RETURN Boolean;
   FUNCTION ">"  (Left, Right : Float) RETURN Boolean;
   FUNCTION ">=" (Left, Right : Float) RETURN Boolean;

   FUNCTION "+"  (Right : Float) RETURN Float;
   FUNCTION "-"  (Right : Float) RETURN Float;
   FUNCTION "ABS"(Right : Float) RETURN Float;

   FUNCTION "+"  (Left, Right : Float) RETURN Float;
   FUNCTION "-"  (Left, Right : Float) RETURN Float;
   FUNCTION "*"  (Left, Right : Float) RETURN Float;
   FUNCTION "/"  (Left, Right : Float) RETURN Float;

   FUNCTION "**" (Left : Float; Right : Integer) RETURN Float;

   ...

END Standard;
```

As another example from `standard`, consider Fig. 11.2, which shows the specification for the predefined type `Integer`. Notice the style in which all the familiar integer operations are listed.

Figure 11.2. Section of Package Standard Describing Integer

```
PACKAGE Standard IS

-- This is the section of the package Standard that describes
-- the predefined type Integer.
-- Excerpted and reformatted from the Ada 95 RM, Section A.1.

   ...

   TYPE Integer IS RANGE Implementation_Defined;

-- The predefined operators for this type are as follows:

   FUNCTION "="  (Left, Right : Integer) RETURN Boolean;
   FUNCTION "/=" (Left, Right : Integer) RETURN Boolean;
   FUNCTION "<"  (Left, Right : Integer) RETURN Boolean;
   FUNCTION "<=" (Left, Right : Integer) RETURN Boolean;
   FUNCTION ">"  (Left, Right : Integer) RETURN Boolean;
   FUNCTION ">=" (Left, Right : Integer) RETURN Boolean;

   FUNCTION "+"  (Right : Integer) RETURN Integer;
   FUNCTION "-"  (Right : Integer) RETURN Integer;
   FUNCTION "ABS" (Right : Integer) RETURN Integer;

   FUNCTION "+"  (Left, Right : Integer) RETURN Integer;
   FUNCTION "-"  (Left, Right : Integer) RETURN Integer;
```

```
FUNCTION "*"   (Left, Right : Integer) RETURN Integer;
FUNCTION "/"   (Left, Right : Integer) RETURN Integer;
FUNCTION "REM" (Left, Right : Integer) RETURN Integer;
FUNCTION "MOD" (Left, Right : Integer) RETURN Integer;

FUNCTION "**"  (Left : Integer; Right : Integer) RETURN Integer;

...

END Standard;
```

The Nature of an ADT

An abstract data type, or ADT, is really just a formal name for a *type:* a set of values and a set of operations that are appropriately applied to those values.

A program that uses an abstract data type is called a *client program*. A client program can declare and manipulate objects of the data type and use the data type's operators without knowing the details of the internal representation of the data type or the implementation of its operators; these details are hidden from the client program (this is called *information hiding* by computer scientists). In this way we separate the *use* of the data and operators (by the client program) from the *representation* of the type and *implementation* of the operators (by the abstract data type). This provides several advantages. It allows us to implement the client program and abstract data type independently of each other. If we decide to change the implementation of an operator (function or procedure) in the abstract data type, we can do this without affecting the client program. Finally, because the internal representation of a data type is hidden from its client program, we can even change the internal representation at a later time without modifying the client.

An ADT is an important kind of *reusable software component*. ADTs are written so as to be usable by a variety of client programs. An ADT needs to have no knowledge of the client programs that will use it; the client programs needs to have no knowledge of the internal details of the ADT. Ideally, ADTs are thought of as being analogous to the various integrated electronic components that are used in modern computers and other devices: One needs to understand only the interface to an ADT to "plug it in" to a program, the way electronic components are plugged into a circuit board.

ADTs facilitate programming in the large because they reside in ever-larger libraries of program resources. Having large libraries of general resources available makes the client programs much simpler because their writers do not have to "reinvent the wheel." The modern software industry is devoting much time and effort to the development of component libraries; your study of ADTs will give you a taste of how this development is done.

ADTs are built in Ada by using packages; ADT packages are very similar to the *class* encapsulations that are used in other object-oriented languages. The remainder of this chapter introduces concepts of ADTs and discusses four ADTs in particular: the predefined package `Ada.Calendar` and four user-written packages for calendar dates, currency quantities, employee records, and multiple spiders.

The Structure of an ADT

Abstract data types are a general concept in programming, independent of any particular programming language. An ADT consists of the specification of one or more data types and a set of operations that are applicable to the type or types. Generally the type is a composite type, often a record of some kind. The operations can be classified into several classes:

- *Constructor:* A constructor creates, or constructs, an object of the type by putting its component parts together into a unified whole.

- *Selector:* A selector selects a particular component of an object.

- *Inquiry:* An inquiry operation asks whether an object has a particular property, for example, whether it is empty.

- *Input/output:* As usual, an input/output operation is the communication link between the value of an object and the world outside the program, usually a human operator at the terminal or a disk file or printer.

Ada Features for ADTs

Ada provides many capabilities to help us develop ADTs. Here is a summary of the abstraction features that we use in this book. We will make use of the first six in this chapter; the last two will be introduced in Chapter 12 and used to advantage in the remaining chapters.

- Ada provides *subtypes*. This feature allows us to define a class of numeric or enumeration values and attach range constraints to it. This allows the compiler to make certain that we never assign an out-of-range value to a variable.

- Ada provides *record field initialization*. This allows us to define a record type in such a way that each field in each variable of that type is initialized to a predetermined value.

- Ada provides *packages*. As we have seen throughout this book, a package is an ideal way of encapsulating—grouping together—resources—types, functions, procedures, important constants, and so on—and making them available to client programs. A package specification acts as a "contract" between the writer of the package and the writer of the client program. Furthermore, the compiler checks to make sure that the contract is followed: Everything that is promised in the specification must be delivered in the package body, and client programs must use the package resources correctly, for example, by calling procedures only with the correct parameters.

- Ada provides *private types*. The private type capability enables us to write a package that provides a new type to client programs, in such a way that the client program cannot accidentally misuse values of the type by referencing information that is most properly kept private, that is, restricted for the internal use of the package body only.

- Ada provides *operator overloading*. This allows us to write new arithmetic and comparison operators for new types and use them just as we use the predefined operators.

- Ada provides *user-defined exceptions*. This enables the writer of a package to provide exceptions to client programs in order to signal to a client when it has done something inappropriate with the package. The writer of the client program can write exception handlers for user-defined exceptions that work exactly like the handlers we write for the predefined exceptions such as `Constraint_Error`.

- Ada provides *attributes* such as the `First` and `Last` attributes that we have used frequently thus far. Attributes make it possible to write subprograms that manipulate data structures without knowing all their details. This is especially useful in the case of arrays, in which a subroutine that manipulates an array parameter can be written without knowing the array bounds: All it needs to do is to inquire about the array bounds by asking for the `First` and `Last` attributes. This will be used to great advantage starting in Chapter 12.

- Finally, Ada provides *generic definition*. Generic definition allows us to write subprograms and packages that are so general that they do not even have to know all the details of the types they manipulate; these types can be passed to the generic unit as parameters when the generic unit is instantiated. We have seen generic instantiation so far only with respect to the `Ada.Text_IO` libraries. Chapter 12 will introduce more about generics and show you how to write generic units of your own.

EXERCISES FOR SECTION 11.1

Self-Check

1. Explain the various kinds of operations in an ADT.

11.2 System Structures: The ADT Package Ada.Calendar

Before learning to write ADTs, it is helpful to study an existing one in detail. We have used the predefined package `Ada.Calendar` in a number of previous examples in this book without paying much attention to the fact that `Ada.Calendar` serves as an excellent example of a well-thought-out ADT. It happens that `Ada.Calendar` is always provided with an Ada compiler (indeed, it *must* be provided), and our own ADTs will often be written in the style of `Ada.Calendar`. Systematic study of `Ada.Calendar` will teach you a lot about the design of ADTs and prepare you to start writing your own.

Resources Provided by Ada.Calendar

Package `Ada.Calendar` uses a type `Duration`, which is actually defined in `Standard`, not here. `Duration` is a measure of *elapsed* time: One duration unit is exactly equal to one elapsed second. Note that this is not the same as the time of day. Time of day, often called "wall clock" time in computing applications, gives a particular instant of time: 12:05 P.M. on January 25, 1980, for example. Duration measures the *passage* of time: Two minutes, or 120 seconds, elapse between 12:05 P.M. and 12:07 P.M. on the same day. Time of day is one of the resources provided by `Ada.Calendar`, in the form of a type `Time`.

The purpose of `Ada.Calendar` is to provide a useful number of operations on time-of-day values. Figure 11.3 shows the entire specification of package `Ada.Calendar`, which we have copied straight from the Ada standard, making changes only in the formatting and comments in the specification.

Figure 11.3. Full Specification of Ada.Calendar

```
PACKAGE Ada.Calendar IS

   -- standard Ada package, must be supplied with compilers
   -- provides useful services for dates and times

   -- type definitions

   TYPE Time IS PRIVATE;

   SUBTYPE Year_Number  IS Integer  RANGE 1901..2099;
   SUBTYPE Month_Number IS Integer  RANGE 1..12;
   SUBTYPE Day_Number   IS Integer  RANGE 1..31;
   SUBTYPE Day_Duration IS Duration RANGE 0.0..86_400;
   -- Duration is a predefined (standard) fixed-point type;
   -- Day_Duration range is the number of seconds in 24 hours

   -- constructor operation

   -- constructs a Time value from its components; note that the
   -- default for Seconds is 0.0, so if Seconds value isn't given,
   -- the time is assumed to be at midnight

   FUNCTION Time_Of (Year : Year_Number;
                     Month : Month_Number;
                     Day : Day_Number;
                     Seconds  : Day_Duration:=0.0) RETURN Time;

   -- selector operations

   FUNCTION Year  (Date : Time)  RETURN Year_Number;
   FUNCTION Month (Date : Time)  RETURN Month_Number;
   FUNCTION Day   (Date : Time)  RETURN Day_Number;
   FUNCTION Seconds (Date : Time) RETURN Day_Duration;

   -- splits a Time value into its component parts

   PROCEDURE Split (Date    : IN  Time;
                    Year    : OUT Year_Number;
                    Month   : OUT Month_Number;
                    Day : OUT Day_Number;
```

```
                    Seconds   : OUT Day_Duration);

    -- read the computer's clock to get the current time of day

    FUNCTION Clock RETURN Time;

    -- arithmetic and comparison operations

    -- note that only the "sensible" operations are defined.
    -- this is possible because Time is a private type with no
    -- predefined operations except := and =

    FUNCTION "<"  (Left, Right : Time)       RETURN Boolean;
    FUNCTION "<=" (Left, Right : Time)       RETURN Boolean;
    FUNCTION ">"  (Left, Right : Time)       RETURN Boolean;
    FUNCTION ">=" (Left, Right : Time)       RETURN Boolean;

    FUNCTION "+" (Left : Time;      Right : Duration) RETURN Time;
    FUNCTION "+" (Left : Duration; Right : Time)      RETURN Time;
    FUNCTION "-" (Left : Time;      Right : Duration) RETURN Time;
    FUNCTION "-" (Left : Time;      Right : Time)      RETURN Duration;

    -- exported exceptions

    -- Time_Error is raised by Time_Of if its actual parameters
    -- don't form a proper date, and also by "+" and "-" if they
    -- can't return a date whose year number is in range,
    -- or if "-" can't return a value that is in the
    -- range of the type Duration.

    Time_Error : EXCEPTION;

PRIVATE

    -- implementation-dependent (the details depend on the computer's
    -- internal clock structure, and are not important because Ada.Calendar
    -- provides all the operations we need)

END Ada.Calendar;
```

The first line of code in `Ada.Calendar` is a partial type definition:

```
TYPE Time IS PRIVATE;
```

The definition is completed at the bottom of the figure, below the word PRIVATE. Ada provides certain rules for the use of private types. First, variables of the type may be declared; for example,

```
MyBirthDay : Ada.Calendar.Time;
LastWeek : Ada.Calendar.Time;
```

are permissible declarations. Second, one variable of a private type may be assigned the value of another variable of the same type, and two variables of a private type may be compared for equality or inequality. For example,

```
LastWeek := MyBirthday;
IF LastWeek /= MyBirthday THEN...
```

are both valid operations. *No other operations are predefined*. Indeed, one of the purposes of private types is to allow the writer of a package to define *exactly* those operations he or she deems appropriate.

Following the definition of Time are four subtype declarations. Three of these give the acceptable ranges for year, month, and day values; the fourth specifies the number of duration units, or seconds, in a 24-hour day: 86,400. The Ada standard says that any time value from midnight on January 1, 1901, to midnight on December 31, 2099, must be treated as a unique valid value by Ada.Calendar; furthermore, two consecutive time values must not differ by more than 20 milliseconds.

Time is treated as a private type for two reasons. First, the internal representation of a time value is dependent on the form that the hardware clock uses for time values. Second, not all operations make sense for time values. If Time were treated as just some sort of integer value, for example, we could multiply two times together; however, multiplying 3 P.M. by 4 P.M. is meaningless! Making Time a private type allowed the designers of Ada to control precisely the set of sensible operations on Time values. What are these operations?

To use time values well, the client program must be able to create time values, for example, by supplying a month, a day, and a year. Ada.Calendar provides a function Time_Of for this purpose. An operation like Time_Of, which *constructs* a value of the new type from its component parts, is called a *constructor* operation. There are also five *selector* operations, Year, Month, Day, Seconds, and Split, which allow the client program to select various components of a time value in a useful form (integer and duration values). The first four of these operations are functions that return individual components; Split is a procedure that produces all four components in a single call. The next operation is Clock, which returns the current time of day as a Time value.

We know from the discussion above that each time value is unique; also, time values are *monotonically increasing;* that is, as time progresses, each new value is greater than the previous one. This conforms to our real-world view of time and the concepts of "earlier" and "later." Because time is monotonically increasing—*totally ordered* is another mathematical term with similar meaning—we can confidently compare two values. As for any private type, Ada already provides equality and inequality operators, so Ada.Calendar provides the others: <, <=, >, and >=. Notice that these are specified as functions; they can be used in function form, for example,

```
IF Ada.Calendar."<="(RightNow, AnotherTime) THEN...
```

or as normal infix operators, for example,

```
IF RightNow <= AnotherTime THEN...
```

(The latter form is permitted *only* if a USE Ada.Calendar appears at the top of the program.)

To do computations with time values, Ada provides some arithmetic operations. Only those operations that make sense are provided by the package, as follows:

```
FUNCTION "+" (Left : Time; Right : Duration) RETURN Time;
FUNCTION "+" (Left : Duration; Right : Time) RETURN Time;
FUNCTION "-" (Left : Time; Right : Duration) RETURN Time;
FUNCTION "-" (Left : Time; Right : Time)     RETURN Duration;
```

For example, adding two times together makes no sense (what does it mean to add 3 P.M. to 4 P.M.?); it is therefore not possible to do so with `Ada.Calendar` operations. It does make sense to add a duration to a time; for example, 3 P.M. plus one hour is 4 P.M. The two `"+"` operations are provided to ensure that the time value can appear on the right or the left. Finally, the subtraction operations are sensible ones: Subtracting 3 P.M. from 4 P.M. gives one elapsed hour; subtracting two hours from 7 A.M. gives 5 A.M. These operations serve as an excellent example of the usefulness of private types in ensuring that a client cannot perform meaningless operations or operations that do not make physical sense.

The final line of code in the specification defines an exception `Time_Error`. This exception is raised whenever a `Time_Of` call would return an invalid time value, for example, if 2 (February), 30, and 1999 were supplied as parameters: February 30 does not exist. `Ada.Calendar` also understands leap years, so `Time_Error` would be raised if 2, 29, and 1999 were supplied to `Time_Of`, because 1999 is not a leap year. `Time_Error` is also raised if the subtraction operator is given two times that are so far apart that the computer cannot represent the number of elapsed seconds that separate them.

CASE STUDY:

WORLD TIMES

As an example of the use of `Ada.Calendar`, consider the problem of determining the time in other time zones around the world.

Problem Specification
Write a program to allow the user to enter the abbreviation of one of a set of cities and display the current time in that city.

Analysis
Given a table of city codes and the number of time zones separating each from the user's home time zone, we can use `Ada.Calendar` to find the current local time, then add or subtract the appropriate number of seconds to find the time elsewhere.

Data Requirements

Problem Inputs

```
City : Cities
```

Design

Algorithm
1. Read the value of `city` from the keyboard.

2. Find the current local time.

3. Find the time in `city` by using the time zone offset table.

4. Display the local time and the time in `city`.

Test Plan
Since you can easily look up the number of hours of offset, test the program for the different allowed cities, and be certain that the time is computed properly. Also test, as usual, for invalid input, that is, a token that is not a city code.

Implementation
Program 11.1 gives the program for `World_Time`. Type `Cities` gives a list of city names or abbreviations; a procedure `ReadCity` reads a city name robustly, refusing to permit an invalid city to be entered; and a procedure `DisplayTime` is used to display a time value in a useful form. `DisplayTime` is a modification of `TimeOfDay`, developed earlier in Program 7.3.

Program 11.1 Time around the World

```
WITH Ada.Text_IO;
WITH Ada.Integer_Text_IO;
WITH Ada.Calendar;
PROCEDURE World_Time IS
-----------------------------------------------------------------
--| Finds the current time in any of several time zones
--| Author: Michael B. Feldman, The George Washington University
--| Last Modified: September 1998
-----------------------------------------------------------------

  TYPE Cities IS (Paris, London, Rio, Caracas, DC,
                  Chicago, Denver, Seattle, Honolulu);

  PACKAGE City_IO IS NEW Ada.Text_IO.Enumeration_IO(Cities);

  TimeHere  : Ada.Calendar.Time;
  TimeThere : Ada.Calendar.Time;
  There     : Cities;

  FUNCTION AdjustTime(T: Ada.Calendar.Time; City: Cities)
    RETURN Ada.Calendar.Time IS

  -- given a time value, finds the corresponding time
  -- in a given time zone

    TYPE TimeDiffs IS ARRAY (Cities) OF Integer;

    -- table of time differences from DC; modify this table if you are
    -- not located in the Eastern U.S. time zone
    Offsets : CONSTANT TimeDiffs :=
       (Paris => +6, London => +5, Rio => +2, Caracas => -1, DC => 0,
        Chicago => -1, Denver => -2, Seattle => -3,  Honolulu => -5);

  BEGIN -- AdjustTime

    RETURN Ada.Calendar."+"(T, Duration(Offsets(City) * 3600));

  END AdjustTime;


  PROCEDURE ReadCity(City : OUT Cities) IS

  -- reads a city name from the terminal, robustly
```

```
      BEGIN -- ReadCity

   LOOP
     BEGIN      -- exception handler block
       Ada.Text_IO.Put_Line
         (Item => "Please enter one of the following:");
       Ada.Text_IO.Put_Line
         (Item => "Paris, London, Rio, Caracas, DC, ");
       Ada.Text_IO.Put(Item =>
          "Chicago, Denver, Seattle, Honolulu >");

       City_IO.Get(Item => City);
       EXIT;   -- good input data
     EXCEPTION -- bad input data
       WHEN Ada.Text_IO.Data_Error =>
         Ada.Text_IO.Skip_Line;
         Ada.Text_IO.Put
           (Item => "Invalid city name; please try again.");
         Ada.Text_IO.New_Line;
     END;        -- exception handler block
   END LOOP;

END ReadCity;


PROCEDURE DisplayTime(T: Ada.Calendar.Time) IS

   SecsPastMidnight : Natural;
   MinsPastMidnight : Natural;
   Secs             : Natural;
   Mins             : Natural;
   Hrs              : Natural;

BEGIN -- Display_Time

   SecsPastMidnight :=
     Natural(Ada.Calendar.Seconds(T));
   MinsPastMidnight := SecsPastMidnight/60;
   Secs             := SecsPastMidnight REM 60;
   Mins             := MinsPastMidnight REM 60;
   Hrs              := MinsPastMidnight / 60;

   Ada.Integer_Text_IO.Put (Item => Hrs, Width => 1);
   Ada.Text_IO.Put (Item => ':');
   IF Mins < 10 THEN
     Ada.Text_IO.Put (Item => '0');
   END IF;
   Ada.Integer_Text_IO.Put (Item => Mins, Width => 1);
   Ada.Text_IO.Put (Item => ':');
   IF Secs < 10 THEN
     Ada.Text_IO.Put (Item => '0');
   END IF;
   Ada.Integer_Text_IO.Put (Item => Secs, Width => 1);

END DisplayTime;

BEGIN -- World_Time

ReadCity(City => There);
```

```
TimeHere := Ada.Calendar.Clock;
TimeThere := AdjustTime(T=>TimeHere, City=>There);

Ada.Text_IO.Put(Item => "Current local time is ");
DisplayTime(T => TimeHere);
Ada.Text_IO.New_Line;
Ada.Text_IO.Put(Item => "Current time in ");
City_IO.Put(Item => There, Width => 1);
Ada.Text_IO.Put(Item => " is ");
DisplayTime(T => TimeThere);
Ada.Text_IO.New_Line;

END World_Time;
```

Sample Run

```
Please enter one of the following:
Paris, London, Rio, Caracas, DC,
Chicago, Denver, Seattle, Honolulu >xxx
Invalid city name; please try again.
Please enter one of the following:
Paris, London, Rio, Caracas, DC,
Chicago, Denver, Seattle, Honolulu >paris
Current local time is 22:46:44
Current time in PARIS is 4:46:44
```

The function `AdjustTime` does the work of computing the new time. It contains a table of offsets, or number of time zones away from local time. `Ada.Calendar."+"` is used to add or subtract the appropriate number of seconds:

```
RETURN Ada.Calendar."+"(T, Duration(Offsets(City) * 3600));
```

The array `Offsets` gives the time zone differences; the number of seconds is computed by multiplying the number of time zones by 3600 (the number of seconds in an hour), then converting to type `Duration`.

It is important to note that on most computers, `Ada.Calendar.Clock` gives the current *local* time, not some universal time value. The array `Offsets` is initialized to the offsets from the authors' home time zone, the Eastern U.S. zone; you will have to change the table values if you are running this program in another zone. An exercise suggests an approach to solving this problem in a more robust manner.

EXERCISES FOR SECTION 11.2

Programming

1. Write a program that tests the operations in package `Ada.Calendar`. Try to add two times together, for example. Also investigate what happens when `Time_Of` is called with parameters that would lead to an invalid time value (February 30, for example, or February 29, 1997). Does `Ada.Calendar` behave correctly?

11.3 System Structures: Writing an ADT for Calendar Dates

Section 11.2 illustrated the use of an ADT. It is now time to consider how we might *write* an ADT of our own.

In Chapter 9 we developed a package `Simple_Dates` for representing, reading, and displaying calendar dates. A difficulty with that package is that the user can enter and store a meaningless date (February 30, for example). In this section we improve the package so that it is more robust and offers more capabilities.

Specification for the Improved Dates Package

The specification for our improved package appears in Program 11.2. We represent a date using the same record form as in `Simple_Dates`, but now it is a private type so that a client program does not manipulate the fields directly. This prevents the user from storing an invalid date in a date variable. We shall also move the input/output operations into a child package `Dates.IO`. This is a style that we shall use in other ADTs as well.

Program 11.2 Specification for Improved Dates Package

```
WITH Ada.Calendar;
PACKAGE Dates IS
-----------------------------------------------------------------
--| Specification for package to represent calendar dates
--| Author: Michael B. Feldman, The George Washington University
--| Last Modified: September 1998
-----------------------------------------------------------------

  TYPE Months IS
    (Jan, Feb, Mar, Apr, May, Jun, Jul, Aug, Sep, Oct, Nov, Dec);

  SUBTYPE Year_Number  IS Ada.Calendar.Year_Number;
  SUBTYPE Day_Number   IS Ada.Calendar.Day_Number;

  TYPE Date IS PRIVATE;
  Date_Error : EXCEPTION;

  -- constructors

  FUNCTION Today RETURN Date;
  -- Pre:  None
  -- Post: Returns today's date; analogous to Ada.Calendar.Clock

  FUNCTION Date_Of(Year  : Year_Number;
                   Month : Months;
                   Day   : Day_Number) RETURN Date;
  -- Pre:    Year, Month, and Day are defined
  -- Post:   Returns a Date value
  -- Raises: Date_Error if the year, month, day triple do not
  --   form a valid date (Feb. 30, for example)
  -- Analogous to Ada.Calendar.Time_Of

  -- selectors
```

```
FUNCTION Year (D: Date) RETURN Year_Number;
FUNCTION Month(D: Date) RETURN Months;
FUNCTION Day  (D: Date) RETURN Day_Number;
-- Pre:  D is defined
-- Post: Return the year, month, or day component, respectively

PRIVATE

  TYPE Date IS RECORD
    Month: Months := Months'First;
    Day:   Day_Number := Day_Number'First;
    Year:  Year_Number := Year_Number'First;
  END RECORD;

END Dates;
```

We define two subtypes `Year_Number` and `Month_Number` as "nicknames" for the ones provided by `Ada.Calendar`. Because `Date` is a private type, a client program has no direct access to its fields. Therefore we need to supply constructors `Today`, as in `Simple_Dates`, and `Date_Of` by analogy with the `Time_Of` constructor in `Ada.Calendar`. Further, we need selectors `Year`, `Month`, and `Day`, by analogy with the corresponding ones in `Ada.Calendar`, each of which selects and returns the given component of the date record. Also by analogy with `Ada.Calendar`, we provide an exception `Date_Error`, raised when `Date_Of` would produce a meaningless date such as February 30 or June 31.

SYNTAX
DISPLAY

Private Type Definition

Form:

```
PACKAGE PackageName IS
...
  TYPE TypeName IS PRIVATE;
...
PRIVATE
  TYPE TypeName IS full type definition (usually a record)
END PackageName;
```

Example:

```
PACKAGE Rationals IS
...
  TYPE Rational IS PRIVATE;
...
PRIVATE
  TYPE Rational IS RECORD
    Numerator: Integer;
    Denominator: Positive;
  END RECORD;
END Rationals;
```

Interpretation:

A private type can be defined only in a package specification. The first occurrence of *TypeName* defines it as a private type; the full type definition appears at the end of the specification, in the private section.

Note:

Do not confuse PRIVATE types with LIMITED PRIVATE ones. A PRIVATE type automatically has the predefined operations :=, =, and /=, in addition to any operations you define in the package. A LIMITED PRIVATE type has no predefined operations at all. LIMITED PRIVATE types are useful in certain situations and are discussed in Chapter 15.

SYNTAX
DISPLAY

User-Defined Exception

Form:

ExceptionName : EXCEPTION;

Example:

ZeroDenominator: EXCEPTION;

Interpretation:

Exceptions are usually defined in a package specification. The exception can be raised by an operation in the corresponding package body by the statement

RAISE ExceptionName ;

A client program can have an exception handler for this exception, of the form

WHEN ExceptionName =>

Body of the Improved Dates Package

Program 11.3 shows the body of package Dates. Because Ada.Calendar already knows how to validate a date, the constructor function Date_Of just uses Ada.Calendar.Time_Of to do this. If Time_Of does not raise Time_Error, the date is valid. The selectors Year, Month, and Day should be obvious, and Today works just as it did in Simple_Dates, calling the appropriate Ada.Calendar operations to produce the date.

Program 11.3 Body of Improved Dates Package

```
WITH Ada.Calendar;
PACKAGE BODY Dates IS
-----------------------------------------------------------------
--| Body for package to represent calendar dates
--| Author: Michael B. Feldman, The George Washington University
--| Last Modified: September 1998
-----------------------------------------------------------------

  FUNCTION Today RETURN Date IS
    -- Finds today's date and returns it as a record of type Date
```

```ada
-- Today's date is gotten from Ada.Calendar

   Right_Now  : Ada.Calendar.Time;        -- holds internal clock value
   Temp       : Date;

BEGIN -- Today

   -- Get the current time value from the computer's clock
   Right_Now := Ada.Calendar.Clock;

   -- Extract the current month, day, and year from the time value
   Temp.Month := Months'Val(Ada.Calendar.Month(Right_Now)- 1);
   Temp.Day := Ada.Calendar.Day  (Right_Now);
   Temp.Year := Ada.Calendar.Year (Date => Right_Now);

   RETURN Temp;

END Today;

FUNCTION Date_Of(Year : Year_Number;
                 Month : Months;
                 Day : Day_Number) RETURN Date IS

-- constructs a date given year, month, and day.

   Temp: Ada.Calendar.Time;

BEGIN -- Date_Of

   Temp := Ada.Calendar.Time_Of(Year=>Year,
                                Month=>Months'Pos(Month)+1, Day=>Day);
   -- assert: M, D, and Y form a sensible date if Time_error not raised

   RETURN  (Month => Month, Year => Year, Day => Day);
   -- assert: a valid date is returned

EXCEPTION

   WHEN Ada.Calendar.Time_Error =>
     RAISE Date_Error;

END Date_Of;

FUNCTION Year (D: Date) RETURN Year_Number IS
BEGIN
   RETURN D.Year;
END Year;

FUNCTION Month (D: Date) RETURN Months IS
BEGIN
   RETURN D.Month;
END Month;

FUNCTION Day (D: Date) RETURN Day_Number IS
BEGIN
   RETURN D.Day;
END Day;

END Dates;
```

The Child Package Dates.IO

As was mentioned earlier, it is a good idea to separate construction of dates and selection of date fields from input and output of dates, and so we provide a child package, Dates.IO, to handle the Get and Put operations. Recall that a child package can be thought of as an extension of its parent package.

Program 11.4 shows the specification of the child package.

Program 11.4 Specification for Dates Child Package for Input/Output

```
WITH Ada.Text_IO;
PACKAGE Dates.IO IS
------------------------------------------------------------------
--| Specification for child package to read and display dates
--| Author: Michael B. Feldman, The George Washington University
--| Last Modified: September 1998
------------------------------------------------------------------

   TYPE Formats IS
     (Full,             -- February 7, 1998
      Short,            -- 07 FEB 98
      Numeric);         -- 2/7/98

   PROCEDURE Get(Item: OUT Date);
   PROCEDURE Get(File: IN Ada.Text_IO.File_Type; Item: OUT Date);
   -- Pre:  File is open
   -- Post: Reads a date in mmm dd yyyy form from standard or input
   --    or an external file, respectively

   PROCEDURE Put(Item: IN Date; Format: IN Formats);
   PROCEDURE Put(File: IN Ada.Text_IO.File_Type;
                 Item: IN Date; Format: IN Formats);
   -- Pre:  File is open; Item and Format are defined
   -- Post: Writes a date in the desired format to standard output
   --    or an external file, respectively

END Dates.IO;
```

In this specification we define an enumeration type, Formats, as follows:

```
TYPE Format IS (Full, Short, Numeric);
```

which we will use in the output procedure to determine which of the four following forms will be used to display a date:

```
February 4, 199
04 FEB 99
2/4/99
```

Program 11.5 gives the body of the child package.

Program 11.5 Body of Dates Child Package for Input/Output

```
WITH Ada.Calendar;
WITH Ada.Text_IO;
WITH Ada.Integer_Text_IO;
```

```ada
PACKAGE BODY Dates.IO IS
-------------------------------------------------------------------
--| Body for child package to read and display calendar dates
--| Author: Michael B. Feldman, The George Washington University
--| Last Modified: September 1998
-------------------------------------------------------------------

  PACKAGE Month_IO IS
    NEW Ada.Text_IO.Enumeration_IO(Enum => Months);

  PROCEDURE Get(File: IN Ada.Text_IO.File_Type; Item: OUT Date) IS

    M:     Months;
    D:     Day_Number;
    Y:     Year_Number;

  BEGIN -- Get

    Month_IO.Get (File => File, Item => M);
    Ada.Integer_Text_IO.Get(File => File, Item => D);
    Ada.Integer_Text_IO.Get(File => File, Item => Y);
    -- assert: M, D, and Y are well-formed and in range
    --          otherwise one of the Get's would raise an exception

    Item := Date_Of (Month => M, Year => Y, Day => D);
    -- assert: Item is a valid date if Date_Error not raised

  EXCEPTION

    WHEN Ada.Text_IO.Data_Error =>
      RAISE Date_Error;
    WHEN Constraint_Error =>
      RAISE Date_Error;
    WHEN Date_Error =>
      RAISE Date_Error;

  END Get;

  PROCEDURE WriteShort
    (File: IN Ada.Text_IO.File_Type; Item: IN Date) IS
  -- Pre: Item is assigned a value
  -- Post: Writes a date in dd MMM yy form

    Last2Digits : Natural;

  BEGIN -- WriteShort

    Last2Digits := Item.Year REM 100;

    IF Item.Day < 10 THEN
      Ada.Text_IO.Put(File => File, Item => '0');
    END IF;
    Ada.Integer_Text_IO.Put
      (File => File, Item => Item.Day, Width => 1);
    Ada.Text_IO.Put(File => File, Item => ' ');
    Month_IO.Put (File => File, Item => Item.Month, Width => 1);
    Ada.Text_IO.Put(File => File, Item => ' ');
    IF Last2Digits < 10 THEN
      Ada.Text_IO.Put(File => File, Item => '0');
    END IF;
```

```
        Ada.Integer_Text_IO.Put
          (File => File, Item => Last2Digits, Width => 1);

    END WriteShort;

    PROCEDURE WriteFull
      (File: IN Ada.Text_IO.File_Type; Item: IN Date) IS
    -- Pre: Item is assigned a value
    -- Post: Writes a date in Monthname dd, yyyy form

    BEGIN

      CASE Item.Month IS
        WHEN Jan =>
          Ada.Text_IO.Put(File => File, Item => "January");
        WHEN Feb =>
          Ada.Text_IO.Put(File => File, Item => "February");
        WHEN Mar =>
          Ada.Text_IO.Put(File => File, Item => "March");
        WHEN Apr =>
          Ada.Text_IO.Put(File => File, Item => "April");
        WHEN May =>
          Ada.Text_IO.Put(File => File, Item => "May");
        WHEN Jun =>
          Ada.Text_IO.Put(File => File, Item => "June");
        WHEN Jul =>
          Ada.Text_IO.Put(File => File, Item => "July");
        WHEN Aug =>
          Ada.Text_IO.Put(File => File, Item => "August");
        WHEN Sep =>
          Ada.Text_IO.Put(File => File, Item => "September");
        WHEN Oct =>
          Ada.Text_IO.Put(File => File, Item => "October");
        WHEN Nov =>
          Ada.Text_IO.Put(File => File, Item => "November");
        WHEN Dec =>
          Ada.Text_IO.Put(File => File, Item => "December");
      END CASE;

      Ada.Text_IO.Put(File => File, Item => ' ');
      Ada.Integer_Text_IO.Put
        (File => File, Item => Item.Day, Width => 1);
      Ada.Text_IO.Put(File => File, Item => ", ");
      Ada.Integer_Text_IO.Put
        (File => File, Item => Item.Year, Width => 1);

    END WriteFull;

    PROCEDURE WriteNumeric
      (File: IN Ada.Text_IO.File_Type; Item: IN Date) IS
    -- Pre: Item is assigned a value
    -- Post: Writes a date in mm/dd/yy form

      Last2Digits : Natural;

    BEGIN

      Last2Digits := Item.Year REM 100;

      Ada.Integer_Text_IO.Put
```

```
      (File => File, Item => Months'Pos(Item.Month)+1, Width => 1);
    Ada.Text_IO.Put(File => File, Item => '/');
    Ada.Integer_Text_IO.Put
      (File => File, Item => Item.Day, Width => 1);
    Ada.Text_IO.Put(File => File, Item => '/');
    IF Last2Digits < 10 THEN
      Ada.Text_IO.Put(File => File, Item => '0');
    END IF;
    Ada.Integer_Text_IO.Put
      (File => File, Item => Last2Digits, Width => 1);

  END WriteNumeric;

  PROCEDURE Put(File: IN Ada.Text_IO.File_Type;
               Item: IN Date; Format: IN Formats) IS
  BEGIN -- Put
    CASE Format IS
      WHEN Short =>
        WriteShort(File => File, Item => Item);
      WHEN Full =>
        WriteFull(File => File, Item => Item);
      WHEN Numeric =>
        WriteNumeric(File => File, Item => Item);
    END CASE;
  END Put;

  PROCEDURE Get(Item: OUT Date) IS
  BEGIN -- Get
    Get(File => Ada.Text_IO.Standard_Input, Item => Item);
  END Get;

  PROCEDURE Put(Item: IN Date; Format: IN Formats) IS
  BEGIN -- Put
    Put(File => Ada.Text_IO.Standard_Output, Item => Item,
        Format => Format);
  END Put;

END Dates.IO;
```

The procedure Dates.IO.Get reads a date a bit more robustly than its counterpart in Simple_Dates. If the date that is read is ill-formed (month, day, or year is not of the proper form), or if the combination would yield a meaningless date, Date_Error is raised and must be handled by the client program. This is analogous to the way in which the various Get procedures in Ada.Text_IO raise Data_Error for ill-formed or out-of-range input.

The procedure Dates.IO.Put displays a date in one of the three forms given previously, depending upon the value of the parameter Format. Put calls one of three local procedures WriteFull, WriteShort, and WriteNumeric, depending on a CASE statement to select the appropriate one. WriteShort and WriteNumeric are based on Todays_Date (Program 4.6) and Todays_Date_2 (Program 4.7); WriteFull needs explanation.

WriteFull uses a CASE statement to write the appropriate month name, depending on the month field of the date record. It would have been nice to use an enumeration type for the full names of the months, because Enumeration_IO is so easy to use. Unfortunately, the Put procedure in Enumeration_IO displays or writes the enumeration literal either in uppercase letters or in lowercase ones; there is no way to get it to display just the first letter as a capital. Because in U.S. correspondence we always capitalize just the first letter of the month, we need to use the CASE statement to control the precise form of the string displayed.

PROGRAM STYLE

> ## Procedures in a Package Body but Not in the Specification
>
> It is worth noting that the three procedures WriteFull, WriteShort, and Write-Numeric appear *only* in the package body; they are *not* given in the specification. This is quite intentional: These procedures are not intended for use by the client program; their only purpose is to refine the procedure Put, which is indeed intended for the client.
>
> When you design a package, you should consider very carefully just which operations to give to the client, list these in the specification, and implement them in the body. It is, of course, a compilation error to list a procedure or function in the specification and *not* put a corresponding body in the package body. This is because the specification is a contract that makes promises to the client that the body must fulfill. However, it is *not* an error to write procedures or functions in the body but not in the specification. Indeed, it is often quite desirable to do this, as the Dates example illustrates.

Program 11.6 shows a test of the Dates and Dates.IO packages. The program displays the current date in all three formats, then asks the user to enter a date and displays that date all three ways.

Program 11.6 Test of Improved Dates Package

```
WITH Ada.Text_IO;
WITH Dates;
WITH Dates.IO;
PROCEDURE Test_Dates IS
-----------------------------------------------------------------
--| Demonstration of Dates package
--| Author: Michael B. Feldman, The George Washington University
--| Last Modified: September 1998
-----------------------------------------------------------------

   D: Dates.Date;

BEGIN -- Test_Dates

   -- first test the function Today
   D := Dates.Today;
   Ada.Text_IO.Put(Item => "Today is ");
   Ada.Text_IO.New_Line;
   Dates.IO.Put(Item => D, Format => Dates.IO.Short);
   Ada.Text_IO.New_Line;
   Dates.IO.Put(Item => D, Format => Dates.IO.Full);
   Ada.Text_IO.New_Line;
   Dates.IO.Put(Item => D, Format => Dates.IO.Numeric);
   Ada.Text_IO.New_Line;

   LOOP
```

```
   BEGIN -- block for exception handler
     Ada.Text_IO.Put("Please enter a date in MMM DD YYYY form > ");
     Dates.IO.Get(Item => D);
     EXIT; -- only if no exception is raised
   EXCEPTION
     WHEN Dates.Date_Error =>
       Ada.Text_IO.Skip_Line;
       Ada.Text_IO.Put
         (Item => "Badly formed date; try again, please.");
       Ada.Text_IO.New_Line;
   END;

 END LOOP;

 Ada.Text_IO.Put(Item => "You entered ");
 Ada.Text_IO.New_Line;
 Dates.IO.Put(Item => D, Format => Dates.IO.Short);
 Ada.Text_IO.New_Line;
 Dates.IO.Put(Item => D, Format => Dates.IO.Full);
 Ada.Text_IO.New_Line;
 Dates.IO.Put(Item => D, Format => Dates.IO.Numeric);
 Ada.Text_IO.New_Line;

END Test_Dates;
```

Sample Run

```
Today is
07 SEP 98
September 7, 1998
9/7/98
Please enter a date in MMM DD YYYY form > Jul 8 1947
You entered
08 JUL 47
July 8, 1947
7/8/47
```

EXERCISES FOR SECTION 11.3

Self-Check

1. Explain the advantages of making the data record a private type.

Programming

1. Write a short program that attempts to access a field of a date record directly. Explain the result you get.

2. Expand Program 11.6 so that the user has a chance to enter a number of dates. Use this to test the dates package with a number of test cases that will show whether Dates is behaving correctly for all inputs.

3. Suppose that package `Ada.Calendar` did not have a date-validating operation. Rewrite the body of `Dates` so that a date supplied to `Date_Of` is validated by your package, raising `Date_Error` if the date would be meaningless. Do not use `Ada.Calendar.Time_Of` to do this.

11.4 System Structures: Writing an ADT for Money Quantities

In this section we develop an ADT for monetary quantities, which we shall call `Currency`. What is important about this ADT is that in writing operations for `Currency` values, we discover that not all operations make sense. An advantage of the ADT approach is that we can control the set of operations to allow only meaningful ones to be done.

Requirements

We require a way to represent monetary values to ensure that calculations with these quantities make sense and are exact. Only sensible operations should be allowed. It is meaningful to compare, add, subtract, and divide monetary quantities but not to multiply them—$4.00/$2.00 is a dimensionless ratio 2.0, but $2.00 × $3.00 has no meaning. On the other hand, it is certainly sensible to multiply a currency value by a "normal" dimensionless quantity, for example, to find 25% of $150.00.

To understand the exact-result requirement, you must realize that not every fractional decimal value can be represented exactly as a binary floating-point quantity, and sometimes operations such as addition and subtraction cause the result to be rounded off. While this approximation to the real numbers is often acceptable, it is unacceptable in monetary calculations—you would not be happy if the bank approximated your account balance.

Analysis

We are asked to construct a software component providing a type and a set of operations. There are no specific problem inputs and outputs, but we shall need to provide input and output operations so that our user—again, another programmer—can write client programs that read and display currency values.

To ensure exact operations, we cannot simply use floating-point values. Because integer arithmetic is exact, we will represent currency as a pair of two nonnegative integer values, `Dollars` and `Cents`, and a `Boolean` value to indicate whether the currency value is positive or not. We will then be able to write an ADT that provides exact operations.

Design

We now look at the important algorithms in currency calculations. We are allowing both positive and negative values and representing a currency value as a pair of integers. Given a currency quantity Q, denote its dollars and cents parts by `Q.Dollars` and `Q.Cents`, respectively; we carry the sign separately as a flag `Q.Positive`. First let us see how to convert a float value to a currency value:

Algorithm for Converting a Float F to a Currency Quantity Q

1. `Q.Dollars` is the integer part of `ABS F`; `ABS` means absolute value, as usual.

2.   Q.Cents is $100 \times$ (ABS F — Q.Dollars)

3.   Q.Positive is True if and only if F >= 0.0

Note how the cents part of a currency value is calculated as the fractional part of the Float value, multiplied by 100.

Now let us look at key algorithms for adding and subtracting two positive currency values.

To Add Two Positive Currency Values Q1 and Q2 to Produce Result

1.   Set TempCents to the sum of Q1.Cents and Q2.Cents

2.   IF TempCents > 99 THEN we have a carry:

   3.   Result.Cents is TempCents — 100

   4.   Result.Dollars is Q1.Dollars + Q2.Dollars + 1

5.   ELSE no carry:

   6.   Result.Cents is TempCents

   7.   Result.Dollars is Q1.Dollars + Q2.Dollars

   END IF;

To Subtract Q2 from Q1 to Produce Result

1.   IF Q1 < Q2 THEN Result is negative:

   2.   Interchange Q1 and Q2

   END IF;

3.   IF Q1.Cents < Q2.Cents THEN we need a borrow:

   4.   Result.Cents is (100 + Q1.Cents) - Q2.Cents

   5.   Result.Dollars is (Q1.Dollars - 1) - Q2.Dollars

6.   ELSE no borrow:

   7.   Result.Cents is Q1.Cents - Q2.Cents

   8.   Result.Dollars is Q1.Dollars - Q2.Dollars

   END IF;

Make sure you understand these algorithms; try some examples by hand to test yourself.

Program 11.7 shows the specification for this ADT package. The type Quantity is declared to be PRIVATE so that we can control all operations on values of this type. Note that we are also providing a subtype CentsType, which has range 0–99.

Program 11.7 Specification for Currency Package

```
PACKAGE Currency IS
-------------------------------------------------------------------
--| Specification of the abstract data type for representing
--| and manipulating Currency numbers.
--| All values of type Currency.Quantity are initialized to 0.0.
--| Author: Michael B. Feldman, The George Washington University
--| Last Modified: September 1998
-------------------------------------------------------------------

   SUBTYPE CentsType IS Integer RANGE 0..99;
   TYPE    Quantity  IS PRIVATE;

   -- Operations

   FUNCTION MakeCurrency (F : Float)    RETURN Quantity;
   -- constructor:
   -- Pre : F is defined
   -- Post: returns a Currency Quantity

   FUNCTION MakeFloat    (Q : Quantity) RETURN Float;
   -- constructor:
   -- Pre:  Q is defined
   -- Post: returns the value of Q in Float form

   FUNCTION Dollars   (Q : Quantity) RETURN Natural;
   FUNCTION Cents     (Q : Quantity) RETURN CentsType;
   FUNCTION IsPositive(Q : Quantity) RETURN Boolean;
   -- selectors:
   -- Pre:  Q is defined
   -- Post: Dollars returns the Dollars part of Q; Cents the Cents part

   FUNCTION "<" (Q1 : Quantity; Q2 : Quantity) RETURN Boolean;
   FUNCTION ">" (Q1 : Quantity; Q2 : Quantity) RETURN Boolean;
   FUNCTION "<="(Q1 : Quantity; Q2 : Quantity) RETURN Boolean;
   FUNCTION ">="(Q1 : Quantity; Q2 : Quantity) RETURN Boolean;
   -- inquiry operators:
   -- Pre : Q1 and Q2 are defined
   -- Post: return Q1 < Q2, Q1 > Q2, Q1 <= Q2, and Q1 >= Q2, respectively

   FUNCTION "+"  (Q  : Quantity) RETURN Quantity;
   FUNCTION "-"  (Q  : Quantity) RETURN Quantity;
   FUNCTION "ABS"(Q  : Quantity) RETURN Quantity;
   -- monadic arithmetic constructors:
   -- Pre:  Q is defined
   -- Post: return Q, -Q, ABS Q respectively

   FUNCTION "+"  (Q1 : Quantity; Q2 : Quantity) RETURN Quantity;
   FUNCTION "-"  (Q1 : Quantity; Q2 : Quantity) RETURN Quantity;
   FUNCTION "*"  (F  : Float;    Q  : Quantity) RETURN Quantity;
   FUNCTION "*"  (Q  : Quantity; F  : Float   ) RETURN Quantity;
   FUNCTION "/"  (Q1 : Quantity; Q2 : Quantity) RETURN Float;
   FUNCTION "/"  (Q  : Quantity; F  : Float   ) RETURN Quantity;
   -- dyadic arithmetic constructors:
   -- Pre : Q1 and Q2 are defined
   -- Post: these are the sensible arithmetic operators on Quantity.
   --    Note that multiplying two monetary values is not sensible.

PRIVATE
```

```
-- A record of type Quantity consists of a pair of Natural values
-- such that the first number represents the Dollars part
-- and the second number represents the Cents part.
-- The sign of a Quantity value is indicated by a Boolean field
-- called Positive.

   TYPE Quantity IS RECORD
     Positive: Boolean    := True;
     Dollars : Natural    := 0;
     Cents   : CentsType := 0;
   END RECORD; -- Quantity

END Currency;
```

Looking at the operations on the currency type, we see first that operators are provided to produce a currency quantity from its dollars and cents components and to convert in both directions between our currency type and `Float` values. The next group of operations are selectors to return the `Dollars` and `Cents` parts and an inquiry operator to determine whether or not a currency value is positive.

The next four operators are the usual comparison operations that we saw in `Ada.Calendar`. Note that we can use predefined equality/inequality with no problem because two currency values are equal if and only if their dollars, cents, and signs are respectively equal. The comparison operators are followed by three monadic arithmetic operators whose meaning should be obvious.

The final six operators are interesting ones. Note that addition and subtraction are defined for currency values, as one would expect. But multiplication is defined only for a currency value and a `Float` value, not for two currency values. This is because the product of two currency values is meaningless, but finding, for example, 0.25 (which might represent 25%) of a currency value is indeed meaningful. The two multiplication operations allow the mixed operands to be presented in either order. Similarly, the division operations are meaningful ones: Dividing one currency value by another gives a normal `Float`; dividing a currency value by a `Float` gives a currency value.

Defining operators as we have done here is called *operator overloading*. Recall the similar group of operators in `Ada.Calendar`; it makes no difference whether the operators are provided by a predefined package such as `Ada.Calendar` or by a user-defined package such as `Currency`. Operators are really nothing more than functions with an unusual syntax, appearing between their parameters instead of preceding them. Because function names can be overloaded, so can operator names. Operator overloading allows us to write operations that are mathematical in nature using the familiar mathematical symbols.

It is important to understand that Ada allows us to overload *only* the operator symbols that are already available in the language; we cannot, for example, define a new operator `"?"` because `"?"` is not already an operator in Ada. Also bear in mind that, for reasons that are beyond the scope of this book to explain, it is *not* possible to overload the two membership operators `"IN"` and `"NOT IN"`.

The last part of the specification is, as usual, the PRIVATE part, in which the currency type is defined in full. Note that it is just a record with three fields and that all three fields are initialized as before.

Implementation

Now Program 11.8 gives the body for `Currency`. The key to understanding the operations is the first four function bodies. The first two, `Add` and `Subtract`, are not provided to client programs; they are there only to make writing the other operators more convenient for us.

Program 11.8 Body of Currency Package

```
PACKAGE BODY Currency IS
------------------------------------------------------------------
--| Body of the abstract data type for representing
--| and manipulating Currency numbers.
--| All values of type Currency.Quantity are initialized to 0.0.
--| Author: Michael B. Feldman, The George Washington University
--| Last Modified: September 1998
------------------------------------------------------------------

-- internal operations, not exported to the client

  SUBTYPE NonNegFloat IS Float RANGE 0.0 .. Float'Last;

  FUNCTION Add (Q1: Quantity; Q2: Quantity) RETURN Quantity IS
  -- Pre:  Q1 >= 0.0 and Q2 >= 0.0.
  -- Post: Returns the sum of Q1 and Q2.
  -- This is just an auxiliary routine used in "+" and "-" below.

    Result    : Quantity;
    TempCents : Natural;

  BEGIN -- Add

    TempCents := Q1.Cents + Q2.Cents;
    IF TempCents > 99 THEN -- we had a carry
      Result.Cents   := TempCents - 100;
      Result.Dollars := Q1.Dollars + Q2.Dollars + 1;
    ELSE
      Result.Cents   := TempCents;
      Result.Dollars := Q1.Dollars + Q2.Dollars;
    END IF;
    RETURN Result;

  END Add;

  FUNCTION Subtract (Q1: Quantity; Q2: Quantity) RETURN Quantity IS
  -- Pre:  Q1 >= 0.0 and Q2 >= 0.0.
  -- Post: Returns the difference of Q1 and Q2.
  -- This is just an auxiliary routine used in "+" and "-" below.

    Result    : Quantity;

  BEGIN -- Subtract

    IF Q1 > Q2 THEN  -- Result is positive
      IF Q2.Cents > Q1.Cents THEN -- we need a borrow
        Result.Cents   := (100 + Q1.Cents) - Q2.Cents;
        Result.Dollars := (Q1.Dollars - 1) - Q2.Dollars;
      ELSE
        Result.Cents   := Q1.Cents   - Q2.Cents;
```

```
            Result.Dollars := Q1.Dollars - Q2.Dollars;
        END IF;
      ELSE              -- Result is negative
        Result.Positive := False;
        IF Q1.Cents > Q2.Cents THEN -- we need a borrow
          Result.Cents   := (100 + Q2.Cents) - Q1.Cents;
          Result.Dollars := (Q2.Dollars - 1) - Q1.Dollars;
        ELSE
          Result.Cents   := Q2.Cents   - Q1.Cents;
          Result.Dollars := Q2.Dollars - Q1.Dollars;
        END IF;
      END IF;
      RETURN Result;

END Subtract;


-- Exported Operators

FUNCTION "+"(Q1 : Quantity; Q2 : Quantity) RETURN Quantity IS
BEGIN
  IF Q1.Positive AND Q2.Positive THEN
    RETURN Add(Q1,Q2);
  ELSIF (NOT Q1.Positive) AND (NOT Q2.Positive) THEN
    RETURN -Add(-Q1, -Q2);
  ELSIF Q1.Positive AND (NOT Q2.Positive) THEN
    RETURN Subtract(Q1, -Q2);
  ELSE -- NOT Q1.Positive AND Q2.Positive;
    RETURN Subtract(Q2, -Q1);
  END IF;
END "+";

FUNCTION "-"(Q1 : Quantity; Q2 : Quantity) RETURN Quantity IS
BEGIN
  RETURN Q1 + (-Q2);
END "-";

FUNCTION MakeCurrency (F : Float)    RETURN Quantity IS
  Result: Quantity;
  T: Float;
BEGIN

  T := Float'Truncation(ABS F); -- get whole-number part
  Result := (Positive => True,
             Dollars =>  Natural(T),    -- just a type change
             Cents   =>  Natural(100.0 * (ABS F -  T)));

  IF F < 0.0 THEN
    Result.Positive := False;
  END IF;

  RETURN Result;
END MakeCurrency;

FUNCTION MakeFloat (Q : Quantity) RETURN Float IS
  Result: Float;
BEGIN
  Result := Float(100 * Q.Dollars + Q.Cents) / 100.0;
  IF Q.Positive THEN
    RETURN Result;
  ELSE
```

```
        RETURN -Result;
     END IF;
  END MakeFloat;

FUNCTION Dollars (Q : Quantity) RETURN Natural IS
BEGIN
   RETURN Q.Dollars;
END Dollars;

FUNCTION Cents (Q : Quantity) RETURN CentsType IS
BEGIN
   RETURN Q.Cents;
END Cents;

FUNCTION IsPositive(Q : Quantity) RETURN Boolean IS
BEGIN
   RETURN Q.Positive;
END IsPositive;

FUNCTION ">" (Q1 : Quantity; Q2 : Quantity) RETURN Boolean IS
BEGIN
   RETURN MakeFloat(Q1) > MakeFloat(Q2);
END ">";

FUNCTION "<" (Q1 : Quantity; Q2 : Quantity) RETURN Boolean IS
BEGIN -- stub
   RETURN True;
END "<";

FUNCTION "<=" (Q1 : Quantity; Q2 : Quantity) RETURN Boolean IS
BEGIN -- stub
   RETURN True;
END "<=";

FUNCTION ">=" (Q1 : Quantity; Q2 : Quantity) RETURN Boolean IS
BEGIN -- stub
   RETURN True;
END ">=";

FUNCTION "+"(Q  : Quantity) RETURN Quantity IS
BEGIN
   RETURN Q;
END "+";

FUNCTION "-"(Q  : Quantity) RETURN Quantity IS
BEGIN
   RETURN (Positive => NOT Q.Positive,
           Dollars  => Q.Dollars,
           Cents    => Q.Cents);
END "-";

FUNCTION "ABS"(Q  : Quantity) RETURN Quantity IS
BEGIN -- stub
   RETURN Q;
END "ABS";

FUNCTION "*"(F  : Float;   Q  : Quantity) RETURN Quantity IS
BEGIN
   RETURN(MakeCurrency(F * MakeFloat(Q)));
END "*";
```

```
FUNCTION "*"(Q  : Quantity; F  : Float   ) RETURN Quantity IS
BEGIN -- stub
  RETURN Q;
END "*";

FUNCTION "/"(Q1 : Quantity; Q2 : Quantity) RETURN Float IS
BEGIN
  RETURN MakeFloat(Q1) / MakeFloat(Q2);
END "/";

FUNCTION "/"(Q  : Quantity; F  : Float   ) RETURN Quantity IS
BEGIN -- stub
  RETURN Q;
END "/";
```

```
END Currency;
```

Add and Subtract are implemented following the algorithms above. The exported addition operator "+", which can handle positive or negative values, uses Add or Subtract according to the signs of its operands; the exported operator "-" just adds a negated value.

The next two operations are our constructors to convert to and from currency values. Note how these are written. In going from Float to currency, we need to find the whole-number part of the float quantity, because this will be the Dollars part of the currency quantity. We do this by using the attribute function Float'Truncation, which does just what we want.

Finally, the remaining operators are given, mostly as stubs. You can complete the package and develop a program to test it, as an exercise. Programs 11.9 and 11.10 give the specification and body for a child package Currency.IO. We do not show a test program; we leave its development as an exercise.

Program 11.9 Specification for Currency.IO Child Package

```
WITH Ada.Text_IO;
PACKAGE Currency.IO IS
----------------------------------------------------------------
--| Specification of the input/output child package for Currency
--| Author: Michael B. Feldman, The George Washington University
--| Last Modified: September 1998
----------------------------------------------------------------

  -- input operations to read a Quantity from terminal or file

  PROCEDURE Get (Item : OUT Quantity);
  PROCEDURE Get (File: IN Ada.Text_IO.File_Type; Item : OUT Quantity);
  -- Pre : File is open
  -- Post: The currency quantity is read as a normal
  --    floating point value.

  -- output operations to display a Quantity on terminal or
  -- write it to an external file

  PROCEDURE Put (Item : IN Quantity; Width: IN Natural:=8);
  PROCEDURE Put (File : IN Ada.Text_IO.File_Type;
                 Item : IN Quantity; Width: IN Natural:=8);
  -- Pre:  File is open, Item is defined
```

```
        -- Post: Displays or writes the currency quantity.
        --       Width is used by analogy with Integer_IO

END Currency.IO;
```

Program 11.10 Body of Currency.IO Child Package

```
WITH Ada.Text_IO;
WITH Ada.Integer_Text_IO;
WITH Ada.Float_Text_IO;
PACKAGE BODY Currency.IO IS
--------------------------------------------------------------------
--| Body of the input/output child package for Currency
--| Author: Michael B. Feldman, The George Washington University
--| Last Modified: September 1998
--------------------------------------------------------------------

  -- input procedures

  PROCEDURE Get (File: IN Ada.Text_IO.File_Type; Item : OUT Quantity) IS
    F: Float;
  BEGIN -- Get

    -- just read it as a Float quantity, then convert
    Ada.Float_Text_IO.Get(File => File, Item => F);
    Item := MakeCurrency(F);

  END Get;

  PROCEDURE Get (Item : OUT Quantity) IS
  BEGIN -- Get
    Get(File => Ada.Text_IO.Standard_Input, Item => Item);
  END Get;

  -- output procedures

  PROCEDURE Put (File : IN Ada.Text_IO.File_Type;
                 Item : IN Quantity; Width: IN Natural:=8) IS
  BEGIN -- Put

    -- dollars first
    IF IsPositive(Item) THEN
      Ada.Integer_Text_IO.Put(File=>File, Item=>Dollars(Item),Width=>1);
    ELSE
      Ada.Integer_Text_IO.Put
        (File=>File, Item=>-Dollars(Item),Width=>1);
    END IF;

    -- then decimal point and cents
    Ada.Text_IO.Put(File => File, Item => '.');
    IF Cents(Item) < 10 THEN
      Ada.Text_IO.Put(File => File, Item => '0');
    END IF;
    Ada.Integer_Text_IO.Put
      (File => File, Item => Cents(Item),Width => 1);

  END Put;

  PROCEDURE Put (Item : IN Quantity; Width: IN Natural:=8) IS
  BEGIN -- Put
```

```
      Put(File => Ada.Text_IO.Standard_Output, Item => Item,
          Width => Width);
   END Put;

END Currency.IO;
```

This example has shown the advantage of using a PRIVATE type not just to encapsulate representation details, but also to give us complete control over the operations a client is permitted to do. As part of developing your test program, you might wish to attempt some operations that are not provided in the package, such as multiplying two currency values. Attempting this will result in a compilation error; this tells you that the compiler is aiding you in controlling the client operations.

The USE and USE TYPE Clauses

The USE clause allows unqualified references to package capabilities. Given three Currency.Quantity variables C1, C2, and C3, a currency addition operation is ordinarily written

```
C3 := Currency."+"(C1,C2);
```

that is, just writing "+" as a function. However, if a client program were preceded by

```
USE Currency;
```

it could be written

```
C1 := C2 + C3;
```

One of the advantages of Ada's permitting operator symbols such as "+" to be defined as functions is that they can be used in expressions in infix form, as in the above line. When the expressions get more complex, this makes programs even more readable. Compare the line

```
Currency.IO.Put(Item => Currency."+"(D, Currency."*"(E,F)));
```

with the line

```
Currency.IO.Put(Item => A + E * F);
```

This is possible, however, only if a USE clause appears in the client program. Otherwise, the operator not only must be qualified (as in Currency."+") but also must be used as a prefix function call like any other function call.

Many in industry recommend against using the USE statement because in a program that WITHS and USES many packages, the USES make so many types and operations directly visible that it is very confusing to the reader. Ada 95 adds the USE TYPE statement as a compromise so that USE can in general be avoided without losing the benefit of user-defined operators. Writing, for example,

```
USE TYPE Currency.Quantity;
```

gives direct visibility to *only* the infix operators that are declared in the package but to nothing else, and specifically not to other operations such as `MakeCurrency`, `Dollars`, and `Cents`.

Operator Overloading

Form

```
FUNCTION " OpSymbol " (Formal1: Type1; Formal2: Type2)
  RETURN ReturnType ;
```

Example

```
FUNCTION "+" (Q1: Quantity; Q2:Quantity) RETURN Quantity;
```

Interpretation:

The function, defined in a package `P`, will be associated with the operator *OpSymbol* and can be called from a client program in one of two ways. If x is of type *ReturnType*,

```
X := Actual1 OpSymbol Actual2;
```

can be used if a USE or USE TYPE statement appears in the client program; otherwise,

```
X := P."OpSymbol"(Actual1, Actual2);
```

is required.

Notes:

1. The quotation marks around the operator are required in the second form above and are not allowed in the first case.
2. The operators `"IN"` and `"NOT IN"` cannot be overloaded. All other predefined operators can be overloaded.
3. The precedence of the operator cannot be changed by an overload; for example, any `"+"` operator will have lower precedence than any `"*"` operator.

The USE Clause Again

The USE clause would allow us to write unqualified references to all the infix operators in `Currency`.

Most Ada experts advise that qualified references should be used wherever possible because they clarify programs by always indicating the name of the package whose operation is being called. These same experts often advocate *never* writing a USE clause because then qualified references are optional. In this book we use the USE where appropriate—for example, to make infix ADT operators possible—but we also use qualified reference in most cases, even where a USE is present and the qualification is optional.

When you have an ADT that provides infix operators, the Ada 95 USE TYPE clause provides a nice compromise because it allows the infix operators to be unqualified, but nothing else.

PROGRAM STYLE

Advantages of Private Types

A client program that uses ADT `Currency` does not need to know the actual internal representation of data type `Quantity` (i.e., a record with two fields). The client can call an operator function of ADT `Currency` to perform an operation (e.g., currency addition) without having this knowledge. In fact, it is better to hide this information from the client program to prevent the client from directly manipulating the individual fields of a rational variable.

It is advantageous for a client program not to have direct access to the representation of a rational quantity for three reasons:

1. It is easier to write and read a client program that treats a currency quantity just like a predefined one, that is, without being cluttered with direct reference to implementation details.

2. The client program cannot directly store values in the fields of a currency variable.

3. If we change the representation—for example, to an array of two elements instead of a record—the client program does not have to be modified in any way, only recompiled.

There is a fourth advantage, which would apply if the type represented something more sophisticated, say, a data base record of some kind. Each record might contain information for "internal use only," that is, for use only by the data management program itself, not for use by clients. Making the record `PRIVATE` ensures that the entire record structure is not made available to the client, only that information which the ADT designer chooses to supply via the ADT operations. This is an important advantage for large, complicated, and secure applications.

11.5 System Structures: Using an ADT to Create a Mini-Data Base

In this section we will develop an ADT for employee records that could be used in a larger data base application. This ADT also uses the `Dates` and `Currency` ADTs from Sections 11.3 and 11.4, respectively, and will be used in a case study in this section to produce an interactive query system for employees.

For our purposes an employee record will contain six fields:

- Identification number, an integer in the range 1111–9999

- Name, up to 30 characters

- Gender, male or female

- Number of dependents, that is, spouse and/or children

- Annual salary, a currency quantity

- Start date, that is, the date when the employee joined the organization

Program 11.11 shows the specification of a package `Employees`. Note that the constant `MaxName`, the subtypes `IDType` and `NameType`, and the types `GenderType` and `Employee` are provided in the specification. For reasons that are discussed several times in this chapter, the record type `Employee` is `PRIVATE` so that client programs do not have direct access to the field names or structure of the record. (A justification for this might be the intention to add more fields in the future that are never accessed by clients but are handled purely internally by the package body.)

Program 11.11 Specification for Employees Package

```
WITH Currency;
WITH Dates;
PACKAGE Employees IS
------------------------------------------------------------------
--| Specification for ADT package to handle Employee records
--| Author: Michael B. Feldman, The George Washington University
--| Last Modified: September 1998
------------------------------------------------------------------

   -- constant and type definitions

   MaxName: CONSTANT Positive := 30;
   SUBTYPE NameType IS String(1..MaxName);

   SUBTYPE IDType IS Positive RANGE 1111..9999;
   TYPE    GenderType IS (Female, Male);

   TYPE Employee IS PRIVATE;

   -- operations

   -- constructor

   FUNCTION MakeEmployee (ID:        IDType;
                          Name:      NameType;
                          Gender:    GenderType;
                          NumDepend: Natural;
                          Salary:    Currency.Quantity;
                          StartDate: Dates.Date)  RETURN Employee;
   -- Pre: all input parameters are defined
   -- Post: returns a value of type Employee

   -- selectors

   FUNCTION RetrieveID       (OneEmp: Employee) RETURN IDType;
   FUNCTION RetrieveName     (OneEmp: Employee) RETURN NameType;
   FUNCTION RetrieveGender   (OneEmp: Employee) RETURN GenderType;
   FUNCTION RetrieveNumDepend (OneEmp: Employee) RETURN Natural;
   FUNCTION RetrieveSalary   (OneEmp: Employee) RETURN Currency.Quantity;
   FUNCTION RetrieveDate     (OneEmp: Employee) RETURN Dates.Date;
   -- Pre: OneEmp is defined
   -- Post: each selector retrieves its desired field

PRIVATE

   TYPE Employee IS RECORD
      ID:        IDType := IDType'Last;
      Name:      NameType := (OTHERS => ' ');
```

```
      Gender:     GenderType := Female;
      NumDepend: Natural := 0;
      Salary:     Currency.Quantity := Currency.MakeCurrency(0.00);
      StartDate: Dates.Date := Dates.Date_Of(1980, Dates.Jan, 1);
    END RECORD;

END Employees;
```

Because a client program cannot get into the details of an employee record, the ADT package must provide a set of constructor and selector operations. These are shown in the specification as the constructor `MakeEmployee` and the selectors `RetrieveName`, `RetrieveGender`, `RetrieveNumDepend`, `RetrieveSalary`, and `RetrieveDate`. The body of this relatively simple package is given in Program 11.12. Additional operations on employee records depend upon how the records will be used, as you will see in the next section.

Program 11.12 Body of Employees Package

```
PACKAGE BODY Employees IS
----------------------------------------------------------------
--| Body of ADT package to handle Employee records
--| Author: Michael B. Feldman, The George Washington University
--| Last Modified: September 1998
----------------------------------------------------------------

  -- operations

  -- constructor

  FUNCTION MakeEmployee (ID:        IDType;
                         Name:      NameType;
                         Gender:    GenderType;
                         NumDepend: Natural;
                         Salary:    Currency.Quantity;
                         StartDate: Dates.Date)  RETURN Employee IS

    TempRecord: Employee;

  BEGIN -- MakeEmployee

    TempRecord :=
      (ID => ID, Name => Name, Gender => Gender,
       NumDepend => NumDepend, Salary => Salary, StartDate => StartDate);
    RETURN TempRecord;

  END MakeEmployee;

  FUNCTION RetrieveID (OneEmp: Employee) RETURN IDType IS
  BEGIN
    RETURN OneEmp.ID;
  END RetrieveID;

  FUNCTION RetrieveName (OneEmp: Employee) RETURN NameType IS
  BEGIN
    RETURN OneEmp.Name;
  END RetrieveName;

  FUNCTION RetrieveGender (OneEmp: Employee) RETURN GenderType IS
```

```
BEGIN
  RETURN OneEmp.Gender;
END RetrieveGender;

FUNCTION RetrieveNumDepend (OneEmp: Employee) RETURN Natural IS
BEGIN
  RETURN OneEmp.NumDepend;
END RetrieveNumDepend;

FUNCTION RetrieveSalary (OneEmp: Employee) RETURN Currency.Quantity IS
BEGIN
  RETURN OneEmp.Salary;
END RetrieveSalary;

FUNCTION RetrieveDate (OneEmp: Employee) RETURN Dates.Date IS
BEGIN
  RETURN OneEmp.StartDate;
END RetrieveDate;
```

```
END Employees;
```

In Programs 11.13 and 11.14 we give the specification and body for a child package for simple employee input and output, providing procedures `ReadEmployee` and `DisplayEmployee`. The read procedure is not robust; invalid input will result in program termination. Similarly, the display procedure merely copies the fields onto the screen, with no additional formatting. As an exercise, you can improve this child package and write a program to test it and the parent package `Employees`.

Program 11.13 Specification for Employees.IO Child Package

```
PACKAGE Employees.IO IS
-----------------------------------------------------------------
--| Child Package for Employee Input/Output
--| Author: Michael B. Feldman, The George Washington University
--| Last Modified: September 1998
-----------------------------------------------------------------

  PROCEDURE ReadEmployee (Item: OUT Employee);
  -- reads an Employee record from the terminal
  -- Pre: none
  -- Post: Item contains a record of type Employee

  PROCEDURE DisplayEmployee (Item: IN Employee);
  -- displays an Employee record on the screen
  -- Pre: Item is defined
  -- Post: displays the fields of Item on the screen

END Employees.IO;
```

Program 11.14 Body of Employees.IO Child Package

```
WITH Ada.Text_IO;
WITH Ada.Float_Text_IO;
WITH Ada.Integer_Text_IO;
WITH Dates.IO;
WITH Currency.IO;
PACKAGE BODY Employees.IO IS
```

```ada
  --------------------------------------------------------------
  --| Body of Child Package for Employee Input/Output
  --| Author: Michael B. Feldman, The George Washington University
  --| Last Modified: September 1998
  --------------------------------------------------------------

    PACKAGE GenderType_IO IS
      NEW Ada.Text_IO.Enumeration_IO(Enum => GenderType);

    PROCEDURE ReadEmployee (Item: OUT Employee) IS

      S: String(1..MaxName);
      Count: Natural;

    BEGIN -- simple, non-robust ReadEmployee

      Ada.Text_IO.Put(Item => "ID > ");
      Ada.Integer_Text_IO.Get(Item => Item.ID);
      Ada.Text_IO.Skip_Line;

      Ada.Text_IO.Put(Item => "Name > ");
      Ada.Text_IO.Get_Line(Item => S, Last => Count);
      Item.Name(1..Count) := S(1..Count);

      Ada.Text_IO.Put(Item => "Gender (Female or Male) > ");
      GenderType_IO.Get(Item => Item.Gender);

      Ada.Text_IO.Put(Item => "Number of dependents > ");
      Ada.Integer_Text_IO.Get(Item => Item.NumDepend);

      Ada.Text_IO.Put(Item => "Salary > ");
      Currency.IO.Get(Item => Item.Salary);

      Ada.Text_IO.Put(Item => "Starting Date, mmm dd yyyy > ");
      Dates.IO.Get(Item => Item.StartDate);

    END ReadEmployee;

    PROCEDURE DisplayEmployee (Item: IN Employee) IS

    BEGIN -- simple DisplayEmployee

      Ada.Integer_Text_IO.Put(Item => Item.ID, Width => 1);
      Ada.Text_IO.New_Line;
      Ada.Text_IO.Put(Item => Item.Name);
      Ada.Text_IO.New_Line;
      GenderType_IO.Put(Item => Item.Gender);
      Ada.Text_IO.New_Line;
      Ada.Integer_Text_IO.Put(Item => Item.NumDepend, Width => 1);
      Ada.Text_IO.New_Line;
      Currency.IO.Put(Item => Item.Salary);
      Ada.Text_IO.New_Line;
      Dates.IO.Put(Item => Item.StartDate, Format => Dates.IO.Full);
      Ada.Text_IO.New_Line;

    END DisplayEmployee;

  END Employees.IO;
```

It is worth mentioning that the input/output procedures are making direct references to the employee fields (e.g., `Item.Gender`) even though `Employee` is a `PRIVATE` type. This shows an essential difference between a *child* package, which can be thought of as a separate part of the original parent, and a *client* package or program, which just uses the package. A child package, being part of a "family," has knowledge of private family details that are not available to clients. Naturally, as is the case with human families, this knowledge of private details must be used with care!

CASE STUDY

EMPLOYEE INQUIRY SYSTEM

To show a useful application of the package `Employees`, we introduce a case study involving an interactive query system that allows the user to build and modify a data base of employee records.

Problem Specification

We have a small company with no more than 25 employees. We wish to allow an interactive user to enter employee information into a computer and be able to do the following kinds of operations:

- Enter a new record into the computer

- Given an employee ID, search for and display that employee's record

- Given an employee ID, retrieve the record, change some of the other fields of the record, and return it to the database

- Delete a record when an employee leaves the company

- Display the entire set of employee records on the screen

Analysis

Because we already have a package that can handle individual employee records, we have two tasks ahead of us:

1. Develop a way of holding a number of records and performing the above operations

2. Develop a way for an interactive user to enter commands into the system

The two tasks are best separated into a set of operations that manipulate the data base without concern for any user interaction and a "user interface" that can handle user interactions without concern for the details of the data base operations. This is a very common approach to separation of concerns in designing a system.

Design

In keeping with the separation outlined above, we design the following system components:

1. A *data base package,* a set of operations in the form of procedures that a client program can call. The user of this part of the system, like the user of the employee package, is a *programmer* who is creating a larger application. The same database package could be used by many different applications, one of which is component 2 below.

2. A *user interface* program, in our case a menu-driven program to allow a user to select from a set of commands to do the functions listed above. Here, the user is an *end user*, a member of the company such as the personnel or payroll manager, not a programmer.

Program 11.15 shows the specification for the data base package. The programmer using this package sees only a set of operations; the data base itself is encapsulated in the body of the package, as we shall see.

Program 11.15 Specification for Data Base Package

```
WITH Employees;
PACKAGE Database IS
----------------------------------------------------------------
--| Specification of the abstract data object for a data base
--| of employee records
--| Author: Michael B. Feldman, The George Washington University
--| Last Modified: September 1998
----------------------------------------------------------------

  -- Exported Exception

  DatabaseFull: EXCEPTION;

  -- Operations

  PROCEDURE Initialize;
  -- Pre : None
  -- Post: Database is emptied of all records

  PROCEDURE Insert (E       : Employees.Employee;
                    Success : OUT Boolean);
  --   Pre   : E is defined
  --   Post  : Inserts new element E into database
  --      Success is True if insertion is performed, and False
  --      if database already has an element with the same ID as E.
  --   Raises: DatabaseFull if the database is full before insertion

  PROCEDURE Replace (E       : Employees.Employee;
                     Success : OUT Boolean);
  --   Pre   : E is defined
  --   Post  : Finds record in database with E's ID, and replaces it
  --      with E. Success is True if replacement is performed, and False
  --      if database has no element with the same ID as E.

  PROCEDURE Retrieve (ID      : IN  Employees.IDType;
                      E       : OUT Employees.Employee;
                      Success : OUT Boolean);
  --   Pre : ID is defined
  --   Post: Copies into E the database record with the given ID
  --      Success is True if the copy is performed, and False
```

```
--      if database has no element with the given ID

PROCEDURE Delete (ID      : IN Employees.IDType;
                  Success : OUT Boolean);
--   Pre : ID is defined
--   Post: Deletes from database the record with the given ID
--      Success is True if deletion is performed, and False
--      if database has no element with the given ID

PROCEDURE Display;
--   Pre : None
--   Post: The database records are displayed in order by ID

END Database;
```

Test Plan

The data base operations can be tested by a simple program consisting of a number of calls to procedures in the package. A number of operations need to be done, just to be certain that they all operate correctly. Specifically, note that the operations all have a "successful" result and a "not successful" result. Test cases must be carefully chosen to be sure that all operations behave correctly whether the result is successful or not.

Implementation

The body of the data base package is given in Program 11.16. As can be seen from the types and other declarations, the data base is a simple structure: We are just using an array to store the employee records; this array is contained in a record along with a field indicating the number of records stored in the array. The entire company's records are stored in the data base variable `Company`.

Program 11.16 Body of Data Base Package

```
WITH Ada.Text_IO;
WITH Employees;
WITH Employees.IO;
PACKAGE BODY Database IS
-----------------------------------------------------------------
--| Body of the abstract data object for a data base
--| of employee records
--| Author: Michael B. Feldman, The George Washington University
--| Last Modified: September 1998
-----------------------------------------------------------------

  -- declarations for the Employee database, TableType

  MaxData: CONSTANT Positive := 25;

  SUBTYPE CompanyIndex IS Natural RANGE 1..MaxData;
  SUBTYPE CompanyRange IS Natural RANGE 0..MaxData;
  TYPE DataArray IS ARRAY(CompanyIndex) OF Employees.Employee;

  TYPE TableType IS RECORD
    Data: DataArray;
    CurrentSize:    CompanyRange := 0;
  END RECORD;

  Company: TableType;
```

```
   PROCEDURE Initialize IS
   BEGIN -- Initialize
     Company.CurrentSize := 0;
   END Initialize;

   PROCEDURE Insert (E        : Employees.Employee;
                     Success : OUT Boolean) IS
   BEGIN -- Insert

     Success := True;

     -- First search database for E's ID; set Success false if found
     FOR Which IN 1..Company.CurrentSize LOOP
       IF Employees.RetrieveID(Company.Data(Which)) =
          Employees.RetrieveID(E) THEN
         Success := False;
         RETURN;
       END IF;
     END LOOP;

     -- we didn't find a matching record, so we can insert this one
     Company.CurrentSize := Company.CurrentSize + 1;
     Company.Data(Company.CurrentSize) := E;

   END Insert;

   PROCEDURE Replace (E        : Employees.Employee;
                      Success : OUT Boolean) IS
   BEGIN -- stub
     Ada.Text_IO.Put(Item => "Replace is still under construction.");
     Ada.Text_IO.New_Line;
   END Replace;

   PROCEDURE Retrieve (ID      : IN  Employees.IDType;
                       E       : OUT Employees.Employee;
                       Success : OUT Boolean) IS
   BEGIN -- stub
     Ada.Text_IO.Put(Item => "Retrieve is still under construction.");
     Ada.Text_IO.New_Line;
   END Retrieve;

   PROCEDURE Delete (ID      : IN Employees.IDType;
                     Success : OUT Boolean) IS
   BEGIN -- stub
     Ada.Text_IO.Put(Item => "Delete is still under construction.");
     Ada.Text_IO.New_Line;
   END Delete;

   PROCEDURE Display IS
   BEGIN -- Display

     FOR Which IN 1..Company.CurrentSize LOOP
       Employees.IO.DisplayEmployee (Item => Company.Data(Which));
       Ada.Text_IO.New_Line;
     END LOOP;

   END Display;

END Database;
```

Three operations are fully coded in this package:

- `Initialize` clears out the array by setting its `CurrentSize` field to zero. There is no need actually to "erase" the records themselves; they will be overwritten by newly arriving records.

- `Insert` loops through the array looking for a record with the given ID. As given in the postconditions for this operation, if a record is found, the insertion *fails*, because otherwise we would be inserting two or more employee records with the same ID. If we search the entire occupied part of the array without finding a record with the same ID, we just store the new record in the next available array cell.

- `Display` loops through the array, calling the employee display procedure repeatedly.

The rest of the operations are left as an exercise. They are coded as stubs; if one is called, it simply displays an "under construction" message.

Given the single constructor and field-by-field selector operations provided by package `Employees`, the best way to change a single field in the record is to retrieve the record with a `Retrieve` call, then retrieve the individual fields, change the desired ones, and construct a new record, calling `Replace` to put it back in the data base. An alternative design would modify the employee package with some new constructor operations, each of which modifies a single field of its record parameter.

Finally, because the records are kept in the array in no particular order, the easiest way to delete a record with a given array subscript is just to copy the *last* record in the array into that position, then to decrement the variable in which you keep track of how many records are present. That is, if there are 20 records in the 100-element array, and you wish to delete record number 7, just copy record number 20 into position 7, and change the number of records to 19.

Program 11.17 gives a simple test program, which you can use as an example to build a more elaborate one. For brevity we omit the sample run.

Program 11.17 Simple Test of Data Base Package

```
WITH Ada.Text_IO;
WITH Employees;
WITH Employees.IO;
WITH Database;
PROCEDURE Test_Database IS
------------------------------------------------------------------
--| Simple Test of Employee Data Base
--| Author: Michael B. Feldman, The George Washington University
--| Last Modified: September 1998
------------------------------------------------------------------

  E: Employees.Employee;
  Success: Boolean;

BEGIN -- Test_Database

  Database.Initialize;

  FOR Count IN 1..3 LOOP
```

```
      Employees.IO.ReadEmployee(Item => E);
      Database.Insert(E => E, Success => Success);
      Ada.Text_IO.Put(Item => "--------------------");
      Ada.Text_IO.New_Line;
      Database.Display;
      Ada.Text_IO.Put(Item => "--------------------");
      Ada.Text_IO.New_Line;

   END LOOP;

END Test_Database;
```

The final step is to build an interactive interface to the data base system. We leave this as an exercise; you can start with the robust menu handler given as Program 7.7 in Section 7.4.

Abstract Data Types and Abstract Data Objects

Our data base implementation is actually what is known as an *abstract data object (ADO)* implementation. An ADO differs from an ADT in that an ADT, as we have seen in the date, currency, and employee cases, provides a type so that client programs can declare variables ("objects") of the type, whereas an ADO encapsulates a single object in the package body, unseen by client programs and manipulated only by calls to the ADO operations.

An alternative data base design would turn the package into an ADT, which would provide a PRIVATE type TableType to client programs. The client then could declare several data bases, for example, one for each of the company's several offices. Each data base operation would have a parameter indicating which data base was being manipulated.

EXERCISES FOR SECTION 11.5

Programming

1. In the package Employees.IO, revise the body of the procedure ReadEmployee to make it robust, and the procedure DisplayEmployee to provide "prettier" formatting of the output. Also, write a program to test the package Employees.

2. Add to package Employees.IO two procedures—GetEmployee and PutEmployee—that read and write employee records using a disk file.

3. Complete the case study in this section by completing the data base operations and by doing a detailed design, structure chart, algorithm specification, and coding for the menu-driven inquiry program.

11.6 Continuing Saga: Writing an ADT for Multiple Spiders

In our continuing study of the spider, all packages and programs have assumed that only one spider lives in the room. How could we emulate a situation in which the room contains an entire village of spiders? As we saw in Chapter 8, the spider package implements what we now know as an abstract data object. To provide for multiple spiders, we need an abstract data *type*. Program 11.18 gives a sketch of a specification for an ADT package `spiders`.

Program 11.18 Package Specification for Multiple Spiders

```
PACKAGE Spiders IS
---------------------------------------------------------------------
--| This package provides procedures to emulate multiple
--| spiders. The spiders can move around
--| the screen drawing simple patterns.
--| Author: John Dalbey, Cal Poly San Luis Obispo, 1992
--| Adapted by: Michael B. Feldman, The George Washington University
--| Last Modified: September 1998
---------------------------------------------------------------------
   ...

TYPE Spider IS PRIVATE;

   ...

   PROCEDURE TurnRight (Which: IN OUT Spider);
   -- Pre:  None
   -- Post: Spider turns 90 degrees to the right.

   FUNCTION  AtWall (Which: Spider) RETURN Boolean;
   -- Pre:  None
   -- Post: Returns True if the spider is standing next to a wall
   --    (edge of the room) and facing it, and False otherwise.

   ...

PRIVATE

   TYPE Spider IS RECORD
      Ink           : ScreenColors;
      Heading       : Directions;
      CurrentColumn : RoomWidth;                -- spider's position
      CurrentRow    : RoomHeight;               --      in the room.
   END RECORD;

END Spiders;
```

Here `Spider` is a PRIVATE type that, like `Employee`, is provided to client programs. The specification shows examples of just two procedures, `TurnRight` and `Step`. Note that each procedure now has a parameter of type `Spider`. A `Spiders` client might then declare

```
Charlotte: Spiders.Spider;
Murgatroyd: Spiders.Spider;
```

and proceed to call spider operations such as

```
Spiders.Step(Which => Charlotte);
Spiders.TurnRight(Which => Murgatroyd);
```

Completing the package is left as an exercise.

11.7 Tricks of the Trade: Common Programming Errors

The most common error in writing and using overloaded operators in Ada is to misunderstand when the operator must be placed in quotation marks. Quotation marks are required if the operator is used in prefix form (e.g., `Currency."+"(C1,C2)`) and not permitted if the operator is used in infix form (e.g., `C1 + C2`). Infix form is of course allowed only in the presence of a USE or USE TYPE statement to eliminate the need for qualification.

In writing an exception handler for a package-defined exception, do not forget that the exception name must be qualified unless a USE is present, for example,

```
EXCEPTION
  WHEN Dates.Date_Error =>
```

A common design error in writing ADTs is to put too much in the specification. Often an ADT has extra functions or procedures in the body that are used only by other operations in the body and not intended to be used by client programs. Putting specifications for these in the package specification provides them to the client, whether or not this was intended.

CHAPTER REVIEW

In this chapter you studied abstract data types, or ADTs, implemented in Ada as packages. ADTs are characterized by a type and a set of operations applicable to that type. In Ada the type in an ADT package is often declared as PRIVATE, which prevents a client program from directly accessing the values stored in variables of the type, requiring instead that the client use package-provided operations.

Operator overloading is another useful Ada feature that was introduced in this chapter. If the ADT is a mathematical type for which addition, for example, is appropriate, this addition operation can be called `"+"`. Similarly, a comparison operation implementing "less than" for the new type can be called `"<"`.

Yet another important concept used in this chapter is the package-provided exception. An exception can be defined to report an unusual condition, such as a client action that violates an assumption of the package. If an exception is provided in the package specification, a client program can handle it with a normal Ada exception handler. Exception handling is thus no different for package-provided exceptions than it is for predefined ones.

New Ada Constructs in Chapter 11

The new constructs introduced in this chapter are given in Table 11.1.

Table 11.1   New Ada Constructs in Chapter 11

Construct	Effect
Private Type Definition	
`PACKAGE ComplexNumbers IS` `   TYPE Complex IS PRIVATE;   ...`	Defines a type `Complex` that has no predefined operations other than copying and equality.

`PRIVATE`
 	
`   TYPE Complex IS RECORD`
`      RealPart: Float;`
`      ImaginaryPart: Float;`
`   END RECORD;`
 	
`END ComplexNumbers;`
	The type definition is completed here in the `PRIVATE` section.

User-Defined Exception	
`SomethingIsWrong: EXCEPTION;`	Usually placed in a package specification; defines an exception that can be raised by an operation in the package body and handled by an exception handler in the client program.
Operator Overloading	
`FUNCTION "+"(Left, Right: Complex)` `   RETURN Complex;`	Creates an additional meaning for the `"+"` operator.

Quick-Check Exercises

1. A(n) _____ operation selects a particular component of an ADT object, a(n) _____ creates an ADT object from its component parts, and a(n) _____ operation asks whether an ADT object has a given property.

2. The syntax for an exception handler depends on whether the exception is a predefined one or a user-defined one (True/False).

3. List all the operator symbols in Ada that can be overloaded. List the ones that cannot.

Answers to Quick-Check Exercises

1. Selector, constructor, inquiry

2. False, the syntax is exactly the same.

3. `+`, `-`, `*`, `/`, `**`, `MOD`, `REM`, `ABS`, `AND`, `OR`, `NOT`, `XOR`, `&`, `=`, `/=`, `<`, `<=`, `>`, and `>=` all can be overloaded; `IN` and `NOT IN` cannot be.

Review Questions

1. Explain the rules for `PRIVATE` types. Which operations can be done on objects of a `PRIVATE` type?

2. Suppose we wrote, and included in `Currency`, an operation called `"*"` that actually *added* its operands instead of multiplying them. Would this be legal in Ada? Explain. Even if it is legal, give some reasons why it is not a good idea to do this.

Programming Projects

1. The `World_Time` program presented in Section 11.2 has a limitation: The array of time zone offsets must be completely redefined if the program user is not in the Eastern U.S. time zone. In many applications, time zone offsets are computed with respect to Greenwich Mean Time, often referred to as GMT or Zulu. This is the local time in Greenwich, England. Modify `World_Time` so that Zulu is used as the "zero point" for the offsets. (Encyclopedias and almanacs usually describe the various official time zones around the world; so do amateur radio guides.) Because your computer's clock normally reports only local time, your program will need to find out from the user the time zone in which he or she is located before it can compute the time elsewhere.

2. Write a program that asks the user to enter a group of currency quantities from the keyboard, reads these numbers into an array, then sorts them and displays the largest, smallest, median, and average values.

3. Complete and test the currency package of Section 11.4.

4. Complete and test the various packages in the employee data base project and the interactive user interface.

5. Refer to Section 9.4 on hierarchical records. Develop an ADT to handle address records. Given the ADTs for address records, employee records (Section 11.5), and dates (Section 11.3), develop an ADT that uses these to provide op-

erations on the hierarchical employee records described in Section 9.4 and modify the inquiry system of Section 11.5 so that hierarchical employee records can be manipulated by the terminal user.

6. Modify the bank account program given in Chapter 10, Programming Project 6. By analogy with Programs 11.11 through 11.17, develop an ADT for a bank transaction, a child package for transaction input/output, and a data base package to store transaction records. Use the dates packages (Programs 11.3 through 11.5) and the currency packages (Programs 11.5 through 11.10) to represent the transaction date and amount, respectively.

7. Complete the `spiders` ADT package of Section 11.6.

CHAPTER 12

Introduction to Unconstrained Array Types and Generics

This chapter introduces you to two features of Ada that make the language extremely useful for developing reusable software components: unconstrained array types and generics. An *unconstrained array type* is one that is declared in such a way that the bounds of the array are not specified in the type declaration; rather, they are supplied only when a variable of the type is declared. Many arrays of the same number of dimensions but differing sizes can be declared from the same type definition. Moreover, subprograms can be written that accept these arrays as parameters and work with them without knowing their sizes in advance. This is extremely helpful in writing general-purpose programs such as sorts and numerical algorithms.

As it happens, we have been using an unconstrained array type all along in this book: Ada's string type is one of these, predefined in standard. In this chapter you will learn how to define and use unconstrained array types of your own. Understanding unconstrained array types is an important part of understanding how to use generics well; that is why the two subjects are together in this chapter.

A *generic component* (package or subprogram) is one that is parametrized at the level of the types with which it works. There are generic formal and actual parameters, just like the "normal" ones that we use with subprograms and variant records. A generic component can be instantiated or "tailored" to work with a specific type. This means that a very general program or package can be written whose code is independent of the type it manipulates. Versions of it can be created with a single statement in each case to handle many different types.

You have been using generic units from the start in this book. You tailored `Ada.Text_IO.Enumeration_IO` for different enumeration types, most recently `Dates.Months` in Section 11.3. Also, in Section 8.3 we tailored `Ada.Numerics.Discrete_Random` for a range of random numbers. This chapter shows you how to create your own generics and tailor them for many interesting purposes.

Through the careful design of generic units, an entire industry of reusable, tailorable, software components can be built up and used for a wide range of applications. Indeed, several small companies have been quite successful in doing exactly that.

12.1 Data Structures: Unconstrained Array Types

The purpose of unconstrained array types is to allow subprograms that operate on arrays to be written without prior knowledge of the bounds of the arrays. Let us start with a type definition:

```
TYPE ListType IS ARRAY (Integer RANGE <>) OF Float;
```

The phrase `Integer RANGE <>` means that the subscript range, or bounds, of any variable of type `ListType` must form an integer subrange; the symbol `<>` is read "box" and means "we'll fill in the missing range when we declare `ListType` variables."

The type `ListType` is said to be *unconstrained*. When variables are declared, the compiler must know how much storage to allocate, and so each variable declaration *must* carry a range constraint, for example:

```
L1 : ListType(1..50);     -- 50 elements
L2 : ListType(-10..10);   -- 21 elements
L3 : ListType(0..20);     -- 21 elements
```

Operations on Unconstrained Array Types

The operations of assignment and equality testing are defined for unconstrained array types, but for either operation to proceed without raising `Constraint_Error`, both operands must be variables of the same unconstrained array type and both operands must have the same number of elements. So

```
L1 := L2;
```

will raise `Constraint_Error`, but the following operations will all succeed:

```
L2 := L3;
L1 (20..40) := L2;
L2 (1..5) := L1 (6..10);
```

These slicing operations were introduced in Chapter 10 in the discussion of Ada strings. Ada's string type is actually defined in `Standard` as follows:

```
TYPE String IS ARRAY (Positive RANGE <>) OF Character;
```

making strings just a special case of unconstrained arrays. The slicing operations work for all one-dimensional arrays just as they do for strings.

Attribute Functions for Unconstrained Arrays

Ada defines a number of attribute functions that can be used to determine the bounds of array variables. Given the type `ListType` above and the variable `L2`,

- `L2'First` returns the low bound of `L2`, or −10 in this case.

- `L2'Last` returns the high bound of `L2`, or 10.

- `L2'Length` returns the number of elements in `L2`, or 21.

- `L2'Range` returns the range `−10..10`.

The last attribute is useful in controlling loops, for instance,

```
FOR WhichElement IN L2'Range LOOP
  Ada.Float_Text_IO.Put
    (Item=>L2(WhichElement), Fore=>1, Aft=>2, Exp=>0);
  Ada.Text_IO.New_Line;
END LOOP;
```

The construct `L2'Range` is a short way of writing `L2'First..L2'Last`, so the same fragment could be written as follows:

```
FOR WhichElement IN L2'First..L2'Last LOOP
  Ada.Float_Text_IO.Put
    (Item=>L2(WhichElement), Fore=>1, Aft=>2, Exp=>0);
  Ada.Text_IO.New_Line;
END LOOP;
```

■ Example 12.1

To show the utility of unconstrained arrays, consider a function to find the maximum value stored in an array of floating-point numbers. For this function to be generally useful and reusable, it needs to be able to work for all kinds of floating-point arrays, no matter what their bounds. Using the type `ListType`, Program 12.1 shows such a function contained in a test program.

The program also contains a procedure `DisplayList`, which displays the contents of a `ListType` variable, whatever its bounds. The main program declares two lists of differing bounds, then displays the lists and tests the function `MaxValue`. From the output of the program, you can see that the maximum is found correctly even though the two lists have different sizes. ■

Program 12.1 A Demonstration of Unconstrained Arrays

```
WITH Ada.Text_IO;
WITH Ada.Float_Text_IO;
```

```
PROCEDURE Test_Max_Value IS
-----------------------------------------------------------------
--| illustrates use of unconstrained array types
--| Author: Michael B. Feldman, The George Washington University
--| Last Modified: September 1998
-----------------------------------------------------------------

   TYPE  ListType IS ARRAY(Integer RANGE <>) of Float;

   L1 : ListType(1..5);      -- 5 elements
   L2 : ListType(-4..3);     -- 8 elements

   -- local procedure to display the contents of a list

   PROCEDURE DisplayList(L: ListType) IS
   -- Pre: L is defined
   -- Post: display all values in the list

   BEGIN -- DisplayList

     FOR Count IN L'Range LOOP
       Ada.Float_Text_IO.Put(Item=>L(Count), Fore=>3, Aft=>1, Exp=>0);
     END LOOP;
     Ada.Text_IO.New_Line;

   END DisplayList;


   FUNCTION MaxValue(L: ListType) RETURN Float IS
   -- Pre: L is defined
   -- Post: returns the largest value stored in L

     CurrentMax : Float;

   BEGIN -- MaxValue

     CurrentMax := Float'First;     -- minimum value of Float

     FOR WhichElement IN L'Range LOOP
       IF L(WhichElement) > CurrentMax THEN
         CurrentMax := L(WhichElement);
       END IF;
     END LOOP;
     -- assert: CurrentMax contains the largest value in L

     RETURN CurrentMax;

   END MaxValue;


BEGIN -- Test_Max_Value

  L1 := (0.0, -5.7, 2.3, 5.9, 1.6);
  L2 := (3.1, -2.4, 0.0, -5.7, 8.0, 2.3, 5.9, 1.6);

  Ada.Text_IO.Put(Item=> "Testing MaxValue for float lists");
  Ada.Text_IO.New_Line;
  Ada.Text_IO.New_Line;
  Ada.Text_IO.Put(Item=> "Here is the list L1");
  Ada.Text_IO.New_Line;
```

```
    DisplayList(L => L1);

    Ada.Text_IO.Put(Item=> "The maximum value in this list is ");
    Ada.Float_Text_IO.Put(Item => MaxValue(L=>L1),
               Fore=>1, Aft=>2, Exp=>0);
    Ada.Text_IO.New_Line;
    Ada.Text_IO.New_Line;

    Ada.Text_IO.Put(Item=> "Here is the list L2");
    Ada.Text_IO.New_Line;
    DisplayList(L => L2);

    Ada.Text_IO.Put(Item=> "The maximum value in this list is ");
    Ada.Float_Text_IO.Put(Item => MaxValue(L=>L2),
               Fore=>1, Aft=>2, Exp=>0);
    Ada.Text_IO.New_Line;

END Test_Max_Value;
```

Sample Run

```
Testing MaxValue for float lists

Here is the list L1
  0.0 -5.7  2.3  5.9  1.6
The maximum value in this list is 5.90

Here is the list L2
  3.1 -2.4  0.0 -5.7  8.0  2.3  5.9  1.6
The maximum value in this list is 8.00
```

SYNTAX DISPLAY

Unconstrained Array Type

Form:

```
TYPE ArrayType IS ARRAY (IndexType RANGE <>) OF ValueType ;
```

Example:

```
SUBTYPE DaysInYear IS Positive RANGE 1..366;
SUBTYPE Temperature IS Float RANGE -100.0 .. 200.0;
TYPE TemperatureReadings IS
  ARRAY (DaysInYear RANGE <>) OF Temperature;
```

Interpretation:

The array type is declared with minimum and maximum bounds given by
IndexType. The actual bounds of an array variable must be supplied, as a subrange of *IndexType,* when that variable is declared. It is therefore illegal to
declare

```
Temps: TemperatureReadings;
```

Rather, the declaration must include bounds:

```
Temps: TemperatureReadings (1..31);
```

Slicing and Unconstrained Arrays

In Section 10.1 we studied array slicing in the context of strings. Slicing is actually more general: It is available for *all* one-dimensional unconstrained arrays in Ada. For example, given the function `MaxValue` from Program 12.1 and a `Float` variable `Y`, it is permissible to call `MaxValue` with a slice as its parameter, as in

```
Y := MaxValue(L => L2(0..2));
```

which would search only the given slice of the array for a maximum value. As an exercise, you can modify Program 12.1 to test this concept.

EXERCISES FOR SECTION 12.1

Programming

1. Modify Program 12.1 to call `MaxValue` with parameters `L1(2..4)`, `L2(0..2)`, and `L2(-4..-1)` and ascertain that the program correctly finds the given maximum values.

12.2 Problem Solving: A General Sorting Program

We introduced the concept of sorting and sort procedures in earlier chapters. The utility of a sort procedure is greatly enhanced if it can be used with a wide variety of arguments. In this section we develop a sort that will work for arrays of the same unconstrained type but differing bounds; in Section 12.4 we will exploit the full generality of Ada's generics to create a sort that will work with any unconstrained array type at all, regardless of its index type or element type.

CASE
STUDY:
SOFTWARE SUPPORT "HOTLINE"

You are employed in the customer-support department of a software company. the toll-free telephone system is open seven days a week, and your supervisor is interested in knowing how many calls arrive each day and also in seeing the data presented in order of increasing number of calls. That is, the day with the fewest calls will appear first, and the day with the most calls will appear last. Your supervisor might also wish to see the data for weekdays or weekend days only.

Analysis

Since you are experienced in data handling, you realize that this is basically a sorting problem, and so you develop a sort program that will work with arrays of call records. The program should handle correctly arrays of one through seven elements, so that, for example, just the weekdays or just the weekend days can be sorted.

Data Requirements

Probem Inputs

a set of up to seven pairs of data, each giving a day of the week (type `Days`) and a number of calls (type `Natural`)

Problem Outputs

a display of the data pairs, sorted in order of increasing number of calls

Design

Here is a good application of unconstrained array types. Let us define the types

```
TYPE Days IS (Mon, Tue, Wed, Thu, Fri, Sat, Sun);
SUBTYPE DayRange IS Natural RANGE 0..6;
TYPE CallRecord IS RECORD
   DayOfWeek    : Days;
   NumberOfCalls: Natural;
END RECORD;
TYPE Callers IS ARRAY(DayRange RANGE <>) OF CallRecord;
```

and write a procedure `Exchange` capable of exchanging two elements of type `Natural`. The procedure `SelectSort` will be a simple modification of the one we did in Section 9.10.

Algorithm

We developed a simple sorting algorithm and procedure `SelectSort` in Section 9.10. We can just adapt the sort procedure to the current record strucure; the algorithm is unchanged.

Implementation

Program 12.2 gives the modified sort procedure `SelectSort`, together with auxiliary procedures `Exchange` and `DisplayCallers`. The main program declares three arrays of type `Callers` with differing bounds and illustrates the sort procedure operating on the three arrays in turn. Note how the attributes are used in `SelectSort` to make the procedure independent of the bounds of the parameter.

Program 12.2 Sorting Unconstrained Arrays

```
WITH Ada.Text_IO;
WITH Ada.Integer_Text_IO;
PROCEDURE Phone_Service IS
-----------------------------------------------------------------
--| Shows sorting of unconstrained arrays and slices
--| Author: Michael B. Feldman, The George Washington University
--| Last Modified: September 1998
-----------------------------------------------------------------
```

```
SUBTYPE DayRange IS Natural  RANGE 0..6;
SUBTYPE Weekdays IS DayRange RANGE 0..4;
SUBTYPE Weekend  IS DayRange RANGE 5..6;

TYPE Days IS (Mon, Tue, Wed, Thu, Fri, Sat, Sun);
TYPE CallRecord IS RECORD
  DayOfWeek    : Days;
  NumberOfCalls: Natural;
END RECORD;

TYPE Callers IS ARRAY(DayRange RANGE <>) of CallRecord;

PACKAGE Days_IO IS NEW Ada.Text_IO.Enumeration_IO(Enum => Days);

ThisWeek:        Callers(DayRange);
WeekdayCallers: Callers(Weekdays);
WeekendCallers: Callers(Weekend);

PROCEDURE DisplayCallers (List: Callers) IS
-- Pre:  List is defined
-- Post: display all elements in the vector

BEGIN -- DisplayCallers
  FOR Count IN List'Range LOOP
    Days_IO.Put  (Item=>List(Count).DayOfWeek, Width=>3);
    Ada.Integer_Text_IO.Put
      (Item=>List(Count).NumberOfCalls, Width=>4);
    Ada.Text_IO.New_Line;
  END LOOP;
  Ada.Text_IO.New_Line;
END DisplayCallers;


PROCEDURE Exchange(Value1, Value2: IN OUT CallRecord) IS
-- Pre:  Value1 and Value2 are defined
-- Post: Value1 and Value2 are interchanged

  TempValue: CallRecord;

BEGIN -- Exchange
  TempValue := Value1;
  Value1    := Value2;
  Value2    := TempValue;
END Exchange;


PROCEDURE SelectSort(List: IN OUT Callers) IS
-- Pre:  List is defined
-- Post: elements of List are arranged in ascending order

  IndexOfMin: DayRange;

BEGIN

  FOR PositionToFill IN List'First..List'Last - 1 LOOP

    IndexOfMin := PositionToFill;

    FOR ItemToCompare IN PositionToFill + 1..List'Last LOOP
      IF List(ItemToCompare).NumberOfCalls
```

```
                    < List(IndexOfMin).NumberOfCalls THEN
                      IndexOfMin := ItemToCompare;
                  END IF;
              END LOOP;

              IF IndexOfMin /= PositionToFill THEN
                Exchange(List(PositionToFill),List(IndexOfMin));
              END IF;

          END LOOP;

      END SelectSort;


    BEGIN -- Phone_Service

      ThisWeek := ((Mon, 12), (Tue, 23), (Wed, 100), (Thu, 40),
                   (Fri, 52), (Sat, 17), (Sun,   2));
      WeekdayCallers := ThisWeek(Weekdays);
      WeekendCallers := ThisWeek(Weekend);

      Ada.Text_IO.Put(Item=> "Testing SelectSort for telephone callers");
      Ada.Text_IO.New_Line;
      Ada.Text_IO.Put(Item=> "Here is ThisWeek before sorting.");
      Ada.Text_IO.New_Line;
      DisplayCallers(List => ThisWeek);
      Ada.Text_IO.New_Line;

      SelectSort(List => ThisWeek);
      Ada.Text_IO.Put(Item=> "Here is ThisWeek after upward sorting.");
      Ada.Text_IO.New_Line;
      DisplayCallers(List => ThisWeek);
      Ada.Text_IO.New_Line;

      Ada.Text_IO.Put(Item=> "Here is WeekdayCallers before sorting.");
      Ada.Text_IO.New_Line;
      DisplayCallers(List => WeekdayCallers);
      Ada.Text_IO.New_Line;

      SelectSort(List => WeekdayCallers);
      Ada.Text_IO.Put
        (Item=> "Here is WeekdayCallers after upward sorting.");
      Ada.Text_IO.New_Line;
      DisplayCallers(List => WeekdayCallers);
      Ada.Text_IO.New_Line;

      Ada.Text_IO.Put(Item=> "Here is the WeekendCallers before sorting.");
      Ada.Text_IO.New_Line;
      DisplayCallers(List => WeekendCallers);
      Ada.Text_IO.New_Line;

      SelectSort(List => WeekendCallers);
      Ada.Text_IO.Put
        (Item=> "Here is WeekendCallers after upward sorting.");
      Ada.Text_IO.New_Line;
      DisplayCallers(List => WeekendCallers);
      Ada.Text_IO.New_Line;

    END Phone_Service;
```

Sample Run

```
Testing SelectSort for telephone callers
Here is ThisWeek before sorting.
MON  12
TUE  23
WED 100
THU  40
FRI  52
SAT  17
SUN   2


Here is ThisWeek after upward sorting.
SUN   2
MON  12
SAT  17
TUE  23
THU  40
FRI  52
WED 100


Here is WeekdayCallers before sorting.
MON  12
TUE  23
WED 100
THU  40
FRI  52


Here is WeekdayCallers after upward sorting.
MON  12
TUE  23
THU  40
FRI  52
WED 100


Here is the WeekendCallers before sorting.
SAT  17
SUN   2


Here is WeekendCallers after upward sorting.
SUN   2
SAT  17
```

Unconstrained arrays and slicing make it easier to write programs that deal with partially filled arrays. Look again at Program 9.15, in which an array of scores is sorted. If the score array type were defined as an unconstrained type similar to `Callers` and the variable `scores` were declared as an array object similar to `v1`, then the procedure `SelectSort` would need only a single parameter—namely, the name of the actual array to be sorted. Once `scores` was partially filled, the slice `scores(1..ClassSize)` could be passed as the single actual parameter. You can make this change as an exercise.

EXERCISES FOR SECTION 12.2

Programming

1. Modify Program 9.15 so that `ScoreArray` is defined as an unconstrained array type and `SelectSort` requires only a single parameter.

12.3 System Structures: Generic Units

Ada's system of types and procedures requires that the type of a procedure's actual parameter always match that of the formal parameter. This means that a procedure or function that needs to do the same thing to values of two different types must be written twice—once for each type. Consider the procedure `Exchange`:

```
PROCEDURE Exchange(Value1, Value2: IN OUT Natural) IS
  TempValue: Natural;
BEGIN
  TempValue := Value1;
  Value1    := Value2;
  Value2    := TempValue;
END Exchange;
```

A procedure to exchange two `Float` values would have the same sequence of statements, but the type references would be different:

```
PROCEDURE Exchange(Value1, Value2: IN OUT Float) IS
  TempValue: Float;
BEGIN
  TempValue := Value1;
  Value1    := Value2;
  Value2    := TempValue;
END Exchange;
```

Obviously, we could modify the first version to give the second version by using an editor. Because we are likely to need the `Natural` version again, we modify a copy of it. This gives two versions of a procedure that are almost the same; because of overloading, the two can both be called `Exchange`. Carrying this to its extreme, we could build up a large library of `Exchange` programs with our editor and be ready for any eventuality. `Exchange` could even be made to work with array or record structures, because Ada allows assignment for any type.

There is a problem with this approach: It clutters our file system with a large number of similar programs. Worse still, suppose that a bug turns up in the statements for `Exchange` or in another program with more complexity. The bug will have turned up in *one* of the versions; the same bug will probably be present in all of them, but we would probably forget to fix all the others! This is, in miniature, a problem that industry has long faced: multiple versions of a program, all similar but not exactly alike, all requiring debugging and other maintenance.

Returning to our simple example, it would be nice if we could create *one* version of Exchange, test it, then put it in the library. When we needed a version to work with a particular type, we could just tell the compiler to use our pretested Exchange but to change the type it accepts. The compiler would make the change automatically, and we would still be left with only a single copy of the procedure to maintain.

It happens that Ada allows us to do exactly this. The solution to this problem is *generics*. A generic unit is a *recipe* or *template* for a procedure, function, or package. Such a unit is declared with *formal parameters* that are *types* and sometimes that are *procedure* or *function names*. An analogy can be drawn with an unusual recipe for a layer cake: all the elements are there *except* that the following items are left as parameters to be plugged in by the baker:

- The number of layers
- The kind of filling between the layers
- The flavor of the cake itself
- The flavor of the icing

This recipe was pretested by the cookbook author, but before we can use it for a three-layer yellow cake with marshmallow filling and chocolate icing, we need to (at least mentally) make all the changes necessary to the ingredients list. Only after this *instance* of the recipe has been created does it make sense to try to make a cake using it.

Generic Type Parameters

■ Example 12.2

Program 12.3 is a specification for a generic exchange program. This specification indicates to the compiler that we wish ValueType to be a formal parameter. The formal parameters are listed between the word GENERIC and the procedure heading. Writing

```
TYPE ValueType IS PRIVATE;
```

tells the compiler that *any* type, *including* a private one, can be plugged in as the kind of element to exchange. We will introduce more examples of type parameters below.

Program 12.3 Specification for Generic Exchange Procedure

```
GENERIC
  TYPE ValueType IS PRIVATE;  -- any type OK except LIMITED PRIVATE
PROCEDURE Swap_Generic(Value1, Value2: IN OUT ValueType);
----------------------------------------------------------------
--| Specification for generic exchange procedure
--| Author: Michael B. Feldman, The George Washington University
--| Last Modified: September 1998
----------------------------------------------------------------
```

The body of `Swap_Generic` appears as Program 12.4. Notice that `Swap_Generic` looks essentially the same as the `Integer` and `Float` versions, except for the use of `ValueType` wherever a type is required. `ValueType` is a *formal type parameter.*

Program 12.4 Body of Generic Exchange Procedure

```
PROCEDURE Swap_Generic(Value1, Value2: IN OUT ValueType) IS
-----------------------------------------------------------------
--| Body of generic exchange procedure
--| Author: Michael B. Feldman, The George Washington University
--| Last Modified: September 1998
-----------------------------------------------------------------

  TempValue: ValueType;

BEGIN -- Swap_Generic

  TempValue := Value1;
  Value1    := Value2;
  Value2    := TempValue;

END Swap_Generic;
```

The specification and body of a generic procedure or function are, syntactically, independent compilation units; as such, they reside (usually) in separate files. Compiling the specification and the body creates a version of the generic that is ready to be `WITH`-ed by a client, then *instantiated,* or tailored by plugging in the desired type. A `WITH`-ing client could, for example, include the following statements:

```
PROCEDURE IntegerSwap IS NEW Swap_Generic (ValueType => Integer);
PROCEDURE CharSwap IS NEW Swap_Generic (ValueType => Character);
```

The notation is familiar; we have used it in creating instances of `Ada.Text_IO`. `Enumeration_IO` and other standard-library generics. Program 12.5 shows how the `Swap_Generic` procedure could be tested and used. The two instantiations above appear in the program. ■

Program 12.5 A Test of the Generic Swap Procedure

```
WITH Swap_Generic;
WITH Ada.Text_IO;
WITH Ada.Integer_Text_IO;
PROCEDURE Test_Swap_Generic IS
-----------------------------------------------------------------
--| Test program for Swap_Generic
--| Author: Michael B. Feldman, The George Washington University
--| Last Modified: September 1998
-----------------------------------------------------------------

  X : Integer;
  Y : Integer;

  A : Character;
  B : Character;
```

```
      PROCEDURE IntegerSwap IS NEW Swap_Generic (ValueType => Integer);
      PROCEDURE CharSwap IS NEW Swap_Generic (ValueType => Character);

BEGIN -- Test_Swap_Generic

  X := 3;
  Y := -5;
  A := 'x';
  B := 'q';

  Ada.Text_IO.Put("Before swapping, X and Y are, respectively ");
  Ada.Integer_Text_IO.Put(Item => X, Width => 4);
  Ada.Integer_Text_IO.Put(Item => Y, Width => 4);
  Ada.Text_IO.New_Line;

  IntegerSwap(Value1 => X,Value2 => Y);

  Ada.Text_IO.Put("After  swapping, X and Y are, respectively ");
  Ada.Integer_Text_IO.Put(Item => X, Width => 4);
  Ada.Integer_Text_IO.Put(Item => Y, Width => 4);
  Ada.Text_IO.New_Line;
  Ada.Text_IO.New_Line;

  Ada.Text_IO.Put("Before swapping, A and B are, respectively ");
  Ada.Text_IO.Put(Item => A);
  Ada.Text_IO.Put(Item => B);
  Ada.Text_IO.New_Line;

  CharSwap(Value1 => A,Value2 => B);

  Ada.Text_IO.Put("After  swapping, A and B are, respectively ");
  Ada.Text_IO.Put(Item => A);
  Ada.Text_IO.Put(Item => B);
  Ada.Text_IO.New_Line;

END Test_Swap_Generic;
```

Sample Run

```
Before swapping, X and Y are, respectively    3  -5
After  swapping, X and Y are, respectively   -5   3

Before swapping, A and B are, respectively xq
After  swapping, A and B are, respectively qx
```

Generic Subprogram Parameters

Sometimes, a generic recipe needs to be instantiated with the names of functions or procedures. To continue the food analogy, a certain fish recipe can be prepared by either baking or broiling; the rest of the recipe is independent. So the action "desired cooking method" would be a parameter of that recipe.

■ Example 12.3

Consider the function `Maximum` from Program 5.6, which returns the larger of its two `Integer` operands:

```
FUNCTION Maximum (Value1, Value2: Integer) RETURN Integer IS

  Result: Integer;

BEGIN

  IF Value1 > Value2 THEN
    Result := Value1;
  ELSE
    Result := Value2;
  END IF;

  RETURN Result;

END Maximum;
```

We would like to make a function that returns the larger of its two operands, *regardless of the types of these operands.* As in the case of `Generic_Swap`, we can use a generic type parameter to indicate that an instance can be created for any type. This is not enough, however. The `IF` statement compares the two input values: Suppose the type that we use to instantiate does not have an obvious, predefined, "greater than" operation? Suppose that the type is a user-defined record with a key field, for example? "Greater than" is not predefined for records! We can surely write such an operation, but we need to inform the compiler to use it; when writing a generic, we need to reassure the compiler that all the operations used in the body of the generic will exist at instantiation time. Let us indicate in the generic specification that a comparison function will exist.

Program 12.6 is the desired generic specification. The `WITH` syntax here takes getting used to, but it works.

Program 12.6 Specification for Generic Maximum Function

```
GENERIC
  TYPE ValueType IS PRIVATE;
  WITH FUNCTION Compare(L, R : ValueType) RETURN Boolean;
FUNCTION Maximum_Generic(L, R : ValueType) RETURN ValueType;
----------------------------------------------------------------
--| Specification for generic maximum function
--| Author: Michael B. Feldman, The George Washington University
--| Last Modified: September 1998
----------------------------------------------------------------
```

The body of the generic function, shown as Program 12.7, looks similar to the one just given for `Maximum`.

Program 12.7 Body of Generic Maximum Function

```
FUNCTION Maximum_Generic(L, R : ValueType) RETURN ValueType IS
----------------------------------------------------------------
--| Body of generic maximum function
```

```
--| Author: Michael B. Feldman, The George Washington University
--| Last Modified: September 1998
-----------------------------------------------------------------

BEGIN -- Maximum_Generic

  IF Compare(L, R) THEN
    RETURN L;
  ELSE
    RETURN R;
  END IF;

END Maximum_Generic;
```

An instantiation for `Float` values might be

```
FUNCTION FloatMax IS
  NEW Maximum_Generic (ValueType=>Float, Compare=> ">");
```

Notice how the "greater than" operator is supplied. It makes no difference that the generic expected a function and we gave it an operator; after all, an operator *is* a function. What is important is that the *structure* of the actual parameter matches the structure of the formal parameter. As long as there is a ">" available for `Float` (of course there is, in `standard`), the instantiation will succeed.

The Ada compiler has no idea what the function `Compare` will do when the generic is instantiated. It turns out, then, that if we just supply "<" as an actual parameter for `Compare`, the instantiation finds the minimum instead of the maximum! Program 12.8 shows a total of six instantiations, giving minimum and maximum functions for `Integer`, `Float`, and `Currency` values. All the minimums are called `Minimum`; all the maximums are called `Maximum`; this is the normal Ada overloading principle in action. ■

Program 12.8 Test of Generic Maximum Function

```
WITH Ada.Text_IO;
WITH Ada.Float_Text_IO;
WITH Ada.Integer_Text_IO;
WITH Currency; USE Currency;
WITH Currency.IO;
WITH Maximum_Generic;
PROCEDURE Test_Maximum_Generic IS
-----------------------------------------------------------------
--| Test program for Generic Maximum, using six instances
--| Author: Michael B. Feldman, The George Washington University
--| Last Modified: September 1998
-----------------------------------------------------------------

  FUNCTION Maximum IS
    NEW Maximum_Generic (ValueType=>Float,    Compare=> ">");
  FUNCTION Minimum IS
    NEW Maximum_Generic (ValueType=>Float,    Compare=> "<");

  FUNCTION Maximum IS
    NEW Maximum_Generic (ValueType=>Integer,  Compare=> ">");
  FUNCTION Minimum IS
    NEW Maximum_Generic (ValueType=>Integer,  Compare=> "<");
```

```
FUNCTION Maximum IS
   NEW Maximum_Generic (ValueType=>Quantity, Compare=> ">");
FUNCTION Minimum IS
   NEW Maximum_Generic (ValueType=>Quantity, Compare=> "<");

BEGIN -- Test_Maximum_Generic

   Ada.Text_IO.Put("Maximum of -3 and 7 is ");
   Ada.Integer_Text_IO.Put(Item => Maximum(-3, 7), Width=>1);
   Ada.Text_IO.New_Line;
   Ada.Text_IO.Put("Minimum of -3 and 7 is ");
   Ada.Integer_Text_IO.Put(Item => Minimum(-3, 7), Width=>1);
   Ada.Text_IO.New_Line(Spacing => 2);

   Ada.Text_IO.Put("Maximum of -3.29 and 7.84 is ");
   Ada.Float_Text_IO.Put
      (Item => Maximum(-3.29, 7.84), Fore=>1, Aft=>2, Exp=>0);
   Ada.Text_IO.New_Line;
   Ada.Text_IO.Put("Minimum of -3.29 and 7.84 is ");
   Ada.Float_Text_IO.Put
      (Item => Minimum(-3.29, 7.84), Fore=>1, Aft=>2, Exp=>0);
   Ada.Text_IO.New_Line(Spacing => 2);

   Ada.Text_IO.Put("Maximum of 23.65 and 37.49 is ");
   Currency.IO.Put
      (Item => Maximum(MakeCurrency(23.65), MakeCurrency(37.49)));
   Ada.Text_IO.New_Line;
   Ada.Text_IO.Put("Minimum of 23.65 and 37.49 is ");
   Currency.IO.Put
      (Item => Minimum(MakeCurrency(23.65), MakeCurrency(37.49)));
   Ada.Text_IO.New_Line(Spacing => 2);

END Test_Maximum_Generic;
```

Sample Run

```
Maximum of -3 and 7 is 7
Minimum of -3 and 7 is -3

Maximum of -3.29 and 7.84 is 7.84
Minimum of -3.29 and 7.84 is -3.29

Maximum of 23.65 and 37.49 is 37.49
Minimum of 23.65 and 37.49 is 23.65
```

Generic Array Parameters

An important use for generics, combined with unconstrained array types, is building very general subprograms to deal with arrays. For a generic to be instantiated for many different array types, we need to specify formal parameters for the index and array types.

■ Example 12.4

Program 12.9 is a specification for a function `Maximum_Array_Generic` that returns the "largest" of all the elements in an array, regardless of the index or element type. "Largest" is in quotes because we know already that we can make it work as a minimum finder as well.

Program 12.9 Specification for Generic Array Maximum Function

```
GENERIC

  TYPE ValueType IS PRIVATE;  -- any nonlimited type
  TYPE IndexType IS (<>);     -- any discrete type
  TYPE ArrayType IS ARRAY(IndexType RANGE <>) OF ValueType;
  WITH FUNCTION Compare(L, R : ValueType) RETURN Boolean;

FUNCTION Maximum_Array_Generic(List: ArrayType) RETURN ValueType;
----------------------------------------------------------------
--| Specification for generic version of array maximum finder
--| Author: Michael B. Feldman, The George Washington University
--| Last Modified: September 1998
----------------------------------------------------------------
```

The syntax of the specification for `IndexType` means "any discrete type is OK as an actual parameter." Recalling that discrete types are the integer and enumeration types and subtypes, this is exactly what we need for the index type of the array. The specification for `ArrayType` looks like a type declaration, but *it is not*. Rather, it is a description to the compiler of the *kind* of array type that is acceptable as an actual parameter. In this case the array type must be indexed by `IndexType` (or a subtype thereof) and have elements of type `ValueType` (or a subtype thereof).

The body of `Maximum_Array_Generic` can be seen in Program 12.10. You can write a test program for it as an exercise. As a hint, consider the following declarations:

```
TYPE FloatVector IS ARRAY(Integer RANGE <>) OF Float;
TYPE CurrencyVector IS ARRAY (Positive RANGE <>) OF Currency.Quantity;
```

and instantiate the generic as follows:

```
FUNCTION Maximum IS
  NEW Maximum_Array_Generic(ValueType=>Float, IndexType=>Integer,
                    ArrayType=>FloatVector, Compare=>">");

FUNCTION Minimum IS
  NEW Maximum_Array_Generic(ValueType=>Currency.Quantity,
                    IndexType=>Positive,
                    ArrayType=>CurrencyVector, Compare=>"<");  ■
```

Program 12.10 Body of Generic Array Maximum Function

```
FUNCTION Maximum_Array_Generic(List: ArrayType) RETURN ValueType IS
----------------------------------------------------------------
--| Body of generic array maximum finder
--| Author: Michael B. Feldman, The George Washington University
--| Last Modified: September 1998
----------------------------------------------------------------
```

```
    Result: ValueType;

BEGIN -- Maximum_Array_Generic

    Result := List(List'First);
    FOR WhichElement IN List'Range LOOP
      IF Compare(List(WhichElement), Result) THEN
        Result := List(WhichElement);
      END IF;
    END LOOP;

    RETURN Result;

END Maximum_Array_Generic;
```

EXERCISES FOR SECTION 12.3

Self-Check

1. Review the ADTs we developed in Chapter 11. For which ones could `Swap_Generic` *not* be instantiated? How about `Maximum_Generic`?

Programming

1. Modify the test program for `Swap_Generic` to instantiate for some other types.

2. Repeat problem 1 for `Maximum_Generic`.

3. Write a test program for `Maximum_Array_Generic` as suggested in the section.

12.4 Problem Solving: A Generic Sorting Program

Let us continue our study of generics with the development of a generic sort procedure that uses much of what we have done in the chapter. We develop a sort procedure that will work correctly for *any* variable of *any* unconstrained array type, regardless of its bounds, index type, or element type.

In Program 12.2 we developed `SelectSort`, which works for any array of a *particular* unconstrained array type. We just need to modify it to make it generic. We also have our procedure `Swap_Generic`, which we can instantiate and use to handle exchanges.

Program 12.11 is the specification for the generic sort routine. This is similar to `Maximum_Array_Generic` from Program 12.9.

Program 12.11 Specification for Generic Sort Procedure

```
GENERIC

    TYPE ElementType IS PRIVATE;   -- any nonlimited type will do
    TYPE IndexType   IS (<>);      -- any discrete type for index
    TYPE ListType    IS ARRAY (IndexType RANGE <>) OF ElementType;
    WITH FUNCTION Compare (Left, Right : ElementType) RETURN Boolean;

PROCEDURE Sort_Generic(List: IN OUT ListType);
-----------------------------------------------------------------
--| Specification for Generic Exchange Sort - will sort input
--| array in order according to Compare
--| Author: Michael B. Feldman, The George Washington University
--| Last Modified: September 1998
-----------------------------------------------------------------
```

With your current knowledge of generics, you can understand this specification easily. The body of the generic sort can be found as Program 12.12. Notice that the body begins with the context clause

```
WITH Swap_Generic;
```

and instantiates this procedure for whatever the element type turns out to be. We have here a case of one generic instantiating another; this is the kind of situation that demonstrates the power of generics to help write very general programs. The rest of the procedure body is very similar to our earlier `SelectSort` procedure (Program 12.2), with the necessary modifications.

Program 12.12 Body of Generic Sort Procedure

```
WITH Swap_Generic;
PROCEDURE Sort_Generic(List: IN OUT ListType) IS
-----------------------------------------------------------------
--| Body of Generic Sort Procedure
--| Author: Michael B. Feldman, The George Washington University
--| Last Modified: September 1998
-----------------------------------------------------------------

   -- we need to make an instance of Swap_Generic for this case
   PROCEDURE Exchange IS NEW Swap_Generic (ValueType => ElementType);

   IndexOfMin: IndexType;

BEGIN -- Sort_Generic

   FOR PositionToFill IN List'First .. IndexType'Pred(List'Last) LOOP

     IndexOfMin := PositionToFill;

     FOR ItemToCompare IN
       IndexType'Succ(PositionToFill) .. List'Last LOOP
       IF Compare(List(ItemToCompare),  List(IndexOfMin)) THEN
         IndexOfMin := ItemToCompare;
       END IF;
     END LOOP;
```

```
    IF IndexOfMin /= PositionToFill  THEN
      Exchange(List(PositionToFill), List(IndexOfMin));
    END IF;

  END LOOP;

END Sort_Generic;
```

Using the Generic Sort to Order an Array of Records

`Sort_Generic` can be especially useful in sorting arrays of records as we did in Programs 9.14 and 12.2. Consider the following declarations:

```
MaxSize : CONSTANT Positive := 250;
MaxScore : CONSTANT Positive := 100;

SUBTYPE StudentName IS String(1..20);
SUBTYPE ClassIndex  IS Positive RANGE 1..MaxSize;
SUBTYPE ClassRange  IS Natural RANGE 0..MaxSize;
SUBTYPE ScoreRange  IS Natural RANGE 0..MaxScore;

TYPE ScoreRecord IS RECORD
Name:  StudentName;
Score: ScoreRange;
END RECORD;

TYPE ScoreArray IS ARRAY (ClassIndex RANGE <>) OF ScoreRecord;
```

Here is a "compare" function that tells us whether one record is "less than" another (in the sense that one score is lower than the other):

```
FUNCTION ScoreLess(Score1, Score2 : ScoreRecord) RETURN Boolean IS
BEGIN
  RETURN Score1.Score < Score2.Score;
END ScoreLess;
```

This function compares the score fields of the two records, returning `True` if the first record is "less than" the second and `False` otherwise. We could have named this function `"<"`, of course, but we chose not to do so in the interest of clarity. Given `Sort_Generic`, it takes only a single instantiation statement to create a sort that will order an array of score records in ascending order:

```
PROCEDURE SortUpScores IS NEW Sort_Generic
  (ElementType => ScoreRecord,
   IndexType   => ClassIndex,
   ListType    => ScoreArray,
   Compare     => ScoreLess);
```

Given variables `Scores` and `ClassSize` as follows:

```
Scores: ScoreArray(ClassIndex'First..ClassIndex'Last);
ClassSize: ClassRange;
```

we see that scores can hold up to 250 records and ClassSize can be used to determine the actual number of records read from a file into the array. The array can easily be put in ascending order by score, just by calling SortUpScores with the appropriate array slice:

```
SortUpScores(List => Scores(1..ClassSize));
```

Program 12.13 demonstrates the sort for two entirely different array types: an array of float values and an array of phone call records as we used in Section 12.2.

Program 12.13 Test of Generic Sort Procedure

```
WITH Ada.Text_IO;
WITH Ada.Integer_Text_IO;
WITH Ada.Float_Text_IO;
WITH Sort_Generic;
PROCEDURE Test_Sort_Generic IS
-----------------------------------------------------------------
--| Demonstrates Sort_Generic using two unrelated kinds of lists;
--| this is not a realistic application but rather just shows that
--| many instances of a generic can occur within one client program.
--| Author: Michael B. Feldman, The George Washington University
--| Last Modified: September 1998
-----------------------------------------------------------------

  SUBTYPE Index IS Integer RANGE 1..10;
  TYPE    FloatVector IS ARRAY(Index RANGE <>) OF Float;

  V1 : FloatVector(1..10);

  SUBTYPE DayRange IS Natural  RANGE 0..6;
  SUBTYPE Weekdays IS DayRange RANGE 0..4;
  SUBTYPE Weekend  IS DayRange RANGE 5..6;

  TYPE Days IS (Mon, Tue, Wed, Thu, Fri, Sat, Sun);
  TYPE CallRecord IS RECORD
    DayOfWeek    : Days;
    NumberOfCalls: Natural;
  END RECORD;

  TYPE Callers IS ARRAY(DayRange RANGE <>) of CallRecord;

  PACKAGE Days_IO IS NEW Ada.Text_IO.Enumeration_IO(Enum => Days);

  ThisWeek:        Callers(DayRange);

  -- if we are going to sort CallRecords,
  -- we need to know how to compare them

  FUNCTION "<" (L, R: CallRecord) RETURN Boolean IS
  BEGIN
    RETURN L.NumberOfCalls < R.NumberOfCalls;
  END "<";

  FUNCTION ">" (L, R: CallRecord) RETURN Boolean IS
  BEGIN
    RETURN L.NumberOfCalls > R.NumberOfCalls;
  END ">";
```

```ada
-- local procedures to display the contents of two kinds of lists

PROCEDURE DisplayCallers (List: Callers) IS
BEGIN -- DisplayCallers
  FOR Count IN List'Range LOOP
    Days_IO.Put  (Item=>List(Count).DayOfWeek, Width=>3);
    Ada.Integer_Text_IO.Put
      (Item=>List(Count).NumberOfCalls, Width=>4);
    Ada.Text_IO.New_Line;
  END LOOP;
  Ada.Text_IO.New_Line;
END DisplayCallers;

PROCEDURE DisplayFloatVector (V: FloatVector) IS
BEGIN
  FOR Count IN V'First..V'Last LOOP
    Ada.Float_Text_IO.Put(Item=>V(Count), Fore=>4, Aft=>2, Exp=>0);
  END LOOP;
  Ada.Text_IO.New_Line;
END DisplayFloatVector;

-- two instances of Sort_Generic for Float vectors;
-- the first sorts in increasing order, the second in decreasing order

PROCEDURE SortUpFloat IS NEW Sort_Generic
  (ElementType => Float,
   IndexType   => Index,
   ListType    => FloatVector,
   Compare     => "<");

PROCEDURE SortDownFloat IS NEW Sort_Generic
  (ElementType => Float,
   IndexType   => Index,
   ListType    => FloatVector,
   Compare     => ">");

-- two instances of Sort_Generic for Callers;
-- the first sorts in increasing order, the second in decreasing order

PROCEDURE SortUpCallers IS NEW Sort_Generic
  (ElementType => CallRecord,
   IndexType   => DayRange,
   ListType    => Callers,
   Compare     => "<");

PROCEDURE SortDownCallers IS NEW Sort_Generic
  (ElementType => CallRecord,
   IndexType   => DayRange,
   ListType    => Callers,
   Compare     => ">");

BEGIN -- Test_Sort_Generic

  V1 := (0.7, 1.5, 6.9, -3.2, 0.0, 5.1, 2.0, 7.3, 2.2, -5.9);
  Ada.Text_IO.New_Line;
  Ada.Text_IO.Put(Item=> "Testing Sort_Generic for float vectors");
  Ada.Text_IO.New_Line;
  Ada.Text_IO.Put(Item=> "Here is the vector before sorting.");
  Ada.Text_IO.New_Line;
```

```
            DisplayFloatVector(V => V1(3..3));
            Ada.Text_IO.New_Line;

            SortUpFloat(List => V1(3..3));
            Ada.Text_IO.Put(Item=> "Here is the vector after upward sorting.");
            Ada.Text_IO.New_Line;
            DisplayFloatVector(V => V1);
            Ada.Text_IO.New_Line;

            SortDownFloat(List => V1);
            Ada.Text_IO.Put(Item=> "Here is the vector after downward sorting.");
            Ada.Text_IO.New_Line;
            DisplayFloatVector(V => V1);
            Ada.Text_IO.New_Line;

            ThisWeek := ((Mon, 12), (Tue, 23), (Wed, 100), (Thu, 40),
                         (Fri, 52), (Sat, 17), (Sun,   2));

            Ada.Text_IO.Put(Item=> "Testing Sort_Generic for telephone callers");
            Ada.Text_IO.New_Line;
            Ada.Text_IO.Put(Item=> "Here is ThisWeek before sorting.");
            Ada.Text_IO.New_Line;
            DisplayCallers(List => ThisWeek);
            Ada.Text_IO.New_Line;

            SortUpCallers(List => ThisWeek);
            Ada.Text_IO.Put(Item=> "Here is ThisWeek after upward sorting.");
            Ada.Text_IO.New_Line;
            DisplayCallers(List => ThisWeek);
            Ada.Text_IO.New_Line;

            SortDownCallers(List => ThisWeek);
            Ada.Text_IO.Put(Item=> "Here is ThisWeek after downward sorting.");
            Ada.Text_IO.New_Line;
            DisplayCallers(List => ThisWeek);
            Ada.Text_IO.New_Line;

END Test_Sort_Generic;
```

Sample Run

```
Testing Sort_Generic for float vectors
Here is the vector before sorting.
    0.70    1.50    6.90   -3.20    0.00    5.10    2.00    7.30    2.20   -5.90

Here is the vector after upward sorting.
   -5.90    0.70    1.50   -3.20    0.00    2.20    2.00    6.90    5.10    7.30

Here is the vector after downward sorting.
    7.30    5.10    6.90    0.70    1.50    2.20    2.00    0.00   -3.20   -5.90

Testing Sort_Generic for telephone callers
Here is ThisWeek before sorting.
MON  12
TUE  23
WED 100
THU  40
FRI  52
SAT  17
SUN   2
```

```
Here is ThisWeek after upward sorting.
SUN    2
MON   12
TUE   23
SAT   17
THU   40
FRI   52
WED  100


Here is ThisWeek after downward sorting.
WED  100
FRI   52
THU   40
TUE   23
SAT   17
MON   12
SUN    2
```

SYNTAX DISPLAY

Generic Specification

Form:

```
GENERIC
  list of generic formal parameters
PROCEDURE pname (list of procedure parameters );

GENERIC
  list of generic formal parameters
FUNCTION fname (list of function parameters ) RETURN ResultType;

GENERIC
  list of generic formal parameters
PACKAGE pname IS
  specifications of resources provided by the package
END pname ;
```

Example:

```
GENERIC
  TYPE ValueType IS PRIVATE;
  TYPE IndexType IS (<>);
  WITH FUNCTION "+"(L,R: ValueType) RETURN ValueType;
  WITH FUNCTION "*"(L,R: ValueType) RETURN ValueType;
  Zero: ValueType;
PACKAGE Vectors IS
  TYPE Vector IS ARRAY(IndexType RANGE <>) OF ValueType;
  Bounds_Error: EXCEPTION;
  FUNCTION "+"(L, R: Vector) RETURN Vector;
  FUNCTION "*"(L, R: Vector) RETURN ValueType;
END Vectors;
```

Interpretation:

The generic specification defines a generic procedure, function, or package, for which a corresponding body must also be provided. The list of generic formal type, procedure or function, and object parameters indicates the structure of the parameters to be supplied at instantiation of the generic.

Here are the forms of the generic type parameters we have seen here and their interpretation. There are other generic type parameters, but their discussion is beyond the scope of this book. This form:

```
TYPE ValueParameterName IS PRIVATE;
```

most commonly used as a value parameter, indicates that any type can be matched at instantiation, including a PRIVATE type, as long as it is not LIMITED PRIVATE. That is, the operations of assignment and equality testing must be defined for the type.

This form:

```
TYPE IndexParameterName IS (<>);
```

indicates that any discrete type—that is, an integer or enumeration type or sub-type—can be matched at instantiation. This form is commonly used to specify the index type of an array type.

Finally, this form:

```
TYPE ArrayParameterName IS
  ARRAY(IndexParameterName RANGE <>) OF ValueParameterName;
```

indicates that any unconstrained array type with the given index and value types can be matched at instantiation.

EXERCISES FOR SECTION 12.4

Self-Check

1. Explain how Sort_Generic could be instantiated to order an array of score records in alphabetical order by the name of the student.

2. Explain how Sort_Generic could be instantiated to order an array of score records in descending order by score.

Programming

1. Modify Test_Sort_Generic so that the element type is aanother type we have defined in this book. Try it for Currency or Date, for example.

12.5 System Structures: A Generic Sets Package

Up to this point we have seen only generic functions and procedures. In this section we develop a generic *package,* namely, one for representing *discrete sets,* or sets of integers or enumeration values.

Sets are very important both in mathematics and in computer applications. Given a universe of objects or values, a set S is just a collection of objects belonging to that universe. Some common universes are the integers, the positive integers, alphabet letters, and sets of values that we could represent as enumeration types. Sets are so important in programming that some languages, especially Pascal, provide sets as a predefined type. Ada does not have a predefined set type; in this section we will show an ADT that will emulate Pascal's predefined type, using a generic package.

Often sets are described just by listing their members between braces, as in the set $\{a, b\}$ taken from the universe of English alphabet letters. In general, there is no ordering associated with a set, so $\{a, b\}$ and $\{b, a\}$ usually describe the same set. Two sets are said to be equal if they have the same members. A set is said to be empty if it has no members. In cases in which there is no ordering, it also makes no difference if we name a member twice, so $\{a, b, a\} = \{b, a, b\} = \{a, b\}$.

Operations on Sets

What are the important operations associated with sets? Certainly, inserting a member in a set and deleting a member from a set are essential; so are testing a set to see whether a given element is a member and testing a set to see whether it is empty. The last two operations are *predicate* or *inquiry* selector operations; they return Boolean values. The most important dyadic constructor operations are as follows:

- The *union* of two sets S and T (written usually as $S \cup T$), which returns the set containing all of S's members and all of T's members

- The *intersection* of S and T ($S \cap T$), which returns the set containing all elements which are members of both S and T

- The *difference* $S - T$, which returns the set containing all elements which are members of S but not of T

An often-used monadic constructor is the complement $-S$, which returns the set containing all elements in the universe which are not members of S.

We will use + and * to represent the union and intersection, respectively, because the union and intersection symbols are not part of the ASCII character set. For example, if the universe is the letters a–k, inclusive, and $S = \{a, d, e, g\}$ and $T = \{b, c, d, e, k\}$, then

$$S + T = \{a, b, c, d, e, g, k\}$$
$$S * T = \{d, e\}$$
$$S - T = \{a, g\} \text{ and } T - S = \{b, c, k\}$$
$$-S = \{b, c, f, h, i, j, k\}$$

Finally, two more inquiry operations are commonly used:

- the *improper subset* operation: S is an improper subset of T if and only if all members of S are also members of T.

- the *proper subset* operation: S is a proper subset of T if and only if all members of S are members of T but at least one member of T is not a member of S.

Because the subset symbols are also missing from the type `Character`, we use `<=` and `<` for improper and proper subset, respectively. For example, {*b*, *c*} < {*a*, *b*, *c*, *d*, *e*} and {*b*, *c*} <= {*a*, *b*, *c*, *d*, *e*} but is not a subset of {*c*, *e*}. Also, {*a*, *b*} <= {*a*, *b*}.

Specifying the Generic Set ADT

Mathematically, sets can be infinite (all the integers, for example). In programming applications, however, it is finite sets that are most interesting. Therefore we confine ourselves to representing finite sets and specifically to sets that are taken from finite universes of integers or enumeration values. As we shall see, it is easy to use Ada's generic facility to build a package that provides a good but more flexible approximation of the predefined set facility of Pascal.

A universe is either an integer subtype or an enumeration type, which means that a universe also happens to be a valid index range for arrays. Choosing a universe, we implement a set as a one-dimensional array of `Boolean` values, with index range corresponding to that universe. Given a set *S* that is represented in this fashion, if a given member of the universe is a member of *S*, we let the corresponding element of *S* be `True`; otherwise we let that element be `False`. This representation is often called the *characteristic function* or *bit map* of a set, and is an especially compact way to represent a large set. For example, suppose we choose the universe a–g. Every set over this universe is represented as a `Boolean` array indexed a–g, and specifically the set *S* = {*a*, *d*, *e*, *g*} is represented as

a	b	c	d	e	f	g
True	False	False	True	True	False	True

Now let us devise a generic Ada package for this ADT. A framework for the generic part of the specification is

```
GENERIC

   TYPE Universe IS (<>);

PACKAGE Sets_Generic IS
   . . .
END Sets_Generic;
```

The second line specifies a generic parameter that can match any discrete type, that is, any enumeration type or integer subtype. This is exactly what we need for our finite, discrete universes.

Program 12.14 gives the desired specification, complete with a private part defining the type `set`. Making sets a `PRIVATE` type allows client programs to copy sets and check them for inequality using the predefined `:=`, `=`, and `/=` operations but prohibits clients from direct access to the implementation of sets. This leaves us, the package writer, the flexibility to change the implementation of sets without requiring any code changes in client programs.

Program 12.14 Specification for Generic Set Package

```
GENERIC

  TYPE Universe IS (<>);  -- any integer or enumeration type

PACKAGE Sets_Generic IS

  -----------------------------------------------------------------------
  --| Generic specification for sets over discrete universes
  --| Author: Michael B. Feldman, The George Washington University
  --| Last Modified: September 1998
  -----------------------------------------------------------------------

    TYPE Set IS PRIVATE;
    Phi: CONSTANT Set; -- empty set

    -- constructors

    FUNCTION "+" (S: Set; E: Universe) RETURN Set;
    FUNCTION "-" (S: Set; E: Universe) RETURN Set;
    -- Pre:  S and E are defined
    -- Post: returns S with E inserted or deleted respectively;
    --   "+" has no effect if IsIn(S,E); "-" has none if NOT IsIn(S,E)

    FUNCTION Singleton(E: Universe) RETURN Set;
    FUNCTION "+" (E1, E2: Universe) RETURN Set;
    -- Pre:  E, E1, and E2 are defined
    -- Post: returns a set made from one or two elements

    FUNCTION "+" (S, T : Set) RETURN Set;
    FUNCTION "*" (S, T : Set) RETURN Set;
    FUNCTION "-" (S, T : Set) RETURN Set;
    -- Pre:  S and T are defined
    -- Post: returns the union, intersection, and difference of
    --   S and T, respectively

    FUNCTION "-"  (S : Set) RETURN Set;
    -- Pre:  S is defined
    -- Post: returns the complement of S


    -- selectors
    FUNCTION IsIn (S : Set; E : Universe) RETURN Boolean;
    -- Pre:  S and E are defined
    -- Post: returns True if and only if E is a member of S

    FUNCTION IsEmpty (S : Set) RETURN Boolean;
    -- Pre:  S is defined
    -- Post: returns True if and only if S is empty


    FUNCTION SizeOf (S : Set) RETURN Natural;
    -- Pre:  S is defined
    -- Post: returns the number of members in S

    FUNCTION "<=" (S, T : Set) RETURN Boolean;
    FUNCTION "<"  (S, T : Set) RETURN Boolean;
    -- Pre:  S and T are defined
    -- Post: returns True if and only if S is
    --   an improper or proper subset of T, respectively
```

```
PRIVATE
  TYPE SetArray IS ARRAY (Universe) OF Boolean;
  TYPE Set IS RECORD
    Store: SetArray := (OTHERS => False);
  END RECORD;
  Phi: CONSTANT Set := (Store => (OTHERS => False));
END Sets_Generic;
```

Note in the type definition that the Boolean array is stored in a record. This is to allow us to initialize all sets by default to the empty set: Recall that Ada allows us to default-initialize only objects of a record type. Note also the constant Phi, which we use to represent the empty set. The constant is partially declared at the top of the specification, then completed in the private part, after the full type definition for the PRIVATE type is given.

The operations to insert and delete a member are shown as operators "+" and "-", respectively, so that given a set s and an element E, the expressions s + E and s - E are meaningful. We include two additional constructor operators: singleton, which creates a singleton set—a set with a single member—from its element parameter, and another "+" operator to create a set from two elements. Specifying all these operations as functions makes it easy to create a set with the desired membership. For example, a client program could instantiate Sets_Generic as follows:

```
SUBTYPE SmallNatural is NATURAL RANGE 0..15);
PACKAGE NaturalSets IS NEW Sets_Generic(Universe => SmallNatural);
```

and then, having declared a variable,

```
S: NaturalSets.Set;
```

can include the odd small naturals in s with

```
S := 7 + 3 + 13 + 5 + 1 + 9 + 11 + 15;
```

Implementing the Generic Set ADT

Program 12.15 shows the body of the package Sets_Generic. Note that the union, intersection, and difference operators construct their results by looping through the sets, finding elementwise AND, OR, and NOT values.

Program 12.15 Body of Generic Set Package

```
PACKAGE BODY Sets_Generic IS
------------------------------------------------------------------
--| Body of generic sets package
--| Author: Michael B. Feldman, The George Washington University
--| Last Modified: September 1998
------------------------------------------------------------------

  -- constructors

  FUNCTION "+" (S: Set; E: Universe) RETURN Set IS
    Result: Set := S;
```

```
BEGIN -- "+"
  Result.Store (E) := True;
  RETURN Result;
END "+";

FUNCTION "-" (S: Set; E: Universe) RETURN Set IS
  Result: Set := S;
BEGIN -- "-"
  Result.Store (E) := False;
  RETURN Result;
END "-";

FUNCTION Singleton(E: Universe) RETURN Set IS
BEGIN -- Singleton
  RETURN Phi + E;
END Singleton;

FUNCTION "+" (E1, E2: Universe) RETURN Set IS
BEGIN -- "+"
  RETURN Phi + E1 + E2;
END "+";

FUNCTION "+" (S, T : Set) RETURN Set IS
  Result: Set;
BEGIN -- "+"
  FOR E IN Universe LOOP
    Result.Store(E) := S.Store(E) OR T.Store(E);
  END LOOP;
  RETURN Result;
END "+";

FUNCTION "*" (S, T : Set) RETURN Set IS
  Result: Set;
BEGIN -- "*"
  FOR E IN Universe LOOP
    Result.Store(E) := S.Store(E) AND T.Store(E);
  END LOOP;
  RETURN Result;
END "*";

FUNCTION "-" (S, T : Set) RETURN Set IS
  Result: Set;
BEGIN -- "-"
  FOR E IN Universe LOOP
    Result.Store(E) := S.Store(E) AND NOT T.Store(E);
  END LOOP;
  RETURN Result;
END "-";

FUNCTION "-" (S : Set) RETURN Set IS
  Result: Set;
BEGIN -- "-"
  FOR E IN Universe LOOP
    Result.Store(E) := NOT S.Store(E);
  END LOOP;
  RETURN Result;
END "-";

-- selectors
```

```
FUNCTION IsIn (S : Set; E : Universe) RETURN Boolean IS
BEGIN -- IsIn
  RETURN S.Store (E);
END IsIn;

FUNCTION IsEmpty (S : Set) RETURN Boolean IS
BEGIN -- IsEmpty
  RETURN S = Phi;
END IsEmpty;

FUNCTION SizeOf (S : Set) RETURN Natural IS
  Result: Natural := 0;
BEGIN -- SizeOf
  FOR E IN Universe LOOP
    IF S.Store(E) THEN
      Result := Result + 1;
    END IF;
  END LOOP;
  RETURN Result;
END SizeOf;

FUNCTION "<=" (S, T : Set) RETURN Boolean IS
BEGIN -- "<="
  RETURN (S + T) = T;
END "<=";

FUNCTION "<" (S, T : Set) RETURN Boolean IS
BEGIN -- "<"
  RETURN S /= T AND THEN S <= T;
END "<";

END Sets_Generic;
```

An Application: Music Makers

Program 12.16 shows an example of how Sets_Generic might be used. An enumeration type Instruments is declared, representing common musical instruments. The generic package is instantiated for these, and variables are created representing different kinds of musical ensembles, depending on the instruments usually found in them. The program shows one local procedure DisplayEnsemble which operates by using an instance of Ada.Text_IO.Enumeration_IO and iterating through an ensemble to display only those instruments present in that ensemble.

Program 12.16 A Music Makers Program

```
WITH Ada.Text_IO;
WITH Sets_Generic;
PROCEDURE Music_Makers IS
-------------------------------------------------------------------------
--| Example of the use of Sets_Generic, to create musical ensembles
--| Author: Michael B. Feldman, The George Washington University
--| Last Modified: September 1995
-------------------------------------------------------------------------

  TYPE Instruments IS
    (Violin, Viola, Cello, BassViol,        -- classical strings
```

```
         Piano, Harpsichord, Organ,               -- classical keyboards
         Clarinet, Saxophone,                     -- single-reed woodwinds
         Oboe, Bassoon,                           -- double-reed woodwinds
         Flute, Piccolo,                          -- flutes
         Trumpet, Trombone, FrenchHorn, Tuba,     -- brass
         Tympani, Snare, TomTom, BassDrum,        -- drums
         Cymbals, Triangle, Bells, Marimba,       -- percussion
         Guitar, Banjo, Ukelele,                  -- folk strings
         Accordion, Keyboard);                    -- miscellaneous

    PACKAGE Music_IO IS
      NEW Ada.Text_IO.Enumeration_IO(Enum => Instruments);
    PACKAGE Ensembles IS NEW Sets_Generic (Universe => Instruments);
    USE Ensembles;

    SUBTYPE Ensemble IS Ensembles.Set; -- nickname for this program

    Strings: CONSTANT Ensemble := Violin + Viola + Cello + BassViol;
    Brasses: CONSTANT Ensemble := Trumpet + Trombone + FrenchHorn + Tuba;
    JazzDrums: CONSTANT Ensemble := Snare + TomTom + BassDrum + Cymbals;

    JazzCombo:         Ensemble;
    StringQuartet:     Ensemble;
    PhillyStringBand:  Ensemble;
    RockBand:          Ensemble;

    PROCEDURE DisplayEnsemble(Band: Ensemble) IS
    BEGIN
      FOR Instrument IN Instruments LOOP
        IF IsIn(Band, Instrument) THEN
          Music_IO.Put(Instrument);
          Ada.Text_IO.New_Line;
        END IF;
      END LOOP;
      Ada.Text_IO.New_Line;
    END DisplayEnsemble;

BEGIN -- Music_Makers

  JazzCombo := JazzDrums + Guitar + BassViol + Trumpet;
  Ada.Text_IO.Put(Item => "Jazz Combo:");
  Ada.Text_IO.New_Line;
  DisplayEnsemble(Band => JazzCombo);

  PhillyStringBand := Guitar + Ukelele + Banjo + Accordion
    + Saxophone + Snare + BassDrum;
  Ada.Text_IO.Put(Item => "Philly String Band:");
  Ada.Text_IO.New_Line;
  DisplayEnsemble(Band => PhillyStringBand);

  StringQuartet := Strings - BassViol;
  Ada.Text_IO.Put(Item => "String Quartet:");
  Ada.Text_IO.New_Line;
  DisplayEnsemble(Band => StringQuartet);

  RockBand := Guitar + Keyboard + JazzDrums;
  Ada.Text_IO.Put(Item => "Rock Band:");
  Ada.Text_IO.New_Line;
  DisplayEnsemble(Band => RockBand);
```

```
END Music_Makers;
```

Sample Run

```
Jazz Combo:
BASSVIOL
TRUMPET
SNARE
TOMTOM
BASSDRUM
CYMBALS
GUITAR

Philly String Band:
SAXOPHONE
SNARE
BASSDRUM
GUITAR
BANJO
UKELELE
ACCORDION

String Quartet:
VIOLIN
VIOLA
CELLO

Rock Band:
SNARE
TOMTOM
BASSDRUM
CYMBALS
GUITAR
KEYBOARD
```

One of the ensembles in the program, `PhillyStringBand`, reveals the author's Philadelphia upbringing: This city is the home of the String Band, which—as can be seen from the instruments—contains more than strings and no violins. A large number of String Bands march in Philadelphia's New Year's Day parade; prizes are awarded to the groups that have the most imaginative costumes as well as the best music.

As an exercise, you can create some of your favorite musical ensembles. Try creating a brass band and a symphony orchestra. This example highlights one of the difficulties in using sets in the pure mathematical sense: Because duplicate elements do not change the set, we cannot, using this representation, keep track of just how many of each instrument are in a particular ensemble—only the instrument *types* are represented.

12.6 Tricks of the Trade: Common Programming Errors

In dealing with unconstrained array types, a common error is neglecting to supply bounds when a variable is declared, which leads to a compilation error. Keep in mind that bounds are generally not supplied in declaring a procedure or function parameter whose type is an unconstrained array type.

In writing generic specifications, it is sometimes difficult to figure out exactly which formal parameters to write. We have studied generic type parameters only briefly, and you will be wise to keep your generic specifications simple, following the examples in the chapter. Neglecting to supply a generic procedure or function parameter will result in a compilation error if the compiler encounters that procedure or function in the body. We always need to reassure the compiler that an appropriate operation will be supplied at instantiation, and the way to do this is by defining appropriate formal parameters.

CHAPTER REVIEW

In this chapter we studied two important concepts in building reusable software components. Unconstrained array types allow us to define array types such that the bounds of a given array are left unspecified until the array variable is declared. Unconstrained array types facilitate writing general-purpose subprograms that deal with arrays, such as vector operations and sort procedures.

Generic definition allows us to create templates, or recipes, for subprograms and packages. These templates allow us to leave such things as parameter types, sizes, and operations unspecified until instantiation time. Once a generic template is compiled, multiple versions of it, called instances, can then be created, each with a single statement. The availability of generic definition and instantiation gives us the potential for building large and powerful libraries of reusable software components with much less effort and with much greater maintainability. In this chapter we saw a number of useful generic components for exchanging values, finding the maximum, sorting, and vector handling.

New Ada Constructs in Chapter 12

The new Ada constructs that were introduced in this chapter are listed in Table 12.1.

Table 12.1 Summary of New Ada Constructs

Construct	*Effect*
Unconstrained Array Type	

```SUBTYPE Weeks IS Positive RANGE 1..52;```
```SUBTYPE Rainfall IS Float RANGE 0.0..500.0;```
```TYPE RainTable IS```
``` ARRAY (Weeks RANGE <>) OF Rainfall;```
```SecondQuarter: RainTable(14..26);```
	Declares an array type whose variables can be indexed by any subrange of `Weeks` and a variable with 13 elements.

Construct	Effect
Generic Specification	

```
GENERIC

  TYPE ValueType IS PRIVATE;
  TYPE IndexType IS (<>);
  TYPE ArrayType IS
    ARRAY(IndexType RANGE <>) OF ValueType;
  WITH FUNCTION Compare(L,R: ValueType)
    RETURN Boolean;

FUNCTION IndexOfMax(A: ArrayType) RETURN IndexType;
```

Specifies a function to find the location of the "largest" value in an array.

Quick-Check Exercises

1. Define an unconstrained array type.

2. How many dimensions can an unconstrained array type have?

3. Explain what is meant by a generic template.

4. What is a generic type parameter? Give examples.

5. What is a generic procedure or function parameter? Give examples.

6. Given a generic parameter

   ```
   WITH FUNCTION Compare(L,R: ValueType) RETURN Boolean;
   ```

   explain why it is legal to match this with an operator "<" or ">" at instantiation.

Answers to Quick-Check Exercises

1. An unconstrained array type is one in which the bounds of array variables are not fixed until the variables are declared.

2. There is no language-defined limit on the number of dimensions; unconstrained array types are no different from other array types in this regard.

3. A specification of a procedure, function, or package that must be instantiated before it can be used.

4. A generic type parameter specifies which class of types is acceptable as a match in creating an instance. Examples are any type that is not limited private, any discrete type, and any unconstrained array type with given index and element types.

5. A generic procedure or function parameter indicates to the compiler that the name of a procedure or function with a matching parameter list will be supplied at instantiation.

6. An operator is just a certain kind of function. Ada does not care whether the name of such a function is an operator symbol or an identifier, as long as there is a correct match of the parameters and result type of the function.

Review Questions

1. Explain how unconstrained array types, and array attributes, facilitate creating general-purpose array-handling programs.

2. One generic parameter form we did not discuss in the chapter is

   ```
   TYPE SomeParameterName IS LIMITED PRIVATE;
   ```

   which allows *any* type, even a LIMITED PRIVATE one, to be supplied as a match at instantiation. Suppose we used one of these type forms in a generic package specification. What limitations would this place on the kinds of statements that could appear in the body of the package?

Programming Projects

1. In Section 9.10 we developed a function Search (Program 9.13) that looks through an array for a particular value. Revise Search to make it generic, and write a test program for several instances.

2. Revise the case study of Section 9.10, in which an array of score records is read from a file, then sorted. Use the generic sort procedure from Section 12.4, instantiating it as suggested there.

3. Demonstrate Maximum_Array_Generic for some interesting instantiations.

4. A useful function similar to Maximum_Array_Generic is one that finds the *location* of the "maximum" value in an array or slice, rather than the value itself. Write such a function as a generic, then write a generic sort program that uses it.

5. A useful function similar to Maximum_Array_Generic is one that finds the *location* of the "maximum" value in an array or slice, rather than the value itself. Write such a function as a generic, then write a generic sort program that uses it.

6. Invent some interesting kinds of sets and instantiate and test the generic sets package for these.

7. Modify Program 12.16 to create some musical ensembles that interest you.

8. Ada provides an interesting feature for working with `Boolean` arrays: The logical operators `NOT`, `AND`, `OR`, and `XOR` (exclusive `OR`) are predefined for these arrays. This allows us to simplify the operators in the sets package by removing the loops and replacing them by expressions of the form `s.Store AND T.Store`. Modify the package to take advantage of this feature.

9. The feature described in exercise 8 can also lead to a very nice code optimization. The `PRAGMA` (compiler directive) `Pack`, applied to a `Boolean` array type, will often allocate space for objects of this type using a single bit per `Boolean` value. Because many computers have hardware logical instructions that operate on binary words, the compiler can often implement an intersection, for example, using a small number of "word-wise" machine instructions. Write a program to examine this issue. The attribute `Size`, applied to a data structure, returns a `Positive` value giving the number of bits allocated for that structure. So you can declare

```
TYPE BitArray IS ARRAY(Character) OF Boolean;
TYPE BitArray2 IS ARRAY(Character) OF Boolean;
PRAGMMA Pack(BitArray2);
```

and then use ordinary integer output procedures to display `SetArray'Size` and `SetArray2'Size`. Is there a difference in the packed and unpacked versions of the type?

If your compiler allows you to examine the machine or assembly code it produces, and if you can understand machine or assembly language, check to see whether your compiler is indeed taking advantage of the optimization we have just described.

CHAPTER 13

Multidimensional Arrays and Variant Records

So far, the arrays that we have seen have been one-dimensional ones, and the record structures have been fairly simple. In this chapter we look at more interesting and complex structured types.

A *multidimensional array* has, as the name suggests, more than one dimension. Instead of being a linear collection of elements, it may have the "shape" of a rectangle (two-dimensional) or even a rectangular solid or cube (three-dimensional). In fact, there is in theory no limit to the number of dimensions an array type can have, and examples with more than three are not uncommon. Multidimensional arrays give us the ability to structure information in useful tabular forms.

A *variant record* is one with several different possible structures, instead of just one structure as we saw in Chapter 9. The structure of the record is determined, at execution time, by the value of a special field called the *discriminant* field; CASE constructs are used both to declare the record type and to process variables of the type.

13.1 Data Structures: Multidimensional Arrays

■ Example 13.1

One two-dimensional object we are all familiar with is a tic-tac-toe board. The declarations

```
SUBTYPE MoveRange IS Positive RANGE 1..3;
TYPE GameSymbol IS (X, O, E); -- for Tic Tac Toe; E indicates empty cell
TYPE BoardArray IS ARRAY (MoveRange, MoveRange) OF GameSymbol;
```

```
Empty     : CONSTANT GameSymbol := E;
TicTacToe : BoardArray;
```

allocate storage for the array `TicTacToe`. This array has nine storage cells arranged in three rows and three columns. A single enumeration value may be stored in each cell. `TicTacToe` is a two-dimensional array as pictured in Fig. 13.1.

Figure 13.1 A Tic-Tac-Toe Board Stored as Array TicTacToe

```
        Column

        1   2   3

    1   X   O   E

Row 2   O   X   O <----- TicTacToe(2,3)

    3   X   X   X
```

This array has nine elements, each of which must be referenced by specifying a row subscript (1, 2, or 3) and a column subscript (1, 2, or 3). Each array element contains a character value. The array element `TicTacToe(2,3)` pointed to in Fig. 13.1 is in row 2, column 3 of the array; it contains the enumeration value O. The diagonal line consisting of array elements `TicTacToe(1,1)`, `TicTacToe(2,2)`, and `TicTacToe(3,3)` represents a win for player X; each cell contains the value X. ∎

SYNTAX DISPLAY

Array Type Declaration (Multidimensional)

Form:

```
TYPE multidim IS
  ARRAY (range1, range2, ... , rangen)
  OF element-type ;
```

Example:

```
TYPE YearByMonth IS ARRAY (1900..1999, Month) OF Real;
TYPE Election IS ARRAY (Candidate, Precinct) OF Integer;
```

Interpretation:

$Range_i$ represents the *subscript-type* of dimension i of array type *multidim*. Each *subscript-type* is a discrete (integer or enumeration) range, which may be written explicitly (as in `1900..1999`) or as a type or subtype name (as in `Month`). The *element-type* may be any predefined type or a previously defined scalar or composite data type.

Although we will focus our discussion on arrays with two and three dimensions, there is no limit on the number of dimensions allowed in Ada. However, there may be a limit imposed by the particular implementation you are using. The amount of memory space allocated for storage of a multidimensional array is the *product* of the ranges and therefore can be quite large.

■ Example 13.2

The array `Table` declared below

```
Table : ARRAY (1..7, 1..5, 1..6) OF Float;
```

consists of three dimensions: the first subscript may take on values from 1 to 7; the second, from 1 to 5; and the third, from 1 to 6. A total of $7 \times 5 \times 6$, or 210, floating-point numbers may be stored in the array `Table`. All three subscripts must be specified in each reference to array `Table` (e.g. `Table(2,3,4)`). ■

Storage of Multidimensional Arrays

Most Ada implementations store multidimensional arrays in adjacent memory cells to simplify accessing the individual elements. The elements of a two-dimensional array are often stored in order by row (i.e., first row 1, then row 2, and so on). This is called *row-major order*. To access a particular array element, the compiler computes the offset of that element from the first element stored. To perform this computation, the compiler must know the size of each element in bytes and the number of elements per row. Both values are available from the array type declaration.

For example, the array `TicTacToe` would be stored in row-major form as shown in Fig. 13.2. There are three elements per row, and each element occupies one byte of storage. The offset for element `TicTacToe(i,j)` is computed from the formula

$$\text{Offset} = (i - 1) \times 3 + (j - 1)$$

This formula gives a value of 0 as the offset for element `TicTacToe(1,1)` and a value of 5 as the offset for element `TicTacToe(2,3)`.

Not all compilers use a row-major form for a multidimensional array; Fortran compilers, for instance, store arrays in a column-by-column, or column-major, form. It is interesting to note that the Ada standard does not require a particular way of storing these structures: an Ada compiler can use row-major, column-major, or some other unusual form. Usually there is no particular reason for you to know the storage method; it is an abstraction just like floating-point numbers are.

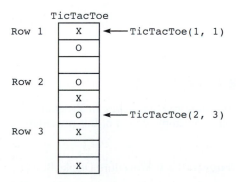

Figure 13.2 Array TicTacToe in Memory, Row–Major Form

Manipulation of Two-Dimensional Arrays

A row subscript and a column subscript must be specified to reference an element of a two-dimensional array. The type of each of the two subscripts must be compatible with the corresponding subscript type specified in the array declaration. Assuming that `Game_IO` is an instance of `Ada.Text_IO.Enumeration_IO` for values of type `GameSymbol`, the loop

```
FOR Column IN MoveRange LOOP
   Game_IO.Put (Item => TicTacToe(1,Column));
END LOOP;
```

displays the first row of array `TicTacToe` (`TicTacToe(1,1)`, `TicTacToe(1,2)`, and `TicTacToe(1,3)`) on the current output line. The loop

```
FOR Row IN MoveRange LOOP
   Game_IO.Put (Item => TicTacToe(Row, 1));
   Ada.Text_IO.New_Line;
END LOOP;
```

displays the second column of `TicTacToe` (`TicTacToe(1,2)`, `TicTacToe(2,2)`, and `TicTacToe(3,2)`) in a vertical line.

■ Example 13.3

We can use aggregates in multidimensional arrays just as we did in one-dimensional arrays. We can use an aggregate assignment

```
TicTacToe := (MoveRange => (MoveRange => EMPTY));
```

or even

```
TicTacToe := (OTHERS => (OTHERS => EMPTY));
```

The double aggregate indicates that for each of the rows, all the columns are to be set to `Empty`.

We can use nested loops to access all elements in a multidimensional array in a predetermined order. In the next examples the outer-loop control variable determines the row being accessed, and the inner-loop control variable selects each element in that row.　■

■ Example 13.4

Procedure `DisplayBoard` in Program 13.1 displays the current status of a tic-tac-toe board. A sample output of this procedure is shown in Fig. 13.3.　■

Program 13.1 Procedure DisplayBoard

```
PROCEDURE DisplayBoard (TicTacToe : BoardArray) IS
-- Pre : Array TicTacToe is defined.
```

```
-- Post: Displays all elements of array TicTacToe.

BEGIN -- DisplayBoard

  Ada.Text_IO.Put(Item => "-------");
  Ada.Text_IO.New_Line;
  FOR Row IN MoveRange LOOP
    -- Display all columns of current row
    FOR Column IN MoveRange LOOP
      Ada.Text_IO.Put(Item => "|");
      Game_IO.Put(Item => TicTacToe (Row,Column));
    END LOOP;
    Ada.Text_IO.Put(Item => "|");
    Ada.Text_IO.New_Line;
    Ada.Text_IO.Put(Item => "-------");
    Ada.Text_IO.New_Line;
  END LOOP;

END DisplayBoard;
```

Figure 13.3 Sample Output of DisplayBoard

```
-------
|X|O|E|
-------
|O|X|O|
-------
|X|E|X|
-------
```

■ Example 13.5

Function `IsFilled` in Program 13.2 returns a value of `True` if a tic-tac-toe board is all filled up; it returns a value of `False` if there is at least one cell that contains the value `Empty`. We are assuming that all cells are initialized to `Empty` before the game begins. To move to a particular cell, the current player replaces the constant `Empty` in that cell with an `X` or an `O`. Function `IsFilled` could be called before making a move to determine whether there were any possible moves left. The `IF` statement

```
IF IsFilled(TicTacToe) THEN
  Ada.Text_IO.Put(Item => "Game is a draw!");
  Ada.Text_IO.New_Line;
END IF;
```

displays an appropriate message when there are no moves.   ■

Program 13.2 Function IsFilled

```
FUNCTION IsFilled (TicTacToe : BoardArray) RETURN Boolean IS
-- Pre : Elements of array TicTacToe are assigned values.
--       An empty cell contains the value Empty
-- Post: Returns True if array is filled; otherwise,
--       returns False.
```

```
BEGIN  -- IsFilled

  -- Set Board_Filled to False and return if any cell is empty.
  FOR Row IN MoveRange LOOP
    FOR Column IN MoveRange LOOP
      IF TicTacToe(Row,Column) = Empty THEN
        RETURN False;        -- board is not filled
      END IF;
    END LOOP;
  END LOOP;

  RETURN True;                    -- board is filled

END IsFilled;
```

■ Example 13.6

Procedure `EnterMove` in Program 13.3 is used to enter a move into the array `TicTac-Toe`. `EnterMove` calls procedure `Robust_Input.Get` (see Program 7.10) twice to enter a pair of values into the move coordinates, `MoveRow` and `MoveColumn`. If the cell selected by these coordinates is empty, its value is reset to the character that is stored in `Player` (x or o). ■

Program 13.3 Procedure EnterMove

```
PROCEDURE EnterMove (Player : GameSymbol;
                     TicTacToe : IN OUT BoardArray) IS
-- Pre : Player is "X" or "O" and array TicTacToe has at least
--       one empty cell.
-- Post: The value of Player is stored in the empty cell of
--       TicTacToe whose coordinates are read in; the rest
--       of array TicTacToe is unchanged.

  MoveRow    : MoveRange;    -- coordinates of selected cell
  MoveColumn : MoveRange;

BEGIN  -- EnterMove

  LOOP
    Ada.Text_IO.Put(Item => "Enter your move row and then the column");
    Ada.Text_IO.New_Line;
    RobustInput.Get (MinVal => 1, MaxVal => 3, Item => MoveRow);
    RobustInput.Get (MinVal => 1, MaxVal => 3, Item => MoveColumn);

    IF TicTacToe(MoveRow, MoveColumn) = Empty THEN
      EXIT;
    ELSE
      Ada.Text_IO.Put(Item => "Cell is occupied - try again");
      Ada.Text_IO.New_Line;
    END IF;
  END LOOP;

  TicTacToe(MoveRow, MoveColumn) := Player;  -- Define cell

END EnterMove;
```

EXERCISES FOR SECTION 13.1

Self-Check

1. Declare a three-dimensional array type in which the first subscript consists of letters from 'A' to 'F', the second subscript consists of integers from 1 to 10, and the third consists of the user defined type Day. Floating-point numbers will be stored in the array. How many elements can be stored in an array with this type?

2. Assuming the declarations below

   ```
   TYPE MatrixType IS ARRAY (1..5, 1..4) OF Float;
   Matrix : MatrixType,
   ```

   answer the following questions:

   a. How many elements are there in array Matrix?

   b. Write a statement to display the element in row 3, column 4.

   c. Assuming row-major storage, what is the offset for this element?

   d. What formula is used to compute the offset for Matrix(i, j)?

   e. Write a loop that computes the sum of elements in row 5.

   f. Write a loop that computes the sum of elements in column 4.

   g. Write a nested loop structure that computes the sum of all array elements.

   h. Write nested loops that display the array after it has been rotated 90 degrees counterclockwise. Your program segment should display column 4 as the first output line, column 3 as the second output line, and so on.

Programming

1. Write a function that determines whether either player has won a game of tic-tac-toe. The function should first check all rows to see whether one player occupies all the cells in that row, then all columns, and then the two diagonals. The function should return a value from the enumeration type (NoWinner, XWins, YWins).

13.2 Problem Solving: Using Multidimensional Arrays

The subscript type for each dimension of the multidimensional array `TicTacToe` is a subrange of type `Integer`. It is not necessary for the subscript types to all have the same base type. The arrays in the next example have a different subscript type for each dimension.

■ Example 13.7

A university offers 50 courses at each of five campuses. The registrar's office can conveniently store the enrollments of these courses in the following array `Enroll`.

```
MaxCourse : CONSTANT Positive := 50;  -- maximum number of courses
SUBTYPE Course IS Positive RANGE 1..50;

TYPE Campus IS (Main, Ambler, Center, Delaware, Montco);
TYPE CourseByCampus IS ARRAY (Course, Campus) OF Natural;

Enroll : CourseByCampus;
```

This array consists of 5 × 50 = 250 elements, as shown in Fig. 13.4. `Enroll(1, Center)` represents the number of students in course 1 at `Center` campus.

If the registrar wanted to break down this enrollment information according to student rank, a three-dimensional array with 1000 elements would be required. The additional declarations for this array follow, and the array is shown in Fig. 13.5.

```
TYPE Rank IS (Freshman, Sophomore, Junior, Senior);
TYPE CourseByCampusByRank IS ARRAY (Course, Campus, Rank) OF Natural;

ClassEnroll : CourseByCampusByRank;
```

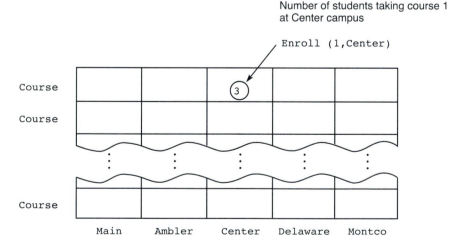

Figure 13.4 Two-Dimensional Array Enroll

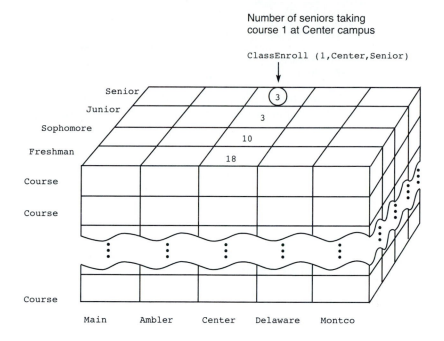

Number of seniors taking
course 1 at Center campus

ClassEnroll (1,Center,Senior)

Figure 13.5 Three-Dimensional Array ClassEnroll

The subscripted variable `ClassEnroll(1, Center, Senior)` represents the number of seniors taking course 1 at `Center` campus. ∎

■ Example 13.8

We can again use aggregates to initialize the entire three-dimensional array to zero, which would need to be done at the beginning of a university registration cycle, for example.

```
ClassEnroll := (OTHERS => (OTHERS => (OTHERS => 0)));
```
∎

■ Example 13.9

Given a variable `Total`, of type `Natural`, the program segment

```
Total := 0;
FOR ClassRank IN Rank LOOP
  Total := Total + ClassEnroll(1, Center, ClassRank);
END LOOP;
```

computes the total number of students of all ranks in course 1 at `Center` campus. The program segment

```
Total := 0;
FOR CurCampus IN Campus LOOP
  FOR ClassRank IN Rank LOOP
    Total := Total + ClassEnroll(1, CurCampus, ClassRank);
  END LOOP;
END LOOP;
```

computes the total number of students in course 1 (regardless of rank or campus). Finally, the total enrollment is computed by the program segment

```
Total := 0;
FOR CurCourse IN Courses LOOP
  FOR CurCampus IN Campus LOOP
    FOR ClassRank IN Rank LOOP
      Total := Total + ClassEnroll(CurCourse,CurCampus, ClassRank);
    END LOOP;
  END LOOP;
END LOOP;
```
■

■ Example 13.10

Suppose we wanted to store and tabulate our student data by gender as well. Given an enumeration type

```
TYPE Gender IS (Female, Male);
```

we could declare a four-dimensional array structure

```
TYPE CourseByCampusByRankByGender IS
  ARRAY (Course, Campus, Rank, Gender) OF Natural;
```

This is difficult to visualize, because our physical world is three-dimensional, but it is quite normal in programming.   ■

EXERCISES FOR SECTION 13.2

Self-Check

1. Declare a three-dimensional array that can be used to keep track of the number of students in the math classes (Math1, Algebra, Geometry, Algebra2, Trigonometry, Calculus) at your old high school according to the grade level and gender of the students. How many elements are in this array?

2. Extend row-major order to three dimensions and show how the array ClassEnroll might be stored in row-major form. What would be the offset for the array element ClassEnroll(1,Center,Senior) and the general formula for ClassEnroll(i,j,k)?

Programming

1. Write program segments that perform the following operations:

   a. Enter the enrollment data.

   b. Find the number of juniors in all classes at all campuses. Students will be counted once for each course in which they are enrolled.

   c. Find the number of sophomores on all campuses who are enrolled in course 2.

   d. Compute and display the number of students at Main campus enrolled in each course and the total number of students at Main campus in all courses. Students will be counted once for each course in which they are enrolled.

   e. Compute and display the number of upper-class students in all courses at each campus, as well as the total number of upper-class students enrolled. (Upper-class students are juniors and seniors.) Again, students will be counted once for each course in which they are enrolled.

2. Starting from Example 13.10, write a program segment that will find the number of female sophomores at all campuses.

13.3 Data Structures: Variant Records

The record types that we have seen so far are such that all records of a given record type have exactly the same form and structure. It is possible and often very useful, however, to define record types that have some fields that are the same for all variables of that type (fixed part) and some fields that may be different (variant part). Such a structure is called a *variant record*.

Consider an application from business information systems. There are three categories of employee in a particular company: One group (professionals) receives a fixed monthly salary, one group (sales) receives a fixed monthly salary plus a commission on their sales, and the third group (clerical) receives an hourly wage and is paid weekly on the basis of the number of hours worked.

How shall we represent a pay record for employees? The record type that we saw in Section 11.5 is oversimplified; it does not take into account the different categories. We require a record type that can represent any of several structures, depending on the category. This is a perfect application for a variant record type.

A pay record for a given pay period has a *fixed part* giving the employee's ID and name, the ending date of the pay period, and a *variant part* giving the pay information according to the pay status. Given these basic type declarations:

```
SUBTYPE NameRange IS Positive RANGE 1..20;
SUBTYPE NameType IS String(NameRange);
SUBTYPE IDType IS Positive RANGE 1111..9999;
SUBTYPE WorkHours IS Float RANGE 0.0..168.0;
```

```
SUBTYPE CommissionPercentage IS Float RANGE 0.00..0.50;
TYPE PayCategories IS (Unknown, Professional, Sales, Clerical);
```

here is a declaration of this variant record type:

```
TYPE Employee (PayStatus : PayCategories := Unknown) IS RECORD
  ID         : IDType;
  NameLength: NameRange;
  Name       : NameType;
  PayPeriod : Dates.Date;

  CASE PayStatus IS
    WHEN Professional =>
      MonthSalary : Currency.Quantity;
    WHEN Sales =>
      WeekSalary   : Currency.Quantity;
      CommRate     : CommissionPercentage;
      SalesAmount : Currency.Quantity;
    WHEN Clerical =>
      HourlyWage   : Currency.Quantity;
      HoursWorked : WorkHours;
    WHEN Unknown =>
      NULL;
  END CASE;

END RECORD;
```

The line at the beginning of the record declaration,

```
TYPE Employee (PayStatus : PayCategories := Unknown) IS RECORD
```

indicates to the compiler that the record is a *discriminated record* that may have a variant part and that the *discriminant* field, which indicates which of several variants is present, is PayStatus. The discriminant is a special field that looks like a parameter of a procedure; indeed, it has many of the aspects of a parameter in that the record is *parametrized,* or varies, according to the value of the discriminant. The reason for having a value Unknown used as a default will be explained shortly.

The fixed part of a record always precedes the variant part. The variant part begins with the phrase

```
CASE PayStatus IS
```

and declares the different forms the variant part can have. The NULL case indicates that there is no variant part for PayStatus equal to Unknown. There are three different pay records, each of a different variant.

For each variable of type PayRecord, the compiler will usually allocate sufficient storage space to accommodate the largest of the record variants shown in Fig. 13.6. However, *only one of the variants is defined at any given time; this particular variant is determined by the discriminant field value.*

Suppose we declare

```
Jane: Employee(PayStatus => Professional);
```

Then Jane's record would look like the fixed part and variant 2 of the record in Fig. 13.6. Because `Jane.PayStatus` is `Professional`, only the variant field `MonthSalary` may be correctly referenced. All other variant fields are undefined. The fragment

```
Ada.Text_IO.Put("Jane's full name is ");
Ada.Text_IO.Put(Jane.Name(1..Jane.NameLength));
Ada.Text_IO.New_Line;
Ada.Text_IO.Put("and her monthly salary is $");
Currency.IO.Put(Jane.MonthSalary);
Ada.Text_IO.New_Line;
```

displays the lines

```
Jane's full name is Jane Smith
and her monthly salary is $5000.00
```

In Ada, the compiler and run-time system are very careful to check the consistency of the discriminant value with the references to fields in the record. If, at execution time, an attempt is made to access a field that is not defined in the current variant (i.e., the variant determined by the current discriminant value), `Constraint_Error` is raised. For this reason, a CASE statement is often used to process the variant part of a record. By using the discriminant field as the CASE selector, we can ensure that only the currently defined variant is manipulated.

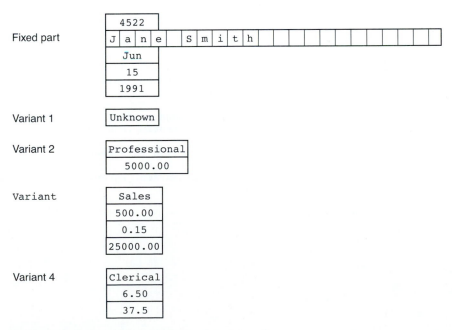

Figure 13.6 Four Variants of a Variant Record

Displaying a Variant Record

The fragment in Fig. 13.7 displays the data stored in the variant part of a record `CurrentEmp`. The value of `CurrentEmp.PayStatus` determines what information will be displayed.

Figure 13.7 Displaying a Variant Record

```
Ada.Text_IO.Put(Item => "Employee ID ");
Ada.Integer_Text_IO.Put(Item => CurrentEmp.ID, Width => 4);
Ada.Text_IO.New_Line;
Ada.Text_IO.Put(Item => "Employee Name ");
Ada.Text_IO.Put(Item => CurrentEmp.Name(1..CurrentEmp.NameLength));
Ada.Text_IO.New_Line;
Ada.Text_IO.Put(Item => "Pay Period Ending ");
Dates.Put(Item => CurrentEmp.PayPeriod, Format => Numeric);
Ada.Text_IO.New_Line;

CASE CurrentEmp.PayStatus IS

  WHEN Unknown =>
    Ada.Text_IO.Put(Item => "Unknown pay status!");
    Ada.Text_IO.New_Line;
  WHEN Professional =>
    Ada.Text_IO.Put("Monthly Salary is $");
    Currency.IO.Put(Item=>CurrentEmp.MonthSalary);
    Ada.Text_IO.New_Line;
  WHEN Sales =>
    Ada.Text_IO.Put("Weekly Salary is $");
    Currency.IO.Put(Item=>CurrentEmp.WeekSalary);
    Ada.Text_IO.New_Line;
    Ada.Text_IO.Put("Commission percent is ");
    Ada.Float_Text_IO.Put
      (Item=>CurrentEmp.CommRate, Fore=>1, Aft=>2, Exp=>0);
    Ada.Text_IO.New_Line;
    Ada.Text_IO.Put("Sales this week $");
    Currency.IO.Put(Item=>CurrentEmp.SalesAmount);
    Ada.Text_IO.New_Line;
  WHEN Clerical =>
    Ada.Text_IO.Put("Hourly wage is $");
    Currency.IO.Put(Item=>CurrentEmp.HourlyWage);
    Ada.Text_IO.New_Line;
    Ada.Text_IO.Put("Hours worked this week ");
    Ada.Float_Text_IO.Put
      (Item=>CurrentEmp.HoursWorked, Fore=>1, Aft=>2, Exp=>0);
    Ada.Text_IO.New_Line;

END CASE;
```

**SYNTAX
DISPLAY**

Record Type with Variant Part

Form:
```
TYPE rec-type (discriminant : disc_type := default) IS RECORD
  ID₁ : type₁;
  ID₂ : type₂;
  .

  .
  fixed part
  .
  IDₙ : typeₙ;
  CASE discriminant IS
    WHEN value₁ =>
      field-list₁
    WHEN value₂ =>
      field-list₂
    .

    .
    variant part

    WHEN valueₙ =>
      field-listₙ;
    WHEN OTHERS =>
      others-field-list
  END CASE;
END RECORD;
```

Example:
```
TYPE Face (Bald : Boolean) IS RECORD
  Eyes : Color;
  Height: Inches;
  CASE Bald IS
    WHEN True =>
      WearsWig : Boolean
    WHEN False =>
      HairColor : Color;
  END CASE;
END RECORD;
```

Interpretation:

The *field-list* for the fixed part is declared first. The variant part starts with the reserved word CASE. The identifer *discriminant* is the name of the discriminant field of the record; the discriminant field name is separated by a colon from its type (*disc-type*), which must be an enumeration type (such as Boolean) or a subrange of an integer type.

The CASE values (*value₁*, *value₂* , ... , *valueₖ*) are lists of values of the discriminant field as defined by *discriminant-type*. *Field-listᵢ* describes the record fields associated with *valueᵢ*. Each element of *field-listᵢ* specifies a field name and its type.

Note 1:

All field names must be unique. The same field name may not appear in the fixed and variant parts or in two field lists of the variant part.

Note 2:

An empty field list (no variant part for that CASE label) is indicated by NULL instead of a field list.

Note 3:

As in all CASE forms, all values of the discriminant must be covered by WHEN clauses. Values not covered otherwise can be covered by a WHEN OTHERS clause.

Note 4:

If := *default* is omitted from the discriminant declaration, all variables of the type must be constrained at the time they are declared; that is, a value for the discriminant must be supplied. If the default is present, unconstrained variables may be declared; that is, variables without an explicit discriminant value.

Constrained and Unconstrained Variant Records

Ada has very strict rules to guarantee two things:

- The discriminant of a variant record is always defined, that is, it always has some value.

- The discriminant value is always consistent with the actual data stored in the record.

The first condition is ensured by requiring that if a default value for the discriminant is *not* present in the record declaration, *all* declarations of variables must supply a value for the discriminant. In the pay status case above, a default of Unknown is supplied; therefore it is possible to declare a record without a discriminant value, as in

```
CurrentEmp : PayRecord;
```

Supplying a discriminant value is not prohibited, however;

```
AnotherEmp : PayRecord(PayStatus=>Professional);
```

is allowed. In the case of the Face record in the preceding syntax display, it would be a compilation error to declare

```
JohnsFace : Face;
```

and in this case a discriminant value is *required:*

```
JohnsFace : Face(Bald=>False);
```

An *unconstrained* record variable is one that has a default discriminant value and none is supplied in the variable declaration. It is permissible to change the discriminant value of an unconstrained record at execution time, under rules to be specified in the next section. This means that the variable CurrentEmp can hold a professional employee at one moment, a sales employee at another. This is a common use of variant records in data processing.

A *constrained* record variable is one whose discriminant value is supplied when the variable is declared. Both `AnotherEmp` and the second `JohnsFace` are constrained. It is *not* permitted to change the discriminant value of a constrained record at execution time; this means that we are "stuck" with the discriminant value. `AnotherEmp` is constrained because we chose to make it so even though the discriminant has a default; `JohnsFace` is constrained because we have no choice, because no default is supplied for `Bald`. `JohnsFace` cannot take into account his losing his hair at a later date.

Storing Values into Variant Records

Ada's rules for variant records might seem cumbersome, but the rules are designed to guarantee that the contents of a variant record are always consistent. Here are the basic rules for storing values into a variant record variable:

- Any field of the variable may be selected and *read* individually, by a field selector, at any time.

- Any field of the variable may be selected and *changed* individually (say, by an assignment statement) *except* a discriminant field; if the change is not consistent with the current discriminant value, `Constraint_Error` is raised.

- The discriminant field of a *constrained* record cannot be changed under any circumstances.

- The discriminant field of an *unconstrained* record can be changed, but only if the *entire* record is changed at the same time. There are two ways to do this: Use a record aggregate or copy another record.

A common application of variant records is to read the value of a discriminant from the terminal or a file, then create a record variable with that variant. By the rules above, the value cannot be stored directly into the discriminant. It, and the other fields of the record, must be held in temporary variables and stored *as a unit* into the variant record using an aggregate.

As we have seen, there is often a distinct advantage in supplying a default value for the discriminant. If we do not, all variables of the type must be constrained when they are declared, and much of the flexibility of variant records—especially their ability to change structure at execution time—is lost.

PROGRAM STYLE

> ### Declaring Variant Records
>
> We recommend that variant record type declarations usually have a default value supplied for the discriminant. Otherwise, all variables of that type will have to be constrained when they are declared, and much of the flexibility of variant records—especially their ability to change structure at execution time—will be lost.

Operations on Variant Records

As always in Ada, assignment and equality testing are defined for variant records. However, certain rules apply:

- A variant record value can always be assigned to an *unconstrained* variable of the same record type. This is possible because it is permissible to change the discriminant of an unconstrained variable.

- A variant record value can be assigned to a *constrained* variable of the same record type *only* if the discriminant values match. This restriction follows from the fact that the discriminant value of a constrained variable cannot be changed, ever.

- Two variant record values can be compared for equality only if the discriminant values agree; otherwise, `Constraint_Error` is raised.

Section 11.5 developed an ADT for handling a data base of employee records. As an exercise, you can modify that ADT, and the associated interactive client program, to handle the more realistic variant employee records described in this section.

EXERCISES FOR SECTION 13.3

Self-Check

1. How many bytes of storage are required for each of the variants of `Employee`? You will probably have to check your Ada compiler documentation to determine the storage required by each of the fields comprising this record.

Programming

1. Write a procedure to display a record of type `Face` as declared in the previous syntax display.

13.4 System Structures: Geometric Figures

In this section we introduce a package to represent, read, and display various geometric figures, including their areas and perimeters.

We need to provide first a representation scheme for geometric figures, with a useful set of operations, and second, a means for interactive users to read and display these figures. As in other ADTs we have developed, it is useful to separate these two concerns.

We first develop an abstract data type that allows a client program to construct a geometric figure. The characteristics for a circle are different from those for a rectangle (a square is a rectangle whose width and height are equal), so we use a record with a variant part. In this case, the fixed part of the record will contain its area and perimeter, which are computed automatically as the figure is constructed. Here is the variant type Figure:

```
SUBTYPE NonNegFloat IS Float RANGE 0.0 .. Float'Last;
TYPE FigKind IS (Rectangle, Square, Circle);

TYPE Figure (FigShape : FigKind := Rectangle) IS RECORD
  Area : NonNegFloat := 0.0;
  Perimeter : NonNegFloat := 0.0;
  CASE FigShape IS
    WHEN Rect | Square =>
      Width : NonNegFloat := 0.0;
      Height : NonNegFloat := 0.0;
    WHEN Circle =>
      Radius : NonNegFloat := 0.0;
  END CASE;
END RECORD;
```

Implementing the Specification of Geometry

The package specification appears as Program 13.4.

Program 13.4 Specification for Geometry Package

```
PACKAGE Geometry IS
-------------------------------------------------------------------
--| Defines an abstract data type for a geometric figure.
--| Operations include constructors for rectangles, circles,
--| and squares, and selectors for width, height, side,
--| area and perimeter.
--| Author: Michael B. Feldman, The George Washington University
--| Last Modified: September 1998
-------------------------------------------------------------------

  -- Data Types

  SUBTYPE NonNegFloat IS Float RANGE 0.0 .. Float'Last;
  TYPE FigKind IS (Rectangle, Square, Circle);

  TYPE Figure (FigShape : FigKind := Rectangle) IS PRIVATE;

  -- Exported Exception

  ShapeError: EXCEPTION;

  -- Constructor Operations

  FUNCTION MakeRectangle (Width, Height : NonNegFloat) RETURN Figure;
  -- Pre : Width and Height are defined
  -- Post: returns a rectangle

  FUNCTION MakeCircle (Radius : NonNegFloat) RETURN Figure;
```

```
    -- Pre : Radius is defined
    -- Post: returns a circle

    FUNCTION MakeSquare (Side : NonNegFloat) RETURN Figure;
    -- Pre : Side is defined
    -- Post: returns a square

    -- selectors
    FUNCTION Shape     (OneFig : Figure) RETURN FigKind;
    FUNCTION Height    (OneFig : Figure) RETURN NonNegFloat;
    FUNCTION Width     (OneFig : Figure) RETURN NonNegFloat;
    FUNCTION Radius    (OneFig : Figure) RETURN NonNegFloat;
    FUNCTION Side      (OneFig : Figure) RETURN NonNegFloat;
    FUNCTION Perimeter (OneFig : Figure) RETURN NonNegFloat;
    FUNCTION Area      (OneFig : Figure) RETURN NonNegFloat;
    -- Pre   : OneFig is defined.
    -- Post  : Returns the appropriate characteristic
    -- Raises: ShapeError if the requested characteristic is
    --           undefined for the shape of OneFig

PRIVATE

    TYPE Figure (FigShape : FigKind := Rectangle) IS RECORD
      Area : NonNegFloat := 0.0;
      Perimeter : NonNegFloat := 0.0;
      CASE FigShape IS
        WHEN Rectangle | Square =>
          Width : NonNegFloat := 0.0;
          Height : NonNegFloat := 0.0;
        WHEN Circle =>
          Radius : NonNegFloat := 0.0;
      END CASE;
    END RECORD;

END Geometry;
```

We have defined the data type `Figure` as a PRIVATE type. Why? If the client program had access to the details of the record representing the figure, it could, for example, change the `Perimeter` field by simply plugging in a new number. Because the figure would no longer make geometric sense, this action would violate the abstraction. Note the syntax for declaring a PRIVATE type with a variant: The discriminant appears first in the partial declaration and later in the complete declaration in the PRIVATE part of the specification.

The following design decisions make the data type safe from accidental misuse:

1. The data type is declared PRIVATE to keep client programs from prying into, and changing, fields of the record, such as the area and the perimeter, or changing the length of the side without changing the area and perimeter fields accordingly.

2. All fields of the type are initialized to 0.0 by default so that every variable of the type is automatically well defined (a figure with sides of 0.0 also has area and perimeter of 0.0).

3. The area and perimeter are calculated automatically when the figure is constructed because these are uniquely determined by the other characteristics.

The operations in the package are three constructors, `MakeRecangle`, `MakeCircle`, and `MakeSquare`, which construct the appropriate variant given the relevant characteristics, and a set of selectors `Shape`, `Width`, `Height`, `Side`, `Radius`, `Area`, and `Perimeter`, which return these characteristics of the figure. Note that even though a square and a rectangle use the same variant, the constructors and selectors are different for them. Also, we export an exception `ShapeError` to prevent a client from applying an inappropriate selector (e.g., finding the radius of a square).

A client program can declare variables of type `Figure` in either constrained or unconstrained form. The variable

```
SomeShape : Figure;
```

can hold, at different moments, a circle, a square, or a rectangle; it is unconstrained. However,

```
BigSquare : Figure (FigShape => Square);
```

can hold only a square, because it is constrained; that is, we plugged a discriminant value into the declaration of the variable and are now "locked in" to that value.

Implementing the Package Body

Program 13.5 shows the package body for `Geometry`.

Program 13.5 Body of Geometry Package

```
WITH Ada.Numerics; USE Ada.Numerics;
PACKAGE BODY Geometry IS
-----------------------------------------------------------------------
--| Body of abstract data type package for geometric figures.
--| Author: Michael B. Feldman, The George Washington University
--| Last Modified: September 1998
-----------------------------------------------------------------------

   -- Internal functions, not exported to client. ComputePerimeter
   -- and ComputeArea are used to ensure that all figures are
   -- constructed with these attributes automatically inserted.
   -- The exported selectors Perimeter and Area assume that these
   -- fields have been set by the internal functions.

   FUNCTION ComputePerimeter (OneFig : Figure) RETURN NonNegFloat IS
   -- Pre : The discriminant and characteristics of OneFig are defined.
   -- Post: Returns Perimeter of OneFig.

   BEGIN -- ComputePerimeter

     CASE OneFig.FigShape IS
       WHEN Rectangle =>
         RETURN 2.0 * (OneFig.Width + OneFig.Height);
       WHEN Square =>
         RETURN 4.0 * OneFig.Width;
       WHEN Circle =>
         RETURN 2.0 * Pi * OneFig.Radius;
     END CASE;
```

```
END ComputePerimeter;

FUNCTION ComputeArea (OneFig : Figure) RETURN NonNegFloat IS
-- Pre : The discriminant and characteristics of OneFig are defined.
-- Post: Returns Area of OneFig.

BEGIN -- ComputeArea

  CASE OneFig.FigShape IS
    WHEN Rectangle =>
      RETURN OneFig.Width * OneFig.Height;
    WHEN Square =>
      RETURN OneFig.Width ** 2;
    WHEN Circle =>
      RETURN Pi * OneFig.Radius ** 2 ;
  END CASE;

END ComputeArea;

-- Exported Operations

FUNCTION MakeRectangle (Width, Height : NonNegFloat) RETURN Figure IS

  Result : Figure(FigShape => Rectangle);

BEGIN -- MakeRectangle

  Result.Height    := Height;
  Result.Width     := Width;
  Result.Area      := ComputeArea(Result);
  Result.Perimeter := ComputePerimeter(Result);

  RETURN Result;

END MakeRectangle;

FUNCTION MakeCircle (Radius : NonNegFloat) RETURN Figure IS

  Result: Figure (FigShape => Circle);

BEGIN -- MakeCircle

  Result.Radius    := Radius;
  Result.Area      := ComputeArea(Result);
  Result.Perimeter := ComputePerimeter(Result);

  RETURN Result;

END MakeCircle;

FUNCTION MakeSquare (Side : NonNegFloat) RETURN Figure IS

  Result: Figure (FigShape => Square);

BEGIN -- MakeSquare

  Result.Height    := Side;
  Result.Width     := Side;
  Result.Area      := ComputeArea(Result);
```

```
      Result.Perimeter := ComputePerimeter(Result);

   RETURN Result;

END MakeSquare;

FUNCTION Shape (OneFig : Figure) RETURN FigKind IS

BEGIN -- Perimeter
   RETURN OneFig.FigShape;
END Shape;

FUNCTION Perimeter (OneFig : Figure) RETURN NonNegFloat IS

BEGIN -- Perimeter
   RETURN OneFig.Perimeter;
END Perimeter;

FUNCTION Area (OneFig : Figure) RETURN NonNegFloat IS

BEGIN -- Area
   RETURN OneFig.Area;
END Area;

FUNCTION Height (OneFig : Figure) RETURN NonNegFloat IS

BEGIN -- Height
   CASE OneFig.FigShape IS
     WHEN Rectangle | Square =>
       RETURN OneFig.Height;
     WHEN OTHERS =>
       RAISE ShapeError;
   END CASE;
END Height;

FUNCTION Width (OneFig : Figure) RETURN NonNegFloat IS

BEGIN -- Width
   CASE OneFig.FigShape IS
     WHEN Rectangle | Square =>
       RETURN OneFig.Width;
     WHEN OTHERS =>
       RAISE ShapeError;
   END CASE;
END Width;

FUNCTION Side (OneFig : Figure) RETURN NonNegFloat IS

BEGIN -- Side
   CASE OneFig.FigShape IS
     WHEN  Square =>
       RETURN OneFig.Height;
     WHEN OTHERS =>
       RAISE ShapeError;
   END CASE;
END Side;

FUNCTION Radius (OneFig : Figure) RETURN NonNegFloat IS

BEGIN -- Radius
```

```
        CASE OneFig.FigShape IS
          WHEN Circle =>
            RETURN OneFig.Radius;
          WHEN OTHERS =>
            RAISE ShapeError;
        END CASE;
      END Radius;

    END Geometry;
```

The constructor functions create the appropriate variant of the record from the relevant components, then calculate the area and perimeter. Local functions ComputeArea and ComputePerimeter are used to assist. These are not given in the specification. The user can find out the area and perimeter by calling the appropriate selector, whose code is straightforward. Note that even though a square is also a rectangle, we distinguish between them in many of the operations. Note in many of these operations how a CASE statement is used to control the processing of the variant data.

The Child Package Geometry.IO

As in the currency and employee ADTs in Chapter 11, we choose to separate the input/output operations into a child package. Programs 13.6 and 13.7 give the specification and body for Geometry.IO. Procedure Get reads in the enumeration value denoting the kind of figure, reads the data required for the kind of figure indicated by the discriminant field, and calls the appropriate constructor. This procedure serves as a good example of how to read a variant record from the interactive user. As before, in the Get and Put procedures, a CASE statement controls the processing of the data in the variant part.

Program 13.6 Specification for Geometry.IO Child Package

```
PACKAGE Geometry.IO IS
-------------------------------------------------------------------------
--| Child Package: Input/Output for Geometric Figures
--| Author: Michael B. Feldman, The George Washington University
--| Last Modified: September 1998
-------------------------------------------------------------------------

  PROCEDURE Get (Item : OUT Geometry.Figure);
  -- Pre : None
  -- Post: Item  contains a geometric figure.

  PROCEDURE Put (Item : IN Geometry.Figure);
  -- Pre : Item is defined.
  -- Post: Item is displayed.

END Geometry.IO;
```

Program 13.7 Body of Geometry.IO Child Package

```
WITH Robust_Input;
WITH Ada.Float_Text_IO;
WITH Ada.Text_IO;
PACKAGE BODY Geometry.IO IS
```

```
----------------------------------------------------------------
--| Body of Input/Output Package for Geometric Figures
--| Author: Michael B. Feldman, The George Washington University
--| Last Modified: September 1998
----------------------------------------------------------------

  MaxSize: CONSTANT NonNegFloat := 1_000_000.0;

  PACKAGE FigKind_IO IS NEW Ada.Text_IO.Enumeration_IO (Enum => FigKind);

  -- Local procedure ReadShape and RobustGet are used only within
  -- the package, therefore not exported.

  PROCEDURE ReadShape (Item : OUT FigKind) IS
  -- Pre:  none
  -- Post: Item contains a figure kind. ReadShape reads robustly.

    TempItem: FigKind;

  BEGIN -- ReadShape

    LOOP
      BEGIN
        Ada.Text_IO.Put
          (Item => "Enter a shape: rectangle, circle, square > ");
        FigKind_IO.Get(Item => TempItem);
        Item := TempItem;
        EXIT;
      EXCEPTION
        WHEN Ada.Text_IO.Data_Error =>
          Ada.Text_IO.Put ("Value not a valid shape. Please try again.");
          Ada.Text_IO.New_Line;
          Ada.Text_IO.Skip_Line;
      END;
    END LOOP;

  END ReadShape;

  PROCEDURE Get (Item : OUT Figure) IS

    Shape  : FigKind;
    Height : NonNegFloat;
    Width  : NonNegFloat;
    Side   : NonNegFloat;
    Radius : NonNegFloat;

  BEGIN  -- Get

    -- Read the shape character and define the discriminant
    ReadShape(Shape);

    -- Select the proper variant and read pertinent data
    CASE Shape IS
      WHEN Rectangle =>
        Ada.Text_IO.Put(Item => "Enter width.");
        Ada.Text_IO.New_Line;
        Robust_Input.Get
          (Item => Width, MinVal => 0.0, MaxVal => MaxSize);
        Ada.Text_IO.Put(Item => "Enter height.");
        Ada.Text_IO.New_Line;
```

```
        Robust_Input.Get
          (Item => Height, MinVal => 0.0, MaxVal => MaxSize);
        Item := MakeRectangle(Width, Height);

    WHEN Square    =>
        Ada.Text_IO.Put(Item => "Enter length of side.");
        Ada.Text_IO.New_Line;
        Robust_Input.Get
          (Item => Side, MinVal => 0.0, MaxVal => MaxSize);
        Item := MakeSquare(Side);

    WHEN Circle    =>
        Ada.Text_IO.Put(Item => "Enter circle radius.");
        Ada.Text_IO.New_Line;
        Robust_Input.Get
          (Item => Radius, MinVal => 0.0, MaxVal => MaxSize);
        Item := MakeCircle(Radius);

  END CASE;

END Get;

PROCEDURE Put (Item: IN Figure) IS

BEGIN -- DisplayFigure

  -- Display shape and characteristics
  Ada.Text_IO.Put(Item => "Figure shape: ");
  FigKind_IO.Put(Item => Shape(Item), Width => 1);
  Ada.Text_IO.New_Line;

  CASE Item.FigShape IS
    WHEN Rectangle =>
      Ada.Text_IO.Put(Item => "height = ");
      Ada.Float_Text_IO.Put
        (Item => Height(Item), Fore=>1, Aft=>2, Exp=>0);
      Ada.Text_IO.Put(Item => "; width = ");
      Ada.Float_Text_IO.Put
        (Item => Width(Item), Fore=>1, Aft=>2, Exp=>0);

    WHEN Square =>
      Ada.Text_IO.Put(Item => "side = ");
      Ada.Float_Text_IO.Put
        (Item => Height(Item), Fore=>1, Aft=>2, Exp=>0);

    WHEN Circle =>
      Ada.Text_IO.Put(Item => "radius = ");
      Ada.Float_Text_IO.Put
        (Item => Radius(Item), Fore=>1, Aft=>2, Exp=>0);

  END CASE;

  Ada.Text_IO.Put(Item => "; perimeter = ");
  Ada.Float_Text_IO.Put
    (Item => Perimeter(Item), Fore=>1, Aft=>2, Exp=>0);
  Ada.Text_IO.Put(Item => "; area = ");
  Ada.Float_Text_IO.Put
    (Item => Area(Item), Fore=>1, Aft=>2, Exp=>0);
  Ada.Text_IO.New_Line;
```

```
      END Put;

END Geometry.IO;
```

Program 13.8 shows a brief and straightforward test program for the package. Note how simple this program is, because we have encapsulated all the details in the parent and child packages.

Program 13.8 Demonstration of Geometry Package

```
WITH Ada.Text_IO;
WITH Ada.Integer_Text_IO;
WITH Geometry;
WITH Geometry.IO;
PROCEDURE Test_Geometry IS
-----------------------------------------------------------------------
--| Program to test package Geometry
--| Author: Michael B. Feldman, The George Washington University
--| Last Modified: September 1998
-----------------------------------------------------------------------

  MyFig : Geometry.Figure;                    -- a figure

BEGIN -- Test_Geometry

  FOR TestTrial IN 1..3 LOOP

    Ada.Text_IO.New_Line;
    Ada.Text_IO.Put(Item => "     Trial #");
    Ada.Integer_Text_IO.Put(Item => TestTrial, Width => 1);
    Ada.Text_IO.New_Line;
    Geometry.IO.Get (Item => MyFig);
    Geometry.IO.Put (Item => MyFig);

  END LOOP;

END Test_Geometry;
```

Sample Run

```
     Trial #1
Enter a shape: rectangle, circle, square > triangle
Value not a valid shape. Please try again.
Enter a shape: rectangle, circle, square > rect
Value not a valid shape. Please try again.
Enter a shape: rectangle, circle, square > rectangle
Enter width.
Enter a floating-point value between 0.00 and 1000000.00 > 3
Enter height.
Enter a floating-point value between 0.00 and 1000000.00 > 5
Figure shape: RECTANGLE
height = 5.00; width = 3.00; perimeter = 16.00; area = 15.00

     Trial #2
Enter a shape: rectangle, circle, square > circle
Enter circle radius.
Enter a floating-point value between 0.00 and 1000000.00 > 4
Figure shape: CIRCLE
```

```
radius = 4.00; perimeter = 25.13; area = 50.27

    Trial #3
Enter a shape: rectangle, circle, square > square
Enter length of side.
Enter a floating-point value between 0.00 and 1000000.00 > 5
Figure shape: SQUARE
side = 5.00; perimeter = 20.00; area = 25.00
```

EXERCISES FOR SECTION 13.4

Programming

1. Add the variant

    ```
    RightTriangle : (Base, Height : Float);
    ```

    to `Figure` and modify the operators to include triangles. Use the formulas

    $$area = 1/2\ base \times height$$

    $$hypotenuse = \sqrt{base^2 + height^2}$$

    where *base* and *height* are the two sides that form the right angle.

13.5 Continuing Saga: Keeping Track of Multiple Spiders

Let's return once again to the spider system, in particular to the multiple-spider package developed in Section 11.6 (Program 11.19). This package is missing an important feature. Each location in the room can hold only one spider. We would like to add a new exception to the `Spiders` package specification,

```
Hit_a_Spider: EXCEPTION;
```

which, by analogy with the exception `Hit_the_Wall`, can be raised by `Jump` and handled by a user's spider program if a second spider tries to move into an occupied location. Although each individual spider's record contains its current location, nothing in the package keeps track of the overall state of the room, so there is no way to know whether any given location is occupied.

Sections 13.1 and 13.2 give us the data and control structures necessary to detect a collision. Let us define, in the *body* of `Spiders`, a type `RoomType` as

```
TYPE RoomType IS ARRAY (RoomHeight, RoomWidth) OF Boolean;
```

where `False` means an empty location and `True` means an occupied one. Now we can declare, in the body of the package, a room variable

```
Occupied: RoomType;
```

Which spider operations must be modified accordingly?

First, we must initialize the room, with all locations unoccupied. We can do this in the `DrawRoom` procedure with the statement

```
Occupied := (OTHERS => (OTHERS => False));
```

Next, when a spider enters the room at a given location, we must mark its square as occupied. We can do this in the `Start` procedure, to which we already pass parameters `Row` and `Col`, with the statement

```
Occupied (Row, Col) := True;
```

Finally, when a spider attempts to move (using the `Jump` procedure), we need to detect a collision. We write the new algorithm for `Jump`, leaving the details of the coding as an exercise. Note that a spider can jump *over,* but not *into,* an occupied location.

Algorithm for Spiders.Jump

1. IF the spider is trying to jump into or through the wall THEN

    2. RAISE Hit_the_Wall

    ELSIF the spider is trying to jump into an occupied location THEN

    3. RAISE Hit_a_Spider

    ELSE
    4. Mark the spider's current location as unoccupied

    5. Mark the spider's new location as occupied

    6. Draw the spider in its new location

    7. Change the spider's own location coordinates

    END IF;

13.6 Tricks of the Trade: Common Programming Errors

When you use multidimensional arrays, make sure the subscript for each dimension is consistent with its declared type. Of course, if any subscript value is out of range, `Constraint_Error` will be raised.

If you use nested FOR loops to process the array elements, make sure that loop control variables used as array subscripts are in the correct order. The order of the loop control variables determines the sequence in which the array elements will be processed.

Understanding variant records is not always easy. In defining variant record structures, remember that the only way to allow for changing the variant stored in a variant record variable is to supply a default value for the discriminant. This action makes the variable unconstrained.

In using variant record variables, keep in mind that the value of the discriminant field determines the form of the variant part that is currently defined; attempting to manipulate any other variant will cause either a compilation error or the raising of `Constraint_Error`. It is the programmer's responsibility to ensure that the correct variant is being processed; consequently, a variant record should always be manipulated in a CASE statement with the discriminant field used as the CASE selector to ensure that the proper variant part is being manipulated.

CHAPTER REVIEW

Multidimensional arrays were used to represent tables of information and game boards. Nested loops are needed to manipulate the elements of a mutidimensional array in a systematic way. The correspondence between the loop-control variables and the array subscripts determines the order in which the array elements are processed.

Also in this chapter, we introduced variant records. A variant record is one that can have one of several structures, depending on the value of a special field called the discriminant. We used variant records to represent employee records and geometric figures.

New Ada Constructs in Chapter 13

The new Ada constructs introduced in this chapter are described in Table 13.1.

Table 13.1 Summary of New Ada Constructs

Construct	*Effect*
Declaring Multidimensional Arrays	
`SUBTYPE Weeks IS Positive RANGE 1..52;`	
`TYPE Days IS` `  (Mon,Tue,Wed,Thu,Fri,Sat,Sun);`	
`TYPE YearMatrix IS` `  ARRAY(Weeks,Days) OF Float;`	`YearMatrix` describes a two-dimensional array with 52 rows and 7 columns
`Sales : YearMatrix;`	`Sales` is an array of this type and can store 364 float numbers.
Multidimensional Array References	
`Sales := (OTHERS=>(OTHERS=>0.0));`	Initializes all elements of `Sales` to zero.
`Ada.Float_Text_IO.Put` `  (Item=>Sales(3, Mon));`	Displays the element of `Sales` for `Monday` of week 3.
`Ada.Float_Text_IO.Get` `  (Item=>Sales(1, Sun));`	Reads the value for the first `Sunday` into `Sales`.

Construct	Effect
| ```
TotalSales := 0.0;
FOR Week IN Weeks LOOP
  FOR Today IN Days LOOP
    TotalSales := TotalSales
      + Sales(Week,Today);
  END LOOP;
END LOOP;
``` | Finds the total sales for the entire year. |

Variant Record Declaration

Construct	Effect
| ```
TYPE KidKind IS (Girl, Boy);
``` | A record type with a variant part is declared. The discriminant is an enumeration value. |
| ```
TYPE Child(Gender: KidKind:=Girl) IS RECORD
  First: Character;
  Last: Character;
  Age: Natural;

  CASE Gender IS
    WHEN Girl =>
      Sugar: Float;
      Spice: Float;
    WHEN Boy =>
      Snakes: Integer;
      Snails: Integer;
      Tails: Integer;
  END CASE;
END RECORD;
``` | Each record variable can store two characters and an integer.

One variant part can store two float values, and the other can store three integer values. |
| ```
Kid : Child;
``` | `Kid` is a `Child` record. |

Referencing a Record Variant

Construct	Effect
| ```
CASE Kid.Gender IS
  WHEN Girl =>
    Ada.Text_IO.Put
      (Item => "Lbs. of sugar>");
    Ada.Float_Text_IO.Get
      (Item=>Kid.Sugar);
  WHEN Boy =>
    Ada.Integer_Text_IO.Put
      (Item=>"No. of snakes>");
    Ada.Integer_Text_IO.Get
      (Item=>Kid.Snakes);
END CASE;
``` | Uses a `CASE` statement to read data into the variant part of the record `Kid`. If discriminant is `Girl`, reads a value into the field `Kid.Sugar`; if the discriminant is `Boy`, reads a value into the field `Kid.Snakes`. |

Quick-Check Exercises

1. How many subscripts can an array have in Ada?

2. What is the difference between row-major and column-major order? Which does Ada use?

3. What does row-major order mean when an array has more than two subscripts?
```

4. What control structure is used to process all the elements in a multidimensional array?

5. Write a program segment to display the sum of the values (type `Float`) in each column of a two-dimensional array, `Table`, with data type `ARRAY(1..5, 1..3) OF Float`. How many column sums will be displayed? How many elements are included in each sum?

6. Write the type declaration for an array that stores the batting averages by position (`Catcher`, `Pitcher`, `FirstBase`, and so on) for each of 12 baseball teams in each of two leagues (`American` and `National`).

7. When should you use a variant record?

8. Explain the use of the discriminant field. Can a variant record have more than one discriminant field?

9. Explain the difference between a constrained variant record and an unconstrained one.

Answers to Quick-Check Exercises

1. There is no specific limit; however, the size of the array is limited by the memory space available, and multidimensional arrays require memory equal to the product of the dimensions, which can be quite large.

2. In row-major order, the first row of the array is placed at the beginning of the memory area allocated to the array. It is followed by the second row, and so on. In column-major order, the first column is placed at the beginning of the array memory area. The Ada standard does not specify an ordering, but many compilers use row-major order.

3. If an array `Table` has `N` subscripts, the array elements are placed in memory in the order `Table(1,1,...,1,1)`, `Table(1,1,...,1,2)`, `Table(1,1, ...,1,3)`, and so on. Then the next-to-last subscript is changed, and the elements `Table(1,1,...,2,1)`, `Table(1,1,...,2,2)`, `Table(1,1... ,2,3)` ... are placed. The first subscript will be the last one that changes.

4. Nested `FOR` loops.

5.

```
ColumnSum := 0.0;
FOR Column IN 1..3 LOOP
  ColumnSum := 0.0;
  FOR Row IN 1..5 LOOP
    ColumnSum := ColumnSum + Table(Row,Col);
  END LOOP;
  Ada.Text_IO.Put(Item=>"Sum for column ");
  Ada.Integer_Text_IO.Put(Item=>Column, Width=>1);
  Ada.Text_IO.Put(Item=>"is ");
  Ada.Integer_Text_IO.Put(Item=>ColumnSum);
END LOOP;
```

Three column sums, five elements added per column.

6.

```
TYPE Position IS
   (Pitcher, Catcher, FirstBase, SecondBase, ThirdBase,
    ShortStop, LeftField, CenterField, RightField);
TYPE League IS (American, National);
SUBTYPE Teams IS Positive RANGE 1..15;
TYPE BAArray IS ARRAY (League, Teams, Position) OF Float;
```

7. When an object has some fields that are always the same and a small number of fields that may be different.

8. The discriminant field is a special field of a variant record, used to distinguish between the variants. A record may have more than one discriminant.

9. A constrained variant record is one in which the discriminant is given a value when the variable is declared, which "locks in" the variant. An unconstrained record is one in which a default value was supplied for the discriminant, which allows the variant to change over the life of the variable.

Review Questions for Chapter 13

1. Define row-major order and column-major order. For an array type whose three dimensions are `1..4`, `2..3`, and `5..7`, draw storage layouts for both row-major and column-major order.

2. Write the variant declaration for `Supplies`, which consists of either `Paper`, `Ribbon`, or `Labels`. For `Paper` the information needed is the number of sheets per box and the size of the paper. For `Ribbon` the size, color, and kind (`Carbon` or `Cloth`) are needed. For `Labels` the size and number per box are needed. For each supply, the cost, number on hand, and reorder point must also be stored. Use whatever data types are appropriate for each field.

3. Write the declaration for `Vehicle`. If the vehicle is a `Truck`, we need to know its `BedSize` and `CabSize`. If the vehicle is a `Wagon`, we need to know whether or not it has a third row of seats (`Boolean`). If the vehicle is a `Sedan`, the information needed is `TwoDoor` or `FourDoor`. For all vehicles we need to know whether the transmission is `Manual` or `Automatic`; whether it has `AirConditioning`, `PowerSteering`, or `PowerBrakes` (all `Boolean`); and the gas mileage. Use whatever data types are appropriate for each field.

Programming Projects

1. Starting with the tic-tac-toe procedures from Section 13.1, develop an interactive program that allows two people to play tic-tac-toe against each other.

2. Starting with the class-enrollment program segments in Section 13.2, develop an interactive program for the registrar to use.

3. Write a set of procedures to manipulate a pair of matrices. You should provide procedures for addition, subtraction, and multiplication. Each procedure should validate its input parameters (i.e., check all matrix dimensions) before performing the required data manipulation.

4. The results from the mayor's election have been reported by each voting district as follows:

Voting District	Candidate A	Candidate B	Candidate C	Candidate D
1	192	48	206	37
2	147	90	312	21
3	186	12	121	38
4	114	21	408	39
5	267	13	382	29

Write a program to do the following:

a. Display the table with appropriate headings for the rows and columns.

b. Compute and display the total number of votes received by each candidate and the percent of the total votes cast.

c. If any one candidate received over 50% of the votes, the program should print a message declaring that candidate the winner.

d. If no candidate received over 50% of the votes, the program should print a message declaring a runoff between the two candidates receiving the highest number of votes; the two candidates should be identified by their letter names.

e. Run the program once with the above data and once with candidate C receiving only 108 votes in precinct 4.

5. Write a program that reads the five cards representing a poker hand into a two-dimensional array (first dimension, suit; second dimension, rank). Evaluate the poker hand by using procedures to determine whether the hand is a flush (all one suit), a straight (five consecutive cards), a straight flush (five consecutive cards of one suit), four of a kind, a full house (three of one kind, two of another), three of a kind, two pair, or one pair.

6. Do Problem 5, but represent a card as a record with two fields representing the suit and the rank, and a poker hand as an array of these records.

7. Modify the package `spiders` as suggested in Section 13.5, to detect spider collisions in the room.

8. Modify the employees and data base packages (Programs 11.11 through 11.17) to accommodate the variant record for `Employee`.

CHAPTER 14

Recursion

This book has shown many examples of procedures and functions, as well as programs that call them. You know that a function can call another function; that is, a statement in the body of a function F contains a call of another function G. What would happen if a statement in F contained a call of F? This situation—a function or procedure calling itself—not only is permitted, but in fact is very interesting and useful. The concept of a subprogram—a function or a procedure—calling itself is a mathematical concept called *recursion,* and a subprogram that contains a call to itself is called a *recursive* subprogram.

Recursion can be an alternative to iteration (looping), although a recursive solution to a given problem uses somewhat more computer time and space than an iterative solution to the same problem; this is due to the overhead for the extra procedure calls. However, in many instances the use of recursion enables us to specify a natural, simple solution to a problem that would otherwise be difficult to solve. For this reason, recursion is an important and powerful tool in problem solving and programming.

14.1 Problem Solving: The Nature of Recursion

Problems that lend themselves to a recursive solution have the following characteristics:

- One or more simple cases of the problem (called *stopping cases*) have a simple, nonrecursive solution.

- For the other cases, there is a process (using recursion) for substituting one or more reduced cases of the problem that are closer to a stopping case.

- Eventually, the problem can be reduced to stopping cases only, all of which are relatively easy to solve.

The recursive algorithms that we write will generally consist of an IF statement with the form shown below:

```
IF  the stopping case is reached  THEN
   Solve it
ELSE
   Reduce the problem using recursion
END IF;
```

Figure 14.1 illustrates what we mean by this. Let's assume that for a particular problem of size N, we can split this problem into one involving a problem of size 1, which we can solve (a stopping case), and a problem of size $N - 1$, which we can split further. If we split the problem N times, we will end up with N problems of size 1, all of which we can solve.

■ Example 14.1

Consider how we might solve the problem of multiplying 6 by 3, assuming that we know the addition tables but not the multiplication tables. The problem of multiplying 6 by 3 can be split into the two problems:

Problem 1. Multiply 6 by 2.

Problem 2. Add 6 to the result of problem 1.

Because we know the addition tables, we can solve problem 2 but not problem 1. However, problem 1 is simpler than the original problem. We can split it into the two problems 1.1 and 1.2, leaving us three problems to solve, two of which are additions.

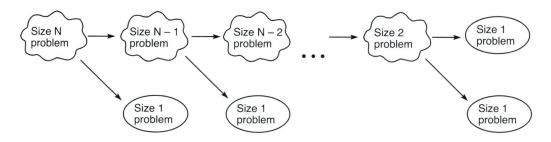

Figure 14.1 Splitting a Problem into Smaller Problems

Problem 1. Multiply 6 by 2.

Problem 1.1 Multiply 6 by 1.

Problem 1.2 Add 6 to the result.

Problem 2. Add 6 to the result of problem 1.

Even though we don't know the multiplication tables, we are familiar with the simple rule that, for any M, $M \times 1$ is M. By solving problem 1.1 (the answer is 6) and problem 1.2, we get the solution to problem 1 (the answer is 12). Solving problem 2 gives us the final answer, 18.

Program 14.1 implements this approach to doing multiplication as the recursive Ada function `Multiply`, which returns the product, $M \times N$, of its two arguments.

Program 14.1 Recursive Multiplication

```
FUNCTION Multiply (M : IN Integer; N : IN Positive)
  RETURN Integer IS
-- Performs multiplication recursively using the + operator
-- Pre : M and N are defined and N > 0
-- Post: returns M * N

  Result: Integer;

BEGIN  -- Multiply

  IF N = 1 THEN
    Result := M;                        -- stopping case
  ELSE
    Result := M + Multiply(M, N-1);  -- recursion
  END  IF;

  RETURN Result;

END Multiply;
```

The stopping case is reached when the condition `N = 1` is `True`. In this case the answer is M ($M \times 1$ is M). If N is greater than 1, the statement

```
Result := M + Multiply(M, N-1) -- recursive step
```

executes, splitting the original problem into the two simpler problems:

Problem 1. Multiply M by $N - 1$.

Problem 2. Add M to the result.

The first of these problems is solved by calling `Multiply` again with `N-1` as its second argument. If the new second argument is greater than 1, there will be additional calls to function `Multiply`. The recursive step in function `Multiply` splits the problem of multiplication by N into an addition problem and a problem of multiplication by $N - 1$.

To demonstrate how this function works, Program 14.2 shows `Multiply` modified to display the values of its parameters each time it is called, and the return value before it returns. The test program prompts the user for two numbers, then calls `Multiply`. ■

Program 14.2 A Test of Recursive Multiplication

```
WITH Ada.Text_IO;
WITH Ada.Integer_Text_IO;
PROCEDURE Test_Multiply IS
----------------------------------------------------------------------
--| Demonstration of recursive Multiply function
--| Author: Michael B. Feldman, The George Washington University
--| Last Modified: September 1998
----------------------------------------------------------------------

  FirstInt  : Integer;   -- inputs
  SecondInt : Positive;
  Answer    : Integer;   -- output

  FUNCTION Multiply (M : IN Integer; N : IN Positive)
    RETURN Integer IS
  -- Performs multiplication recursively using the + operator
  -- Pre : M and N are defined
  -- Post: returns M * N

    Result: Integer;

  BEGIN   -- Multiply

    Ada.Text_IO.Put(Item => "Multiply called with parameters");
    Ada.Integer_Text_IO.Put(Item => M, Width => 2);
    Ada.Integer_Text_IO.Put(Item => N, Width => 3);
    Ada.Text_IO.New_Line;

    IF N = 1 THEN
      Result := M;                       -- stopping case
    ELSE
      Result := M + Multiply(M, N-1);  -- recursion
    END  IF;

    Ada.Text_IO.Put(Item => "Returning from Multiply with result ");
    Ada.Integer_Text_IO.Put(Item => Result, Width => 1);
    Ada.Text_IO.New_Line;

    RETURN Result;

  END Multiply;

BEGIN -- Test_Multiply

  Ada.Text_IO.Put(Item => "Please enter a integer > ");
  Ada.Integer_Text_IO.Get(Item => FirstInt);
  Ada.Text_IO.Put(Item => "Please enter a positive integer > ");
  Ada.Integer_Text_IO.Get(Item => SecondInt);

  Answer := Multiply(M => FirstInt, N => SecondInt);

  Ada.Text_IO.Put(Item => "The product of the two integers is ");
```

```
      Ada.Integer_Text_IO.Put(Item => Answer, Width => 1);
      Ada.Text_IO.New_Line;

END Test_Multiply;
```

Sample Run

```
Please enter a integer > 6
Please enter a positive integer > 3
Multiply called with parameters 6   3
Multiply called with parameters 6   2
Multiply called with parameters 6   1
Returning from Multiply with result 6
Returning from Multiply with result 12
Returning from Multiply with result 18
The product of the two integers is 18
```

EXERCISES FOR SECTION 14.1

Self-Check

1. Show the problems that are generated by the function call `Multiply(5,4)`. Use a diagram similar to Fig. 14.1.

14.2 Tricks of the Trade: Tracing a Recursive Function

Hand-tracing an algorithm's execution provides us with valuable insight into how that algorithm works. We can also trace the execution of a recursive procedure or function. We will illustrate how to do this by studying a recursive function next.

In Section 14.1 we wrote the recursive function `Multiply` (see Program 14.1). We can trace the execution of the function call `Multiply(6,3)` by drawing an *activation frame* corresponding to each call of the function. An activation frame shows the parameter values for each call and summarizes its execution.

The three activation frames generated to solve the problem of multiplying 6 by 3 are shown in Fig. 14.2. Each downward arrow indicates a recursive call of the function; the arrow is drawn starting from the line of the activation frame in which the recursive call is made. The value returned from each call is shown alongside each upward arrow. The upward arrow from each function call points to the operator + because the addition is performed just after the return.

Figure 14.2 shows that there are three calls to function `Multiply`. Parameter M has the value 6 for all three calls; parameter N has the values 3, 2, and finally 1. Because N is 1 in the third call, the value of M (i.e., 6) is returned as the result of the third and last call. After returning to the second activation frame, the value of M is added to this result

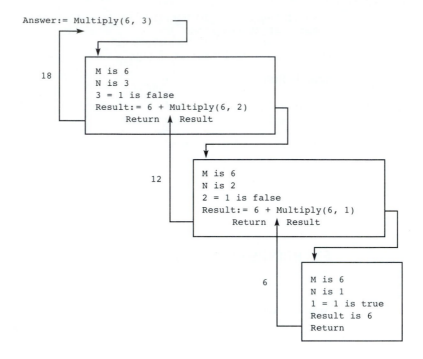

Figure 14.2 Trace of Function Call Answer := Multiply(6,3)

and the sum (i.e., 12) is returned as the result of the second call. After returning to the first activation frame, the value of M is added to this result, and the sum (i.e., 18) is returned as the result of the original call to function Multiply.

Parameter and Local Variable Stacks

To keep track of the values of M, N, and Result at any given point, a special data structure, called a *stack*, is used. Think of the times you have stood in line in a cafeteria. Clean dishes are always placed on top of a stack of dishes. When you need a dish, you remove the one that was most recently placed on the stack; the next to last dish that was placed on the stack moves to the top of the stack.

Similarly, whenever a new function call occurs, the parameter values associated with that call are placed ("pushed") on the top of the parameter stack. Also, a new cell whose value is initially undefined is placed on top of the stack for the local variable Result. Whenever M, N, or Result is referenced, the value at the top of the corresponding stack is always used. When a subprogram return occurs, the value that is currently at the top of each stack is removed ("popped"), and the value just below it moves to the top, just as in the cafeteria stack.

As an example, let's look at the three stacks right after the first call to Multiply (but before Multiply does any work). There is one cell on each stack, as shown below. Result has no value yet, because Multiply computes it.

After first call to Multiply:

```
 M        N       Result
|6|      |3|       |?|
```

Just after the second call to `Multiply`, the number 2 is placed on top of the stack for N, and the top of the stack for `Result` becomes undefined again as shown below. The top cells represent the top of each stack.

After second call to `Multiply`:

```
 M        N       Result
|6|      |2|       |?|
|6|      |3|       |?|
```

`Multiply` is called again, and this time the number 1 is placed on top of the stack.

After third call to `Multiply`:

```
 M        N       Result
|6|      |1|       |?|
|6|      |2|       |?|
|6|      |3|       |?|
```

Because 1 is the stopping case, `Result` can be computed.

After first computation of `Result`:

```
 M        N       Result
|6|      |1|       |6|
|6|      |2|       |?|
|6|      |3|       |?|
```

The function can now return, which causes the values at the top of the stack to be removed. Because `Multiply` was called in a statement that computes `Result`, a new value of `Result` is placed on top of the stack.

After first return and second computation of `Result`:

```
 M        N       Result
|6|      |2|      |12|
|6|      |3|       |?|
```

The function can now return yet again and compute a new value of `Result`.

After second return and third computation of `Result`:

```
 M        N       Result
|6|      |2|      |18|
```

Finally, we return to the main program; the final value of `Result` is left on top of the stack, where it can be picked up and copied into `Answer`.

After third return:

```
 M        N       Result
|?|      |?|      |18|
```

We can write recursive subprograms without being concerned about stacks; the stacks and instructions to manipulate them are automatically placed in your program by the compiler.

For illustrative purposes we have used separate stacks for each parameter in our discussion; however, the compiler actually maintains a single stack. Each time a call to a subprogram occurs (even a nonrecursive one), all its parameters and local variables are pushed onto the stack along with the memory address of the calling statement. The latter gives the computer the return point after execution of the procedure or function. Although multiple copies of a procedure's parameters may be saved on the stack, there is only one copy of the procedure body in memory.

Stacks are used by most programming languages to implement *all* subprogram calls, not just recursive ones. Indeed, recursive calls are really just a special case in which the calling and called subprograms are the same.

EXERCISES FOR SECTION 14.2

Self-Check

1. Trace the execution of `Multiply(5,4)` and show the stacks after each recursive call.

14.3 Problem Solving: Recursive Mathematical Functions

Many mathematical functions are defined recursively. An example is the factorial of a number n ($n!$).

- $0!$ is 1.

- $n!$ is $n \times (n-1)!$, for $n > 0$.

Thus $4!$ is $4 \times 3 \times 2 \times 1$, or 24. It is quite easy to implement this definition as a recursive function in Ada.

■ Example 14.2

Function `Factorial` in Program 14.3 computes the factorial of its argument N.

Program 14.3 Recursive Factorial Function

```
FUNCTION Factorial (N : IN Natural) RETURN Positive IS
-- Computes the factorial of N (N!) recursively
-- Pre : N is defined and N >= 0
-- Post: returns N!

BEGIN  -- Factorial
```

```
IF N = 0 THEN
   RETURN 1;                         -- stopping case
ELSE
   RETURN N * Factorial(N-1);   -- recursion
END  IF;

END Factorial;
```

The recursive step

```
Result := N * Factorial(N-1);
```

implements the second line of the factorial definition above. This means that the result of the current call (argument N) is determined by multiplying the result of the next call (argument N-1) by N.

A trace of

```
Answer := Factorial(N => 3);
```

is shown in Fig. 14.3.

The value that is returned from the original call, Factorial(N => 3), is 6, and this value is assigned to Answer. Be careful when using the factorial function; its value increases very rapidly and could lead to an integer overflow exception (e.g., 10! is 24,320).

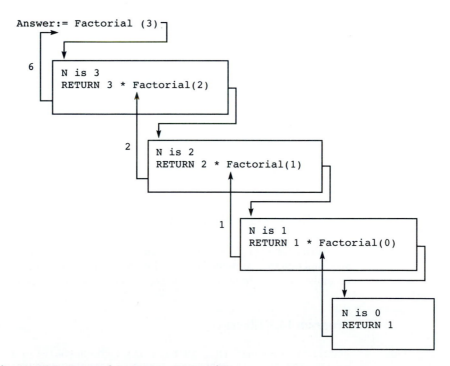

Figure 14.3 Trace of Answer := Factorial(3)

Although the recursive implementation of function `Factorial` follows naturally from its definition, this function can be implemented easily using iteration. The iterative version is shown in Program 14.4; it is in fact the same function that appeared back in Program 5.19, as one of the useful functions there.

Program 14.4 Factorial, Iterative Version

```
FUNCTION Factorial_Iterative (N : IN Natural) RETURN Positive IS
-- Computes the factorial of N (N!) iteratively
-- Pre : N is defined and N >= 0
-- Post: returns N!

  Result : Positive;                       -- holds the product

BEGIN  -- Factorial_Iterative

  Result := 1;
  FOR Count IN 2 .. N LOOP
    Result := Result * Count;
  END LOOP;

  RETURN Result;

END Factorial_Iterative;
```

Note that the iterative version contains a loop as its major control structure, whereas the recursive version contains an `IF` statement. ∎

■ Example 14.3

The Fibonacci numbers are a sequence of numbers that have many varied uses. They were originally intended to model the growth of a rabbit colony. The Fibonacci sequence 1, 1, 2, 3, 5, 8, 13, 21, 34, ... increases rapidly: Each number in the sequence is the sum of the two previous ones. The fifteenth number in the sequence is 610 (that's a lot of rabbits). The Fibonacci sequence is defined below:

- Fib_1 is 1.

- Fib_2 is 1.

- Fib_n is $Fib_{n-2} + Fib_{n-1}$, for $n > 2$.

Verify for yourself that the sequence of numbers shown above is correct. A recursive function that computes the Nth Fibonacci number is shown as Program 14.5. Each recursive step generates two recursive calls to function `Fibonacci`. ∎

Program 14.5 Fibonacci

```
FUNCTION Fibonacci (N : IN Natural) RETURN Positive IS
-- Returns the Nth Fibonacci number, computed recursively
-- Pre : N is defined and N >= 0
```

```
-- Post: returns N!

BEGIN   -- Fibonacci

  IF (N = 1) OR (N = 2) THEN
    RETURN 1;
  ELSE
    RETURN Fibonacci(N-2) + Fibonacci(N-1);
  END IF;

END Fibonacci;
```

■ Example 14.4

The *greatest common divisor* (GCD) of two positve integers is the largest integer that divides them both; Euclid's algorithm for finding the GCD is defined recursively:

- GCD(M, N) is N if $N <= M$ and N divides M.

- GCD(M, N) is GCD(N, M) if $M < N$.

- GCD(M, N) is GCD(N, remainder of M divided by N) otherwise.

   This algorithm states that the GCD is N if N is the smaller number and N divides M. If M is the smaller number, the GCD determination should be performed with the arguments transposed. If N does not divide M, the answer is obtained by finding the GCD of N and the remainder of M divided by N. The function GCD is shown as Program 14.6. ■

Program 14.6 Greatest Common Divisor, Recursive Version

```
FUNCTION GCD (M, N : IN Positive) RETURN Positive IS
-- Pre : M and N are defined.
-- Post: Returns the greatest common divisor of M and N.

  Result: Positive;

BEGIN -- GCD

  IF (N <= M) AND (M REM N = 0) THEN
    Result := N;
  ELSIF M < N THEN
    Result := GCD(N, M);
  ELSE
    Result := GCD(N, M REM N);
  END IF;

  RETURN Result;

END GCD;
```

EXERCISES FOR SECTION 14.3

Self-Check

1. If Ada did not have an exponentiation operation (**), we could write our own. Complete the following recursive function, which calculates the value of a number (Base) raised to a power (Power).

```
FUNCTION PowerOf (Base: Integer; Power: Positive)
   RETURN Integer IS

   Result: Integer;

BEGIN -- PowerOf

   IF Power = _____ THEN
     Result := _____ ;
   ELSE
     Result := _____ * _____ ;
   END IF;

END PowerOf;
```

2. What is the output of the following program? What does function strange compute?

```
WITH Ada.Text_IO;
WITH Ada.Integer_Text_IO;
PROCEDURE TestStrange IS

   FUNCTION Strange (N : Integer) RETURN Integer IS
     Result: Integer;
   BEGIN
     IF N = 1 THEN
       Result := 0;
     ELSE
       Result := 1 + Strange (N / 2);
     END IF;
   END Strange;

BEGIN -- TestStrange

   Ada.Integer_Text_IO.Put(Item => Strange(8);
   Ada.Text_IO.New_Line;

END TestStrange;
```

3. Explain what would happen if the terminating condition for the Fibonacci function were just ($N = 1$).

Programming

1. Write a recursive function, FindSum, that calculates the sum of successive integers starting at 1 and ending at N (i.e., FindSum(N) = $(1 + 2 + ... + (N - 1) + N)$).

2. Write an iterative version of the Fibonacci function.

14.4 Problem Solving: More Recursive Programs

This section examines three familiar problems and implements a recursive procedure or function to solve each.

CASE STUDY

PRINTING AN ARRAY BACKWARD

Problem Specification
Provide a recursive solution to the problem of displaying the elements of an array in reverse order.

Analysis
If the array x has elements with subscripts x'First..x'Last, the element values should be displayed in the sequence X(X'Last), X(X'Last-1), X(X'Last-2), ..., X(X'First+1),X(X'First). The stopping case is displaying an array with one element; the solution is to display that element. For larger arrays the recursive step is to display the last array element (X(X'Last)) and then display the subarray with subscripts X'First..X'last-1 backward.

Data Requirements

Problem Inputs
an array of integer values (x : IntArray)

Problem Outputs
the array values in reverse order (X(X'Last), X(X'Last-1), ... , X(X'First+1), X(X'First))

Algorithm
1. IF X'First = X'Last (i.e., if slice x has only one element), THEN

    2. Display X(X'Last)

    ELSE

    3. Display X(X'Last)
    4. Display the subarray with subscripts X'First..X'Last-1

    END IF;

Implementation

Program 14.7 implements the recursive algorithm and gives a test program.

Program 14.7 Printing an Array Backward

```
WITH Ada.Text_IO;
WITH Ada.Integer_Text_IO;
PROCEDURE Test_Print_Backward IS
-------------------------------------------------------------------
--| Demonstration of recursive procedure to print an array backward
--| Author: Michael B. Feldman, The George Washington University
--| Last Modified: September 1998
-------------------------------------------------------------------

  TYPE IntArray IS ARRAY(Integer RANGE <>) OF Integer;
  Test: IntArray(1..10);

  PROCEDURE PrintBackward (X : IntArray) IS

    -- Prints a slice of an integer array X with bounds X'First..X'Last.
    -- Pre : Array X is defined and X'First <= X'Last.
    -- Post: Displays X(X'Last), X(X'Last-1), ... , X(X'First)

  BEGIN -- PrintBackward

    IF X'First = X'Last THEN -- stopping case - slice has only one element
        Ada.Integer_Text_IO.Put(Item => X(X'Last), Width => 3);
      ELSIF X'First > X'Last THEN    -- error in specifying slice bounds
        Ada.Text_IO.Put(Item => "Error in bounds of array slice");
        Ada.Text_IO.New_Line;
      ELSE
        -- recursive step
        Ada.Integer_Text_IO.Put(Item => X(X'Last), Width => 3);
        PrintBackward (X => X(X'First..X'Last-1));
      END IF;

  END PrintBackward;

BEGIN -- Test_Print_Backward

  Test := (1,3,5,7,9,11,13,15,17,19);
  PrintBackward(X => Test(1..3));
  Ada.Text_IO.New_Line;

END Test_Print_Backward;
```

Sample Run

```
5  3  1
```

Given the following array type and variable:

```
TYPE IntArray IS ARRAY(Integer RANGE <>) OF Integer;
Test: IntArray(1..3);
```

the procedure call PrintBackward(Test(1..3)) results in the three Put statements being executed in the order indicated below, and the elements of Test will be printed backward as desired.

```
Ada.Integer_Text_IO.Put (Item => Test(3));
Ada.Integer_Text_IO.Put (Item => Test(2));
Ada.Integer_Text_IO.Put (Item => Test(1));
```

To verify this, we trace the execution of the procedure call statement above in Fig. 14.4.

Each rightward arrow indicate a recursive procedure call; each leftward arrow indicates a return to the previous level.

Call PrintBackward with parameter Test(1..3).

> Display Test(3).

> Call PrintBackward with parameter Test(1..2).

>> Display Test(2).

>> Call PrintBackward with parameter Test(1..1).

>>> Display Test(1).

>>> Return from third call.

>> Return from second call.

> Return from original call.

As shown, there are three calls to procedure PrintBackward, each with different parameters. The procedure returns always occur in the reverse order of the procedure calls; in other words, we return from the last call first, then we return from the next to last call, and so on. This time there are no statements left to execute after the returns, because the recursive call

```
PrintBackward (X(X'First..X'Last-1))
```

occurs at the end of the recursive step.

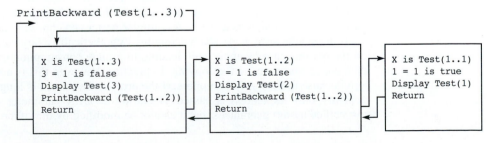

Figure 14.4 Trace of PrintBackward(Test(1..3))

CASE
STUDY

DISPLAYING AN ARRAY IN NORMAL ORDER

Problem Specification
Provide a recursive procedure that displays the elements of an array in normal order.

Analysis
We can use the approach just followed to display the elements of an array in normal order. Again the stopping case is an array with just one element.

Data Requirements

Problem Inputs
an array of integer values (X : IntArray)

Problem Outputs
the array values in normal order (X(X'First), X(X'First+1), ... , X(X'Last-1), X(X'Last))

Algorithm
1. IF X'First = X'Last (i.e., if slice x has only one element) THEN

    2.   Display X(X'Last)

    ELSE

    3.   Display the subarray with subscripts X'First..X'Last-1

    4.   Display X(X'Last)

    END IF;

The only difference between this algorithm and the one shown earlier is that steps 3 and 4 are transposed.

Implementation
The implementation and testing is left as an exercise.

You might be wondering whether there are any special performance problems associated with passing arrays through a series of recursive calls. Recall that the Ada standard does not specify whether an array is passed to a subprogram by creating a local copy or by just passing its address. A compiler writer can choose to do it either way.

If indeed the array is passed by copying, hypothetically a large array might be copied many times in a recursive call, leading to a huge consumption of space for all the local copies and time for the copying. In practice, however, this is not a cause for concern because in most Ada compilers, if the array to be passed is longer than just a few elements, only its address is passed. Declaring an array parameter with mode IN (or unspecified mode) guarantees that it cannot be modified by the subprogram.

CASE
STUDY

DISCOVERING WHETHER A STRING IS A PALINDROME

Problem Specification
A *palindrome* is a string or sentence that reads the same backward and forward. RADAR is a palindrome. When the Biblical first man met the Biblical first woman, he might have said "Madam, I'm Adam," which is a palindrome if one neglects the punctuation. (Adam, in his first fit of anger, might also have said "Mad am I, Madam.") The problem is to write a program that discovers whether a string of 80 characters or less is a palindrome.

Analysis
Our program can discover whether a string is a palindrome by first finding the reverse of the string, then checking whether the string is the same as its reverse.

Data Requirements

Problem Inputs
the input string (s: String)

Problem Outputs
a message to the user indicating whether s is a palindrome

Algorithm
1. Find the reverse R of the given string s

2. IF R is equal to s THEN

   the original string is a palindrome

   ELSE

   the original string is not a palindrome

   END IF;

Step 1 Refinement
1.1. IF s is empty or has only one character THEN

   1.2. R is the same as s

   ELSE

   1.3. Remove the first character of s, and concatenate it to the reverse of the rest of s

   END IF;

Step 1.3 contains the words "to the reverse of the rest of s". Because the purpose of the step is to find the reverse, this suggests a recursive algorithm. Step 1.1 tests for the stopping case; step 1.2 implements the stopping case. We can write this as a recursive code fragment:

```
IF S'Length <= 1 THEN
  RETURN S;
ELSE
  RETURN StringReverse(S(S'First+1..S'Last)) & S(S'First);;
END IF;
```

The recursive call passes the tail of s, that is, s with the first character removed. We call our recursive function StringReverse and not Reverse because the latter is a reserved word in Ada, which we cannot use for anything else.

Implementation

Program 14.8 shows the program Palindrome, which uses the recursive function StringReverse just described. To make the output illustrate the recursion better, we have included an output statement in StringReverse that just displays the value of the parameter to this function. In the sample run you can observe that the string passed to StringReverse is shorter and shorter. Note also that we are using Get_Line to read the string, then passing only the useful slice to StringReverse.

Program 14.8 Palindrome

```
WITH Ada.Text_IO;
PROCEDURE Palindrome IS
--------------------------------------------------------------------
--| Display the reverse of a string of 80 characters or less, and
--| indicate whether the string is a palindrome
--| Author: Michael B. Feldman, The George Washington University
--| Last Modified: September 1998
--------------------------------------------------------------------

  Input: String(1..80);  -- the input string
  Last : Natural;        -- index of input string's last character
  R    : String(1..80);  -- the reverse of the input string

  -- local function StringReverse

  FUNCTION StringReverse(S: String) RETURN String IS
    -- returns the reverse of a string
    -- Pre: S is defined
    -- Post: returns the reverse of S

  BEGIN -- StringReverse

    -- these are just to illustrate the recursion
    Ada.Text_IO.Put(S);
    Ada.Text_IO.New_Line;

    IF S'Length <= 1 THEN
      RETURN S;
    ELSE
      RETURN StringReverse(S(S'First+1..S'Last)) & S(S'First);
    END IF;

  END StringReverse;

BEGIN -- Palindrome

  FOR Trial IN 1..5 LOOP
```

```
      Ada.Text_IO.Put
         (Item => "Please enter a string of 80 characters or less.");
      Ada.Text_IO.New_Line;
      Ada.Text_IO.Get_Line(Item => Input, Last => Last);

      R(1..Last) := StringReverse(Input(1..Last));
      Ada.Text_IO.Put("The reverse of the string is ");
      Ada.Text_IO.New_Line;
      Ada.Text_IO.Put(Item => R(1..Last));
      Ada.Text_IO.New_Line;

      IF R (1..Last) = Input (1..Last) THEN
         Ada.Text_IO.Put(Item => "The string is a palindrome.");
         Ada.Text_IO.New_Line;
      ELSE
         Ada.Text_IO.Put(Item => "The string is not a palindrome.");
         Ada.Text_IO.New_Line;
      END IF;

      Ada.Text_IO.New_Line;

   END LOOP;

END Palindrome;
```

Sample Run

```
Please enter a string of 80 characters or less.
radar
radar
adar
dar
ar
r
The reverse of the string is
radar
The string is a palindrome.

Please enter a string of 80 characters or less.
Madam, I'm Adam
Madam, I'm Adam
adam, I'm Adam
dam, I'm Adam
am, I'm Adam
m, I'm Adam
, I'm Adam
 I'm Adam
I'm Adam
'm Adam
m Adam
 Adam
Adam
dam
am
m
The reverse of the string is
madA m'I ,madaM
The string is not a palindrome.
```

```
Please enter a string of 80 characters or less.
madamimadam
madamimadam
adamimadam
damimadam
amimadam
mimadam
imadam
madam
adam
dam
am
m
The reverse of the string is
madamimadam
The string is a palindrome.

Please enter a string of 80 characters or less.
abc
abc
bc
c
The reverse of the string is
cba
The string is not a palindrome.

Please enter a string of 80 characters or less.
X
X
The reverse of the string is
X
The string is a palindrome.
```

As you can see from the second and third test cases, this program treats blanks and punctuation marks as ordinary characters and so does not discover that "Madam, I'm Adam" is a palindrome. As an exercise, you can improve this program so that blanks and punctuation are ignored and uppercase letters are treated the same as lowercase ones.

EXERCISES FOR SECTION 14.4

Self-Check

1. Trace the execution of `PrintNormal` and `PrintBackward` on an array that has the integers 5, 8, 10, 1 stored in consecutive elements.

Programming

1. Provide an iterative procedure that is equivalent to `PrintBackward`.

2. Write a recursive procedure that reverses the elements in an array `x(1..N)`. The recursive step should shift the slice `x(2..N)` down one element into the subarray `x(1..N-1)` (i.e., `x(1)` gets `x(2)`, `x(2)` gets `x(3)`, ... `x(N-1)` gets `x(N)`), store the old `x(1)` in `x(N)`, and then reverse the subarray `x(1..N-1)`.

14.5 Problem Solving: More Case Studies in Recursion

This section presents two more case studies in recursion: Tower of Hanoi and picture processing with recursion.

CASE STUDY

TOWERS OF HANOI

The Towers of Hanoi problem is a representation of an old Asian puzzle. It involves moving a specified number of disks from one tower (or peg) to another. The disks are arranged on the first tower in order of increasing size, with the largest disk on the bottom. Legend has it that the world will come to an end when the problem is solved for 64 disks. In the version of the problem shown in Fig. 14.5 there are five disks (numbered 1 through 5) and three towers or pegs (lettered A, B, C). The goal is to move the five disks from peg A to peg C subject to the following rules:

1. Only one disk may be moved at a time, and this disk must be the top disk on a peg.

2. A larger disk may never be placed on top of a smaller disk.

Problem Specification
Solve the Towers of Hanoi Problem for N disks, where N is a parameter.

Analysis
The solution to the Towers of Hanoi problem consists of a printed list of individual disk moves. We need a recursive procedure that can be used to move any number of disks from one peg to another, using the third peg as an auxiliary.

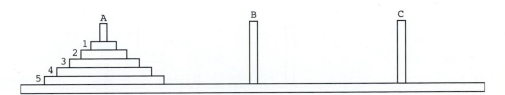

Figure 14.5 Towers of Hanoi

Data Requirements

Problem Inputs
the number of disks to be moved (N : Integer)
the *from* peg (FromPeg : 'A'..'C')
the *to* peg (ToPeg : 'A'..'C')
the *auxiliary* peg (AuxPeg : 'A'..'C')

Problem Outputs
a list of individual disk moves

Design
The stopping cases of the problem involve moving one disk only (e.g., "move disk 2 from peg A to peg C"). A simpler problem than the original would be to move four disks subject to the conditions above, or three disks, and so on. Therefore we want to split the original five-disk problem into one or more problems involving fewer disks. Let's consider splitting the original problem into the following three problems:

1.   Move four disks from peg A to peg B.

2.   Move disk 5 from peg A to peg C.

3.   Move four disks from peg B to peg C.

Step 1 moves all disks but the largest to tower B, an auxiliary tower that was not mentioned in the original problem. Step 2 moves the largest disk to the goal tower, tower C. Then step 3 moves the remaining disks from B to the goal tower, where they will be placed on top of the largest disk. Let's assume that we will be able to perform step 1 and step 2 (a stopping case); Fig. 14.6 shows the status of the three towers after completion of these steps. At this point, it should be clear that we can solve the original five-disk problem if we can complete step 3.

Unfortunately, we still don't know how to perform step 1 or step 3. However, both these steps involve four disks instead of five, so they are simpler than the original problem. We should be able to split *them* into even simpler problems. Step 3 involves moving four disks from tower B to tower C, so we can split it into two three-disk problems and a one-disk problem:

3.1. Move three disks from peg B to peg A.

3.2. Move disk 4 from peg B to peg C.

3.3. Move three disks from peg A to peg C.

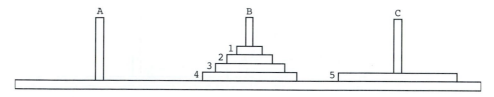

Figure 14.6 Towers of Hanoi after Steps 1 and 2

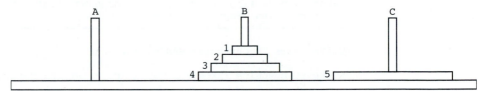

Figure 14.7 Towers of Hanoi after Steps 1, 2, 3.1, and 3.2

Figure 14.7 shows the status of the towers after completion of steps 3.1 and 3.2. We now have the two largest disks on peg C. Once we complete step 3.3, all five disks will be on peg C as required.

By splitting each N-disk problem into two problems involving $N - 1$ disks and a one-disk problem, we will eventually reach all cases of one disk, which we know how to solve.

Initial Algorithm

1.   IF N is 1, THEN

2.   Move disk 1 from the *from* peg to the *to* peg

ELSE

3.   Move $N - 1$ disks from the *from* peg to the auxiliary peg using the *to* peg

4.   Move disk N from the *from* peg to the *to* peg

5.   Move $N - 1$ disks from the auxiliary peg to the *to* peg using the *from* peg

END IF;

If N is 1, a stopping case is reached. If N is greater than 1, the recursive step (following ELSE) splits the original problem into three smaller subproblems, one of which is a stopping case. Each stopping case displays a move instruction. Verify that the recursive step generates the three problems listed after Fig. 14.5 when N is 5, the *from* peg is A, and the *to* peg is C.

Implementation

The implementation of this algorithm is shown as procedure Tower in Program 14.9. Procedure Tower has four parameters. The procedure call statement

```
Tower (N => 5, FromPeg => 'A',ToPeg => 'C',AuxPeg => 'B');
```

solves the problem posed earlier of moving five disks from peg A to peg C using B as an auxiliary. An auxiliary procedure MoveDisk is included.

Program 14.9 A Test of Towers of Hanoi

```
WITH Ada.Text_IO;
WITH Ada.Integer_Text_IO;
PROCEDURE Test_Tower IS
---------------------------------------------------------------------
--| Demonstration of the recursive procedure Tower,
--| which solves a 3-peg Towers of Hanoi problem
```

```
--| Author: Michael B. Feldman, The George Washington University
--| Last Modified: September 1998
-----------------------------------------------------------------------

   SUBTYPE Pegs IS Character RANGE 'A'..'C';

   PROCEDURE MoveDisk (FromPeg, ToPeg: Pegs; Which: Natural) IS

   -- Auxiliary procedure implementing a 1-disk move

   BEGIN
     Ada.Text_IO.Put(Item => "Move disk ");
     Ada.Integer_Text_IO.Put(Item => Which, Width => 1);
     Ada.Text_IO.Put(Item => " from peg ");
     Ada.Text_IO.Put(Item => FromPeg);
     Ada.Text_IO.Put(Item => " to peg ");
     Ada.Text_IO.Put(Item => ToPeg);
     Ada.Text_IO.New_Line;
   END MoveDisk;

   PROCEDURE Tower (FromPeg, ToPeg, AuxPeg: Pegs; N: Natural) IS

   -- Moves N disks from FromPeg to ToPeg
   -- using AuxPeg as an auxiliary.

   BEGIN  -- Tower

     IF N = 1 THEN
       -- stopping case
       MoveDisk(FromPeg, ToPeg, 1);
     ELSE
       -- recursive step
       Tower (FromPeg, AuxPeg, ToPeg, N-1);
       MoveDisk(FromPeg, ToPeg, N);
       Tower (AuxPeg, ToPeg, FromPeg, N-1);
     END IF;

   END Tower;

BEGIN -- Test_Tower

   Tower (FromPeg => 'A', ToPeg => 'B', AuxPeg => 'C', N => 5);

END Test_Tower;
```

Sample Run

```
Move disk 1 from peg A to peg B
Move disk 2 from peg A to peg C
Move disk 1 from peg B to peg C
Move disk 3 from peg A to peg B
Move disk 1 from peg C to peg A
Move disk 2 from peg C to peg B
Move disk 1 from peg A to peg B
Move disk 4 from peg A to peg C
Move disk 1 from peg B to peg C
Move disk 2 from peg B to peg A
Move disk 1 from peg C to peg A
Move disk 3 from peg B to peg C
Move disk 1 from peg A to peg B
```

```
Move disk 2 from peg A to peg C
Move disk 1 from peg B to peg C
Move disk 5 from peg A to peg B
Move disk 1 from peg C to peg A
Move disk 2 from peg C to peg B
Move disk 1 from peg A to peg B
Move disk 3 from peg C to peg A
Move disk 1 from peg B to peg C
Move disk 2 from peg B to peg A
Move disk 1 from peg C to peg A
Move disk 4 from peg C to peg B
Move disk 1 from peg A to peg B
Move disk 2 from peg A to peg C
Move disk 1 from peg B to peg C
Move disk 3 from peg A to peg B
Move disk 1 from peg C to peg A
Move disk 2 from peg C to peg B
Move disk 1 from peg A to peg B
```

In Program 14.9 the stopping case (move disk 1) is implemented as a call to procedure MoveDisk. Each recursive step consists of two recursive calls to Tower with a call to MoveDisk sandwiched between them. The first recursive call solves the problem of moving $N-1$ disks to the auxiliary peg. The call to MoveDisk displays a message to move disk N to the to peg. The second recursive call solves the problem of moving the $N-1$ disks back from the auxiliary peg to the to peg.

Testing
The procedure call statement

```
Tower (FromPeg => 'A', ToPeg => 'C', AuxPeg => 'B', N => 3);
```

solves a simpler three-disk problem: Move three disks from peg A to peg C. Its execution is traced in Fig. 14.8. Verify for yourself that this list of steps does indeed solve the three-disk problem.

Comparison of Iteration and Recursive Procedures

It is interesting to consider that procedure Tower in Program 14.9 will solve the Tower of Hanoi Problem for any number of disks. The three-disk problem results in a total of seven calls to procedure Tower and is solved by seven disk moves. The five-disk problem results in a total of 31 calls to procedure Tower and is solved in 31 moves. In general, the number of moves required to solve the n-disk problem is $2^n - 1$: We say that it is a $O(2^n)$ problem. Because each procedure call requires the allocation and initialization of a local data area in memory, the computer time increases exponentially with the problem size. For this reason, be careful about running this program with a value of N that is larger than 10.

The dramatic increase in processing time for larger towers is a function of this problem, not recursion. In general, however, if there are recursive and iterative solutions to the same problem, the recursive solution requires more time and space because of the extra procedure calls.

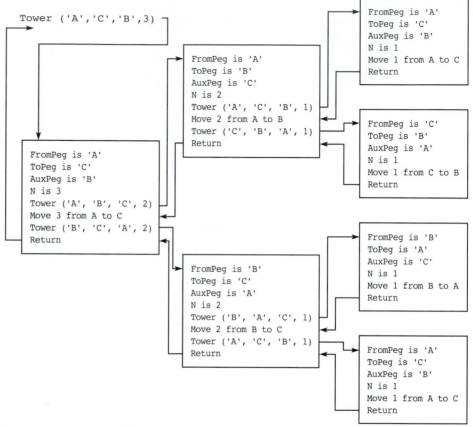

Figure 14.8 Trace of Tower ('A', 'B', 'C', 3)

Although recursion was not really needed to solve the simpler problems in this chapter, it was extremely useful in formulating an algorithm for Towers of Hanoi. For certain problems, recursion leads naturally to solutions that are much easier to read and understand than their iterative counterparts. In those cases the benefits gained from increased clarity far outweigh the extra cost in time and memory of running a recursive program.

Many would argue that the recursive programs are esthetically more pleasing. They are indeed often more compact. Once you are accustomed to thinking recursively, the recursive form is somewhat easier to read and understand than the iterative form.

Some programmers like to use recursion as a conceptual tool. Once they have written the recursive form of a function or procedure, they can translate it into an iterative version if run-time efficiency is a major concern.

PICTURE PROCESSING WITH RECURSION

The next problem is a good illustration of the power of recursion. As for the Towers of Hanoi problem, its solution is relatively easy to write recursively; however, the problem would be much more difficult without using recursion. Unlike Towers of Hanoi, which is a cute and popular exercise, picture-processing algorithms have real applications.

Problem Specification

We have a two-dimensional grid G of cells, each of which may be empty or filled. The filled cells that are connected form a *blob*. There may be several blobs on the grid. We would like a function that accepts as input the coordinates of a particular cell and returns the size of the blob containing the cell.

There are three blobs in the sample grid in Fig. 14.9. If the function parameters represent the x and y coordinates of a cell, the result of BlobSize(G,3,4) is 5, the result of BlobSize(G,1,2) is 2, the result of BlobSize(G,5,5) is 0, and the result of Blob-Size(G,5,1) is 4.

Figure 14.9 Grid with Three Blobs

```
      1   2   3   4   5
    ---------------------
1 |   | X |   |   | X |
    ---------------------
2 | X |   |   | X | X |
    ---------------------
3 |   |   | X | X |   |
    ---------------------
4 | X |   |   |   |   |
    ---------------------
5 | X | X | X |   |   |
    ---------------------
```

Analysis

Function BlobSize must test the cell specified by its arguments to see whether it is filled. There are two stopping cases: The cell (x, y) is not on the grid, or the cell (x, y) is empty. In either case the value returned by BlobSize is 0. If the cell is on the grid and filled, the value returned is 1 plus the size of the blobs containing each of its eight neighbors. To avoid counting a filled cell more than once, we will mark it as empty once we have visited it.

Data Requirements

Problem Inputs

the grid (Grid: BlobArray)
the x and y coordinates of the point being visited (x, y : Integer)

Problem Outputs

the number of the cells in the blob containing point (x, y)

Algorithm

1.   IF cell (x, y) is not in the array THEN

2.   Return a count of 0

ELSIF cell (x, y) is empty, THEN

3.   Return a count of 0

ELSE

4.   Mark cell (x, y) as empty

5.   Add 1 and see whether the blob contains any of the eight neighbors of cell (x, y)

END IF;

Function BlobSize is shown in Program 14.10, assuming the declarations below. The array type BlobArray has element values Filled or Empty. The array G has, as usual, bounds G'Range(1) for the rows and G'Range(2) for the columns.

Program 14.10 Computing the Size of Blobs in a Grid

```
WITH Ada.Text_IO;
WITH Ada.Integer_Text_IO;
PROCEDURE Test_Blob_Size IS
-----------------------------------------------------------------------
--| Illustrates the recursive function BlobSize, which computes
--| size of a "blob" or group of filled cells on a grid.
--| Author: Michael B. Feldman, The George Washington University
--| Last Modified: September 1998
-----------------------------------------------------------------------

  TYPE Fill IS (Empty, Filled);
  TYPE BlobArray IS ARRAY (Integer RANGE <>,Integer RANGE <>) OF Fill;

  Test: BlobArray(1..5,1..5);

  PROCEDURE DisplayGrid(Grid: BlobArray) IS
  -- Pre:  Grid is defined
  -- Post: displays Grid on the screen

  BEGIN -- DisplayGrid

    FOR Column IN Grid'Range(2) LOOP -- top border
      Ada.Text_IO.Put(Item => "----");
    END LOOP;
    Ada.Text_IO.Put(Item => '-');
    Ada.Text_IO.New_Line;

    FOR Row IN Grid'Range(1) LOOP
      FOR Column IN Grid'Range(2) LOOP
        IF Grid(Row, Column) = Filled THEN
          Ada.Text_IO.Put(Item => "| X ");
        ELSE
          Ada.Text_IO.Put(Item => "|   ");
        END IF;
      END LOOP;
```

```ada
      Ada.Text_IO.Put(Item => '|');
      Ada.Text_IO.New_Line;

      FOR Column IN Grid'Range(2) LOOP -- after each row
         Ada.Text_IO.Put(Item => "----");
      END LOOP;
      Ada.Text_IO.Put(Item => '-');
      Ada.Text_IO.New_Line;
   END LOOP;

END DisplayGrid;

FUNCTION BlobSize(Grid : BlobArray; X, Y: Integer) RETURN Natural IS
-- Counts the number of filled cells in the blob containing
-- point (X, Y).
-- Pre : Blob array Grid and point (X,Y) are defined.
-- Post: Returns the size of the blob containing point (X, Y).
--       Resets the status of each cell in the blob to Empty.

   CopyOfGrid : BlobArray(Grid'Range(1),Grid'Range(2));
                            -- because functions can't modify
                            -- their parameters, in Ada

   FUNCTION Blob (X, Y : Integer) RETURN Natural IS

   -- Inner function that performs the counting operation for BlobSize
   -- Pre : Global array CopyOfGrid and point (X,Y) are defined.
   -- Post: Returns the size of the blob containing point (X, Y).
   --       Resets the status of each cell in the blob to Empty.

   Result: Natural;

   BEGIN -- Blob

      IF (X NOT IN CopyOfGrid'Range(1)) OR
         (Y NOT IN CopyOfGrid'Range(2)) THEN
         Result := 0;                        -- cell not in grid
      ELSIF CopyOfGrid(X, Y) = Empty THEN
         Result := 0;                        -- cell is empty
      ELSE -- cell is filled
         -- recursive step
         CopyOfGrid(X, Y) := Empty;
         Result := 1 + Blob(X-1, Y+1) + Blob(X, Y+1) +
                       Blob(X+1, Y+1) + Blob(X+1, Y) +
                       Blob(X+1, Y-1) + Blob(X, Y-1) +
                       Blob(X-1, Y-1) + Blob(X-1, Y);
      END IF;

      RETURN Result;

   END Blob;

BEGIN

   CopyOfGrid := Grid;
   RETURN Blob(X,Y);

END BlobSize;

BEGIN -- Test_Blob_Size
```

```
Test := ((Empty,   Filled,  Empty,   Empty,   Filled),
         (Filled,  Empty,   Empty,   Filled,  Filled),
         (Empty,   Empty,   Filled,  Filled,  Empty ),
         (Filled,  Empty,   Empty,   Empty,   Empty ),
         (Filled,  Filled,  Filled,  Empty,   Empty ));

DisplayGrid (Grid => Test);

Ada.Text_IO.Put(Item => "BlobSize(3,4) is ");
Ada.Integer_Text_IO.Put(Item => BlobSize(Test,3,4), Width => 1);
Ada.Text_IO.New_Line;

Ada.Text_IO.Put(Item => "BlobSize(1,2) is ");
Ada.Integer_Text_IO.Put(Item => BlobSize(Test,1,2), Width => 1);
Ada.Text_IO.New_Line;

Ada.Text_IO.Put(Item => "BlobSize(5,5) is ");
Ada.Integer_Text_IO.Put(Item => BlobSize(Test,5,5), Width => 1);
Ada.Text_IO.New_Line;

Ada.Text_IO.Put(Item => "BlobSize(5,1) is ");
Ada.Integer_Text_IO.Put(Item => BlobSize(Test,5,1), Width => 1);
Ada.Text_IO.New_Line;

END Test_Blob_Size;
```

Sample Run

```
---------------------
|   | X |   |   | X |
---------------------
| X |   |   | X | X |
---------------------
|   |   | X | X |   |
---------------------
| X |   |   |   |   |
---------------------
| X | X | X |   |   |
---------------------
BlobSize(3,4) is 5
BlobSize(1,2) is 2
BlobSize(5,5) is 0
BlobSize(5,1) is 4
```

The auxiliary function Blob in Program 14.10, declared within BlobSize, implements the counting algorithm; function BlobSize simply calls the recursive function Blob, passing on its arguments, and returns the count computed by function Blob as its own result. The purpose of the auxiliary function is to protect the actual array from being modified when filled cells are reset to empty by function Blob. We will come back to this point shortly.

If the cell that is being visited is off the grid or is empty, a value of zero is returned immediately. Otherwise, the recursive step executes, causing function Blob to call itself eight times; each time, a different neighbor of the current cell is visited. The cells are visited in a clockwise manner, starting with the neighbor above and to the left. The function result is defined as the sum of all values returned from these recursive calls plus 1 (for the current cell).

The sequence of operations performed in function Blob is important. The IF statement tests whether the cell (x, y) is on the grid before testing whether (x, y) is empty. If the order were reversed, Constraint_Error would be raised whenever (x, y) was off the grid.

Also, the recursive step resets Grid(X,Y) to Empty before visiting the neighbors of cell (x, y). If this were not done first, cell (x, y) would be counted more than once because it is a neighbor of all its neighbors. A worse problem is that the recursion would not terminate. When each neighbor of the current cell is visited, Blob is called again with the coordinates of the current cell as arguments. If the current cell is Empty, an immediate return occurs. If the current cell is still Filled, the recursive step would be executed erroneously. Eventually, the program will run out of time or memory space; the latter is signaled in Ada by the raising of Storage_Error.

A side effect of the execution of function Blob is that all cells that are part of the blob being processed are reset to Empty. This is the reason for using two functions. Because the array is passed as a parameter to function BlobSize, a local copy CopyOf-Grid is saved when BlobSize is first called. Only this local array is changed by function Blob, not the actual array. If the counting operation were performed in function BlobSize instead of in function Blob, eight copies of this array would be made each time the recursive step was executed. Using the function Blob and the array that is global to all recursive calls of Blob (but still local to BlobSize) prevents the unnecessary copying.

EXERCISES FOR SECTION 14.5

Self-Check

1. How many moves are needed to solve the six-disk problem?

2. Estimate the size of the largest Towers of Hanoi problem that could be solved in less than one day. Assume that one disk can be moved each second.

3. Estimate the size of the largest Towers of Hanoi problem that could be solved in less than one year. Assume that one disk can be moved each second.

4. Trace the execution of function BlobSize for the coordinate pairs (1, 1) and (1, 2) in the sample grid.

5. Is the order of the two tests performed in function BlobSize critical? What happens if we reverse them or combine them into a single condition?

Programming

1. Modify TestTower to read in a data value for *N* (the number of disks).

14.6 Problem Solving: Recursive Searching

CASE
STUDY

RECURSIVE BINARY SEARCH

In Section 9.10 we discussed one technique for searching an array, and we wrote a function that returned the index of a target key in an array if the target was present. To do this, it was necessary to compare array element keys to the target key, starting with the first array element. The comparison process was terminated when the target key was found or the end of the array was reached. We must make N comparisons to determine that a target key is not in an array of N elements. On the average, we must make $N/2$ comparisons to locate a target key that is in the array. The number of comparisons is directly proportional to the number of elements in the array, so we say that this search method is O(N).

Often we want to search an array whose elements are arranged in order by key field. We can take advantage of the fact that the array keys are in ascending order and terminate the search when an array key greater than or equal to the target key is reached. There is no need to look any further in the array; all other keys will also be larger than the target key.

Both these search techniques are called *sequential search* because we examine the array elements in sequence. The modified algorithm discussed above is a sequential search of an ordered array. On the average, a sequential search of an ordered array requires $N/2$ comparisons to locate the target key or determine that it is not in the array; so we still have an O(N) process.

The array searches described above are considered *linear searches* because their execution time increases linearly (in direct proportion) with the number of array elements. This can be a problem in searching very large arrays (for example, $N > 1000$). Consequently, we often use the *binary search algorithm* described below for large sorted arrays.

Problem Specification
Your employer has a directory of customers that she keeps in alphabetical order. Since business has been very good, this list has become too large to search efficiently using a linear search. Write an improved search algorithm that takes advantage of the fact that the array is sorted.

Analysis
The binary search algorithm takes advantage of the fact that the array is ordered to eliminate half of the array elements with each probe into the array. Consequently, if the array has 1000 elements, it will either locate the target value or eliminate 500 elements with its first probe, 250 elements with its second probe, 125 elements with its third probe, and so on. Only 10 probes are necessary to completely search an array of 1000 elements. (Why?) You can use the binary search algorithm to find a name in a large metropolitan telephone directory using 30 or less probes, so this algorithm should be suitable for your employer.

The number of probes to completely search an *N*-element array obviously varies with the number of elements *N*. Can we find a formula for this variation? Because each probe eliminates half the elements, the maximum number of probes is determined by the number of times we can "cut the array in half" before we are left with only one element.

Let's consider some values of *N* corresponding to powers of 2. If *N* is 8 (2^3), for example, we first search an eight-element array, then a four-element array, then a two-element array, and finally a one-element array. We cut the array three times. If *N* is 32 (2^5), we cut the array five times; if *N* is 256 (2^8), we cut the array 8 times; if *N* is 1024 (2^{10}), we cut it 10 times. Indeed, we make a maximum of only 16 cuts even if *N* is 32,768 (2^{16})! If *N* is not an exact power of 2, the number of probes is determined by the next higher power of 2: If *N* is 1000, 1024, or 2^{10}, is the determining power of 2.

An equivalent way of saying "1024 is 2^{10}" is "10 is the logarithm, to the base 2, of 1024," or "$\log_2 1024 = 10$." The formula that we are looking for is that the number of binary search probes into an array of *N* elements is $\log_2 N$. Another way of saying this is that binary search is an O($\log_2 N$) algorithm. This is much faster than sequential search, isn't it?

Now let's develop the binary search algorithm. Because the array is ordered, all we have to do is compare the target key with the middle element of the subarray we are searching. If their keys are the same, we are done. If the middle value is larger than the target, we should search the left half of the array next; otherwise, we should search the right half of the array.

The subarray to be searched, `Slice`, has subscripts `Slice'First..Slice'Last`. The variable `Middle` is the subscript of the middle element in this range. The right half of the array (subscripts `Middle..Slice'Last`) is eliminated by the first probe as shown in Fig. 14.10. The new subarray to be searched is `Slice(Slice'First..Middle-1)`, as shown in Fig. 14.11. The target value, 35, is found on this probe.

The binary search algorithm can be stated clearly by using recursion. The stopping cases are:

- The array has no elements (`Slice'First>Slice'Last` or `Slice'Length=0`).

- The middle value is the target value.

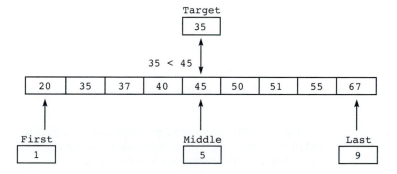

Figure 14.10 First Probe of Binary Search

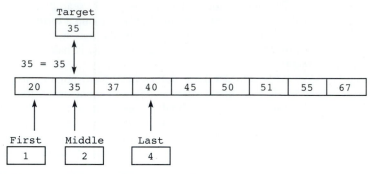

Figure 14.11 Second Probe of Binary Search

In the first case the function result is 0 (we'll require that arrays submitted to this algorithm have positive subscript ranges); in the second case the function result is Middle. The recursive step is to search the appropriate subarray.

Data Requirements

Problem Inputs
array to be searched (Slice : SearchArray)
target being searched for (Target : KeyType)

Problem Outputs
the location of Target, or 0 if not found

Algorithm

1. Compute the subscript of the middle element

2. IF the slice has zero length THEN

   3. Return a result of 0

   ELSIF the target is the middle value THEN

   4. Return the subscript of the middle element

   ELSIF the target is less than the middle value THEN

   5. Search the subarray with subscripts Slice'First..Middle-1

   ELSE

   6. Search the subarray with subscripts Middle+1..Slice'Last

   END IF;

In each of the recursive steps (steps 5 and 6), the bounds of the slice are listed as a part of the actual table parameter in the recursive call. The actual parameters define the search limits for the next probe into the array.

Test Plan

You should test the binary search function very carefully. Besides verifying that it locates target values that are present in the array, verify that they also determine when a target value is missing. Use target values that are within the range of values stored in the array, a target value that is less than the smallest value in the array, and a target value that is greater than the largest value in the array. Make sure that the binary search function terminates regardless of whether the target is missing or where it is located if it is not missing.

Implementation

In the initial call to the recursive procedure, the entire array is normally given. For example, given the following declarations:

```
SUBTYPE KeyType IS Integer;
TYPE SearchArray IS ARRAY(Positive RANGE <>) OF KeyType;

Test: SearchArray(1..9);
Location: Natural;
```

the procedure call statement

```
Location := BinarySearch (Test, 35);
```

could be used to search an array `Test` for the target key `35`. Function `BinarySearch` is shown in Program 14.11.

The assignment statement

```
Middle := (Slice'First + Slice'Last) / 2;
```

computes the subscript of the middle element by finding the average of `Slice'First` and `Slice'Last`.

Program 14.11 A Test of Recursive Binary Search

```
WITH Ada.Text_IO;
WITH Ada.Integer_Text_IO;
PROCEDURE Test_Binary_Search IS
-----------------------------------------------------------------------
--| Test program for Recursive Binary Search
--| Author: Michael B. Feldman, The George Washington University
--| Last Modified: September 1998
-----------------------------------------------------------------------

  TYPE SearchArray IS ARRAY(Positive RANGE <>) OF Integer;
  Test: SearchArray(1..9);

  FUNCTION BinarySearch
    (Slice: SearchArray; Target: Integer) RETURN Natural IS
  -- Performs a recursive binary search of an ordered array of
  -- keys with bounds Slice'First..Slice'Last.
  -- Pre : Target and Slice are defined.
  --       0 < Slice'First <= Slice'Last
  -- Post: Returns the subscript of Target if found in array Slice;
  --       otherwise, returns 0
```

```
      Middle : Natural;       -- the subscript of the middle element

  BEGIN -- BinarySearch

    Middle := (Slice'First + Slice'Last) / 2; -- define Middle

    -- Determine if Target is found or missing or redefine subarray.

    IF Slice'Length = 0 THEN
      RETURN 0;                              -- stopping case: Target missing
    ELSIF Slice(Middle) = Target THEN
      RETURN Middle;                         -- stopping case: Target found
    ELSIF Slice(Middle) > Target THEN    -- search lower subarray
      RETURN BinarySearch (Slice(Slice'First..Middle-1),Target);
    ELSE                                 -- search upper subarray
      RETURN BinarySearch (Slice(Middle+1..Slice'Last),Target);
    END IF;

  END BinarySearch;

BEGIN -- Test_Binary_Search

  Test := (20,35,37,40,45,50,51,55,67);

  Ada.Text_IO.Put(Item => "BinarySearch(Test,35) is");
  Ada.Integer_Text_IO.Put(Item => BinarySearch(Test,35));
  Ada.Text_IO.New_Line;
  Ada.Text_IO.Put(Item => "BinarySearch(Test,19) is");
  Ada.Integer_Text_IO.Put(Item => BinarySearch(Test,19));
  Ada.Text_IO.New_Line;
  Ada.Text_IO.Put(Item => "BinarySearch(Test,75) is");
  Ada.Integer_Text_IO.Put(Item => BinarySearch(Test,75));
  Ada.Text_IO.New_Line;
  Ada.Text_IO.Put(Item => "BinarySearch(Test,20) is");
  Ada.Integer_Text_IO.Put(Item => BinarySearch(Test,20));
  Ada.Text_IO.New_Line;
  Ada.Text_IO.Put(Item => "BinarySearch(Test,67) is");
  Ada.Integer_Text_IO.Put(Item => BinarySearch(Test,67));
  Ada.Text_IO.New_Line;
  Ada.Text_IO.Put(Item => "BinarySearch(Test,54) is");
  Ada.Integer_Text_IO.Put(Item => BinarySearch(Test,54));
  Ada.Text_IO.New_Line;

END Test_Binary_Search;
```

Sample Run

```
BinarySearch(Test,35) is        2
BinarySearch(Test,19) is        0
BinarySearch(Test,75) is        0
BinarySearch(Test,20) is        1
BinarySearch(Test,67) is        9
BinarySearch(Test,54) is        0
```

The binary search function is written to return 0 if the target is not found. This works only because we have required that the array bounds be positive, because otherwise, 0 could be a valid subscript. Binary search would be more general if it could accept arrays with arbitrary integer bounds; in that case it would be better to convert the binary search function to a procedure with two OUT parameters: the index of the target if found and a program flag indicating whether the target was found. This modification is left as an exercise.

14.7 Tricks of the Trade: Debugging Recursive Subprograms

The most common problem with a recursive procedure or function is that it might not terminate properly. For example, if the terminating condition is not correct or incomplete, the procedure may call itself indefinitely or until all available memory is used up. Normally, a "stack overflow," or Storage_Error exception, is an indicator that a recursive procedure is not terminating. Make sure that you identify all stopping cases and provide a terminating condition for each one. Also be sure that each recursive step leads to a situation that is closer to a stopping case and that repeated recursive calls will eventually lead to stopping cases only.

Sometimes it is difficult to observe the result of a recursive procedure execution. If each recursive call generates a large number of output lines and there are many recursive calls, the output will scroll down the screen more quickly than it can be read. On most systems it is possible to stop the screen temporarily by pressing a control character sequence (e.g., Control-S). If this cannot be done, it is still possible to cause your output to stop temporarily by displaying a prompting message followed by a Ada.Text_IO.Get(NextChar) operation. Your program will resume execution when you enter a data character.

CHAPTER REVIEW

This chapter provides many examples of recursive procedures and functions. Studying them should give you some appreciation of the power of recursion as a problem-solving and programming tool and should provide you with valuable insight regarding its use. It may take some time to feel comfortable thinking in this new way about programming, but it is certainly worth the effort.

Quick-Check Exercises

1. Explain the use of a stack in recursion.

2. Which control statement do you always find in a recursive procedure or function?

3. Why would a programmer conceptualize the problem solution using recursion and implement it using iteration?

4. What causes a stack overflow error, indicated in Ada by Storage_Error?

5. What can you say about a recursive algorithm that has the following form?

```
IF condition THEN
   Perform recursive step
END IF;
```

Answers to Quick-Check Exercises

1. The stack is used to hold all parameter and local variable values and the return point for each execution of a recursive procedure.

2. IF statement.

3. When its solution is much easier to conceptualize using recursion but its implementation would be too inefficient.

4. Too many recursive calls.

5. Nothing is done when the stopping case is reached.

Review Questions for Chapter 14

1. Explain the nature of a recursive problem.

2. Discuss the efficiency of recursive procedures.

3. Differentiate between stopping cases and a terminating condition.

4. Convert the following program from an iterative process to a recursive function that calculates an approximate value for e, the base of the natural logarithms, by summing the series

$$1 + 1/1! + 1/2! + ... + 1/N!$$

until additional terms do not affect the approximation.

```
PROCEDURE ELog IS

   ENL:   Float;
   Delta: Float;
   Fact:  Float;
   N:     Float;

BEGIN -- Elog

   ENL := 1.0;
   N := 1.0;
   Fact := 1.0;
   Delta := 1.0;

   LOOP
      ENL := ENL + Delta;
      N := N + 1.0;
      Fact := Fact * N;
      Delta := 1.0 / Fact;
   EXIT WHEN ENL = (ENL + Delta);
```

```
Ada.Text_IO.Put(Item => "The value of e is ");
Ada.Float_Text_IO.Put
   (Item => ENL, Fore => 3, Aft => 15, Exp => 0);

END Elog;
```

Programming Projects

1. Give a recursive definition of the integer addition operation. Write and test a recursive function to produce the sum of two integers. (*Hint:* Use the built-in "+" operation only to add 1 to a number.)

2. Write a procedure that reads each row of an array as a string and converts it to a row of Grid (see Fig. 14.9). The first character of row 1 corresponds to Grid(1,1), the second character to Grid(1,2), and so on. Set the element value to Empty if the character is blank; otherwise, set it to Filled. The number of rows in the array should be read first. Use this procedure in a program that reads in cell coordinates and prints the number of cells in the blob containing each coordinate pair.

3. The expression for computing $C(n, r)$, the number of combinations of n items, taken r at a time, is

$$C(n, r) = \frac{n!}{r!(n - r)!}$$

where ! means factorial. Write and test a function for computing $C(n, r)$.

4. Write a recursive function that returns the value of the following recursive definition:

$$F(X, Y) = X - Y \text{ if } X \text{ or } Y < 0$$
$$F(X, Y) = F(X - 1, Y) + F(X, Y - 1) \text{ otherwise}$$

5. Write a recursive procedure that lists all of the two-letter subsets for a given set of letters. For example:

```
('A', 'C', 'E', 'G') => ('A', 'C'), ('A', 'E'), ('A', 'G'),
                        ('C', 'E'), ('C', 'G'), ('E', 'G')
```

6. Write a procedure that accepts an 8×8 array of characters that represents a maze. Each position can contain either an 'x' or a blank. Starting at position $(1, 1)$, list any path through the maze to get to location $(8, 8)$. Only horizontal and vertical moves are allowed (no diagonal moves). If no path exists, write a message indicating this. Moves can be made only to locations that contain a blank. If an 'x' is encountered, that path is blocked and another must be chosen. Use recursion.

7. We can use a merge technique to sort two arrays. The *merge sort* begins by taking adjacent pairs of array values and ordering the values in each pair. It then forms groups of four elements by merging adjacent pairs (first pair with

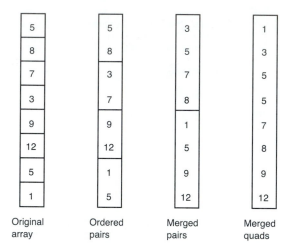

Figure 14.12 Merge Sort

second pair, third pair with fourth pair, and so on) into another array. It then takes adjacent groups of four elements from this new array and merges them back into the original array as groups of eight, and so on. The process terminates when a single group is formed that has the same number of elements as the array. Figure 14.12 shows a merge sort for an array with eight elements. Write a recursive merge sort procedure.

8. Improve the palindrome-finding program (Program 14.8) so that blanks and punctuation are ignored and the program is case-insensitive. (*Hint*: Use operations from `Ada.Characters.Handling` to write a function that takes a string s as a parameter and returns a string representing s with all letters converted to uppercase, as well as blanks and punctuation removed. `"Madam, I'm Adam"` would be converted to `"MADAMIMADAM"`. Use the result of calling this function as the input to `StringReverse`.)

9. Modify `BinarySearch` into a procedure with two output parameters: the location of the key if found and a flag indicating whether or not the key was found.

10. Using the modified `BinarySearch` of Programming Project 8 as a starting point, write a generic binary search procedure that can handle any array with any nonlimited element type and any index type.

CHAPTER 15

Access Types and Dynamic Data Structures

Dynamic data structures are data structures that expand and contract as a program executes. A dynamic data structure is a collection of elements—called *nodes*—that are generally implemented as records. Whereas an array always contains storage for a fixed number of elements, in a dynamic data structure the programmer can increase or reduce the storage allocated, as elements are added to or deleted from the structure.

Dynamic data structures are extremely flexible. It is relatively easy to add new information by creating a new node and inserting it between two existing nodes. It is also relatively easy to delete a node. In this chapter we introduce dynamic data structures and a new kind of Ada type called an *access type*. Access types—often called *pointer types*—are an essential part of using dynamic data structures.

Also introduced in this chapter are the stack and queue data structure, implemented using linked lists.

15.1 Data Structures: Access Types and the NEW Operator

You know how to use arrays to store collections of data. You also know that it is possible for each array element to be a record and have seen a number of examples of such data structures. One characteristic of data collections is that they can vary in size considerably from one run of a program to the next or even during a run. In such cases, an array is not the best structure in which to store the records, because the array size is fixed and therefore must be estimated before the records are read in. If only a few records are present, much space is wasted. Worse, the array cannot expand to hold a number of records greater than its size.

There is a solution to this problem, called *dynamic data structures* or *linked data structures*. Using dynamic data structures, the programmer can increase or decrease the allocated storage to add or delete data items in the collection. In languages like Ada that provide built-in support for linked structures, the compiler associates with an executable program a special storage area, called the *dynamic storage pool,* or sometimes just *pool,* which it initially leaves unassigned to any program variable. A system module called the *storage allocator* is linked into the program and assumes responsibility for allocating blocks of storage from the pool, and returning extra blocks to the pool, *at execution time*. The pool is like a "storage account" from which a program can "borrow" storage to expand a structure, returning the storage when it is no longer needed. The storage allocator can then use that storage to satisfy another storage request from the program.

A special kind of variable is provided for referencing space allocated dynamically from the pool. In Ada these are called *access variables;* in other languages, such as Pascal and C, they are referred to as *pointer variables*. Ada allows us to declare *access types,* and each access variable is an object of an access type. The values of each access type are called *access values* or, informally, *pointers*. A pointer or access value is an abstraction for a hardware address but often does not have the same form.

Consider a record type called `RecType`, defined as

```
TYPE RecType IS RECORD

    ... fields ...

END RECORD;
```

The type definition

```
TYPE RecPointer IS ACCESS RecType;
```

gives us the ability to declare access variables of type `RecPointer`, that is, variables that can *designate,* or hold pointers to, things of type `RecType`. For example, a declaration

```
P1, P2, P3: RecPointer;
```

allocates storage for three such variables.

When an access variable is created in Ada, its value is always initialized to a special, unique internal value known as NULL. This indicates that the pointer doesn't point to anything (yet). It is important to realize that declaring such variables does not cause any records to be allocated; each variable is given just enough space to hold the address of a record.

How do the records themselves come into being? The Ada operator NEW creates them. An assignment statement such as

```
P1 := NEW RecType;
```

causes the storage allocator to search the pool, looking for a block of space large enough to hold a record of type `RecType`. When such a block is found, an access value designating (pointing to) this block is stored in the variable `P1`. Figure 15.1 shows diagrammatically how dynamic allocation works. The cloudlike shape represents the pool, arrows represent pointers, and diagonal lines represent `NULL`.

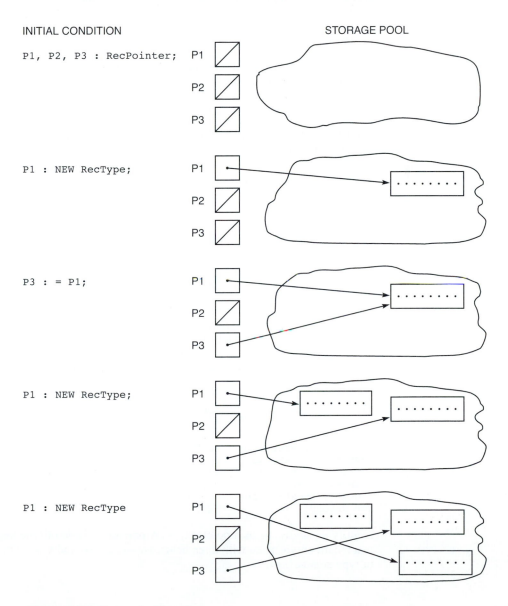

Figure 15.1 Dynamic Allocation

An access variable can acquire a value in only two ways: A value can be delivered by a NEW operation, as above, or it can be copied from another access value. For example,

```
P3 := P1;
```

causes P3 to point to the same record to which P1 points. *An assignment statement to an access variable copies only an access value; it does not copy the designated value!*

If we write

```
P1 := NEW RecType;
```

a second time, space for another record is found in the pool, its address is stored in P1, and P3 is left pointing to the "old" record. If we write

```
P1 := NEW RecType;
```

a third time, the record previously pointed to by P1 is left with nothing pointing to it, thus making it *inaccessible*. This space, in general, remains allocated and unavailable for other use. This situation is often called, picturesquely, a "storage leak," because the storage "leaks away" and can no longer be used. We will return to this subject later in the chapter.

Creating a Linked Structure

Much of the usefulness of dynamic allocation comes from our ability to link together blocks in the storage pool. When we do this, we refer to the result as a *linked structure,* and to the linked blocks as *nodes* (sometimes called *cells).* One very common linked structure is the *singly linked list,* in which each node is connected to the next node by a single pointer. This is analogous to the links in a chain. If you have ever constructed a chain of paper clips, in which you repeatedly add a clip to the end of the chain, you've made a physical singly linked list.

We can connect two nodes if we include a pointer field in each node. The declarations

```
TYPE ElectricityType IS (DC, AC);

TYPE Node;
TYPE NodePointer IS ACCESS Node;
TYPE Node IS RECORD
  Power : ElectricityType;
  Volts : Natural;
  Next : NodePointer;
END RECORD;
```

identify NodePointer as a pointer type. A pointer variable of type NodePointer points to a record of type Node with three fields: Power, Volts, and Next. The Next field is also of type NodePointer.

Note that the first declaration of Node is *incomplete;* it just mentions the name Node without filling in the details. This device is used to inform the compiler of the existence of the type Node so that the next type definition can use it. Using an incomplete type definition meets Ada's requirement that types must be defined before they can be used.

Now let us declare some pointer variables:

```
P : NodePointer;
Q : NodePointer;
R : NodePointer;
```

As in the previous example, P, Q, and R are automatically given initial NULL values. The assignment statements

```
P := NEW Node;
Q := NEW Node;
```

allocate storage for two records of type Node, storing their addresses in P and Q. Initially the Power and Volts fields of these records are as yet undefined; the Next fields of both are initially NULL. Pointer initialization is one of the few cases in Ada in which objects are automatically given initial values at declaration.

In Ada terminology a nonnull access object *designates* (points to) a value. The block of space that P points to is P's designated value. We can refer to the designated value of P using the expression P.ALL, and to the Power field of P.ALL by the expression P.ALL.Power. The assignment statements

```
P.ALL.Power := AC;
P.ALL.Volts := 115;
Q.ALL.Power := DC;
Q.ALL.Volts := 12;
```

define the nonlink fields of these nodes, as shown in Fig. 15.2. Here and in later figures we have left out the cloud symbol for simplicity. The Next fields are still NULL.

The .ALL construct is the way Ada represents a *dereferencing* operation, that is, an operation to find that value to which a pointer points. To simplify the syntax necessary to select a field of a designated value, Ada allows us to omit the .ALL part and just select the field directly. Therefore the following four assignment statements are equivalent to the ones just given: We will use the abbreviated form throughout this chapter. Because P is an access variable, we can read the expression P.Power as "find the value designated by P and select its Power field."

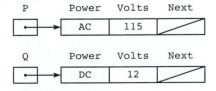

Figure 15.2 Nodes P.ALL and Q.ALL

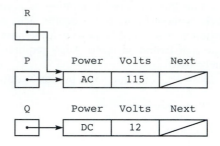

Figure 15.3 Nodes R.ALL/P.ALL and Q.ALL

```
P.Power := AC;
P.Volts := 115;
Q.Power := DC;
Q.Volts := 12;
```

Let us do some more pointer manipulation. The assignment statement

```
R := P;
```

copies the value of pointer variable P into pointer variable R. This means that pointers P and R contain the same access value and, therefore, point to the same node, as shown in Fig. 15.3.

The pointer assignment statements

```
P := Q;
Q := R;
```

have the effect of exchanging the nodes pointed to by P and Q, as shown in Fig. 15.4. The statements

```
Electricity_IO.Put(Item => Q.Power, Width => 4);
Electricity_IO.Put(Item => P.Power, Width => 4);
```

display the Power fields of the records designated by Q and P.

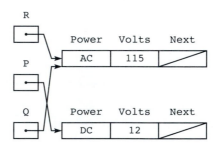

Figure 15.4 Nodes R.ALL/Q.ALL and P.ALL

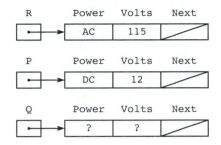

Figure 15.5 Nodes R.ALL, P.ALL, and Q.ALL

For the situation depicted in Fig 15.4 the line

```
AC   DC
```

would be displayed. (As usual, we assume that `Electricity_IO` is an instance of `Ada.Text_IO.Enumeration_IO`.)

The statement

```
Q := NEW Node;
```

changes the value of Q to designate a new node, thereby disconnecting Q from its previous node. The new values of pointer variables P, Q, and R are shown in Fig. 15.5. The data fields of the new node designated by Q are, of course, initially undefined.

It is important to understand the difference between P and P's designated value. P is an access variable (type `NodePointer`) and is used to store the address of a data structure of type `Node`. P can be assigned a new value either by calling `NEW` or by copying another access value of the same type. `P.ALL` is the pool-allocated record designated by P and can be manipulated like any other Ada record. The field selectors `P.Power` and `P.Volts` may be used to reference data (in this case an enumeration value and an integer) stored in this record.

Connecting Nodes

Now we can grow data structures of varying size by connecting nodes together in a singly linked list. If we look at the nodes allocated in the last section, we see that their `Next` fields are currently `NULL`. Since the link fields are type `NodePointer`, they can themselves be used to designate values. The assignment statement

```
R.Next := P;
```

copies the value stored in P (an access value) into the `Next` field of node `R.ALL`. In this way, nodes R and P become connected. Similarly, the assignment statement

```
P.Next := Q;
```

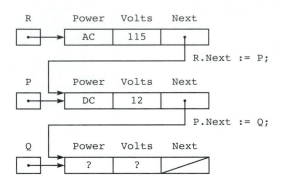

Figure 15.6 Connecting Nodes R.ALL, P.ALL, and Q.ALL

copies the access value stored in access variable Q into the link field of node P.ALL, thereby connecting nodes P and Q. The situation after execution of these two assignment statements is shown in Fig. 15.6.

The data structure pointed to by R has now grown to form a chain of all three nodes. The first node is referenced by R.ALL. The second node can be referenced by P.ALL or R.ALL.Next.ALL, since they both have the same value. Finally, the third node may be referenced by Q.ALL or P.ALL.Next.ALL or even R.ALL.Next.ALL.Next.ALL.

Summary of Operations on Access Values

Let us summarize the operations available for access values. Access types are actually similar to private types. Given types

```
TYPE Something IS ... ;
TYPE PointerToSomething IS ACCESS Something;
```

if P1 and P2 are variables of type PointerToSomething and S is a variable of type Something, the available operations are *allocation*, for example,

```
P1 := NEW Something;
```

which allocates a block of type Something, returning to P1 an access value designating the new block; *assignment*, for example,

```
P2 := P1;
```

which copies the access value from P1 to P2; *dereferencing*, for example,

```
S := P1.ALL;
```

which copies the value designated by P1 into S; and *equality/inequality*, for example,

```
IF P1 = P2 THEN ...
```

which is True if and only if P1 and P2 are equal. Be sure you understand the difference between the line above and

```
IF P1.ALL = P2.ALL THEN ...
```

which compares the designated values.

You may be aware that in some other programming languages, especially C, other operations, for example, incrementation and decrementation, are available for pointer values. These operations are *not* available in Ada.

Returning Dynamic Storage to the Pool

In Fig. 15.1 we allocated a block of storage from the pool but later caused its pointer to point elsewhere (see the last two diagrams in Fig. 15.1). Because no other access value designated it, the block became inaccessible. What happens to a inaccessible block?

In theory the Ada storage allocator could include a module that automatically keeps track of inaccessible blocks and makes them available to be reallocated. Such a module is often called a *garbage collector* because it keeps track of discarded memory blocks. Garbage collectors are provided in some languages, such as Lisp, Snobol, and Java, but are very rarely included in Ada systems. This is because Ada was designed for use in real-time systems in which program timing is very important. Garbage collection is a complex process whose time performance can be unpredictable because it depends on how badly fragmented the storage pool is. For this reason, many Ada users prefer not to have a garbage collector, and therefore compiler implementers usually do not provide it.

An Ada program that continually allocates blocks, then discards them just by making them inaccessible, could well run out of pool storage at some point in operation. Because an Ada system is unlikely to provide an automatic garbage collector, the programmer is responsible for recycling the garbage. Ada provides a standard operation, Unchecked_Deallocation, to return dynamically allocated storage to the pool. This is a generic procedure, with the specification

```
GENERIC
   TYPE Object IS LIMITED PRIVATE;
   TYPE Name IS ACCESS Object;
PROCEDURE Unchecked_Deallocation (X: IN OUT Name);
```

To use this procedure, it must be WITH-ed in a context clause and instantiated by using the access type and the designated type as actual parameters. For example,

```
PROCEDURE Dispose IS
   NEW Unchecked_Deallocation (Object => Node, Name => NodePointer);
```

creates an instance for the types used in this section, and the procedure call statement

```
Dispose (X => P);
```

will return P's designated block to the pool. Paraphrasing the Ada standard, we describe this operation as follows:

- After executing the `Dispose` call, the value of P is NULL.

- If P is already NULL, the call has no effect (in particular, it is not an error).

- If P is not NULL, then the call indicates that P.ALL is no longer needed and may be returned to the pool.

Because we can copy access values, the situation can arise in which more than one access value designates the same block of storage. This situation is known as *aliasing*. For this reason we must be careful when returning storage to the pool. Errors will result if the block returned is later referenced by another access value that still designates them; indeed, the Ada standard says specifically that the effect of doing so is unpredictable. Suppose P designates a node. If we write

```
Q := P;
Dispose(X => P);
```

then the cells designated by P are returned to the pool and the meaning of Q.ALL is unpredictable. In this situation, a variable like Q is usually called a *dangling pointer*. It is important to be sure that there is no need for a particular block before returning the storage occupied by it. Also, we must be careful when coding not to create dangling pointers; these lead to execution errors that will not always give rise to nice Ada exceptions.

Running Out of Dynamic Storage?

It is possible to exhaust the supply of cells in the pool. If this happens in Ada, the storage allocator raises the predefined exception `Storage_Error`.

Normally, we can assume that enough memory cells are available in the pool. However, in writing large programs that create sizable dynamic data structures, it is advisable to code an exception handler for `Storage_Error` in the part of the program that does the allocation. Later in the chapter we will discuss some methods for avoiding unnecessary calls to the allocator.

PROGRAM
STYLE

Programs Should Clean Up after Themselves

When a program that allocates memory dynamically ends, generally the operating system will release all the memory that program used, including the dynamic memory. However, this is not always the case: In some environments, dynamic memory is taken from a systemwide storage pool, often called the *system heap*. In such a situation, if a program does not deallocate all its dynamic memory before it ends, that memory remains inaccessible to other programs. It is therefore good programming practice for programs always to deallocate any dynamic memory they have allocated.

EXERCISES FOR SECTION 15.1

Self-Check

1. For Fig. 15.6, indicate whether each assignment statement is legal, and explain the effect of each legal one.

   a. `R.ALL.Power := "CA";`

   b. `P.ALL := R.ALL;`

   c. `P.ALL.Power := "HT";`

   d. `P := 54;`

   e. `R.ALL.Next.ALL.Volts := 0;`

   f. `P := R;`

   g. `R.ALL.Next.ALL.Next.ALL.Power := "XY";`

   h. `Q.ALL.Volts := R.ALL.Volts;`

2. The assignment statements

   ```
   R := P;
   P := Q;
   Q := R;
   ```

   are used to exchange the values of pointer variables R and Q (type `NodePointer`). What do the following assignment statements do?

   ```
   R.Power := P.Power;
   P.Power := Q.Power;
   Q.Power := R.Power;
   ```

15.2 Data Structures: Linked Lists and Their Operations

A *linked list* is a sequence of list elements or *nodes* in which each node is linked or connected to the node following it. A linked list with three nodes follows:

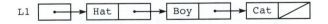

Each node in this list has two fields: The first field contains data, and the second field is a pointer to the next node. There is a pointer (Head) to the first node or *list head*. The last node always has a NULL pointer value, indicated as usual by a diagonal line.

Lists are an important data structure because they can be modified easily, regardless of how many elements may be in the list. For example, a new node containing the string `"Bye"` can be inserted between the strings `"Boy"` and `"Cat"` by changing only one pointer value (the one from `"Boy"`) and setting the pointer from the new node to point to `"Cat"`:

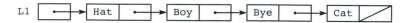

Similarly, it is easy to delete a list element. Only one pointer value has to be changed—the pointer that currently points to the element being deleted. For example, we can delete the string `"Boy"` from the previous linked list by changing the pointer from the node `"Ace"`. The node containing string `"Boy"` is effectively disconnected from the list since there is no longer a pointer to it. The new list consists of the strings `"Hat"`, `"Bye"`, `"Cat"`:

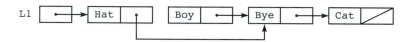

In Section 15.1 we saw how to connect three nodes with pointer fields. The data structure shown in Fig. 15.6 could be considered a list of three nodes with pointer variable R as the pointer to its head. Each node has two data fields (`Power` and `Volts`) and one pointer field (`Next`). The pointer value `NULL` is once again drawn as a diagonal line:

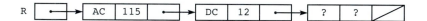

Some Linked List Operations

This section and the ones that follow will treat some common list-processing operations and describe how they are implemented using access types and variables. We will start out with a simple package specification shown in Program 15.1.

Program 15.1 Specification for Linked List Package

```
PACKAGE Linked_Lists IS
-------------------------------------------------------------------
--| Specification for simple linked lists with a single pointer
--| Author: Michael B. Feldman, The George Washington University
--| Last Modified: September 1998
-------------------------------------------------------------------

  SUBTYPE WordType IS String(1..3);

  TYPE List IS PRIVATE;

  PROCEDURE AddToFront (L: IN OUT List; Word: IN WordType);
```

```
-- Pre:  Word is defined; L may be empty
-- Post: Word is inserted at the beginning of L

PROCEDURE AddToEnd (L: IN OUT List; Word: IN WordType);
-- Pre:  Word is defined; L may be empty
-- Post: Word is appended to the end of L

FUNCTION Copy (L: IN List) RETURN List;
-- Pre:  L may be empty
-- Post: returns a complete copy of the list L

PROCEDURE Display (L: IN List);
-- Pre:  L may be empty
-- Post: displays the contents of L's Word fields, in the
--    order in which they appear in L

PRIVATE

  TYPE ListNode;
  TYPE List IS ACCESS ListNode;
  TYPE ListNode IS RECORD
    Word: WordType := "###";
    Next: List;
  END RECORD;

END Linked_Lists;
```

This package provides a PRIVATE type List:

```
SUBTYPE WordType IS String(1..3);
TYPE List IS PRIVATE;
```

The type declarations in the PRIVATE part are as follows:

```
TYPE ListNode;
TYPE List IS ACCESS ListNode;
TYPE ListNode IS RECORD
  Word: WordType := "###";
  Next: List;
END RECORD;
```

The package provides four operations:

- AddToFront, which adds a new node to the beginning of a list,

- Display, which displays all the values in the list, in the order in which the nodes occur,

- AddToEnd, which adds a new value to a list by first storing the value in a node, then connecting this node to the end of the list, and

- Copy, which returns a complete copy of the list.

Given a list L1 as follows:

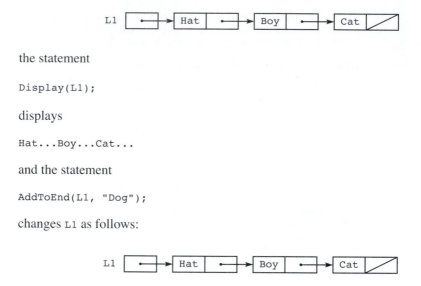

the statement

```
Display(L1);
```

displays

```
Hat...Boy...Cat...
```

and the statement

```
AddToEnd(L1, "Dog");
```

changes L1 as follows:

Program 15.2 is an illustration of these linked list operations.

Program 15.2 A Demonstration of the Linked List Package

```
WITH Ada.Text_IO; USE Ada.Text_IO;
WITH Linked_Lists; USE Linked_Lists;
PROCEDURE Test_Lists IS
-------------------------------------------------------------------
--| Illustrates the singly linked list package operations
--| Author: Michael B. Feldman, The George Washington University
--| Last Modified: September 1998
-------------------------------------------------------------------

   L1: List;
   L2: List;

BEGIN -- Test_Lists

   -- first test the traverse and copy operations for empty list

   Ada.Text_IO.Put_Line(Item => "--------");
   Display(L1);
   Ada.Text_IO.New_Line;
   L2 := Copy(L1);
   Display(L2);
   Ada.Text_IO.New_Line;
   Ada.Text_IO.Put_Line(Item => "--------");

   -- add to end of empty list

   AddToEnd(L1, "Hat");
   Display(L1);
   Ada.Text_IO.New_Line;
```

```
   L2 := Copy(L1);
   Display(L2);
   Ada.Text_IO.New_Line;
   Ada.Text_IO.Put_Line(Item => "--------");

   -- add to end of nonempty list

   AddToEnd(L1, "Boy");
   Display(L1);
   Ada.Text_IO.New_Line;
   Ada.Text_IO.Put_Line(Item => "--------");

   -- add again to end of nonempty list

   AddToEnd(L1, "Cat");
   Display(L1);
   Ada.Text_IO.New_Line;
   Ada.Text_IO.Put_Line(Item => "--------");

   -- add to front of nonempty list and copy result

   AddToFront(L1, "Top");
   Display(L1);
   Ada.Text_IO.New_Line;
   L2 := Copy(L1);
   Display(L2);
   Ada.Text_IO.New_Line;
   Ada.Text_IO.Put_Line(Item => "--------");

END Test_Lists;
```

Sample Run

```
--------


--------
Hat...
Hat...
--------
Hat...Boy...
--------
Hat...Boy...Cat...
--------
Top...Hat...Boy...Cat...
Top...Hat...Boy...Cat...
--------
```

Program 15.3 gives the body of the package. To show the bodies of the various operations as separate programs, we have used Ada *subunits*. Subunits provide a way to write the subprograms of a package as a collection of separate files. In the package body we indicate by the words IS SEPARATE that each procedure or function body is given in a separate file.

Program 15.3 Body of Linked List Package

```
WITH Ada.Text_IO;
PACKAGE BODY Linked_Lists IS
```

```
-------------------------------------------------------------------
--| Skeleton of package body for singly-linked lists;
--| the operations are provided as subunits of the package.
--| Author: Michael B. Feldman, The George Washington University
--| Last Modified: September 1998
-------------------------------------------------------------------

   PROCEDURE AddToFront (L: IN OUT List; Word: IN WordType) IS SEPARATE;

   PROCEDURE AddToEnd (L: IN OUT List; Word: IN WordType) IS SEPARATE;

   FUNCTION Copy (L: IN List) RETURN List IS SEPARATE;

   PROCEDURE Display (L: IN List) IS SEPARATE;

END Linked_Lists;
```

We are now ready to examine how the various linked list operations are implemented. For absolute clarity in this set of program illustrations we include the explicit dereferencing operations (the .ALLs). Be certain that you understand exactly how each operation works before moving to the next.

Program 15.4 shows the implementation of AddToFront. We need to indicate to the Ada compiler that this procedure is indeed the subunit referred to in the package body. The first line of the program,

```
SEPARATE (Linked_Lists)
```

accomplishes this.

Program 15.4 Implementation of AddToFront

```
SEPARATE (Linked_Lists)
PROCEDURE AddToFront (L: IN OUT List; Word: IN WordType) IS
-------------------------------------------------------------------
--| subunit of singly linked list package
--| Author: Michael B. Feldman, The George Washington University
--| Last Modified: September 1998
-------------------------------------------------------------------

  Temp: List;

BEGIN -- AddToFront

  Temp := NEW ListNode;
  Temp.ALL.Word := Word;
  Temp.ALL.Next := L;
  L := Temp;

END AddToFront;
```

This procedure is simple and straightforward, but one must be very careful, in writing operations like this, to get the order of statements exactly right:

1. Allocate a new node, returning an access value in Temp.

2. Store the word value in the new node.

3. Copy the access value in L—pointing to the first node in the list, if any—to the Next field of our new node.

4. Copy Temp's value back into L, which makes L point to the new first node.

Suppose we wrote these statements in the wrong order, for example, we copied Temp to L before copying L to Temp. This would overwrite L's old value, and we'd lose access to the entire list!

In writing linked list operations, one must always ask whether the operation behaves properly if its list parameter is empty. In this case, if L is initially empty, its NULL value is copied into the Next field of the new node, and all is well.

In the next two sections we implement the remaining three operations, first recursively and then iteratively.

SYNTAX DISPLAY

Subunit Stub

Form:

```
SEPARATE(Package Name)
PROCEDURE P(Parameters) IS ...

SEPARATE(Package Name)
FUNCTION F (Parameters) RETURN ReturnType IS ...
```

Example:

```
SEPARATE(Singly_Linked_Lists)
PROCEDURE AddToFront(L: IN OUT List; Word: IN WordType) IS ...
```

Interpretation:

A subunit is a separate file containing a procedure or function that was given as a subunit stub in an earlier package body.

Note:

The line beginning with SEPARATE does *not* end with a semicolon.

Recursive Implementations of Linked List Operations

Linked lists are sometimes called *recursive data structures* because each node contains a pointer to a node of the same type, which is a bit like a recursive procedure containing a call to the same procedure. Indeed, linked list operations can be easily implemented as recursive subprograms.

Program 15.5 gives the implementation of Display.

Program 15.5 Recursive Implementation of Linked List Display

```
SEPARATE (Linked_Lists)
PROCEDURE Display(L: IN List) IS
-----------------------------------------------------------------
--| Recursive implementation of Display
--| subunit of singly linked list package
--| Author: Michael B. Feldman, The George Washington University
```

```
--| Last Modified: September 1998
------------------------------------------------------------------------

BEGIN -- Display

  IF L = NULL THEN
    RETURN;                          -- stopping case
  ELSE
    Ada.Text_IO.Put(Item => L.ALL.Word);
    Ada.Text_IO.Put(Item => "...");

    Display(L => L.ALL.Next); -- recursion
  END IF;

END Display;
```

Note carefully that like every recursive subprogram, `Display` has a stopping case, namely, the end of the list is reached when a `NULL` link is encountered. If the link is not `NULL`, we are not yet at the end of the list, so we display the value in the node, then invoke `Display` recursively for a smaller set of the data, that is, the remainder of the list following the first node.

Program 15.6 shows the recursive implementation of `AddToEnd`.

Program 15.6 Recursive Implementation of AddToEnd

```
SEPARATE (Linked_Lists)
PROCEDURE AddToEnd (L: IN OUT List; Word: IN WordType) IS
------------------------------------------------------------------------
--| Recursive implementation of AddToEnd
--| subunit of singly linked list package
--| Author: Michael B. Feldman, The George Washington University
--| Last Modified: September 1998
------------------------------------------------------------------------

BEGIN

  IF L = NULL THEN
    L := NEW ListNode'(Word,NULL);    -- stopping case
  ELSE
    AddToEnd(L.ALL.Next, Word);       -- recursive case
  END IF;

END AddToEnd;
```

Note again that it has the required stopping case, namely, that its parameter is `NULL`. In this stopping case, the `IN OUT` parameter representing the list is simply made to point to a new list node containing the desired word. The syntax of the line

```
L := NEW ListNode'(Word,NULL);
```

warrants explanation. Here we are calling `NEW` and plugging in the fields of the newly allocated block with a record aggregate `(Word,NULL)`. The apostrophe preceding the aggregate it is required; the construct

```
ListNode'(Word,NULL)
```

is called a *qualified aggregate*.

Returning to Program 15.6, if we are not at the stopping case, that is, not yet at the end of the list, we make a recursive call of AddToEnd, which attempts to add the new value to the end of a list that is shorter by one node.

Now consider the Copy operation. You might think that Copy is a very simple, almost trivial operation. Suppose we implemented Copy with the following body:

```
SEPARATE (Linked_Lists)
FUNCTION Copy(L: IN List) RETURN List IS
BEGIN

  RETURN L;

END Copy;
```

Would a client program with the line

```
L2 := Copy(L1);
```

receive a correct result in L2? No indeed! Simply copying the access value in L1 does *not* copy the list—it copies only the pointer to the beginning of the list! The result would be that L1 and L2 would both point to the same node. This is called a *shallow copy*. Now suppose a modification is made to L1, for example, a new node is added to its end. Since L2 points to the same list, changing the list headed by L1 would also change the list headed by L2 because they are exactly the same list.

This is not what "copying" a value usually means in programming. If you copy an array A into another one B of the same type, A and B are distinct, and changing a value in A does not change B at all. To get a faithful copy of a list, we must copy the entire list, that is, the word in each node of the original must be copied to a newly allocated node of the result. L2 will be a *deep copy* of L1.

Program 15.7 shows a recursive implementation of Copy. In the stopping case the parameter is NULL, so we just return that value. If the parameter is nonnull, the result of the recursive call is a node whose word value is copied from the original and whose link is a pointer to a copy of the remainder of the original.

Program 15.7 Recursive Implementation of Copy

```
SEPARATE (Linked_Lists)
FUNCTION Copy(L: IN List) RETURN List IS
-------------------------------------------------------------------
--| Recursive implementation of Copy
--| subunit of singly linked list package
--| Author: Michael B. Feldman, The George Washington University
--| Last Modified: September 1998
-------------------------------------------------------------------

BEGIN

  IF L = NULL THEN
    RETURN NULL;                      -- stopping case
  ELSE
    RETURN                            -- recursive case
      NEW ListNode'(L.ALL.Word, Copy(L.ALL.Next));
  END IF;
```

```
END Copy;
```

If you are having any trouble understanding this, there is nothing more effective than pretending you are the copy function and drawing a picture of the input list and the result list as it is constructed at each level of recursion.

It is still possible with our package to write, for two lists L1 and L2, a statement like

```
L2 := L1;
```

This is very misleading because it implies that the list is copied, whereas in fact only the pointer to the first node is copied. Indeed, modifying a node in the list pointed to by L2 will also modify that node in the list pointed to by L1 because the two pointers point to the same list! In Section 15.5 we will present an approach using LIMITED PRIVATE types that prohibits a package user of a package from writing such a misleading copy operation.

Iterative Implementation of Linked List Operations

Recursively implemented linked list operations are clean and sometimes even elegantly simple. On the other hand, in most real applications of linked lists, iterative operations are used, so we show iterative versions in this section. The price we pay for eliminating the recursion is that the iterative versions are often more complicated, and sometimes more difficult to understand, than their recursive counterparts.

Program 15.8 shows an iterative version of AddToEnd.

Program 15.8 Iterative Implementation of AddToEnd

```
SEPARATE (Linked_Lists)
PROCEDURE AddToEnd (L: IN OUT List; Word: IN WordType) IS
-----------------------------------------------------------------------
--| Iterative implementation of AddToEnd
--| we must do a linear search to find the end of the list
--| Author: Michael B. Feldman, The George Washington University
--| Last Modified: September 1998
-----------------------------------------------------------------------

   Current: List;  -- designates each node of input list in turn

BEGIN -- AddToEnd

  IF L = NULL THEN

    L := NEW ListNode'(Word,NULL);

  ELSE

     -- initialize the loop
     Current := L;

     -- search until the end
     WHILE Current.ALL.Next /= NULL LOOP
       Current := Current.ALL.Next;
     END LOOP;
```

```
        -- we found the end; Current designates last node
        -- so attach a new node to the node Current designates
        Current.ALL.Next := NEW ListNode'(Word, NULL);

    END IF;

END AddToEnd;
```

Iterative list operations generally consist of a main WHILE loop and, in fact, are generally quite similar to many array algorithms. Recall from Chapter 7 that every WHILE loop must contain three distinct features:

- *Initialization*, which appears before the WHILE

- A *condition*, given in the WHILE statement itself, for continuing the loop

- *Incrementation*, in which some variable is modified to keep the loop moving forward toward completion

These three features are present in Program 15.8: A pointer Current, declared to serve as the loop variable, is initialized by

```
Current := L;
```

which sets Current to point to the beginning of the list. The test to continue the loop is

```
WHILE Current.ALL.Next /= NULL LOOP
```

because, after the loop is finished, we need Current not to be null but rather to be pointing to the last node of the list. This is so that we can connect the new node to the last node's Next field. This is accomplished by the statement

```
Current.ALL.Link := NEW ListNode'(Word, NULL);
```

Finally, the incrementation step is

```
Current := Current.ALL.Next;
```

in which Current is dereferenced and set to the Next value in the designated node.

Program 15.8 contains a special case to see whether the head pointer L itself needs to be modified; this will happen only if L is initially empty. Assuming that L is non-empty, we have another WHILE loop, with Current initialized as in Display to the start of the list. In this case the loop body consists only of the incrementation step because we are simply searching to find the end of the list.

To be certain you understand AddToEnd, practice tracing its execution. Draw a pointer variable Current and move it down the list during each loop iteration. Start with the following list and add "Art" to its end:

EXERCISES FOR SECTION 15.2

Programming

1. Write procedure `Display` as an iterative procedure.

2. Write an iterative version of the function `Copy`.

3. Write a recursive function that returns the length of a list, that is, the number of nodes in the list.

4. Write a recursive function that finds the length of a list.

15.3 Data Structures: Linked Lists with Head and Tail Pointers

The operations `AddToFront` and `AddToEnd` are two of the most common and important list operations. We have seen that `AddToFront` is very simple: A node is allocated and a few values are copied. On the other hand, we saw in the previous section that `AddToEnd` must search the entire list in order to find the last node.

We can make `AddToEnd` independent of the list length by making a very simple change to our data structures: Keep track of the last node by building in a pointer to it. All we need to do is change the declarations in the PRIVATE part to

```
TYPE ListNode;
TYPE ListPtr IS ACCESS ListNode;
TYPE ListNode IS RECORD
  Word: WordType := "###";
  Next: ListPtr;
END RECORD;

TYPE List IS
  Head: ListPtr;
  Tail: ListPtr;
END RECORD;
```

This introduces a new type `ListPtr`, which serves the role of our former `List` type, and also changes our `List` type from a simple pointer into a *header record* containing two pointers, one to the head of the list and one to the tail. This gives a list like the following:

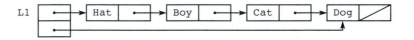

The various operations must be modified to reflect the changed data structures. The key change is to AddToEnd, which is shown as Program 15.9. Note that the WHILE loop or recursive call is gone; no search is necessary because we know immediately where the last node is. This is a very good example of how a small change to a data structure can result in a large change in performance. Here we have used a bit more space for the extra pointer but have eliminated the list search.

Program 15.9 AddToEnd with Head and Tail Pointers

```
SEPARATE (Linked_Lists)
PROCEDURE AddToEnd (L: IN OUT List; Word: IN WordType) IS
-----------------------------------------------------------------------
--| AddToEnd using head and tail pointers
--| Author: Michael B. Feldman, The George Washington University
--| Last Modified: September 1998
-----------------------------------------------------------------------

BEGIN -- AddToEnd

  IF L.Head = NULL THEN

    L.Head := NEW ListNode'(Word,NULL);
    L.Tail := L.Head;

  ELSE -- L.Tail points to a node; new node goes after it

    L.Tail.ALL.Next := NEW ListNode'(Word,NULL);
    L.Tail := L.Tail.ALL.Next;

  END IF;

END AddToEnd;
```

EXERCISES FOR SECTION 15.3

Programming

1. Modify the list package of Section 15.3 to implement a list as a record containing head and tail pointers.

15.4 Problem Solving: Ordered Insertions in Linked Lists

A linked list is often used as an implementation for an ordered sequence of elements which appear in order according to some key. This can be thought of as a linked list analogy to a sorted array. It is therefore important to understand how to insert a new value into a linked list that is already sorted.

The insertion process has four distinct cases:

1. An inserted node is the first one to be added to an empty list.

2. The inserted node's key is less than those of all others in the list; therefore the node goes at the beginning of a nonempty list.

3. The key is greater than all the others; therefore the node goes at the end of the list.

4. The key lies between two others; therefore the node goes in the middle of the list somewhere.

For the list representation we have been using, these four cases are illustrated in Fig. 15.7. A iterative procedure `InsertInOrder` is shown as Program 15.10. We leave it to you to develop a recursive version, which you will find to be a much simpler procedure.

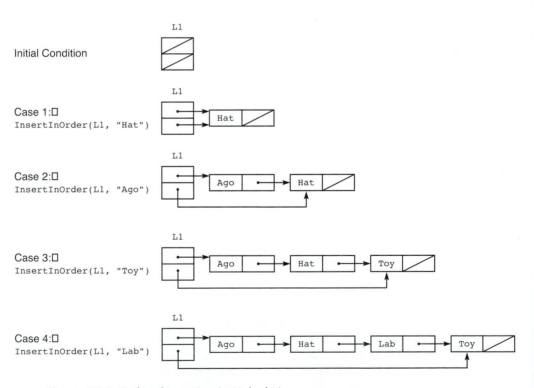

Figure 15.7 Ordered Insertion in Linked List

Program 15.10 Ordered Linked List Insertion

```
SEPARATE (Linked_Lists)
PROCEDURE InsertInOrder (L: IN OUT List; Word: IN WordType) IS
-------------------------------------------------------------------
--| Iterative implementation of InsertInOrder;
--| if Word already in list, second occurrence must follow first one
--| Author: Michael B. Feldman, The George Washington University
--| Last Modified: September 1998
-------------------------------------------------------------------

   Current:  ListPtr;  -- designates each node of input list in turn
   Previous: ListPtr;  -- trailer - one node behind Current
   Temp:     ListPtr;  -- holds pointer to newly allocated node

BEGIN -- InsertInOrder

  IF L.Head = NULL THEN               -- case (1)
    AddToFront (L, Word);

  ELSIF Word < L.Head.ALL.Word THEN   -- case (2)
    AddToFront (L, Word);

  ELSIF Word >= L.Tail.ALL.Word THEN  -- case (3)
    AddToEnd (L, Word);

  ELSE                                -- case (4)

    -- at this point, we know L not empty and
    -- first word <= Word < last word

    Temp     := NEW ListNode'(Word, NULL);
    Previous := L.Head;              -- first node
    Current  := Previous.ALL.Next;  -- second node, if any

    WHILE Word >= Current.ALL.Word LOOP

      Previous := Current;
      Current  := Current.ALL.Next;

    END LOOP;
    -- assert: Previous.ALL.Word <= Word < Current.ALL.Word

    -- insert new node between Previous and Current
    Temp.ALL.Next := Current;
    Previous.ALL.Next := Temp;

  END IF;

END InsertInOrder;
```

Notice how the each of the four cases is handled; only case 4 requires a search through the list. Note also that two pointers are used to search the list because the new node is inserted between two others, in this case those designated by `Previous` and `Current`, respectively. Make sure you understand exactly how the procedure operates by tracing its actions on the example cases shown in the figure. This succession of calls to `InsertInOrder` builds and maintains a sorted list.

EXERCISES FOR SECTION 15.4

Programming

1. Write a recursive version of `InsertInOrder`.

15.5 System Structures: A Generic Version of the Linked List Package

We now build a generic version of our list package so that the element type is not restricted to three-character strings. The specification for `Lists_Generic` is given as Program 15.11.

Program 15.11 Generic Linked List Package

```
GENERIC
  TYPE ElementType IS PRIVATE;
  WITH PROCEDURE DisplayElement (Item: IN ElementType);
PACKAGE Lists_Generic IS
-----------------------------------------------------------------------
--| Specification for generic singly-linked lists
--| Author: Michael B. Feldman, The George Washington University
--| Last Modified: September 1998
-----------------------------------------------------------------------

  TYPE List IS LIMITED PRIVATE;

  ListEmpty: EXCEPTION;

  PROCEDURE MakeEmpty (L : IN OUT List);
  -- Pre:    L is defined
  -- Post:   L is empty

  FUNCTION IsEmpty (L : IN List) RETURN Boolean;
  -- Pre:    L is defined
  -- Post:   returns True if L is empty, False otherwise

  PROCEDURE AddToFront (L: IN OUT List; Element: IN ElementType);
  -- Pre:  Element is defined; L may be empty
  -- Post: Element is inserted at the beginning of L

  FUNCTION RetrieveFront (L: IN List) RETURN ElementType;
  -- Pre:    L is defined; L may be empty
  -- Post:   returns a complete copy of the list L
  -- Raises: ListEmpty if the list is empty before the retrieval

  PROCEDURE RemoveFront (L: IN OUT List);
  -- Pre:    L is defined; L may be empty
  -- Post:   The first node of L is removed
  -- Raises: ListEmpty if the list is empty before the removal
```

```
PROCEDURE AddToEnd (L: IN OUT List; Element: IN ElementType);
-- Pre:  Element is defined; L may be empty
-- Post: Element is appended to the end of L

PROCEDURE Copy (Target: OUT List; Source: IN List);
-- Pre:  Source may be empty
-- Post: Returns a complete copy of Source in Target

PROCEDURE Display (L: IN List);
-- Pre:  L may be empty
-- Post: displays the contents of L's Element fields, in the
--   order in which they appear in L

PRIVATE

   TYPE ListNode;
   TYPE ListPtr IS ACCESS ListNode;
   TYPE ListNode IS RECORD
     Element: ElementType;
     Next: ListPtr;
   END RECORD;

   TYPE List IS RECORD
     Head: ListPtr;
     Tail: ListPtr;
   END RECORD;

END Lists_Generic;
```

The generic parameters are `ElementType`, the element to be contained in each list node, and `DisplayElement`. The latter parameter is needed because the `Display` operation needs to know exactly how to display each element of the list. It cannot simply call `Ada.Text_IO.Put` as in the nongeneric version because the element type is not necessarily a string. For example, if we had

```
SUBTYPE NameType IS String (1..20);
```

we could instantiate the package as

```
PACKAGE NameLists IS
   NEW Lists_Generic
     (ElementType => NameType, DisplayElement => Ada.Text_IO.Put);
```

Of course, this would display all the names on the list on a single line. To tailor the `DisplayElement` operation better, we could write, in our client program,

```
PROCEDURE DisplayName (Item: NameType) IS
BEGIN
  Ada.Text_IO.Put (Item => Item);
  Ada.Text_IO.New_Line;
END DisplayName;
```

and instantiate the list package as

```
PACKAGE NameLists IS
   NEW Lists_Generic
     (ElementType => NameType, DisplayElement => DisplayName);
```

Similarly, if `ElementType` were some record type, we would need only to provide a procedure to display one record and then instantiate the list package with that procedure supplied as the parameter.

Now look at the type declaration for the list type:

```
TYPE List IS LIMITED PRIVATE;
```

We have changed the list from `PRIVATE` to `LIMITED PRIVATE`. This is because while a `PRIVATE` type allows assignment and equality test, a `LIMITED PRIVATE` type has no predefined operations at all, prohibiting even these two. As was mentioned in Section 15.3, it is desirable to disallow these operations for linked lists because they are misleading, copying and comparing only the header pointers instead of the list itself.

Operations in the Generic Linked List Package

Declaring the list type as `LIMITED PRIVATE` necessitates changing the list `Copy` operation from a function to a procedure:

```
PROCEDURE Copy (Target: OUT List; Source: IN List);
```

because writing

```
L2 := Copy (L1);
```

is no longer allowed (the `:=` is prohibited). Copying is done now by writing

```
Copy (Target => L2, Source => L1);
```

that is, as a procedure call.

To give us more flexibility in using the package, we have added four additional operations:

```
PROCEDURE MakeEmpty (L : IN OUT List);
FUNCTION IsEmpty (L : IN List) RETURN Boolean;
FUNCTION RetrieveFront (L: IN List) RETURN ElementType;
PROCEDURE RemoveFront (L: IN OUT List);
```

The behavior of these operations is obvious from the postconditions. `RemoveFront` results in a list like the following:

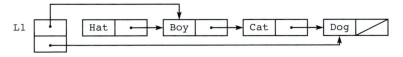

while `MakeEmpty` produces a list like the following:

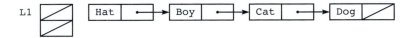

We show `MakeEmpty` and `RemoveFront` as Programs 15.12 and 15.13, respectively. Note that these operations, as written, do not use `Unchecked_Deallocation` to return the discarded nodes to the storage pool. Therefore they remain allocated but completely inaccessible. Over a long program execution, if these operations were done repeatedly, the storage pool would be exhausted and `Storage_Error` would be raised. We leave it as an exercise to correct this design flaw and to complete the other operations in the package.

Program 15.12 Procedure MakeEmpty

```
SEPARATE (Lists_Generic)
PROCEDURE MakeEmpty (L : IN OUT List) IS
----------------------------------------------------------------------
--| MakeEmpty - subunit of Lists_Generic
--| Author: Michael B. Feldman, The George Washington University
--| Last Modified: September 1998
----------------------------------------------------------------------
BEGIN
  L.Head := NULL;
  L.Tail := NULL;
END MakeEmpty;
```

Program 15.13 Procedure RemoveFront

```
SEPARATE (Lists_Generic)
PROCEDURE RemoveFront (L: IN OUT List) IS
----------------------------------------------------------------------
--| RemoveFront; subunit of Lists_Generic
--| Author: Michael B. Feldman, The George Washington University
--| Last Modified: September 1998
----------------------------------------------------------------------

  Temp: ListPtr;

BEGIN -- RemoveFront

  IF L.Head = NULL THEN

    RAISE ListEmpty;

  ELSE -- L.Head points to a node; remove it

    Temp := L.Head;
    L.Head := L.Head.ALL.Next;   -- jump around first node
    Dispose (X => Temp);

  END IF;

END RemoveFront;
```

EXERCISES FOR SECTION 15.5

Programming

1. Complete the generic linked list package.

15.6 Problem Solving: Stacks and Queues

A *stack* is a data structure in which only the top element can be accessed. To illustrate, the plates stored in the spring-loaded device in a buffet line perform like a stack. A customer always takes the top plate; when a plate is removed, the plate beneath it moves to the top. The last plate placed on the stack is the first removed; a stack is therefore a *last-in, first-out (LIFO) structure*.

A *queue* is a data structure that models a real-life queue in a bank or other service situation. New arrivals get on at the end of the queue; customers are removed from the front of the queue as they are served. The earliest arrival in a queue is the first to be served, so the queue is a *first-in, first out (FIFO) structure*.

Implementing Stacks Using Linked Lists

The following diagram shows a stack of three characters. The letter C, the character at the top of the stack, is the only one we can access. We must remove C from the stack to access the symbol +. Removing a value from a stack is called *popping the stack,* and storing a data item in a stack is called *pushing* it onto the stack.

We can implement a stack as a linked list in which all insertions and deletions are performed at the list head. A list representation of the stack containing C, +, and 2 is as follows:

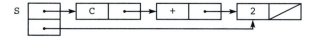

Next we draw the stack after we push the symbol * onto it:

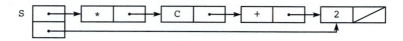

If we pop this stack, we restore the stack to its earlier state.

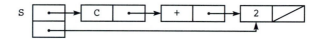

Implementing a Generic Stack ADT

Program 15.14 gives a specification for a generic stack package.

Program 15.14 Generic Stack Package

```
WITH Lists_Generic;
GENERIC
  TYPE StackElement IS PRIVATE;
PACKAGE Stacks_Generic IS
-------------------------------------------------------------------
--| Generic package for LIFO stacks
--| Author: Michael B. Feldman, The George Washington University
--| Last Modified: September 1998
-------------------------------------------------------------------

  -- type definition

  TYPE Stack IS LIMITED PRIVATE;

  -- exported exceptions

  StackEmpty : EXCEPTION;

  -- constructors

  PROCEDURE MakeEmpty (S : IN OUT Stack);
  -- Pre:    S is defined
  -- Post:   S is empty

  PROCEDURE Push (S : IN OUT Stack; E : IN StackElement);
  -- Pre:    S and E are defined
  -- Post:   S is returned with E as the top StackElement

  PROCEDURE Pop (S : IN OUT Stack);
  -- Pre:    S is defined
  -- Post:   S is returned with the top StackElement discarded
  -- Raises: StackEmpty if S contains no StackElements

  -- selector

  FUNCTION Top (S : IN Stack) RETURN StackElement;
```

```
-- Pre:    S is defined
-- Post:   The top StackElement of S is returned
-- Raises: StackEmpty if S contains no StackElements

-- inquiry operations

FUNCTION IsEmpty (S : IN Stack) RETURN Boolean;
-- Pre:    S is defined
-- Post:   returns True if S is empty, False otherwise

PRIVATE

  PROCEDURE Dummy (Item: StackElement);

  PACKAGE Lists IS
    NEW Lists_Generic(ElementType => StackElement,
                      DisplayElement => Dummy);

  TYPE Stack IS RECORD
    Store : Lists.List;
  END RECORD;

END Stacks_Generic;
```

This package takes a single generic parameter, StackElement, and represents a stack as a LIMITED PRIVATE type, implemented as a record containing a linked list as its only field. The package provides an exception, StackEmpty, which is raised if a client program attempts to pop, or retrieve the top element of, an empty stack. The operations are easily understood from the postconditions.

The PRIVATE section of Program 15.14 warrants explanation. Because Lists_Generic requires two generic parameters, we must supply these when we instantiate. The element parameter in the instantiation of Lists_Generic is obvious; the second parameter is a procedure Dummy whose specification is given in the PRIVATE section. We are not interested in displaying the full contents of the stack, so the stack package contains no call to the linked list Display procedure. We therefore provide a do-nothing procedure, just to satisfy the requirements of the list package. The body of Dummy, which is never called but must be given in the body of Stacks_Generic, is just

```
PROCEDURE Dummy (Item: StackElement) IS
BEGIN
  NULL;
END Dummy;
```

As an exercise, you can complete the stack package. Doing so is easy because you have the list package already available. Push will contain a call to AddToFront, Pop will contain a call to RemoveFront, and Top will contain a call to RetrieveFront.

Stack Applications

In Section 14.2 we showed how compilers use stacks to store procedure and function parameters. Compilers also use stacks for data storage while translating expressions. In general, we use stacks in a program to remember a sequence of data objects or actions in the reverse order from that in which they were encountered. Stacks are often an alternative to recursion. To show this, consider a nonrecursive version of `StringReverse`, which was given as a recursive function in Program 14.8. The algorithm for this function is as follows:

Algorithm for Nonrecursive String Reverse

1. Create an empty stack.

2. Push each data character in the input string onto the stack.

3. Retrieve each character from the stack, copy it into the output string, then pop the stack.

Step 2 Refinement

2.1 FOR each character in the input string LOOP

2.2   Push the character onto the stack

END LOOP;

Step 3 Refinement

3.1 FOR each character in the stack LOOP

3.2   Copy the character into the output string

3.3   Pop the stack

END LOOP;

Try carrying out this algorithm by hand. Draw a picture of the stack, then push into it the letters of the word `house`. Popping the characters into the output string will produce the string `esuoh`. Make sure you understand the algorithm. Program 15.15 shows a function implementing this algorithm.

Program 15.15 A Nonrecursive String Reverse Function

```
WITH Stacks_Generic;
FUNCTION StringReverse(S: String) RETURN String IS
-------------------------------------------------------------------
--| Returns the reverse of a string, using a stack instead of recursion
--| Author: Michael B. Feldman, The George Washington University
--| Last Modified: September 1998
-------------------------------------------------------------------

  PACKAGE Char_Stacks IS
    NEW Stacks_Generic(StackElement => Character);
  USE Char_Stacks;

  OneStack: Stack;
  Result: String (S'Range);

BEGIN -- StringReverse

  IF S'Length <= 1 THEN
    RETURN S;
  END IF;
```

```
   MakeEmpty (OneStack);

   FOR Count IN S'Range LOOP
     Push (OneStack, S(Count));
   END LOOP;

   FOR Count IN Result'Range LOOP
     Result (Count) := Top (OneStack);
     Pop (OneStack);
   END LOOP;

   RETURN Result;

END StringReverse;
```

In this function, which might be included in a program like `Palindrome` (Program 14.8), `Stacks_Generic` is instantiated for the type `Character`, then the algorithm is translated straightforwardly into Ada.

CASE STUDY

CHECKING FOR BALANCED PARENTHESES

Another application of a stack is to determine whether the parentheses in an expression are balanced. For example, the expression

```
(a + b * (c / (d - e))) + (d / e)
1         2   3         321   1       1
```

has balanced parentheses. We can solve this problem without using a stack by ignoring all characters except the symbols (and). We start a counter at 1 and add 1 for each open parenthesis that follows another open parenthesis and subtract 1 for each closed parenthesis that follows another closed parenthesis. Because we are ignoring all other symbols, the parentheses that are being considered do not have to be consecutive characters. If the expression is balanced, the final count will be 1, and it will always be positive.

This task becomes more difficult if we expand our notion of parentheses to include braces and brackets. For example, the expression

```
(a + b * {c / [d - e]}) + (d / e)
```

is balanced, but the expression

```
(a + b * {c / [d - e}) + (d / e)
```

is not because the subexpression [d - e} is incorrect.

Problem Specification

The set of open parenthesis symbols is {, [, and (. An expression is balanced if each subexpression that starts with the symbol { ends with the symbol }; the same is true for the symbol pairs [ ] and ( ). In other words, the unmatched open parenthesis nearest to each closed parenthesis must have the correct shape (e.g., if } is the closed parenthesis in question, the symbol { must be the nearest unmatched open parenthesis).

Analysis

Solving this problem without stacks would be fairly difficult, but with stacks it becomes easy. First, scan the expression from left to right, ignoring all characters except for parenthesis symbols (including braces and brackets). Push each open parenthesis symbol onto a stack of characters. For a closed parenthesis symbol, pop an open parenthesis from the stack and see whether it matches the closed parenthesis. If the symbols don't match or the stack is empty, there is an error in the expression. If they do match, continue the scan.

Data Requirements

Problem Input

expression to be checked for balanced parentheses (`Expression: String`)

Problem Output

the function result indicating whether the parentheses in `Expression` are balanced

Program Variables

stack of open parentheses (`ParenStack: Stack`)
next character in input expression (`NextChar : Character`)
open parenthesis at top of stack (`OpenParen : Character`)
index to `Expression` (`Index : Positive`)
program flag (`Balanced   : Boolean`)

Algorithm

1   Create an empty stack of characters.

2.   Assume that the expression is balanced (`Balanced` is `True`).

3.   `WHILE` we are still in the expression and the expression is balanced `LOOP`

    4.   Get the next character in the expression.

    5.   `IF` the next character is an open parenthesis `THEN`

        6.   Push it onto the stack.

    `ELSIF` the next character is a closed parenthesis `THEN`

        7.   Pop the top of the stack.

    `END IF;`

    8.   `IF` stack was empty or its top was incorrect `THEN`

        9.   Set `Balanced` to `False`.

    `END IF;`

`END LOOP;`

10.   The expression is balanced if `Balanced` is `True` and the stack is empty.

The IF statement in step 5 tests each character in the expression, ignoring all characters except for open and closed parenthesis symbols. If the next character is an open parenthesis symbol, it is pushed onto the stack. If the next character is a closed parenthesis symbol, the nearest unmatched open parenthesis is retrieved (by popping the stack) and compared to the closed parenthesis (steps 7 and 8). If the next character is not an open or closed parenthesis symbol, it is ignored.

Implementation

Program 15.16 shows a function that determines whether its input parameter (an expression) is balanced.

Program 15.16 Function IsBalanced

```
WITH Stacks_Generic;
FUNCTION IsBalanced (Expression: String) RETURN Boolean IS
-----------------------------------------------------------------------
--| Determines whether a string is balanced with respect to
--| parentheses () [] and {}
--| Author: Michael B. Feldman, The George Washington University
--| Last Modified: September 1998
-----------------------------------------------------------------------

   PACKAGE Char_Stacks IS NEW Stacks_Generic(StackElement => Character);
   USE Char_Stacks;

   ParenStack: Stack;          -- stack of open parentheses
   NextChar   : Character;     -- next character in input expression
   OpenParen : Character;      -- open parenthesis at top of stack
   Index     : Positive;       -- index to Expression
   Balanced  : Boolean;        -- program flag

BEGIN -- IsBalanced

   MakeEmpty (ParenStack);
   Balanced := True;
   Index := Expression'First;

   WHILE Index <= Expression'Last AND THEN Balanced LOOP

     NextChar := Expression (Index);
     CASE NextChar IS

       WHEN '(' | '[' | '{' =>
         Push (ParenStack, NextChar);       -- Push open parenthesis

       WHEN ')' | ']' | '}' =>
         IF IsEmpty (ParenStack) THEN
           Balanced := False;
         ELSE
           OpenParen := Top (ParenStack); -- Get nearest open paren
           Pop (ParenStack);
           CASE NextChar IS                 -- Do open and close match?
             WHEN ')' =>
               Balanced := OpenParen = '(';
             WHEN ']' =>
               Balanced := OpenParen = '[';
             WHEN '}' =>
               Balanced := OpenParen = '{';
```

```
            WHEN OTHERS =>
                NULL;
            END CASE;
          END IF;

      WHEN OTHERS =>
          NULL;

   END CASE;
      Index := Index + 1;                    -- move on to next character
   END LOOP;

   RETURN Balanced AND IsEmpty (ParenStack);

END IsBalanced;
```

The IF statement from step 5 of the algorithm is in fact written as a CASE statement, which more easily tests for open and closed parentheses. Each open parenthesis is pushed onto stack ParenStack. For each closed parenthesis, Top retrieves the nearest unmatched open parenthesis from the stack, and Pop pops the stack. If the stack is empty, Balance is set to False, causing the WHILE loop exit. Otherwise, the CASE statement sets Balanced to indicate whether the character popped matches the current closed parenthesis symbol. After loop exit occurs, the function result is returned. It is True only when the expression is balanced and the stack is empty.

Implementing Queues as Linked Lists

A queue can be used to model any kind of queueing situation, such as a line of customers waiting at a checkout counter or a stream of jobs waiting to be printed by a printer. For example, here is a linked list representing a queue of three students waiting to speak to their advisor, who insists on strict FIFO order in student conferences:

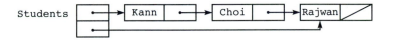

The name of the student who has been waiting the longest is Kann (pointed to by the head pointer); the name of the most recent arrival is Rajwan (pointed to by the tail pointer). Kann will be the first one to leave the queue when the advisor becomes available, and the head pointer will be reset to point to Choi. Any new students will be added to the end of the queue after Rajwan. Here is the queue after Kann leaves it:

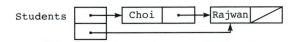

Here is the queue after Perez arrives:

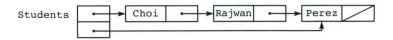

Program 15.17 gives the specification for a generic queue package. It is similar to the stack package in its structure.

Program 15.17 Generic Queue Package

```
WITH Lists_Generic;
GENERIC

  TYPE QueueElement IS PRIVATE;

PACKAGE Queues_Generic IS
-----------------------------------------------------------------------
--| Generic package for FIFO queues
--| Author: Michael B. Feldman, The George Washington University
--| Last Modified: September 1998
-----------------------------------------------------------------------

  -- type definition

  TYPE Queue IS LIMITED PRIVATE;

  -- exported exceptions

  QueueEmpty : EXCEPTION;

  -- constructors

  PROCEDURE MakeEmpty (Q : IN OUT Queue);
  -- Pre:    Q is defined
  -- Post:   Q is empty

  PROCEDURE Enqueue (Q : IN OUT Queue; E : IN QueueElement);
  -- Pre:    Q and E are defined
  -- Post:   Q is returned with E as the top QueueElement

  PROCEDURE Dequeue (Q : IN OUT Queue);
  -- Pre:    Q is defined
  -- Post:   Q is returned with the top QueueElement discarded
  -- Raises: QueueEmpty if Q contains no QueueElements

  -- selector

  FUNCTION First (Q : IN Queue) RETURN QueueElement;
  -- Pre:    Q is defined
  -- Post:   The first QueueElement of Q is returned
  -- Raises: QueueEmpty if Q contains no QueueElements

  -- inquiry operations

  FUNCTION IsEmpty (Q : IN Queue) RETURN Boolean;
  -- Pre:    Q is defined
```

```
-- Post:    returns True if Q is empty, False otherwise
PRIVATE

  PROCEDURE Dummy (Item: QueueElement);

  PACKAGE Lists IS
    NEW Lists_Generic(ElementType => QueueElement,
                      DisplayElement => Dummy);

  TYPE Queue IS RECORD
    Store : Lists.List;
  END RECORD;

END Queues_Generic;
```

We leave it as an exercise to complete the package body for this package. As in the stack package, the queue operations are easily written in terms of the list ones. Enqueue will call AddToEnd, Dequeue will call RemoveFront, and so on.

EXERCISES FOR SECTION 15.6

Programming

1.   Complete the generic stack package given in this section.

2.   Complete the generic queue package given in this section.

15.7 Tricks of the Trade: Debugging Programs with Linked Lists

The three most common errors in writing programs using dyamic structures are dereferencing a null pointer, infinite loops and infinite recursion, and off-by-one problems.

Dereferencing a Null Pointer

When processing linked data structures, make sure that the pointer to the next node is not NULL. If pointer P has the value NULL, the record P.ALL is undefined. Therefore, the condition

```
(P.ALL.ID /= 9999) AND (P /= NULL)
```

will cause Constraint_Error to be raised when P is NULL. You can prevent this by writing the expression using the short-circuit operator AND THEN:

```
(P /= NULL) AND THEN (P.ALL.ID /= 9999)
```

This causes the left side to be evaluated first and evaluates the right side only if the left side is `True`.

Infinite Loops and Infinite Recursion

A linked list program can get into an infinite loop in two ways. First, if you write a `WHILE` loop and forget to write an incrementation step, the loop has no way to progress toward completion. In this case the program will either appear to "hang" or possibly will display the same value over and over.

Second, your program could get stuck in an infinite loop or infinite recursion while creating a dynamic data structure. If this happens, it is quite possible that the program will keep allocating new blocks and consume all the memory cells in the storage pool. If this happens, `Storage_Error` is raised. For both of these reasons, be especially careful in writing the `WHILE` condition and the loop incrementation statement. Be certain the loop is always initialized properly and incremented each time through. Also be careful that your recursive programs will eventually reach a stopping case.

Off-by-One Errors

Off-by-one errors are common in linked list programs. In traversing a list with K elements, for example, sometimes only the first $K - 1$ elements or the last $K - 1$ are displayed. These logic errors will not raise exceptions but will give incorrect results. They are usually caused by careless loop initialization or termination conditions. Note that a program that tries to go one step too far will generally "fall off the end of the list," causing `Constraint_Error` to be raised upon dereferencing a null pointer.

Some debugging tools allow you to display the value of a pointer variable, but such a value cannot normally be displayed with `Ada.Text_IO` procedures. It is therefore difficult to debug programs that manipulate pointers. You will have to trace the execution of such a program by printing an information field that uniquely identifies the list element being processed instead of the pointer value itself. In doing a trace, drawing a picture of the list as it is built and manipulated is enormously helpful.

In writing driver programs, it is often helpful to create a sample linked structure using the technique shown in Section 15.1. The data and pointer fields of the structure can be defined using assignment statements.

CHAPTER REVIEW

Access types and dynamic data structures are used to create linked lists, which are an extremely important data structure in computing. Linked lists are found in nearly every kind of computer application: Spreadsheet processing, operating system modules, compilers, and many others commonly employ linked lists and other dynamic data structures.

New Ada Constructs in Chapter 15

The new Ada constructs introduced in this chapter are described in Table 15.1.

Table 15.1   Summary of New Ada Constructs

Statement	Effect
```TYPE NodePointer IS ACCESS ListNode;```	Declares an access (pointer) type whose variables can point to values of type `ListNode`
```P: NodePointer; Q: NodePointer;```	and two variables of the access type
```PROCEDURE Dispose IS NEW Unchecked_Deallocation (Object => ListNode, Name => NodePointer);```	Instantiates a predefined generic procedure to give an operation to return tree nodes to the storage pool
```P := NEW ListNode;```	Allocates a node and stores a pointer to it in `P`
```Q := P;```	Copies one pointer value to another
```Q.ALL := P.ALL;```	Copies one record's contents to the other

Review Questions for Chapter 15

1. Differentiate between dynamic and nondynamic data structures.

2. Define a simple linked list. Indicate how the pointers are used to establish a link between nodes. Also indicate any other variables that would be needed to reference the linked list.

3. Write a procedure that links a node into an existing list. Parameters are a pointer to the head of the linked list and a pointer to the node to be inserted. Assume that dummy sentinel records exist at the beginning and end of the linked list and there are no duplicate records.

   Given the following type definitions, insert the new element, preserving ID order:

   ```
   TYPE Node;
   TYPE Ptr IS ACCESS Node;
   TYPE Node IS RECORD
      ID : INTEGER;
      Name : String(1..10);
      GPA : NonNegFloat;
      Link : PTR
   END RECORD;
   ```

4. Write an algorithm to remove a node (identified by `TargetID`) from an ordered list that does not contain a dummy record at the beginning.

5. Write the necessary procedures to duplicate all elements in one linked list that have a Grade Point Average (GPA) of 3.5 or above in another linked list. The original list is ordered by ID number; the new list should be ordered by GPA. Do not remove nodes from the existing list. Assume that the list nodes are type `Node` as described in question 3. Parameters will be a pointer to the head of the existing list and to the head of the new linked list (`GPAHead`).

6. Declare a node for a two-way, or doubly linked, list, and indicate how a traversal would be made in reverse order (from the last list element to the list head). Include any variables or fields that are necessary.

Programming Projects

1. Write a procedure that attaches one list to the end of another. Note that this procedure destroys the original lists.

2. Write a function that returns the concatenation of two lists `L1` and `L2`, that is, a list containing copies of all the nodes of `L1` followed by copies of all the nodes of `L2`. Note that this function does *not* destroy either `L1` or `L2`.

3. Write a procedure that deletes from an ordered list `L` the *first* node containing a given word.

4. Write a procedure that deletes from an ordered list `L` the *last* node containing a given word.

5. Write a procedure that deletes from an ordered list `L` *all* nodes containing a given word.

6. Write a function that takes two ordered lists as inputs, then returns a list in which the two input lists are merged. That is, if `L1` contains `"ABC"`, `"HIJ"`, and `"PQR"` and `L2` contains `"DEF"`, `"HIJ"`, `"MNO"`, and `"STU"`, the result list contains `"ABC"`, `"DEF"`, `" HIJ"`, `"HIJ"`, `"MNO"`, `"PQR"`, and `"STU"`.

7. Complete the generic package given in Section 15.5, writing the body and the remaining operations. Also correct the design flaw in `MakeEmpty` and `Remove-Front`, so that the latter returns the discarded node to the storage pool and the former returns *all* nodes in the list to the storage pool. (*Hint:* `MakeEmpty` must loop through the list, returning each node one at a time.)

8. Sometimes a list node is declared to have *two* pointers, one to the next node and one to the previous node. Develop a package for such doubly linked lists, and write the operations so that advantage is taken of the fact that each node points to its predecessor as well as its successor. Specifically, how does having the extra pointers simplify operations like ordered insertion and deletion?

9. Modify your employee data base system from Section 11.5 so that the data base is represented as an instance of the generic list package from Section 15.5.

CHAPTER 16

Programming with Objects: Tagged Record Types

The variant records that we studied in Chapter 13 provide much expressive power to create complex types with several different parts. However, they have an important limitation: A variant record must be fully defined and compiled, and CASE statements are used to control processing its various parts.

In this chapter we look at *tagged types*, a generalization of variant records that allows new variants to be added without recompiling the packages in which the original variants are declared. Tagged types implement *type extension*, a kind of *inheritance*. Inheritance is an important concept used in many object-oriented programs.

We also discuss *general access types*, a generalization of the access types in Chapter 15. General access types allow the programmer to create a pointer to a statically declared variable, not just a dynamically allocated block. The combination of general access types and tagged types gives a very interesting and powerful style of object-oriented programming.

16.1 System Structures: Object-Oriented Programming

Object-oriented programming (OOP) is a programming methodology that relies on a number of language features. These are:

- *Encapsulation*, provided very well by Ada's packages and especially by private types

- *Genericity*, provided by Ada's generics capability

- *Inheritance,* through which a new type takes on some or all of the properties of an existing one. This is provided by Ada's derived types, and extended considerably in tagged types, both of which are subjects of this chapter.

- *Polymorphism,* partially supported by Ada's procedure and function overloading, and extended significantly through the concept of *dynamic dispatching*

In OOP, an object has two important characteristics:

1. It has *state,* that is, it has a value that may change over time.

2. It has *behavior,* that is, it has a set of operations that act on it, and these operations are the only ones that can change its state (value).

In working with this book you have been using OOP concepts since the earliest chapters. You have been working with Ada variables; *object* is just a more modern name for variable. As you know, each variable has a type and can take on only values from that type's set of values.

Also, each type has a set of operations associated with it. The predefined types, such as `Integer` or `Ada.Calendar.Time`, all have predefined operations, and *only* the given operations are valid for values of the given type. Throughout the book we have emphasized Ada compilers' concern for validity of operations: they give compilation errors wherever they can, and compile run-time checks into the program wherever they cannot.

Further, you have used packages right along, starting with the input/output packages and other predefined packages such as `Ada.Calendar` and `Ada.Numerics`. You have used other packages and perhaps even written one or two yourself. Having reached this point, you are quite accustomed to encapsulation.

In Chapter 11 you explored the idea of doing your own encapsulation, writing new types and sets of operations, and implementing these in ADT packages. Most of the ADTs in Chapter 11 defined PRIVATE record types; PRIVATE types allowed us to control precisely which predefined and programmer-defined operations were valid. This precision of control over operations is a very important aspect of OOP.

Chapter 12 introduced you to writing generic packages; in earlier chapters you used a few generic packages, such as `Ada.Text_IO.Enumeration_IO` and `Ada.Numerics. Discrete_Random`. You are therefore at least a bit familiar with genericity.

Some writers use the term *object-based programming* to describe programming that uses "only" encapsulation and genericity but not inheritance and polymorphism. These writers believe inheritance and polymorphism to be of paramount importance and that any program that doesn't take advantage of these two concepts is simply not object-oriented. We think the distinction is somewhat artificial; encapsulation and genericity are just as important in developing good object-oriented designs.

16.2 System Structures: Tagged Types

The variant records we studied in Chapter 13 provide much expressive power to create complex types with several different parts. However, they have an important limitation: A variant record must be fully defined and compiled, and `CASE` statements are used to control processing its various parts.

Now suppose a new variant must be added. Consider the employee record of Section 13.4, which we repeat here for clarity:

```
TYPE PayCategories IS (Unknown, Professional, Sales, Clerical);

TYPE Employee (PayStatus : PayCategories := Unknown) IS RECORD
   ID        : IDType;
   Name      : NameType;
   PayPeriod : Dates.Date;

   CASE PayStatus IS
     WHEN Professional =>
       MonthSalary : Currency.Quantity;
     WHEN Sales =>
       WeekSalary  : Currency.Quantity;
       CommRate    : CommissionPercentage;
       SalesAmount : Currency.Quantity;
     WHEN Clerical =>
       HourlyWage  : Currency.Quantity;
       HoursWorked : WorkHours;
     WHEN Unknown =>
       NULL;
   END CASE;

END RECORD;
```

Suppose a new category of employee is added, `Manager`, for example. The enumeration type `PayCategories` must be modified, and the variant type declaration must be changed, adding a choice `WHEN Manager`, to account for the new variant. All operations on objects of the type must be similarly changed.

Further, if the type declaration happened to appear in a package specification, every client of that package must at least be recompiled and perhaps even modified. It would be nice if we could somehow extend a type, adding new fields and operations but without modifying or recompiling existing packages or programs. This is called *type extension* and is provided in Ada by *tagged types*. A tagged type is analogous to a variant record, but it can be extended without changing the original type declaration.

Tagged Types

A record type can be declared as `TAGGED` to indicate that it will potentially be extended by adding additional fields. Each object of a tagged type is given a tag by the compiler; you can think of a tag as analogous to a hidden discriminant. Whereas with ordinary variant records the programmer must write explicit code to use a discriminant, a tag is manipulated automatically in the executing program.

As an example of a tagged type, consider representing a person with three general characteristics: a name, a gender, and a date of birth. We can declare this as follows:

```
TYPE Person IS TAGGED RECORD
   Name: NameType;
   Gender: Genders;
   BirthDate: Date;
END RECORD;
```

where `Genders` has been declared as:

```
TYPE Genders IS (Female, Male);
```

and the name and birth date fields are, respectively, some string type and a date from our package `Dates`.

Now suppose we declare `Person` in the specification of a package `Persons`, together with a number of operations that are implemented in the package body. We then write one or more client programs that use `Persons`. At a later date we discover a need to represent personnel, or people who work in a company. An employee is a person with a company identifier and a second date indicating when she or he joined the company. Note the "is a" relationship: An employee *is a* person with additional characteristics. Without tagged types, we would either develop an entire new personnel type, or go back and modify our original person type. Using tagged types, we can derive a new type based on the existing one:

```
TYPE Employee IS NEW Person WITH RECORD
   ID: IDRange;
   StartDate: Date;
END RECORD;
```

This declares a new type and reflects the "is a" relationship directly. Each employee now has five fields: the two new ones and the three it *inherited* from the person type. Furthermore, the new type can be declared in a new package, with a new set of operations, *without disturbing the existing package or any programs that use it*. This technique is called *programming by extension*.

We can carry this further, of course. The payroll department in our company wishes to extend our employee type for payroll purposes and so needs three special categories of employees. The new types can be derived from the employee type:

```
TYPE Professional IS NEW Employee WITH RECORD
   MonthSalary : Quantity;
END RECORD;

TYPE Sales IS NEW Employee WITH RECORD
   WeekSalary  : Quantity;
   CommRate    : CommissionPercentage;
END RECORD;

TYPE Clerical IS NEW Employee WITH RECORD
   HourlyWage  : Quantity;
END RECORD;
```

where the `Quantity` values are taken from package `Currency`. In a further refinement of the "is a" relationship, a professional is an employee, who in turn is a person. As before, the new types can be declared and used in one or more new packages, without causing any modification of the older packages or any of their clients.

It is instructive to note that in Ada 83 new types can be derived from ordinary Ada 83 types. The new type has the same structure (set of values) as the original, and the operations of the original type are generally inherited by the new one. Ada 95 adds to this the ability to extend the type.

Converting among Derived Tagged Types

The five types declared above form a *type hierarchy:*

```
Person
  Employee
    Professional
    Sales
    Clerical
```

Ada allows us to convert explicitly from a lower type to a higher one. If P is a `Person`, E is an `Employee`, and R is a `Professional`, we can write an aggregate

```
R := (Name => "Nancy",
      Gender => Female,
      BirthDate => Date_Of(1950, Oct, 21),
      ID => 2345,
      StartDate => Date_Of(1990, Jul, 1),
      MonthSalary => 5000.00);
```

and can "up-convert" to P

```
P := Person(R);
```

which is a familiar conversion construct. In the case of tagged types, the conversion "strips off" the extra fields.

How do we "down-convert"? Since a conversion to a lower type generally adds fields, we use a special aggregate structure for this. If we had

```
P := (Name => "Nancy",
      Gender => Female,
      BirthDate => Date_Of(1950, Oct, 21);
```

we could make E by writing

```
E := (P WITH ID => 2345, StartDate => Date_Of(1990, Jul, 1));
```

The text following WITH is called an *extension aggregate.* Generally, of course, client programs will not use the aggregate form because types like these will, in general, be PRIVATE. This brings us to the subject of operations on tagged types.

Primitive and Nonprimitive Operations on Tagged Types

The operations on tagged types are rather special. A fundamental Ada 95 notion is the *primitive operation.* Put simply, a primitive operation of a type is either a predefined operator on the type—such as the operators on Integer, for example—or an operation (function, subprogram, or operator) that is declared just below the type in the same package specification and has a parameter of that type. Nearly all the operations in the packages thus far in this book have been, in Ada 95 terminology, primitive. The term becomes important in the context of tagged types. Each primitive operation of a tagged type T is inherited by all types derived from T; sometimes we desire the inheritance, but sometimes we do not.

We shall explain this in the context of three package specifications, `Persons`, `Personnel`, and `Payroll`, which appear as Programs 16.1, 16.2, and 16.3, respectively.

Program 16.1 Specification for Persons Package

```
WITH Dates; USE Dates;
PACKAGE Persons IS
-------------------------------------------------------------------
--| Specification for Persons. This package provides a root type
--| Person, with the fields Name, Gender, and BirthDate. Person
--| is a tagged private type, which means that it has all the
--| characteristics of an ordinary private type but also that it
--| can be extended by derivation.
--| Author: Michael B. Feldman, The George Washington University
--| Last Modified: September 1998
-------------------------------------------------------------------

  TYPE Genders IS (Female, Male);

  SUBTYPE NameRange IS Positive RANGE 1..20;
  SUBTYPE NameType  IS String(NameRange);

  TYPE Person IS TAGGED PRIVATE;

  -- selectors

  FUNCTION NameOf  (Whom: Person) RETURN NameType;
  FUNCTION GenderOf(Whom: Person) RETURN Genders;
  FUNCTION DOBOf   (Whom: Person) RETURN Date;
  -- Pre:  Whom is defined
  -- Post: returns the appropriate field value

  PROCEDURE Put(Item: IN Person);
  -- Pre:  Item is defined
  -- Post: Item's fields are displayed

  PACKAGE Constructors IS

    -- this inner package is necessary so that MakePerson is not a
    -- "primitive" function, that is, so that it is not inherited
    -- by types derived from Person.

    FUNCTION MakePerson(Name     : String;
                        Gender   : Genders;
                        BirthDate: Date) RETURN Person;
    -- Pre:  Name, Gender, and BirthDate are defined
    -- Post: returns a Person with the given field values

  END Constructors;

PRIVATE
```

```
TYPE Person IS TAGGED RECORD
  NameLength: NameRange := 1;
  NameField : NameType := (OTHERS => ' ');
  Gender    : Genders := Female;
  BirthDate : Date;
END RECORD;

END Persons;
```

In Program 16.1, `Person` is a `PRIVATE` type with initialized fields, as in most of our packages. Note, in the visible part of the specification (above the `PRIVATE` line), the declaration

```
TYPE Person IS TAGGED PRIVATE;
```

which is consistent with our understanding of private declarations, with the addition of `TAGGED`. The package specification further gives four operations in the selector category; this style is familiar to you from earlier packages. However, the constructor operation is not declared here, but rather in an inner package, `Constructors`. Why the unfamiliar structure?

Our intention in writing `Persons` is to allow new types to be derived and extended from `Person`. Consider the type `Employee` introduced earlier. An employee is a person with additional fields; the type `Employee` inherits all the primitive operations of `Person`, that is, for each primitive `Person` operation, there is a similar one for `Employee`, with a similar parameter profile. So the `Employee` type also has operations `NameOf`, `GenderOf`, and `DOBOf`.

Inheritance is fine for the selectors: For example, a client will certainly wish to find out an employee's name, and an inherited operation just like the `Person` selector is a perfectly good operation to return the name. The constructor is a different story, however, because we need to pass all the field values into it. A person has three fields; an employee has five. If we wrote a person constructor as a primitive operation (e.g., `MakePerson`), it would be inherited by the employee type, so a client could call `Make-Person` with a parameter of type `Employee`. But this would be wrong! The object would be constructed with only three of its fields filled in!

Writing a separate constructor for `Employee` is a useful thing to do, and we shall do it shortly. However, it does not solve our problem because `MakePerson` would still be available for the client to call.

Because it would be very unsafe and therefore unwise to allow `MakePerson` to be inherited by derived types, we need to take preventive action. There are several ways to do this; here we handle the problem by realizing that—by Ada's rules of primitive operations—an operation that is declared in an inner package, such as `Persons.Constructors` in Program 16.1, is *not* primitive and is therefore *not* inherited. Putting the constructor in an inner package puts a small burden on the client programmer, who can write `Persons.NameOf` but must write `Persons.Constructors.MakePerson`. This is a small price to pay for the added safety.

Deriving New Tagged Types

Program 16.2 gives the specification for `Personnel`.

Program 16.2 Specification for Personnel Package

```
WITH Persons; USE Persons;
WITH Dates; USE Dates;
PACKAGE Personnel IS
--------------------------------------------------------------------
--| Specification for Personnel, which provides a type Employee,
--| a derivative of Persons.Person. Note that the operations on
--| objects of type Persons.Person are inherited by objects of
--| type Employee, so we need selectors only for the new
--| fields! As in the case of Persons, we place the constructor
--| in an inner package.
--| Author: Michael B. Feldman, The George Washington University
--| Last Modified: September 1998
--------------------------------------------------------------------

   TYPE Employee IS NEW Person WITH PRIVATE;
      -- Here is where Employee is derived; the extension fields are
      -- also PRIVATE, so clients cannot access them directly.

   TYPE IDType IS NEW Positive RANGE 1111..9999;

   -- selectors

   FUNCTION StartOf (Whom: Employee) RETURN Date;
   FUNCTION IDOf    (Whom: Employee) RETURN IDType;
      -- Pre:  Whom is defined
      -- Post: return the appropriate field values

   PROCEDURE Put(Item: Employee);
      -- Pre:  Item is defined
      -- Post: Item is displayed

   PACKAGE Constructors IS

      -- as in Persons, we use an inner package to prevent the
      -- constructor from being inherited by further derivatives
      -- of Employee

      FUNCTION  MakeEmployee(Name    : String;
                             Gender  : Genders;
                             BirthDate: Date;
                             StartDate: Date;
                             ID      : IDType) RETURN Employee;
      -- Pre:  Name, Gender, BirthDate, StateDate, and ID are defined
      -- Post: Whom contains the desired field values

   END Constructors;

PRIVATE

   TYPE Employee IS NEW Person WITH RECORD
      ID        : IDType := 1111;
      StartDate : Date;
   END RECORD;
```

```
END Personnel;
```

Its structure is similar to that of `Persons`, but note how the type `Employee` is declared:

```
TYPE Employee IS NEW Person WITH PRIVATE;
```

The syntax `WITH PRIVATE` indicates a private extension; it allows `Employee` to be a `PRIVATE` type just as `Person` is. `Personnel` also provides selectors `StartOf` and `IDOf` and a constructor `MakeEmployee` in an inner package.

The type `Employee` inherits the primitive operations of `Person`: `NameOf`, `GenderOf`, and `DOBof`. This is fine; employees also have these fields. What about `Put`? `Persons.Put` displays the fields of a person. If `Put` were inherited by `Employee`, it would, of course, display *only* the fields that `Employee` and `Person` have in common, which is not what we desire. We therefore supply another `Put` for the employee type. Because it has a similar parameter profile, the only difference being the substitution of `Employee` for `Person`, this new employee operation is said to *override* the corresponding person operation. The body of `Personnel.Put`—we will show this shortly—displays all five fields of an employee.

Why were we able to override `Person.Put` so simply, without using an inner package? The key is that the two `Put` parameter profiles are so similar. The constructors' parameter profiles are very different from one another, so writing a `MakePerson` in `Personnel`, with a profile appropriate for `Employee`, simply would not have solved that problem.

Program 16.3 gives the specification for `Payroll`, which gives the three pay categories we sketched earlier.

Program 16.3 Specification for Payroll Package

```
WITH Currency; USE Currency;
WITH Dates; USE Dates;
WITH Persons; USE Persons;
WITH Personnel; USE Personnel;
PACKAGE Payroll IS
-------------------------------------------------------------------
--| Specification for Payroll, a set of payroll categories
--| derived from Personnel. Each type has a primitive operation
--| Put, which overrides the one inherited from Employee.
--| Author: Michael B. Feldman, The George Washington University
--| Last Modified: September 1998
-------------------------------------------------------------------

  SUBTYPE CommissionPercentage IS Float RANGE 0.00..0.50;

  TYPE Professional IS NEW Employee WITH PRIVATE;
  TYPE Sales IS NEW Employee WITH PRIVATE;
  TYPE Clerical IS NEW Employee WITH PRIVATE;

  PROCEDURE Put(Item: Professional);
  PROCEDURE Put(Item: Sales);
  PROCEDURE Put(Item: Clerical);

  PACKAGE Constructors IS
```

```
                      -- constructors for the three new types
                      FUNCTION MakeProfessional(Name       : String;
                                                Gender     : Genders;
                                                BirthDate  : Date;
                                                StartDate  : Date;
                                                ID         : IDType;
                                                MonthSalary: Quantity)
                                                RETURN Professional;

           FUNCTION MakeSales (Name       : String;
                               Gender     : Genders;
                               BirthDate  : Date;
                               StartDate  : Date;
                               ID         : IDType;
                               WeekSalary : Quantity;
                               CommRate   : CommissionPercentage)
                               RETURN Sales;

           FUNCTION MakeClerical (Name       : String;
                                  Gender     : Genders;
                                  BirthDate  : Date;
                                  StartDate  : Date;
                                  ID         : IDType;
                                  HourlyWage : Quantity)
                                  RETURN Clerical;

      -- Pre:  All input fields are defined
      -- Post: Returns an initialized value of the respective type

   END Constructors;

PRIVATE

   -- full extensions for the three types

   TYPE Professional IS NEW Employee WITH RECORD
     MonthSalary : Quantity;
   END RECORD;

   TYPE Sales IS NEW Employee WITH RECORD
     WeekSalary  : Quantity;
     CommRate    : CommissionPercentage;
   END RECORD;

   TYPE Clerical IS NEW Employee WITH RECORD
     HourlyWage  : Quantity;
   END RECORD;

END Payroll;
```

The three types are closely related—all are used by the payroll department—so it is sensible to collect them into a single package as we have done here. Note the three derived PRIVATE type declarations, the three overriding Put operations, and the three constructors in the inner package. We have not included field selectors, preferring to leave that as an exercise.

Before going on to the package bodies, look at Program 16.4, which illustrates the use of these packages.

Program 16.4 Creating a Company of Employees

```
WITH Ada.Text_IO; USE Ada.Text_IO;
WITH Currency; USE Currency;
WITH Dates; USE Dates;
WITH Persons; USE Persons;
WITH Personnel; USE Personnel;
WITH Payroll; USE Payroll;
PROCEDURE Use_Payroll IS
-------------------------------------------------------------------------
--| Demonstrates the use of tagged types
--| Author: Michael B. Feldman, The George Washington University
--| Last Modified: September 1998
-------------------------------------------------------------------------

  -- demonstrates the use of tagged types

  George: Person;
  Mary  : Employee;
  Martha: Professional;
  Virginia: Sales;
  Herman: Clerical;

BEGIN

  -- first construct all the people

  George := Persons.Constructors.MakePerson(
            Name     => "George",
            Gender   => Male,
            BirthDate => Date_Of(1971,Nov,2));

  Mary := Personnel.Constructors.MakeEmployee(
            Name      => "Mary",
            Gender    => Female,
            BirthDate => Date_Of(1950,Oct,21),
            ID        => 1234,
            StartDate => Date_Of(1989,Jul,1));

  Martha := Payroll.Constructors.MakeProfessional(
            Name       => "Martha",
            Gender     => Female,
            BirthDate  => Date_Of(1947,Jul,8),
            ID         => 2222,
            StartDate  => Date_Of(1985,Jun,6),
            MonthSalary => MakeCurrency(50000.00));

  Virginia := Payroll.Constructors.MakeSales(
            Name       => "Virginia",
            Gender     => Female,
            BirthDate  => Date_Of(1955,Feb,1),
            ID         => 3456,
            StartDate  => Date_Of(1990,Jan,1),
            WeekSalary => MakeCurrency(2500.00),
            CommRate   => 0.25);

  Herman := Payroll.Constructors.MakeClerical(
            Name       => "Herman",
            Gender     => Male,
            BirthDate  => Date_Of(1975,May,13),
```

```
                  ID         => 1557,
                  StartDate  => Date_Of(1991,Jul,1),
                  HourlyWage => MakeCurrency(7.50));

   -- Now display them all. Note that each Put is a different
   -- primitive operation.

   Put(Item => George);
   Ada.Text_IO.Put_Line(Item => "-----------------------");
   Put(Item => Mary);
   Ada.Text_IO.Put_Line(Item => "-----------------------");
   Put(Item => Martha);
   Ada.Text_IO.Put_Line(Item => "-----------------------");
   Put(Item => Virginia);
   Ada.Text_IO.Put_Line(Item => "-----------------------");
   Put(Item => Herman);
   Ada.Text_IO.Put_Line(Item => "-----------------------");

END Use_Payroll;
```

Sample Run

```
Name: George
Gender: male
Birth Date: November 2, 1971
-----------------------------
Name: Mary
Gender: female
Birth Date: October 21, 1950
ID Number: 1234
Start Date: July 1, 1989
-----------------------------
Name: Martha
Gender: female
Birth Date: July 8, 1947
ID Number: 2222
Start Date: June 6, 1985

Category: Professional
Monthly Salary: 50000.00
-----------------------------
Name: Virginia
Gender: female
Birth Date: February 1, 1955
ID Number: 3456
Start Date: January 1, 1990

Category: Sales
Weekly Salary: 2500.00
Commission Rate: 0.25
-----------------------------
Name: Herman
Gender: male
Birth Date: May 13, 1975
ID Number: 1557
Start Date: July 1, 1991

Category: Clerical
Hourly Wage: 7.50
-----------------------------
```

Each of the five variables is of a different type; in each case the appropriate constructor is called—an Ada compiler would reject an attempt to call an inappropriate one—and the appropriate Put is used to display the contents.

Bodies of the Tagged Type Packages

The bodies of Persons, Personnel, and Payroll are given as Programs 16.5, 16.6, and 16.7, respectively.

Program 16.5 Body of Persons Package

```
WITH Ada.Text_IO;
WITH Ada.Integer_Text_IO;
WITH Dates.IO;
PACKAGE BODY Persons IS
-------------------------------------------------------------------------
--| Body of Persons package
--| Author: Michael B. Feldman, The George Washington University
--| Last Modified: September 1998
-------------------------------------------------------------------------

  PACKAGE Gender_IO IS NEW Ada.Text_IO.Enumeration_IO(Enum => Genders);

  FUNCTION NameOf(Whom: Person) RETURN NameType IS
  BEGIN
    RETURN Whom.NameField;
  END NameOf;

  FUNCTION GenderOf(Whom: Person) RETURN Genders IS
  BEGIN
    RETURN Whom.Gender;
  END GenderOf;

  FUNCTION DOBOf(Whom: Person) RETURN Date IS
  BEGIN
    RETURN Whom.BirthDate;
  END DOBOf;

  PROCEDURE Put(Item: Person) IS
  BEGIN
    Ada.Text_IO.Put(Item => "Name: ");
    Ada.Text_IO.Put(Item => Item.NameField(1..Item.NameLength));
    Ada.Text_IO.New_Line;

    Ada.Text_IO.Put(Item => "Gender: ");
    Gender_IO.Put(Item => Item.Gender, Set => Ada.Text_IO.Lower_Case);
    Ada.Text_IO.New_Line;

    Ada.Text_IO.Put(Item => "Birth Date: ");
    Dates.IO.Put(Item => Item.BirthDate, Format => Dates.IO.Full);
    Ada.Text_IO.New_Line;
  END Put;

  PACKAGE BODY Constructors IS

    FUNCTION MakePerson(Name     : String;
                        Gender   : Genders;
```

```
                              BirthDate: Date) RETURN Person IS
        Temp: NameType;
     BEGIN -- MakePerson

       Temp(1..Name'Length) := Name;  -- copy into slice of Temp

       RETURN (NameLength => Name'Length,
               NameField => Temp,
               Gender    => Gender,
               BirthDate => BirthDate);
     END MakePerson;

   END Constructors;

END Persons;
```

Program 16.6 Body of Personnel Package

```
WITH Ada.Text_IO;
WITH Ada.Integer_Text_IO;
WITH Dates.IO;
PACKAGE BODY Personnel IS
-------------------------------------------------------------------------
--| Body of Personnel package
--| Author: Michael B. Feldman, The George Washington University
--| Last Modified: September 1998
-------------------------------------------------------------------------

   PACKAGE BODY Constructors IS

     FUNCTION  MakeEmployee(Name     : String;
                           Gender    : Genders;
                           BirthDate: Date;
                           StartDate: Date;
                           ID        : IDType) RETURN Employee IS
     BEGIN
       -- note how the Persons constructor is used, with an
       -- aggregate for the Person fields and an
       -- extension aggregate to add in the extra fields.
       RETURN (Persons.Constructors.MakePerson(
         Name          => Name,
         Gender        => Gender,
         BirthDate     => BirthDate)
         WITH
           StartDate => StartDate,
           ID => ID);
     END MakeEmployee;

   END Constructors;

   FUNCTION StartOf (Whom: Employee) RETURN Date IS
   BEGIN
     RETURN Whom.StartDate;
   END StartOf;

   FUNCTION IDOf (Whom: Employee) RETURN IDType IS
   BEGIN
     RETURN Whom.ID;
   END IDOf;
```

```
   PROCEDURE Put(Item: Employee) IS
   BEGIN
     -- Note that we can convert Employee to Person and
     -- call Persons.Put for the common fields
     Persons.Put(Item => Persons.Person(Item));

     Ada.Text_IO.Put(Item => "ID Number: ");
     Ada.Integer_Text_IO.Put(Item => Positive(Item.ID), Width => 1);
     Ada.Text_IO.New_Line;

     Ada.Text_IO.Put(Item => "Start Date: ");
     Dates.IO.Put(Item => Item.StartDate, Format => Dates.IO.Full);
     Ada.Text_IO.New_Line;
   END Put;

END Personnel;
```

Program 16.7 Body of Payroll Package

```
WITH Ada.Text_IO;
WITH Ada.Float_Text_IO;
WITH Currency.IO;
PACKAGE BODY Payroll IS
-----------------------------------------------------------------------
--| Body of Payroll package
--| Author: Michael B. Feldman, The George Washington University
--| Last Modified: September 1998
-----------------------------------------------------------------------

   PACKAGE BODY Constructors IS

     -- constructors for the three new types

     FUNCTION  MakeProfessional (Name     : String;
                                 Gender    : Genders;
                                 BirthDate : Date;
                                 StartDate : Date;
                                 ID        : IDType;
                                 MonthSalary: Quantity)
                                 RETURN Professional IS
     BEGIN
       RETURN  (Personnel.Constructors.MakeEmployee(
         Name            => Name,
         Gender          => Gender,
         BirthDate       => Birthdate,
         StartDate       => StartDate,
         ID              => ID)
         WITH MonthSalary => MonthSalary);
     END MakeProfessional;

     FUNCTION MakeSales (Name      : String;
                         Gender    : Genders;
                         BirthDate : Date;
                         StartDate : Date;
                         ID        : IDType;
                         WeekSalary: Quantity;
                         CommRate  : CommissionPercentage)
                         RETURN Sales IS
     BEGIN
       RETURN (Personnel.Constructors.MakeEmployee
```

```
                     (Name              => Name,
              Gender             => Gender,
              BirthDate          => Birthdate,
              StartDate          => StartDate,
              ID                 => ID)
              WITH WeekSalary => WeekSalary, CommRate => CommRate);
       END MakeSales;

       FUNCTION MakeClerical (Name      : String;
                              Gender    : Genders;
                              BirthDate : Date;
                              StartDate : Date;
                              ID        : IDType;
                              HourlyWage: Quantity)
                              RETURN Clerical IS
     BEGIN
       RETURN  (Personnel.Constructors.MakeEmployee
         (Name              => Name,
          Gender             => Gender,
          BirthDate          => Birthdate,
          StartDate          => StartDate,
          ID                 => ID)
          WITH HourlyWage => HourlyWage);
     END MakeClerical;

END Constructors;

PROCEDURE Put(Item: Professional) IS
BEGIN
  Put(Item => Employee(Item));
  Ada.Text_IO.New_Line;

  Ada.Text_IO.Put(Item => "Category: Professional");
  Ada.Text_IO.New_Line;
  Ada.Text_IO.Put(Item => "Monthly Salary: ");
  Currency.IO.Put(Item => Item.MonthSalary);
  Ada.Text_IO.New_Line;
END Put;

PROCEDURE Put(Item: Sales) IS
BEGIN
  Put(Item => Employee(Item));
  Ada.Text_IO.New_Line;

  Ada.Text_IO.Put(Item => "Category: Sales");
  Ada.Text_IO.New_Line;
  Ada.Text_IO.Put(Item => "Weekly Salary: ");
  Currency.IO.Put(Item => Item.WeekSalary);
  Ada.Text_IO.New_Line;
  Ada.Text_IO.Put(Item => "Commission Rate: ");
  Ada.Float_Text_IO.Put(Item => Item.CommRate, Fore=>1,Aft=>2,Exp=>0);
  Ada.Text_IO.New_Line;
END Put;

PROCEDURE Put(Item: Clerical) IS
BEGIN
  Put(Item => Employee(Item));
  Ada.Text_IO.New_Line;

  Ada.Text_IO.Put(Item => "Category: Clerical");
```

```
   Ada.Text_IO.New_Line;
   Ada.Text_IO.Put(Item => "Hourly Wage: ");
   Currency.IO.Put(Item => Item.HourlyWage);
   Ada.Text_IO.New_Line;
 END Put;

END Payroll;
```

In Program 16.7, in the body of the constructor `MakeEmployee` we up-convert the employee to a person, then use `MakePerson` to fill in the person fields. Finally, we use an extension aggregate to fill in the remaining fields. Similarly, in the `Put` procedure we up-convert as before and reuse the `Persons.Put` to display the person fields, and then we display the additional employee fields.

Variables of Tagged Types

Throughout this development we have declared each variable to be of a *specific* tagged type. This is analogous to declaring *constrained* variant variables, as in Chapter 13. A plausible question is, then, whether there exists something analogous to *unconstrained* variant types and variables. The answer to the question is Yes, and we shall show how to do this in Section 16.4. A related question is whether, and how, we can create a "data base" or table of tagged records (e.g., an array of them). The answer to this question is also Yes, and the details are also shown in Section 16.4. Before we can complete the explanation, we must digress into presentation of a different variety of pointer type, namely, the *general access type,* which, like the tagged type, is new in Ada 95.

16.3 Data Structures: General Access Types

The access types that we saw in Chapter 15 can acquire values in only two ways: as the result of an allocator (`NEW`) operation or as a copy of another access value. In particular, there is no direct way to cause an access value to designate a declared variable or constant. As it happens, there are really two kinds of access types:

- *Pool-specific access types,* which are just the access types we worked with in Chapter 15

- *General access types,* which can designate variables, constants, and dynamically allocated values.

Here are three versions of an access type declaration:

```
TYPE IntegerPointer IS ACCESS Integer;
TYPE IntegerPointer IS ACCESS ALL Integer;
TYPE IntegerPointer IS ACCESS CONSTANT Integer;
```

The first declares a familiar access type, which we now call pool-specific. It can designate only an `Integer` value allocated from the pool. The second declares a general access type that can designate an integer variable, integer constant, or pool value. The third is a restricted "read-only" form of the second: If P is of this type, it can be derefer-enced only to *read* the designated value, not to *write* it. That is, P.ALL is not valid on the left side of an assignment statement. This is analogous to an IN parameter.

Given a general access type of the second kind, can its values point to *any* integer variable or constant? No. In keeping with Ada's general philosophy of explicitness in operations, Ada requires that the programmer indicate explicitly that a variable or con-stant is intended to be "pointed to." For example, the integer variable X, declared as

```
X :Integer;
```

cannot be designated by an access value, but the variable Y, declared as

```
Y: ALIASED Integer;
```

can indeed be so designated. In everyday English, an *alias* is a nickname, or a name that a person uses in addition to his or her given name. (A criminal might use a number of aliases to avoid detection.) In programming, the term *aliased* is a fairly standard one and means, by analogy, that the variable can be referred to not only by its name but by any number of aliases (access values).

Suppose P is a general access type as above. How does P acquire a value? Of course, P can still be copied from another access variable or assigned the result of a NEW, but we are interested in designating *variables*. We can cause P to designate Y, for exam-ple, by writing

```
P := Y'Access;
```

The 'Access attribute returns an access value designating Y, or, informally, a pointer to Y.

Program 16.8 illustrates general access types. An array, PromptTable, is made to contain access values that designate strings of different lengths. The four prompts are declared as ALIASED to allow them to be designated. If we wished the prompts to be CONSTANT strings, the access type would then be written as follows:

```
TYPE StringPointer IS ACCESS CONSTANT String;
```

Program 16.8 Illustration of General Access Types

```
WITH Ada.Text_IO;
PROCEDURE General_Access_Types IS
-------------------------------------------------------------------------
--| Illustrates general access types
--| Author: Michael B. Feldman, The George Washington University
--| Last Modified: September 1998
-------------------------------------------------------------------------

  TYPE StringPointer IS ACCESS ALL String;
  -- ALL makes StringPointer a "general access type" as opposed to
  -- a "pool-specific access type." StringPointer values
  -- can designate declared variables and constants,
  -- as well as dynamically allocated (NEW) values

  Prompt1: ALIASED String := "Enter a command >";
  Prompt2: ALIASED String := "Thank you.";
  Prompt3: ALIASED String := "Invalid; try again.";
```

```
Prompt4: ALIASED String := "Bye now.";
-- ALIASED means
--    "able to be designated by a general access value"

PromptTable: ARRAY (1..4) OF StringPointer :=
  (Prompt1'Access, Prompt2'Access,
   Prompt3'Access, Prompt4'Access);
-- We fill the array with access values: for example,
-- Prompt1'Access returns an access value designating Prompt1

BEGIN -- General_Access_Types

  -- display all the prompts in the table
  FOR Which IN PromptTable'Range LOOP
    Ada.Text_IO.Put(Item => PromptTable(Which).ALL); -- dereference
    Ada.Text_IO.New_Line;
  END LOOP;

END General_Access_Types;
```

Sample Run

```
Enter a command >
Thank you.
Invalid; try again.
Bye now.
```

Armed with this introduction to general access types, we are ready to use them in a more elaborate discussion of tagged types.

16.4 System Structures: Class-Wide Types

We used Programs 16.1 through 16.7 to illustrate a hierarchy of tagged types, defining `Person`, `Employee`, `Professional`, `Sales`, and `Clerical`. We declared one variable of each type, `George`, `Mary`, `Martha`, `Virginia`, and `Herman`, demonstrating the appropriate constructors and selectors for each. The time has come to answer two questions left open in Section 16.2:

- How can we declare a variable that can hold a value of *any* type in the hierarchy?

- How can we declare an array, each of whose elements can be a value of any type in the hierarchy?

Class-Wide Types

Each tagged type `T` has an attribute `T'Class`, which represents the entire type hierarchy for which `T` is the parent. In our example a variable of type `Person'Class` can hold a value of any of our five types or indeed of any type derived from any of these in the future. `Person'Class` is known as a *class-wide type,* and the variable is known as a *class-wide variable.*

We are getting closer to answering our questions. However, there is a small catch: A class-wide variable cannot simply be declared but must be *immediately* initialized to a specific value of one of the types, and thereafter, the variable can change its value but not its type.

This rule is analogous to the rules for constrained variant records. A tagged type can be extended indefinitely, with an unknown number derived types, each with an unknown number of extension fields. The compiler cannot possibly know which types might be derived—added to T'Class—in the future, so it cannot even guess at the size of a variable of such an unknown type. This problem does not arise with ordinary variant records because all the possible variants are known when the type declaration is compiled—an ordinary variant record cannot be extended later without rewriting and recompiling the original type declaration.

This is not very helpful when we contemplate setting up a "data base"—an array, say—of tagged objects such as employees. Since there are different types of employee, each element of the array could be of a different type. Furthermore, these elements could not all be immediately initialized because we might obtain the employee data interactively or from an external file. Moreover, we might later wish to add new types of employees without having to modify the data base structure. Indeed, the possibility of future modifications is exactly what first motivated our use of tagged types.

Continuing the analogy with variant records, is there a tagged-type analogue to an *unconstrained* variant record, that is, a variable whose type—within a class—can be left initially unspecified and can change over time?

The answer here is Yes, but the solution is not quite as simple as that for variant records. The difference is that by the time an unconstrained variant object is declared, the compiler knows *all* the possible variants and can therefore know how to arrange for the space to be allocated. In contrast, as we have just seen, a class-wide variable can be declared and the class *later* extended.

Class-Wide General Access Types and Heterogeneous Arrays

We solve the problem in Program 16.9, using general access types. We omit the output of this program because it is identical to that of Program 16.4.

Program 16.9 Creating an Array of Payroll Records

```
WITH Ada.Text_IO; USE Ada.Text_IO;
WITH Currency; USE Currency;
WITH Dates; USE Dates;
WITH Persons; USE Persons;
WITH Personnel; USE Personnel;
WITH Payroll; USE Payroll;
PROCEDURE Payroll_Array IS
------------------------------------------------------------------------
--| Demonstrates the use of classwide general access types
--| and dispatching operations
--| Author: Michael B. Feldman, The George Washington University
--| Last Modified: September 1998
------------------------------------------------------------------------

  George  : ALIASED Person;
  Mary    : ALIASED Employee;
```

```
Martha  : ALIASED Professional;
Virginia: ALIASED Sales;
Herman  : ALIASED Clerical;
-- These values can now be designated by general access values

TYPE PayrollPointer IS ACCESS ALL Person'Class;
-- a PayrollPointer value can designate a value of type
-- Person, or of any type derived from Person, such as
-- Employee, Sales, Professional, or Clerical

TYPE PayrollArray IS ARRAY (1..5) OF PayrollPointer;
-- We can put all our employees in an array by designating
-- them with PayrollPointer values

Company: PayrollArray;

BEGIN

   -- first construct all the people, as before

   George := Persons.Constructors.MakePerson(
              Name       => "George",
              Gender     => Male,
              BirthDate  => Date_Of(1971,Nov,2));

   Mary := Personnel.Constructors.MakeEmployee(
              Name       => "Mary",
              Gender     => Female,
              BirthDate  => Date_Of(1950,Oct,21),
              ID         => 1234,
              StartDate  => Date_Of(1989,Jul,1));

   Martha := Payroll.Constructors.MakeProfessional(
              Name        => "Martha",
              Gender      => Female,
              BirthDate   => Date_Of(1947,Jul,8),
              ID          => 2222,
              StartDate   => Date_Of(1985,Jun,6),
              MonthSalary => MakeCurrency(50000.00));

   Virginia := Payroll.Constructors.MakeSales(
              Name        => "Virginia",
              Gender      => Female,
              BirthDate   => Date_Of(1955,Feb,1),
              ID          => 3456,
              StartDate   => Date_Of(1990,Jan,1),
              WeekSalary  => MakeCurrency(2500.00),
              CommRate    => 0.25);

   Herman := Payroll.Constructors.MakeClerical(
              Name        => "Herman",
              Gender      => Male,
              BirthDate   => Date_Of(1975,May,13),
              ID          => 1557,
              StartDate   => Date_Of(1991,Jul,1),
              HourlyWage  => MakeCurrency(7.50));

   -- Now put the people into the company; each array element is
   -- a different type!
```

```
Company := (Herman'Access, Martha'Access, Virginia'Access,
            Mary'Access, George'Access);

-- Now display them all. Note that each time Put is invoked,
-- precisely the appropriate Put is "dispatched".

FOR Which IN Company'Range LOOP
  Put(Company(Which).ALL);
  Ada.Text_IO.Put_Line(Item => "-----------------------");
END LOOP;

END Payroll_Array;
```

Here our five people are declared as in Program 16.4, but now they are ALIASED. We further declared a general access type PayrollPointer and an array of values of this type:

```
TYPE PayrollPointer IS ACCESS ALL Person'Class;
TYPE PayrollArray IS ARRAY (1..5) OF PayrollPointer;
```

The access type can designate any type in Person'Class; each array element is a value of that access type. We can now declare a variable

```
Company: PayrollArray;
```

and, after constructing all the people as in Program 16.4, we can put them into the company, using an array aggregate:

```
Company := (Herman'Access, Martha'Access, Virginia'Access,
            Mary'Access, George'Access);
```

The type PayrollArray is an example of how Ada allows you to create a *heterogenous array,* that is, an array, each of whose values is a different type. Strictly speaking, the values in Company are all just class-wide access values, but each *designated* value is a different type, so the desired behavior is obtained. Our questions are answered.

16.5 System Structures: Dynamic Dispatching

Given the array of values in Program 16.9, we display the entire company just by looping through the array, dereferencing each pointer to obtain the value to display:

```
FOR Which IN Company'Range LOOP
  Put(Company(Which).ALL);
  Text_IO.Put_Line(Item => "-----------------------");
END LOOP;
```

There is more to the Put in the above loop than meets the eye. Note that each value being displayed is of a *different* type, each of which has its own Put as defined in the three packages of Section 16.2. If we had used variant records, we would need a CASE to decide which variant to display. Here, the appropriate Put is selected, at execution time, automatically. This is called *dynamic dispatching,* and it is a very important technique in object-oriented programming. The correct Put is said to be *dispatched.*

Dispatching is closely related to primitive operations. In our example, `Put` is a primitive operation of `Person`. For `Person` and each type derived from `Person`, that is, each type in `Person'Class`, `Put` is inherited by default or, as in our situation, overridden. The five `Put`s have the same name and parameters differing only by the type within `Person'Class`. The correct `Put` can thus be dispatched.

We note that the values designated by `Company(Which)` could have been placed in `Company` by dynamic allocation instead of using `ALIASED` variables. In fact, the next section shows how to make `Company` fully dynamic.

16.6 Heterogeneous Linked Lists

To end our discussion of tagged types and also of linked lists, we show in Program 16.10 a fully dynamic example. Once again we omit the output, which is again identical to that of Program 16.4.

Program 16.10 Creating a Linked List of Payroll Records

```
WITH Ada.Text_IO; USE Ada.Text_IO;
WITH Currency; USE Currency;
WITH Dates; USE Dates;
WITH Persons; USE Persons;
WITH Personnel; USE Personnel;
WITH Payroll; USE Payroll;
WITH Lists_Generic;
PROCEDURE Payroll_List IS
-----------------------------------------------------------------------
--| Demonstrates the use of a heterogeneous list.
--| Author: Michael B. Feldman, The George Washington University
--| Last Modified: September 1998
-----------------------------------------------------------------------

  TYPE PayrollPointer IS ACCESS ALL Person'Class;
  -- as before, this can designate a Person or anything
  -- derived from Person

  PROCEDURE PutPerson (Item: IN PayrollPointer) IS
  BEGIN
    Put(Item => Item.ALL);  -- dispatch to the appropriate Put
    Ada.Text_IO.Put_Line(Item => "-----------------------");
  END PutPerson;

  PACKAGE PayrollLists IS NEW Lists_Generic
    (ElementType => PayrollPointer, DisplayElement => PutPerson);
  USE PayrollLists;
  -- The list element type is now a classwide pointer

  Company: List;
  Temp   : PayrollPointer;

BEGIN -- Payroll_List

  -- Construct all the people dynamically, and add each one
  -- to the end of the list as it is constructed. We no longer
  -- need an explicit variable for each person.
```

```
        Temp := NEW Person'(Persons.Constructors.MakePerson(
                  Name       => "George",
                  Gender     => Male,
                  BirthDate => Date_Of(1971,Nov,2)));
     AddToEnd(Company, Temp);

        Temp := NEW Employee'(Personnel.Constructors.MakeEmployee(
                  Name       => "Mary",
                  Gender     => Female,
                  BirthDate => Date_Of(1950,Oct,21),
                  ID         => 1234,
                  StartDate => Date_Of(1989,Jul,1)));
     AddToEnd(Company, Temp);

        Temp := NEW Professional'(Payroll.Constructors.MakeProfessional(
                  Name        => "Martha",
                  Gender      => Female,
                  BirthDate   => Date_Of(1947,Jul,8),
                  ID          => 2222,
                  StartDate   => Date_Of(1985,Jun,6),
                  MonthSalary => MakeCurrency(50000.00)));
     AddToEnd(Company, Temp);

        Temp := NEW Sales'(Payroll.Constructors.MakeSales(
                  Name        => "Virginia",
                  Gender      => Female,
                  BirthDate   => Date_Of(1955,Feb,1),
                  ID          => 3456,
                  StartDate   => Date_Of(1990,Jan,1),
                  WeekSalary  => MakeCurrency(2500.00),
                  CommRate    => 0.25));
     AddToEnd(Company, Temp);

        Temp := NEW Clerical'(Payroll.Constructors.MakeClerical(
                  Name        => "Herman",
                  Gender      => Male,
                  BirthDate   => Date_Of(1975,May,13),
                  ID          => 1557,
                  StartDate   => Date_Of(1991,Jul,1),
                  HourlyWage  => MakeCurrency(7.50)));
     AddToEnd(Company, Temp);

     -- Now we can display the list.

     Display (Company);

END Payroll_List;
```

Here we use our generic singly linked list package from Section 15.5, instantiating it for our class-wide access type and declaring a few useful variables:

```
TYPE PayrollPointer IS ACCESS ALL Person'Class;
-- as before, this can designate a Person or anything
-- derived from Person

PROCEDURE PutPerson(Item: IN PayrollPointer) IS
BEGIN
  Put(Item => Item.ALL);   -- This will dispatch to the proper Put
  Ada.Text_IO.Put_Line(Item => "------------------------");
```

```
END PutPerson;

PACKAGE PayrollLists IS NEW Lists_Generic
  (ElementType => PayrollPointer, DisplayElement => PutPerson);
USE PayrollLists;
-- The list element type is now a classwide pointer

Company: List;
Temp   : PayrollPointer;
```

Note that the element type in each list node is one of our class-wide pointers. We can now use `Temp` as a "holding area" for a dynamically allocated `Professional`, for example, and then add it to the end of our company list:

```
Temp := NEW Clerical'(Payroll.Constructors.MakeClerical(
          Name       => "Herman",
          Gender     => Male,
          BirthDate  => Date_Of(1975,May,13),
          ID         => 1557,
          StartDate  => Date_Of(1991,Jul,1),
          HourlyWage => MakeCurrency(7.50)));
AddToEnd(Company, Temp);
```

Note also the `PutPerson` procedure with which we instantiate `Lists_Generic`. The first line of the procedure body calls `Put` with a parameter gotten by dereferencing the pointer. Since the pointer type is classwide, the `Put` that is actually called depends on the type of the pointer's designated value. This is another example of dispatching.

After building a linked list of five people constructed in this manner, `Display` is called. This list procedure dispatches the appropriate `Put` to display each person:

```
Display (Company);
```

This presentation has only scratched the surface of the facilities Ada provides for object-oriented programming; a full treatment is beyond the scope of this book. The discussion here should give you an indication of the power of type extension and dynamic dispatching and perhaps an appreciation of why object-oriented programming has become such a popular technique for building software systems.

No technique is perfect, and there is a price to be paid for inheritance. Large, deep type hierarchies, while very powerful, can also be difficult to work with and maintain because all the derived types and operations depend very intimately on types and operations that are higher in the hierarchy. A change at the top can cause a "ripple effect" through the hierarchy; this may be an advantage, but the high degree of coupling among types might also have unanticipated effects.

As an example of why a large type hierarchy constructed with inheritance is often difficult to use and maintain, consider a variable `Virginia` of type `Sales` and an expression

```
GenderOf(Virginia)
```

Now suppose a problem arises that leads you to suspect a bug in `GenderOf`. How do you know where to look for the definition and body of `GenderOf`? It is not defined in the same package with `Sales`; indeed, it is defined in `Persons`, at the top of the type hierarchy. To discover this, you must look in every package specification all the way up the hierarchy, because the operation could have been defined, like Idof, in an intermediate package. The deeper the hierarchy, the more difficult it is to locate the definition of any given operation.

This is clearly quite different from the other ADTs that we have seen, in which the type provided by the package and all its operations were defined in full in that package.

Like any other powerful tool, inheritance must be used with common sense and moderation, and the tradeoffs must be carefully considered. Use it to build hierarchical structures of types that are truly related in some obvious way; avoid the trap of using it solely because it is there.

CHAPTER REVIEW

In this chapter we presented some introductory material on tagged types. The latter is a very important capability of Ada because it provides inheritance and therefore facilitates object-oriented programming. Closely related to tagged types is general access types, which are pointers that can designate declared variables as well as dynamically allocated ones.

New Ada Constructs in Chapter 16

The new Ada constructs introduced in this chapter are described in Table 16.1.

Table 16.1   Summary of New Ada Constructs

Construct	Effect
Tagged Type	

`TYPE MotorVehicle IS TAGGED RECORD`
`   Axles: Positive;`
`   EngineSize: Positive;`
`   Weight: Positive;`
`END RECORD;`
	Declares a tagged type, which can be extended by derivation to produce dynamic variants

`FUNCTION AxlesOf(M: MotorVehicle)` `   RETURN Positive;`	If AxlesOf is declared just below MotorVehicle in the same package spec, it is a primitive operation.
`TYPE TopType IS (Soft, Hard);`	

`TYPE Automobile IS NEW MotorVehicle`
`   WITH RECORD`
`      Doors: Positive;`
`      Top: TopType;`
`   END RECORD;`
	Automobile is derived from MotorVehicle and inherits its primitive operations

`FUNCTION TopOf(A: Automobile)` `   RETURN TopType;`	DoorsOf is a primitive operation of Automobile

Construct	Effect
Extension Aggregate	
`A: Automobile;`	A is an `Automobile` that inherits several of its fields from `MotorVehicle`

`A := (MakeVehicle`
`  (Axles => X,`
`   EngineSize => E,`
`   Weight => W)`
`   WITH`
`     Doors => 4,`
`     Top => Soft);`	

Class-Wide Type	
`V: MotorVehicle'Class;`	V can be a `MotorVehicle`, an `Automobile`, or anything else derived from `MotorVehicle`.
General Access Type	
`TYPE V_Pointer IS` `  ACCESS ALL MotorVehicle'Class;`	Can designate (point to) a value of MotorVehicle or anything derived from it.
Aliased Variable	

`V: ALIASED MotorVehicle;`
`VP: V_Pointer;`
`VP := V'Access;`
	Can be pointed to by a value of type `V_Pointer`. `VP` contains a pointer to `V`.

Quick-Check Exercises

1. What is a tagged type? How is it related to a variant record?

2. What is a primitive operation?

3. What is a derived tagged type?

4. What is the difference between a pool-specific and a general access type?

5. What is an aliased variable?

Answers to Quick-Check Exercises

1. A type that is extensible, that is, one from which new types can be derived that have additional fields.

2. An operation on a tagged type that is declared just below it in the same package specification and has a parameter of the tagged type.

3. A type that has been derived from a previously defined tagged type, possibly with an extension consisting of one or more new fields.

4. A pool-specific access type can acquire a value only by a call to NEW or by a copy of another access value; a general access type can acquire a value either by a NEW call or by taking the 'Access attribute of an aliased variable.

5. An aliased variable is one that may be designated (pointed to) by a general access value.

Review Questions for Chapter 16

1. Write the tagged type declarations for Supplies. For each supply, the cost, number on hand, and reorder point must be stored. For Paper the information needed is the number of sheets per box and the size of the paper. For Ribbon the size, color, and kind (Carbon or Cloth) are needed. For Labels the size and number per box are needed. Use whatever data types are appropriate for each field.

3. For the motor vehicle example begun in Table 16.1, complete a reasonably full set of tagged type declarations that describe different types of vehicles, epecially motorcycles, automobiles, and large trucks.

Programming Projects

1. Modify the geometric shapes example from Section 13.5 so that the basic shape is a tagged type with perimeter and area fields, and other shapes are derived from the basic one. Use the style of the employees example from Section 16.2.

2. Modify the employees and data base packages (Programs 11.11 through 11.17) to accommodate the tagged record hierarchy described in this chapter.

3. Develop a data base structure for motor vehicles, similar to the employees data base of Programs 11.11 through 11.17, starting with the tagged types in Table 16.1 and adding a realistic set of derived types.

4. Develop a tagged record structure for the different kinds of people in a university: undergraduates, graduate students, faculty, and staff. The detailed design of the different record types is up to you; use your imagination and experience to determine which fields and operations each type ought to have. Then develop a university data base that is similar to the employee data base.

CHAPTER 17

Introduction to Concurrent Programming

17.1   Problem Solving: What Is Concurrent Programming?

17.2   System Structures: Task Types and Task Objects

17.3   System Structures: Protected Types and Protected Objects

17.4   Continuing Saga: Multiple Concurrent Spiders

Chapter Review

Each program that we have seen so far has been a *sequential*, or *single-threaded*, one; that is, it has consisted of a series of steps that are executed in sequence, one after the other. In this chapter we introduce the idea of a *concurrent*, or *multithreaded*, program, one in which several things can happen—or at least appear to happen—simultaneously.

Concurrent actions are really a part of most interesting programs. For example, a time-shared operating system must deal with a number of human users working simultaneously at their terminals. Further, many real-time applications, especially those controlling physical processes, are composed of concurrent program segments, each responsible for its own physical subsystem. Finally, the world is concurrent, filled with people doing different things all at the same time, and a program that would model that world is best seen as comprising concurrent program segments.

This chapter introduces you to the fascinating field of *concurrent programming*, which is the writing of concurrent programs. Ada provides an especially rich and interesting set of structures for concurrent programming; this chapter presents some of these structures. In particular, we introduce Ada *task types* and *protected types*. A task object is an active program, carrying on its activities independently of other tasks and interacting with others only where necessary. A protected object is passive; its purpose is to encapsulate a data structure and provide services to tasks upon request, allowing many tasks to view the structure simultaneously but authorizing only one task at a time to modify the structure.

17.1 Problem Solving: What Is Concurrent Programming?

Much of the programming world involves concurrent applications. Here are some examples from operating systems, real-time systems, and simulation.

Operating Systems

When you and your colleagues all log in to terminals connected to the same time-sharing system, each of you works separately, but you are all using the same computer. Each of you has the feeling that the computer is working only on your task, yet many of you are working simultaneously. How is this seeming paradox possible?

The illusion that you are alone on the time-shared computer is caused by a combination of fast computers and clever programming. Suppose you are using the computer to edit a program or read electronic mail. You read and type at human speed. A very fast typist can enter 100 words per minute, or—at an average of six characters per word—about 10 characters per second. In the tenth of a second between two of your keystrokes, a modern computer can execute hundreds of thousands of machine instructions. If those "extra" machine instructions could be put to productive use, the computer would have plenty of time between your keystrokes to service other human users. It is not unusual for a modern time-shared computer to handle 100 or more simultaneous users, each working at human speed.

Managing all those instructions and users is part of the responsibility of a modern operating system. An operating system is, as you know by now, just a sophisticated program; in fact, it is a *concurrent* program, capable of managing many devices and human users to give the illusion of simultaneity.

Some time-shared computers consist of a single CPU; others consist of a set of identical CPUs. With more than one CPU, programs can be executed in *parallel*—that is, literally at the same time. With a single CPU, no real parallel execution is possible, but that one CPU can be shared in such a way that many programs *seem* to be executing in parallel. Concurrent programming is the creation of programs that consist of segments that have the potential for parallel execution; depending upon the actual number of CPUs available, execution of a concurrent program may be literally parallel, entirely time-shared, or some combination of the two.

Real-Time Systems

Many computer systems exist to control physical systems of one kind or another. Examples abound in medical technology, manufacturing and robotics, and transportation. In the latter domain, real-time computer programs control modern automotive fuel systems, aircraft such as the Boeing 777, and railroads such as the Channel Tunnel between France and England and the subway system in Washington, D.C. These are, of necessity, concurrent programs: They must manage a number of electronic devices simultaneously; these devices, in turn, are connected to physical machines such as an automobile's fuel injection system or a railroad's "turnout" (a movable section of track that allows a train to enter one or the other of two rail lines).

Modeling and Simulation

Concurrent programming is useful in modeling or simulating physical systems, even if those systems are not directly controlled by a computer. For example, the waiting and service times in a bank, supermarket, or other service organization can be studied by writing a program in which each customer and each server—bank teller, supermarket checker, airline reservation clerk—is represented by its own program segment, which interacts with the other segments.

Similarly, a subway system can be modeled by a program in which each train, station, turnout, and block (section of track that is permitted to hold at most one train) is represented by a program segment. The flow of simulated customers in the bank, or of trains in the subway, can be controlled or varied at will.

Simulation is an important tool in optimizing physical systems—for example, choosing the most effective number of open checkout lanes in a supermarket or the frequency and maximum speed of trains in a subway. Studying the computer model provides information and insight into the behavior of the physical system if the former is a faithful representation of the latter; concurrent programming provides a natural way of assigning program segments to represent physical objects and therefore aids greatly in developing good simulations.

Ada is one of only a few programming languages—and the only popular one—to provide built-in structures for concurrent programming. In this chapter, we use a series of examples to present a few of the basic Ada structures and end with a spider program, namely, a simulation of a family of spiders, all trying simultaneously to move around the room without bumping into walls or other spiders.

Ada Structures for Concurrent Programming

In concurrent programming, an execution of a program segment is called a *process*. For example, when, logged into a time-sharing system, you invoke the electronic mail program, a process is created. The mail program itself is just a file on disk; when it is loaded into memory and executed, that execution is a process. If you and several friends all log in at the same time and invoke the e-mail program, several copies of that program are executing simultaneously on the same computer. One *program* has given rise to multiple simultaneous *processes*. Ada's term for process is *task;* Ada provides *task types* to allow the creation of multiple processes—which Ada calls *task objects*—resulting from a single program declaration.

Generally, your incoming e-mail is stored in a system file called the electronic mail box, or just mailbox. Suppose you are reading your mail when a friend sends you a message. The new message must be added to your mailbox file; your reading must be momentarily suspended while the file is modified (you might not notice the temporary suspension, but it happens anyway). Now suppose that two incoming messages arrive at the same time. Not only must your reading be suspended, but something in the mail software must update your mailbox one message at a time. If this protection were not provided—if two messages could update the mailbox literally at the same time—the mailbox would become hopelessly garbled and therefore useless.

The e-mail situation is an example of a *readers-writers problem,* a category of computing problems in which multiple readers of, and multiple writers to, a data structure must be prevented from interfering with one another. The prevention technique is called *mutual exclusion;* update actions on the data structure are handled one at a time while other actions are excluded. Ada's *protected types* provide mutual exclusion. We can declare a protected type, and variables of that type, with read operations called *pro-*

tected functions and update operations called *protected procedures*. Ada guarantees that these protected operations execute correctly. Specifically, multiple calls to a protected procedure are executed one at a time.

Section 17.2 introduces task types and task objects; Section 17.3 introduces protected types and protected objects.

17.2 System Structures: Task Types and Task Objects

An Ada task is an interesting structure. It has aspects of a package, a procedure, and a data structure but is really none of these; it is something different altogether:

- Like a package, a task has a specification and a body. Unlike a package, it must be declared in an enclosing structure, not put in a separate file and compiled separately.

- Like a procedure, a task has a declaration section and a sequence of executable statements. However, it is not called like a procedure; rather, it starts executing implicitly, automatically, as a part of its enclosing block.

- Like a data structure, it has a type and is brought into existence by declaring a variable of the type. Indeed, like a variant record, it can have one or more discriminants.

Program 17.1 illustrates these aspects of tasks.

Program 17.1 A Task within a Main Program

```
WITH Ada.Text_IO;
PROCEDURE One_Task IS
-----------------------------------------------------------------------
--| Show the declaration of a simple task type and one
--| variable of that type.
--| Author: Michael B. Feldman, The George Washington University
--| Last Modified: September 1998
-----------------------------------------------------------------------

  -- A task type has a specification
  TASK TYPE SimpleTask (Message: Character);

  -- A task type has a body
  TASK BODY SimpleTask IS

  BEGIN -- SimpleTask

    FOR Count IN 1..10 LOOP
      Ada.Text_IO.Put("Hello from Task " & Message);
      Ada.Text_IO.New_Line;
    END LOOP;

  END SimpleTask;

  Task_A: SimpleTask(Message => 'A');
```

```
BEGIN -- One_Task

-- Unlike procedures, tasks are not "called" but are activated
-- automatically.

-- Task_A will start executing as soon as control reaches this
-- point, just after the BEGIN but before any of the main program's
-- statements are executed.

  NULL;

END One_Task;
```

Sample Run

```
Hello from Task A
Hello from Task A
Hello from Task A
Hello from Task A
Hello from Task A
Hello from Task A
Hello from Task A
Hello from Task A
Hello from Task A
Hello from Task A
```

First note the overall structure of the program. A task type, `SimpleTask`, is declared with a discriminant, `Message`. This task specification is followed by a task body in which the message is displayed ten times. Next, `Task_A` is declared as a task variable, usually called a task object, with a discriminant value of `'A'`.

Reaching the main `BEGIN` of this program, we discover that the program has no executable statements, just a `NULL` statement to satisfy the rule that a procedure must have at least one statement. Yet the sample run shows the task actually displaying `Hello from Task A` ten times. The task was never called from the main program, yet it executed anyway.

In fact, the task began its execution just after the main `BEGIN` was reached. In Ada this is called "task activation": All tasks that are declared in a given block are activated just after the `BEGIN` of that block. Here there is only one task, `Task_A`.

Multiple Task Objects of the Same Type

Program 17.2 shows the declaration of two task objects, `Task_A` and `Task_B`. Further, the task type is modified to allow two discriminants: the message and the number of times the message is to be displayed. A discriminant acts here like a parameter of the task, but it is not a fully general parameter; like a variant-record discriminant, it must be of a discrete—integer or enumeration—type. A string, for example, cannot be used as a task discriminant.

Program 17.2 Two Tasks within a Main Program

```
WITH Ada.Text_IO;
PROCEDURE Two_Tasks IS
```

```
------------------------------------------------------------------
--| Show the declaration of a simple task type and two
--| variables of that type.
--| Author: Michael B. Feldman, The George Washington University
--| Last Modified: September 1998
------------------------------------------------------------------

    -- A task type has a specification
    TASK TYPE SimpleTask (Message: Character; HowMany: Positive);

    -- A task type has a body
    TASK BODY SimpleTask IS

    BEGIN -- SimpleTask

      FOR Count IN 1..HowMany LOOP
        Ada.Text_IO.Put("Hello from Task " & Message);
        Ada.Text_IO.New_Line;
      END LOOP;

    END SimpleTask;

    -- Now we declare two variables of the type
    Task_A: SimpleTask(Message => 'A', HowMany => 5);
    Task_B: SimpleTask(Message => 'B', HowMany => 7);

BEGIN -- Two_Tasks

-- Task_A and Task_B will both start executing as soon as control
-- reaches this point, again before any of the main program's
-- statements are executed. The Ada standard does not specify
-- which task will start first.

    NULL;

END Two_Tasks;
```

Sample Run

```
Hello from Task B
Hello from Task B
Hello from Task B
Hello from Task B
Hello from Task B
Hello from Task B
Hello from Task B
Hello from Task A
Hello from Task A
Hello from Task A
Hello from Task A
Hello from Task A
```

As in Program 17.1, Task_A and Task_B are activated just after the main BEGIN. Now there are two tasks; in which order are they activated? The Ada standard does not specify this, leaving it instead up to the compiler implementer. In a short while, we shall see how to control the order in which tasks start their work.

Looking at the sample run from Program 17.2, we see that `Task_B` evidently started—and completed—its work before `Task_A` even started its own work. This tells us first that the compiler we used activated `Task_B` first, and also that, once scheduled for the CPU, `Task_B` was allowed to continue executing until it completed its run. This seems odd: The tasks do not really execute as though they were running in parallel; there is, apparently, no time-sharing. If there were, we would expect `Task_A` and `Task_B` output to be interleaved in some fashion.

In fact, the Ada standard allows, but does not require, *time-slicing.* Time-slicing, implemented in the run-time support software, supports "parallel" execution by giving each task a slice, usually called a *quantum,* which is a certain amount of time on the CPU. At the end of the quantum the run-time system steps in and gives the CPU to another task, allowing it a quantum, and so on, in "round-robin" fashion.

Cooperating Tasks

If Program 17.2 were compiled for a computer with several processors, in theory `Task_A` and `Task_B` could have been executed—truly in parallel—on separate CPUs, and no time-slicing would be needed. With a single CPU, we would like to emulate the parallel operation, ensuring concurrent execution of a set of tasks even if the Ada run-time system does not time-slice.

To get "parallel" behavior portably, using one CPU or many, with or without time-slicing, we code the tasks in a style called *cooperative multitasking;* that is, we design each task so that it periodically "goes to sleep," giving up its turn on the CPU so that another task can execute for a while.

Program 17.3 shows how this is done, using a DELAY statement in each iteration of the task body's FOR loop. The DELAY causes the task to suspend its execution, or "sleep." Now while `Task_A` is "sleeping," `Task_B` can be executing, and so on. The cooperating nature of the two tasks is easily seen in the sample output.

Program 17.3 Using DELAY to Achieve Cooperation

```
WITH Ada.Text_IO;
PROCEDURE Two_Cooperating_Tasks IS
-------------------------------------------------------------------
--| Show the declaration of a simple task type and two
--| variables of that type. The tasks use DELAYs to cooperate.
--| The DELAY causes another task to get a turn in the CPU.
--| Author: Michael B. Feldman, The George Washington University
--| Last Modified: September 1998
-------------------------------------------------------------------

   -- A task type has a specification
   TASK TYPE SimpleTask (Message: Character; HowMany: Positive);

   -- A task type has a body
   TASK BODY SimpleTask IS

BEGIN -- SimpleTask

   FOR Count IN 1..HowMany LOOP
     Ada.Text_IO.Put(Item => "Hello from Task " & Message);
     Ada.Text_IO.New_Line;
```

```
        DELAY 0.1;              -- lets another task have the CPU
      END LOOP;

  END SimpleTask;

  -- Now we declare two variables of the type
  Task_A: SimpleTask(Message => 'A', HowMany => 5);
  Task_B: SimpleTask(Message => 'B', HowMany => 7);

BEGIN -- Two_Cooperating_Tasks

-- Task_A and Task_B will both start executing as soon as control
-- reaches this point, again before any of the main program's
-- statements are executed. The Ada standard does not specify
-- which task will start first.

  NULL;

END Two_Cooperating_Tasks;
```

Sample Run

```
Hello from Task B
Hello from Task A
Hello from Task B
Hello from Task A
Hello from Task B
Hello from Task A
Hello from Task B
Hello from Task A
Hello from Task B
Hello from Task A
Hello from Task B
Hello from Task B
```

Controlling the Starting Order of Tasks

We know that the Ada standard does not specify an order of activation for multiple tasks in the same program. Each compiler can use a different order; indeed, a compiler is—theoretically—free to use a different starting order each time the program is run, though practical compilers rarely if ever take advantage of this freedom.

Although we cannot control the actual activation order of tasks, we can gain control of the order in which these tasks start to do their work by using a so-called "start button." This is a special case of a *task entry,* which is a point in a task at which it can *synchronize* with other tasks. This is illustrated in Program 17.4.

Program 17.4 Using "Start Buttons" to Control Tasks' Starting Order

```
WITH Ada.Text_IO;
PROCEDURE Start_Buttons IS
-------------------------------------------------------------------
--| Show the declaration of a simple task type and three
--| variables of that type. The tasks use DELAYs to cooperate.
--| "Start button" entries are used to to control starting order.
--| Author: Michael B. Feldman, The George Washington University
--| Last Modified: September 1998
```

```
   TASK TYPE SimpleTask (Message: Character; HowMany: Positive) IS

      -- This specification provides a "start button" entry.
      ENTRY StartRunning;

   END SimpleTask;

   TASK BODY SimpleTask IS

   BEGIN -- SimpleTask

      -- The task will "block" at the ACCEPT, waiting for the "button"
      -- to be "pushed" (called from another task, Main in this case).
      ACCEPT StartRunning;

      FOR Count IN 1..HowMany LOOP
         Ada.Text_IO.Put(Item => "Hello from Task " & Message);
         Ada.Text_IO.New_Line;
         DELAY 0.1;              -- lets another task have the CPU
      END LOOP;

   END SimpleTask;

      -- Now we declare three variables of the type
      Task_A: SimpleTask(Message => 'A', HowMany => 5);
      Task_B: SimpleTask(Message => 'B', HowMany => 7);
      Task_C: SimpleTask(Message => 'C', HowMany => 4);

BEGIN -- Start_Buttons

-- Tasks will all start executing as soon as control
-- reaches this point, but each will block on its ACCEPT
-- until the entry is called. In this way we control the starting
-- order of the tasks.

   Task_B.StartRunning;
   Task_A.StartRunning;
   Task_C.StartRunning;

END Start_Buttons;
```

Sample Run

```
Hello from Task B
Hello from Task A
Hello from Task C
Hello from Task B
Hello from Task A
Hello from Task C
Hello from Task B
Hello from Task A
Hello from Task C
Hello from Task B
Hello from Task A
Hello from Task C
Hello from Task B
Hello from Task A
Hello from Task B
```

```
Hello from Task B
```

In this program, the task specification is expanded to include an entry specification:

```
ENTRY StartRunning;
```

This is, syntactically, similar to the subprogram specifications that usually appear in package specifications. The task body includes, immediately after its BEGIN, the corresponding line

```
ACCEPT StartRunning;
```

According to the rules of Ada, a SimpleTask object, upon reaching an ACCEPT statement, must *wait* at that statement until the corresponding entry is called by another task. In Program 17.4, then, each task—Task_A, Task_B, and Task_C—is activated just after the main program's BEGIN, but—before it starts any work—each reaches its respective ACCEPT and must wait there (in this simple case, possibly forever) until the entry is called.

How is the entry called? In our first three examples the main program had nothing to do. In this case its job is to "press the start buttons" of the three tasks, with the entry call statements

```
Task_B.StartRunning;
Task_A.StartRunning;
Task_C.StartRunning;
```

These statements are syntactically similar to procedure calls. The first statement "presses the start button" of Task_B. Since Task_B was waiting for the button to be pressed, it accepts the call and proceeds with its work.

The main program is apparently executing—in this case, pressing the start buttons—in "parallel" with the three tasks. In fact, this is true. In a program with multiple tasks, the Ada run-time system treats the main program as a task as well.

SYNTAX DISPLAY

Task Type Specification

Form:

```
TASK TYPE tname (optional list of discrimnents ) IS
  ENTRY e1;
  ENTRY e2;
  . . .
END tname;
```

Example:

```
TASK TYPE Philosopher (Name: Natural) IS
  ENTRY Come_to_Life (First, Second: Chopstick);
END Philosopher;
```

Interpretation:

The task type specification gives a list of the entries to be provided by the task objects.

SYNTAX
DISPLAY

Task Body

Form:

```
TASK BODY tname IS
  local declaration-section
BEGIN
  statement sequence
END tname;
```

Example:

The `SimpleTask` bodies shown in this section serve as examples; we need not repeat them here.

Interpretation:

The task body contains the local declarations and statement sequence of the task. Multiple task objects of the type can be declared; each task object has, in effect, a copy of the task body.

A task body can contain code that is much more interesting than we have seen. Ada provides the SELECT statement to give a programmer much flexibility in coding task bodies. For example, using the SELECT,

- The ACCEPT statement can be written to "time out" if a call is not received within a given time interval.

- The task can be made to terminate—end its execution—if the call is never received.

- The task specification can provide a number of entries and its body can be made to respond to whichever of a set of different entry calls occurs first, then loop around and respond again.

The SELECT construct is one of the most interesting in all of programming; entire books can be written about the possibilities it offers. Space does not permit a full discussion of the SELECT here; we hope this brief discussion has sparked your curiosity to learn more about it.

In this section we have seen the basics of task types and objects. We now proceed to introduce protected types and objects.

17.3 System Structures: Protected Types and Protected Objects

In Section 17.1 we discussed mutual exclusion using the example of an e-mail reader. Here we look at an analogous, but simpler, situation. Suppose we have a three-task program like Program 17.4, but we want each task to write its output in its own area of the screen. The desired output is

```
Hello from Task A        Hello from Task B        Hello from Task C
Hello from Task A        Hello from Task B        Hello from Task C
```

```
Hello from Task A        Hello from Task B        Hello from Task C
Hello from Task A        Hello from Task B        Hello from Task C
Hello from Task A        Hello from Task B
                         Hello from Task B
                         Hello from Task B
```

This simple example is representative of *multiwindow* programs. We modify the task specification to read

```
TASK TYPE SimpleTask (Message: Character;
                      HowMany: Screen.Depth;
                      Column:  Screen.Width) IS . . .
```

adding a third discriminant, Column, to indicate which screen column each task should use for the first character of its repeated message. Further, we modify the main loop of the task body as follows:

```
FOR Count IN 1..HowMany LOOP
  Screen.MoveCursor(Row => Count, Column => Column);
  Ada.Text_IO.Put(Item => "Hello from Task " & Message);
  DELAY 0.5;              -- lets another task have the CPU
END LOOP;
```

That is, the task positions the screen cursor to the proper column before writing the message. Program 17.5 shows the full program.

Program 17.5 Several Tasks Using the Screen

```
WITH Ada.Text_IO;
WITH Screen;
PROCEDURE Columns IS
-------------------------------------------------------------------------
--| Shows tasks writing into their respective columns on the
--| screen. This will not always work correctly, because if the
--| tasks are time-sliced, one task may lose the CPU before
--| sending its entire "message" to the screen. This may result
--| in strange "garbage" on the screen.
--| Author: Michael B. Feldman, The George Washington University
--| Last Modified: September 1998
-------------------------------------------------------------------------

   TASK TYPE SimpleTask (Message: Character;
                         HowMany: Screen.Depth;
                         Column:  Screen.Width) IS

   -- This specification provides a "start button" entry.
   ENTRY StartRunning;

   END SimpleTask;

   TASK BODY SimpleTask IS

   BEGIN -- SimpleTask

      -- Each task will write its message in its own column
      ACCEPT StartRunning;
```

```
    FOR Count IN 1..HowMany LOOP
      Screen.MoveCursor(Row => Count, Column => Column);
      Ada.Text_IO.Put(Item => "Hello from Task " & Message);
      DELAY 0.5;              -- lets another task have the CPU
    END LOOP;

  END SimpleTask;

  -- Now we declare three variables of the type
  Task_A: SimpleTask(Message => 'A', HowMany => 5, Column => 1);
  Task_B: SimpleTask(Message => 'B', HowMany => 7, Column => 26);
  Task_C: SimpleTask(Message => 'C', HowMany => 4, Column => 51);

BEGIN -- Columns

  Screen.ClearScreen;
  Task_B.StartRunning;
  Task_A.StartRunning;
  Task_C.StartRunning;

END Columns;
```

Sample Run

```
Hello from Task A        Hello from Task B        Hello from Task C
                                                  2Hello from Task
C;26f[2;1fHello from Task AHello from Task B                [[3;1fHello
 from Task A3;26fHello from Task BHello from Task C4;4;1fHello from Task
 A51fHello from Task C26fHello from Task B5;526;f1fHello from Task BHello
 from Task A
                         Hello from Task B
                         Hello from Task B
```

The output from running this program is not exactly what we intended! Instead of the desired neat columns, we got messages displayed in seemingly random locations, interspersed with apparent "garbage" like

```
C;26f[2;1f
```

What happened here? To understand this, recall the body of `Screen.MoveCursor` (included in Program 4.9):

```
PROCEDURE MoveCursor (Column : Width; Row : Depth) IS
BEGIN
  Ada.Text_IO.Put (Item => ASCII.ESC);
  Ada.Text_IO.Put ("[");
  Ada.Integer_Text_IO.Put (Item => Row, Width => 1);
  Ada.Text_IO.Put (Item => ';');
  Ada.Integer_Text_IO.Put (Item => Column, Width => 1);
  Ada.Text_IO.Put (Item => 'f');
END MoveCursor;
```

Positioning the cursor requires an instruction, up to eight characters in length, to the ANSI terminal software: the ESC character, then '[', followed by a possibly two-digit Row, then ';', then a possibly two-digit Column value, and finally 'F'. Once it receives the entire instruction, the terminal actually moves the cursor on the screen.

Suppose the `MoveCursor` call is issued from within a task, as in the present example. Suppose further that in this case the Ada run-time system *does* provide time-slicing to give "parallel" behavior of multiple tasks. It is quite possible that the task's quantum will expire after only some of the eight characters have been sent to the terminal, and then another task will attempt to write something to the terminal. The terminal never recognized the first instruction, because it received only part of it, so instead of obeying the instruction, it just displays the characters. The "garbage" string above, `c;26f[2;1f`, consists of pieces from several different intended instructions.

This problem arose because a task was interrupted in mid-instruction, and then another task was allowed to begin its own screen instruction. This is called a *race condition* because two tasks are, effectively, in a race to write to the screen, with unpredictable results. It is actually a readers-writers problem: Multiple tasks are interfering with each other's attempts to write to the screen.

To prevent this problem from ruining our columnar output, we must *protect* the screen so that—whether or not we have time-slicing—a task is allowed to finish an entire display operation before another task can begin one. We can do this in Ada with a protected type, as shown in Program 17.6.

Program 17.6 Using a Protected Type to Ensure Completion of a Screen Action

```
WITH Ada.Text_IO;
WITH Screen;
PROCEDURE Protect_Screen IS
-------------------------------------------------------------------------
--| Shows tasks writing into their respective columns on the
--| screen. This time we use a protected type, whose procedure
--| can be executed by only one task at a time.
--| Author: Michael B. Feldman, The George Washington University
--| Last Modified: September 1998
-------------------------------------------------------------------------

   PROTECTED TYPE ScreenManagerType IS

   -- If multiple calls of Write are made simultaneously, each is
   -- executed in its entirety before the next is begun.
   -- The Ada standard does not specify an order of execution.

      PROCEDURE Write (Item:   IN String;
                       Row:    IN Screen.Depth;
                       Column: IN Screen.Width);

   END ScreenManagerType;

   PROTECTED BODY ScreenManagerType IS

      PROCEDURE Write (Item:   IN String;
                       Row:    IN Screen.Depth;
                       Column: IN Screen.Width) IS
      BEGIN -- Write

         Screen.MoveCursor(Row => Row, Column => Column);
         Ada.Text_IO.Put(Item => Item);

      END Write;

   END ScreenManagerType;
```

```
Manager: ScreenManagerType;

TASK TYPE SimpleTask (Message: Character;
                         HowMany: Screen.Depth;
                         Column:  Screen.Width) IS

   -- This specification provides a "start button" entry.
   ENTRY StartRunning;

END SimpleTask;

TASK BODY SimpleTask IS

BEGIN -- SimpleTask

   -- Each task will write its message in its own column
   -- Now the task locks the screen before moving the cursor,
   -- unlocking it when writing is completed.

   ACCEPT StartRunning;

   FOR Count IN 1..HowMany LOOP

      -- No need to lock the screen explicitly; just call the
      -- protected procedure.
      Manager.Write(Row => Count, Column => Column,
                    Item => "Hello from Task " & Message);

      DELAY 0.5;                -- lets another task have the CPU
   END LOOP;

END SimpleTask;

-- Now we declare three variables of the type
Task_A: SimpleTask(Message => 'A', HowMany => 5, Column => 1);
Task_B: SimpleTask(Message => 'B', HowMany => 7, Column => 26);
Task_C: SimpleTask(Message => 'C', HowMany => 4, Column => 51);

BEGIN -- Protect_Screen

   Screen.ClearScreen;
   Task_B.StartRunning;
   Task_A.StartRunning;
   Task_C.StartRunning;

END Protect_Screen;
```

In this program, we declare a type

```
PROTECTED TYPE ScreenManagerType IS

   PROCEDURE Write (Item:   IN String;
                    Row:    IN Screen.Depth;
                    Column: IN Screen.Width);

END ScreenManagerType;

Manager: ScreenManagerType;
```

An object of this type in this case `Manager`, provides a procedure `Write` to which are passed all the parameters of the desired screen operation: the string to be written, the row, and the column. Any task wishing to write to the screen must do so by passing these parameters to the screen manager. The `SimpleTask` body now contains a call

```
Manager.Write(Row => Count, Column => Column,
            Item => "Hello from Task " & Message);
```

as required. The body of the protected type is

```
PROTECTED BODY ScreenManagerType IS

  PROCEDURE Write (Item:   IN String;
                   Row:    IN Screen.Depth;
                   Column: IN Screen.Width) IS
  BEGIN -- Write

    Screen.MoveCursor(Row => Row, Column => Column);
    Ada.Text_IO.Put(Item => Item);

  END Write;

END ScreenManagerType;
```

and the `Write` procedure encapsulates the `MoveCursor` and `Put` operations.

What is the difference between this protected write procedure and an ordinary procedure? Ada guarantees that each call of a protected procedure will complete before another call can be started. Even if several tasks are running, trading control of the CPU among them, a task will not be allowed to start a protected procedure call if another call of the same procedure, or any other procedure of the same protected object, is still incomplete. In our case, this provides the necessary mutual exclusion for the screen.

Protected types can provide functions and entries in addition to procedures. Protected functions allow for multiple tasks to examine a data structure simultaneously but not to modify the data structure. Protected entries have some of the properties of both task entries and protected procedures. A detailed discussion of these is beyond our scope here.

The next section will introduce a more interesting use of protected types.

17.4 Continuing Saga: Multiple Concurrent Spiders

In Section 11.6 we developed the package specification `Spiders` for multiple spiders (Program 11.18); we left the body as an exercise. However, we could not, at that time, consider how to program the spiders so that they acted independently of each other, crawling at will around the room. In this section we show how to develop multiple concurrent spiders.

Developing a Task Type for Drunken Spiders

Recall the "drunken spider" program from Program 2.15. There the spider, in a state of inebriation, lurched around its room, taking a random number of steps and occasionally hitting the wall. Here we see a number of drunken spiders trying to get around, occasionally hitting the wall and sometimes bumping into each other. Suppose a spider refers to itself as Me. The main loop of that spider's life is given by the following:

```
LOOP

  FOR Count IN 1..Random_20.Random (Gen => G) LOOP

    BEGIN    -- to handle exception
      Spiders.Step(Me);
    EXCEPTION
      WHEN Spiders.Hit_the_Wall =>   -- turn around
        Spiders.Right (Me);
        Spiders.Right (Me);
      WHEN Spiders.Hit_a_Spider =>   -- turn right
        Spiders.Right (Me);
    END;

  END LOOP;

  Spiders.Right (Me);

END LOOP;
```

In an endless loop, the spider first selects a random number of steps in the range 1..20, then tries to step forward that number of times. If it hits the wall (Spiders.Hit_the_Wall is raised), it turns around and keeps stepping in the opposite direction; if it bumps into another spider (Spiders.Hit_a_Spider is raised), it turns right and continues its walk.

Program 17.7 shows a full program in which this loop is incorporated in a task type Drunken_Spider_Task, with a discriminant MyColor and a "start button" entry called Hatch. The discriminant has a default value Spiders.Black; this means that if a spider object declaration fails to provide a value for the discriminant, the default value will be taken.

Program 17.7 Three Drunken Spiders

```
WITH Spiders;
WITH Ada.Text_IO;
WITH Ada.Numerics.Discrete_Random;
PROCEDURE Three_Drunken_Spiders IS
-----------------------------------------------------------------------
--| Multiple drunken spiders try to tour their room.
--| The spiders are represented as task objects.
--| Author: Michael B. Feldman, The George Washington University
--| Last Modified: September 1998
-----------------------------------------------------------------------

  -- Now a spider is a task object, as defined by this type.
  -- Note: default color is black.
  TASK TYPE Drunken_Spider_Task
    (MyColor: Spiders.Colors := Spiders.Green) IS
```

```
      -- one "start button" entry to bring spider to life
      ENTRY Hatch;

   END Drunken_Spider_Task;

   TASK BODY Drunken_Spider_Task IS

      Me: Spiders.Spider;

   BEGIN -- Drunken_Spider_Task

      ACCEPT Hatch;    -- come to life here

      -- Randomize all starting parameters
      Spiders.Start (Which => Me,
                     Row => Spiders.RandomStep,
                     Col => Spiders.RandomStep,
                     WhichColor => MyColor,
                     WhichWay => Spiders.RandomDirection);

         LOOP

            -- Spider will count steps correctly but might change direction
            FOR Count IN 1..Spiders.RandomStep LOOP

               BEGIN    -- to handle exception
                  Spiders.Step(Me);
               EXCEPTION
                  WHEN Spiders.Hit_the_Wall =>  -- turn around
                     Spiders.TurnRight (Me);
                     Spiders.TurnRight (Me);
                  WHEN Spiders.Hit_a_Spider =>  -- turn right
                     Spiders.TurnRight (Me);
               END;

            END LOOP;

            Spiders.TurnRight (Me);

         END LOOP;

      EXCEPTION

         WHEN OTHERS =>
            Ada.Text_IO.Put(Item => "This spider is dying.");
            Ada.Text_IO.New_Line;

   END Drunken_Spider_Task;

   -- Now declare some spider objects
   Charlotte : Drunken_Spider_Task(MyColor => Spiders.Green);
   Murgatroyd: Drunken_Spider_Task(MyColor => Spiders.Red);
   Arachne   : Drunken_Spider_Task(MyColor => Spiders.Blue);

BEGIN -- Three_Drunken_Spiders

   Spiders.Draw_Room;

   -- Bring the spiders to life, then stand back and watch!
```

```
Charlotte.Hatch;
Murgatroyd.Hatch;
Arachne.Hatch;
```

```
END Three_Drunken_Spiders;
```

Within the task body is a local variable

```
Me: Spiders.Spider;
```

which is referred to further in the task body. If we declare multiple objects of type `Drunken_Spider_Task`, each one will have its own `Me` variable.

The rest is straightforward: Each spider waits at its ACCEPT to be hatched, then calls `Spiders.Start` with random values for the starting direction and position. At this point, the spider starts executing its main loop.

Three `Drunken_Spider_Task` objects are declared with their respective color discriminants. After the main BEGIN, each spider is brought to life, and nothing is left for the main program to do but watch the action.

Protecting the Spider Move Operation

We are not quite finished with the multiple spider example. Consider the algorithm for detecting a possible collision between spiders and acting accordingly:

Algorithm for Spider Move

1. Compute location into which spider is trying to move

2. IF the spider is trying to move to an occupied square THEN

    3. RAISE Hit_a_Spider

    ELSE

    4. Step out of the current space into the unoccupied square

    END IF;

Step 4 can be refined into

Step 4 Refinement

4.1 Draw a colored mark in the current square

4.2 Mark the current space as unoccupied

4.3 Mark the new space as occupied

4.4 Draw a spider symbol in the new square

There are therefore several operations to be done to record the spider's move, involving both the screen and the room board in which we keep track of occupancy. Because several spiders are crawling around concurrently, we must be sure that steps 4.1 through 4.4 are done as a single operation. Consider a situation in which Murgatroyd executes its step 4.1 and 4.2, vacating its square. but then—before Murgatroyd actually moves to its new space in steps 4.3 and 4.4—Charlotte is able to move into that same square because it is not yet marked as occupied. This is not a very good situation—it leaves Murgatroyd without a square.

This is another example of a situation in which mutual exclusion is necessary. We can handle this by analogy with the screen protector from Program 17.6. We will define a protected type that "owns" the room array, with a procedure Move to encapsulate steps 4.1 through 4.4 in one protected operation.

Let us add to the body of Spiders the following declarations:

```
TYPE Status IS (Unoccupied, Occupied);
TYPE BoardType IS ARRAY (RoomHeight, RoomWidth) OF Status;

PROTECTED TYPE Room_Type IS

  PROCEDURE Move (Which: IN OUT Spider; HowMany: IN Natural);

PRIVATE

  RoomBoard: BoardType := (OTHERS => (OTHERS => Unoccupied));

END Room_Type;

PROTECTED BODY Room_Type IS SEPARATE;

Room: Room_Type;
```

Our protected type Room_Type has some memory, RoomBoard, that belongs to it exclusively, as indicated in the PRIVATE section. Move is a protected operation; a given call of Move will be executed in its entirety before another Move can be started. The declarations above show the protected body as a separate subunit; the subunit is given in full as Program 17.8.

Program 17.8 Protecting the Room Board from Multiple Accesses

```
SEPARATE (Spiders)
PROTECTED BODY Room_Type IS
-----------------------------------------------------------------
--| Body of protected type for the spider's room.
--| The room array is protected from concurrent access by
--| requiring all access to be via the protected procedure Move.
--| Author: Michael B. Feldman, The George Washington University
--| Last Modified: September 1998
-----------------------------------------------------------------

  PROCEDURE Move (Which: IN OUT Spider; HowMany: IN Natural) IS
    Row:    RoomHeight;
    Column: RoomWidth;
  BEGIN -- Move

    -- If out of bounds raise exception.
    IF NearWall (Which, HowMany) THEN
      RAISE Hit_the_Wall;
    END IF;

    Row    := Which.CurrentRow;
    Column := Which.CurrentColumn;
```

```
    -- Compute new proposed location
    CASE Which.Heading IS
      WHEN North =>
        Row := Which.CurrentRow - HowMany;
      WHEN East  =>
        Column := Which.CurrentColumn + HowMany;
      WHEN South =>
        Row := Which.CurrentRow + HowMany;
      WHEN West  =>
        Column := Which.CurrentColumn - HowMany;
    END CASE;

    -- Is this space occupied?
    IF RoomBoard(Row, Column) = Occupied THEN
      RAISE Hit_a_Spider;
    ELSE

      -- put a block down where spider is standing; vacate space
      DrawSymbol(Which => Which, WhichChar => ColorSymbols(Which.Ink));
      RoomBoard(Which.CurrentRow, Which.CurrentColumn) := Unoccupied;

      -- occupy new space
      RoomBoard(Row, Column) := Occupied;
      Which.CurrentRow    := Row;
      Which.CurrentColumn := Column;
      ShowSpider (Which);

    END IF;

  END Move;

END Room_Type;
```

All that remains is to modify the bodies of those operations in the `spiders` package body that involve a move. Here is `Jump`, for example:

```
PROCEDURE Jump (Which: IN OUT Spider; HowMany: IN Positive) IS
BEGIN

  -- Concurrent spiders now, so move must be protected.
  Room.Move(Which, HowMany);

  IF Debugging = On THEN    -- if debug mode,
    Ada.Text_IO.Skip_Line; -- wait for user to press ENTER
  ELSE
    DELAY 0.1;
  END IF;

END Jump;
```

We leave it to you as an exercise to complete the package body.

SYNTAX
DISPLAY

Protected Type Specification

Form:
```
PROTECTED TYPE pname (optional list of discriminants ) IS
   specifications of functions, procedures, and entries
   . . .
PRIVATE
   declarations of encapsulated data structures
END pname;
```

Example:

See the `Room_Type` and `ScreenManagerType` specifications in this chapter.

Interpretation:

The protected type specification gives a list of the procedures, functions, and entries to be provided by the protected objects. The PRIVATE part is optional.

SYNTAX
DISPLAY

Protected Body

Form:

```
PROTECTED BODY pname IS
BEGIN
   entry, procedure, and function bodies
END pname;
```

Example:

See the `Room_Type` and `ScreenManagerType` bodies in this chapter.

Interpretation:

The protected body contains the bodies of the protected operations.

Arrays of Task Objects

Finally, we show an example of how tasks really do have aspects of data objects. Program 17.9 shows how we could create an array of spider objects.

Program 17.9 Creating an Array of Spiders

```
WITH Spiders;
WITH Ada.Text_IO;
WITH Ada.Numerics.Discrete_Random;
PROCEDURE Drunken_Spiders_Family IS
-----------------------------------------------------------------
--| Multiple drunken spiders try to tour their room.
--| The spiders are represented as task objects;
--| a spider family is represented by an array of spiders.
--| Author: Michael B. Feldman, The George Washington University
--| Last Modified: September 1998
-----------------------------------------------------------------
```

```
SUBTYPE RandomSteps IS Positive RANGE 1..20;

PACKAGE Random_20 IS NEW Ada.Numerics.Discrete_Random
  (Result_Subtype => RandomSteps);

G: Random_20.Generator;

PACKAGE RandomHeading IS NEW Ada.Numerics.Discrete_Random
  (Result_Subtype => Spiders.Directions);

D: RandomHeading.Generator;

-- Now a spider is a task object, as defined by this type.
TASK TYPE Drunken_Spider_Task
  (MyColor: Spiders.ScreenColors := Spiders.Black) IS

  -- one "start button" entry to bring spider to life
  ENTRY Hatch;

END Drunken_Spider_Task;

TASK BODY Drunken_Spider_Task IS

  Me: Spiders.Spider;

BEGIN -- Drunken_Spider_Task

  ACCEPT Hatch;     -- come to life here

  -- Randomize all starting parameters
  Spiders.Start (Which => Me,
                 Row => Random_20.Random(Gen => G),
                 Col => Random_20.Random(Gen => G),
                 WhichColor => MyColor,
                 WhichWay => RandomHeading.Random(Gen => D));

    LOOP

      -- Spider will count steps correctly but might change direction
      FOR Count IN 1..Random_20.Random (Gen => G) LOOP

        BEGIN   -- to handle exception
          Spiders.Step(Me);
        EXCEPTION
          WHEN Spiders.Hit_the_Wall =>  -- turn around
            Spiders.Right (Me);
            Spiders.Right (Me);
          WHEN Spiders.Hit_a_Spider =>  -- turn right
            Spiders.Right (Me);
        END;

      END LOOP;

      Spiders.Right (Me);

    END LOOP;

EXCEPTION
```

```
        WHEN OTHERS =>
          Ada.Text_IO.Put(Item => "This spider is dying.");
          Ada.Text_IO.New_Line;

    END Drunken_Spider_Task;

    SUBTYPE FamilyRange IS Positive RANGE 1..10;
    TYPE FamilyType IS ARRAY (FamilyRange) OF Drunken_Spider_Task;

    Family: FamilyType;    -- now we have an entire array of spiders

BEGIN -- Drunken_Spiders_Family

    Spiders.DrawRoom;

    -- Bring the spiders to life, then stand back and watch!
    FOR Which IN FamilyRange LOOP
     Family(Which).Hatch;
    END LOOP;

END Drunken_Spiders_Family;
```

Instead of declaring named spider variables as we did in Program 17.7, we give a few new declarations:

```
SUBTYPE FamilyRange IS Positive RANGE 1..10;
TYPE FamilyType IS ARRAY (FamilyRange) OF Drunken_Spider_Task;
Family: FamilyType;    -- now we have an entire array of spiders
```

Here we declare `Family` as a ten-element array of spider task objects. As in the case of ordinary task variables, the entire array of spiders is activated just after the main BEGIN. We then cause all the spiders to hatch by using a simple FOR loop:

```
FOR Which IN FamilyRange LOOP
   Family(Which).Hatch;
END LOOP;
```

Varying the bounds of `FamilyRange` is sufficient to change the size of the spider family.

CHAPTER REVIEW

In this chapter we introduced Ada tasks and protected types. These are used to support concurrent programming, which is the writing of programs with multiple threads of control or processes.

Tasks are active program units that act as processes; in a given program, each task is separately activated and executes independently of the others. A task is an interesting kind of program unit: It has a specification and a body like a package, contains a declaration section and a sequence of statements like a procedure, and has a type like a data structure. Tasks are declared like other variables; they can also be array elements. We have seen a few examples of task discriminants and entries; other tasking statements, especially the SELECT statement, are very interesting but beyond the scope of our discussion here.

A protected type is a way to create an encapsulated data structure with operations that are protected in a concurrent environment. Protected operations can be functions, procedures, or entries; in this brief presentation we have introduced only procedures. The Ada 95 standard provides that multiple concurrent calls of a protected procedure are fully executed one at a time, preventing the multiple calls from interfering with each other and modifying the data structure unpredictably.

We have hardly begun to explore the richness of concurrent programs in Ada; we hope this brief introduction has sparked your interest in the subject and that you will continue to learn more about concurrent programming in general and its Ada implementation in particular.

New Ada Constructs in Chapter 17

The new Ada constructs introduced in this chapter are described in Table 17.1.

Table 17.1 Summary of New Ada Constructs

Construct	*Effect*
Task Type	

<pre>TASK TYPE SimpleTask
          (Message: Character;
          HowMany: Positive) IS
  ENTRY StartRunning;
END SimpleTask;</pre>
	SimpleTask is a type; Message and HowMany are discriminants whose values are passed to the task objects when they are activated. StartRunning is a "start button" entry.

<pre>TASK BODY SimpleTask IS
 	
BEGIN -- SimpleTask
 	
  ACCEPT StartRunning;</pre>
	Each task object waits here for its entry to be called, and then continues on its own.

<pre> FOR Count IN 1..HowMany LOOP
    Ada.Text_IO.Put
      (Item => "Hello from Task " & Message);
    Ada.Text_IO.New_Line;
    DELAY 0.1;
  END LOOP;
END SimpleTask;</pre>
	Here is the task's main loop.

Construct	Effect
Task Object	
| ```
Task_A: SimpleTask
        (Message => 'A', HowMany => 5);
Task_B: SimpleTask
        (Message => 'B', HowMany => 7);
``` | Two task objects are declared with discriminant values. |
| *Entry Call* | |
| ```
Task_B.StartRunning;
Task_A.StartRunning;
``` | The two tasks' "start button" entries are called. |
| *Protected Type* | |
| ```
PROTECTED TYPE ScreenManagerType IS
  PROCEDURE Write (Item:   IN String;
                   Row:    IN Screen.Depth;
                   Column: IN Screen.Width);
PRIVATE
  -- a data structure could be declared here
END ScreenManagerType;
``` | ScreenManagerType provides a protected procedure Write. Multiple calls to Write are guaranteed to be processed one at a time. This provides mutual exclusion on operations that modify the protected structure. |
| ```
PROTECTED BODY ScreenManagerType IS
  PROCEDURE Write (Item:   IN String;
                   Row:    IN Screen.Depth;
                   Column: IN Screen.Width) IS
  BEGIN -- Write
    Screen.MoveCursor
      (Row => Row, Column => Column);
    Ada.Text_IO.Put(Item => Item);
  END Write;
END ScreenManagerType;
``` | This is the body of the protected type. |
| *Protected Object* | |
| ```
Manager: ScreenManagerType;
``` | Manager is a protected object. |

Quick–Check Exercises

1. How is a task different from a procedure?

2. When are tasks activated? What is the order of activation?

3. If multiple tasks are active, how do they share the CPU?

4. How does a task handle an ACCEPT in its task body?
```

5. What happens when a task calls an entry in another task?

6. How does a protected procedure differ from an ordinary procedure?

Answers to Quick-Check Exercises

1. A procedure is called, but a task is activated implicitly and has its own thread of control.

2. Tasks are activated just after the BEGIN of the block in which they are declared. Ada does not predefine an order of activation.

3. The run-time system may or may not time-slice the tasks; if it does not, the first task to get the CPU will keep it until that task reaches a DELAY or other statement that causes it to block.

4. The task waits at the ACCEPT until another task calls the entry.

5. It waits at the point of call until the called task accepts the call at an ACCEPT statement.

6. An ordinary procedure can be called simultaneously by several tasks. Multiple calls of a protected procedure are executed one at a time.

Review Questions for Chapter 17

1. Explain, in as much detail as you can provide, how multiple tasks can share a single computer.

2. Explain why protected types are necessary.

Programming Projects

1. Investigate whether your Ada implementation supports time-slicing and, if it does, whether time-slicing can be turned on and off at will. Experiment with doing so, using Program 17.2 as a test program.

2. Experiment with using different starting orders in Program 17.4. Is there any difference in the behavior?

3. Develop a program that uses two tasks to write two lines of asterisks repeatedly across the screen. One task will write 80 asterisks from left to right in row 5 and then "erase" the line by writing 80 blanks from right to left in that row. The other task will write 80 asterisks from right to left in row 10 and then "erase" that line by writing blanks from left to right. Use DELAY statements in the tasks to ensure that the output is interleaved. The visual effect will be interesting.

4. Section 17.4 suggests a modification to the body of the `Spiders` package (Program 7.11, modified according to the specification in Program 11.19) using a protected type to keep track of the spiders on the board. Modify the package accordingly and test it using Program 2.13 or 2.14. Now remove the protection from the `Move` procedure, that is, declare it as an ordinary procedure and the board as an ordinary data structure. Test again; is there any difference in the behavior?

5. (Thanks to Chet Lund for this challenging adaptation of Edsger Dijkstra's famous "Dining Philosophers" problem published in 1971.) This project involves five students over a weekend; each student alternately eats Chinese food and sleeps. That's it. The five students are sitting at a large round table in the student union building. They eat and sleep at the table (these students are not in condition to leave the table after eating). This project simulates their behavior over the weekend. The weekend is 48 hours long. Use one second on the computer to represent one hour of weekend time. The simulation rules are as follows:

   - There are five students, each represented by a task object.

   - There are five chopsticks, each represented by a protected object with `PickUp` and `PutDown` procedures, in an array of five chopsticks.

   - Between each pair of students is a single chopstick. To eat, a student must pick up her left chopstick and her right chopstick. After eating, a student puts down both chopsticks, freeing them for the adjacent students.

   - Only one student can have a chopstick at a time.

   - There is enough food in the center of the table for the entire weekend.

   - Each student eats for periods of 1, 2, 3, or 4 hours at a time; the length of an eating period is determined randomly. Each student sleeps for random periods of 1, 2, 3, or 4 hours at a time.

   - If all five students hold just one chopstick and are waiting for the other one, everything deadlocks and they all starve.

   - After the 48 hours is over, each student must be allowed to complete her current eating and sleeping cycle.

   - Your program will use discriminants to assign each student a pair of chopsticks in the declaration for that student.

   Here is some sample output from a run.

```
Nikki is eating.
Nikki finished eating.
Nikki is sleeping.
Nikki is finished sleeping.
        . . .
Passing quit to diner tasks
Nikki is finished sleeping.
Nikki TASK is terminating
        . . .
All tasks have quit.  Program completed.
```

APPENDIX A

High-Resolution Color Graphics

Many beginning students of Ada ask whether it is possible to do computer graphics with Ada. The answer is very simple: Of course it is! In fact, in this book we have actually done some: Our `Screen` package is a very simple computer graphics package, and its operations `ClearScreen` and `MoveCursor` are very similar to operations that are found in all graphics packages.

Computer graphics is almost never a part of a programming language. Rather, graphics capabilities are provided through libraries. These libraries are generally platform-specific; that is, they are specific to a certain combination of CPU, operating system, and display type. Indeed, our Ada `Screen` package is not part of Ada; it is an added package that is specific to platforms that support the ANSI 24-row, 80-column monochrome display emulator.

In the body of this book, we have focused on software development using standard Ada 95; we have not wished to distract the reader with discussions of platform-dependent issues such as graphics. On the other hand, color graphics is interesting and exciting. The purpose of this appendix is to introduce the reader to high-resolution color graphics using a particular graphics package, `AdaGraph`. We describe this package in Section A.1. In Section A.2 we show a sine-wave plotting example that illustrates many `AdaGraph` operations. In Section A.3 we show a new version of the `Spider` package in which the spider draws in color on a high-resolution display. Finally, in Section A.4 we show two interesting spider programs that use the new package.

A.1   AdaGraph: A Basic High-Resolution Graphics Package

`AdaGraph` was originally developed for the Microsoft Windows 95, 98, and NT platforms by Jerry van Dijk, an Ada developer in the Netherlands. The package is quite simple to understand and to use but provides many useful capabilities. The interface (package specification) for AdaGraph is not very Windows-specific; therefore, others, specifically Martin Carlisle, James Hopper, and Michael Feldman, have developed `AdaGraph` adaptations for several other platforms, including Apple Macintosh, Tcl/Tk, XLib, and Java Virtual Machine (JVM).

The result is a collection of packages that provide very similar graphics functions for multiple platforms; in other words, we have provided a platform-independent high-resolution color graphics capability for Ada 95. The examples in this appendix are entirely platform-independent. All the package versions and examples are provided on the CD-ROM that accompanies this book.

Figure A.1 gives an extract from the `AdaGraph` package specification. For brevity, we will omit detailed descriptions of the various operations; we prefer to let the preconditions and postconditions speak for themselves. We note only that the specification provides for opening and closing a graphics window, drawing lines and polygons in the window, displaying text in the window, and responding to mouse actions, especially button clicks.

Figure A.1 Specification for the AdaGraph package

```
PACKAGE Adagraph IS
------------------------------------------------------------------------
--| Basic 16-color High-Resolution Graphics Package
--| Selected Types and Operations
--| Author: Jerry van Dijk, Leiden, Netherlands
--| Adapted by M. B. Feldman, The George Washington University
--| Last Modified: November 1998
------------------------------------------------------------------------

   -- Output Types

   -- 16-Color Palette; more colors could be used if we were sure
   --    that the display supported them
   TYPE Color_Type IS (Black, Blue, Green, Cyan, Red, Magenta, Brown,
     Light_Gray, Dark_Gray, Light_Blue, Light_Green,
     Light_Cyan, Light_Red, Light_Magenta, Yellow, White);

   -- Indicates whether a graphic shape will be drawn as an outline
   --    or as a filled area
   TYPE Fill_Type IS (Fill, No_Fill);

   -- Graphic Window Management Operations

   PROCEDURE Get_Max_Size (X_Size, Y_Size : OUT Integer);
   -- Pre:  None
   -- Post: X_Size and Y_Size contain the maximum X (horizontal) and Y
   --       (vertical) coordinates, respectively, of graphics windows on
   --       the display. The coordinates are in the range 0..X_Size and
   --       0..Y_Size

   PROCEDURE Create_Graph_Window (
                                   X_Max,  Y_Max  : OUT Integer;
                                   X_Char, Y_Char : OUT Integer);
   -- Pre:    None
   -- Post:   Opens a graphic window on the display, of the maximum size.
   --         The OUT parameters X_Max and Y_Max contain the maximum
   --         horizontal and vertical cordinates, respectively; X_Char
   --         and Y_Char contain the width and height, respectively,
   --         in pixels, of characters to be displayed
   -- Raises: Window_Already_Open if the graphic window is already open

   PROCEDURE Ext_Create_Graph_Window (
                                   X_Max,  Y_Max  : OUT Integer;
```

```
                              X_Char, Y_Char : OUT Integer);
-- Pre:  None
-- Post: Like Create_Graph_Window, but guarantees that the display
--       area of the window is of the maximum size possible

PROCEDURE Create_Sized_Graph_Window (X_Size, Y_Size : IN Integer;
                                     X_Max,  Y_Max  :    OUT Integer;
                                     X_Char, Y_Char :    OUT Integer);
-- Pre:  X_Size and Y_Size are defined
-- Post: Like the previous two operations, but also sets the display
--       area of the window to the size given by X_Size and Y_Size

PROCEDURE Destroy_Graph_Window;
-- Pre:  None
-- Post: Closes the graphic window
-- Raises: Window_Already_Closed if the window is already closed


FUNCTION Is_Open RETURN Boolean;
-- Pre:  None
-- Post: Returns True if the graphic window is active, False otherwise

PROCEDURE Set_Window_Title (Title : IN String);
-- Pre:  Title is defined
-- Post: Sets the title to be displayed at the top of the window

-- Graphic Operations

PROCEDURE Clear_Window (Hue : IN Color_Type := Black);
-- Pre:  Hue is defined
-- Post: Erases the contents of the graphic window and clears it to
--       the given color, Black by default

FUNCTION Get_Pixel (X, Y : IN Integer) RETURN Color_Type;
-- Pre:  X and Y are defined
-- Post: Returns the color of the pixel at the <X, Y> coordinates

PROCEDURE Put_Pixel (X, Y : IN Integer; Hue : IN Color_Type := White);
-- Pre:  X, Y, and Hue are defined
-- Post: Colors a single pixel at the <X, Y> coordinates

PROCEDURE Draw_Line (X1, Y1, X2, Y2 : IN Integer;
                     Hue : IN Color_Type := White);
-- Pre:  X1, Y1, X2, Y2, and Hue are defined
-- Post: Draws a line 1 pixel wide, in the given color,
--       from <X1, Y1> to <X2, Y2>

PROCEDURE Draw_Box (X1, Y1, X2, Y2 : IN Integer;
                    Hue    : IN Color_Type := White;
                    Filled : IN Fill_Type  := No_Fill);
-- Pre:  X1, Y1, X2, Y2, Filled, and Hue are defined
-- Post: Draws a rectangle, in the given color,
--       from <X1, Y1> to <X2, Y2>. If Fill_Type is No_Fill,
--       draws an outline in the given color; if Fill_Type is
--       Fill, draws a filled box.

PROCEDURE Draw_Circle (X, Y, Radius : IN Integer;
                       Hue : IN Color_Type := White;
                       Filled  : IN Fill_Type  := No_Fill);
-- Pre:  X, Y, Hue, and Filled are defined
```

```
                    -- Post: Draws a circle centered at <X, Y> with radius Radius

                    PROCEDURE Draw_Ellipse (X1, Y1, X2, Y2 : IN Integer;
                                            Hue    : IN Color_Type := White;
                                            Filled : IN Fill_Type  := No_Fill);
                    -- Pre:  X1, Y1, X2, Y2, Filled, and Hue are defined
                    -- Post: Draws an ellipse whose bounding rectangle is given by
                    --       <X1, Y2> and <X2, Y2>

                    PROCEDURE Flood_Fill (X, Y : IN Integer;
                                          Hue : IN Color_Type := White);
                    -- Pre:  X, Y, and Hue are defined
                    -- Post: Reads the color at <X, Y> and then replaces this color
                    --       by Hue in all directions until another color is encountered

                    PROCEDURE Display_Text (X, Y : IN Integer;
                                            Text : IN String;
                                            Hue  : IN Color_Type := White);
                    -- Pre:  X, Y, Text, and Hue are defined
                    -- Post: Displays the given text string in the graphics window.
                    --       The character size is the default one in the system; it
                    --       is returned by the window-creating operations

                    -- Polydraw Support

                    FUNCTION Where_X RETURN Integer;
                    FUNCTION Where_Y RETURN Integer;
                    -- Pre:  None
                    -- Post: Return the horizontal and vertical positions, respectively,
                    --       of the current drawing point

                    PROCEDURE Goto_Xy (X, Y : IN Integer);
                    -- Pre:  X and Y are defined
                    -- Post: Moves the current drawing point to <X, Y>

                    PROCEDURE Draw_To (X, Y : IN Integer; Hue : IN Color_Type := White);
                    -- Pre:  X, Y, and Hue are defined
                    -- Post: Draws a line 1 pixel wide, in the given color,
                    --       from the current drawing point to <X, Y>, and moves
                    --       the current drawing point to <X, Y>

                    -- Input Types

                    TYPE Event_Type IS
                      (None, Moved, Left_Up, Left_Down, Right_Up, Right_Down);

                    TYPE Mouse_Type IS RECORD
                      Event : Event_Type;  -- indicates which mouse event occurred;
                      X_Pos : Integer;     -- gives the location of the cursor when
                      Y_Pos : Integer;     -- the mouse event occurred
                    END RECORD;

                    -- Input Operations

                    FUNCTION Key_Hit RETURN Boolean;
                    -- Pre:  None
                    -- Post: Returns True if a character is available (i.e., if a
                    --       key has been pressed)

                    FUNCTION Get_Key RETURN Character;
```

```
-- Pre:  None
-- Post: Waits until a character is available and returns it

FUNCTION Mouse_Event RETURN Boolean;
-- Pre:  None
-- Post: Returns True if a mouse event in the graphic window has
--       become available

FUNCTION Get_Mouse RETURN Mouse_Type;
-- Pre:  None
-- Post: Waits for a mouse event in the graphical window to occur,
--       and returns a record containing the event type and the
--       coordinates of the mouse pointer

   . . .

PRIVATE

   . . .

END Adagraph;
```

A.2   Using AdaGraph Operations

Recall Program 8.4, which plots a sine curve using character graphics. Program A.1 is an adaptation of Program 8.4, in which AdaGraph operations are used to plot a more realistic sine wave.

Program A.1 Drawing a High-Resolution Sine Curve

```
WITH AdaGraph;
USE AdaGraph;
WITH Ada.Text_IO;
WITH Ada.Numerics;
WITH Ada.Numerics.Elementary_Functions;
USE  Ada.Numerics;
USE  Ada.Numerics.Elementary_Functions;
PROCEDURE Sine_Wave IS

----------------------------------------------------------------------
--| Plots a sine curve, using high-resolution graphics.
--| Author: M. B. Feldman, The George Washington University
--| Last Modified: November 1998
----------------------------------------------------------------------

   XMax    : Integer;               -- width of graphic window
   YMax    : Integer;               -- height of graphic window
   XChar   : Integer;               -- width of character font
   YChar   : Integer;               -- height of character font
   Mouse: AdaGraph.Mouse_Type;      -- click to quit program

   RadiansPerDegree : CONSTANT Float := Pi / 180.0;
                                     -- radians per degree
                                     -- Pi in Ada.Numerics

   MinAngle :  CONSTANT Integer := 0;    -- smallest angle
```

```
              MaxAngle :   CONSTANT Integer := 360;   -- largest angle

              MaxAmplitude : Float;                    -- max plot height
              Sine         : Float;                    -- current sine value
              Height       : Integer;                  -- height of plot pixel
          BEGIN

              AdaGraph.Create_Graph_Window(X_Max => XMax, Y_Max => YMax,
                                           X_Char => XChar, Y_Char => YChar);
              MaxAmplitude := Float(YMax / 6);
              AdaGraph.Set_Window_Title(Title => "Sine Wave");
              AdaGraph.Clear_Window(Hue => AdaGraph.White);
              AdaGraph.Draw_Line(X1 => 1,          X2 => XMax,
                                 Y1 => YMax / 2, Y2 => YMax / 2,
                                 Hue => AdaGraph.Black);
              AdaGraph.Goto_XY(X => 0, Y => YMax / 2);

              FOR Degrees IN MinAngle .. MaxAngle LOOP
                IF Degrees REM 2 = 0 THEN
                  Sine := Sin(Float(Degrees) * RadiansPerDegree);
                  Height := YMax / 2 + Integer(MaxAmplitude * Sine);
                  AdaGraph.Draw_To(X   => Degrees / 2,
                                   Y   => Height,
                                   Hue => AdaGraph.Blue);
                  DELAY 0.01;
                END IF;
              END LOOP;

              LOOP
                IF AdaGraph.Mouse_Event THEN
                  Mouse := AdaGraph.Get_Mouse;
                  EXIT WHEN
                  Mouse.Event = AdaGraph.Left_Down OR
                  Mouse.Event = AdaGraph.Right_Down;
                END IF;
              END LOOP;

              AdaGraph.Destroy_Graph_Window;

          END Sine_Wave;
```

The output of this program is shown in Figure A.2. The program first creates a graphic window using the `AdaGraph` operation

```
AdaGraph.Create_Graph_Window(X_Max => XMax, Y_Max => YMax,
                             X_Char => XChar, Y_Char => YChar);
```

The four output parameters `XMax`, `YMax`, `XChar`, and `YChar` are set by this operation; they represent the maximum display area of the window and the size of any displayed text. Next, the statement

```
MaxAmplitude := Float(YMax / 6);
```

computes the maximum height (amplitude) of the sine wave. We intend to plot the curve above and below a horizontal line through the center of the window; the curve will be one-third the height of the window itself. We draw a black center line on a white background as follows:

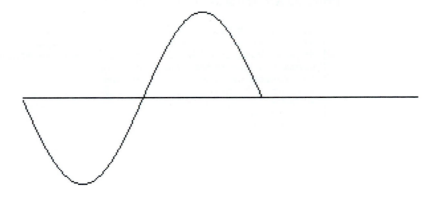

Figure A.2   A High-Resolution Sine Curve

```
AdaGraph.Clear_Window(Hue => AdaGraph.White);
AdaGraph.Draw_Line(X1 => 1,           X2 => XMax,
                   Y1 => YMax / 2, Y2 => YMax / 2,
                   Hue => AdaGraph.Black);
```

We then position the drawing point at the left end of this line:

```
AdaGraph.Goto_XY(X => 0, Y => YMax / 2);
```

which is similar to a `Screen.MoveCursor` call. Finally, the following loop actually plots the sine wave, by drawing short line segments. Each common point represents a 2-degree increment plotted against its sine value.

We encourage you to experiment with `AdaGraph`. For example, consider modifying the histogram-plotting program described in the case study of Section 10.4.

A.3   A High-Resolution Color Spider Package

The `Spider` package that we first presented in Chapter 2 provides an imaginary spider that crawls around its room—a 20 × 20 grid—and draws in monochrome characters, using letters to represent its colored tracks. Program A.2 gives a more exciting version of the package which we call `Spider_Hires` (for "Spider, High Resolution"). This time, the spider lives in a 200 × 200 grid and leaves multicolored tracks. Each spider step is now a very small one, 1/200th of the screen window, and the spider is no longer limited to 90-degree turns but can make more precise turns in increments of 1 degree.

The new spider package is implemented using `AdaGraph`; that is, the operations in the body of the package use `AdaGraph` operations to carry out the graphics manipulations. Therefore, `Spider_Hires` is just as platform-independent as `AdaGraph` is.

Program A.2 The Spider Goes "Hi-Res"

```
PACKAGE Spider_Hires IS
-----------------------------------------------------------------
--| This package provides procedures to emulate "Spider"
--| commands. The spider can move around
--| the screen drawing simple patterns.
--| This is a high-resolution color version of the package.
--| Author: John Dalbey, Cal Poly San Luis Obispo, 1992
--| Adapted by M. B. Feldman, The George Washington University
--| Last Modified: November 1998
-----------------------------------------------------------------
  -- These are the spider's simple parameterless methods

  PROCEDURE Start;
  -- Pre:  None
  -- Post: Spider's room appears on the screen
  --    with spider in the center.

  PROCEDURE Quit;
  -- Pre:  None
  -- Post: End the drawing

  -- now some types, and methods that use the types

  TYPE Directions IS (North, East, South, West);
  TYPE Colors     IS (Red, Green, Blue, Black, None);
  SUBTYPE Steps IS Integer RANGE 1..200;
  SUBTYPE Degrees IS Float RANGE 0.0..360.0;

  PROCEDURE Step(HowMany: Steps := 1);
  -- Pre:  None
  -- Post: Spider takes HowMany steps forward in the direction
  --       it is facing; default is 1.
  -- Raises: Hit_the_Wall if spider tries to step into a wall.

  FUNCTION RandomStep RETURN Steps;
  -- Pre:  None
  -- Post: Returns a random step in the range 1..200

  PROCEDURE TurnRight(HowFar: Degrees := 90.0);
  -- Pre:  None
  -- Post: Spider turns HowMany degrees to the right;
  --        default is 90.

  FUNCTION RandomTurn RETURN Degrees;
  -- Pre:  None
  -- Post: Returns a random angle of turn

  PROCEDURE Face (WhichWay: IN Directions);
  -- Pre:  WhichWay has been assigned a value
  -- Post: Spider turns to face the given direction.

  FUNCTION IsFacing RETURN Directions;
  -- Pre:  None
  -- Post: Returns the nearest direction the spider is facing.
  --         (Rounds the spider's heading to the nearest direction)

  FUNCTION RandomDirection RETURN Directions;
  -- Pre:  None
```

```
-- Post: Returns a random direction

PROCEDURE ChangeColor (NewColor: Colors);
-- Pre:  NewColor has been assigned a value
-- Post: Spider leaves its tracks in the new color

FUNCTION IsPainting RETURN Colors;
-- Pre:  None
-- Post: Returns the color in which the spider is painting

FUNCTION RandomColor RETURN Colors;
-- Pre:  None
-- Post: Returns a random color

FUNCTION AtWall RETURN Boolean;
-- Pre:  None
-- Post: Returns True if the spider is standing next to a wall

Hit_The_Wall: EXCEPTION;

TYPE Switch IS (On, Off);

PROCEDURE Debug (Setting: IN Switch);
-- Pre:  None
-- Post: Turns on or off single stepping through the program.

FUNCTION  Debugging RETURN Switch;
-- Pre:  None
-- Post: Returns on or Off depending on Debug setting

TYPE Speeds IS (Slow, Medium, Fast);

PROCEDURE SetSpeed (Speed: IN Speeds);
-- Pre:  Speed is defined
-- Post: Execution speed is set as desired

PROCEDURE Wait;
-- Pre:  None
-- Post: Causes the program to wait for a mouse click
--          before proceeding
```

```
END Spider_Hires;
```

Most of the spider operations are unchanged from the low-resolution version. We have designed the new package so that your old spider programs will still work with minimal change. To use an old program, you need only change all the `Spider` references to `Spider_Hires` and recompile.

Here we mention some of the new operations. First, the `Step` and `TurnRight` commands now have parameters with default values:

```
PROCEDURE Step(HowMany: Steps := 1);
PROCEDURE TurnRight(HowFar: Degrees := 90);
```

A command such as

```
Spider_Hires.Step;
```

causes the spider to take one step forward, and a command such as

```
Spider_Hires.TurnRight;
```

causes a 90-degree right turn. Thus these commands in an old program will behave properly with the new package.

The new package also has a speed control feature:

```
TYPE Speeds IS (Slow, Medium, Fast);
PROCEDURE SetSpeed (Speed: IN Speeds);
```

The spider starts out moving `Fast`. A command such as

```
Spider_Hires.SetSpeed (Speed => Spider_Hires.Medium);
```

causes the spider to draw somewhat more slowly.

Still another change is

```
PROCEDURE Wait;
```

Calling this procedure, as in

```
Spider_Hires.Wait;
```

causes the spider to pause until the mouse is clicked.

Finally, the debugging option is changed. With the debug mode set to `on`, a mouse click controls the single step operation instead of an ENTER keypress.

A.4   Using the High-Resolution Spider Package

In this section we present two examples of interesting patterns drawn by the high-resolution spider.

Drawing High-Resolution Spirals

First, Program A.3 is an almost exact copy of Program 2.9. The only difference is that the spider now draws 120 lines instead of ten.

Program A.3 A Spider Program to Draw a High-Resolution Spiral

```
WITH Spider_Hires;
PROCEDURE Spiral IS
-------------------------------------------------------------
--| Draw spiral pattern with spider - use nested loops
--| High-resolution version
--| Author: M. B. Feldman, The George Washington University
--| Last Modified: November 1998
-------------------------------------------------------------
BEGIN -- Spiral

  Spider_Hires.Start;
  Spider_Hires.Face(WhichWay => Spider_Hires.RandomDirection);
```

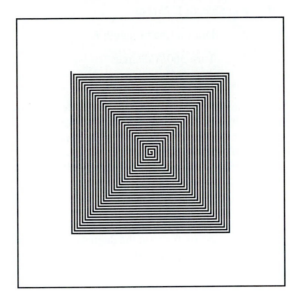

Figure A.3 The Spider Draws a High-Resolution Spiral

```
-- draw 120 lines, starting in a random direction
FOR Line IN 1..120 LOOP

   -- inner loop takes its bound from outer count
   FOR Count IN 1..Line LOOP
     Spider_Hires.Step;
   END LOOP;

   Spider_Hires.TurnRight;
END LOOP;

Spider_Hires.Quit;

END Spiral;
```

Figure A.3 shows the output of this program. This is a prettier pattern than the lower resolution one, isn't it?

Drawing Regular Polygons

Now let's investigate how the spider can draw regular polygons. Recall from your study of plane geometry that the interior angles of a polygon must add up to 360 degrees. Further, in an N-sided regular polygon, all the angles must be the same size, namely, $360/N$ degrees. For example, the angles in a square are all 90 degrees, the angles in an equilateral triangle are all 120 degrees, and those in a pentagon are all 72 degrees. The algorithm for drawing an N-sided polygon with sides of length L is then

1.   FOR Side IN 1..*N* LOOP

    2.   Draw a line of length *L*

    3.   Turn 360/*N* degrees

END LOOP

The old spider can make only 90-degree turns. It can draw rectangular boxes, but it can't draw other polygons. On the other hand, the new spider can turn an arbitrary number of degrees, and therefore it can draw polygons of an arbitrary number of sides.

In Program A.4 the spider does exactly this. The program contains a procedure `Polygon`, which carries out the algorithm we just presented. Note that the turn command contains a type conversion:

```
TurnRight(HowFar => 360.0/Float(Sides));
```

This is necessary because the degrees are given as a floating-point quantity and we cannot legally divide it directly by an integer.

Program A.4 A Spider Program That Draws Some Regular Polygons

```
WITH Spider_Hires;
USE  Spider_Hires;
PROCEDURE Polygons IS
----------------------------------------------------------------
--| Draw regular polygon pattern with spider
--| High-resolution version
--| Author: M. B. Feldman, The George Washington University
--| Last Modified: November 1998
----------------------------------------------------------------

   PROCEDURE Polygon(Length: IN Steps; Sides: Positive) IS
   BEGIN
     FOR Side IN 1..Sides LOOP
       Step(HowMany => Length);
       TurnRight(HowFar => 360.0/Float(Sides));
     END LOOP;
   END Polygon;

BEGIN
  Start;
  Polygon(Length => 15, Sides => 5);
  Wait;
  Face(WhichWay => West);
  Polygon(Length => 25, Sides => 11);
  Quit;
END Polygons;
```

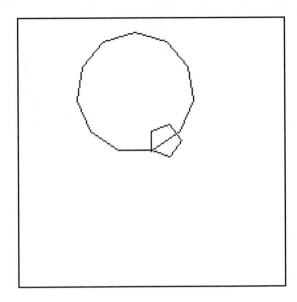

Figure A.4   The Spider Draws Regular Polygons

In the main program, `Polygon` is called twice, first to draw a pentagon, then to draw an 11-sided regular polygon. Figure A.4 shows the output.

Drawing Polystars

Finally, we consider a variation of polygons, called *polystars*. A polystar is a regular figure, but the angles are very sharp ones, so the lines cross each other to produce a star shape. Specifically, the polystar algorithm is

1.   FOR Side IN 1..*N* LOOP

    2.   Draw a line of length *L*

    3.   Turn 180 – 180/*N* degrees

    END LOOP

To draw a six-pointed star, we would turn 150 degrees; to draw a ten-pointed one, we'd turn 162 degrees, and so on. Figure A.5 shows a 17-pointed polystar; Program A.5 is a spider program that produces it.

It is worth experimenting with polygons and polystars; try various numbers of sides and various lengths. It's fun!

Figure A.4   The Spider Draws a 17-Pointed Polystar

Program A.5 A Spider Program to Draw a 17-Sided Polystar

```
WITH Spider_Hires;
USE  Spider_Hires;
PROCEDURE Polystars IS
----------------------------------------------------------------
--| Draw polystar pattern with spider
--| High-resolution version
--| Author: M. B. Feldman, The George Washington University
--| Last Modified: November 1998
----------------------------------------------------------------

  PROCEDURE Polystar(Length: IN Steps; Sides: IN Positive) IS
  -- Pre:  Length and sides are defined
  -- Post: Draws a polystar pattern with the spider
  BEGIN
    FOR Side IN 1..Sides LOOP
      Step(HowMany => Length);
      TurnRight(HowFar => 180.0 - 180.0/Float(Sides));
    END LOOP;
  END Polystar;

BEGIN -- Polystars
  Start;
  Polystar(Length => 80, Sides => 17);
  Quit;
END Polystars;
```

APPENDIX B

████████████

The Ada Character Set, Delimiters, and Reserved Words

B.1   The Ada Character Set

B.2   Delimiters

B.3   Reserved Words

This appendix is adapted from the Ada 95 Reference Manual, Sections 2.1, 2.2, and 2.9.

B.1   The Ada Character Set

The Ada 95 standard uses the ISO 8859-1 (Latin-1) character set. This character set includes the usual letters A–Z, but also a number of additional characters to provide for the additional letters used in non-English languages. For example, French uses accented letters such as é and à; German has letters using the umlaut such as ü, the Scandinavian languages have dipthongs such as æ, and so forth. For purposes of this book, we use just the 26 letters of English; if you are in another country and wish to use the additional letters, you can find out locally how to do so on your computer or terminal. The following characters are used in constructing programs in this book:

(a) uppercase letters

   A B C D E F G H I J K L M N O P Q R S T U V W X Y Z

(b) lowercase letters

   a b c d e f g h i j k l m n o p q r s t u v w x y z

(c) digits

   0 1 2 3 4 5 6 7 8 9

(d) special characters

   " # & ' ( ) * + , - . / : ; < = > _ | ! $ % ? @ [\ ] ^ ` { } ~

(e) the space character

Format effectors are the characters called horizontal tabulation, vertical tabulation, carriage return, line feed, and form feed.

The following names are used in referring to special characters:

symbol	name	symbol	name
"	quotation	>	greater than
#	sharp	_	underline
&	ampersand	|	vertical bar
'	apostrophe, tick	!	exclamation point
(	left parenthesis	$	dollar
)	right parenthesis	%	percent
*	star, multiply	?	question mark
+	plus	@	commercial at
,	comma	[	left square bracket
-	hyphen, minus	\	backslash
.	dot, point, period	]	right square bracket
/	slash, divide	^	circumflex
:	colon	`	grave accent
;	semicolon	{	left brace
<	less than	}	right brace
=	equal	~	tilde

B.2   Delimiters

A *delimiter* is either one of the following special characters:

& ' ( ) * + , - . / : ; < = > |

or one of the following *compound delimiters,* each composed of two adjacent special characters:

=>   ..   **   :=   /=   >=   <=   <<   >>   <>

The following names are used in referring to compound delimiters:

delimiter	name
=>	arrow
..	double dot
**	double star, exponentiate

delimiter	name
:=	assignment (pronounced: "becomes")
/=	inequality (pronounced: "not equal")
>=	greater than or equal
<=	less than or equal
<<	left label bracket
>>	right label bracket
<>	box

B.3   Reserved Words

The identifiers listed below are called *reserved words* and are reserved for special significance in the language. In this book the reserved words always appear in uppercase.

ABORT	ELSE	NEW	RETURN
ABS	ELSIF	NOT	REVERSE
ABSTRACT	END	NULL	
ACCEPT	ENTRY		SELECT
ACCESS	EXCEPTION		SEPARATE
ALIASED	EXIT	OF	SUBTYPE
ALL		OR	
AND	FOR	OTHERS	TAGGED
ARRAY	FUNCTION	OUT	TASK
AT			TERMINATE
	GENERIC	PACKAGE	THEN
BEGIN	GOTO	PRAGMA	TYPE
BODY		PRIVATE	
	IF	PROCEDURE	
CASE	IN	PROTECTED	UNTIL
CONSTANT	IS		USE
		RAISE	
DECLARE		RANGE	WHEN
DELAY	LIMITED	RECORD	WHILE
DELTA	LOOP	REM	WITH
DIGITS		RENAMES	
DO	MOD	REQUEUE	XOR

A reserved word must not be used as a declared identifier.

APPENDIX C

Ada's Predefined Environment: Package Standard

This appendix, adapted from the Ada 95 Reference Manual, Section A.1, outlines the specification of the package `standard` containing all predefined identifiers in the language. The corresponding package body is not specified by the language.

The operators that are predefined for the types declared in the package Standard are given in comments since they are implicitly declared. Italics are used for pseudonames of anonymous types (such as *root_real*) and for undefined information (such as *implementation-defined*).

```
PACKAGE Standard is
   PRAGMA Pure(Standard);

   TYPE Boolean IS (False, True);

   -- The predefined relational operators for this type are as follows:

   -- FUNCTION "="   (Left, Right : Boolean) RETURN Boolean;
   -- FUNCTION "/="  (Left, Right : Boolean) RETURN Boolean;
   -- FUNCTION "<"   (Left, Right : Boolean) RETURN Boolean;
   -- FUNCTION "<="  (Left, Right : Boolean) RETURN Boolean;
   -- FUNCTION ">"   (Left, Right : Boolean) RETURN Boolean;
   -- FUNCTION ">="  (Left, Right : Boolean) RETURN Boolean;

   -- The predefined logical operators and the predefined logical
   -- negation operator are as follows:

   -- FUNCTION "AND" (Left, Right : Boolean) RETURN Boolean;
   -- FUNCTION "OR"  (Left, Right : Boolean) RETURN Boolean;
   -- FUNCTION "XOR" (Left, Right : Boolean) RETURN Boolean;

   -- FUNCTION "NOT" (Right : Boolean) RETURN Boolean;

   -- The integer type root_integer is predefined.
   -- The corresponding universal type is universal_integer.

   TYPE Integer IS RANGE implementation-defined;

   SUBTYPE Natural  IS Integer RANGE  0.. Integer'Last;
   SUBTYPE Positive IS Integer RANGE  1.. Integer'Last;

   -- The predefined operators for type Integer are as follows:

   -- FUNCTION "="   (Left, Right : Integer) RETURN Boolean;
   -- FUNCTION "/="  (Left, Right : Integer) RETURN Boolean;
   -- FUNCTION "<"   (Left, Right : Integer) RETURN Boolean;
   -- FUNCTION "<="  (Left, Right : Integer) RETURN Boolean;
   -- FUNCTION ">"   (Left, Right : Integer) RETURN Boolean;
   -- FUNCTION ">="  (Left, Right : Integer) RETURN Boolean;
```

```
-- FUNCTION "+"   (Right : Integer) RETURN Integer;
-- FUNCTION "-"   (Right : Integer) RETURN Integer;
-- FUNCTION "ABS" (Right : Integer) RETURN Integer;

-- FUNCTION "+"   (Left, Right : Integer) RETURN Integer;
-- FUNCTION "-"   (Left, Right : Integer) RETURN Integer;
-- FUNCTION "*"   (Left, Right : Integer) RETURN Integer;
-- FUNCTION "/"   (Left, Right : Integer) RETURN Integer;
-- FUNCTION "REM" (Left, Right : Integer) RETURN Integer;
-- FUNCTION "MOD" (Left, Right : Integer) RETURN Integer;

-- FUNCTION "**"  (Left : Integer; Right : Natural) RETURN Integer;

-- The specification of each operator for the type
-- root_integer, or for any additional predefined integer
-- type, is obtained by replacing Integer by the name of the type
-- in the specification of the corresponding operator of the type
-- Integer. The right operand of the exponentiation operator
-- remains as subtype Natural.

-- The floating point type root_real is predefined.
-- The corresponding universal type is universal_real.

TYPE Float IS DIGITS implementation-defined;

-- The predefined operators for this type are as follows:

-- FUNCTION "="   (Left, Right : Float) RETURN Boolean;
-- FUNCTION "/="  (Left, Right : Float) RETURN Boolean;
-- FUNCTION "<"   (Left, Right : Float) RETURN Boolean;
-- FUNCTION "<="  (Left, Right : Float) RETURN Boolean;
-- FUNCTION ">"   (Left, Right : Float) RETURN Boolean;
-- FUNCTION ">="  (Left, Right : Float) RETURN Boolean;

-- FUNCTION "+"   (Right : Float) RETURN Float;
-- FUNCTION "-"   (Right : Float) RETURN Float;
-- FUNCTION "ABS" (Right : Float) RETURN Float;

-- FUNCTION "+"   (Left, Right : Float) RETURN Float;
-- FUNCTION "-"   (Left, Right : Float) RETURN Float;
-- FUNCTION "*"   (Left, Right : Float) RETURN Float;
-- FUNCTION "/"   (Left, Right : Float) RETURN Float;

-- FUNCTION "**"  (Left : Float; Right : Integer) RETURN Float;

-- The specification of each operator for the type root_real, or
-- for any  additional predefined floating point type, is
-- obtained by replacing Float by the name of the type in the
-- specification of the corresponding operator of the type Float.

-- In  addition, the following operators are predefined for the
-- root numeric types:

FUNCTION "*" (Left : root_integer; Right : root_real)
  RETURN root_real;

FUNCTION "*" (Left : root_real;    Right : root_integer)
  RETURN root_real;
```

```
FUNCTION "/" (Left : root_real;    Right : root_integer)
  RETURN root_real;

-- The type universal_fixed is predefined.
-- The only multiplying operators defined between
-- fixed point types are

FUNCTION "*" (Left : universal_fixed; Right : universal_fixed)
  RETURN universal_fixed;

FUNCTION "/" (Left : universal_fixed; Right : universal_fixed)
  RETURN universal_fixed;


-- The declaration of type Character is based on the standard ISO
-- 8859-1 character set.

-- There are no character literals corresponding to the positions
-- for control characters.
-- They are indicated in italics in this definition.

TYPE Character IS

  (nul,  soh,  stx,  etx,     eot,  enq,  ack,  bel,    -- 0..7
   bs,   ht,   lf,   vt,      ff,   cr,   so,   si,      -- 8..15

   dle,  dc1,  dc2,  dc3,     dc4,  nak,  syn,  etb,     -- 16..23
   can,  em,   sub,  esc,     fs,   gs,   rs,   us,      -- 24..31

   ' ',  '!',  '"',  '#',     '$',  '%',  '&',  ''',     -- 32..39
   '(',  ')',  '*',  '+',     ',',  '-',  '.',  '/',     -- 40..47

   '0',  '1',  '2',  '3',     '4',  '5',  '6',  '7',     -- 48..55
   '8',  '9',  ':',  ';',     '<',  '=',  '>',  '?',     -- 56..63

   '@',  'A',  'B',  'C',     'D',  'E',  'F',  'G',     -- 64..71
   'H',  'I',  'J',  'K',     'L',  'M',  'N',  'O',     -- 72..79

   'P',  'Q',  'R',  'S',     'T',  'U',  'V',  'W',     -- 80..87
   'X',  'Y',  'Z',  '[',     '\',  ']',  '^',  '_',     -- 88..95

   '`',  'a',  'b',  'c',     'd',  'e',  'f',  'g',     -- 96..103
   'h',  'i',  'j',  'k',     'l',  'm',  'n',  'o',     -- 104..111

   'p',  'q',  'r',  's',     't',  'u',  'v',  'w',     -- 112..119
   'x',  'y',  'z',  '{',     '|',  '}',  '~',  del,     -- 120..127


   reserved_128,     reserved_129, bph,  nbh,
   reserved_132,     nel,      ssa,  esa,

   hts,  htj,  vts,  pld,     plu,  ri,   ss2,  ss3,

   dcs,  pu1,  pu2,  sts,     cch,  mw,   spa,  epa,

   sos, reserved_153, sci, csi,
   st,   osc,  pm,   apc,

   ... );
```

```
-- The predefined operators for the type Character are the same as
-- for any enumeration type.


-- The declaration of type Wide_Character is based on the standard
-- ISO 10646 BMP character set.
-- The first 256 positions have the same contents as type
-- Character.

TYPE Wide_Character IS (nul, soh ... FFFE, FFFF);


PACKAGE ASCII IS ... END ASCII;   --Obsolescent; see J.


-- Predefined string types:

TYPE String IS ARRAY(Positive RANGE <>) OF Character;
  PRAGMA Pack(String);

-- The predefined operators for this type are as follows:

--FUNCTION "="  (Left, Right: String) RETURN Boolean;
--FUNCTION "/=" (Left, Right: String) RETURN Boolean;
--FUNCTION "<"  (Left, Right: String) RETURN Boolean;
--FUNCTION "<=" (Left, Right: String) RETURN Boolean;
--FUNCTION ">"  (Left, Right: String) RETURN Boolean;
--FUNCTION ">=" (Left, Right: String) RETURN Boolean;

--FUNCTION "&" (Left: String;    Right: String)    RETURN String;
--FUNCTION "&" (Left: Character; Right: String)    RETURN String;
--FUNCTION "&" (Left: String;    Right: Character) RETURN String;
--FUNCTION "&" (Left: Character; Right: Character) RETURN String;

TYPE Wide_String IS ARRAY(Positive RANGE <>) OF Wide_Character;
  PRAGMA Pack(Wide_String);

-- The predefined operators for this type correspond to
-- those for String

TYPE Duration IS
  DELTA implementation-defined RANGE implementation-defined;

-- The predefined operators for the type Duration are the same
-- as for any fixed point type.

-- The predefined exceptions:

      Constraint_Error: EXCEPTION;
      Program_Error   : EXCEPTION;
      Storage_Error   : EXCEPTION;
      Tasking_Error   : EXCEPTION;

END Standard;
```

APPENDIX D

Specification of the Package Ada.Text_IO

This appendix, adapted from the Ada 95 Reference Manual, Section A.10.1, gives the specification for `Ada.Text_IO`. Note that the numeric subpackages `Integer_IO` and `Float_IO` are given here as generic. The standard also provides for the preinstantiated packages `Ada.Integer_Text_IO` and `Ada.Float_Text_IO` as we have used in this book. These last two packages are part of the standard libraries and do not need to be created or compiled by the user.

Explanations of the most common input/output exceptions are given in Appendix F, along with the other exceptions that a student is likely to encounter.

```
WITH Ada.IO_Exceptions;
PACKAGE Ada.Text_IO IS

  TYPE File_Type IS limited private;

  TYPE File_Mode IS (In_File, Out_File, Append_File);

  TYPE Count IS RANGE  0.. implementation-defined;
  SUBTYPE Positive_Count IS Count RANGE  1 .. Count'Last;
  Unbounded : CONSTANT Count :=  ; -- line and page length

  SUBTYPE Field      IS Integer RANGE  0 .. implementation-defined;
  SUBTYPE Number_Base IS Integer RANGE  2 .. 16;

  TYPE Type_Set IS (Lower_Case, Upper_Case);

  -- File Management

  PROCEDURE Create (File : IN out File_Type;
                    Mode : IN File_Mode := Out_File;
                    Name : IN String    := "";
                    Form : IN String    := "");

  PROCEDURE Open  (File : IN out File_Type;
                   Mode : IN File_Mode;
                   Name : IN String;
                   Form : IN String := "");

  PROCEDURE Close  (File : IN out File_Type);
  PROCEDURE Delete (File : IN out File_Type);
  PROCEDURE Reset  (File : IN out File_Type; Mode : IN File_Mode);
  PROCEDURE Reset  (File : IN out File_Type);

  FUNCTION  Mode   (File : IN File_Type) RETURN File_Mode;
  FUNCTION  Name   (File : IN File_Type) RETURN String;
  FUNCTION  Form   (File : IN File_Type) RETURN String;

  FUNCTION  Is_Open(File : IN File_Type) RETURN Boolean;
```

```
-- Control of default input and output files

PROCEDURE Set_Input (File : IN File_Type);
PROCEDURE Set_Output(File : IN File_Type);
PROCEDURE Set_Error (File : IN File_Type);

FUNCTION Standard_Input  RETURN File_Type;
FUNCTION Standard_Output RETURN File_Type;
FUNCTION Standard_Error  RETURN File_Type;

FUNCTION Current_Input   RETURN File_Type;
FUNCTION Current_Output  RETURN File_Type;
FUNCTION Current_Error   RETURN File_Type;

TYPE File_Access IS ACCESS CONSTANT File_Type;

FUNCTION Standard_Input  RETURN File_Access;
FUNCTION Standard_Output RETURN File_Access;
FUNCTION Standard_Error  RETURN File_Access;

FUNCTION Current_Input   RETURN File_Access;
FUNCTION Current_Output  RETURN File_Access;
FUNCTION Current_Error   RETURN File_Access;

  --Buffer control
PROCEDURE Flush (File : IN OUT File_Type);
PROCEDURE Flush;

-- Specification of line and page lengths

PROCEDURE Set_Line_Length(File : IN File_Type; To : IN Count);
PROCEDURE Set_Line_Length(To   : IN Count);

PROCEDURE Set_Page_Length(File : IN File_Type; To : IN Count);
PROCEDURE Set_Page_Length(To   : IN Count);

FUNCTION  Line_Length(File : IN File_Type) RETURN Count;
FUNCTION  Line_Length RETURN Count;

FUNCTION  Page_Length(File : IN File_Type) RETURN Count;
FUNCTION  Page_Length RETURN Count;

-- Column, Line, and Page Control

PROCEDURE New_Line   (File    : IN File_Type;
                      Spacing : IN Positive_Count :=  );
PROCEDURE New_Line   (Spacing : IN Positive_Count :=  );

PROCEDURE Skip_Line  (File    : IN File_Type;
                      Spacing : IN Positive_Count :=  );
PROCEDURE Skip_Line  (Spacing : IN Positive_Count :=  );

FUNCTION  End_Of_Line(File : IN File_Type) RETURN Boolean;
FUNCTION  End_Of_Line RETURN Boolean;

PROCEDURE New_Page   (File : IN File_Type);
PROCEDURE New_Page;

PROCEDURE Skip_Page  (File : IN File_Type);
```

```
PROCEDURE Skip_Page;

FUNCTION  End_Of_Page(File : IN File_Type) RETURN Boolean;
FUNCTION  End_Of_Page RETURN Boolean;

FUNCTION  End_Of_File(File : IN File_Type) RETURN Boolean;
FUNCTION  End_Of_File RETURN Boolean;

PROCEDURE Set_Col (File : IN File_Type; To : IN Positive_Count);
PROCEDURE Set_Col (To   : IN Positive_Count);

PROCEDURE Set_Line(File : IN File_Type; To : IN Positive_Count);
PROCEDURE Set_Line(To   : IN Positive_Count);

FUNCTION Col (File : IN File_Type) RETURN Positive_Count;
FUNCTION Col  RETURN Positive_Count;

FUNCTION Line(File : IN File_Type) RETURN Positive_Count;
FUNCTION Line RETURN Positive_Count;

FUNCTION Page(File : IN File_Type) RETURN Positive_Count;
FUNCTION Page RETURN Positive_Count;

-- Character Input-Output

PROCEDURE Get(File : IN  File_Type; Item : OUT Character);
PROCEDURE Get(Item : OUT Character);

PROCEDURE Put(File : IN  File_Type; Item : IN Character);
PROCEDURE Put(Item : IN  Character);

PROCEDURE Look_Ahead (File        : IN  File_Type;
                      Item        : OUTCharacter;
                      End_Of_Line : OUT Boolean);
PROCEDURE Look_Ahead (Item        : OUT Character;
                      End_Of_Line : OUT Boolean);

PROCEDURE Get_Immediate(File      : IN  File_Type;
                        Item      : OUT Character);
PROCEDURE Get_Immediate(Item      : OUT Character);

PROCEDURE Get_Immediate(File      : IN  File_Type;
                        Item      : OUT Character;
                        Available : OUT Boolean);
PROCEDURE Get_Immediate(Item      : OUT Character;
                        Available : OUT Boolean);

-- String Input-Output

PROCEDURE Get(File : IN  File_Type; Item : OUT String);
PROCEDURE Get(Item : OUT String);

PROCEDURE Put(File : IN  File_Type; Item : IN String);
PROCEDURE Put(Item : IN  String);

PROCEDURE Get_Line(File : IN  File_Type;
                   Item : OUT String;
                   Last : OUT Natural);
PROCEDURE Get_Line(Item : OUT String; Last : OUT Natural);
```

```
PROCEDURE Put_Line(File : IN  File_Type; Item : IN String);
PROCEDURE Put_Line(Item : IN  String);

  -- Generic packages for Input-Output of Integer Types

GENERIC
   TYPE Num IS RANGE <>;
PACKAGE Integer_IO IS

   Default_Width : Field := Num'Width;
   Default_Base  : Number_Base := 10;

   PROCEDURE Get(File  : IN  File_Type;
                 Item  : OUT Num;
                 Width : IN Field := 0);
   PROCEDURE Get(Item  : OUT Num;
                 Width : IN  Field := 0);

   PROCEDURE Put(File  : IN File_Type;
                 Item  : IN Num;
                 Width : IN Field := Default_Width;
                 Base  : IN Number_Base := Default_Base);
   PROCEDURE Put(Item  : IN Num;
                 Width : IN Field := Default_Width;
                 Base  : IN Number_Base := Default_Base);
   PROCEDURE Get(From : IN  String;
                 Item : OUT Num;
                 Last : OUT Positive);
   PROCEDURE Put(To   : OUT String;
                 Item : IN Num;
                 Base : IN Number_Base := Default_Base);

END Integer_IO;


-- Generic PACKAGEs for Input-Output of Real Types

GENERIC
   TYPE Num IS digits <>;
PACKAGE Float_IO IS

   Default_Fore : Field := 2;
   Default_Aft  : Field := Num'Digits-1 ;
   Default_Exp  : Field := 3;

   PROCEDURE Get(File  : IN  File_Type;
                 Item  : OUT Num;
                 Width : IN  Field := 0);
   PROCEDURE Get(Item  : OUT Num;
                 Width : IN  Field := 0);

   PROCEDURE Put(File : IN File_Type;
                 Item : IN Num;
                 Fore : IN Field := Default_Fore;
                 Aft  : IN Field := Default_Aft;
                 Exp  : IN Field := Default_Exp);
   PROCEDURE Put(Item : IN Num;
                 Fore : IN Field := Default_Fore;
                 Aft  : IN Field := Default_Aft;
                 Exp  : IN Field := Default_Exp);
```

```
                  PROCEDURE Get(From : IN String;
                               Item : OUT Num;
                               Last : OUT Positive);
                  PROCEDURE Put(To   : OUT String;
                               Item : IN Num;
                               Aft  : IN Field := Default_Aft;
                               Exp  : IN Field := Default_Exp);
            END Float_IO;

            -- Generic package for Input-Output of Enumeration Types

            GENERIC
               TYPE Enum IS (<>);
            PACKAGE Enumeration_IO IS

               Default_Width   : Field := 0;
               Default_Setting : Type_Set := Upper_Case;

               PROCEDURE Get(File : IN  File_Type;
                            Item : OUT Enum);
               PROCEDURE Get(Item : OUT Enum);

               PROCEDURE Put(File  : IN File_Type;
                            Item  : IN Enum;
                            Width : IN Field    := Default_Width;
                            Set   : IN Type_Set := Default_Setting);
               PROCEDURE Put(Item  : IN Enum;
                            Width : IN Field    := Default_Width;
                            Set   : IN Type_Set := Default_Setting);

               PROCEDURE Get(From : IN  String;
                            Item : OUT Enum;
                            Last : OUT Positive);
               PROCEDURE Put(To   : OUT String;
                            Item : IN  Enum;
                            Set  : IN  Type_Set := Default_Setting);
            END Enumeration_IO;

               -- Exceptions

            Status_Error : EXCEPTION RENAMES IO_Exceptions.Status_Error;
            Mode_Error   : EXCEPTION RENAMES IO_Exceptions.Mode_Error;
            Name_Error   : EXCEPTION RENAMES IO_Exceptions.Name_Error;
            Use_Error    : EXCEPTION RENAMES IO_Exceptions.Use_Error;
            Device_Error : EXCEPTION RENAMES IO_Exceptions.Device_Error;
            End_Error    : EXCEPTION RENAMES IO_Exceptions.End_Error;
            Data_Error   : EXCEPTION RENAMES IO_Exceptions.Data_Error;
            Layout_Error : EXCEPTION RENAMES IO_Exceptions.Layout_Error;

         PRIVATE
            ... -- not specified by the language
         END Ada.Text_IO;
```

APPENDIX E

Specifications of the Ada Math Libraries

This appendix, adapted from the Ada 95 Reference Manual, Sections A.5.1 and A.5.2, give the specifications for the packages `Ada.Numerics`, `Ada.Numerics.Float_Random`, `Ada.Numerics.Elementary_Functions`, and the generic package `Ada.Numerics.Discrete_Random`.

```
PACKAGE Ada.Numerics IS

   Argument_Error : EXCEPTION;
   Pi : CONSTANT :=
      3.14159_26535_89793_23846_26433_83279_50288_41971_69399_37511;
   e  : CONSTANT :=
      2.71828_18284_59045_23536_02874_71352_66249_77572_47093_69996;

END Ada.Numerics;


PACKAGE Ada.Numerics.Elementary_Functions IS

   FUNCTION Sqrt     (X             : Float)        RETURN Float;
   FUNCTION Log      (X             : Float)        RETURN Float;
   FUNCTION Log      (X, Base       : Float)        RETURN Float;
   FUNCTION Exp      (X             : Float)        RETURN Float;
   FUNCTION "**"     (Left, Right   : Float)        RETURN Float;

   FUNCTION Sin      (X             : Float)        RETURN Float;
   FUNCTION Sin      (X, Cycle      : Float)        RETURN Float;
   FUNCTION Cos      (X             : Float)        RETURN Float;
   FUNCTION Cos      (X, Cycle      : Float)        RETURN Float;
   FUNCTION Tan      (X             : Float)        RETURN Float;
   FUNCTION Tan      (X, Cycle      : Float)        RETURN Float;
   FUNCTION Cot      (X             : Float)        RETURN Float;
   FUNCTION Cot      (X, Cycle      : Float)        RETURN Float;

   FUNCTION Arcsin   (X             : Float)        RETURN Float;
   FUNCTION Arcsin   (X, Cycle      : Float)        RETURN Float;
   FUNCTION Arccos   (X             : Float)        RETURN Float;
   FUNCTION Arccos   (X, Cycle      : Float)        RETURN Float;
   FUNCTION Arctan   (Y             : Float;
                      X             : Float := . )  RETURN Float;
   FUNCTION Arctan   (Y             : Float;
                      X             : Float := . ;
                      Cycle         : Float)        RETURN Float;
   FUNCTION Arccot   (X             : Float;
                      Y             : Float := . )  RETURN Float;
   FUNCTION Arccot   (X             : Float;
                      Y             : Float := . ;
                      Cycle         : Float)        RETURN Float;
```

```
    FUNCTION Sinh    (X              : Float)          RETURN Float;
    FUNCTION Cosh    (X              : Float)          RETURN Float;
    FUNCTION Tanh    (X              : Float)          RETURN Float;
    FUNCTION Coth    (X              : Float)          RETURN Float;
    FUNCTION Arcsinh (X              : Float)          RETURN Float;
    FUNCTION Arccosh (X              : Float)          RETURN Float;
    FUNCTION Arctanh (X              : Float)          RETURN Float;
    FUNCTION Arccoth (X              : Float)          RETURN Float;

END Ada.Numerics.Elementary_Functions;


PACKAGE Ada.Numerics.Float_Random IS

  -- Basic facilities

  TYPE Generator IS limited private;
  SUBTYPE Uniformly_Distributed IS Float RANGE 0.0 .. 1.0;
  FUNCTION Random (Gen : Generator) RETURN Uniformly_Distributed;

  PROCEDURE Reset (Gen       : IN Generator;
                   Initiator : IN Integer);
  PROCEDURE Reset (Gen       : IN Generator);

  -- Advanced facilities

  TYPE State IS private;

  PROCEDURE Save  (Gen        : IN  Generator;
                   To_State   : OUT State);
  PROCEDURE Reset (Gen        : IN  Generator;
                   From_State : IN  State);

  Max_Image_Width : constant := implementation-defined integer value;

  FUNCTION Image (Of_State    : State)  RETURN String;
  FUNCTION Value (Coded_State : String) RETURN State;

PRIVATE
  ... -- not specified by the language
END Ada.Numerics.Float_Random;


GENERIC
  TYPE Result_SubTYPE IS (<>);
PACKAGE Ada.Numerics.Discrete_Random IS

  -- Basic facilities

  TYPE Generator IS limited private;

  FUNCTION Random (Gen : Generator) RETURN Result_SubTYPE;

  PROCEDURE Reset (Gen       : IN Generator;
                   Initiator : IN Integer);
  PROCEDURE Reset (Gen       : IN Generator);

  -- Advanced facilities

  TYPE State IS private;
```

```
PROCEDURE Save  (Gen       : IN  Generator;
                 To_State  : OUT State);
PROCEDURE Reset (Gen       : IN  Generator;
                 From_State : IN  State);

Max_Image_Width : constant := implementation-defined integer value;

FUNCTION Image (Of_State    : State)  RETURN String;
FUNCTION Value (Coded_State : String) RETURN State;

PRIVATE
  ... -- not specified by the language
END Ada.Numerics.Discrete_Random;
```

APPENDIX F

Summary of Ada Execution-Time Exceptions

This appendix summarizes the predefined Ada exceptions. Ada distinguishes exceptions defined in the language from those defined in standard packages. The summary should help students to write exception handlers and to interpret run-time messages that report unhandled exceptions propagated out of a main program.

F.1   Exceptions Defined in the Language

The following exceptions are predefined in the Ada language:

- `Constraint_Error` is raised if an attempt is made to store a value in a variable that is out of range for that variable, that is, out of the range of the variable's type or subtype. It will also be raised if an attempt is made to dereference a null access value (pointer), to copy a string or similar array into another of a different size, or to copy a variant record object into another that is constrained to a different value of the discriminant.

- `Program_Error` is raised in a number of situations that are unlikely to arise in courses that use this book. For example, WITH-ing a number of packages could cause an attempted call of a subprogram whose body has not yet been elaborated. This occurrence is rare in student projects with simple package dependencies but arises occasionally in industry.

- `Storage_Error` is raised if the storage pool is exhausted by dynamic allocation, typically in an infinite loop in whose body a NEW call is executed. The exception is also raised if the run-time stack is exhausted by subprogram calls, for example, by an infinite recursion.

- `Tasking_Error` is raised if two concurrent Ada tasks are unable to communicate.

F.2 Exception Defined in Ada.Calendar

One exception is defined in the package `Ada.Calendar`:

- `Ada.Calendar.Time_Error` is raised if the actual parameters in a call of `Ada.Cal-endar.Time_Of` do not form a valid date or if subtracting two values of type `Ada.Calendar.Time` results in a value that lies outside the range of the predefined type `Duration`.

F.3 Exception Defined in Ada.Numerics

One exception is defined in the package `Ada.Numerics`:

- The `Argument_Error` exception is raised by a subprogram in a child unit of `Ada.Numerics` to signal that one or more of the actual subprogram parameters are outside the domain of the corresponding mathematical function.

F.4 Exceptions Defined in Ada.Text_IO

The following exceptions can be raised by `Ada.Text_IO` operations:

- `Ada.Text_IO.Status_Error` is raised by an attempt to operate upon a file that is not open and by an attempt to open a file that is already open.

- `Ada.Text_IO.Mode_Error` is raised by an attempt to read from, or test for the end of, a file whose current mode is `Out_File` and also by an attempt to write to a file whose current mode is `In_File`. This exception is also raised by specifying a file whose current mode is `Out_File` in a call of `Set_Input`, `Skip_Line`, `End_Of_Line`, `Skip_Page`, or `End_Of_Page` or by specifying a file whose current mode is `In_File` in a call of `Set_Output`, `Set_Line_Length`, `Set_Page_Length`, `Line_Length`, `Page_Length`, `New_Line`, or `New_Page`.

- `Ada.Text_IO.Name_Error` is raised by a call of `Create` or `Open` if the string given for the parameter `Name` does not allow the identification of an external file. For example, this exception is raised if the string is improper or, alternatively, if either none or more than one external file corresponds to the string. In student programs, this exception is often raised if the *case* of the file name given in the procedure call does not agree with the case of the name in the student's directory. This is especially common in UNIX, in which file names are case-sensitive.

- `Ada.Text_IO.Use_Error` is raised if an operation is attempted that is not possible for reasons that depend on characteristics of the external file. For example, this exception in raised by the procedure `Create`, among other circumstances, if the given mode is `Out_File` but the form specifies an input-only device, if the parameter `Form` specifies invalid access rights, or if an external file with the given name already exists and overwriting is not allowed.

- `Ada.Text_IO.Device_Error` is raised if an input-output operation cannot be completed because of a malfunction of the underlying system. This should rarely occur in a student program.

- `Ada.Text_IO.End_Error` is raised by an attempt to skip (read past) the end of a file. In student programs this may happen if the file terminator is immediately preceded by a line terminator. In this case a solution is to include a handler for this exception in the file input section of the program. Sometimes, inserting a `Ada.Text_IO.Skip_Line` call in the file input loop will work as well.

- `Ada.Text_IO.Data_Error` is raised by a procedure `Get` if the input character sequence fails to satisfy the required syntax or if the value input does not belong to the range of the required type or subtype. Common causes are entering an integer or character literal where a `Float` literal is required and entering an invalid enumeration literal.

- `Ada.Text_IO.Layout_Error` is raised by `Col`, `Line`, or `Page` if the value returned exceeds `Count'Last`. The exception `Layout_Error` is also raised on output by an attempt to set column or line numbers in excess of specified maximum line or page lengths, respectively (excluding the unbounded cases). It is also raised by an attempt to `Put` too many characters to a string.

APPENDIX G

The Ada 95 Educational Resources CD-ROM

The Ada 95 Educational Resources CD-ROM is a collection of materials assembled by Michael Feldman. It is an ISO-9660 CD-ROM that can be read under Apple Macintosh OS, MS-DOS/PC-DOS, Windows 95/98/NT, and Linux and other UNIX variants. The collection includes compilers, interactive development environments (IDEs), program libraries (including all the example programs from this book), and a set of Ada 95 reference documents that will be helpful to students and educators. This material is freely distributable, with the exception of the Tenon MachTen CodeBuilder installer, which is included here by special permission of Tenon Intersystems.

The CD-ROM is organized into five folders: documents (DOCUMENT), Macintosh OS (MACOS), Windows 95/98/NT (WINDOWS), Linux (LINUX), and MS-DOS/PC-DOS (DOS). The contents of these folders is decribed briefly here; refer to the README file on the CD-ROM for last-minute details and changes.

The DOCUMENT Folder

This folder contains:

- installers for Adobe Acrobat Reader for Macintosh, Windows, and Linux, which can be installed and used for reading all the PDF-format documentation on the CD-ROM;

- the Ada 95 Reference Manual, Annotated Reference Manual, and Rationale, in plain text, Portable Data Format (PDF), and browsable HTML, forms;

- documentation for the GNU Ada 95 Compiler (GNAT) in plain text, HTML and PDF forms;

- Ada 95 quick reference card and syntax summary, in PDF; and

- Ada 95 graphical syntax charts, in HTML and Graphical Input Format (GIF) form.

The MACOS Folder

This folder contains:

- an installer for Tenon Intersystems' MachTen CodeBuilder for the Apple Power Macintosh computer family. CodeBuilder is an implementation of UNIX that runs as a MacOS application; it includes many software tools and compilers for various languages, including the GNU Ada 95 Compiler (GNAT) for the Macintosh;

- a CodeBuilder user manual in PDF format;
- the GRASP multilanguage, multiplatform editor and IDE, developed at Auburn University;
- all the programs from this book, suitable for compilation under CodeBuilder; and
- a MacOS version of the `AdaGraph` basic graphics package, suitable for compilation using GNAT under CodeBuilder.

The WINDOWS Folder

This folder contains

- GNAT for Windows 95/98/NT, including the AdaGIDE IDE;
- all the programs from this book, suitable for compilation under Windows;
- the Windows version of `AdaGraph`; and
- GRASP for Windows.

The LINUX Folder

This folder contains

- GNAT for Linux;
- all the programs from this book, for compilation under Linux; and
- GRASP for Linux.

The DOS Folder

This folder contains

- GNAT for MS-DOS/PC-DOS, including the AdaCAPS IDE;
- all the programs from this book, for compilation under DOS; and
- a basic Ada 95 VGA graphics package similar to `AdaGraph` and a `Spider` package that uses it.

INDEX OF SYNTAX DISPLAYS

INDEX OF STYLE DISPLAYS

INDEX OF EXAMPLE PROGRAMS

GENERAL INDEX